6 sixth edition

D0701386

JUVENILE JUSTICE
an introduction

John T. Whitehead
East Tennessee State University

Steven P. Lab
Bowling Green State University

 LexisNexis™

anderson publishing
A member of the LexisNexis Group

Juvenile Justice: An Introduction, Sixth Edition

Copyright © 1990, 1996, 1999, 2004, 2006, 2009
        Matthew Bender & Company, Inc., a member of the LexisNexis Group

        Phone 877-374-2919
    Web Site www.lexisnexis.com/anderson/criminaljustice

LexisNexis and the Knowledge Burst logo are trademarks of Reed Elsevier Properties, Inc.
Anderson Publishing is a registered trademark of Anderson Publishing, a member of the LexisNexis Group.

Library of Congress Cataloging-in-Publication Data

Whitehead, John T.
    Juvenile justice : an introduction / John T. Whitehead, Steven P. Lab. -- 6th ed.
        p. cm.
    Includes index.
    ISBN 978-1-59345-613-9 (softbound)
    1. Juvenile delinquency. 2. Juvenile justice, Administration of. 3. Juvenile justice,
    Administration of--United States. I. Lab, Steven P. II. Title.

    HV9069.W46 2009
    364.36--dc22   2009002511

Cover design by Tin Box Studio, Inc.

EDITOR Ellen S. Boyne
ACQUISITIONS EDITOR Michael C. Braswell

Dedication
to
Pat, Danny & Tim Whitehead
and
Danielle, Madison, Rylee & Bryce

FOREWORD

For this Sixth Edition of *Juvenile Justice: An Introduction* we have updated materials. We have included the latest available statistics on juvenile crime and victimization, drug use, court processing, and corrections. In the police chapter and the institutions and probation chapters we have included recent research on the effectiveness of the police and treatment interventions. In the last chapter we have added a section on life without parole for juveniles in addition to the previous discussion of the death penalty for juveniles (including the *Roper* case).

In each chapter we have added a section entitled "What You Need to Know." This is a list that summarizes key pieces of information. Along with the Important Terms list, this section should help students focus on the key concepts and information in each chapter. We have also included web site information at key points in the text showing students where they can go to get the latest information from such sources as the FBI *Uniform Crime Reports* and the Office of Juvenile Justice and Delinquency Prevention.

A test bank and PowerPoint slides are available to professors who adopt the text.

We thank all of the people at LexisNexis Matthew Bender (Anderson Publishing) for their support and hard work. We are especially grateful to Ellen Boyne, our editor, for her excellent work in editing and producing the book, and to Mickey Braswell for his continuing support.

JTW
SPL

TABLE OF CONTENTS

Chapter 5
Gang Delinquency   **101**

Chapter 14
Future Directions in Juvenile Justice   **377**

INTRODUCTION – THE DEFINITION AND EXTENT OF DELINQUENCY

Important Terms

dark figure of crime

delinquency

Index crimes

juvenile

Monitoring the Future (MTF)

National Incident-Based Reporting System (NIBRS)

National Youth Survey (NYS)

offense rate

panel design

self-report measures

Short–Nye instrument

status offense

transfer

Uniform Crime Reports (UCR)

waiver

What You Need to Know

- Delinquency can be defined in terms of criminal laws just like for adults; status offenses, which are applied only to youths; or sociological/criminological definitions, which take on a specific meaning depending on the interests of the individual or group studying delinquency.

- Defining delinquency requires one to define who is a juvenile. Most states outline minimum and maximum ages as well as exceptions in which the youth can be handled as an adult.

- Measures of delinquency include official records of the juvenile justice and criminal justice system and self-report surveys.

- According to the UCR, roughly 15 percent of all arrests are of youths under the age of 18, with one-quarter of all property arrests being of youths.

- Court and correctional statistics also provide insight to the extent of delinquency, although the magnitude of the problem appears much less due to the funneling effect of system involvement.

- Self-report measures reveal that virtually all youths offend, although this is true only when status offenses are included. Otherwise, the results are remarkably similar to official figures when serious crimes are considered.

- Regardless of the measure used, the trend in delinquency has been one of large increases since the 1960s with some leveling off and decreases since the late 1990s.

INTRODUCTION

Discussions of the juvenile justice system cannot proceed without a clear understanding of the behaviors that it is tasked to address. As will be seen in Chapter 2, the juvenile court and the juvenile justice system are relatively recent inventions, tracing their history back to the late 1800s. Prior to that time, youths who broke the law were handled in the same system and in the same ways as adults. It was not until the 1800s that crime and misbehavior by youths were redefined as separate and distinct from adult offending. "Delinquency" was born, and new mechanisms of social control were developed to address problem children.

In the relatively short time period since "delinquency" and the juvenile court were initiated, society has developed a separate system for handling youthful offenders. Youthful offenders who used to be seen as simply young "criminals" have been transformed into "delinquents." The label of "delinquent," however, represents a variety of different behaviors and means different things at different places and points in time. It is important to understand the diversity in definitions of delinquency in order to examine the workings of the juvenile justice system adequately.

DEFINING DELINQUENCY

As already noted, **delinquency** has a number of different meanings. These various interpretations appear both in state statutes and criminological discussions of juvenile behavior. State statutes typically offer two sets of definitions for delinquency—a criminal law definition and a status offense definition. Beyond the codified legal definitions are social/criminological definitions that are used in research on juvenile misconduct.

Criminal Law Definitions

A criminal law definition of delinquency delineates activity that is illegal regardless of the age of the offender. "Delinquency" is simply a substitute label for criminal behavior by a juvenile. The only distinction between being a delinquent and being a criminal is the age of the individual.

You can go to your state's statutes and look up the definitions of "delinquency," "status offense," and "juvenile."

Criminal law definitions of delinquency typically define a delinquent as someone who violates the criminal laws of the jurisdiction (see Figure 1.1). The key to these statutes is the idea that a juvenile violated the criminal law. The fact that a juvenile committed the offense means that a different label will be imposed (delinquent versus criminal) and a different system will handle the individual (juvenile versus adult). A criminal law definition explicitly extends the criminal statutes to the juvenile population.

FIGURE 1.1 A Criminal Law Definition of Delinquency

(F) "Delinquent child" includes any of the following:

   (1) Any child, except a juvenile traffic offender, who violates any law of this state or the United States, or any ordinance of a political subdivision of the state, that would be an offense if committed by an adult;

   (2) Any child who violates any lawful order of the court . . .

   (3) Any child who violates [prohibitions against purchasing or owning a firearm or handgun (Section 2321.211)];

   (4) Any child who is a habitual truant and who previously has been adjudicated an unruly child for being a habitual truant;

   (5) Any child who is a chronic truant.

Source: Ohio Revised Code (2008). Section 2152.02. Available at: http://codes.ohio.gov/orc

Status Offense Definitions

Besides criminal actions that can be committed by a juvenile, there are other behaviors for which only juveniles can be held accountable. This type of behavior is usually referred to as **status offense** because they are only illegal if they are committed by persons of a particular "status." Thus, juvenile status offenses represent acts that are illegal only for juveniles. Adults who take part in these acts are not subject to sanctioning by the formal justice system.

While "status offender" is the most common term for those who violate these acts, a variety of other names are applied to these individuals. Among the more common names are "unruly," "dependent," and "incorrigible," as well as acronyms such as PINS (person in need of supervision) or CHINS (child in need of supervision). One common criticism of status offense definitions is that they are ambiguous and the language is so vague that they allow wide latitude in interpreting what is and is not a violation (see Figure 1.2). Such statutes allow the juvenile justice system to intervene in the life of almost any youth.

FIGURE 1.2 A Status Offense Definition of Delinquency

Ohio Chapter 2151.022 defines an "unruly child" as:

   (A) Any child who does not submit to the reasonable control of the child's parents, teachers, guardian, or custodian, by reason of being wayward or habitually disobedient;

   (B) Any child who is an habitual truant from school and who previously has not been adjudicated an unruly child for being an habitual truant;

   (C) Any child who behaves in a manner as to injure or endanger the child's own health or morals or the health or morals of others;

   (D) Any child who violates a law . . . that is applicable only to a child.

Source: Ohio Revised Code (2008). Section 2151.022. Available at: http://codes.ohio.gov/orc

The behaviors outlined by status offense statutes make virtually any behavior of a juvenile sanctionable by the state. The definitions are all-encompassing and have been criticized for being overly broad (see, for example, President's Commission on Law Enforcement and the Administration of Justice, 1967). Arguments for eliminating such overly broad language have resulted in some courts ruling that the statutory language, such as that referring to "leading an idle, dissolute, lewd, or immoral life," is unconstitutionally vague (*Gonzalez v. Mailliard*, 1971).

Actions that typically fall under the heading of status offenses include truancy; smoking; drinking; curfew violations; disobeying the orders of parents, teachers, or other adults; swearing; running away; and other acts that are allowable for adults. All juveniles violate these statutes at one time or another. Normal youthful behavior includes many of these activities. It is possible that all youths could be subjected to system intervention under these types of "status" definitions.

Social/Criminological Definitions

The study of delinquency and juvenile justice often relies on definitions of delinquency that do not conform precisely to the legal definitions of delinquent or status offenses. The definition of delinquency often takes on a specific meaning depending on the interests of the group or individual examining juvenile misconduct. The 1967 President's Commission on Law Enforcement and the Administration of Justice took a broad view by defining delinquency as a combination of delinquent and status offense statutes:

> Delinquency comprises cases of children alleged to have committed an offense that if committed by an adult would be a crime. It also comprises cases of children alleged to have violated specific ordinances or regulatory laws that apply only to children . . . (President's Commission, 1967:4).

Cloward and Ohlin (1960) define delinquent acts as those "that officials engaged in the administration of criminal justice select ... from among many deviant acts, as forms of behavior proscribed by the approved norms of society" (Cloward and Ohlin, 1960:2-3). This means that the police, court officials, corrections officers, and others determine which actions are to be considered delinquent when they decide to take action. This definition limits the discussion of delinquency to those actions that are handled by the justice system. Juvenile behavior that is ignored by the system is not to be considered delinquent.

Most definitions of delinquency present juvenile behavior as either delinquent or nondelinquent, with no middle ground. In reality, most individuals fall in between these extremes, having violated some laws and conformed to others. Most juveniles are involved, to varying degrees, in some form of delinquent behavior. Cavan and Ferdinand (1981) offer a continuum of behavior that ranges from extreme delinquency on one end to extreme "goodness" on the other (see Figure 1.3). The shape of the continuum, a bell curve, represents the proportional distribution of juveniles along the continuum. It is assumed that the largest group of youths would fall into the middle category of "normal conformity." The left-hand portion of the curve represent youths who run the risk of being apprehended and labeled delinquent. Minor underconformity may include such acts as status and victimless offenses while the delinquent contraculture category includes serious acts such as murder and rape and suggests organized involvement in deviance. The right side of the curve represents individuals who do not become involved in delinquency. Few juveniles appear in either of the "contraculture" categories of extreme delinquent or extreme goodness.

FIGURE 1.3 Behavior Continuum

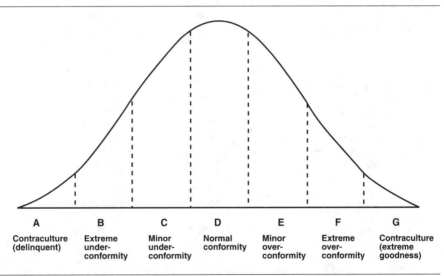

A	B	C	D	E	F	G
Contraculture (delinquent)	Extreme under-conformity	Minor under-conformity	Normal conformity	Minor over-conformity	Extreme over-conformity	Contraculture (extreme goodness)

Source: Figure 2.1 from *Juvenile Delinquency*, 4th ed. by Ruth Shonle Cavan and Theodore N. Ferdinand. Copyright © 1981 by Ruth Shonle Cavan and Theodore N. Ferdinand. Reprinted by permission.

Today, most criminological research considers delinquency in terms of Cavan and Ferdinand's continuum. It does not limit the researcher to a simple legal definition or an either/or dichotomy. Instead, it allows the inspection of various types of delinquent activity as well as activity that is highly overconforming. Seen as a continuum, juvenile activity can be subdivided into various parts and phases that change over time and can be compared to one another.

DEFINING A JUVENILE

In every definition of delinquency there is an implicit assumption of what constitutes a **juvenile**. Interestingly, the legal definition of a juvenile varies from jurisdiction to jurisdiction. This means that persons subject to the juvenile statutes in one location may not be in another place. Table 1.1 presents the age at which the adult court assumes responsibility for the actions of individuals in different jurisdictions. Under these ages the individual is considered a juvenile and is handled in the juvenile justice system. The majority of states (37) and the District of Columbia recognize juveniles as individuals below the age of 18. In three states juveniles are age 15 or younger, and 10 states define juveniles as those under 17 years old.

TABLE 1.1 Ages at Which Criminal Courts Gain Jurisdiction over Young Offenders

Age 16	Age 18	
Connecticut	Alabama	Mississippi
New York	Alaska	Montana
North Carolina	Arizona	Nebraska
	Arkansas	Nevada
	California	New Jersey
	Colorado	New Mexico
Age 17	Delaware	North Dakota
	District of	Ohio
Georgia	Columbia	Oklahoma
Illinois	Florida	Oregon
Louisiana	Hawaii	Pennsylvania
Massachusetts	Idaho	Rhode Island
Michigan	Indiana	South Dakota
Missouri	Iowa	Tennessee
New Hampshire	Kansas	Utah
South Carolina	Kentucky	Vermont
Texas	Maine	Virginia
Wisconsin	Maryland	Washington
	Minnesota	West Virginia
		Wyoming

Source: M. King and L. Szymanski (2006). "National Overviews." *State Juvenile Justice Profiles.* Pittsburgh: National Center for Juvenile Justice. Available at: http://www.ncjj.org/stateprofiles

Besides setting an upper age for juvenile status, other factors influence whether an individual can be handled in the juvenile justice system. First, some states set a lower age limit in outlining who can be treated by the juvenile justice process. These ages range from age six to age 10 (see Table 1.2), although 34 states and the District of Columbia have no lower age limit. In those states with a lower age level, any juvenile below the minimum age who exhibits deviant behavior is simply returned to his or her parents or guardian for handling.

TABLE 1.2 Lower Age Limits for Juvenile Court Jurisdiction

Age 6	Age 10	No Specified Age		
North Carolina	Arkansas	Alabama	Indiana	North Dakota
	Colorado	Alaska	Iowa	Ohio
	Kansas	California	Kentucky	Oklahoma
Age 7	Louisiana	Connecticut	Maine	Oregon
	Minnesota	Delaware	Michigan	Rhode Island
Maryland	Mississippi	District of	Missouri	South Carolina
Massachusetts	Pennsylvania	Columbia	Montana	Tennessee
New York	South Dakota	Florida	Nebraska	Utah
	Texas	Georgia	Nevada	Virginia
Age 8	Vermont	Hawaii	New Hampshire	Washington
	Wisconsin	Idaho	New Jersey	West Virginia
Arizona		Illinois	New Mexico	Wyoming

Source: M. King and L. Szymanski (2006). "National Overviews." *State Juvenile Justice Profiles.* Pittsburgh: National Center for Juvenile Justice. Available at: http://www.ncjj.org/stateprofiles

A second age consideration is the termination of the juvenile system's intervention with an individual. Many state statutes allow the juvenile system to continue supervision and intervention with individuals who have passed the maximum age limit (see Table 1.3). In three states the juvenile court retains jurisdiction until the disposition is completed. The most common maximum age at which juvenile court jurisdiction is relinquished is age 20. Maintaining jurisdiction occurs mainly when that person committed his or her act as a juvenile and/or is being handled as an extension of intervention begun when he or she was a juvenile.

TABLE 1.3 Maximum Ages at Which Juvenile Courts May Maintain Jurisdiction over Youthful Offenders

Age 18	Age 20			Age 21
Alaska	Alabama	Maine	Ohio	Florida
Iowa	Arizona	Maryland	Pennsylvania	
Kentucky	Arkansas	Massachusetts	Rhode Island	
Nebraska	Connecticut	Michigan	South Carolina	**Age 22**
Oklahoma	Delaware	Minnesota	South Dakota	
Tennessee	District of	Missouri	Texas	Kansas
Vermont	Columbia	Nevada	Utah	
	Georgia	New Hampshire	Virginia	
	Idaho	New Mexico	Washington	**Age 24**
	Illinois	New York	West Virginia	
Age 19	Indiana	North Carolina	Wyoming	California
	Louisiana			Montana
Mississippi				Oregon
North Dakota	**Until the Full Term of Disposition Order**			Wisconsin
	Colorado	New Jersey	Hawaii	

Source: M. King and L. Szymanski (2006). "National Overviews." *State Juvenile Justice Profiles*. Pittsburgh: National Center for Juvenile Justice. Available at: http://www.ncjj.org/stateprofiles/

A final factor influencing juvenile court jurisdiction involves **waiver** or **transfer** provisions that may send a youth to adult court. Waiver is a process by which an individual who is legally a juvenile is sent to the adult criminal system for disposition and handling. While in the past ages 15 and 16 typically constituted the youngest ages at which waiver could occur, recent years have seen a move toward waiving younger individuals to the adult system. As of 2006, 22 states and the District of Columbia set no minimum for waiver, two set it at age 10, three set it at age 12, and another four states allow waiver of 13-year-olds to the adult court (see Table 1.4).

TABLE 1.4 Minimum Ages for Transfer to Criminal Court

Age 10	Age 14	Age 15	
Kansas	Alabama	New Mexico	
Vermont	Arkansas		
	California		
Age 12	Connecticut	**No Minimum Age**	
	Iowa		
Colorado	Kentucky	Alaska	Nebraska
Missouri	Louisiana	Arizona	Nevada
Montana	Massachusetts	Delaware	Oklahoma
	Michigan	District of	Oregon
	Minnesota	Columbia	Pennsylvania
Age 13	New Jersey	Florida	Rhode Island
Illinois	North Dakota	Georgia	South Carolina
Mississippi	Ohio	Hawaii	South Dakota
New Hampshire	Texas	Idaho	Tennessee
New York	Utah	Indiana	Washington
North Carolina	Virginia	Maine	West Virginia
Wyoming		Maryland	Wisconsin

Source: P. Griffin (2007). "National Overviews." *State Juvenile Justice Profiles*. Pittsburgh: National Center for Juvenile Justice. Available at: http://www.ncjj.org/stateprofiles

The varying definitions of delinquency and the consideration of what age constitutes being a "juvenile" have a major impact on any study of juvenile justice. The definitions alter the type of behavior with which we are concerned, the practices and interventions used in the treatment of delinquency, and the number of problems and youths subjected to intervention and study. It is the effect of the definition of delinquency on the measurement of delinquency to which we now turn.

THE EXTENT OF DELINQUENCY

There are various ways to measure delinquency, each of which produces a different picture of the delinquency problem. The different methods for measuring delinquency result in different absolute levels of delinquency as well as different information on the offense, the offender, and the victim. The two basic approaches to measuring delinquency are the use of official records and the administration of self-report surveys.

Official Measures of Delinquency

Official measures of delinquency are based on the records of various justice system agencies. Consequently, the level of delinquency reflects both the activity of juveniles and the activity of the agency that is dealing with the youths. The degree of detail in the records also varies by agency. The police, courts, and corrections each have different sets of priorities and mandates under which they operate. As a result, the data compiled by the agencies differ from one another. The following pages will consider data from each of these official sources.

Uniform Crime Reports

The **Uniform Crime Reports (UCR)** provide information on the number of offenses coming to the attention of the police, the number of arrests police make, and the number of referrals by the police to the juvenile court. This data is collected yearly by the Federal Bureau of Investigation and provides information on 29 categories of offenses. These counts reflect only crimes known to the police. Actions that are not reported to the police are not included in the yearly crime figures. The UCR is comprised of two offense subgroups. The first eight offenses are known as the Part I crimes or **Index crimes**. Included in this group are the more serious crimes (as delineated by the FBI) of murder, rape, robbery, aggravated assault, burglary, larceny, motor vehicle theft, and arson. All remaining offenses fall within the Part II category. Extensive information, including demographic data on the victim and offender (if known), circumstances of the offense, the use of a weapon, and the time and place of the offense, is gathered for the Part I offenses. For Part II offenses, only information on offenses for which a suspect has been arrested are tabulated.

Age Distribution. Due to the fact that only about 20 percent of all crimes are cleared by an arrest each year, little information is known about the offender in most crimes. Some idea about the participation of juveniles in delinquent/criminal behavior, however, can be gathered from

Up-to-date and more extensive UCR data can be found at http://www.fbi.gov/ucr/cius2007/index.html

an inspection of those cases in which an offender can be identified and/or arrested. Table 1.5 presents arrest data for 2006. More than 10 million arrests were reported to the FBI. Of these arrests, 1,626,523 or 15.5 percent of the total were of juveniles under the age of 18.

TABLE 1.5 Distribution of Juvenile Arrests, 2006

Offense Charged	Number		Percent Under 18	Percent of Juvenile Arrestees					
	All Ages	Under 18		Males	Females	White	Black	Am. Indian or Alaskan Native	Asian or Pacific Islander
Total	10,472,432	1,626,523	15.5	71.1	28.9	67.1	30.3	1.1	1.4
Murder and nonnegligent manslaughter	9,815	956	9.7	94.7	5.3	39.1	59.2	0.6	1.0
Forcible rape	17,112	2,519	14.7	98.0	2.0	63.5	34.4	1.2	0.9
Robbery	93,527	26,092	27.9	90.5	9.5	31.0	67.4	0.4	1.2
Aggravated assault	327,478	44,424	13.6	76.7	23.3	55.7	42.1	1.0	1.2
Burglary	222,192	61,155	27.5	88.7	11.3	66.3	31.5	1.1	1.1
Larceny-theft	801,633	206,187	25.7	59.1	40.9	67.5	29.5	1.1	1.9
Motor vehicle theft	100,775	25,338	25.1	83.3	16.7	53.7	43.4	1.0	1.9
Arson	12,002	5,888	49.1	86.1	13.9	79.2	18.3	0.8	1.7
Violent crimes	447,932	73,991	16.5	82.5	17.5	47.0	51.0	0.8	1.2
Property crimes	1,136,602	298,568	26.3	67.8	32.2	66.3	30.9	1.1	1.7
Other assaults	952,741	181,965	19.1	66.4	33.6	58.9	39.0	1.0	1.1
Forgery and counterfeiting	79,477	2,583	3.2	67.1	32.9	73.7	24.0	0.8	1.5
Fraud	197,722	5,681	2.9	65.8	34.2	64.1	34.3	0.6	1.1
Embezzlement	14,769	1,037	7.0	55.4	44.6	60.2	37.7	0.6	1.4
Stolen property	90,084	15,649	17.4	85.4	14.6	56.2	41.9	0.8	1.1
Vandalism	220,422	86,170	39.1	86.8	13.2	78.6	19.1	1.0	1.3
Weapons; carrying, possessing, etc.	147,623	34,700	23.5	89.9	10.1	61.1	36.8	0.8	1.3
Prostitution and commercialized vice	59,724	1,208	2.0	26.2	73.8	44.2	53.9	0.8	1.1
Sex offenses (except forcible rape)	63,243	11,516	18.2	90.2	9.8	71.4	26.9	0.7	1.0
Drug abuse violations	1,379,887	143,639	10.4	84.2	15.8	68.3	30.1	0.8	0.9
Gambling	9,018	1,620	18.0	96.6	3.4	8.6	90.8	0.1	0.5
Offenses against family and children	92,065	3,633	3.9	62.5	37.5	75.6	22.7	0.7	1.0
Driving under the influence	1,038,633	14,292	1.4	76.8	33.2	93.7	3.6	1.6	1.1
Liquor laws	469,186	102,755	21.9	63.8	36.2	91.3	4.9	2.6	1.2
Drunkenness	409,490	12,057	2.9	75.1	24.9	89.4	8.1	1.7	0.8
Disorderly conduct	519,046	153,231	29.5	67.0	33.0	57.8	40.2	1.2	0.8
Vagrancy	27,053	3,734	13.8	69.7	30.3	76.9	22.0	0.5	0.6
All other offenses	2,917,803	279,991	9.6	73.4	26.6	72.0	25.4	1.1	1.5
Suspicion	1,725	316	18.3	78.5	21.5	64.9	34.2	0.0	0.9
Curfew and loitering law violations	114,313	14,313	100.0	68.9	31.1	61.0	37.2	0.7	1.1
Runaways	83,874	83,874	100.0	43.4	56.6	68.5	25.0	1.8	4.7

Source: Federal Bureau of Investigation (2007). Compiled by authors.

A closer inspection of the arrest data reveals the extent to which youths were involved in serious offending. For the violent crimes of murder, rape, robbery, and aggravated assault, youths comprised 16.5 percent of the total arrests. This represents almost 74,000 offenses. More striking is the fact that youths were arrested for almost 300,000 property offenses. This reflects more than 26 percent of all property offense arrests in 2006. Taken by themselves, these figures are large. The problem is exacerbated, however, when you consider that youths between the ages of 10 and 17 (inclusive) make up only 11.6 percent of the total U.S. population (U.S. Bureau of the Census, 2005). Youthful offenders are contributing more than their share to the level of arrests in the nation.

Sex Distribution. The UCR routinely presents breakdowns of crime by sex of the offender. UCR data for 2006 show that juvenile females made up 29 percent of all juvenile arrests. Adult females, however, constitute only 22 percent of adult arrests. While males commit a greater percentage of violent crimes than property crimes (82.5% compared to 67.8%), roughly one-quarter of both male and female juvenile arrests are for Index crimes. A much greater percentage of males are arrested for every Index offense category, as well as most Part II offenses. The only offenses for which females are more often arrested are prostitution and runaway offenses.

Race Distribution. The UCR also provides information on the race of juvenile arrestees. Table 1.5 presents data on arrests for white, black, Native American, and Asian/Pacific Island youths. White youths make up the vast majority of all arrestees (67.1%), and account for two-thirds (66%) of the Part I property offenses. Black youths, however, are greatly overrepresented in violent personal offenses (murder, rape, robbery, and aggravated assault). This overrepresentation of blacks in violent offenses (51%) is even more dramatic in light of the fact that blacks comprise only 14.6 percent of the youthful U.S. population (U.S. Bureau of the Census, 2005).

An examination of individual Part I offenses provides a more detailed look at the data. While a greater percentage of white youths commit every type of offense than blacks, except for murder and robbery (blacks and whites commit almost exactly the same number of murders and blacks commit many more robberies), offending by black youths far surpasses their population representation for all Part I offenses except arson.

Trends in Delinquency. The trend in youthful crime has changed in recent years. The change in the number of violent offenses since 1986 appears in Figure 1.4. Arrests for both murder and rape remained relatively stable, while robbery and aggravated assault arrests increased from 1986 to 1995, dropped until 2003, and rose again in recent figures. Data on property crimes (see Figure 1.5) show general declines since 1986, except for an increase in larceny arrests in 1995.

FIGURE 1.4 Trend in Juvenile Violent Crime, 1986-2006

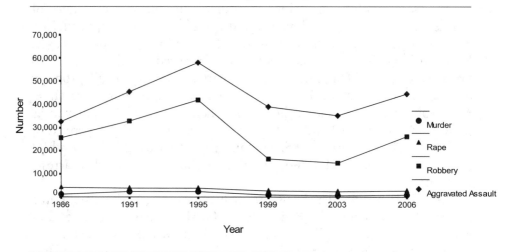

Source: Constructed by authors from UCR data.

FIGURE 1.5 Trend in Juvenile Property Crime, 1986-2006

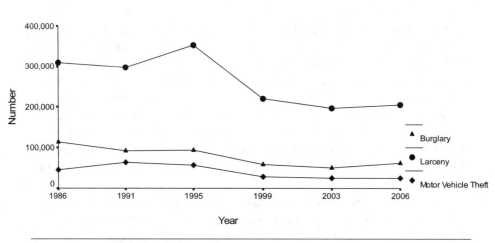

Source: Constructed by authors from UCR data.

Perhaps a better way to examine change over time is to consider the **offense rate** (typically the number of offenses per 100,000), which elimi-nates the influence of any changes in the number of potential offenders on the delinquency data. Juvenile arrest rates showed a steady increase throughout the 1960s and mid-1970s, leveled off and showed some decline in the late-1970s and 1980s, increased in the late 1980s and early 1990s, and has abated since the mid-1990s. One thing that is clear in both the raw number of arrests and the arrest rate figures is that official juvenile offending is higher today than 40 years ago, although the recent trend has been toward lower arrests.

A Critique of the UCR. The UCR is the longest running and most widely known and cited method of collecting information on crime in the United States. It began in 1931 and has continued on a yearly basis since that time. Despite this longevity and notoriety, the UCR has a number of flaws that must be considered when using the data (see O'Brien, 1985). The most frequent criticism is the fact that it reflects only those offenses known to the police. Many individuals, for whatever reason, opt not to contact the police when they are a victim or a witness to a crime. This failure to bring crimes to the attention of the police results in an under-count of crime in the United States. The unreported crimes are typically referred to as the **dark figure of crime**.

A second concern with the UCR is that it is voluntary, and it relies on the individual agencies to report their data accurately. Each agency tabulates and forwards its own data to the FBI. Political and economic pressures have been known to influence the accuracy of counts submitted to the UCR system. For example, changes in police procedure due to political decisions can alter the amount of attention a police department pays to a certain form of crime. Similarly, the simple reclassification of offenses from one category to another (i.e., listing "rapes" as "other sex offenses," or "aggravated assaults" as "simple assaults") can alter the reported crime rates. Decisions like these can greatly alter the annual offense counts and have an impact on trend data over time.

Another concern in using the UCR is the lack of information on offenders in much of the data. UCR arrest data reflect only those offenders who were caught in the course of the crime or ensuing investigation. The fact that only about 20 percent of all crimes are cleared by an arrest means that little is known about the offenders in most crimes. It is possible that UCR figures are distorted in terms of the age, race, and sex distribution of the total offending population. The UCR provides no information about the offender in roughly 80 percent of the crimes committed each year.

Another serious problem entails the fact that the UCR counts offenses and not offenders. It would be easy to claim that the number of offenders is equal to the number of reported offenses, but unfortunately, this would provide a highly inaccurate picture. Many offenders commit more than one offense over a period of time. Alternatively, some individuals may commit a single act (such as bank robbery) that legally constitutes more than one offense (robbery, assault, and possibly kidnapping). These problems make it difficult to estimate the number of offenders over any period of time using the UCR. The number of offenders is clearly not equal to the number of offenses.

A variety of other concerns must be considered in using the UCR data. Among these are the fact that legal definitions of crime change over time and vary from place to place. In addition, the methods of data collection have changed over time (particularly from hand to computer tabulation). A further concern is the fact that any selective enforcement of the law or bias in making arrests can result in an overrepresentation of certain individuals (such as lower-class youths) in the UCR figures.

Concerns over the UCR have led to the introduction of the **National Incident-Based Reporting System (NIBRS)**. The NIBRS system grew out of a report completed in the mid-1980s that examined the changing needs for data collection and analysis that could assist law enforcement in combating crime. The NIBRS data has several major advantages over the traditional UCR data. First, NIBRS collects detailed information on 22 categories of offenses with 46 specific crimes rather than just the eight Index offenses. Second, rather than count only the most serious Index offense committed, NIBRS reports on all of the offenses that occur during a criminal incident. Third, NIBRS data includes a wide array of information not found in the traditional UCR data and collects that data on each crime incident. Among the information included in this expanded data collection process is detailed information on the offenders (if known), the victim, the victim-offender relationship, injuries, and property loss.

Information on NIBRS can be found at http://www.fbi.gov/ucr/ucr.htm#nibrs

The great advantage of the NIBRS data is the ability of law enforcement and researchers to gain a more in-depth picture of the crime problem and to use that information to decide on appropriate courses of action. Unfortunately, participation in the NIBRS system requires increased data-entry requirements and data-processing abilities on the part of local law enforcement. The agencies must also meet stringent guidelines for participation. Because of these requirements, NIBRS has not been implemented nationally, and no nationally representative data are available for study. Local agencies using the NIBRS system, however, are able to undertake more sophisticated analyses of their crime problems.

The most problematic aspect of official police data for the study of delinquency is the combined issues of the dark figure of crime and the failure to identify offenders in the vast majority of all cases. It is due to these problems that alternative methods of unofficial crime and delinquency data have been developed. Before turning to these types of data collection, we will look at two additional official measures of delinquency.

Juvenile Court Statistics

Juvenile court data present a picture of the cases and the juveniles who reach the adjudication stage of the system. The numbers of juveniles who appear in these records are smaller than those found in police data. This is due primarily to the fact that most juveniles reach the court through contact with the police who filter and screen cases. Relatively few youths are referred to court directly by their families, schools, or other associates. In 2000, the police referred 84 percent of the cases in juvenile court (Puzzanchera et al., 2004). Table 1.6 presents data on delinquency cases in juvenile court. In 2002, approximately 1,615,400 youths reached the juvenile court for delinquent offenses. This translates into a rate of 52 out of every 1,000 youths. Data since 1960 (not presented) show a steady increase in the rate of youths entering the court. In 1960, the rate was 20.1. The 2002 rate represents a greater than 250 percent increase.

TABLE 1.6 Number and Rates of Youths in Juvenile Court—1991, 1994, 1997, 2000, 2002

	1991	1994	1997	2000	2002
Offense Type	**Number of Offenses**				
Delinquency					
Person	278,151	360,574	392,568	375,592	387,500
Property	848,896	867,770	847,556	668,588	624,900
Drugs	65,422	131,141	194,457	194,187	193,200
Public Order	221,051	306,375	385,122	394,975	409,800
Offense Type	**Rate per 1,000 Population**				
Delinquency					
Person	10.0	12.1	12.5	11.5	12.4
Property	30.5	29.1	27.0	20.5	20.0
Drugs	2.4	4.4	6.2	5.9	6.2
Public Order	7.9	10.3	12.3	12.1	13.1

Source: Constructed by authors from data presented by C. Puzzanchera, A.L. Stahl, T.A. Finnegan, N. Tierney, and H.N. Snyder (2004). *Juvenile Court Statistics 2000.* Pittsburgh: National Center for Juvenile Justice; A. Stahl, T. Finnegan, and W. Kang (2003). *Easy Access to Juvenile Court Statistics: 1985-2000.* Washington, DC: U.S. Department of Justice; and A. Stahl, C. Puzzanchera, S. Livsey, A. Sladky, T. Finnegan, N. Tierney, and H.N. Snyder (2007). *Juvenile Court Statistics: 2003-2004.* Pittsburgh: National Center for Juvenile Justice.

Information on type of offense, sex, and race is also available in the court statistics. Like the UCR data, males dominate throughout the juvenile court statistics. The number of both male and female delin-

quency cases increased since 1985. While the number of male cases peaked in 1996-1997 and has fallen since that time, the number of female

> Additional juvenile court statistics are available at http://ncjj.servehttp.com/ NCJJWebsite/publications_detail.asp?n =NCJ218587

cases increased from 1985 to 1997 and has remained relatively stable since 1997 (Puzzanchera et al., 2004). The number of person, public order, and drug cases has clearly increased since 1985, but property crime cases have been decreasing since the mid-1990s after increasing from 1985 and the early 1990s (Puzzanchera et al., 2005).

Similar to UCR figures, court data show that property offenses dominate at about 40 percent of all delinquency cases. Public order offenses (such as disorderly conduct and liquor violations) and offenses against persons each contribute approximately 25 percent to the juvenile court caseload. Not surprisingly, older youths are referred at a much greater rate than are younger youths for delinquency offenses (rate of 109.1 for 17-year-olds; 4.6 for 10-year-olds) (Puzzanchera et al., 2005).

In terms of race, raw court numbers are dominated by white youths (78% of all petitions). Despite the fact that more white youths appear in juvenile court, blacks are overrepresented given their proportion in the population. The 2002 delinquency case rate for white youths is 44.4 per 1,000, while the rate for black youths is more than double at 94.0, and the rate for other races is 30.9 (Puzzanchera et al., 2005).

Juvenile Corrections Statistics

A third official source of information on juveniles coming into contact with the juvenile justice system is records kept on juvenile correctional facilities. The U.S. Justice Department routinely conducts a census of the population of juvenile facilities. As with juvenile court statistics, the numbers of youths who appear in these statistics are smaller than the UCR and court figures. Juvenile facilities rely heavily upon the juvenile court for their clients, and few of the youths coming into contact with the court are sentenced to confinement. Therefore, the figures found in data from juvenile facilities represent only a fraction of all the youths having contact with the juvenile system.

Table 1.7 presents data on youths in public and private juvenile facilities in 2003. The data in the table represent a one-day count, and the daily totals would vary around these figures. For 2003, public facilities handled more than 66,000 youths, and private institutions dealt with an additional 30,000 on any one day (Snyder and Sickmund, 2006). Information on the sex of offender and type of offense is also provided in correctional data. Not unlike UCR or court statistics, correctional figures show that most offenders are male. Table 1.7 shows that females make up only 17 percent of the private and 14 percent of the public institutions' clients.

Few differences appear in the reason for admission when comparing public and private institutions. Each type of institution handles roughly the same proportion of youths committing different types of offenses. The only significant difference appears in status offenses, where 11 percent of the youths in private institutions are there for these violations, compared with only 2 percent of the youths in public facilities.

TABLE 1.7 Characteristics of Juveniles in Correctional Facilities: Average One-Day Count—2003

Characteristic	Public Facility		Private Facility	
Number of Juveniles	66,210		30,321	
Sex:				
Male	58,265	(88%)	26,470	(83%)
Female	7,945	(12%)	4,851	(17%)
Reason for Admission:				
Person Offense	23,499	(35%)	9,671	(32%)
Property Offense	18,740	(28%)	9,073	(27%)
Drug Offense	4,851	(7%)	3,137	(10%)
Public Order Offense	6,782	(10%)	3,866	(9%)
Status Offense	1,548	(2%)	3,312	(11%)
Technical Violation	10,790	(16%)	3,262	(11%)

Source: Compiled from H.N. Snyder and M. Sickmund (2006). *Juvenile Offenders and Victims: 2006 National Report.* Pittsburgh: National Center for Juvenile Justice.

The trend in correctional figures is somewhat interesting. Figures indicate that the number of incarcerated youths steadily increased until the late 1990s, with reductions since. The one-day count of youths in public and private facilities increased from 80,091 in 1983 to 99,008 in 1993 (a 24% increase) to 108,757 in 1999 (a further 10% increase), although the number decreased by 11 percent to 96,531 in 2003. The earlier increases may be due to the increased violence and drug problems in the late 1980s and early 1990s. Recent moderation in incarceration mirrors the reduction in arrest statistics.

Correctional data is available at http://www.ncjrs.gov/pdffiles1/ojjdp/202885.pdf

Summary of Official Statistics

Each of the various official measures of delinquency presents a slightly different view of juvenile offending. In terms of numbers of offenses, the UCR presents the most disturbing picture due to the large numbers of offenses it reflects. In addition to the number of offenses, the UCR provides detailed information on a variety of demographic and crime-related characteristics. Unfortunately, as noted earlier, this source of data has a number of inherent defects that limit its usefulness, in particular its reliance upon offenses known to the police.

Juvenile court statistics and correctional facility data also present a picture of juvenile misconduct that is somewhat narrow. A large part of the problem with these figures lies in the fact that they are greatly dependent on the productivity of the police. Most youths entering the courts and institutions initiate their journey by way of police contact. Any failure at the police level, therefore, carries over to these other counts. The increased levels of status offenses in court and correctional data is one point where discrepancies with the arrest data appear. This is probably due to court referrals from sources other than the police. The problems and differences do not make the information useless, though. Rather, the data can be used to assess the workings of the institutions over time and provide insight into the juvenile system. They cannot be used to portray the extent of the juvenile crime problem accurately.

Self-Report Measures of Delinquency

Self-report measures attempt to gauge the level of delinquency by asking individuals to tell of their participation in deviant activity. This approach has a number of advantages. First, it is possible to measure both actions "known to the police" and those that are not known by official agents of social control. Second, it becomes possible to gather information on all offenders and not just those few who are arrested for an offense. Self-reports do not need an arrest in order to have information on the perpetrator. Third, self-report surveys can ask a variety of questions designed to elicit information useful in understanding why an individual violates the law. Information routinely collected includes data on family background (such as broken home, parental affection), economic status (occupation, income), education, attitudes (toward school, family or work), friends' behavior, and many others as well as direct questions about the deviant behavior. This type of information is not available from most official delinquency measures. For these and other reasons, self-report methods have proliferated in recent years.

Self-report surveys have a fairly long history in juvenile justice. One of the earliest surveys was developed by James Short and Ivan Nye (see Figure 1.6). This survey asked youths to note the frequency with which they committed each of 23 items. The items in the scale were dominated by status and minor offenses. The few serious crimes included in the original list (such as stealing over $50) were deleted in subsequent forms of the scales, which included only the seven starred items.

Self-report scales like the **Short–Nye instrument** invariably uncover a great deal of delinquent activity. Indeed, various studies using these types of scales show that virtually every person is a delinquent. This is due to the type of questions asked in the scale. It is hard to conceive of anyone saying they never committed any of the behaviors asked. Defying parental authority or trying alcohol at some time are rather universal activities by juveniles. Asking if the individual has "ever" committed an act contributes to the high levels of positive responses. Compared to official counts of delinquency, such self-reports show a great deal more deviance.

FIGURE 1.6 Short and Nye Self-Reported Delinquency Items

Defied parents' authority*
Driven too fast or recklessly
Taken little things (worth less than $2) that did not belong to you*
Taken things of medium value ($2-$50)
Taken things of large value ($50)
Used force (strong-arm methods) to get money from another person
Taken part in "gang fights"
Taken a car for a ride without the owner's knowledge
Bought or drank beer, wine, or liquor (including drinking at home)*
Bought or drank beer, wine, or liquor (outside your home)
Drank beer, wine, or liquor in your own home
Deliberate property damage*
Used or sold narcotic drugs
Had sex relations with another person of the same sex (not masturbation)*
Had sex relations with a person of the opposite sex
Gone hunting or fishing without a license (or violated other game laws)
Taken things you didn't want
"Beat up" on kids who hadn't done anything to you
Hurt someone to see them squirm

* Commonly used items in subsequent self-report studies.

Source: J.F. Short and I. Nye (1958). "Extent of Unrecorded Delinquency: Tentative Conclusion." *Journal of Criminal Law, Criminology and Police Science* 49:296-302.

More recent self-report surveys, such as the **Monitoring the Future (MTF)** survey (see Table 1.8), include many more serious offenses and elicit significantly fewer positive responses. The MTF project includes questions on hitting teachers, group fighting, use of weapons, robbery, and aggravated assault. The data in Table 1.8 show the great differences in response rates between less serious and more serious offenses. For example, arguing or fighting with your parents is reported by 90 percent of the total respondents, while only 3 percent report hitting an instructor and 4 percent report using a knife or gun in a robbery or setting fire to someone's property. An inspection of the MTF data by sex reveals similar levels of offending by males and females. Only for "arguing or having a fight" with one's parents do more females report offending. Males exceed females by more than 10 percent only for

More detailed MTF data can be found at http://www.monitoringthefuture.org/

getting into a serious fight at school, theft under $50, burglary, and damaging school property. In the remaining offense categories, males and females are within 10 percentage points of one another. In terms of racial breakdown, in only one category (arguing or having a fight with parents) do whites and blacks differ by more than 10 percent. For most categories the difference is less than 5 percent.

These self-report data show that, although many persons commit various deviant acts, the majority of subjects confine their activity to minor offenses. Indeed, when major, serious offenses are included, there is a great decrease in the level of reported offending. The figures become much more similar to those in official statistics.

One problem with many self-report surveys is the fact that they are one-shot studies. That is, they take a single measurement on one sample of youths. There is no second sample to compare the results to and no repeat measurement taken on the same or similar persons at a later point in time. Several notable exceptions to this are the Monitoring the Future (MTF) project and the **National Youth Survey (NYS)**.

Each of these surveys are (or have been) undertaken on a regular basis. The MTF project surveys a national sample of youths and young adults each year, primarily about drug use. While different respondents participate each year, it is possible to examine general trends and changes over time. The NYS used a **panel design**, which means the same set of individuals were interviewed repeatedly over an extended number of years. The NYS began with a group of 11- to 17-year-olds from across the United States and reinterviewed them over a period of years. This allowed researchers to compare the number of offenses and changes in offending over time. These and other self-report surveys find high levels of delinquency when minor and less serious behaviors are considered, but show reduced levels of serious offenses and behaviors.

Age Distribution

The age distribution of offending in self-report data generally mirrors that of official data. Offending increases as individuals reach later teen and young adult years. Some variation emerges when the contact of the self-report survey changes. Surveys dominated by minor and status offenses reveal that criminal activity is largely a juvenile problem. Likewise, younger respondents tend to report less offending when serious offenses (such as aggravated assault and felony theft) are considered. Older youths report more serious offending and substance use.

Race Distribution

Unlike in official data, most differences in offending by race are modest in size. Data from the MTF project show only minor variation between black respondents and white respondents. Similarly, NYS data reveal a greater percentage of blacks involved in felony assaults, some minor assaults, and robbery, while white percentages exceed black figures for hitting parents, minor theft offenses, damage offenses, and most other categories of crime (Elliott et al., 1983). These differences, however, are generally very small and range in the area of one to five percentage points.

Sex Distribution

Self-report surveys display sex differences similar to those found in official data. Almost without exception, males report higher involvement in offending than females, although the differences are dependent on the type of behavior. Table 1.8 includes data on the sex differential in the MTF. Like the race findings, many of the differences in the male data and female data are small and appear mainly in the more serious offenses.

TABLE 1.8 Percent Reporting One or More Delinquent Acts in Last 12 Months, Class of 2003—Monitoring the Future Survey

Delinquent Activity	Total	Sex		Race	
		Males	Females	Whites	Blacks
Argued or had fight with either of your parents	89.7	87.6	92.4	93.1	75.7
Hit an instructor or supervisor	3.2	5.2	0.9	2.5	1.5
Gotten into a serious fight in school or at work	14.3	19.4	8.8	12.1	18.4
Taken part in a fight where a group of your friends were against another group	19.8	24.6	14.9	17.8	21.4
Hurt someone badly enough to need bandages or a doctor	12.0	8.9	5.1	10.2	14.4
Used a knife or gun of some other thing (like a club) to get something from a person	3.9	6.5	0.9	2.4	2.8
Taken something not belonging to you worth under $50	27.7	34.2	21.1	26.9	21.2
Taken something not belonging to you worth over $50	9.6	13.7	5.1	8.4	7.0
Taken something from a store without paying for it	26.8	30.9	22.8	23.4	30.3
Taken a car that didn't belong to someone in your family without permission of the owner	5.3	8.0	2.4	4.0	5.0
Taken part of a car without permission of the owner	5.6	9.0	2.1	4.3	5.2
Gone into some house or building when you weren't supposed to be there	23.0	29.0	17.3	22.9	19.6
Set fire to someone's property on purpose	3.8	6.7	0.9	3.4	2.7
Damaged school property on purpose	13.2	19.9	6.4	12.6	9.2
Damaged property at work on purpose	6.8	11.1	2.6	6.7	4.7
Been arrested and taken to a police station	8.0	11.6	4.1	7.1	8.6

Source: Adapted by authors from A.L. Pastore and K. Maguire (2008). *Sourcebook of Criminal Justice Statistics, Online*. Available at: http://www.albany.edu/sourcebook

Critique of Self-Report Data

Self-report studies paint a different picture of offending compared to official figures and pose separate problems for researchers. The most common concern with self-report data involves the truthfulness of the respondents. Interestingly, most investigations into the validity of the self-report data show that the figures are fairly accurate. This assessment is based on studies that compare self-report results to lie-detector tests, repeated measures, and cross checks with other forms of data (Clarke and Tifft, 1966; Gold, 1970; Hardt and Peterson-Hardt, 1977; Hindelang et al., 1981; Lab and Allen, 1984). The greatest discrepancies between self-report and official figures can be attributed to the different domains of behavior that are tapped by the two methods. Official records focus more on serious offenses, while self-reports often probe more minor offending.

An additional shortcoming of self-report data is the focus on juveniles. Due to the problems of locating accessible groups of adults, most self-report research has been carried out on youths. Although the data are rich with information on kids, there is little opportunity to compare the findings to those found on adults. Typical adult samples found in self-report surveys deal with institutionalized adults or young adults in college settings. Neither of these two groups are representative of the general adult population. The method of selecting youths for self-report surveys may also bias the results. The typical use of school students in surveys may inadvertently miss high-rate offenders who are truants or dropouts and not present at the time of data collection.

Despite these shortcomings/concerns, there are great advantages to using self-report data. First, these data provide information on offenses not known by the police. Second, the method is able to probe the number of times each individual commits an offense. Much official data (especially police records) are not readily set up to track an individual over time. Self-reports, however, can simply ask about the number and frequency of offending. Third, self-report surveys often ask a variety of questions about the individual's background, which provides a rich base of information on the demographic and social factors related to delinquent activity. Finally, the richness of the data allows for a more complete discussion of the reasons why an individual acts in a certain way than the data found in official records.

Comparing the Delinquency Measures

The different types of delinquency measures (official and self-report) show both similarities and differences. In general, they show that delinquency is a widespread problem. It is not restricted to any one group, area, or type of offense. The level of offending increased throughout the 1960s and early 1970s, leveled off and showed some decreases in the late 1970s and 1980s, increased in the late 1980s and early 1990s (particularly in serious personal offenses), and has been decreasing until the last several years. There is a clear diversity in offending. Youths are involved in all types of behavior—from status offenses to serious personal crimes. Property crimes dominate in all measures, and personal offenses are the least common.

Most differences in the measures appear in the relative magnitude of offending and by offending subgroups in the population. Self-report measures uncover more offending than official measures. Official measures themselves differ in magnitude, with police figures leading court and correctional data. In terms of demographics, official figures show a much larger number of black offenders than self-report measures. Self-report statistics find little racial difference in offending. Similar discrepancies emerge when considering the sex of the offenders. While males dominate in magnitude of offending, official figures show the sexes committing different types of offenses. Self-report data, however, tend to portray the sexes as participating in the same types of behavior.

The differences between the measures are a result of the measurement techniques. Official records provide an ongoing look at the level and change in delinquency from year to year according to the formal justice system. These records reflect offenses that are brought to the attention of the authorities. Actions that are not reported but are withheld from public officials are lost to these records. Self-reports typically portray a larger delinquency problem than official figures. The cause of this is the type of activities that are probed in the survey. Surveys that inquire about minor status offenses will always find high delinquency levels. When more serious offenses form the core of the questionnaire, however, the number of delinquents falls to lower levels.

No single method of measuring delinquency should be considered better than the others. The usefulness of the measures depends entirely on the question that is being answered. Each method provides a different set of information about delinquency. Official records are useful for noting change in official processing and handling of youths over time. They also provide a long-term set of data that allows the inspection of changes over time. Official data are also rich in information about various demographic and offense factors not found in other measures. Self-reports provide a measure of delinquency based on the offender's viewpoint. They are capable of addressing behaviors that may not result in arrests and lead to official records. These measures are rich in data on minor crimes, the number of offenses an individual commits, demographics on offenders, and why an individual acts in a certain way.

SUMMARY

The study of delinquency depends heavily on the definition of delinquency and the measurement of the problem. The definition is not clear-cut and varies greatly from one study to another. Delinquency can be limited to those acts that are violations of the criminal code, signify those actions that are illegal only for juveniles, represent some combination of both criminal and status offenses, or be molded to fit the criminological question of each researcher.

The outcome of this search for a definition of delinquency is a vast array of different measures of delinquency and resultant claims about the level of delinquent activity. The major methods of measuring delinquency—official and self-report—rely on somewhat different conceptions of what constitutes delinquency. The UCR, for example, is oriented more toward a criminal law point of view and considers only two very broad status offense categories (runaway, curfew, and loitering) among the 29 offense categories. Conversely, self-reports often rely heavily on status offenses in their surveys and include only a few (mostly property) criminal offenses. Throughout this great confusion of definitions and measures there is no clear sign of arriving at a consensus on the issues.

Perhaps the reason behind the great discrepancies in definitions and measures can be found in the history of juvenile justice. The juvenile system has grown quickly over the past century and has seen many changes. Part of this is due to changes in the view society holds of youthful offenders. It may also be attributable to changes in the field of criminology and corrections. The changes in the juvenile system and the impact of various factors on the definition and extent of delinquency make up the substance for the next chapter on the history of juvenile justice.

DISCUSSION QUESTIONS

1. You have been appointed to write a definition of delinquency for the state legislature. You can either propose a new definition or rely on the existing definition. What is your definition? Why is it best, and why should it be accepted?

2. You have been asked to research each of the following questions or issues. What type of delinquency measure(s) will you use and why?
   - How much delinquency is there in the country?
   - What characterizes the typical juvenile offender?
   - What are some of the causes for delinquency?
   - Has the delinquency rate increased or decreased over the past 15 years?

3. A discussion has arisen over the best measure of delinquency. As an expert on such matters, you are asked to present an unbiased view of the strengths and weaknesses of official and self-report measures. Be as thorough as possible.

Chapter 2

THE HISTORY OF JUVENILE JUSTICE

Important Terms

abandonment

apprenticeship

Chancery Court

child savers

Commonwealth v. Fisher

dowry

Ex parte Crouse

houses of refuge

infanticide

involuntary servitude

Kent v. United States

nullification

parens patriae

right to intervention

wet-nursing

What You Need to Know

- Throughout most of history, youthful offenders were handled under the same laws and system as adults.

- The early institutions for handling juveniles (houses of refuge and reformatories) emerged in the 1800s as an outgrowth of concern over poverty and the need to train youths to be productive members of society.

- The first recognized juvenile court was in Cook County, Illinois, in 1899 with a focus on helping youths and not punishment.

- *Parens patriae* became the philosophical basis for the new juvenile court with a focus on handling youths as parents would handle their children.

- The early court cases of *Ex parte Crouse* and *Commonwealth v. Fisher* affirmed the right of the state to intervene in a child's life even if the parents objected.

- Platt and others argue that the juvenile court was not developed solely out of the benevolent intentions of those involved, rather it was developed as a tool of capitalism to ensure a complacent work force.

- Today, juvenile courts operate under a number of different rationales besides *parens patriae*, including punishment, deterrence, child welfare, restorative justice, and rehabilitation.

INTRODUCTION

There is no question that juvenile misbehavior is a major concern in modern American society. No matter which definition of delinquency or which form of measurement is used, the level of delinquent activity is high. Any understanding of the juvenile justice system must begin with an analysis of delinquency in a historical framework. Interestingly, the history of juvenile delinquency and juvenile justice is a relatively short one. While deviance on the part of young persons has always been a fact of life, societal intervention and participation in the handling of juvenile transgressors has gained most of its momentum in the last 100-150 years. This chapter will discuss the state of affairs leading to the development of a juvenile justice system and briefly examine the early workings of that system.

PROPERTY AND PERSON

An understanding of the development of juvenile justice must begin with an understanding of the place of children in society. Throughout most of history, there was no such status as "child." Youthful members of society did not enjoy a separate status that brought with it a distinct set of expectations, behaviors, and/or privileges. Rather, the young were considered either property or people. The very young, from birth to age five or six, held much the same status as any other property in society. They were subject to the same dictates as other property—bought, sold, and disposed of according to the needs of the owner. Once the individual reached the age of five or six, he or she became a full-fledged member of society and was expected to act according to the same mandates placed on all "adult" members of society (Aries, 1962).

The state of indifference toward the young and the absence of any separate status are easy to understand within a historical setting. First, the life expectancy of the average person was short. More importantly, the infant mortality rate exceeded 50 percent. The failure to develop a personal, caring attitude for infants, therefore, can be viewed as a defense mechanism. Indifference reduced or eliminated the pain and sorrow that would accompany the loss of the infant. A second explanation for the lack of concern over the young entailed the inability of many families to provide for the young. Families lived from day to day on what they could produce. Each child represented an increased burden to the already overburdened family.

The inability to provide economically for a child led to a variety of practices. **Infanticide,** or the killing of young children, was a common response to the appearance of an unwanted and demanding child prior to the fourth century (and continued in some places into the fourteenth century) (Mause, 1974). Mothers would kill their young in order to alleviate the future needs of providing for the child. The great chances that the infant would die anyway from disease or illness made this practice easier for the parents.

The killing of female offspring was especially prominent. Females were considered more burdensome than males. This was because they would not be as productive as a male if they lived and because of the **dowry** practice. The marriage of a daughter often necessitated the provision of goods by the female's family to the groom. The basic rationale was that the groom and his family were assuming the burden of caring for a marginally productive female. The dowry practice was especially problematic for the poor, who could not provide a sufficient enticement for a prospective husband. The killing of a female infant, therefore, not only removed the immediate needs of caring for the infant but also eliminated the future need of a dowry.

A practice similar to infanticide was **abandonment**. Parents would abandon their children to die for the same reasons underlying infanticide. Abandonment grew to be the more acceptable practice in the fourth to thirteenth centuries and appeared as late as the seventeenth and eighteenth centuries. Infanticide and abandonment were not restricted to the poor members of society. Historical records show that even the affluent accepted the killing of infants. One prime example of this is the story of Oedipus the king. Oedipus, the son of the Greek king and queen, was destined to kill his father and marry his mother. In order to avoid this fate, the parents had the infant Oedipus bound at the ankles, taken to the mountains, and abandoned.

Another method that appeared for handling youths was **wet-nursing**. A wet-nurse was a surrogate mother paid to care for a child (Mause, 1974). Wealthy families would hire other women to raise their children until they had reached the stage of "adulthood," at which time the child would return and assume a productive role in the family. Poor women, who assumed the role of wet nurses, would kill their natural offspring in order to save their mother's milk for the "paying" youths. The arrangement served a monetary purpose for the poor while relieving the wealthy of an unwanted responsibility.

Children who survived the first few years of life became subjected to a new set of activities. These new actions, however, retained the economic concerns that allowed for infanticide and other practices. The inability to provide for the needs of the family prompted the development of **involuntary servitude** and **apprenticeship** for the young. In essence, these actions were nothing more than the sale of youths by the family. The father, by selling the children, accomplished two things. First, he alleviated the burden of having to feed and clothe the person. Second, he gained something of "greater" value in return—money, a farm animal, food, or some other necessity of life. Such practices also were promoted as a means of providing labor for those in need. The rise of industrialization created a need for skilled labor, which could be learned by children through apprenticeships.

A second set of reasons behind the apprenticeship and servitude of youths was the general view that individuals who survived the years of infancy were simply "little adults." Indeed, children participated in the same activities as adults. Children worked at trades, drank alcohol, dueled, and participated in sex with adults and other young people. Part of this can be attributed to the lack of distinct expectations for youths. There was no period of schooling or education that separated the young from the actions of adults. Additionally, the living conditions of the family placed all ages within the same set of social conditions. The family home was typically a single room used for all activities. Eating, sleeping, and entertaining occurred in the same place and in view of everyone. The youthful members of society, therefore, learned and participated early in life.

The general view that children were the same as adults extended to the realm of legal sanctioning. Children were viewed as adults and were subject to the same rules and regulations as adults (Empey, 1982). There did not exist a separate system for dealing with youthful offenders. At best, the father was responsible for controlling the child and his choices for punishment had no bounds. Additionally, society could sanction youths in the same way as adults. The law made no distinction based on the age of the offender. In fact, youths could be (and were) sentenced to death for various deviant actions. While the law allowed for and prescribed harsh punishments, there is some question as to how frequently the more serious actions were actually used. Platt (1977) suggested that, while many youths could be sentenced to death, few received such a sentence, and most of those who did were never put to death. Similarly, Faust and Brantingham (1979) claimed that a process of **nullification**, or refusal to enforce the law against children, took place because of the lack of penalties geared specifically for juvenile offenders.

Throughout most of history, children held no special status in society. They did not receive any special, protected treatment. If anything, they were subjected to harsher treatment than adults. In terms of legal proscriptions, children could be held liable for the same actions and in the same fashion as adults. There was no legal term of "delinquency" under which the state could intervene with youths. Youths fell under the same statutes and guidelines that were used with adult offenders.

The concept of childhood began to emerge in the sixteenth and seventeenth centuries. It was during this time that medical advancements brought about a lengthening of the life expectancy of youths. Youths also began to be viewed as different from adults. They were in need of protection, assistance, and guidance in order to grow up uncorrupted by the world. This movement was led by clergy and scholars of the time. These leaders saw the young as a source of attack on the immoral and sinful aspects of society. Youths, who were not yet corrupted, had to be shielded from society and trained for their future role in the world. Children were seen as a catalyst for general social change. Childhood came to be seen as a period of time during which the young could receive an education and moral training without the pressures of adulthood.

Accompanying these changes were alterations in how youthful offenders should be disciplined. Responses to misbehavior began to be tailored to fit the age of the offender. In England, youths under the age of seven could not be held responsible for their actions, individuals between eight and 14 could be held responsible only when it could be shown they understood the consequences of their actions, and youths age 14 and over were considered adults (Empey, 1982). While these types of changes began to recognize the difference between juveniles and adults, the actions taken against offenders remained the same, regardless of the age of the offender.

TABLE 2.1 Highlights in the Development of Juvenile Justice

16th-17th century	concept of "childhood" begins to emerge
1825	first House of Refuge opened in New York
1838	*Ex parte Crouse* established "*parens patriae*" as basis for state intervention with youths
1841	probation started in Boston by John Augustus
mid-1800s	development of cottage reformatories for juveniles
1892	New York legislation enacted providing for separate trials for youthful offenders
1899	first juvenile court in Cook County (Chicago), Illinois
1905	*Commonwealth v. Fisher*—reaffirmation of *parens patriae* philosophy for juvenile court
1912	U.S. Children's Bureau established to oversee juvenile justice
1920	all but three states with juvenile court; 320 separate juvenile courts in the United States
1920-1960	growth of juvenile justice system—separate institutions, few legal challenges, new agencies and treatments
1966	*Kent v. United States*—beginning of legal challenges to *parens patriae* and juvenile justice processing
1970s–present	increasing growth of due process in juvenile justice and emphasis on punishment in juvenile and criminal justice systems

THE RISE OF JUVENILE INSTITUTIONS

Changes in the methods of dealing with problem youths corresponded to the changes occurring in American society of the early 1800s. During this time, there was a great movement toward the cities.

Industrialization was drawing families out of the countryside and to the cities. The cities were growing in both size and density. In addition, the individuals moving to the cities brought with them a variety of outlooks and ideas. This growing diversity in the population was especially true of the cities in the United States, which were attracting immigrants from a wide range of European countries. The promise of a better life in the new world also brought with it a great deal of poverty.

Methods for dealing with problem youths grew out of the establishment of ways to handle poor people in the cities (see Rothman, 1971, 1980). The poor were seen both as a threat to society and in need of help. The primary response for dealing with the poor entailed the training of the poor. It was assumed that these people could be made into productive members of society. Unfortunately, there was little that could be done with the adult poor. They were beyond the training stage and were set in their ways. The children of the poor, however, were viewed as trainable. A key aspect of this training was the removal of the child from the bad influences and substandard training of the poor parents. While this view became prominent in the 1800s, Krisberg and Austin (1978) noted that as early as 1555 the English established the Bridewell Institution in London to handle youthful beggars. The primary emphasis of the institution was the handling of poor and destitute youths, although in practice the institution handled all problem youths, including delinquents. The Bridewell Institution was envisioned as a place where the youths would be trained in a skill that they could use after they were released.

The establishment of institutions in the early 1800s in the United States closely followed the ideas of the Bridewell Institution. The institutions were viewed as places for training those individuals who were not productive and who seemed to pose a threat to society. There was a heavy emphasis on the problems of the poor. The establishment of institutions for the poor and delinquent also reflected a shift in the view of causes of deviance. Throughout most of history, deviance was viewed as a result of problems inherent in the individual. The 1800s, meanwhile, witnessed a growth in the belief that deviance was a result of poor environmental conditions. A change in the environment, therefore, should result in changed behavior. The earlier the individual was placed into a new environment, the better the chances of having a positive impact on the person's actions. The establishment of new institutions also provided the court with an alternative to doing nothing with juveniles or placing them in adult institutions.

Houses of Refuge

The establishment of institutions for children in the 1800s clearly conformed to these ideas. These early institutions were called **houses of refuge** and were envisioned as a place for separating the youth from the detrimental environment of the city. The first house of refuge was established in New York in 1825 and was followed by institutions in Boston (1826) and Philadelphia (1828). The rationale and setup of the houses of refuge closely followed the concern for the poor and the need for training discussed above.

Central aspects in the handling of youths were indeterminate sentences, education, skills training, hard work, religious training, parental discipline, and apprenticeships (Pisciotta, 1983). The use of education, skills training, hard work, and apprenticeships were clear indications that the goal was to produce a productive member of society. Indeterminate sentences allowed the institution to work with each person on an individual basis. Where one youth may benefit from a short period of intervention, another child may require extended work and assistance. The interest in religious training and parental discipline carried over the historical ideas that the best methods of training lay in the realm of the family and the church. The families of the youths in the institution were considered to be lacking in the ability to provide these basic needs. The houses of refuge were envisioned as shelters and sanctuaries that would protect and nurture their wards away from the corrupting influences of the city and the poor family (Rothman, 1971).

The establishment of the houses of refuge also was seen as a means of removing children from the criminogenic influences of the workhouses and adult jails (Krisberg and Austin, 1978). Reformers saw the prior methods of handling youths through the adult system as nothing more than placing poor and problem juveniles in contact with adult criminal offenders. The natural outcome would be "schools for crime" that produced more problems than they solved. The houses of refuge supposedly differed by offering education and training in useful skills within a setting that allowed for control and discipline of the children.

While the rationale and the goals of the houses of refuge were laudable, the daily operations and the impact of the institutions were questionable. Many of the activities were far removed from the real world. Inmates had little, if any, contact with members of the opposite sex. Military behavior was the norm. This included enforced silence, marching to and from different activities, the wearing of uniforms, and swift and habitual corporal punishment (Rothman, 1971). Apprenticeships often failed to be more than simple slave labor. Many of the apprenticeships were on farms in the country. Problem youths were apprenticed to ship captains and sent to sea. In general, there was no quality control or oversight for the apprenticeships. The institutional labor was often dictated by contractual obligations that led to exploitation of the youths by the institutional masters. Children were bribed, beaten, and even subjected to extended incarceration if the monetary interests of the administrators were at stake (Pisciotta, 1982).

Besides failing to provide the basic tools that they promised, the houses of refuge also failed in other respects. For the most part, these institutions were nothing but new prisons. They were tremendously overcrowded. This overcrowding was partly due to the admission of persons not suited for the goals of the institutions. The houses of refuge served the poor and destitute, and the delinquent youths. At the same time, they handled poverty-stricken adults and adult offenders. The overcrowding of the facilities by such diverse groups of inmates changed the focus of daily operations from the goals of education and training to that of simple custody and discipline. The establishment of institutions like the Lyman School for Boys in 1848 by the state of Massachusetts eliminated the housing of adult and juvenile offenders in the same facility but carried on the tradition of overcrowding and related problems. In general, the early houses of refuge failed to provide their stated goals and settled into a process very reminiscent of that of the adult prisons and jails that had previously been the norm for handling youths.

New Reformatories

The failure of the early houses of refuge did not lead to the end of juvenile institutions. The problems of the houses of refuge were well known by the mid-1800s. While the practice of the institutions had failed, proponents argued that the principles underlying intervention were correct. The issue, therefore, was in proper implementation of intervention. Emphasis on education, training, and parental discipline led to the establishment of "cottage" reformatories.

The cottage setup was intended to closely parallel a family. Concerned surrogate parents would oversee the training and education of a small number of problem youths. Discipline would be intermixed with the care and concern typical of family life. Most of the cottages were located in the country and emphasized work on the farm. This was supposed to separate the youth from the criminogenic features of the urban environment and instill a sense of hard, honest work in the charges. The idea of indeterminate sentencing carried over to the cottage approach.

Other changes in the handling of youths accompanied the growth of these cottage reformatories. Foremost among these features was the development of probation in 1841 by John Augustus. While the early use of probation was centered on adult offenders, by 1869 the state of Massachusetts dictated that the State Board of Charities would participate in, and take charge of, court cases involving youthful offenders (Krisberg and Austin, 1978). Probation officers would assist in the gathering of information on the youths, suggest alternative means of intervention, and oversee the placement of juveniles in reformatories and apprenticeships. Another method of dealing with youths, in accordance with the cottage idea, entailed the "placing out" of juveniles into foster homes. For the most part, these placements were the same as apprenticeships.

Such placements were seen as an alternative to institutionalization and allowed for the training of youths in a worthwhile occupation.

Unfortunately, like the earlier houses of refuge, these new alternatives for handling youths faced many of the same problems. The institutions and cottages became terribly overcrowded to the point that custody became the primary concern. Apprenticeships proved to be little more than slave labor, and youths often fled at the first opportunity. One analysis of 210 apprenticed individuals found that 72 percent of the youths either ran away or returned to the institution (Pisciotta, 1979). The harsh treatment of the youths in the institutions led to running away, the setting of fires, and various sexual problems (Pisciotta, 1982). The inability to handle some youths prompted the establishment of special facilities such as the Elmira Reformatory in 1876. Unfortunately, Elmira accepted both juveniles and young adults and negated the premise of separating youths from criminogenic older offenders. A final problem with the institutions was the continued mixing of both deviant and destitute youths in the same facilities. The institutions considered that being poor was closely tied to deviant activity and, as a result, intervened in the lives of lower-class individuals regardless of the existence (or lack) of a delinquent or criminal act.

Institutions for Females

Throughout the development of alternatives for handling boys, little attention was paid to females. Problem girls were dealt with in the same institutions as males and adults. Part of the reason for this was the relatively small number of females officially handled by agents of social control. Exceptions to this situation began to appear in the mid-1800s with the establishment of separate institutions for girls. One of the most well known facilities for females was the Lancaster State Industrial School for Girls in Massachusetts. The girls committed to Lancaster had the same basic background as boys found in other institutions. They were mostly from poor, immigrant families who were faced with the vagaries and problems of the urban environment (Brenzel, 1983). The institutions were set up as family cottages in order to deal with these problems.

The hoped-for end product of the institutions for girls was the production of females capable of fulfilling their place in society. Where boys were to become productive laborers, females were to learn how to be good housewives and mothers (Brenzel, 1983). Success with the girls was gauged by successful marriage and parenthood. Much of the concern centered on the plight of future generations that were to be raised by the problem girls and not on the girls themselves. Unfortunately, these institutions fared no better than those handling boys. While some girls successfully graduated from the institutions, married, and became mothers, others did not realize the goals set by the institutions. In addition, Lancaster and similar institutions tended to be little more than prisons for youths. They were characterized by overcrowding, lack of treatment, and strict discipline. The differing focus from male institutions did not result in different outcomes.

THE ESTABLISHMENT OF THE JUVENILE COURT

The juvenile court arose in response to the failure of the earlier interventions with juveniles and to address the issues of the era. The late 1800s continued to experience great levels of immigration by lower-class Europeans to the industrial cities of the United States. Environmental factors remained at the head of the list of causes for deviant behavior. In addition, the emergence of psychological and sociological explanations for behavior suggested that the problems of society could be fixed. Finally, middle- and upper-class individuals (primarily women) were interested in doing something to help the poor and destitute. The new court system utilized many of the earlier intervention ideas. Consequently, the expansion of juvenile justice was subjected to many of the same problems of the earlier interventions, as well as new concerns.

The Growth of the Juvenile Court

The first recognized individual juvenile court was established in Cook County, Illinois, in 1899. While this represented the first official juvenile court, a variety of jurisdictions implemented and experimented with similar institutions. Between 1870 and 1877, the state of Massachusetts established separate court dockets, separate hearings, and separate record keeping for cases involving juveniles under the age of 16 (Ryerson, 1978). New York passed legislation in 1892 that provided for separate trials for juvenile offenders, although juveniles continued to be held in the adult system (Platt, 1977). Similarly, Judge Ben Lindsey of Colorado, a leading advocate of juvenile court, operated a quasi-juvenile court for a number of years prior to the establishment of the court in Illinois (Parsloe, 1978). Regardless of the initial beginnings, by 1920 all but three states had juvenile courts, and there were more than 320 separate juvenile courts in the United States (Ryerson, 1978).

The legislation that established the Illinois court reflected the general belief in the ability to alter youthful behavior. First, the court was to operate in a highly informal manner without any of the trappings of the adult court. Lawyers and other adversarial features of the adult system (such as rules of evidence and testimony under oath) were discouraged. The judge was to take a paternal stance toward the juvenile and provide whatever help and assistance was needed. The emphasis was on assisting the youth rather than on punishing an offense. Second, all juveniles under the age of 16 could be handled by the new court. The court was not restricted to dealing with youths who committed criminal acts. Rather, the court could intervene in any situation in which a youth was in need of help. In practical terms, this allowed intervention into the lives of the poor and immigrants, whose child-raising practices did not conform to the ideas of the court. Third, the new court relied extensively on the use of probation. Probation continued to serve both administrative functions for the court as well as supervisory actions with adjudicated youths.

While no two juvenile courts could claim to have the same program, the courts all held the same general principles of providing assistance for the juveniles. Julian W. Mack of the Chicago juvenile court aptly portrayed the role and methods of the court when he stated:

> Most of the children who come before the court are, naturally, the children of the poor. In many cases the parents are foreigners, frequently unable to speak English, and without an understanding of American methods and views. What they need, more than anything else, is kindly assistance; and the aim of the court, in appointing a probation officer for the child, is to have the child and the parents feel, not so much the power, as the friendly interest of the state; to show them that the object of the court is to help them to train the child right... (Mack, 1909).

Within this statement, Mack noted the minor concern over the deviant act in the court, the goal of providing assistance to both the youth and the family, the place of probation in the court, and the typical youth who was subjected to court intervention.

The progressive reforms that led to the establishment of the juvenile courts also had other influences. One of the impacts was a gradual widening of the juvenile court's mandate. The original Illinois statute allowed intervention for criminal activity, dependency, and neglect. In 1903, Illinois added such actions as curfew violation and incorrigibility (status offenses) to the situations allowing intervention. A second area of change involved the development of new institutions for handling youths who needed to be removed from their families. One of the first new institutions was the Illinois State School at St. Charles, Illinois, which was funded in 1901 and opened in 1905 (Platt, 1977). These institutions closely followed the family/cottage model used throughout the late 1800s. The greatest distinction was in the administrative unit (the juvenile court vs. the adult court) and not in orientation. A move toward using full-time, paid probation officers also occurred shortly after the court's beginnings. By 1912, the federal government established the U.S. Children's Bureau to oversee the expanding realm of juvenile justice (Ryerson, 1978).

A final major movement coming from the progressive reforms was the institution of court-affiliated guidance clinics. The first of these was established in Chicago by William Healy, a leading proponent of the juvenile court, in 1909. These clinics relied on the new psychological and sociological explanations emerging during this time. Central to these explanations was the need for the expert analysis of each juvenile in order to identify the unique factors contributing to the individual's behavior. Following Healy's example, 232 clinics were established by 1931 (Krisberg and Austin, 1978).

The Legal Philosophy of the Court

Perhaps the greatest challenge to the growth of the juvenile system entailed debate over the philosophy of the court and the question of a juvenile's constitutional rights. Critics of the court and earlier interventions often claimed that the state was subjecting juveniles to intervention without regard to their rights and those of the family. In many instances the state was forcibly removing a youth from his or her parents' custody. These new interventions were viewed as an abrogation of the family's position in society. The problems of constitutional rights and the new juvenile justice system were deemed inconsequential compared to the possible benefits that could accrue from intervention. Indeed, the state relied on the doctrine of **parens patriae** for justification of its position. Table 2.2 presents key factors in the growth of *parens patriae* and its application to the juvenile court.

TABLE 2.2 Factors in the Growth of *Parens Patriae*

English Chancery Court (Middle Ages)	Basis of state intervention for welfare of children, particularly in cases of property rights and orphans
Ex parte Crouse (1838)	Pennsylvania Supreme Court rules that *parens patriae* is sufficient basis for intervening in the lives of juveniles without parental consent
People v. Turner (1870)	Illinois Supreme Court rules against *parens patriae* in favor of parental rights to raise and care for offspring; largely ignored by the courts
Commonwealth v. Fisher (1905)	Pennsylvania Supreme Court rules that the court can intervene without impunity when the objective is to help the youth, i.e., if the intent is good the juvenile court can act
Kent v. United States (1966)	*Parens patriae* is seriously questioned in light of the lack of adequate help and treatment provided by the juvenile court coupled with the lack of due process applied in juvenile cases

Parens patriae, or the state as parent, was based on the actions of the English **Chancery Court.** The Chancery Court was primarily concerned

with property matters in feudal England. One aspect of the court's function was to oversee the financial affairs of juveniles whose parents had
died and who were not yet capable of handling their own matters. The
court acted as a guardian until such time that the youth could assume
responsibility. In practice, the court dealt only with matters involving
more well-to-do families. The offspring of the poor did not have any
property to protect. As an arm of the state, the Chancery Court often
converted much of the property to the ownership of the state. There
would be little to gain in overseeing the needs of the poor. Regardless of
the intention of the Chancery Court, the precedent was set for intervention into the lives of children.

Movements to intervene into the lives of children in the United States
were quick to rely on *parens patriae* for justification. The earliest example
of this involved the case **Ex parte Crouse**. Mary Ann Crouse was incarcerated upon her mother's request but against her father's wishes. Her father
argued that it was illegal to incarcerate a child without the benefit of a jury
trial. In rejecting the father's argument, the court denied that the Bill of
Rights applied to youths. The Pennsylvania Supreme Court ruled in 1838:

> May not the natural parents, when unequal to the task of edu-
> cation, or unworthy of it, be superseded by the *parens patriae*,
> or common guardian of the community? It is to be remem-
> bered that the public has a paramount interest in the virtue and
> knowledge of its members, and that of strict right the business
> of education belongs to it. That parents are ordinarily entrust-
> ed with it, is because it can seldom be put in better hands; but
> where they are incompetent or corrupt, what is there to pre-
> vent the public from withdrawing their faculties, held as they
> obviously are, at its sufferance? The right of parental control is
> a natural, but not an inalienable one. It is not excepted by the
> declaration of rights out of the subject of ordinary legislation
> (*Ex parte Crouse*, 1838).

The *Crouse* opinion set the tone for intervention with juveniles in
the United States. In essence, the state could intervene, regardless of the
reason, if it found that the child was in need of help or assistance that the
parents and family could not provide. The decision relied solely on the
good intentions of the state and the need to provide the proper training
for the child.

Intervention based on *parens patriae* did not go completely unchallenged. Critics charged that the state was overextending its rights by
intervening in many minor matters that should be simply ignored. More
importantly, the argument was made that the state provided little more
than incarceration and was not providing the education, training, and
benevolent care that was required under the *parens patriae* doctrine. In
People v. Turner (1870), the Illinois Supreme Court stated:

> In our solicitude to form youths for the duties of civil life, we should not forget the rights which inhere both in parents and children. The principle of the absorption of the child in, and its complete subjection to the despotism of, the State, is wholly inadmissible in the modern civilized world.
>
> The parent has the right to the care, custody, and assistance of his child. The duty to maintain and protect it, is a principle of a natural law.

In this instance the court affirmed the rights of the parent to care for the child. The intervention of the state was to be reserved for instances in which the youth had violated a criminal law and after the application of due process concerns. The good intentions of the state and the needs of the youth were not enough to warrant unfettered intervention into the family unit. Despite this apparent shift in legal concerns, most jurisdictions ignored the opinion and continued to follow the general guidelines set forth in the *Crouse* decision.

The issues of a child's and parent's rights were largely settled in the 1905 case, **Commonwealth v. Fisher**. In this case the Pennsylvania Supreme Court directly addressed the question of a juvenile's behavior, his or her constitutional rights, and the intent of the juvenile system in intervention. The court said:

> The design is not punishment, nor the restraint imprisonment, any more than is the wholesome restraint which a parent exercises over his child. The severity in either case must necessarily be tempered to meet the necessities of the particular situation. There is no probability, in the proper administration of the law, of the child's liberty being unduly invaded. Every statute which is designed to give protection, care, and training to children, as a needed substitute for parental authority, and performance of parental duty, is but a recognition of the duty of the state, as the legitimate guardian and protector of children where other guardianship fails. No constitutional right is violated (*Commonwealth v. Fisher*, 1905).

The key concern was over the intent of the intervention and not the rights of the juvenile, his or her parents, or the effectiveness of the system. In essence, the child had a **right to intervention** and not a right to freedom. Moreover, the parents had little, if any, rights in the disposition of the child. The juvenile court was viewed as providing help in the most benevolent fashion possible. The Pennsylvania Supreme Court was granting the juvenile system a free hand in dealing with youths.

The basic constitutionality of the juvenile system went largely unchallenged after the *Fisher* decision. Those cases that did arise were met with the same rationale and outcome of the earlier case. It was not until the mid-1960s that the courts began to alter their views and grant some constitutional rights to juveniles. Indeed, not until 1966 was the benevolent premise of the juvenile system adequately challenged. In the U.S. Supreme Court case of **Kent v. United States**, Justice Abe Fortas said:

> There is evidence, in fact, that there may be grounds for concern that the child receives the worst of both worlds: that he gets neither the protections accorded to adults nor the solicitous care and regenerative treatment postulated for children (*Kent v. United States*, 1966).

As will be seen in Chapter 9, the constitutional rights provided to juveniles in the last two decades are not equal to those provided to adults. The courts have continued to reserve various powers for the state and treat juveniles as a separate class of citizens with different rights and expectations.

Problems of the Court

Despite the swift adoption of the juvenile court and its related components, the new system was faced with a number of problems and failures. A major problem involved the extent to which the various operations were initiated. Many of the courts and agencies relied solely on untrained volunteers. The number of full-time, paid juvenile court judges, probation officers, and trained clinicians was small. Ryerson (1978) cited one survey (Beldon, 1920) that found that only 55 percent of the courts provided regular probation services and, of those with probation, less than 50 percent of the officers were full-time employees. The same survey reported that there were only 23 full-time juvenile court judges in the United States in 1918 (Beldon, 1920). The child guidance clinics experienced the same shortage of trained professionals. As a result, most youths did not receive any evaluation. Most evaluations that occurred took place after a child was incarcerated (Ryerson, 1978). This lack of adequate staff was accompanied by inadequate facilities and resources. While the juvenile court retained the use of institutionalization, the choice of placement usually rested on those institutions that had existed prior to the court's establishment. The problems of these institutions were the same as before. Harsh treatment, military regimentation, lack of training and education, high recidivism, and running away all continued. The new agencies, such as the child guidance clinics, similarly failed to provide the treatment and supervision they promised.

Criticism of the court also focused on its expanded jurisdiction. As noted above, new statutes outlined juvenile behavior that had previously been left to the family for correction. The expanded jurisdiction of the court based on *parens patriae* also led to an increase in unofficial dispositions and handling of youths. There is evidence that many proceedings took place without the presence of a judge or the keeping of records. Such actions were justified on the basis of relieving the burden

of the court and the desire to avoid the stigma of a more formal procedure. While these reasons may have been laudatory, they encouraged the
handling of more juveniles with very minor transgressions. Many trivial
actions, such as making noise, sledding in the street, playing in the street,
riding bicycles on the sidewalk, and throwing paper into the sewers,
became the subject of these unofficial cases (Rothman, 1980).

BENEVOLENCE OR SELF-INTEREST?

The institution of the juvenile court has generally been held as a
progressive, humanitarian development. Most historians refer to the
time period from about 1880 to the 1920s as the Progressive Era. It
was during this time that many laws were passed mandating apparently
humanitarian reforms. Actions such as mandatory schooling, regulations
on working conditions for both adults and juveniles, concern over the
plight of the poor and immigrants, the growth of agencies dealing with
health concerns, and the establishment of the juvenile court were listed
as examples of the benevolent actions of the reformers and society. Coercion within the juvenile justice system, and other forms of intervention,
were considered a necessary evil for improving the lot of those who did
not know any better (Rothman, 1980). Schlossman (1977) went so far
as to label the benevolent movement in juvenile justice as an exercise in
love. He plainly stated that institutions and the court needed to provide
the type of love, affection, and concern found in the family setting.

According to other writers, however, benevolence was not the driving factor. Anthony Platt (1977) referred to the persons involved in the
development of the juvenile court as **child savers**. The issue he addressed
was the rationale for saving the youths. Platt viewed the growth of juvenile justice as a part of larger social movements that attempted to solidi-
fy the position of corporate capitalism in the United States. Rather than
being a humanistic endeavor to help the less fortunate societal members,
intervention through the courts allowed the powerful classes of society
to mold a disciplined, complacent labor force. The juvenile court was a
means of preserving the existing class system in the United States (Platt,
1977). Krisberg and Austin (1978) essentially made the same argument.
They saw the system as a vehicle of the upper classes for controlling the
"dangerous" (lower) classes in society.

Both Platt (1977) and Krisberg and Austin (1978) pointed to a
variety of factors in support of their contentions. First, the driving force
behind the growth of the juvenile system, especially the juvenile court,
were middle- and upper-class individuals. Middle-class women formed
one key group in the system's development (Platt, 1977). These women
were the wives and daughters of the industrialists and landed gentry who
controlled production and had the greatest say in government. A second

form of support rested on the fact that the system grew during the time when the lower-class ranks were swelling with new, poor immigrants. In essence, the lower class was growing to a point at which it could pose a threat to the status quo. Third, and related to the second, was the establishment of new laws that addressed the activity of the lower classes. Statutes governing youthful behavior primarily addressed the actions of the poor and immigrants. The government extended control over entirely new classes of behaviors in the juvenile justice statutes. A fourth indication of the juvenile system's inherent bias was the exploitive use of children who were incarcerated or under the care of the system. Youths were placed in involuntary servitude, indentured, and apprenticed, all under the argument that they would benefit from learning a trade. Realistically, according to Platt (1977) and Krisberg and Austin (1978), these actions supplied immediate cheap labor and indoctrinated the youths in the capitalistic ideology of the upper classes. It was upon these, and similar, arguments that various writers question the benevolent intentions of those individuals involved in the juvenile justice system movement.

Additional support for the argument that the system lacked the benevolence purported in many studies comes from an evaluation of the treatment of females and blacks. Pisciotta (1983) offered evidence that the juvenile justice system had been both racist and sexist. The author noted that most residential institutions in the early 1800s refused to admit blacks. Instead, black youths were subjected to continued incarceration in adult facilities until special institutions for blacks could be built. One of the earliest separate black institutions was opened in Philadelphia in 1848. Exceptions to this rule of separating whites and blacks were restricted to instances in which the admittance of blacks was economically advantageous to those in charge. Once admitted to an institution, little education was supplied. Intervention with blacks revolved around training them in menial labor and to learn their "proper place" in society. Females were handled in a similar fashion (Pisciotta, 1983). Academic education was minimized while religious, moral, and domestic training was emphasized. This view of proper training for women rested on the expectation that females were to stay in the home and raise the next generation of children (Brenzel, 1983; Pisciotta, 1983).

One possible problem with the proposal that the juvenile court was a self-serving invention of the powerful involves the place of the new professionals in the growth of the system. As noted earlier, the emergence of the new psychological and sociological explanations for behavior played a major role in the direction of the juvenile institutions and court. Why did these professionals not criticize the growth of juvenile justice if, indeed, it was simply a means for the powerful to control the masses? Platt (1977) addressed this issue by pointing out that the professionals received a great deal of benefit from juvenile justice, regardless of the driving forces. These individuals gained the reputation as experts, secured employment as either full-time employees or paid consultants, gained access to data and information otherwise denied to them, and found a forum willing to let them advance their theories and ideas. It was not that these professionals may not have objected to the biased premise of the system, they simply found more personal benefits in allowing the system to be instituted and advanced.

The debate over the intent of those forming the juvenile court has not been resolved. The usefulness of recognizing the difference in opinion is in opening the way for varied suggestions about dealing with problem youths. Individuals who assume the benevolence point of view turn to a variety of theoretical explanations and the accompanying forms of intervention. Advocates of the self-interest perspective focus on the actions of society and not the individual offender. Instead of looking for ways to help the youth, these writers suggest that changes in the social structure account for variation in the levels of deviance. This approach will be further explored in Chapter 4.

Ellen S. Boyne

Detention facilities for juveniles take several forms. The Western Maryland Children's Center is a detention facility with a medical suite, an intake area, a school, a full-size kitchen and dining area, a maintenance shop, indoor and outdoor recreation areas, and three dormitories. The center's mission statement says that the detention environment should maximize the restorative process and truly impact the development of the juveniles detained.

JUVENILE JUSTICE FROM 1920 TO THE 1960S

Most of the great movements and changes in juvenile justice were completed by the early 1920s. By this time, the juvenile court was solidly entrenched as the proper institution for dealing with problem youths. The problems and criticisms directed at the court and its institutions were passed off as the failure to implement the programs properly. The shortcomings were not inherent features of the system. Advocates called for increased resources, time, and patience. Society and the legal system were content to leave the juvenile justice system alone to search for effective interventions, provided the system continued to act in the best interests of its youthful clients. Changes in the handling of youths over the next few decades, therefore, were restricted to generating new theories of behavior, attempting new types of treatment, and evaluating their efforts.

Various new institutions were established for handling problem youths. These were necessitated both by increased numbers of youths entering the system and differing approaches to treating youths. Psychological explanations and perspectives led to the growth of various training and counseling (group and individual) programs. Psychotherapeutic interventions gained prominence in the 1940s and led to private and public institutions based on these ideas. The use of such interventions as guided group interaction and peer pressure formed the basis of programs such as the Highfields Project in 1950. Highfields was a short-term, residential facility that allowed the youths to visit their families and remain a part of the community. This type of program helped form the basis for halfway houses and other community interventions. Later chapters will address such actions in more detail.

CHANGES SINCE THE 1970S

Challenges to the *parens patriae* doctrine through a growing number of court cases in the late 1960s and early 1970s were early signals of major changes in society's approach to both juvenile misbehavior and adult criminality. The strong reliance on and belief in rehabilitation and treatment that dominated throughout the twentieth century has given way to more punitive responses (Garland, 2001). Retribution, just deserts, and deterrence have emerged as the watchwords for both the juvenile and criminal justice systems. Rather than look for the causes of deviant behavior in the inequities of society or the surroundings of the offender, there is a stronger belief that individuals of all ages choose to commit offenses and need to be held responsible for their actions.

Garland (2001) views these changes in social control as a result of numerous changes and forces over the past 30 years. Among those influences have been rising crime rates, changing economic conditions that marginalize greater number of individuals, challenges to the welfare state, growing concern for victims, the diversification of the population, the perceived inability of the state to control the citizenry, and the perception that families and other institutions have lost their ability to control the behavior of their members. Passing new laws, increasing the use of punishment, and similar responses have emerged as responses to these and other perceived problems. Changes in the juvenile justice system and society's response to youths is a clear reflection of these broad social changes.

> You can read more about the general purpose clauses for juvenile courts at http://www.ncjj.org/stateprofiles/overviews/faq9.asp

Despite the movement to include greater emphasis on retribution and punishment in the juvenile justice system, *parens patriae* remains the key philosophy underlying juvenile courts in the United States. This is illustrated in an analysis of the "purpose clauses" for juvenile courts found in state statutes. Griffin and associates (2006) identify five general categories of juvenile court purpose clauses (see Table 2.3). In only one of the five categories is *parens patriae* largely excluded and the emphasis shifted to an adult court/criminal law orientation for the juvenile court. The other four categories maintain *parens patriae* as at least a key component (if not directly named) in addressing problem youths.

TABLE 2.3 Categories of Juvenile Court General Purpose Clauses

Balanced and Restorative Justice Clauses:
- juvenile court is to focus on balancing the needs of the youth, the victim, and public safety
- typically includes an emphasis on treatment, care, and guidance of the youths
- found in 17 states

"Standard Juvenile Court Act" Clauses:
- emphasis on "care, guidance, and control" to ensure the welfare of the youth
- offer care similar to that which would normally be supplied by the parents
- found in 9 states

"Legislative Guide" Clauses:
- provide care, protection, supervision, and rehabilitation to children
- maintain children in the home if at all possible
- provide institutional protection to youths
- found in 6 states

Punishment, Deterrence, Accountability, and/or Public Safety Clauses:
- criminal court orientation
- focus on community safety and offender accountability
- found in 6 states

Traditional Child Welfare Clauses:
- emphasis on welfare and best interests of child
- focus on *parens patriae* philosophy
- found in 3 states

Source: Adapted by authors from P. Griffin, L. Szymanski, and M. King (2006). "National Overviews." *State Juvenile Justice Profiles*. Pittsburgh: National Center for Juvenile Justice. Available at http://www.ncjj.org/stateprofiles

SUMMARY

The growth of juvenile justice from the 1920s to the early 1960s followed a pattern of new programs, all within the original mandate and scope of the early reformers. The issues that fueled debate in the early years have returned to be debated in recent years. While there has been an increased emphasis on punishment and due process in the system, many of the rehabilitation and treatment ideas are still being tried and adapted in an attempt to live up to the *parens patriae* ideals that still underlie the juvenile justice system. The remainder of the text will look at the varied issues and the operation of the juvenile system, primarily since the early 1960s. Questions of theory, implementation, practice, and evaluation form the core of the discussion.

DISCUSSION QUESTIONS

1. Concern over child abuse has greatly increased over the past two decades. Many people argue that society's young are treated worse today than at any time in history. Based on your knowledge, place this view within a historical framework. That is, outline the historical view of children and some of the major practices for handling kids.

2. You are an administrator of an early house of refuge and are asked to give a dispassionate view of your institution. What are the strengths and weaknesses of this type of institution? What problems do you face, and how can you correct them?

3. The legislature is proposing to abolish the juvenile court. Argue in favor of the legal philosophy that is the basis for the court. What is the philosophy, why has it been legally upheld throughout the years, and why should it be maintained?

Chapter 3

EXPLAINING DELINQUENCY—BIOLOGICAL AND PSYCHOLOGICAL APPROACHES

Important Terms

atavistic

biosociology

Classicism

concordance

determinism

ego

free will

hedonistic calculus

id

Interpersonal Maturity
    Levels (I-levels)

IQ

medical model

meta-analysis

Minnesota Multiphasic
    Personality Inventory (MMPI)

modeling

moral development

multiple causation

nature–nurture controversy

Neoclassicism

neurotransmitters

operant conditioning

orthomolecular factors

Positivism

psychoanalysis

psychopharmacological perspective

reactive hypoglycemia

soft determinism

somatotypes

spiritualistic or
    demonologic explanations

superego

theory

What You Need to Know

- The Classical school of thought believes humans are free-willed and choose their behavior, while the Positivist school sees behavior as dictated by outside causes beyond the control of the individual. Neoclassicism takes a middle ground where choices can be made from limited options.

- Early theories of behavior relied on biological explanations. Lombroso and others relied on physical features to identify criminals.

- Studies of genetics-inheritance and behavior find that there is some degree of heritability in behavior, although it is small and subject to a great deal of external influence.

- Modern biological theories are best considered as biosociology, which refers to the fact that there are both biological and environmental influences on behavior, and it is necessary to consider the interaction of these factors.

- While psychological theories have a long history, they are limited by three common features—they focus largely on early life experiences to the exclusion of other variables, they are highly individualistic, and they are most useful in treatment settings.

- Freudian psychoanalysis seeks the cause of behavior in the unconscious/instinctual parts of humankind, particularly in the battle between the id, ego, and superego.

- Developmental explanations argue that everyone develops through certain stages, with each stage contributing to the knowledge a person needs to be a successful conforming member of society. Deviance results when an individual fails to advance successfully through all the stages.

- Attempts to identify antisocial personalities have been common but have not succeeded in being able to assess adequately who will and will not be deviant.

- Low IQ has often been used as an argument for why some people break the law; however, a key unknown is the extent to which IQ is inherited or is a result of one's environment.

INTRODUCTION

Throughout the history of juvenile justice, criminologists and others interested in deviant behavior have sought to explain why certain individuals act in certain ways at certain times. The number of theories for deviant behavior has grown considerably over the past 100 years as the field of criminology has progressed and the level of research has improved. A **theory** can be described as an attempt to answer the question "Why?" Why does an individual violate the norms of society? Why do certain conditions seem to accompany deviant behavior? Why does deviance occur when it does? These and other "why" questions form the basis for the theories that have been proposed for explaining delinquent behavior.

The types of factors that have been used to explain delinquency take a wide variety of forms. Early **spiritualistic** or **demonologic explanations** reflected the belief that deviant acts were the result of the battle between good and evil—God and the devil. Individuals who committed crimes were possessed by the devil. Consequently, the solution to deviance involved exorcising the devil and delivering the individual back to God. Often times this could only be accomplished through the death of the devil's vessel—the individual. The soul would then be freed to join God.

These nonscientific explanations gave way in the 1700s with the advent of Classicism and the movement into Positivistic approaches in the later 1800s. Classicism and Positivism are "schools of thought" rather than specific theories of behavior. These schools lay out general beliefs about people and the world that shape the form that individual theories will take.

THEORETICAL SCHOOLS OF THOUGHT

Every explanation of behavior, whether it be conventional or deviant behavior, rests on a number of implicit assumptions about individuals and the world within which they operate. These beliefs form the core of many arguments about the causes of crime and how to deal with offenders. For example, differences in opinions about the death penalty often boil down to different beliefs about whether punishment can deter people. Every science has schools of thought that organize its ideas. In criminology the two schools are Classicism and Positivism.

The Classical School

Classicism finds its roots in the writings of Cesare Bonesana Marchese de Beccaria (1738-1794) and Jeremy Bentham (1748-1832). Beccaria was an Italian aristocrat who broke with the ruling classes to condemn the methods of dealing with crime and morals in society. In outlining a new set of criminal and penal practices, he set forth a number of beliefs about humankind and the function of society in dealing with deviance.

Under Classicism, humans are viewed as having **free will**. That is, individuals choose to act the way that they do after calculating the pros and cons of an activity. Coupled with the idea of free will is the belief that humans are hedonistic. Under the **hedonistic calculus,** individuals seek to maximize pleasure and minimize pain (Bentham, 1948). Individuals, therefore, choose activities and behaviors based on their calculation of the amount of pleasure and pain that will result. Pleasurable behaviors will be undertaken and repeated, while painful activities will cease. Under Classicism, individuals make a conscious, *rational* decision to commit crime based on the expectation of a pleasurable outcome.

These beliefs about free will and hedonism suggest that the solution to crime requires altering the outcome of the hedonistic calculation. That is, increasing pain and reducing pleasure can reduce, and possibly eliminate, deviant behavior. Beccaria and other Classicists, therefore, focused their efforts on making laws and setting punishments that would alter the choices of individuals. Beccaria felt that individuals could not make an informed decision to avoid crime unless they were presented with a clear set of laws and punishments. The emphasis must be on the offense and the legal system, not the offender. There must be a set punishment for each crime, and the level of punishment must be sufficient to offset any pleasurable consequence of an individual's behavior.

Cesare Beccaria wrote his booklet, *Dei Delitti Delle Pene*, in Italian in 1764 as a critique of the administration of justice in Europe in the middle of the eighteenth century. Soon translated into French and English, it became a major influence on legal reforms in Europe and America, read by the likes of Thomas Jefferson and John Adams.

en.wikipedia.org

Classicism seeks to prevent and deter crime by punishing the offender for the offense. Ideally, individuals should be deterred from crime by knowing the pain that would come from being caught and punished. Punishment is not meant to be a form of retribution or retaliation by society. Instead, punishment is solely for the purpose of altering the outcome of the "hedonistic calculus."

Classicism dominated discussions of crime, deviance, and the law in the 1800s. Indeed, changes in laws reflected the general belief in free will and attempts to deter individuals from becoming involved in crime. Unfortunately, crime did not disappear, and new ideas about behavior began to emerge in the late 1800s. Much of this movement toward a new "school of thought" grew out of the developing medical sciences.

TABLE 3.1 Major Elements of Classicism and Positivism

Classicism	Positivism	Neoclassicism
Free will	Determinism	Soft determinism
Hedonism	Multiple causation	Free will with limited choices
Rational offender Emphasis on offense	Emphasize offender/ situation differences	Punishment or treatment
Legal responses— Clear laws and procedures	Medical model— Crime as "symptom" Individualized response	
Punishment for prevention and deterrence	Rehabilitation and treatment	

The Positivistic School

The basic tenets of **Positivism** are diametrically opposed to those of Classicism. Rather than hold the individual responsible for his or her actions, Positivists claim that behavior is *determined* (caused) by factors beyond the control of the individual. Altering behavior, therefore, cannot be brought about through simply raising the amount of pain a person will receive if caught and punished. Rather, changing behavior can be accomplished only by identifying and eliminating the factors that are causing the individual to act in a certain way.

Positivism typically recognizes that there are multiple causes of behavior. Deviance may be the result of a single factor, multiple causes, or a series of events or situations occurring over a period of time. The same deviant act committed by different people may be the outcome of totally different causes. The fact that there is no single cause of crime requires examining each individual case for reasons behind that behavior. The approach used by Positivists to identify causes follows a **medical model** or uses a medical analogy.

Using a medical model, the scientist approaches deviance the same way that a doctor approaches a sickness. Just like a doctor considers coughs and fevers as symptoms of other problems, the Positivist views deviant acts, like burglary and rape, as symptoms of other underlying causes or conditions. The Positivist attempts to identify what causes an individual to commit a deviant act and prescribes a tailored response to the person and circumstances. For example, two burglars may have committed their acts for different reasons, thus necessitating totally different interventions. The emphasis in Positivism, therefore, is not on the offense. Rather, the emphasis is on the offender, the unique situation, and the various factors causing the individual to be an offender.

The logical extension of the focus on **determinism** and **multiple causation** is the belief in rehabilitation and treatment. Instead of punishing an individual for his or her actions, Positivism seeks to remove the root causes of the deviant behavior. The proper rehabilitation or treatment strategies may be as diverse as the number of clients. For example, one burglar may need financial assistance for his or her family because the offense served to provide food for the family, while another burglar may need group counseling to address the specific animosity toward the victim that caused the action. Treatment and rehabilitation need to be tailored to the circumstances of the individual.

Positivism emerged from the 1800s as the dominant school of thought. Advances in medicine, psychology, and sociology presaged a more scientific approach to explaining and understanding deviance. The emerging juvenile justice system focused on identifying the causes of delinquency and sought ways to correct the inadequacies that led to delinquency. While the criminal justice system retained vestiges of Classicism and deterrence, the juvenile justice system and the emerging field of criminology embraced the ideas of Positivism.

Neoclassicism and a Summary

In recent years, the juvenile justice system has shifted back to a more Classical viewpoint, with mandatory punishments, deterrence, and the waiver of youths to the adult system. While Positivism has not totally disappeared, the dominant approach better fits a label of **Neoclassicism**. Neoclassicism takes the position that an individual exercises some degree of free will. The choices, however, are limited by factors both within and outside of the individual. Sometimes referred to as **soft determinism**, an individual can make decisions only based on the available choices. The available options determine the extent to which the person can exercise his or her free will. This compromise gives both the Classicist and Positivist a stake in the criminal and juvenile justice systems.

The balance of this chapter, as well as the entire next chapter, discuss a wide range of theories. The biological and psychological theories appearing in this chapter are primarily Positivistic in orientation. For the most part, they approach deviance as the outcome of forces beyond the control of the individual. The sociological theories appearing in Chapter 4, however, more often incorporate elements of free will in their arguments.

BIOLOGICAL AND SOCIOBIOLOGICAL THEORIES

Explanations of deviance based on biological factors are among the earliest and the most recent theories in criminology. Medical advances, particularly in the 1800s, led to explanations of behavior that focused on the biological makeup of the individual. The underlying assumption made by the early biological theorists was that if the biological makeup of the individual dictated his or her physical capabilities, these characteristics could also contribute to the type of behavior exhibited by the person.

Physical Appearance

Early biological explanations focused heavily on observable physical features of offenders. The basic argument was that offenders could be identified by their appearance, which often was described in terms that suggested an ape-like appearance. The leading name in this area of early research was Cesare Lombroso. Lombroso, who is considered the father of modern criminology, based his ideas on Charles Darwin's theory of the survival of the species and viewed criminals as throwbacks to an earlier state of human existence. These individuals were not as physically or mentally advanced as the rest of society. Lombroso (1876) identified a number of **atavistic**, or ape-like, qualities that generally reflected the physical features of the apes from whom man was a descendant (see Table 3.2). In a study of incarcerated offenders, Lombroso (1876) noted that more than 40 percent of the criminals had five or more atavistic traits. These "born criminals" were a direct result of the lack of evolutionary progression found in the person. The remaining criminals fell into categories of "criminaloids" and "insane" criminals. Criminaloids were individuals who entered criminal activity due to a variety of factors including mental, physical, and social conditions that, when occurring at the same time, would trigger deviant behavior (Vold and Bernard, 1986). Insane criminals included idiots and mentally deranged individuals.

TABLE 3.2 Lombrosian Atavistic Characteristics

Physical Characteristics	Nonphysical characteristics
Protruding jaw	Sensitivity to temperature changes
High forehead	Agility
Asymmetrical face	Lacking a sense of right or wrong
Bad teeth	Fondness for animals
Deep, close-set eyes	Tolerance of pain
Excessively long arms or legs	
Abnormal nasal features	
Exaggerated sex organs	

Unfortunately, much of Lombroso's research looked only at incarcerated criminals. His failure to include a control group of noncriminals (or even nonincarcerated criminals) meant that he was unable to state whether the results would be different if he studied people in the general public. Indeed, subsequent research by Lombroso, which added control groups, pointed out this weakness and led him to consider a second set of nonphysical atavistic qualities, as well as environmental and social factors for explaining deviance.

Lombroso's work led to a great deal of controversy. Goring (1913), in an early critique of Lombroso's ideas, found only minor differences in the physical makeup of convicts and a control group of noncriminal citizens. Conversely, Hooton (1931) claimed to find a great deal of physical difference between 14,000 convicts and 3,000 noncriminal subjects. Hooton also claimed that various physical features could be used to identify persons participating in different types of offenses. A number of criticisms, however, have been leveled at Hooton's work (Vold and Bernard, 1986). Foremost among these are the facts that Hooton did not consider the past offense history of his subjects and he ignored information that clearly contradicted his conclusions.

Despite the criticisms of Lombroso and his contemporaries, the relation between physical appearance and deviance has appeared in twentieth-century research as **somatotypes,** or body types. Perhaps the best known of these studies was one by Sheldon (1949), who identified three basic somatotypes and related temperaments (see Table 3.3). Sheldon (1949), classifying delinquents in a residential facility, found that mesomorphic characteristics were most prevalent and ectomorphic features were the least common. Based on his observations he concluded that mesomorphic individuals were more likely to commit delinquent acts than were other youths. Support for the relationship between mesomorphy and delinquency is also found in the studies of Sheldon Glueck and Eleanor Glueck (1956) and Juan Cortes (1972).

TABLE 3.3 Sheldon's Physiques and Temperaments

Physique	Temperament
Endomorph: short, fat, round, soft	Viscerotonic: soft, easygoing, extrovert
Mesomorph: muscular, large, barrel-chested, thick, hard	Somotonic: dynamic, active, athletic, aggressive, talkative
Ectomorph: bony, thin, skinny, small, delicate	Cerebrotonic: nervous, complainer, introvert

Source: Constructed from W.H. Sheldon (1949). *Varieties of Delinquent Youth: An Introduction to Correctional Psychiatry.* New York: Harper and Brothers.

Not unexpectedly, somatotype studies share similar methodological problems. First, much of the research is based on subjective determinations of body type, often by simply looking at photographs of the youths. Second, the researchers do not consider changes in body type as the youths grow older. Third, the researchers ignore the possibility that mesomorphic youths are more often recruited into delinquency because of their physical build, rather than having a natural propensity to commit delinquent acts. Fourth, considering delinquents as only incarcerated youths may bias the results if mesomorphic delinquents are institutionalized more often because they are perceived as greater threats than are smaller youths. Finally, the determination that mesomorphs were somotonic (aggressive, active, etc.) rests on the fact that many delinquents are mesomorphs and delinquent behavior is considered aggressive. Based on these problems, physical type theories have fallen out of favor and are rarely addressed in contemporary juvenile justice.

Genetic-Inheritance Studies

Biological explanations often assume a strong genetic contribution to behavior. The fact that physical features are clearly passed on from generation to generation has led some to extend that same propensity to nonphysical factors, such as behavioral tendencies. Two basic methods for inspecting this possibility are comparing the behavior of twins and comparing the behavior of offspring to their biological parents. In both sets of studies, it is not the criminal behavior that is considered to be inherited. Rather, it is factors such as low self-control, sensation-seeking, and temperament that are inherited, which lead to criminality (Eysenck and Gudjonsson, 1989; Mednick and Christiansen, 1977; Rowe, 2002).

Twin Studies

Studying twins for the genetic propensity to be deviant requires knowing whether the siblings are monozygotic (MZ)(identical) or dizygotic (DZ)(fraternal) twins. Monozygotic (MZ) twins are the product of a single fertilized egg that separates into two individuals with an identical genetic makeup. Dizygotic (DZ) twins are the result of two separate eggs fertilized by separate sperm. While genetically similar, the two offspring will not be genetically identical and are no more genetically similar than any two siblings born at different points in time. An examination of the genetic propensity for deviant behavior rests on finding greater **concordance**, or similarity, in behavior for MZ twins than for DZ twins or common siblings.

Several studies of twins claim to find a genetic component to behavior. Newman and associates (1937), for example, reported much higher concordance in behavior for the MZ twins than DZ twins. This is interpreted as evidence of a genetic factor in delinquency. Similarly, using a registry of 6,000 pairs of twins in Denmark, Christiansen (1974) uncovered three times as much concordance between MZ twins than between DZ twins when criminal records were inspected. More recently, Lyons (1996), in a large-scale analysis of subjects from a registry of Vietnam-era veterans born between 1939 and 1957, reports higher concordance for MZ twins than DZ twins, especially for adult criminality. Each of these studies concludes that genetic factors have an influence on the actions of the individuals.

While other reviews find support for a genetic component to behavior (see, for example, Ellis, 1982; Wilson and Herrnstein, 1985), a number of problems plague the studies. First, most of the observed relationships are small and insignificant (Reiss and Roth, 1993). Second, several studies show that DZ twins are more concordant than normal siblings, which would not be expected from a genetic argument (Rutter, 1996). Third, most studies lack control over any environmental influences impacting on the individuals (Katz and Chamblis, 1995; Reiss and Roth, 1993). The levels of concordance may be due to similarity in rearing practices or imitation between siblings. Identical twins may be expected to act more similarly by family and friends as a result of the "identical" label. Fraternal twins may be expected to be more individual and not so similar. Finally, distinguishing between MZ and DZ twins can only be done using laboratory tests. Unfortunately, in most studies the determination is based on how similar the siblings look, what they have been told throughout their lives, or the visual determination of a doctor (often at the time of birth). The failure to distinguish the two types of twins adequately could greatly affect the study results.

Adoption Studies

A second method of investigating the genetic contribution to deviance is through the comparison of the behavior of adopted offspring and their biological parents. Adoption studies assume that any similarity between the adopted offspring and the biological parent must be due to the genetic similarity between the subjects because the child has been raised in a different environment from the parent.

Various adoption studies provide support similar to that found in twins studies. Schulsinger (1972) finds that psychopathic subjects have more psychopathic biological relatives than do nonpsychopaths. The difference, however, is not great (7%) and is based on a total of only 114 observations. Crowe (1972), analyzing females and their offspring, reports only a 13 percent difference in the arrests of offspring of offending and nonoffending mothers. The results, however, reflect a total difference of only six fewer offenders with nonoffending mothers. The results in both of these studies offer a weak genetic argument. Hutchings and Mednick (1977), using a much larger sample, reported that 49 percent of criminal boys have criminal biological fathers while only 31 percent of noncriminal boys have a criminal biological father. Whether the adoptive father is criminal or not does not eliminate this relationship, although it does temper the results.

One important qualifier that must be considered in adoption studies involves the separation of the genetic and environmental influences on the individuals. The assumption throughout the research is that the simple fact of adoption is enough to guarantee that the environment of the biological parents is being controlled. Ellis (1982) points out, however, that one overwhelming consideration in many adoptions is the matching of the adopting environment to that from which the individual is being taken. This would seriously impair a study's ability to distinguish the effects of genetics and environment. A related factor deals with the time point of the adoption. Few studies can substantiate when the adoptions actually took place. Adoptions close to birth would have the best chance of eliminating the environmental influence of the biological parents. Adoptions after that point in time could carry a good deal of environmental impact to the new environment. While each of these qualify and temper the results of adoption studies, they do not negate the fact that most such studies show a tendency toward a genetic component in behavior.

In an attempt to clarify the varied findings from twin and adoption studies, Walters (1992) undertook a meta-analysis of 38 projects dating from 1930 to 1989. In a **meta-analysis**, the researcher uses the reported data from past studies and computes a common statistic for all studies, thereby allowing a direct comparison of the different results. Walters (1992) reported that there is a "low-moderate" correlation between heredity and crime. The significance of this finding, however, is problematic because the stronger methodological studies provided less support for the relationship. This was especially true for the adoption studies, which have the best chance of separating genetics from the environment (Walters, 1992).

To date, theorists have not provided strong support for their genetic arguments. This is not to say that genetics hold no influence on behavior. Genetic research is still in its infancy, and future advances may reveal contributors to a wide range of behaviors. Nevertheless, the problem of separating the environmental influences from a genetic component will remain a serious concern.

Biosocial Factors

The recent trend in seeking biological explanations of behavior involves what is known as biosocial approaches. **Biosociology,** or sociobiology, refers to the idea that the biological makeup of the organism and the surrounding environment are intimately related. The environment plays a part in shaping the organism, and the organism, through its daily activity and interpretation of the world, shapes the environment. In terms of deviant behavior, the old belief that deviance is a direct result of a biological condition is no longer tenable. Instead, biosociology sees deviance occurring when specific biological conditions coincide with appropriate sociological or environmental factors. For example, an individual with a congenital hormonal defect may be overly aggressive in situations that force him or her into a choice between fight and flight. This individual, however, does not seek out such situations or become aggressive without the external stimulus. The more modern biological explanations of behavior, therefore, accommodate both biological and sociological factors.

Testosterone and Aggression

Among the normal functions of the body is the production and secretion of various hormones. These natural chemicals control many of the basic bodily functions, including growth, reproduction, and functioning of the central nervous system. In terms of deviant behavior, most attention has focused on reproductive hormones (Shah and Roth, 1974). Androgen, the male sex hormone present in testosterone, has been found to be related to aggressive behavior, particularly in animal studies. Studies on human subjects, typically of incarcerated offenders, have found higher testosterone levels among more aggressive and more serious offenders (Booth and Osgood, 1993; Ehrnkranz et al., 1974; Kreuz and Rose, 1972; Rada et al., 1976). While such studies suggest that testosterone leads to greater levels of aggression, the evidence is not totally convincing. Among the problems are the fact that testosterone levels vary over even short time periods; testosterone is affected by diet, stress, exercise, and social factors (Booth and Osgood, 1993; Katz and Chamblis, 1995; Nassi and Abramowitz, 1976; Reiss and Roth, 1993); and aggressive behavior may cause testosterone levels to increase, rather than the other way around (Harris, 1999).

Orthomolecular Factors

Orthomolecular factors refer to chemicals that are introduced to the body or altered through diet or other influences. One commonly discussed potential problem is the influence of sugar on behavior. Hypoglycemia is the term most often used in these discussions. However, hypoglycemia, a condition of low blood sugar, manifests itself in a lack of energy, lethargy, nervousness, and, in the extreme, a coma. It is difficult to imagine these individuals taking aggressive deviant actions against anyone or anything. The proper term for the relationship between blood sugar levels and criminal activity is **reactive hypoglycemia**, which refers to changes in the blood sugar level, both higher and lower, as a result of dietary intake.

While various researchers claim to have found support for a relationship between hypoglycemia and crime (Bonnett and Pfeiffer, 1978; Geary, 1983; Hippchen, 1978, 1981; Podolsky, 1964; Schauss, 1980), their conclusions rest upon suspect research methodology (Gray and Gray, 1983). Much of the support comes from anecdotal accounts of physicians and psychologists who simply compare a person's diet to his or her behavior without establishing the different bodily needs or processes of the different individuals. What constitutes an overconsumption of sugar by one individual may be minor for another individual. In addition, the commonly used Oral Glucose Tolerance Test is not a definitive measure of blood sugar (Gray and Gray, 1983). When more accurate measures are used, the studies fail to support reactive hypoglycemia as an explanation for deviance. Most studies also fail to note that nutrition and diet are highly related to social class, which may be the operant factor in the relationship with deviance (Katz and Chamblis, 1995). Given the state of the evidence, reactive hypoglycemia is considered a minor cause of deviance (American Dietetics Association, 1984; Gray and Gray, 1983; National Dairy Council, 1985).

Alcohol and other drugs are other substances linked to deviant behavior. That alcohol correlates with delinquency and criminality is indisputable. What is questionable is the mechanism at work. Many would argue that alcohol is a disinhibitor, making it easier for an individual to commit crime. Reiss and Roth (1993) suggest a more biological connection in which alcohol alters the processing of information and, depending on the dosage, may prompt aggression and irritability, or more passivity and sluggishness. The use of other licit and illicit drugs may also lead to criminal behavior. The mechanism underlying the correlation between drugs and deviance, however, is not clear. From a **psychopharmacological perspective**, drugs have a direct causal impact on crime by inducing the user to act out in a certain way (Goldstein, 1989). At the same time, drug use may be related to deviance as a result of crime and violence related to the need to purchase drugs in uncontrolled settings. Such systemic crime is the result of competition between drug dealers or the need to commit property crimes in order to obtain money for drug purchases (Goldstein, 1989). Whether the drugs–crime relationship is psychopharmacological or systemic may be a function of the type of drug and related factors (its addictive properties, its cost, etc.).

The Central Nervous System

A wide range of factors related to the brain and central nervous system have received attention in studies of deviant behavior. Recognition that different parts of the brain are related to different behaviors has led some researchers to look at brain abnormalities and functioning and deviance. Various methods are available for such analyses, including magnetic resonance imaging (MRI), positron emission tomography (PET scans), and electronencephalography (EEG). An MRI can show the physical makeup of the brain and reveal any physical problems (Rowe, 2002). A PET scan, however, reveals differing levels of brain activity when faced with varying stimuli (Rowe, 2002). Similarly, an EEG measures a person's electrical brain waves, which can be compared to those of other individuals (Rowe, 2002). Based on these new technologies, Raine et al. (1995) conclude that there is clear evidence relating brain functioning, especially frontal and temporal lobe problems, to deviant activity. The impact of these factors relative to other variables, such as the environment, however, is not clear.

A related topic deals with whether different **neurotransmitters** (chemicals involved in the transmission of electrical impulses through the nervous system) are capable of altering an individual's behavior. Among the neurotransmitters that have been investigated are dopamine, norepinephrine, and serotonin. Goldman et al. (1996) report that dopamine is directly related to aggressive behavior. Similarly, Virkkunen et al. (1996) note that serotonin levels influence impulse control, hyperactivity, and other behavior related to deviance. Research has shown that it is possible to alter various neurotransmitters, both purposefully with drugs and inadvertently through the use of alcohol and other substances. Such changes can alter social behavior (Brunner, 1996). While still in its early stages, this research suggests that there is a relationship between different neurotransmitters and deviance (Brennan et al., 1995; Reiss and Roth, 1993).

Most of the recent biosocial approaches suffer from similar problems. First, the identification of correlations is often touted as clear evidence of a causal relationship. Second, there may be reversed time order in many of the relationships (Reiss and Roth, 1993). For example, aggressive behavior may lead to physical confrontations that involve head injuries and alterations in the functioning of the brain. Third, the ability to generalize results of studies based on animals to human beings is questionable. Finally, the studies typically fail to consider other spurious factors, such as social status, diet, and the environment, in the consideration of biosocial influences. It is possible that these other factors are influencing both deviance and neurological functioning.

Implications for Juvenile Justice

At the present time there is still relatively little known about the relationships between biological influences and deviant behavior. Despite methodological problems, studies have provided qualified support for biosocial explanations. At the same time, they raise many more questions.

The modern biosocial approaches have engendered interest in biological influences on behavior. Conditions that have a genetic component or behaviors related to hormonal or orthomolecular problems can be altered or modified by changes in diet or drug therapy. Depo-Provera, for example, is a drug that inhibits the production of testosterone and has been used with sex offenders. As biosocial research progresses, additional practical uses for curbing deviance will emerge.

While biological explanations have yet to gain prominence in juvenile justice, there is reason to believe that they will continue to draw increased attention in the future. As Brennan and associates note:

> Understanding of the interaction of genetic and environmental factors in the causes of crime may lead to the improvement of treatment and prevention. Partial genetic etiology does not in

the least imply pessimism regarding treatment or prevention. Quite the contrary! Several genetically based conditions are treated very successfully by environmental intervention (Brennan, Mednick, and Volavka, 1995:90).

At the same time, caution must be taken when implementing programs based on biosocial research. These activities may also bring about more harm than good. For example, altering a diet to do away with "problem" foods may inadvertently damage an otherwise good diet. The most prudent direction for biosocial advocates to pursue at the present time would be expanded research.

PSYCHOLOGICAL EXPLANATIONS

A second general area of explanations for delinquency entails psychological theories. As with other types of theories, psychological explanations take a variety of forms and include a wide range of factors. The early base for psychological theories was biological/physical factors. Indeed, psychiatry, which is usually seen as a part of the general psychological field, is distinguished by its strong commitment to finding physiological bases for aberrant behavior. Psychiatrists are medical doctors who have specialized in the general area of mental disorders.

Many psychological explanations, however, do not look for a physical explanation. Instead, the psychological orientation can be seen as having a few distinctive characteristics. First, and foremost, these approaches generally view problems as arising out of early life experiences. Deviance is seen as a result of problems and flaws that were not recognized and corrected during the adolescent years. Second, psychological explanations are highly individualistic. While many individuals may display the same or similar behavior, different explanations or factors (such as incomplete socialization or poor personality development) may be at work for each person. Finally, because of the individualistic orientation, psychological explanations lend themselves to a treatment orientation. Rather than focus on who will become deviant, the emphasis is on working with individuals who are already having problems and assisting them to overcome the problem.

Psychoanalytic Explanations

Perhaps one of the most widely recognized names in psychology is Sigmund Freud (1856-1939). Freud pioneered the psychoanalytic approach to understanding human behavior. The major premise of **psychoanalysis** is that unconscious, and perhaps instinctual, factors account for much of the behavior displayed by individuals. In particular, deviance is the result of unconscious desires and drives being manifested in behavior. Some individuals are unable to exert control over their desires due to faulty or incomplete training during the early years of life. The goal of psychoanalysis is to identify the unconscious, precipitating factors and then develop conscious methods for dealing with them.

TABLE 3.4 The Freudian Personality

Id	unconscious desires, drives, instincts
Superego	learned values, behaviors; moral character of the individual; outlines the acceptable and unacceptable; may be conscious or unconscious
Ego	social identity of individual; actual behavior; conscious activity

Freudian psychoanalysis outlines three distinct parts to the personality that are involved in behavior (see Table 3.4). The **id** reflects the unconscious desires, drives, and instincts within the individual. In simple terms, the id can be seen as the selfish, "I want" part of the individual. The **superego** entails values that the individual learns from others. These values form the moral character of the individual and help dictate what the person considers acceptable or unacceptable behavior. The superego is a result of early moral training and provides the rationale for refraining from various types of behavior. Where the id looks for satisfaction of desires, the superego responds with either a "can't have" orientation or a "must do" response. That is, the superego helps orient the individual's behavior away from simple desires and toward the value system that the person has incorporated. The actions of the superego may be both conscious and unconscious. The final part of the personality, the **ego**, is the social identity that is exhibited through behavior. It is often the manifestation of the conflict between the id and the superego. The ego is the conscious attempt to satisfy the needs of the id while continuing to abide by the mandates of the superego. This aspect is always conscious because it is the solution to the question of whether the individual follows his or her drives or the morally correct line of activity.

Psychoanalysis seeks to uncover the causes of behavior by bringing the unconscious conflict between the id and the superego to consciousness. Often, psychoanalysis is only undertaken when an individual develops criminally deviant behavior. The conflict between the id and the superego, however, will not always appear as deviance. Instead, the internal conflict can be manifested in various ways. Table 3.5 outlines eight possible "defense mechanisms." Deviance may appear in some mechanisms (such as repression, rationalization, or displacement), while other mechanisms may lead to socially acceptable behaviors.

TABLE 3.5 Psychoanalytic Defense Mechanisms

REPRESSION	An active attempt to push desires and thoughts out of one's consciousness or to keep material from reaching consciousness. Example: You forget that you owned a pet that was run over by a car when you were a child.
DISPLACEMENT	A change in the primary object of a feeling or desire to a secondary one that is less threatening. Example: You are angry at your boss but you yell at your husband or wife instead.
SUBLIMATION	Here the displacement is more long-term and the object chosen is socially acceptable. Example: You want to hit and hurt your father, but you become a professional boxer or football player.
DENIAL	The truth of certain facts or experiences is denied, rather than forgotten as in repression. Example: Your daughter dies but you act as if she is alive, keeping a bed made up for her.
REACTION FORMATION	A desire is changed or transformed into the opposite feeling or desire. Example: You hate or deeply resent your father, but you tell everyone how much you love him and act toward him in a loving manner.
PROJECTION	You have an unconscious desire or thought, but you attribute it to someone else instead of acknowledging it in yourself. Example: You no longer love someone, but instead accuse him or her of no longer loving you.
RATIONALIZATION	The process of finding an acceptable reason for doing something unacceptable. Example: You punish your child harshly, but say "I'm doing this for your own good."
REGRESSION	You replace your desires or thoughts with those from an earlier stage of your development. Example: You are under stress and get angry at someone who works for you, so you throw a temper tantrum.

Source: P. Van Voorhis, M. Braswell, and D. Lester (2007). *Correctional Counseling and Rehabilitation*, 6th ed. Newark, NJ: LexisNexis Matthew Bender, p. 44.

Where Freud did not specifically address criminality, other researchers have tried to apply psychoanalysis to delinquent behavior. Erikson (1968) suggests that some youths fail to develop an identity (or ego) of their own. Instead, they gather much of their self-image from the peers with whom they associate. Delinquent peers, therefore, would lead the individual to delinquency. Where Erikson (1968) focuses on the failure to develop an ego, Abrahamson (1944) and Aichhorn (1963) target the poor development of a superego. The absence of an adequate superego leaves the id unchecked, which results in behavior reflective of a person's uncontrolled instincts, drives, and desires.

Despite the development of a large body of literature, the psychoanalytic approach is subjected to strong criticism. One of the most problematic concerns is that psychoanalysis relies on vaguely defined terms and constructs to represent its key concepts. Consequently, it is very hard to undertake empirical tests of the theory. There is no clear method for measuring the id, ego, or superego. A second major criticism involves the fact that psychoanalysis is totally retrospective. That is, it is useful only for looking at what has already happened. It is geared toward uncovering the reasons why something happened and working to correct those reasons. A third area deals with the emphasis on early childhood. With few exceptions, it is assumed that little change occurs after adolescence. Adult behavior is viewed only as a result of poor childhood socialization and not from factors appearing in adult life. Finally, psychoanalysis is criticized for ignoring social-structural factors in the determination of behavior. Indeed, with the heavy emphasis on the unconscious, psychoanalysis examines the social setting of the individual only to the extent that it failed to provide the necessary moral atmosphere during early adolescence.

Developmental Approaches

A number of writers identify the source of deviance in interrupted or arrested developmental patterns during childhood. The basic assumption behind these explanations is that all individuals develop through a number of stages. Each stage provides an integral part of the total knowledge and understanding that a person needs to operate in society. The failure of an individual to complete any one of these stages or steps successfully may lead to some form of socially unacceptable behavior. This basic argument can be seen in Freud's psychoanalytic explanation in which the failure to develop appropriate superego and ego responses to the id takes place in early childhood. The child is born with the id but must learn and internalize the moral dictates of society as he or she grows.

Interpersonal Maturity

One of the most well-known developmental approaches in delinquency research is the **Interpersonal Maturity Levels (I-levels)**. The I-levels represent a continuum from the most basic stage of development through the most advanced stage (see Table 3.6). The interruption of any stage makes the attainment of later stages difficult, if not impossible.

Most delinquency and deviance occurs in Levels 2, 3, and 4. Level 2 individuals operate primarily on the basis of their own need and use others only as a source of enjoyment or fulfillment. While Level 3 individuals begin to integrate rules, they are still oriented toward their own needs. As a result, they may realize what they are doing is wrong but cannot justify the rules with their desires. Finally, persons in Level 4 may resort to delinquent behavior as a means of striking out against what they perceive as contradictory demands. The inability to cope with competing demands may result in choosing delinquent activity. Individuals at any level try to balance their own needs against the expectations and needs of others. Operating at the lower maturity levels, however, leads to behavior that is counter to societal demands, with or without the cognizant understanding of those demands.

TABLE 3.6 Interpersonal Maturity Levels

Level 1:	The individual learns to discriminate between themselves and others.
Level 2:	The individual starts to separate things into persons and objects, partly on the basis of their own needs and what they can control.
Level 3:	At this level the individual begins to learn rules and can start to manipulate the environment for their own benefit.
Level 4:	The individual begins to perceive things from the standpoint of others. He/she sees conflicts between expectations of others and their own needs.
Level 5:	Here the individual becomes aware of patterns of behavior and relationships. There becomes an awareness of distinctions made between events, objects, and roles in society.
Level 6:	The individual is able to distinguish between himself/herself and the roles they play. These are not one and the same and can accommodate one another.
Level 7:	At this level, the individual begins to perceive a variety of methods for dealing with the world and makes choices based on his/her and other's past experiences and for the benefit of everyone.

Source: Compiled from C. Sullivan, M.Q. Grant, and J.D. Grant (1957). "The Development of Interpersonal Maturity: Applications to Delinquency." *Psychiatry* 20:373-385.

Moral Development

A second well known developmental approach is Kohlberg's (1981) **moral development**. Kohlberg's model notes that individuals progress through six stages of "moral development," which are arranged into three levels (Table 3.7). The Preconventional Level is characteristic of young children, while most adults fall into the Conventional Level. Only a small proportion of adults reach the Postconventional or Principled Level. Deviant individuals typically fail to display the same level of moral development as noncriminals with the same or similar characteristics. As in the I-level classification scheme, Kohlberg views deviance as a result of interrupted or incomplete development. For example, an individual at Stage 2 sees his or her own needs and feels that he or she does not get enough in return for what they do or want. As a result, that person may turn to deviance to "balance" the exchange.

Both the I-level and moral development perspectives, as well as others, are limited primarily to treatment. As with psychoanalysis, the identification of developmental stages and problems typically occurs *after* a problem has become manifest. The individual then undergoes a one-on-one evaluation in which the potential for subjective evaluation becomes a problem. In instances in which developmental typologies have been used for prediction (such as with I-levels), the predictive capacity of the tools has been found to be weak. Further, developmental approaches have been criticized as imprecise, contradictory, and not necessarily sequential (see, for example, Rich and DeVitis, 1985; Simpson, 1974; Williams and Williams, 1970). In general, developmental arguments have proved much more useful in treatment of deviant individuals.

TABLE 3.7 Kohlberg's Moral Development

Level I. Preconventional Level

Stage 1 Right is obedience to authority and rules, and avoiding punishment. There is clear concern for one's own physical well-being.

Stage 2 Right corresponds to seeing one's own needs, taking responsibility for one's self, and allowing others to do the same. At issue is a fair exchange with others.

Level II. Conventional Level

Stage 3 Right is avoiding the disapproval of others, having good intentions and motives, and being concerned for others. Individuals are aware of others and their needs.

Stage 4 Right is doing one's duty to society and others, and upholding the social order. The individual is capable of looking at things from society's viewpoint.

Level III. Postconventional or Principled Level

Stage 5 Right is based on upholding the rules and values agreed upon by society. The individual feels obligated to society. There is a recognized social contract between the individual and society that outlines acceptable behavior.

Stage 6 Right is a reflection of universal ethical principles. The individual recognizes the moral rightness of behavior and acts accordingly.

Source: Compiled from L. Kohlberg (1981). *The Philosophy of Moral Development*. San Francisco: Harper and Row.

Learning Theories

Implicit in developmental discussions is the idea that people learn right from wrong, and learning takes place over a long period of time. There is a cumulative nature to learning. In learning theories, the emphasis is on how an individual learns and what factors are effective in promoting learning. The failure of an individual to complete a developmental stage successfully, therefore, may be due to a problem in the learning process.

Modeling is perhaps the simplest form of learning. According to Bandura and Walters (1963), children learn by copying the behavior of others. Most modeling follows the behavior of significant others, particularly parents, siblings, peers, and other individuals close to the child. Modeling, however, is not limited to the people around the youth. Children also can learn from characters, both real and fictional. If the child continuously sees deviance, either real or fictional, the child may begin to copy that behavior. The child may not know whether it is right or wrong. He or she only knows that this is how people act. (Further discussion of modeling and identification will be taken up in Chapter 4.)

A more classical psychological learning theory is that of **operant conditioning**. Operant conditioning deals with the reinforcement of behavior through a complex system of rewards. Skinner (1953) and others view subsequent behavior as a consequence of past responses to behavior. Specifically, an individual repeats (or does not repeat) a behavior based on what happened when the behavior in question appeared in the past. For example, a child who does as he or she is told by his or her parents is given a treat for being good. The treat becomes a reinforcer for future good behavior. In operant conditioning the reinforcement comes after the behavior or action of the individual. Actions that result in a pleasurable response (positive reinforcer) or that eliminate painful or unpleasant situations (negative reinforcer) will be repeated. Learning, therefore, becomes an ongoing process, with every choice made by the individual resulting in some form of response. Future actions are based on the reinforcement, or lack thereof, of past behavior.

Bandura and Walters (1963) have combined conditioning and modeling in a general discussion of learning. They note that the degree to which a child models his or her behavior is mitigated by the level of reward or punishment that the model receives. For example, a child observing an act of aggression by another person or a fictional character is more likely to copy that act if the aggressive person is rewarded or not punished. Therefore, the process of learning through operant conditioning can take a vicarious route through observation of the experiences of others. Two key concerns have been raised in relation to psychological learning theories. First, while modeling and operant conditioning make intuitive sense and receive support from anecdotal and case studies, most of the supportive studies rely on correlational analyses and contain serious methodological flaws. A second problem is that modeling and operant conditioning approaches ignore the potential contribution of the individual to behavior. The basic assumption is that the individual is a product of the environment and has little influence over his or her choice of activity.

Personality and Delinquency

Various researchers have proposed that deviants display certain personality characteristics that can be used to explain deviant and criminal behavior. Psychologists have developed a wide array of personality classifications and measures for uncovering personality traits. Indeed, the *Diagnostic and Statistical Manual of Mental Disorders* (4th ed.) of the American Psychiatric Association (known as the DSM-IV) includes the classification of "antisocial personality disorder," which refers to individuals who show a continuing pattern of behavior harmful to others.

One of the early attempts to distinguish delinquents from nondelinquents using personality factors was conducted by

> You can read more about the DSM-IV at http://www.psych.org/MainMenu/Research/DSMIV.aspx

Sheldon Glueck and Eleanor Glueck (1956). Comparing 500 delinquents to 500 matched nondelinquents, Glueck and Glueck claimed that

> delinquents are more extroverted, vivacious, impulsive, . . . less self-controlled . . . are more hostile, resentful, defiant, suspicious, . . . destructive . . . and are less fearful of failure or defeat than the nondelinquents. They are less concerned about meeting conventional expectations and are more ambivalent toward or far less submissive to authority. They are, as a group, more socially assertive (Glueck and Glueck, 1956: 275).

This picture of the delinquent was meant to summarize their overall personality pattern and indicate differences from conventional youths.

While the work of Glueck and Glueck still draws attention today, several concerns have been raised about the findings. First, not all the traits associated with the delinquents are undesirable. For example, being extroverted, assertive, less fearful of failure, and less submissive are traits that many individuals would find valuable. Second, the authors assume that the individuals had these traits before they exhibited delinquent behavior. It could be argued, however, that the delinquents were hostile, resentful, defiant, and ambivalent to authority due to their contact with the justice system. These feelings may come after contact with the system, not before the delinquent act. If so, they cannot be a cause of the antisocial behavior. Finally, the individuals who evaluated the youths were aware of which youths were delinquent and which were not delinquent. It is possible that knowing an individual is delinquent and in an institution may prompt an evaluator to expect the subject to be more assertive, more hostile, or have less self-control. Despite these concerns, interest in personality types continues.

A major change in personality research has been to try and develop standardized measures of personality. Such an effort would avoid some of the pitfalls seen in Glueck and Glueck's study. The **Minnesota Multiphasic Personality Inventory (MMPI)** is one standardized method for uncovering personality traits in individuals. The MMPI is an inventory of 556 true/false questions that are designed to tap 10 personality dimensions identified in past clinical analyses (Megargee and Bohn, 1979) without the need for extended clinical observation. The MMPI assumes that everyone answers some questions in a deviant manner.

Therefore, no single scale question is associated with deviant behavior. Instead, deviance is considered more likely as the individual answers in a deviant fashion on a number of questions. The key, therefore, is the overall tendency in the scales.

While the MMPI has been used extensively, it has been challenged on a number of grounds. First, to the extent that the prior clinical evaluations are in error, poorly conceived, or invalid, the MMPI results also are questionable. The results are only as good and useful as the underlying clinical factors. Second, the MMPI is useful primarily in the treatment of offenders, and not for predicting or explaining deviance prior to its occurrence. Finally, because the MMPI has been refined using institutionalized subjects, it is possible that it reflects factors related to institutional life and experiences, rather than a deviant personality. The inventory has been subjected to relatively few tests outside of the institutional setting.

Waldo and Dinitz (1967) and Tennenbaum (1977) present a number of problems with the studies of personality. Perhaps the most damaging problem is that many studies fail to probe whether personality leads to delinquency or whether delinquency and system processing produces the observed personalities. A second problem is the fact that personality scores and studies often rely on subjective evaluations by clinical workers. Knowledge that the incarcerated subjects have committed certain types of actions may lead to identifying personality traits that fit that behavior. A final concern reflects the poor research methodology used in many analyses. Typical problems are the failure to draw adequate (or random) samples, the lack of control groups for comparison, and the failure to consider other (spurious) variables that may be more important in explaining the phenomenon under question. While these criticisms make the results problematic for the identification and prediction of behavior, they do not negate the potential usefulness of the techniques in the rehabilitative setting.

Mental Deficiency and Delinquency

Since the late 1800s, low intelligence has been offered as a prime cause of deviant behavior. The scientific interest in the relation between intelligence and deviance can be traced to the development of IQ testing. **IQ**, or intelligence quotient, was developed by Alfred Binet in the early 1900s as a numerical representation of the mental ability of the individual. The formula for IQ is rather simple:

$$IQ = (mental\ age/chronological\ age) \times 100$$

The mental age of an individual is determined by performance on a standardized test. The test consists of questions geared toward different aged individuals. Persons age 10 and up are expected to be able to answer a certain level of questioning and all those from the easier levels. More difficult questions are assumed to be beyond the ability of the average 10-year-old. Once an individual's mental age is determined, the researcher simply divides that figure by the respondent's actual age and multiplies by the base of 100.

Since the development of the IQ test, many researchers have attempted to show that delinquency and deviance are related to low intelligence. The assumption that IQ is related to crime is not a surprising one given the knowledge that most incarcerated offenders tend to be less educated and display below-average scores on academic achievement tests. The major source of debate concerning IQ revolves around the question of whether IQ is due to nature or nurture.

The **nature–nurture controversy** refers to the question of whether intelligence is inherited (nature) or whether it is an outcome of environmental influences (nurture). The nature argument views IQ as set at birth and not subject to outside influences. The social and physical environment, including education, has little or no influence on a person's IQ. Conversely, the nurture side of the debate proposes that an individual's IQ is the outcome of complex interactions between the genetic makeup of the person and the environment to which the individual is exposed. This view suggests that IQ can be altered through education and other environmental interventions.

The view that intelligence is genetically determined received a great deal of support in the United States, where low IQ scores were used as a means of denying immigrants entry to the country. This position rested on the work of Goddard (1920), who found that most criminals were "feebleminded" (IQ of less than 75). The government's position was that excluding such individuals was in the best interests of the country. Unfortunately, Goddard (1920) examined only incarcerated "criminals" and did not use a comparison group in the analysis. Consequently, he had no way of knowing whether they were more or less "intelligent" than anyone else. Wilson and Herrnstein (1985) and Herrnstein and Murray (1994) also have argued that IQ is substantially due to genetics and that IQ is a strong predictor of criminal activity. The authors also assert that minorities, particularly blacks, score lower on IQ. Tied to the genetic argument, this opens the door for claims of racism and obscures the rest of their argument.

Hirschi and Hindelang (1977) provide the most widely cited argument in the IQ-delinquency literature. The authors argue that IQ is at least as important in predicting delinquency as social class or race, and is related to delinquency regardless of the race or social class of the individual. Their opinion is that IQ is an indirect cause of delinquency. Low IQ, through genetics and/or environment, leads to poor school performance, which prompts a lack of concern for education, a rebellious attitude toward the school and societal demands, and, eventually, a heightened chance of deviant behavior. To the extent that environment has a role, individuals with a low IQ who can be encouraged to stay in school, receive special help, or otherwise enhance their abilities may not experience the problems and frustrations that precipitate deviant activity.

Implications for Juvenile Justice

Before addressing the impact of psychological theories, it is important to point out some of the criticisms leveled at these explanations. As has been noted throughout the above discussions, psychologically oriented explanations are not particularly good for the prediction of behavior. Many are formulated after the fact and seek, primarily, to explain the observed behavior retrospectively. The emphasis is on why something happened and not predicting what will happen in the future. A second concern with psychological studies is the reliance on subjective interpretations. Most psychological endeavors rest on the opinion of individuals who have been trained in the field of psychology. Unfortunately, there is no single orientation or perspective that drives the entire field, or even subfields, of psychology. The subjective nature of psychology, therefore, often leads to conflicting opinions, even when individuals are looking at the exact same information.

Some commentators criticize what they see as the individualistic nature of psychological explanations. Indeed, many psychological endeavors examine individual subjects, and the precise explanation for deviance could vary from subject to subject. This criticism may be shortsighted, however, given the fact that these individualistic approaches form the basis of other, more general theories. For example, operant conditioning is a key component of differential association-reinforcement theory, and hedonism is at the heart of Gottfredson and Hirschi's general theory of crime (see Chapter 4 for discussions of both of these theories).

Psychological explanations have their greatest impact on the correctional end of the juvenile justice system. Psychology's emphasis on identifying the cause of an individual's behavior fits the general treatment orientation of juvenile justice. As a result, juvenile corrections places heavy emphasis on counseling, education, and other rehabilitative methods. Techniques such as I-level classifications and the MMPI are used to gain insight into a juvenile's problems and subsequently design a response to those problems. Additionally, behavior modification techniques are used to set up token economies in detention centers and training schools. Psychology will more than likely remain primarily a correctional tool in juvenile justice until such time that more precise methods of evaluation are generated or the predictive ability of psychological findings are enhanced.

SUMMARY

The biological and psychological explanations discussed in this chapter represent theories and perspectives developed over many decades. While some have been discounted because of their lack of rigor and relevance, they have engendered discussions that may lead to more applicable and useful theories. Psychological explanations have found a clear place in the juvenile justice system. This is particularly true in the juvenile court and in the correctional phase of processing. Biological explanations have not fared so well. This is due mainly to the poor quality of the early explanations and the current lack of expertise in the physical sciences held by criminologists and criminal justicians. The next chapter turns to a discussion of sociological explanations that hold the dominant position in modern discussions of delinquency and criminality.

DISCUSSION QUESTIONS

1. Compare and contrast the Classical and Positivist schools of thought. What are the basic assumptions each hold about the individual and behavior? What implications do each have for the juvenile justice system?

2. There is a movement to shift the emphasis in the juvenile justice system from the sociological theories and explanations for delinquency to the biosocial perspective. Point out and explain what you see as the more promising biosocial approaches. In addition, project the problems or shortcomings that will result if the emphasis is shifted (that is, what are the problems with the biosocial approach)?

3. Identifying a "criminal or delinquent personality" has proven to be quite difficult. Outline some of the more well-known methods for isolating this personality and what problems exist in these approaches. Which method would you use if you had to pick one and why?

4. Psychological theories are common in correctional practice. Pick specific psychological approaches and illustrate their usefulness and shortcomings for use in correcting juvenile delinquents (i.e., critique the approaches).

Chapter 4

SOCIOLOGICAL EXPLANATIONS OF DELINQUENCY

Important Terms

anomie
bond to society
Chicago School
containment theory
culture conflict
developmental theories
differential association
differential identification
differential reinforcement
drift
ecological fallacy
ecological perspective
elaboration model
focal concerns
general strain theory
generic control theory
inner containment
invasion, domination,
    and succession
labeling
life-course theories
looking-glass self
modes of adaptation
outer containment
primary deviance
rational choice theory
reintegrative shaming
role-taking
routine activities perspective
secondary deviance
self-control theory
social control theories
social disorganization
strain theory
subculture
symbolic interactionism
tautological
techniques of neutralization
transfer of evil

What You Need to Know

- Shaw and McKay found that crime and delinquency was concentrated in the center of cities, where lower-SES individuals and immigrants or African Americans lived. The reason they offer for this finding was "social disorganization," meaning the residents did not exert control, thus allowing crime to flourish.

- Differential association argues that deviance is learned just as other behavior is learned. Modifications of differential association include differential identification (which adds the idea of learning from images in the media) and differential reinforcement (which argues we learn from the results of our actions).

- Subcultural theories suggest that youths often act in accordance with a different set of values and beliefs that invariably conflict with the dictates of the larger society, thus leading them to be considered deviant.

- The techniques of neutralization presented by Sykes and Matza allow youths to violate the law while maintaining a positive self-image as a conforming member of society

- Routine activities theory argues that a criminal act requires a motivated offender and a suitable target to coincide where there is an absence of capable guardianship.

- Strain theory suggests that crime is a logical outcome of the disjunction between the socially prescribed goals and the means available for achieving those goals.

- Hirschi's social control theory states that "delinquent acts result when an individual's bond to society is weak or broken." Bond is composed of attachment, commitment, involvement, and belief.

- Self-control theory argues that behavior is controlled by factors an individual internalizes early in life. Good self-control keeps an individual from violating the law.

- The labeling perspective proposes that involvement in the juvenile justice system leads to more deviant behavior by labeling the individual as a deviant and forcing him or her to act in accordance with that label.

- Attempts to integrate theories into more unified, coherent explanations of deviance have met only limited success in advancing sociological theory.

INTRODUCTION

The most prevalent explanations of delinquent behavior are sociologically oriented theories. Indeed, criminology, criminal justice, and juvenile justice have grown around sociological perspectives. The reasons for this are understandable. First, the great changes in society during and after the industrial revolution were accompanied by increased levels of deviant behavior. This behavior, however, was more prevalent in the cities. This led to a natural view that deviant behavior was an outgrowth of social relationships, especially those in urban areas. Second, sociological theories hold a great deal of intuitive appeal. Many of the ideas, as will be seen, are based on common sense and do not require a great deal of education or training for simple understanding. A third reason behind the dominance of sociological explanations entails the ability to test such theories. While tests of biologically oriented theories fail to provide empirical support, and psychological theories often defy empirical testing or are restricted to only individuals, most sociological explanations are accompanied by attempts at empirical research and often find some degree of support.

Sociological theories and perspectives reflect elements of both Classicism and Positivism. From the positivistic view, sociological theories consider a wide array of social and environmental factors as explanations of deviant behavior. Delinquency is a response to the setting in which the individual finds himself or herself. The neighborhood in which an individual grows up, one's peers, the views of others, social and moral training, the organization of society, economic conditions, and the effect of being processed in the criminal justice system are among the many factors considered in sociological theories. Classical elements appear in discussions of deterrence, control, and routine activities theories where the individual is presumed to have some degree of choice in his or her behavior. This chapter attempts to outline the major points of each theory or view and draw out similarities and differences in the sociological explanations for deviance.

THE CHICAGO SCHOOL

Perhaps the earliest sociological explanation to gain importance in criminology, the **ecological perspective** (or "**Chicago School**," so named because of the research done using the city of Chicago as a focus) sought to explain deviance as a natural outgrowth of the location in which it occurs, particularly large cities and places within large cities. Research in the early twentieth century recognized the great growth in the number and size of large cities. European immigrants and Southern blacks were flocking to the industrial cities of the north and northeast. These new urban areas were densely populated, and many of the new residents were uneducated, unemployed, and could not speak English. Along with this great influx of people came increases in various social problems— including criminal activity.

Shaw and McKay: Social Disorganization

Clifford Shaw and Henry McKay (1942) analyzed where delinquency occurred in Chicago. The researchers identified the location of every recorded delinquent act in the city for two different time periods roughly 20 years apart. Based on where it occurred, Shaw and McKay (1942) reported that crime and delinquency was highest:

  1) in and around the central business district,

  2) in poor areas of the city, and

  3) in areas dominated by immigrants and African Americans.

All three conclusions pointed to the same physical location in the city, specifically the city center where economic conditions were poorest and new arrivals were able to find affordable housing.

The stability of the delinquency levels in the same areas over time led Shaw and McKay (1942) to examine what it was about these areas that could explain the findings. What they uncovered was a continuing process of **invasion, domination, and succession** taking place. These areas were undergoing constant change. Over a period of time, poor foreign-born and Southern immigrants would invade the central city areas due to their economic situation and the availability of cheap living conditions in the areas. Over time, one group would gain some degree of dominance in the area. As the residents gained employment and were assimilated into American society, however, they would leave these inner-city areas for the more desirable outer zones. Meanwhile, new groups of poor people would take their place.

The delinquency problem was a result not of specific people, but of the constant turnover of people in the area. This turnover caused a problem referred to as **social disorganization** (Shaw and McKay, 1942). The people in these core areas were unable to exert control over the behavior of those living there. The major concern for the people was to better themselves and move on to other areas. As a result, people did not concern themselves with improving the area, getting to know one another, or taking control of conditions. There was a lack of social organization that could bring about improvements.

Sources of Control

Analyses since the 1950s have consistently uncovered concentrations of crime in certain residential areas. Analyses of Baltimore, Indianapolis, and Detroit all found that poor economic conditions, social heterogeneity, and an inability of residents to exert control and conformity among area residents was related to higher levels of delinquency in neighborhoods (Bordua, 1958; Chilton, 1964; Lander, 1954). Bursik and Grasmick (1993) claim that neighborhood control requires input from private, parochial and public sources (see Table 4.1). Unfortunately, lower-class, transient, high-crime neighborhoods have trouble developing these sources of control. Areas undergoing a great deal of change will have an unstable base for private and parochial control mechanisms, while even in stable neighborhoods with strong private and parochial networks the residents may not be able to marshal the public support needed for effective delinquency control (Bursik and Grasmick, 1993). Hope (1997) refers to this as a problem of vertical integration. That is, some neighborhoods are left out when it comes to working with those in power.

TABLE 4.1 Sources of Neighborhood Control

Private	interpersonal relationships: family, friends, and close associates
Parochial	neighborhood networks and institutions: schools, churches, businesses, social organizations/groups
Public	agencies and institutions of the city, state, or other governmental unit

Source: See A. Hunter (1985) "Private, Parochial and Public School Orders: The Problem of Crime and Incivility in Urban Communities." In G.D. Suttles and M.N. Zald (eds.), *The Challenge of Social Control: Citizenship and Institution Building in a Modern Society* (pp. 230-242). Norwood, NJ: Ablex; and R.J. Bursik and H.G. Grasmick (1993). *Neighborhoods and Crime: The Dimensions of Effective Community Control.* New York: Lexington.

Critique of the Ecological Approach

While the ecological approach and the Chicago School shifted attention away from the biological views of Lombroso to a more sociological orientation, these new ideas also suffered from various problems. First, despite the frequent use of "social disorganization" as a theoretical base, the ecological perspective borrowed various theories and themes (such as anomie) when the occasion arose. This lack of a single coherent theory hampered the growth and use of the ecological approach. Second, many researchers fell into the trap of invoking the ecological fallacy. The **ecological fallacy** refers to attributing results based on grouped data to an individual. For example, a researcher would find that delinquency was highest in areas of low income, low average education, and high density. He or she would then state that an uneducated individual from a poor family living in a two-bedroom home with nine people would be delinquent. In doing so, the researcher commits an ecological fallacy. The fact that an area with certain characteristics has a high rate of delinquency does not mean that an individual exhibiting similar personal characteristics will be delinquent. In fact, many of the delinquents in the identified area may exhibit the exact opposite traits. Knowledge about an area would not tell anything about a specific individual.

A third area of concern dealt with the heavy reliance on official records of delinquency. The finding that delinquency was highest in low socioeconomic areas found a great deal of support in official records. Various examinations using self-report studies (Dentler and Monroe, 1961; Hindelang, Hirschi, and Weis, 1981; Short and Nye, 1958; Tittle, Villemez, and Smith, 1978), however, found little difference in delinquency between the social classes. The findings of many ecological studies, therefore, could have been attributable to biased official records.

Despite problems with the ecological approach, this early work brought crime and delinquency theory squarely into the sociological tradition. For the most part, these early sociological explanations provided a clean break from the biological work of Lombroso and his followers. The ecological studies also provided much of the framework for subsequent theoretical advances.

LEARNING THEORY

Just as under the psychological banner, many sociological theorists see deviance as a result of learning. A variety of factors contribute to the learning process, including with whom an individual has contact, what the individual observes, and the consequences of one's behavior. The most prominent of the social learning theories is differential association, which forms the basis of other learning theories.

Sutherland: Differential Association

Sutherland's (1939) **differential association** views learning as the culmination of various social inputs faced by individuals throughout their lives. Sutherland observed, as did Shaw and McKay, that delinquency was concentrated in the inner-city areas. Instead of attributing this to the area and the problem of social disorganization, Sutherland proposed that deviance was more easily learned in these areas. The disorganization of the area provided a degree of instability that led to the growth of deviant lifestyles and points of view. Juveniles came into daily contact with both deviant and conventional ideas. As a result, children could just as easily learn to accept deviance as they could conventional behavior.

In explaining his views, Sutherland proposed nine specific points to differential association (see Table 4.2). Underlying these nine points is the idea that deviance is learned in the same fashion as conforming behavior. The major sources of that learning are the people with whom an individual comes in contact, particularly the family, peers, and religious institutions. Explicit in the theory is the idea that everyone is exposed to both deviant and conforming information. The choice of activity depends on the relative amount of influence favoring either deviant or conventional behavior.

TABLE 4.2 Sutherland's Differential Association Theory

1. Criminal behavior is learned.

2. Criminal behavior is learned in interaction with other persons in a process of communication.

3. The principal part of the learning of criminal behavior occurs within intimate personal groups.

4. When criminal behavior is learned, the learning includes (a) techniques of the crime, which are sometimes very complicated, sometimes very simple; (b) the specification of motives, drives, rationalizations, and attitudes.

5. The specific direction of motives and drives is learned from definitions of the legal codes as favorable or unfavorable.

6. A person becomes delinquent because of an excess of definitions favorable to violation of law over definitions unfavorable to violation of law.

7. Differential associations may vary in frequency, duration, priority, and intensity.

8. The process of learning criminal behavior by association with criminal and anticriminal patterns involves all of the mechanisms that are involved in any other learning.

9. While criminal behavior is an expression of general needs and values, it is not explained by those general needs and values, because noncriminal behavior is an expression of the same needs and values.

Source: Compiled from E.H. Sutherland and D.R. Cressey (1974). *Criminology*, 9th ed. Philadelphia: Lippincott, pp. 75-76.

The basic formula for differential association has been criticized from a variety of perspectives. One of the criticisms revolves around Sutherland's failure to define or operationalize his terms. For example, he failed to define frequency, duration, priority, and intensity of associations. The common definitions of frequency (number of contacts), duration (length of a contact), priority (temporal order of the contacts), and intensity (significance of the contact) have been supplied by other researchers. Sutherland also failed to explicitly define "an excess of definitions." A second problem, stemming from the first, entails the lack of convincing empirical support for the theory. Although there have been a large number of studies focusing on differential association (for example, Adams, 1974; DeFleur and Quinney, 1966; Reiss and Rhodes, 1961; Short, 1960), most of the empirical support is indirect and highly qualified. A final problem deals with the fact that Sutherland explicitly discounted the influence of factors other than social, face-to-face contacts. While reasonable for the early 1900s, changes in the modern world have prompted researchers to modify and extend the original ideas of differential association.

Modifications of Differential Association

One of the most logical modifications to make in differential association is the inclusion of the mass media and non-face-to-face communication in the theory. Glaser's (1956) **differential identification** proposes that personal association is not always necessary for the transmission of behavioral cues. He sees real and fictional presentations on television and in other mass media as providing information concerning acceptable behavior, especially to children. The basic idea is one of imitation or modeling. An individual observes the activity of a character and begins to copy that character. Another term for this is **role-taking**. The child assumes the role that is portrayed. This is especially problematic because many children fail to realize that the media portrayals are in themselves roles and not the actual behavior of the actor playing the role. Youthful observers may see the behavior as lifelike and may not realize the fictional nature of the material. A youth might observe a glorified version of crime from a desirable fictional character and, thus, act in accordance with that portrayal.

Edwin Sutherland (1883-1950) proposed the theory of differential association, a learning theory of delinquency. Sutherland's theory can be considered the first truly sociological effort to explain crime.

Indiana University Archives

A second set of modifications of differential association revolves around the ideas of operant conditioning. **Differential reinforcement** (Jeffery, 1965) and differential association-reinforcement (Burgess and Akers, 1968) theories propose that an individual can learn from a variety of sources, both social and nonsocial. Social factors include the ideas of both differential association and differential identification. Nonsocial factors, on the other hand, can refer to the outcome of the behavior. If the behavior results in a pleasurable payoff (e.g., useful stolen goods), the behavior will be repeated. The absence of an acceptable return on the behavior or the receipt of an adverse stimulus (an undesirable outcome such as being caught and imprisoned) would prompt avoidance of the activity in the future. Burgess and Akers (1968) rewrote differential association using operant conditioning terminology.

SUBCULTURAL THEORIES

Subcultural explanations owe a great deal to the same research that prompted the early ecological and social learning theories. A key to the discussions of Shaw and McKay (1942), Sutherland (1939), and others was the diversity of people in the cities. It was this cultural diversity that prompted the idea of social disorganization and that provided different inputs to the learning process. Subcultural theorists took these ideas and focused directly on the fact of diversity in the population.

Defining subculture is not an easy task. In the simplest sense, a **subculture** is a smaller part of a larger culture. While it must vary to some degree from the larger culture, it is not totally different. The subculture exists within and is part of the larger culture. More detailed definitions typically refer to a set of values, beliefs, ideas, views, and/or meanings that a group of individuals holds and that are to some degree different from those of the larger culture.

From a subcultural perspective, delinquency and criminality are the result of individuals attempting to act in accordance with subcultural norms. This can occur in two ways. First, an individual acts according to subcultural mandates that, unfortunately, may be considered deviant by the larger society. This problem could be common for new immigrants who have traditionally acted according to one set of cultural proscriptions and are now faced with a different set of expectations in a new cultural setting. Second, deviance may result from the inability to join or be assimilated into a new culture. Consequently, the individual may strike out against society because of the frustration faced in attempting to live according to the new cultural expectations.

The Work of Cohen and Miller

Albert Cohen (1955), recognizing the concentration of delinquency among lower-class boys, proposed that these youths feel ill-equipped to compete in and deal with a middle-class society. Lower-class youths cannot succeed in a middle-class society. This is compounded by the fact that they are expected to follow the goals and aspirations of the middle class. All youths are measured against a middle-class measuring rod. A key component to this problem is the failure of lower-class families to assimilate their children into the middle-class value system.

The failure to succeed in terms of middle-class values leads to feelings of failure and diminished self-worth among the lower-class youths. As a result, these boys join together in groups and act in concert with the group (subcultural) norms instead of with the mandates of the larger culture. While this provides the youths with some degree of self-worth, status, and success, it also leads to **culture conflict**. That is, by following one set of cultural (or subcultural) practices, the individual is violating the proscriptions of another culture. In Cohen's study, adherence to the subcultural group's mandates means violating the laws of middle-class society.

Cohen (1955) identifies three aspects of the emergent "lower-class gang delinquency." He claims that the subculture is malicious, negativistic, and nonutilitarian. In support of this contention, Cohen points out that the youths often steal items, with the intent of causing trouble and harm for another person, not because they want the item. He sees much of the deviant activity as a means of tormenting others. The behavior brings about an immediate "hedonistic" pleasure instead of supplying any long-term need or solution to a problem. In general, there appears to be little point in the behavior besides causing trouble for the larger middle-class culture.

Walter Miller's (1958) subcultural explanation goes beyond the behavior of juveniles to include all lower-class males. Miller views the lower class as operating under a distinct set of cultural values, or **focal concerns** (see Table 4.3). These are: trouble, toughness, smartness, excitement, fate, and autonomy. Adherence to these lower-class focal concerns or values provides status, acceptance, and feelings of belonging for the lower-class individual (Miller, 1958).

TABLE 4.3 Miller's Lower-Class Focal Concerns

Trouble	Refers to the fact that lower-class males spend a large amount of time preoccupied with getting into and out of trouble. Trouble may bring about desired outcomes such as attention and prestige.
Toughness	Emphasis on physical prowess, athletic skill, masculinity, and bravery. Partly a response of lower-class males raised in [single] female-headed households.
Smartness	Basically the idea of being "streetwise." The concern is on how to manipulate the environment and others to your own benefit without being subjected to sanctions of any kind.
Excitement	Refers to the idea that lower-class individuals are oriented around short-term hedonistic desires. Activities, such as gambling and drug use, are undertaken for the immediate excitement or gratification that is generated.
Fate	The belief that, in the long run, individuals have little control over their lives. Luck and fortune dictate the outcome of behavior. Whatever is supposed to happen will happen regardless of the individual's wishes. This allows for a wide latitude in behavior.
Autonomy	While the individual believes in fate, there is a strong desire to resist outside control imposed by other persons. Individuals want total control over themselves until fate intervenes.

Source: Need

At the same time that these values provide positive reinforcement in the lower-class world, they bring about a natural conflict with middle-class values. The goal of the lower-class individual is not to violate the law or the middle-class norms. Instead, the goal is to follow the focal concerns of their class and peers. Deviant behavior, therefore, is a by-product of following the subcultural focal concerns (Miller, 1958). This is different from the view of Cohen (1955), in which deviance is a conscious method of striking out against the middle-class society and value system. Where Cohen (1955) sees the origins of the subcultural behaviors in the reaction of lower-class individuals faced with a middle-class world, Miller (1958) views the focal concerns as an integral part of the lower class.

Sykes and Matza: Techniques of Neutralization

Throughout the discussion of subcultural explanations there is a subtle failure to address the fact that no individual operates in just the subculture. Rather, every individual must deal with both the subcultural and the larger cultural expectations. Indeed, many individuals attempt to abide by both sets of values—those of the subculture and those of the larger culture. Juveniles, in particular, often act in accordance with one set of values or rules and still maintain a positive self-image in which they believe they fit into the acceptable behavior of the larger culture.

Accommodating different lifestyles and behaviors, however, requires individuals to find justifications for the discrepancies. For example, juveniles who commit delinquent acts often see themselves no better and no worse than anyone else, despite recognizing their deviant activity. Sykes and Matza (1957) outlined five **techniques of neutralization** that allow the juvenile to accommodate the deviant behavior while maintaining a self-image as a conformist (see Table 4.4). Each technique requires the individual to admit to the behavior under question. The youth invokes one of the techniques in order to justify his or her behavior in light of confrontation with conventional cultural values. While an exact understanding of how, when, and by whom neutralization techniques are used is not known, evidence shows that such techniques are used in various settings (Agnew, 1994; Agnew and Peters, 1986; Minor, 1981; Thurman, 1984).

Critique of the Subcultural Approach

The attempt to explain deviance through the use of subcultures faces a number of problems. The greatest problem entails identifying a subculture. As noted earlier, the typical process of identifying subcultures through the behavior of the individuals tends to be **tautological**. That is, it leads to a good deal of circular reasoning. The behavior indicates that a subculture exists, and the subculture is used to explain why the behavior occurs. The use of behaviors for identifying subcultures also faces the problem of substituting behaviors for values. A subculture entails a difference in values, beliefs, and norms from those held by the larger culture. It is questionable to what extent you can impute values from behaviors. Two separate forms of activity may reflect the same basic value. For example, in order to feed their families (basic value), one individual takes a low-paying job while another robs the local grocery store (different behaviors).

TABLE 4.4 Sykes and Matza's Techniques of Neutralization

Denial of Responsibility	The youth may claim that the action was an accident or, more likely, assert that he or she was forced into the action by circumstances beyond his or her control.
Denial of Injury	Focuses on the amount of harm caused regardless of violating the law. The absence of harm to an individual may involve pointing to a lack of physical injury, the action was a prank, or the person or business could afford the loss.
Denial of the Victim	The juvenile can deny the existence of a victim by claiming self-defense or retaliation, the absence of a victim (such as involving a business and not a person), and/or that characteristics of the victim brought the harm on himself or herself (such as hazing a homosexual).
Condemnation of the Condemnors	The youth turns the tables on those individuals who condemn his or her behavior by pointing out that the condemnors are no better than he or she. In essence, the condemnors are also deviant.
Appeal to Higher Loyalties	Conflict between the dictates of two groups will be resolved through adherence to the ideas of one group. The juvenile may see greater reward and more loyalty to the subcultural group on some issues which, in turn, lead to deviant behavior.

Source: Constructed from G.M. Sykes and D. Matza (1957). "Techniques of Neutralization: A Theory of Delinquency." *American Sociological Review* 22:664-670.

A second problem entails finding ways of identifying which set of values (subcultural or cultural) is being followed at any given time. This becomes especially problematic when the values are similar to one another. Assuming that there is variability in values and beliefs from group to group, how many values and how great a difference must exist in order to consider the group a subculture? Additionally, not all values can have the same degree of importance. Further, to what extent can an individual be deviant without belonging to a subculture?

Third, there is a possible middle-class bias in many subcultural explanations. Many authors construct their arguments by observing the behavior of lower-class individuals (e.g., Cohen and Miller). Then, these middle-class researchers impute values and beliefs (the core ideas for a subculture) to those behaviors. From their point of view, the behaviors could appear to be malicious, negativistic, and nonutilitarian (à la Cohen), or indicators of trouble, toughness, or similar traits (à la

Miller). The lower-class individuals, however, may be acting as they do for entirely different reasons from those assumed by the researchers. There is ample evidence that middle- and upper-class individuals also partake in deviance. Subcultural theorists have spent little, if any, time addressing the behavior of these individuals. Clearly, subcultural explanations require a good deal of additional research before they can be accepted or rejected.

ROUTINE ACTIVITIES AND RATIONAL CHOICE

Yet another theoretical area with ties to the ecological school is that dealing with routine activities and rational choice. While the two areas have developed out of different backgrounds, they both accept the basic premise that the movement of offenders and victims over space and time places them in varying situations in which criminal activity will be more or less possible. Within these different situations, individuals will make choices about what to do and what not to do (see Clarke and Felson, 1993). Routine activities and rational choice arguments, therefore, rest in the arena of Neoclassicism, in which there is an element of choice.

The **routine activities perspective** assumes that the normal behavior of individuals contributes to deviant events. Cohen and Felson (1979) outline three criteria necessary for the commission of a crime: (1) the presence of a suitable target; (2) a motivated offender; and (3) an absence of guardians. The possibility for deviance is enhanced when these three elements coincide. Changes in family life over the past several decades offer one example of how routine activities may impact delinquency. The increase in the number of two-earner households means that many youths are unsupervised after school and at other times. This situation results in a lack of guardianship, while also offering suitable targets (such as other unsupervised youths or unoccupied homes) for potential offenders. Another example appears in schools, particularly large secondary schools, where motivated offenders and suitable targets (both students) are required to be in close proximity with relatively few teachers or staff (guardians) available to oversee what takes place. Research has shown that the routine activities of individuals are related to a wide array of both personal and property offenses (Belknap, 1987; Kennedy and Forde, 1990; Miethe, Stafford, and Long, 1987; Roncek and Maier, 1991).

Closely tied to routine activities is **rational choice theory**. Rational choice theory assumes that potential offenders make choices based on various factors in the physical and social environments. Among the factors influencing choices are the payoff, effort, support, and risks involved in the potential behavior (Cornish and Clarke, 1986). In essence, the individual chooses if, when, and where to commit a crime based on the opportunities that are presented to him or her. There is ample evidence that offenders make choices. Studies of burglars demonstrate that burglars consider an array of factors when deciding to commit a crime, including financial or emotional need, the availability of concealment, effort required to gain entry, the presence of potential observers, the anticipated payoff, and familiarity with the area (Bennett, 1986; Bennett and Wright, 1984a; Cromwell, Olson, and Avery, 1991; Decker, Wright, and Logie, 1993; Rengert and Wasilchick, 1985; Reppetto, 1974; Taylor and Nee, 1988; Wright and Decker, 1994). This does not mean that offenders plan their behavior in detail. Rather, unplanned, spontaneous behavior may rest on past observations and experiences that lay the foundation for unconscious decisionmaking.

The support for rational choice, however, is not without qualification. The factors identified as important in decisionmaking can vary greatly from situation to situation. Rational choice theory is also criticized for its inability to explain impulsive acts and actions that clearly take place in high-risk settings. This may reflect the fact that individuals can make choices only from available alternatives. It is possible that some individuals will make what appears to be an irrational choice because of limited choices or an inability to identify other options. The neoclassical nature of the theory does not assume total volition by the individual. Finally, Akers (1990) argues that rational choice is little more than an extension of learning theory in which individuals respond to rewards and punishments. Rather than argue its uniqueness, most researchers see rational choice as an extension of and complement to various ideas, including learning theories (see, for example, Fattah, 1993; Harding, 1993; Trasler, 1993).

Rational choice poses an interesting conundrum for juvenile justice. If one assumes that youths do not have the capacity to make truly informed decisions, to what extent can it be claimed that they are making rational choices? The traditional view of the juvenile justice system is that youths cannot form the requisite intent to be held accountable for their actions. Thus, they are not rational. Instead, their behavior is determined by other factors. At the same time, it is naive to assume no rationality by youths. Coupled with routine activities, rational choice may be helpful for explaining increased delinquency during after-school hours (when there are fewer targets but less supervision) or why theft is more common than robbery.

ANOMIE AND STRAIN

Strain theory views deviance as a direct result of a social structure that stresses achievement but fails to provide adequate legitimate means of succeeding. Unlike many other theories, strain theory removes the onus for deviance from the individual and places it on society. Unacceptable behavior by an individual is seen as a natural (and expected) response to the problems posed by the social structure.

An understanding of strain theory begins with an examination of two basic facts. First, humankind is inherently egoistic (Durkheim, 1933). Happiness is the result of realizing one's expectations. Second, society does not provide equal access to the means of reaching those wishes and desires. Modern society does not provide everyone with the education and training they need to succeed. It also requires different specialized jobs to be performed. Each job is important to the whole, but the compensation for different jobs is not the same. As a result, some individuals receive more than others while everyone aspires to reach the top. The mismatch between the expectations or goals of the individual and the availability of the means to achieve those goals is called anomie. Loosely translated, **anomie** refers to a state of normlessness or inadequate regulation. More specifically, it is the inability of the individual to regulate his or her expectations in accordance with the societal structure. Anomie may result in various forms of deviant behavior, including crime.

Merton: Modes of Adaptation

In 1938, Robert Merton took the basic ideas of anomie and expanded the discussion to what is known as **strain theory**. Merton (1938) saw anomie as the lack of correspondence between culturally accepted *goals* and socially institutionalized *means* to achieve those goals. The problem is that American society presents everyone with the goals of achieving material success and reaching the top. At the same time, however, society limits access to the means for achieving those goals. For example, while higher education is a necessary prerequisite for entrance into many professions, not all individuals have the money or opportunity to receive this education. Thus, the means to succeed have been blocked for some societal members. The disjuncture between goals and means is a property of the social structure. Merton argues that what is needed is equal access to the means of achieving the goals.

Merton (1938) outlines five **modes of adaptation**, or ways an individual may respond, to the strain between goals and means (see Table 4.5). Each mode of adaptation reflects an individual's acceptance or rejection of culturally prescribed goals and socially institutionalized means of achieving those goals. *Conformity* represents the acceptance of both the goals and means, regardless of whether he or she succeeds. *Innovation* reflects acceptance of the prescribed goals but, when faced with an inability to succeed via acceptable means, the individual resorts to unacceptable or illegitimate methods of achieving success. In *ritualism*, the exact opposite occurs. While the individual gives up on achieving the goals, he or she continues to act in a socially acceptable fashion. A *retreatist* rejects both the goals and the means. This individual retreats from society through such means as alcohol or other drug use, vagrancy, or psychological withdrawal. The final mode of adaptation, *rebellion*, reflects an attempt to replace the existing societal goals and means with a new set that provides more opportunity for everyone in society.

TABLE 4.5 Merton's Modes of Adaptation

Mode of Adaptation	Cultural Goals	Institutionalized Means
Conformity	+	+
Innovation	+	–
Ritualism	–	+
Retreatism	–	–
Rebellion	±	±

+ means acceptance, – means rejection, ± means rejection and substitution

Source: R.K. Merton (1938). "Social Structure and Anomie." *American Sociological Review* 3:672-682.

The choice of adaptation varies from individual to individual. The most common response, according to Merton (1938), is conformity. This line of action presents the individual with the least amount of resistance and does not add the problems of deviance to the problem of not succeeding. In the remaining modes, individuals can be considered deviant either in their outlook or in their actions. Delinquency appears in innovation, retreatism, and rebellion, in which accepted modes of behavior (means) are replaced by unacceptable actions. While the root problem of anomie is structurally determined, the choice of adaptation can be understood only in light of individual circumstances.

General Strain Theory

Critics of strain theory have argued that not everyone aspires to the societally prescribed goals underlying Merton's discussion. Rather than focus only on the inability to achieve the societally prescribed goals, Agnew (1992) has proposed a **general strain theory** that suggests that strain can arise from two other sources. The first entails the removal of desired or valued stimuli. Examples may include restricting a youth's normal activities, moving to another city and away from friends, canceling a long-planned trip, or being forced to quit a sports team. A second source of strain may be the presentation of negative stimuli, which may cause an individual to become angry or frustrated. Having to walk to school through a dangerous neighborhood, being bused to a distant school, living in an abusive household, or being harassed by other youths are all potential forms of negative stimuli. These two sources of strain may prompt individuals to respond with delinquent or criminal behavior (Agnew, 1992). There are also many nondeviant coping mechanisms that an individual can utilize (Agnew, 1997). Agnew and White (1992) provide empirical support for general strain theory. They report finding a positive relationship between measures of generalized strain and delinquent behavior.

Assessing Strain Theory

The practical implication of traditional strain theory (Merton's view) would appear to be changing the structural barriers to success that underlie deviant activity. Unfortunately, problems with strain theory suggest that such activity would be premature. One major issue entails the problem of operationalizing the key concepts, such as anomie, aspirations, opportunity, and perceptions. Differing definitions of these terms lead to conflicting empirical support for the theory.

Studies by Kornhauser (1978), Quicker (1974), Agnew (1984), and others have noted that the assumed relationship between strain and deviant behavior is not clear. In some instances, deviance appears to be related to low aspirations, while in others deviance may actually cause changes in aspirations instead of the reverse (Kornhauser, 1978). For example, some individuals may substitute immediate gratification and goals in place of the long-term, societal goals. This may be a direct result of the recognized inability to achieve the societal goal.

A second problem stems from the fact that many studies focus on middle- and upper-class youths, while the Mertonian strain theory appears more applicable to lower-class and gang activity. Third, strain theory fails to present any explanation for the choice of adaptation. Little attention is directed to why one person chooses deviance and another does not. Finally, Mertonian strain assumes that all deviance is a result of unfulfilled aspirations. Agnew's (1992) theory addresses some of these issues. It appears that future research should take the broader approach offered by Agnew.

SOCIAL CONTROL THEORY

Where most theories look to identify factors that lead or push a juvenile into delinquency, **social control theories** seek to find factors that keep an individual from becoming deviant. Control theorists ask why many people refrain from violating the law even though they are presented with ample opportunity to commit crimes. Reckless (1967) views the main issue as explaining why one individual becomes deviant and another does not when both are faced with the same situations. The explanation they offer deals with the degree of control exerted on the individual.

Hirschi: Control Theory

Hirschi's (1969) theory states that "delinquent acts result when an individual's bond to society is weak or broken" (p. 16). The underlying assumption is that the individual's behavior is controlled by the connections the person has to conventional social order. Deviance shows up when a person's **bond to society** is weak or broken. According to Hirschi (1969), bond is developed through socialization during early childhood and consists of four elements: attachment, commitment, involvement, and belief (see Table 4.6). The failure of an individual to care about what others think about his or her behavior and views (attachment), to work toward acceptable goals (commitment), to use one's energies and time in socially acceptable behaviors (involvement), and/or to accept the common value system in society (belief) opens the door for deviant and delinquent behavior. Weak or broken bond does not *cause* deviance. Rather, *it allows for* deviance. In other words, weak or broken bond could be viewed as necessary for deviance, but not sufficient. An individual with weak bond may or may not choose to commit deviant acts.

TABLE 4.6 Elements of Hirschi's Bond

Attachment	"sensitivity to the opinion of others" (p. 16)
	The more an individual cares about what others think of himself/herself, the less likely he/she will choose behavior that brings about negative input.
Commitment	a "person invests time, energy, himself, in a certain line of activity" (p. 20)
	As a person builds an investment in conventional endeavors, any choice of deviant behavior will place that investment at risk.
Involvement	"engrossment in conventional activities" (p. 22)
	Because time and energy are limited, once they are used in the pursuit of conventional activities, there is no time or energy left for deviant behavior.
Belief	"the existence of a common value system within the society or group" (p. 23)
	As a person is socialized into and accepts the common belief system, he/she will be less likely to violate those beliefs through deviant activity.

Source: Constructed by authors from T. Hirschi (1969). *Causes of Delinquency*. Berkeley: University of California Press.

Numerous tests of Hirschi's social control theory have been undertaken. Hirschi (1969) surveyed more than 4,000 high school boys about their delinquent activity and elements of bond. Consistent with the theory, he found that delinquency was related to weaker attachment to parents, education, and school; lower aspirations (i.e., lacking commitment); more time spent "joy riding" in cars or being bored (involvement); and less respect for the police and the law (belief). Other studies (Hindelang, 1973; Krohn and Massey, 1980; Poole and Regoli, 1979; Wiatrowski, Griswold, and Roberts, 1981) report similar supportive findings.

Despite support for the theory, a number of problematic issues remain. First, the theory does not adequately explain how bond becomes weak or broken. The theory tries to explain why individuals are deviant and not how they became that way. While poor socialization is the easiest explanation, the theory fails to demonstrate how this occurs. Second, the relative impact of the four elements of bond is left unresolved. For example, if attachment is strong and commitment is moderate but involvement and belief are weak, will this permit deviance or not? As a result of this problem, the theory cannot directly offer suggestions on how to avoid the weakening of bond or how to repair bond.

Another area of concern deals with episodic deviance. Many youths vacillate between delinquent and conventional behavior. This **drift** cannot be explained using control theory. While an individual chooses to commit deviance, the theory does not explain the vacillation in choices over time and place. Such drift can only be adequately explained by proposing that the bond is strengthened and weakened both easily and often. Finally, the theory assumes that all bonding is to conventional, nondeviant lifestyles. It may be possible that a juvenile is raised in a household in which the parents are deviant and espouse nontraditional behaviors. A juvenile in these circumstances should be bonded to deviance. Indeed, Jensen and Brownfield (1983) report that juveniles will follow the deviant behaviors of their parents as well as the nondeviant themes.

Reckless: Containment Theory

Reckless's (1962) **containment theory** differs from Hirschi's bond argument in two fundamental ways. First, containment theory proposes that the individual may have some control over his or her own behavior, rather than having controls imposed by others. Second, while there are factors that promote conformity, there are also forces promoting deviance.

Reckless (1962) outlines two types of containment: outer containment and inner containment (Table 4.7). **Outer containment** offers direct control over the individual from outside sources. These include family members, friends, teachers, and others who provide supervision, training, and pressure to conform. Conversely, **inner containment** is necessary due to the fact that an individual is not always under the direct control of outer containment. Thus, internalized moral codes, tolerance of frustration, and other factors help the individual refrain from deviance. The combination of these two factors should provide an effective means of avoiding deviant behavior. The factors that promote deviant behavior include *internal pushes*, *external pressures*, and *external pulls* (Reckless, 1962). Each of these influences an individual's activity. Poverty, unemployment, discontent, anxiety, deviant peers, and other factors may lead or push people into deviant activity as a viable form of behavioral response. These three factors make deviance an acceptable alternative, while inner and outer containment work to offset their influence.

TABLE 4.7 Elements of Reckless's Containment Theory

Forces promoting conformity:

Outer Containment	The influence of family, peers, and environment on behavior; social pressure, supervision, training, and group membership
Inner Containment	Individual factors such as self-concept, tolerance of frustration, goal-directedness, internalized moral codes

Forces promoting deviance:

Internal Pushes	Restlessness, discontent, anxiety, hostility
External Pressures	Poverty, unemployment, minority status, social inequality
External Pulls	Deviant peers, subcultures, media presentations

Source: Compiled from W.C. Reckless (1962). "A Noncausal Explanation: Containment Theory." *Excerpta Criminologica* 1:131-134.

Containment theory has received both support and criticism. Much of the support revolves around the fact that the theory includes factors related to both society and the individual. Additional support comes from the fact that Reckless proposes a theory to explain conforming behavior occurring amidst great amounts of deviance. The major criticism of containment theory has come in the form of methodological critiques centering on the ability to operationalize the key ideas. Schrag (1971) argues that many of the terms are vague and fall within more than one category. For example, peers work as both constraining forces in outer containment and deviance-producing features of external pulls. Such inconsistency makes the theory hard to test empirically. This may be one cause of the lack of empirical support uncovered by other researchers (Schwartz and Tangri, 1965; Tangri and Schwartz, 1967). Another criticism of containment theory centers around the idea of positive self-concept as an "insulator" against deviance. Indeed, research has failed to find a self-concept/deviance connection.

Self-Control Theory

Control theory has undergone its greatest change with the introduction of **self-control theory**. Rather than assume that behavior is controlled by outside forces throughout an individual's life, Gottfredson and Hirschi

(1990) argue that self-control, internalized early in life, can serve to keep a person from involvement in deviant behavior. Self-control serves as a restraint from choosing the short-term gratification endemic to most criminal behavior. Gottfredson and Hirschi (1990:90) claim that

> people who lack self-control will tend to be impulsive, insensitive, physical (as opposed to mental), risk-taking, short-sighted, and nonverbal, and they will tend therefore to engage in criminal and analogous acts.

Self-control theory assumes that people are hedonistic and make choices emphasizing immediate, short-term pleasure.

The primary source of self-control is good parenting (Gottfredson and Hirschi, 1990). Poor self-control is the result of ineffective child-rearing practices by the parents. Good parenting requires exhibiting concern for the child, consistent monitoring of the child's behavior, the ability to identify problematic behaviors, appropriate reactions to inappropriate behavior, and the time and energy to carry through with parental responsibilities. Should the parents fail to build self-control, other social institutions, such as schools, may influence its formation but are typically poor substitutes for the family (Gottfredson and Hirschi, 1990). Once self-control is internalized, it serves to modify an individual's behavior throughout his or her life.

Self-control theory has received both support and criticism. A number of studies have found evidence that a lack of self-control is related to deviant behavior (Grasmick et al., 1993; Piquero, MacIntosh, and Hickman, 2000; Wood, Pfefferbaum, and Arneklev, 1993). Indeed, both a global measure of self-control as well as individual components (such as risk-taking, self-centeredness, and immediate gratification) are related to various forms of deviance, with the more global measure having the greatest consistency and impact (Wood, Pfefferbaum, and Arneklev, 1993). At the same time, the theory has been criticized for its inability to explain significant changes in behavior later in life and to consider the basic social structure as a contributor to parenting and self-control (Lilly, Cullen, and Ball, 1995). In addition, Akers (1991) argues that the theory is tautological. That is, low self-control is determined by the commission of deviant acts, and the deviant acts are the result of low self-control.

THE LABELING PERSPECTIVE

Another approach that places the blame for deviance on society is the **labeling** perspective. The basic assumption of labeling is that being labeled as deviant by social control agents forces the person to act according to the label. Further deviance is a result of being contacted and sanctioned by the system. Consequently, continued deviance is a response to the actions of society. For example, being labeled a "delinquent" may lead to exclusion from participation in extracurricular school activities. This inability to participate in conforming activities may prompt further deviant behavior.

The Construction of Self-Image

The labeling perspective owes much to the ideas of **symbolic interactionism**. Symbolic interactionism proposes that every individual develops his or her self-image through a process of interaction with the surrounding world (Mead, 1934). How an individual sees himself or herself is determined by how that person thinks others see him or her. That is, a person's self-concept comes out of interaction with other people and the environment. Interaction with other people provides an individual with input about his or her own self. If an individual perceives a positive image of himself or herself from others, the person will hold a positive self-image. A simple way of viewing this process is through what Cooley (1902) calls the **looking-glass self**. The idea is that individuals view themselves in the way other people look at them. The individual attempts to see what other people see and acts accordingly.

Labeling takes these ideas and proposes that individuals mold their behavior in accordance with the perceptions of others. Tannenbaum (1938) saw the sanctioning of deviant behavior as a step in altering a juvenile's self-image from that of a normal, conventional youth to that of being a delinquent. System processing identifies a youth as delinquent, emphasizes the label, and ultimately segregates the youth from normal juvenile behavior. Juveniles begin to view themselves as deviant, which leads to actions consistent with the self-image. Basically, the process of labeling entails a **transfer of evil** from the act to the actor (Tannenbaum, 1938). Instead of viewing the act as deviant and bad, the actor becomes bad and the focus for social action. No longer is the individual someone who committed a crime; the individual is a criminal.

Lemert: Primary and Secondary Deviance

Edwin Lemert (1951) distinguished between two types of deviance—primary and secondary. **Primary deviance** comprises those actions that "are rationalized or otherwise dealt with as functions of a socially acceptable role" (Lemert, 1951). These deviant acts are common and garner minimal attention and mild sanctions. As a result, the individual is not labeled, and his or her self-image is not altered. **Secondary deviance**, however, occurs when an individual "begins to employ his deviant behavior or a role based upon it as a means of defense, attack, or adjustment to the overt and covert problems created by the consequent societal reaction to him" (Lemert, 1951). This means that society has successfully labeled the individual. The individual now views himself or herself as different and/or deviant, and will act accordingly.

TABLE 4.8 Lemert's Labeling Perspective

Primary Deviance	Actions that are rationalized as a result of socially acceptable roles; deviance is considered an aberration and results in only minor sanctions; the offender continues to see self as a normal member of society.
Secondary Deviance	Actions that are taken by an individual as a result of accepting the label, i.e., fulfilling the role proscribed by the label; individual commits deviance as a defense against the negative connotation of being seen as a "deviant."

It is important to note that primary and secondary deviant acts entail the same types of behavior. What distinguishes secondary from primary deviance is the reason behind the action. The behavior is secondary if the act cannot be rationalized as the outcome of a nondeviant social role *and* is committed as an attack or defense against societal reaction. Secondary deviance, therefore, is a *mentalistic construct*. That is, it relies on the mind-set and attitude of the individual involved.

The reasons for conforming to the label are simple. First, a deviant label makes participation in conventional activity difficult. Societal members expect deviance and react to the individual as a deviant, regardless of whether specific behavior is deviant or conforming. Second, by accepting the label, the individual blunts the impact of any negative feedback provided by society. For example, young children cry when told they are bad because the information is counter to their beliefs. Children would not be affected, however, if they saw themselves as bad. Negative input would simply point out what they already knew and accepted. Finally, individuals conform to labels as a means of striking out against those who are condemning them. Using a kind of "if that is what you think" attitude, individuals decide to show society just how bad they can really be if that is what society wants.

The process by which an individual assumes a negative label is not simple. A single deviant act generally will not lead to the successful application of a label. Lemert (1951) proposes an outline of the process that culminates in secondary deviance:

> (1) primary deviation; (2) social penalties; (3) further primary deviation; (4) stronger penalties and rejections; (5) further deviation, perhaps with hostilities and resentment beginning to focus upon those doing the penalizing; (6) crisis reached in the

tolerance quotient...; (7) strengthening of the deviant conduct as a reaction to the stigmatizing and penalties; (8) ultimate acceptance of deviant social status and efforts at adjustment on the basis of the associated role (p. 77).

Lemert notes that this process is not set with any definite number of steps or particular sequence of events. Rather, the process is an illustration of the types of factors that occur.

The Impact of the Labeling Perspective

The assumptions of labeling suggest that youths who have contact with the juvenile justice system are successfully labeled and act accordingly. This view led to major changes in the juvenile justice system in the 1970s. Most of the changes involved diverting youths away from system processing and attempting to find alternatives to incarcerating youths, particularly minor and status offenders. Empirical research presents conflicting evidence on whether a label leads to more delinquency.

Most support for labeling comes from studies that report higher recidivism for youths with prior system contact. The assumption is that the later deviance is due to successful labeling. However, there is no measure of the individual's self-concept in these studies. It is impossible, therefore, to identify the recidivistic behavior as secondary deviance (the result of labeling) or further primary deviance.

Studies that directly examine changes in self-concept after system intervention present conflicting results. Various studies (Foster, Dinitz, and Reckless, 1972; Lipsett, 1968; Snyder, 1971) report little or no effect of system contact on self-image. Other researchers uncover lower self-concept (Ageton and Elliott, 1973; Jensen, 1972; Street, Vinter, and Perrow, 1966). Any inability to find changes in a person's self-image would interrupt the proposed causal chain and raise doubt about the impact of the labeling.

Part of the failure of the labeling perspective may be due to the lack of attention paid to the impact of family, friends, and peer groups. For example, a youth may report no change in self-concept after contact with the formal justice system because he or she actually aspires to gain the label of "gang member." The youth pursues system contact in order to legitimize his or her gang affiliation. Formal system labeling also may fail if the individual receives accolades from family and friends. Conversely, a youth may be labeled by peers even if the system decides not to act. Each of these cases demonstrates that system intervention may be neither necessary nor sufficient for imposing a label. Most evaluations of labeling ignore the many potential confounding factors that may be at work (see, Palamara, Cullen, and Gersten, 1986).

THE INTEGRATION AND ELABORATION OF THEORIES

One trend in criminological theorizing is the attempt to integrate various theories into more unified, coherent explanations of deviance. Many writers feel that, rather than attempt to show that any single theory is appropriate in all situations, each theory should be viewed as applicable to different domains of behavior. A number of authors have experimented with linking different explanations into an integrated theory of deviance. This process, also referred to as an **elaboration model**, attempts to take components of various theories and construct a single explanation that incorporates the best parts of the individual theories. Delbert Elliott and his colleagues (Elliott, 1985; Elliott, Ageton, and Canter, 1979; Elliott, Huizinga, and Ageton, 1985), working with extensive longitudinal data, have constructed and tested a model that includes elements of social control, strain, and differential association theories. In their studies, the authors provide a rough sequential process leading to deviance. Strain is seen as leading to a weakened bond to conventional society, which in turn leads to increased bonding with deviants and subsequent deviant behavior. Mediating this entire process is the influence of learning.

Other authors also report on attempts at linking social control (bond) and differential association theories (see Marcos, Bahr, and Johnson, 1986; Massey and Krohn, 1986; Thornberry, 1987; Thornberry et al., 1994) and control and subcultural theories (Giordano, Cernkovich, and Pugh, 1986). In general, these investigations uncover a dynamic process in which different effects influence deviance at various points in the process. These attempts at building more elaborate explanations have not gone unchallenged. The challenges, however, are not widespread and often appear to reflect rhetorical positions based on defense of favored theories that may not fare well in the new models.

Recent interest in **developmental theories**, or **life-course theories**, generally reflects efforts that incorporate ideas from several theories and perspectives. Conger and Simmons (1997), for example, point out that biological factors play a role in cognitive ability, which impacts on how family, friends, and schools may treat a person, which may then impact on an individual's success in school or in making choices. Throughout this process, the individual faces different demands and opportunities, for which he or she may or may not be adequately prepared. Similarly, Moffitt (1997) offers a sequence in which neuropsychological deficits alter an individual's temperament, speech, learning ability, and other factors, which may cause withdrawal, rejection by others, poor self-concept, failure at school, and a host of other problems. Each of these problems appears as a key factor in several individual theories. The key for Moffitt (1997) is the sequential and cumulative nature of the various factors.

LeBlanc (1997) offers a **generic control theory** that draws on ideas from a variety of perspectives. He proposes that control can come from several sources that vary over time and situation. He offers four primary categories of control mechanisms. The first, *bonding*, deals with how individuals are integrated to and act as part of the community. A second source is *unfolding*, which reflects the growth and development of individuals, especially in terms of internalizing values. *Modeling*, the third type, incorporates patterns that the person can emulate in order to conform. Finally, *constraining* refers to regulation imposed by others. Each of these mechanisms interacts to enhance the level of control. In support of his propositions, LeBlanc (1997) offers a multilayered model that simultaneously discusses criminal acts, the criminal, and criminality. LeBlanc notes, however, that the model requires more work before it can be operationalized for testing. For the purposes of this text, the value of the theory is in its use of concepts and ideas from a wide range of individuals theories.

A final example of the integration/elaboration approach involves the idea of **reintegrative shaming**. Braithwaite (1989) offers shaming as a key mechanism for showing societal disapproval. The shaming, however, needs to be imposed in such a fashion as to draw the offending party into conforming society. Elements of several theories are incorporated in Braithwaite's argument. Labeling and symbolic interaction are important for understanding the risk in shaming someone without concern for reintegration. Social control elements appear in the need to bond the person to society. Additionally, the family is a key actor in teaching proper behavior (learning theory). Braithwaite (1989) also argues that a great deal of shaming takes place vicariously through stories and examples (modeling and imitation ideas).

Many of these "new" theories have yet to undergo rigorous testing. This is partly due to the complexity of the proposed theoretical models and the lack of appropriate data for testing the full explanation. The advantages of the elaboration/integration approach appear in the attempt to draw together long theoretical traditions, each of which has demonstrated some empirical support. The fact that no single theory has adequately explained deviance suggests that this new direction should be continued.

THE IMPACT OF THEORIES ON JUVENILE JUSTICE

While a good deal of theorizing has been devoted to the causes of delinquent activity, the extent to which these explanations have an impact on the daily operations of the juvenile justice system is highly variable. Court dispositions and correctional treatments display the closest relationships between the theories and justice system action. As noted in Chapter 2, the rhetoric of the juvenile court has consistently emphasized the importance of learning and benevolent care of youths. Social learning theory provides support for interventions that focus on providing proper role models and environments conducive to conforming behavior. Trends toward deinstitutionalization rely on the arguments of labeling theory as well as learning principles. Thus, the past 20 years or so have experienced movements to community corrections and less restrictive interventions (see Chapter 12). Recent movements toward incarceration and deterrence of juveniles clearly rely on Classical and Neoclassical assumptions of free will and hedonistic choice.

On a larger scale, various theoretical perspectives have helped influence general social movements. The Great Society reforms that began in the mid-1960s attempted to address the social inequities that lead to deviance. Educational programs, economic assistance, vocational training, physical improvement of inner cities, and other efforts can be traced to strain, subcultural, learning, and ecological explanations of social ills. In many of these social actions, delinquency and criminality were only two of many social problems being addressed. The impact of these specific programs is a matter of debate. The consistency in crime, delinquency, and recidivism rates suggests that there was little impact on these problems, but why they did not have an impact is not clear. Some authors argue that the interventions were too short-lived to alter long-standing social problems. Others claim that the implementation of the programs was incomplete or inappropriate. Still others deny the adequacy of the theoretical explanation being utilized. Regardless of past failures, the various theories continue to find their way into the policies and procedures of the juvenile justice system.

SUMMARY

Explanations of delinquent and criminal behavior, whether biological, psychological, or sociological in nature, provide some insight into the reasons for deviance. The diversity in perspectives, however, illustrates the lack of understanding that still exists. Indeed, the search for a single theory that explains all—or almost all—deviance appears to be an effort in futility. The most reasonable consideration is to view deviance as multifaceted. The explanation, therefore, must consider a wide range in variables and influences. Juvenile justice must not ignore theory simply because until this point in time it has failed to arrive at a totally adequate explanation. Rather, the system must take care to select, implement, and evaluate ideas in light of expanding knowledge and research. While the remainder of the text deals with various interventions and system actions, theory forms an implicit base for all discussions.

DISCUSSION QUESTIONS

1. Sociological explanations for deviance are currently the most well known. Pick any sociological theory, outline the argument, and translate those ideas into practical applications for dealing with juveniles.

2. The President has called for a study that will set the tone for future directions in juvenile justice. As a member of the Commission, you have the opportunity to advocate an underlying theory. Which sociological theory will you fight for, and why is it the best possible approach for guiding the juvenile justice system? Present strengths and weaknesses of your choice.

3. A recent trend in delinquency explanations is the integration or elaboration model. Discuss how you can integrate subculture, learning, and control theories. How are they related, and what will the new explanation provide that any single theory cannot?

Chapter 5

GANG DELINQUENCY

Important Terms

Boston Gun Project

Community-Wide Approach
   to Gang Prevention, Intervention,
   and Suppression Program

detached worker programs

enhancement model

foray

gang

ganging

Gang Resistance Education and
   Training (G.R.E.A.T.) Program

group hazard hypothesis

hybrid gangs

interstitial areas

National Youth Gang Survey
   (NYGS)

near group

pulling levers

rumble

selection model

social facilitation model

STEP Act

wilding gangs

What You Need to Know

- Many studies note that delinquency is often committed in groups, and that such offending is more recognized by agents of social control

- There is no one accepted definition of a gang, although common elements of most definitions include persistence over time, congregating in public, self-identifying as a gang, claims over turf, and participation in illegal activity.

- Thrasher provided one of the earliest studies on gangs and viewed them as mainly "spontaneous play groups" in lower-class areas of town.

- Measuring the extent of gang membership is not easy and generally is reliant on reports from police or other social control agencies.

- In the most recent estimates, there are 26,500 active gangs with roughly 785,000 members in the United States.

- Most gang members are young, male, and Hispanic.

- One of the most frequent concerns is that gangs are migrating from the large cities to other locations. There is little evidence of any planned migration, and most movement is actually due to chance or relocation of gang members for non-gang reasons.

- Youths join gangs primarily for a sense of belonging, status, success, self-esteem, and cohesion.

- While most portrayals show gangs as violent and very criminal, actual gang behavior is mainly social and noncriminal. Criminal activity, however, is an important part of gang membership.

- Most gang violence is isolated and between gang members rather than directed at the general public.

- Among intervention strategies with gangs, suppression is the most used but considered the least effective, while opportunities provision is the least used but considered the most effective.

- Programs that attempt to place workers in the gangs to help direct their behaviors (i.e., detached workers) have little positive impact and may actually draw youths to the gang.

- Law enforcement crackdowns on ganging, such as the Boston Gun Project, can be highly successful, but that success typically lasts only as long as the project operates.

- Classroom-based anti-gang programs such as G.R.E.A.T. have had little impact on gang behavior.

101

INTRODUCTION

For many individuals, agencies, and communities, the problem of youthful misbehavior is most notably gang delinquency. Indeed, a great deal of early research shows that juveniles commit more deviant acts while in the company of other youths than when they are alone (see, for example, Erickson, 1971; Hindelang, 1971). Research on group delinquency dates back to the early twentieth century and the work of Thrasher (1936), Sutherland (1939), and Shaw and associates (1929).

Early delinquency research often focused on the idea that youthful misconduct was a result of peer influences. Differential association theory (Sutherland, 1939) proposed that much delinquent activity was the result of learning that took place in interactions between youths. Shaw and associates (Shaw et al., 1929; Shaw and McKay, 1942) focused heavily on the idea that juvenile misbehavior took place in groups. This theme of group behavior has persisted throughout the study of delinquency.

While studies claim a propensity for juveniles to act in groups, it is possible that much of the group dimension in offending is due to differential responses by society (Erickson, 1973; Feyerherm, 1980). The **group hazard hypothesis** proposes that delinquency committed in groups has a greater chance of being detected and acted upon by the juvenile and criminal justice systems (Erickson, 1973). In a study of 336 youths, Erickson (1973) reports that the group hazard hypothesis holds for select types of delinquent acts, especially more serious offenses. Group behavior simply may make recognition of a problem easier, thus more youths involved in group delinquency become involved with the juvenile justice system. The finding of high levels of group behavior in self-report surveys, however, suggests that the group hazard hypothesis is not a complete explanation of the group nature of delinquent activity.

Much of the interest in group delinquency revolves around the idea of juvenile gangs. Popular concern about gangs can be attributed to the finding that many youthful offenses are committed in concert with other juveniles. Another source for the public's concern may be the portrayal of gang behavior in the mass media. Movies and plays such as *The Blackboard Jungle*, *West Side Story*, and *Colors* dramatize the lure of gangs for youths and the aggressive nature of these groups of youths.

Interest in gangs has waxed and waned over the years. From the 1950s to the early 1960s there was a great deal of attention paid to gang delinquency. This interest subsided in the late 1960s, possibly due to the shift in attention to broader concerns over the social order, such as the Vietnam War, the economy, and racial unrest (Bookin-Weiner and Horowitz, 1983). New theoretical orientations also shifted interest from the offenders to the structure of society and its systems of social control. As a result, gang problems did not retain their priority as research issues. Not until the late 1980s did we see a renewed interest in gangs and gang behavior. Gang researchers attribute the renewed interest to the escalation of gang violence and the belief that gangs are the driving force behind growing drug problems, particularly crack cocaine.

GANGS DEFINED

While there has been a great deal of interest and research in gang activity, no single definition of a gang has developed. In general, the term **gang** has referred to groups that exhibit characteristics setting them apart from other affiliations of juveniles. Various researchers have proposed different definitions of a gang.

In one of the earliest gang definitions, Thrasher (1936) defined a gang as:

> an interstitial group originally formed spontaneously, and then integrated through conflict. It is characterized by the following types of behavior: meeting face to face, milling, movement through space as a unit, conflict, and planning. The result of this collective behavior is the development of tradition, unreflective internal structure, esprit de corps, solidarity, morale, group awareness, and attachment to a local territory (p. 57).

This definition introduced a number of key ideas. First, a gang was a specific form of a group. Second, what made these groups different from others was a system of activity and behavior that included conflict and mutual support of members. Finally, gangs were found in those areas of a city that were deteriorating and in a state of disorganization (**interstitial areas**). Gangs, therefore, were seen by Thrasher as a unique phenomenon of the poor, inner-city, immigrant areas of the early twentieth century.

The National Youth Gang Center has a wealth of information on defining and identifying gangs, as well as data on gang behavior. Go to http://www.iir.com/nygc/

Today, most definitions include the need for society to recognize the group as a threat and for the group to be involved in some degree of criminal/delinquent activity. The need for official recognition as a threat is evident in the definition used by the **National Youth Gang Survey (NYGS)** (2000), which defines a youth gang as:

> a group of youths or young adults in [the] jurisdiction that you or other responsible persons in your agency or community are willing to identify or classify as a "gang."

The NYGS specifically excludes motorcycle gangs, hate groups, prison gangs, or gangs composed exclusively of adults from its work.

Klein and Maxson (2006) offer a definition based on input from American and European researchers and policymakers. They note that

> a street gang is any durable, street-oriented youth group where involvement in illegal activity is part of its group identity.

This definition outlines several key elements. First, the group persists over time despite possible turnover in membership (durability). Second, the group spends a great deal of time outside on the street, in parks, or other public places. Third, the gang membership is composed primarily of youths, although this does not restrict membership to juveniles. Fourth, there is some degree of illegal activity. Finally, the group sees itself as having an identity. This definition, however, has not been universally adopted. and different jurisdictions continue to make up and rely on various definitions.

Curry and Decker (1998) identify six elements typical in most gang definitions: group, symbols, communication, permanence, turf, and crime (see Table 5.1). Being a group is perhaps the easiest of the elements to understand, although most definitions require a minimum number of members. Symbols serve to provide the group with an identity. These elements often are developed for internal use and may not convey meaning outside the group. The symbols also may be used in communication between and among gangs, their members, and others. The development of symbols and unique forms of communication can contribute to the longevity or permanence of the gang. As groups gain permanence they become harder to combat and dismantle. The element of turf, while common, is not as universal as the other elements because there are many examples of gangs that do not claim a physical territory. The final element, crime, is the most important, because group involvement in criminal activities is key to distinguishing a gang from other groups of people who may use the other elements, such as college fraternities and the Boy Scouts (Curry and Decker, 1998).

TABLE 5.1 Typical Elements of a "Gang" Definition

GROUP	usually a specified minimum number of members, certainly more than two
SYMBOLS	clothes, hand signs, colors, etc., which serve to indicate membership
COMMUNICATION	verbal and nonverbal forms, such as made up words, graffiti, hand signals, etc.
PERMANENCE	gangs must persist over time, generally at least one year or more
TURF	territory claimed and/or controlled by the gang (not as common in many definitions)
CRIME	involvement in criminal behavior

Source: Compiled from G.D. Curry and S.H. Decker (1998). *Confronting Gangs: Crime and Community.* Los Angeles: Roxbury.

That a single definition of a gang has not been agreed upon should be clear to the reader. The term "gang" has different meanings to different individuals, in different locations, at different times. What is common about gangs is the perception that they pose some form of threat to the safety of others.

EARLY GANG RESEARCH

Interest in gangs formed a good portion of the empirical and theoretical research prior to the mid-1960s. Much of the early research on gangs focused on describing the gangs and examining the daily workings of these groups. The research relied to a great extent on participant observation techniques. This research approach involved going out and observing the gangs on a daily basis. Such analysis provided a firsthand look at the structure and behavior of the gangs under study.

Thrasher's Gangs

Perhaps the most noted of the early studies of gangs was that of Frederick Thrasher. Thrasher (1936) studied 1,313 gangs with roughly 25,000 members in Chicago. He noted that the beginnings of gangs were found in spontaneous play groups within the interstitial areas of town that were characterized by a large amount of transience, great numbers of immigrant youths, poor living conditions, and a state of social disorganization. These ideas were simple extensions of the early work of Shaw et al. (1929), Shaw and McKay (1942), and the Chicago School. The gangs supplied needed interaction and social contact for the youths, which were not supplied by families or other social institutions.

Thrasher also viewed gangs as an outgrowth of innocent, everyday behavior among adolescents. Spontaneous play groups provided the basis and possibility for conflict. The groups provided a feeling of belonging and togetherness for the participants. The development of leadership, cohesion, and conflict served to strengthen the spontaneous groups and the establishment of a gang.

Thrasher (1936) did not see gangs as a stable or permanent entity. The development of gangs, or **ganging**, was a continuous process. Gangs were comprised mostly of juveniles between the ages of 11 and 17, and few members remained in gangs past young adulthood due to the movement into marriage and legitimate employment. Change in gangs was due to the maturing of individual members, the movement of members out of the immediate community, and the ability of the gang to provide meaningful activity for its members. While the specific makeup of the gang changed, many gangs would survive by replacing old members with

new recruits. The recruits would come from those youths residing in the
territory controlled by the gang.

Gang activity very often centered on conflict within the individual
gang and between different gangs. According to Thrasher (1936), conflict helped build esprit de corps and unity among the gang's members.
Within group disputes settled through conflict provided a basis for common values, loyalty, and cohesion among the membership. Successful
conflict also provided the individual group member with prestige and
status. Conflict with other gangs brought about increased cohesion
among group members and helped to draw the gang into a more formal,
organized, and long-term system of interaction.

The gang was a means for youths in disorganized, inner-city areas to
gain acceptance and exert some power over their situation. Gangs were
not a planned response to problems in the neighborhoods by the youths.
Instead, gangs were formed from the spontaneous play groups in which
the youths found themselves.

Bloch and Neiderhoffer: Gangs as a Natural Response

Twenty years after Thrasher's (1936) monumental work, Bloch and
Neiderhoffer (1958) expanded on many of his ideas. Where Thrasher
viewed gangs as primarily a lower-class juvenile phenomenon, Bloch
and Neiderhoffer proposed that gangs were different from other juvenile
groups simply by a matter of degree. The gang provided its members with
status, success, and feelings of belonging that they were not being provided
by the larger society (Bloch and Neiderhoffer, 1958). Lower-class youths,
who made up most gangs, were simply striving to succeed in the same sense
as middle- and upper-class youths. Their social position, however, led them
into situations that made gang behavior an acceptable alternative.

The organization of the gang was not greatly different from that portrayed by Thrasher (1936). Gangs developed leadership, cohesion, loyalty,
and support through their daily activities. Bloch and Neiderhoffer (1958),
however, saw gangs as somewhat more fragile in terms of their longevity. The loss of a leader was seen as bringing about the dissolution of the
gang. The gang was viewed as having less permanence than those studied
by Thrasher. Despite this departure in views, both studies saw the gang as
providing needed social support and status for participating youths.

Yablonsky: Near Groups

A different view of gangs is found in Yablonsky's (1962) explanation
of gang formation and participation. First, he concentrates mainly on violent gangs whose activity focuses on violence and aggression. The violent

gang strives for emotional gratification through hostile actions toward gang members and nonmembers. It also provides a sense of power for the participating individuals. Second, Yablonsky repudiates the idea that a gang is a well-organized group. Instead, he sees the violent gang as a **near group**, characterized by a relatively short lifetime, little formal organization, a lack of consensus between members, a small core of continuous participants, self-appointed leadership (as opposed to group-approved), and limited cohesion. Most "members" of the gang participate on the fringe and become involved only when individual or group violence is indicated. Self-aggrandizement, not group issues, is the major concern for gang members. This near-group view is restricted only to the violent gangs in Yablonsky's (1962) discussion. Other gangs may reflect the more classic portrayal found in other writings, although Yablonsky would argue that the violent "near group" is the dominant form of gang in society.

THE EXTENT OF GANG MEMBERSHIP

Measuring gang delinquency and/or gang involvement is not an easy task. A number of problems arise when attempting to assess the extent of gang membership. First, there is no single, accepted definition of what constitutes a gang. Any attempt to measure gang membership across jurisdictions, therefore, runs the risk of collecting data that reflect different problems or groups. This problem persists even when a survey (such as the NYGS) provides a definition for agencies to use, because the agency records typically reflect a local definition and the information is not reclassified to correspond to the desired definition before it is submitted. Second, many agencies classify individuals as gang members only if the individual self-identifies as such (Egley et al., 2004). Many youths may not claim gang membership, even if they fit a legal or other definition of a gang member.

Third, many jurisdictions may actively deny the existence of gangs and not collect any data on gangs, thus any count would be an undercount. Similarly, jurisdictions may fail to respond to surveys because they do not collect data (even if they recognize they have a problem) or do not keep special enumerations of "gang crime" separate from general crime. Despite these and other problems/issues, many attempts have been made to assess the extent of gangs and gang membership.

Estimates of gang membership typically rely on surveys of key informants, most often criminal justice system personnel. The earliest of these surveys, which was conducted by Miller (1975) and looked at only six cities, found a low estimate of 700 gangs with roughly 28,000 members. Beginning in 1995, the National Youth Gang Center (NYGC) began conducting annual surveys to gauge the extent of gang behavior and responses to that activity. The NYGC surveys the police departments of all cities with a population over 25,000, sheriff and police departments of all suburban counties in the United States, and randomly selected police and sheriff's departments serving small towns (between 2,500 and 24,999 population) and rural counties. More than 2,000 law enforcement agencies are surveyed each year. Based on the 2006 National Youth Gang Survey (NYGS), 33 percent of the U.S. jurisdictions experience youth gang problems (Egley and O'Donnell, 2008).

TABLE 5.2 Reporting of Gang Problems, 2006

Rural Counties	14.9%
Smaller Cities (2,500-49,999 pop)	37.6%
Suburban Counties	51.0%
Large Cities (50,000+ pop)	86.4%

Source: Constructed from A. Egley, A., and C.E. O'Donnell (2008). *Highlights of the 2006 National Youth Gang Survey*. Washington, DC: Office of Juvenile Justice and Delinquency Prevention.

It is estimated that there are 26,500 active gangs with roughly 785,000 members. The number of gangs and gang members vary greatly from area to area, but they appear in virtually all areas of the country. Table 5.3 provides figures based on the maximum number of reported gangs and gang members in different-size jurisdictions in the 2002-2005 NYGS.

More information on the NYGS can be found at http://www.iir.com/nygc/nygsa/

TABLE 5.3 Number of Gangs and Gang Members, 2002-2005

	Large Cities	Suburban Counties	Smaller Cities	Rural Counties
# of Gangs				
< 4	13.0%	26.0%	48.3%	56.3%
4-6	20.5	19.2	26.7	23.5
7-15	30.8	21.4	12.9	10.9
16-30	15.4	8.9	2.9	3.4
> 30	17.6	14.9	0.0	0.0
# of Members				
< 51	7.6	26.2	24.6	23.5
51-200	17.6	27.9	52.5	54.6
201-500	15.6	12.0	8.3	0.8
501-1,000	12.7	5.0	0.0	0.0
> 1,000	18.5	10.6	0.0	0.0

Source: Constructed by authors from National Youth Gang Center (2007). *National Youth Gang Survey Analysis*. Washington, DC: Office of Juvenile Justice and Delinquency Prevention. Available at: http://www.iir.com/nygc/nygsa/

Despite the development of standardized surveys and growing interest in documenting gang membership, the figures are suspect. The problems and issues noted earlier have the potential of biasing any results. Spokespersons for the Gang Investigators Network suggest that nonresponse by many police agencies may be reducing the reported number of gang members by 200,000 or more (Johnson, 2005).

Klein and Maxson (2006) suggest that a better means of measuring gang participation is to survey youths. An important factor to consider in using surveys to gauge gang membership is whether the survey is conducted in areas with higher-than-typical concentrations of gangs and gang members. The use of nationally representative samples would provide more meaningful estimates, although most surveys are conducted using city-wide or county-wide samples. Based on their review of survey studies since 1990, Klein and Maxson (2006) find 33 different gang prevalence rates, ranging from roughly 5 percent to 20 percent reporting gang membership, with many of the larger figures relating to "ever" belonging to a gang and the smaller figures reflecting younger respondents reporting membership "in the past year."

A group of youths demonstrate some signs that are generally used by gang members. While the proportion of youths claiming membership to gangs varies from place to place, it is clear that a small but significant portion of youths are involved in gangs.

Mark C. Ide

Three clear results emerge from attempts to measure gang participation. First, gangs are found throughout the United States, in both large and small cities, and both urban and rural areas. Second, the scope of the gang problem is large. Finally, the majority of youths do not belong to gangs and probably never will. While the proportion claiming membership varies from one site to another, a small but significant percentage of youths do claim gang membership.

CHARACTERISTICS OF GANGS

Research over the past 30 years has provided a great deal of information on gangs. Unfortunately, there is as much disagreement as agreement on many issues. As with the definition of a gang, questions

still exist concerning characteristics of gang membership, gang organizational structure, and gang migration. The following pages attempt
to synthesize the diverse literature and provide a general view of gangs
in today's society.

Age

Most early research portrayed the typical gang member as a teenage adolescent (Cooper, 1967; Kanter and Bennett, 1968; Klein, 1971;
Miller, 1975; Robin, 1967; Short and Strodbeck, 1965). Miller's (1975)
national survey showed that the peak age years tend to fall in the mid-
teen age group. This fact is borne out in more recent surveys that show
that the peak ages for participation are 14 and 15 (Klein and Maxson,
2006). Gangs often use schools as recruiting grounds (Hutchinson and
Kyle, 1993), adding to the youthful dominance in most gangs. This
does not mean, however, that younger or older individuals have been
excluded from gang membership.

Research since the mid-1980s (see, for example, Hagedorn, 1988;
Horowitz, 1983; Howell, 1997a; Klein and Maxson, 1989; Moore, 1993;
Spergel et al., 1990; Toy, 1992) shows that the age range of gang members has expanded, particularly at the older end. NYGS data show that
individuals age 18 or older made up more than 60 percent of all gang
members in the years from 2001 to 2004. This suggests that gangs are
retaining their members into young adulthood. The lack of meaningful
employment opportunities, coupled with potentially lucrative gang
behavior, is one reason for individuals to retain their gang membership
into their twenties and thirties (Moore, 1991).

Social Class

Most studies find that the vast majority of gangs are found in lower-
class areas and are comprised of lower-class juveniles. The lower-class
nature of gangs finds a great deal of support in the early examinations
and explanations of ganging behavior. Thrasher's (1936) definition of
gangs relies heavily on the physical location of the groups in the lower-
class, deteriorating areas of the city. Subsequent analyses paint a similar picture of gang behavior through explanations of deviance heavily
reliant on the conflict between lower-class individuals and dominant
middle-class society (Cloward and Ohlin, 1960; Cohen, 1955; Miller,
1958). More recent studies suggest that gang delinquency is no longer
restricted to the inner city (Johnstone, 1981; Spergel, 1984). The growth
of gangs in suburban and rural areas provides further evidence that gang
behavior is not restricted to lower-class, inner-city areas.

A separate phenomenon appearing in the literature involves middle-
class gangs. Such gangs are in opposition to the usual view of gang

membership and causes of ganging. Middle-class youths are not faced with the same degree of blocked success as lower-class juveniles. Lowney (1984) views the middle-class gang more as a "near group" along the lines of Yablonsky (1962). **Wilding gangs** fit this "near group" image and, while not as disadvantaged as other youths, these groups strike out at what they perceive as inequalities and infringements on their rights by other ethnic groups (Cummings, 1993). Such middle-class gangs typically do not have well-defined roles, they lack cohesion, and much of the group activity revolves around casual interaction. While many middle-class groups do not fit the traditional image of a gang, the similarity between members and the participation in group-organized behavior leads some to conclude that the youths are a gang (Lowney, 1984). These gangs tend to be less numerous and typically are centered around less violent behavior than their lower-class counterparts.

Race and Ethnicity

Gangs do not appear to be reserved for any particular ethnic or racial groups. Virtually all races and ethnic groups have provided gang delinquents over the years, although different racial/ethnic groups have dominated at different points in time. Thrasher's (1936) gangs consisted mainly of white youths of European descent. Evaluations in the 1950s and 1960s tended to report greater numbers of black gangs. The most recent NYGC (2007) statistics show that Hispanics comprise about 50 percent of all gang members, with African Americans contributing another 35 percent. Whites make up less than 10 percent of the gang population.

Traditionally, gangs tended to be homogeneous in terms of race and ethnicity (Klein, 1971; Short and Strodbeck, 1965; Spergel, 1966; Thrasher, 1936). That is, there were relatively few gangs that had white, black, Hispanic, and Asian members all in the same gang. Part of the reason for this was the similarity between the youths that prompted them to come together as a group. If, as some theorists suggested, gangs are an outgrowth of spontaneous play groups, it would be natural for like individuals to join together and participate in joint activities. Gang delinquency can be seen as a simple extension of other daily activities.

Today, there is a developing trend toward hybrid gangs. The term **hybrid gangs** generally refers to gangs that are mixed racially or ethnically, but these gangs also can be characterized in other ways. For example, members may belong to more than one gang, or different gangs may cooperate with one another in some endeavor (Starbuck, Howell, and Lindquist, 2001). These gangs also may not fit the traditional definition of a gang and may not claim turf or utilize colors, signs, or other symbols typically considered important in recognizing gang behavior. While most gangs remain racially and ethnically homogeneous, Starbuck,

Howell, and Lindquist (2001) note that roughly one-third of the gangs identified in the 1998 NYGS fit the definition of a hybrid gang.

Females and Gangs

Traditional research on gangs has been devoted almost exclusively to the role of males. This is due primarily to the failure of females to contribute to any large extent to gang membership or activity. Thrasher's (1936) pathbreaking study of 1,313 gangs found only five or six female gangs over the course of his study. Surveys of youths uncover the same basic results, with roughly 10 percent of females reporting gang membership (Klein and Maxson, 2006). The NYGC (2007) reports that less than 10 percent of all gang members are female.

The overwhelming dominance of male gangs found in law enforcement data (such as the NYGS) is not mirrored in other sources of information. Other research shows that while there are still more male gangs and gang members, there is a greater presence of females in gangs. Esbensen and Huizinga (1993) report that at least 20 percent of the gang membership in Denver is female. Fagan (1990), Campbell (1990), and Esbensen and Osgood (1997) claim that females comprise roughly one-third of gang members. Curry et al. (1993) uncovered more than 7,000 female gang members in 27 cities. In many cases the females are still part of auxiliary groups (Monti, 1993) and respond to the mandates and activities of their male counterparts (Campbell, 1984, 1990). This auxiliary status of female gangs is most clearly seen in the adoption of similar names to the dominant male gangs (i.e., Disciples and Lady Disciples).

There are indications of growing numbers of autonomous female gangs with their own leadership and separate meetings, which operate independently from the male gang in many instances (Campbell, 1984; Fishman, 1988; Moore, 1991). Female gang members are known to act as lookouts and to carry weapons for male members, as well as participate in their own deviant activities (Fishman, 1988). Indeed, female gang members tend to participate in many of the same forms of deviance as males, including drug use and violence (Bjerregaard and Smith, 1993; Campbell, 1990; Decker and Van Winkle, 1994; Fishman, 1988).

Organization and Size

Gangs tend to have some type of internal organization that affects the activities of its members, the status of those members, and the decision-making processes of the group (Bloch and Neiderhoffer, 1958; Curry and Decker, 1998; Thrasher, 1936; Yablonsky, 1962). The degree of formality and control exercised by the gang varies greatly from gang to gang. Gangs that are more entrepreneurial tend to have a more formal hierarchical structure. Territorial gangs are more loosely organized and have an informal structure (see, for example, Sanders, 1994). Klein and Maxson (2006) outline five gang types (see Table 5.4). These types indicate that gangs are not all mirror images of one another, and they can be diverse in size, structure, and activity. The most common gang form is the compressed type, followed by the neotraditional (Klein and Maxson, 2006).

TABLE 5.4 Klein and Maxson's Gang Types

TRADITIONAL	Very large (over 100 members) with various subgroups; have been in existence for 20+ years; wide range of ages among members; territorial-based; wide range of criminal activity.
NEOTRADITIONAL	Similar to traditional but not as old; typically 50-100 members; territorial; subgroups.
COMPRESSED	Small gang with no subgroups (less than 50 members); members are close in age; short history; not necessarily territorial.
COLLECTIVE	Like the compressed but larger (50+); wider age ranges of members, 10-15 years old; not necessarily territorial.
SPECIALTY	Small gang with no subgroups; narrow age range; short history; very territorial; specializes in few types of crimes.

Source: Constructed from M.W. Klein and C.L. Maxson (2006). *Street Gang Patterns and Policies.* New York: Oxford University Press.

At the heart of most gangs is a single core of devoted members. This core may vary in size but is always much smaller than the purported size of the entire gang. The majority of the gang usually reflects a large body of fringe members who rarely take part in decisionmaking and participate in gang activities only at selected times. Gangs that claim memberships of 100 and greater are probably counting a large number of fringe members.

The core of the gang provides the leadership and decision-making body of the group. Not all gangs, however, have the same leadership structure (Kelling, 1975). In some groups, leadership is provided by a single individual determined according to the talents of the core members. Physical prowess usually determines who becomes the leader of the gang, but this is only a general statement. Other gangs have highly differentiated leadership roles in which different talents call for varied leadership according to the present needs of the group. Fights and violence will call on the best fighter. Criminal activity for profit may require the efforts of another youth who knows more about committing the crime and fencing the goods. Internal conflict may necessitate the efforts of someone who can negotiate and come up with alternative solutions. The extent of such specialization is determined by the abilities of the core members and the needs of the group. Still other gangs may vest leadership in different individuals for each subgroup of the gang or may have a very informal leadership structure in which no clear leaders can be identified (Sanders, 1994).

Besides the core group, many gangs include a range of different subgroups (Miller, Geertz, and Cutter, 1961). This is especially true in recent years as we see gang members from different age groups, as well as more intergenerational gangs (Hutchinson and Kyle, 1993; Moore, 1991, 1993). Often, the subgroups are based on the age of the gang members. A simple form of organization may have only three membership groups—young "wannabes," the core of the gang, and "old guard" members. The different subgroups of a gang may be identified by various names or labels such as PeeWees, Juniors, Seniors, or Old Heads. It is important to note that this tripartite view of a gang is only a simple presentation. Various gangs may have a more complicated system of subgroups, including female auxiliaries or affiliations with gang chapters in other areas of a city. The actual organization varies greatly from gang to gang and place to place.

Gang Migration

One of the oft-mentioned "facts" about recent gang behavior is that of gangs migrating from place to place. Typically, this discussion centers around the idea that gangs are deliberately moving and setting up chapters in other places for the purpose of selling drugs. Support for this assertion is most often anecdotal and relies on the simple observation of the same or similar gang names, colors, graffiti, or behavior from place to place. Solid proof of gang migration, however, is not available.

For the most part, the apparent migration is more accidental than planned. Skolnick, Bluthenthal, and Correl (1993) note that most gang travel and migration begins with non-gang, non-crime-related activities. Visits to family members in other places or the relocation of a family are typical means by which gang members find themselves in a new environment (Klein and Maxson, 2006). In essence, the gang migration is an unintended consequence of normal family behavior. The connection between gangs in different cities, usually considered a result of planned migration, is also more illusory than real (Huff, 1993; Spergel et al., 1990; Valdez, 2000). Survey respondents note that most cities experience gang problems before any significant level of migration is apparent (Maxson, Woods, and Klein, 1996). While gangs in different cities may have the same name, colors, and symbols, these are borrowed from other places. The appearance of established gangs, such as the Crips and Bloods, in cities with no history of gang problems can often be attributed to the arrival of a single gang member who is displaced through family migration.

That there may be gang "chapters" in different cities cannot be totally discounted. Indeed, as competition for drug territory has increased, some gangs have attempted to move operations into smaller cities. This movement, however, is typically limited and does not indicate state-wide or country-wide organizations of juvenile gangs (Klein and Maxson, 2006). One possible, and plausible, explanation for the apparent "franchising" of gangs in different cities is that more sophisticated drug dealers and organizations recruit youths and emerging gangs as local "employees" in the drug trade. Migration for drug selling, therefore, is more an illusion than a reality. Indeed, low migration levels result in relatively small impacts on a city's existing drug problems (Maxson, Woods, and Klein, 1996). For the most part, juvenile gangs are not as entrepreneurial as the public likes to think.

Summary

Attempts to delineate what a gang looks like are doomed to failure. We must recognize that gangs, like any other collective of individuals, will take on different characteristics based on the desires of the members and the underlying goal of the group. Some gangs may be highly structured with many members, clear leadership, and set agendas. Other gangs may be loose confederations of a few individuals who interact on a sporadic basis. Names, colors, territory, leadership, and other components of gangs are in themselves only potential indicators of ganging. Just as the general characteristics of gangs vary, so do the behavioral tendencies of these groups.

WHY DO YOUTHS JOIN GANGS?

Gang members come together and associate with one another for a wide array of reasons. The early work of Thrasher (1936) suggests that the gang provides inner-city youths with a sense of belonging and acceptance. Several early writers (Bloch and Neiderhoffer, 1958; Cohen, 1955; Miller, 1958) argue that the relative disadvantages of being a lower-class youth faced with middle-class goals leads youths to joining gangs as a response to their inability to succeed through normal channels. The lower-class youths find support and unity with others facing similar problems, and gang activity can offer status and a sense of success not available elsewhere. The extent to which the gang is entrepreneurial may provide the members with an income (possibly significant) that is otherwise not available.

More recent research on gangs, particularly that dealing with different racial and ethnic gangs (Chin, 1990; Chin, Fagan, and Kelly, 1992; Horowitz, 1983; Huff, 1993; Joe and Robinson, 1980; Moore, 1991, 1993; Sanders, 1994; Toy, 1992; Vigil, 1993, 1997; Zatz, 1985) also portray gang membership and activity as a result of life in lower-class communities. Many gang members are recent immigrants or are first-generation Americans. The youths often face problems with success in schools and other social situations. Gang behavior is seen as an alternative to the lack of success and status faced by youths. Lower-class youths, regardless of ethnic or racial background, spend a good deal of time on the streets where they meet and interact with other youths. Education is provided through daily street activity. The gang offers its members a sense of belonging and self-esteem, which may not be forthcoming at home (Moore, 1991; Vigil, 1993, 1997).

TABLE 5.5 Reasons for Gang Membership

A Sense of Belonging
Financial Gain/Rewards
Status
Social Support
Improved Self-esteem
Feelings of Family
Group Cohesion
Acceptance
Social Activities

Similarly, explanations for female ganging have been rare but generally follow the same pattern of logic found for male gangs. Brown (1978), Short and Strodbeck (1965), and others have pointed to many of the same social factors associated with male gangs. Blocked opportunity, lack of success at school and home, lack of status, desire for belonging, abuse and family problems at home, and community disorganization were among the cited reasons for female gang participation (Bowker and Klein, 1983; Campbell, 1990; Miller, 2000; Moore, 1988). The welfare reform of the mid-1990s was particularly problematic for females who are already marginalized in the work force and also have to care for children (Moore and Hagedorn, 2001). Gang membership and participation is one possible response to these increased pressures.

The increased intergenerational nature of gang membership also contributes to the growth and construction of gangs. Younger members are often siblings or offspring of current or past gang members. "Apprenticeship" periods for "wannabes" and initiation rituals help build the sense of belonging. The gang provides its members with things they do not get at home, school, or elsewhere.

The importance of a gang to its members can be seen in the level of group cohesion often found among the group. Many of the early writers view cohesion as an essential element of gangs (e.g., Bloch and Neiderhoffer, 1958; Thrasher, 1936; Vigil, 1993; Zevitz, 1993). Cohesion may arise out of different factors that lead to gang membership and activities of the gangs. Gang behavior, particularly conflict activity, is considered essential to building cohesion. Fights in defense of territory, a gang's honor, or an individual member can all strengthen a gang's organization and cohesion.

The extent of gang cohesion can be found in the names, territory, and other identifiers associated with different gangs. Many gangs choose identifying names for themselves that reflect their ethnic or racial backgrounds. Examples of such names include the Black Assassins and the Latin Kings. Names can also reflect the territory claimed by different gangs. Many gangs award the right to wear distinctive clothing to their members. This clothing typically includes the wearing of "colors" or jackets emblazoned with the group name or symbol. Graffiti is used for a variety of reasons, ranging from promoting an individual gang member's reputation to demarcating the territory controlled by a gang. It must be recognized, however, that these outward symbols do not in themselves guarantee cohesion. Indeed, use of names, colors, or graffiti only provide an indicator of cohesion. These features of a gang, however, demonstrate that the gang provides something of value to its members—a sense of belonging, status, feelings of success, financial gain, or something else.

GANG BEHAVIOR

The typical view of gang activity, especially as it has been portrayed in the media, has not changed much over the years. Gangs are portrayed as in constant violent confrontation with one another and with the general public. Contrary to this media portrayal, gangs participate in a variety of different behaviors. This does not mean that the gang fights and drive-by shootings are fictional. Such confrontations have taken place in the past and continue to occur today. The image, however, is distorted. Past and present research suggests that such violent confrontations are rare relative to other gang behavior. Indeed, gangs are involved in many nonviolent activities. Thrasher (1936) noted that many gangs supplied leisure activities, a forum for talk and play, and even gambling. Jankowski (1991) points out that gangs provide a forum for recreation, partying, and companionship.

When gang aggression does occur, it is not necessarily physical in nature. Miller, Gertz, and Cutter (1961) note that less than 7 percent of one gang's aggressive acts involved physical attacks, and none of those actions involved a weapon. Almost 94 percent of the aggression was verbal, and most did not contain anger (Miller, Gertz, and Cutter, 1961). Miller (1966) reported that gang sentiments in favor of violence are rarely manifested in actual physical expression.

While physical aggression may not dominate gang behavior, gangs are involved in significant numbers of crimes. One source of information involves surveys of law enforcement agencies. Estimates from law enforcement data reveal that almost 17,000 gangs were responsible for more than 580,000 offenses in 122 cities and eight counties in 1992 (Curry, Ball, and Decker, 1996).

That gangs are involved in criminal activity is an indisputable fact. Indeed, except for robbery, more than 50 percent of the law enforcement respondents in the 1998 NYGS claimed that some, most, or all of the gang members in their jurisdictions are involved in aggravated assaults, burglaries, motor vehicle thefts, larcenies, and drug sales (National Youth Gang Center, 2000). Similarly, the NAGIA (National Alliance of Gang Investigators Associations) survey (2005) noted high or moderate gang involvement in a significant percent of crimes in all regions of the United States (see Table 5.6). Clearly, criminal behavior by gangs and gang members is evident in data supplied by law enforcement agencies.

TABLE 5.6 Percent of Jurisdictions Reporting High or Moderate Gang Involvement in Crime by Region

Crime	Northeast	South	Midwest	West
Street Drug Sales	60.8%	53.2%	52.0%	73.5%
Firearms Possession	37.2%	35.3%	41.0%	
Vandalism/Graffiti	53.0%	44.5%	54.5%	82.5%
Felony Assault	43.2%	34.1%	43.2%	71.4%
Homicide	27.5%	20.2%	26.2%	44.1%
Burglary	31.4%	33.0%	37.5%	60.9%
Firearms Trafficking	29.4%	22.0%	30.7%	37.5%
Auto Theft	31.3%	33.5%	30.7%	67.9%
Intimidation/Extortion	21.6%	24.3%	30.7%	48.3%

Source: Compiled by authors from National Alliance of Gang Investigators Associations (2005). *National Gang Threat Assessment.* Washington, DC: Bureau of Justice Assistance.

The extent of criminal behavior by gang members also can be addressed through self-report surveys. Thornberry (1998) reported on gang crime as uncovered in the Rochester, Pittsburgh, and Denver youth studies. In every case, gang members accounted for at least eight out of every 10 violent crimes and seven out of 10 drug offenses. Gang members do not confine their offending to serious violent crime. They also participate in a large portion of all property crime (Thornberry, 1998). Similarly, Spergel and associates (1990) pointed out that gang members are more criminally active than nonmembers, and commit three times the level of violence.

The National Alliance of Gang Investigators Associations offers a number of services and information dealing with gangs. See http://www.nagia.org/

Do Gangs Cause Delinquency?

Based on the level of gang-member delinquency, one could argue that the elimination of gangs would significantly reduce the level of youthful deviance. An alternative possibility, however, is that gangs simply attract already delinquent youths, rather than causing increased deviance. The delinquency, therefore, is independent of gang membership. Following this argument, Thornberry and colleagues (1993) identify three possible models of the delinquency–gang relationship: selection, social facilitation, and enhancement. The **selection model** maintains that gangs recruit or attract already delinquent youths. In this model the level of delinquency would be independent of gang status. Under the **social facilitation model**, belonging to a gang is the cause of increased deviance. Periods of gang membership, therefore, will result in delinquent activity not found during nonmembership. Finally, the **enhancement model** strikes a middle ground in which gangs recruit delinquency-prone youths and enhance their deviance.

Two studies have sought to test these models of gang influence directly. Using panel data from the Denver Youth Survey, Esbensen and Huizinga (1993) report that gang members are indeed more delinquent while they are actively involved in the gang. At the same time, however, these youths also report higher levels of offending both before and after active gang participation. Thornberry and colleagues (1993) find that the gang–delinquency relationship varies according to the type of offense and the level of commitment to the gang. The social facilitation model fits for personal and drug-related offenses, while property offenses do not fit any of the models very well. In addition, youths who remain in the gangs for a longer period of time tend to increase their offending (the enhancement model) more than do transient gang members (Thornberry et al., 1993). What these two studies suggest is that the gang is not necessarily the cause of delinquent behavior. Rather, gang membership appears to add to an already established level of deviance by participating youths.

Drug Activity

Drug activity is a major topic of discussion in relation to gang behavior. The National Alliance of Gang Investigators Associations (2005:1) notes that "gangs ... are the primary distributor of drugs throughout the United States." There is no doubt that many gang members use and sell drugs, and that drug sales are an integral part of some organized gangs. The degree to which gangs are involved in drugs, however, is highly variable. For example, drug sales in one gang may involve sales only among its own members, while another gang may be deeply involved in the drug trade throughout the community. Fagan (1990), in a survey of Los Angeles, San Diego, and Chicago gang members, found that roughly 28 percent are rarely involved in drug use, while 35 percent are seriously involved in both use and sales. Much of the distribution of drugs may be tied to more organized, older gangs. Two examples of this would be outlaw motorcycle gangs (NAGIA, 2005) and Jamaican posses (Gay and Marquart, 1993), which have emerged as organized forces for the distribution and sale of marijuana, cocaine, and other drugs in the United States. Research also shows that, while there is a great deal of drug use among youth gangs, the sale of drugs for profit by local gangs is highly variable (Decker and Van Winkle, 1994; Hagedorn, 1994; Mays, Fuller, and Winfree, 1994; Padilla, 1993).

Gang Violence

One clear trend in gang behavior has been an increase in the level of violence and physical aggression in recent years. Where much of the early research attempted to dispel the dominant myth of the centrality of violence in the gangs, more recent studies note that violence is on the rise. Miller (1975, 1982) notes that as early as the late 1970s there was a clear increase in the use of weapons and participation in physical confrontation. While confrontations appeared in the past, they were not a dominant activity and often occurred within the confines of the gang (Miller, Gertz, and Cutter, 1961). While recent research suggests that violence is now a more open activity directed at a greater array of targets, both inside and outside the immediate gang, the bulk of violence is still aimed at other gang members.

The seriousness of the violence is also high, as demonstrated by the number of gang-related killings. In 1994, Chicago and Los Angeles together experienced more than 1,000 gang-related homicides (Howell, 1997). Data from the FBI Supplemental Homicide Reports show that more than 5 percent of all homicides from 1993-2003 were gang-related, and that between 7.1 and 9.9 percent of homicides committed with firearms were gang-related (Harrell, 2005). Table 5.7 presents data on gang-related homicides reported in 2002-2005. In cities of more than 50,000 population, 11 percent reported 10 or more gang-related homicides, and an additional 48 percent reported one to nine gang-related homicides (National Youth Gang Center, 2007). These figures are probably low estimates due to the lack of adequate data-collection methods used by law enforcement in relation to gang problems (National Youth Gang Center, 2005).

TABLE 5.7 Gang-related Homicides, 2002-2005

Number	Large Cities	Suburban Counties	Smaller Cities	Rural Counties
0	36.2%	59.4%	80.4%	75.6%
1-2	28.3	15.9	12.5	13.4
3-9	19.6	10.3	5.0	2.5
10+	11.1	3.8	0.0	0.0

Source: Constructed by authors from National Youth Gang Center (2007). *National Youth Gang Survey Analysis*. Washington, DC: Office of Juvenile Justice and Delinquency Prevention. Available at http://www.iir.com/nygc/nygsa/

Gang violence no longer conforms to the typical image of a **rumble** or gang fight. Rather, most violence appears as forays. A **foray** typically entails an attack by two or three youths upon a single member (or possibly a few members) of a rival gang. A typical form of attack is a "drive-by" shooting. For example, three members of the Bloods drive around a corner, where a member of the Crips lives, they shoot from the car, and then speed away from the scene. A similar retaliatory foray by the Crips is the consequence of the Bloods' action. The foray becomes a self-perpetuating activity. Indeed, gang homicides typically take place on the street and involve both firearms and motor vehicles (Klein and Maxson, 2006).

Modern gang violence differs from the earlier portrayals in a number of ways. First, the violence appears to be more random, partly due to the use of automobiles and the willingness to attack when innocent bystanders are present. Second, the violence occurs more frequently through constant small forays rather than in the occasional large rumble. Third, the hit-and-run tactics of the foray make the violence appear more impersonal. Non-gang peers and other individuals who become victims may often be injured as a result of a foray that occurs on the street. Finally, gangs use lethal weapons, particularly firearms, more often.

Firearms and Gang/Delinquent Behavior

The role of firearms in increased levels of violence, whether by gang members or individual youths, is very clear. Sheppard and colleagues (2000) note that the great increases in juvenile homicides in the mid- to late-1980s and early-1990s was due to the increased availability and use of firearms by youths. From 1984 to 1993, there was a 158 percent increase in the age 15-24 homicide rate involving handguns (Sheppard et al., 2000). According to UCR data, almost nine out of 10 murder victims are age 18 or younger, and 65 percent of the murder victims are killed with a firearm (Snyder, 2000).

Besides looking at data on gun use in crime, it is possible to examine the extent to which juveniles carry or own weapons. According to a Centers for Disease Control and Prevention survey, 14 percent of all male youths claim to have carried a gun outside their home in the prior month (Office of Juvenile Justice and Delinquency Prevention, 1999). Several studies report that significant numbers of youths are threatened with a weapon at school or carry weapons to school for protection (see Kaufman et al., 1998; Lab and Clark, 1996; Sheley and Wright, 1993). Most studies place the level firearms in schools at better than 10 percent of the student body. Given the above, it is not surprising that there are a large number of juvenile offenses that involve firearms.

An even greater problem is firearms use by gang members. According to the 1998 NYGS, more than one-half of the law enforcement respondents claim that gang members use firearms often (21%) or sometimes (32%)

in assault crimes (National Youth Gang Center, 2000). Gang members are the most likely to own guns (Decker, Pennel, and Caldwell, 1997), and recruit youths who already own guns, and they are more likely to carry guns than are non-gang youths (Bjerregaard and Lizotte, 1995). As noted earlier, access to firearms has altered the confrontational approach of gangs from more face-to-face personal interaction to more impersonal drive-by shootings. The result of this use of lethal weapons by gangs is a much higher mortality rate among gang members when compared to the general population (Decker and Van Winkle, 1996; Morales, 1992).

Gang Behavior and Types of Gangs

Not all gangs participate in the same types of deviant behavior as other gangs. Indeed, recent research shows that some gangs tend to specialize in some form of criminal activity. That same research even suggests that a few gangs exist primarily as a forum for criminal behavior, as opposed to a forum for more generalized group behavior. The identification of specific types of offending by gangs, however, is as elusive as identifying a single gang definition. Each gang may do something slightly different from every other gang.

Asian gangs exemplify the type of gang that appears to serve a definitive purpose for their members, and does so through a more narrow selection of criminal acts. A number of studies (Chin, Fagan, and Kelly, 1992; Huff, 1993; Toy, 1992) report that Asian gangs appear to be very profit-oriented and tend to restrict their deviant activities to those that bring a monetary return. Both Huff (1993) and Chin, Fagan, and Kelly (1992) claim that these gangs often have strong ties to organized crime, which directs both the financial dealings and the use of violence in the Asian communities. Analyses of Chicano youths suggest they are strongly territorial-based (Moore, 1991; Sanders, 1994; Vigil, 1993, 1997), which provides the gang with a delineated area for which it has almost exclusive rights to gang recruitment. Besides the territorial nature of Chicano gangs, these groups tend to be more heavily involved in drug use (Moore, 1991, 1993) and general deviance (Vigil, 1993).

In recent years, more atypical gangs have appeared in the literature. Two of these are skinhead gangs and tagger gangs. Skinheads advocate white supremacy and are portrayed as very violent and racist, although this is not true of all skinheads. They also often take an anti-government stance and advocate withdrawal from the dictates of the government, including taxes and all regulatory laws. Skinheads use violence primarily against those who are perceived as a threat to white supremacy (Wooden and Blazak, 2001). At the other extreme are tagger gangs, whose members often view themselves as urban artists. These youths try to have their art seen by as many people as possible, and do not view the graffiti as vandalism, denoting ownership of turf, or harmful to others. It is solely an expression of individuality and a means of gaining status (Wooden and Blazak, 2001).

Explaining Gang Behavior

The reasons behind gang behavior and violence are varied. An examination of different research studies provides different insights. The most prevalent reasons appear to be status, control of turf or territory, and financial gain. Each of these factors are interrelated. As noted earlier, most gang members are from the lower classes. Opportunities for legitimate success and for gaining status in the community are limited by the realities of the world—jobs are few, education seems irrelevant, many must quit school before graduation to help support the family, and male role models are missing due to the absence of fathers in the home, among other factors. The gang serves to provide a means of gaining status. Gang members can prove themselves on the street and are accepted for their contributions to the gang. They can gain honor through their allegiance to other gang members. They are provided with a sense of family and belonging that does not come from the broken, female-headed household. The need for belonging and status also appears in "wilding" gang activity, in which youths randomly attack individuals from a different ethnic background as a form of retaliation for reduced opportunities and perceived injustice (Cummings, 1993; Pinderhughes, 1993). Often, wilding gangs are composed of nonminority youths striking out at minorities.

Turf or territory, a second reason for violence, provides a sense of ownership and control, which often is denied the gang youth (Vigil, 1993). Overcrowded living conditions, frequent movement from place to place, lack of finances to purchase personal property, and other factors lead youths to feel a lack of control. The turf is a means of exerting control and ownership. While it is not ownership in the legal sense of the term, such control helps provide the feelings of status desired by the gang youth. Attacks on the turf are seen as an attack on the property, honor, and status of the individual gang members, and violence is used to protect the turf (Hutchinson and Kyle, 1993).

Financial gain is a third major reason for gang membership and activity. The lower-class gang youth is faced with a lack of legitimate job opportunities. The gang can provide training in criminal activity (such as robbery and burglary), the opportunity for such criminal actions, and support for this behavior. Trafficking in illegal drugs is a lucrative activity for the gangs. It also brings about contact and opportunities with organized crime and a means of increasing status in the gang and community. At the same time that the drug trade has opened new doors for the gang members, it has also added to the stakes in control of turf and the level of violence between gangs.

Drugs and gang violence are typically portrayed as going hand in hand. Whether drug involvement is a driving force behind gang violence, however, is not clear. Klein, Maxson, and Cunningham (1991) report little evidence that drugs are more prevalent in gang homicides than non-gang homicides, and violence is rare in both gang and non-gang drug arrests. Similarly, Maxson (1995) notes that violence in drug sales is rare, occurring in roughly 5 percent of the cases. A recent review of studies also finds little support for a drug–homicide connection in gang behavior (Howell, 1997b). Despite these findings, there is no doubt that conflicts over drugs and sales territories do escalate to violence. It is the extent to which such instances occur that needs further exploration.

While the outward appearance of gang behavior is different from socially acceptable activity, the reasons for the behavior are not much different from those of most other persons. The gang youth values status, belonging, ownership, control, and financial gain. These are major reasons behind the behavior of nondeviant youths and adults. The gang has simply supplied alternative methods for achieving its ends.

INTERVENTION WITH GANGS

Responding to gangs and gang problems is an area in which much work remains to be done. Unfortunately, the first response by many cities to an emerging gang problem is one of denial (Hagedorn, 1988). Cities often do not want to admit that they have gangs. The outcome of such denial is the emergence of a full-blown problem before the authorities are prepared to deal with it. Once the problem is identified, a number of different responses have been used to address the problem.

Spergel and Curry (1993), in the National Youth Gang Survey (NYGS), identified five common intervention strategies (see Table 5.8). The approach listed by 44 percent of the respondents as their primary form of response is suppression, or the use of arrest, prosecution, incarceration, and other criminal justice system procedures. The intervention ranked second in primacy is social interventions (31.5%), followed by organizational change and development (10.9%) and community organization (8.9%). The approach listed as having the lowest ranking is opportunities provision. These results indicate that traditional criminal justice system responses are the most common responses to gang problems, while efforts to alter the social conditions that cause ganging are addressed the least. Interestingly, in an analysis of the perceived effectiveness of the five types of intervention strategies, Spergel and Curry (1993) report that opportunities provision is viewed as the most effective/promising approach, while suppression is seen as the least effective.

TABLE 5.8 Gang Intervention Strategies

Suppression	Includes any form of social control in which the criminal justice system (police, courts, or corrections) or society attempt to impose formal or informal limits on behavior
Social Intervention	Basically a social work approach to working with gangs in the neighborhoods (such as detached worker programs)
Organizational Change and Development	Deals with altering the organization(s) that respond(s) to gang problems, such as through the establishment of gang units or specialized training of its personnel
Community Organization	Efforts aimed at mobilizing the community toward self-improvement and change, including both physical and social alterations
Opportunities Provision	Recognizing the lack of meaningful jobs and the training needed to succeed, and taking steps to change the problems; education, vocational training, and job placement are elements

Source: I.A. Spergel and G.D. Curry (1993). "The National Youth Gang Survey: A Research and Development Process." In Goldstein, A.P., and C.R. Huff (eds.), *The Gang Intervention Handbook* (pp. 359-400). Champaign, IL: Research Press.

Historically, criminal and juvenile justice system personnel have had the primary responsibility for addressing gang behavior. At one extreme this has been done through the simple application of the criminal code against offending youths. At the other end of the spectrum, law enforcement agencies have involved themselves in more social work functions, such as "midnight basketball" leagues and youth clubs. In between these extremes fall specialized gang units, conflict resolution/response teams, and similar activities. The following pages will address four approaches to gang problems, including detached worker programs, legal/law enforcement avenues, the G.R.E.A.T. program, and recent comprehensive initiatives.

Detached Worker Programs

Detached workers have been an integral part of many programs dealing with youths over the years. **Detached worker programs** place gang workers into the community and free the workers from heavy paperwork and administrative requirements (Klein, 1969). The workers are expected to spend considerable time in the neighborhoods, maintain consistent contact with the gangs, and provide immediate assistance and input to the youths. Many programs rely on past gang members for workers. Klein (1971) notes that the strength of the program includes the ability to reach youths who normally are not contacted, the flexibility of workers to handle situations in unique ways, and the ability to establish confidential relationships with youths.

The impact of detached workers on gangs has been mixed. Klein (1969), in perhaps the most noted evaluation of such programs, claimed that the detached workers in Los Angeles organized 113 sporting events, 90 outings, 16 service projects, and 14 self-help programs. However, in assisting the groups to find alternative behaviors, the project inadvertently caused greater cohesiveness and, indirectly, delinquent behavior (Klein, 1969). Greater contact between the gangs and a worker led to gangs becoming closer and more unified, and the gangs were more successful at recruiting new members. Additionally, these groups participated in greater numbers of delinquent acts after the intervention of the detached workers.

More recent proposals for intervention with gangs typically include a heavy detached worker component, although they may not use that terminology. Spergel's (1984, 1986) and Fox's (1985) discussions of gang interventions reveal a striking similarity with detached worker programs. Emphasis is placed on intimate contact with gang members, providing alternative lines of behavior, and serving as a resource for gangs. Based on Klein's earlier work, it could be argued that this approach is ill-fated.

Legal and Law Enforcement Changes

Increased concern about gangs has prompted the development of new organizational structures and the passage of new legislation as means of combating gang problems. Many police departments, particularly in large cities, have established specialized gang crime units (Curry et al., 1992). In support of such efforts, many states have passed legislation making gang affiliation a crime, or increasing penalties for gang-related criminal behavior. California's **STEP Act** (Street Terrorism Enforcement and Prevention) of 1988 effectively criminalizes membership in a street gang. Under STEP, the police can invoke civil penalties against gang members for associating with one another in public, promoting their gang, displaying gang symbols, and being involved in other similar gang behavior. Many states have enhanced the penalties for crimes committed as a result of or in connection to gang membership. Statutes such as those in Florida (Florida Statutes 874.01) and Georgia (Georgia Code 16-16-3) require harsher penalties for gang-related crimes. Despite such efforts, ganging has not abated.

Two recent evaluations look at the operations and effectiveness of specialized gang units. Katz and Webb (2003) report on units in Albuquerque, Las Vegas, Phoenix, and Inglewood (CA). Weisel and Shelly (2004) consider units in San Diego and Indianapolis. In all locations the formation of the units was in response to political pressure, and the operations of the units were generally separate from the rest of the police activities. Katz and Webb (2003) find the units rely mostly on routine police responses and receive little training specific to gangs and gang problems. In both analyses, activities to prevent the formation of gangs is lacking. Rather, most attention seems to be directed at intelligence gathering and investigations aimed at crimes committed by gangs. In general, in neither analysis is there evidence of the units having any significant impact on gangs, gang formation, or gang crime.

One approach that has received a great deal of attention in recent years is to have the police strictly enforce any and all codes and regulations (basically a suppression approach) in an attempt to change the behavior of a target group. This approach, referred to as **pulling levers**, is most notable in the **Boston Gun Project**, which targeted firearms use by gangs. Pulling levers simply seeks to deter behavior by taking a zero-tolerance stance with regard to any transgressions (Cook, Moore, and Braga, 2002). For example, if a single gang member commits an offense with a firearm, the police inform the entire gang that they are subject to increased attention from police and the criminal justice system. Officers and other system personnel will enforce trespassing laws and curfews, frequently stop and question gang members, enforce vagrancy and loitering ordinances, check on and enforce probation and parole rules, seize illegal goods obtained through illegal activities, restrict plea bargaining, and impose the highest penalties possible for even the most minor transgressions (Kennedy, 1998). All of this represents a form of "legal harassment" that is meant to influence gangs and gang members to avoid the use of firearms. An evaluation of the Boston Gun Project reveals significant decreases in several offenses, including homicides, assaults with firearms, and other weapons offenses (Braga et al., 2001). The success of this approach has prompted several other jurisdictions to adopt similar programs (such as Project Excite in Richmond, Virginia).

The G.R.E.A.T. Program

The **Gang Resistance Education and Training (G.R.E.A.T.) Program** is the most recognizable prevention program targeting gangs. The program began in 1991 under a grant from the Bureau of Alcohol, Tobacco, and Firearms (ATF) (now called the Bureau of Alcohol, Tobacco, Firearms, and Explosives) to the Phoenix, Arizona, Police Department. Not unlike the Drug Abuse Resistance Education (D.A.R.E.) program, G.R.E.A.T. is taught by local police officers in middle schools. The original curriculum consisting of nine lessons was expanded to 13 one-hour lessons and is presented in middle schools. The goal of the program is to:

> More information on G.R.E.A.T. can be found at the program's web site: http://www.great-online.org/

> Prevent youth crime, violence, and gang involvement while developing a positive relationship among law enforcement, families, and our young people to create safer communities (Bureau of Justice Assistance, 2005).

The thrust of the program is to provide youths with the necessary skills for identifying high-risk situations and resisting the pressure/allure of taking part in gangs and gang activity. Beyond targeting just ganging, program curricula are geared toward increasing self-esteem, changing attitudes, and eliminating participation in violent behavior. A key component of G.R.E.A.T. is to teach nonviolent conflict resolution techniques to the youths. The program has been adopted by schools throughout the United States. There is also a six-week program for fourth and fifth grades, a six-session family program, and a summer component that reinforces the materials learned in school and provides alternative activities to gang participants.

A longitudinal evaluation shows positive outcomes of G.R.E.A.T. participation. Esbensen and colleagues (2004) evaluated the program using more than 1,750 students in schools from six different cities. Using data for the four years following program participation, the authors report finding less victimization, less risk-taking behavior, improved attitudes toward the police, increased numbers of prosocial peers, and more negative views about gangs among those youths receiving the G.R.E.A.T. lessons (Esbensen et al., 2004). Unfortunately, the evaluation failed to find any impact on the more important target of the project—reduced gang participation. While this is disappointing, the promising results led the sponsors of the G.R.E.A.T. program to undertake a revision of the curriculum, which resulted in the current 13-lesson scheme. No evaluations of the new curriculum are available.

A Planned Comprehensive Response to Gangs

In the mid-1990s, the Office of Juvenile Justice and Delinquency Prevention (OJJDP) initiated the **Community-Wide Approach to Gang Prevention, Intervention, and Suppression Program**. In essence, the program aimed to initiate a comprehensive set of strategies mirroring the five strategies outlined by Spergel and Curry (1993) (see Table 5.8). OJJDP funded program implementation and evaluation in five cities (Bloomington-Normal, Illinois; Mesa, Arizona; Riverside, California; Tucson, Arizona; and San Antonio, Texas).

Several factors emerged across the evaluations. First, in San Antonio, the program was never fully implemented (Spergel, Wa, and Sosa, 2004a). Second, suppression remains the primary response in at least three cities (Spergel, Wa, and Sosa, 2001, 2002, 2003, 2004b). Third, several cities struggled with building programs that included grassroots community organizations. Most of the participants remained official criminal justice agencies and other social service providers (Spergel, Wa, and Sosa, 2001, 2002, 2004a, 2004b). Finally, the more successful programs offered a wider array of activities that could be considered opportunities provision and social interventions, such as counseling, referrals, and job training.

FIGURE 5.1 G.R.E.A.T. Middle School Curriculum

1. Welcome to G.R.E.A.T.
   - Program Introduction
   - Relationship Between Gangs, Violence, Drugs, and Crime

2. What's the Real Deal?
   - Message Analysis
   - Facts and Fiction About Gangs and Violence

3. It's About Us
   - Community
   - Roles and Responsibilities
   - What You Can Do About Gangs

4. Where Do We Go From Here?
   - Setting Realistic and Achievable Goals

5. Decisions, Decisions, Decisions
   - G.R.E.A.T. Decision-Making Model
   - Impact of Decisions on Goals
   - Decision-Making Practice

6. Do You Hear What I Am Saying?
   - Effective Communication
   - Verbal vs. Nonverbal

7. Walk In Someone Else's Shoes
   - Active Listening
   - Identification of Different Emotions
   - Empathy for Others

8. Say It Like You Mean It
   - Body Language
   - Tone of Voice
   - Refusal-Skills Practice

9. Getting Along Without Going Along
   - Influences and Peer Pressure
   - Refusal-Skills Practice

10. Keeping Your Cool
    - G.R.E.A.T. Anger Management Tips
    - Practice Cooling Off

11. Keeping It Together
    - Recognizing Anger in Others
    - Tips for Calming Others

12. Working It Out
    - Consequences for Fighting
    - G.R.E.A.T. Tips for Conflict Resolution
    - Conflict Resolution Practice
    - Where to Go for Help

13. Looking Back
    - Program Review
    - "Making My School a G.R.E.A.T. Place" Project Review

Source: Bureau of Justice Assistance (2005). *Gang Resistance Education and Training.* Available at: http://great-online.org/Components/MiddleSchool.Aspx

The program's impact on gang membership and crime is also mixed. The evaluations of the Bloomington-Normal, Mesa, and Riverside programs report reduced offending and reduced arrests among youths in the experimental neighborhoods (Spergel, Wa, and Sosa, 2001, 2002, 2003). While the Bloomington-Normal program appears to have reduced the level of gang participation (Spergel, Wa, and Sosa, 2001), there was no apparent impact in Riverside, Tucson, or San Antonio (Spergel, Wa, and Sosa, 2003, 2004a, 2004b). Despite the mixed results of the programs, the evidence suggests that a successfully implemented program that targets a wider array of interventions than just suppression activities has the ability to impact positively on the level of gang crime and gang membership.

Overview of Interventions

Evidence concerning the effectiveness of dealing with gangs mirrors the research concerning interventions with individual offenders. The basic conclusion is that many methods of intervention have had little impact on deviant activity. Indeed, some evaluations suggest that intervention exacerbates the problem. A large part of past failures may be due to what Klein (1995) refers to as "conceptually misguided, poorly implemented, half-heartedly pursued" responses and programs.

We must recognize that most programs do not address the major underlying cause of ganging and gang behavior—the lack of social opportunities. Despite the recognition that opportunity provision has the most promise, there are few programs that target this area. The more recent OJJDP community-wide approach is an exception to this problem. The lack of education, training, and jobs receives little attention in most gang interventions. Rather, arrest, prosecution, and incarceration remain the mainstay of society's response. Many authors (see, for example, Cummings and Monti, 1993; Goldstein, 1993; Hagedorn, 1988; Huff, 1990, 1993; Moore, 1991) claim that until major changes are made in the basic social structure, gangs will persist and thrive.

There is room for some hope in dealing with gangs, largely due to recent initiatives that transcend typical narrowly focused local programs. The establishment in 1994 of the National Youth Gang Center has helped coordinate research and knowledge about gangs. Similarly, programs such as the Chicago Gang Violence Reduction Project and the OJJDP Comprehensive Community-Wide Approach to Gang Prevention, Intervention, and Suppression Program are relying on multiple interventions to address gangs and ganging. These programs incorporate elements of suppression, community organization, social interventions, and other efforts into a unified approach to the problems (Thornberry and Burch, 1997).

SUMMARY

Interest in gang activity has a long history in juvenile justice and appears to have engendered renewed interest in the last few years. The research efforts to date provide striking similarities to one another. The form and explanations for ganging have changed little since Thrasher's (1936) early work. The most clear difference in recent work has been the finding of more serious violence directed against a wider range of victims. Despite the persistent and increasingly dangerous problem, there do not appear to be any clearly successful methods for dealing with gangs.

DISCUSSION QUESTIONS

1. Gang delinquency is apparently on the rise and you are called on to explain to the public about gangs and gang behavior. How would you define a gang? What is the typical gang like? How much danger do gangs pose to the average citizen?

2. Gangs are typically accused of dominating violence and drug use/sales. What can you tell about gang involvement in these actions? How does this compare to the general impression about gangs? What is the G.R.E.A.T. program, and how does it relate to these problems?

3. Due to the apparent increase in gang violence, the police are called on to do something about the problem. As a member of the police department, what programs, interventions, or actions would you suggest for dealing with gangs and/or the public's perception? Be as specific as possible. If past programs form the basis of your suggestions, provide information on the strengths and weaknesses of those programs and how you would improve on them.

Chapter 6

DRUGS AND DELINQUENCY

Important Terms

affective interventions

Breaking the Cycle
(BTC) program

detoxification

Drug Abuse Resistance
Education (D.A.R.E.)

drug court

incidence

"Just Say No"

knowledge approach

life skills training

maintenance programs

Monitoring the Future
(MTF) Project

Multi-dimensional Family
Therapy (MDFT)

National Survey on Drug
Use and Health

outpatient drug-free programs

prevalence

reciprocal relationship

spurious relationship

systemic violence

therapeutic communities

use, abuse, addiction

What You Need to Know

- The Monitoring the Future Project surveys eighth-, tenth-, and twelfth-grade students every year to measure drug use. The results show very little drug use beyond alcohol and suggest that most use is experimental.

- Trend data for drug use over time show fairly consistent reductions in use.

- The relationship between drug use and delinquency is not entirely clear, with some studies showing that use precedes delinquency and others showing that delinquency precedes drug use. The actual relationship is probably a reciprocal one, with each behavior contributing to the other.

- No one type of drug treatment is effective for every individual or every drug. Treatment needs to vary by the individual circumstances.

- Gauging the effectiveness of drug treatment is very difficult due to the fact that most clients drop out before completion of treatment. What is clear is that treatment can be effective at reducing the need for and abuse of drugs.

- The "Just Say No" approach to prevention is shortsighted and has failed to show any impact on drug use.

- One positive approach is life skills training, which focuses on developing resistance skills for individuals. Evaluations show that this approach can be effective at curbing drug use.

- The popular D.A.R.E. program has failed to have any impact on drug use or abuse.

- Drug courts represent one of the more recent movements for addressing drug use and crime. These courts couple formal court action and intervention with individualized treatment plans involving the offender and his or her family.

INTRODUCTION

Youthful drug use continues to be a societal concern. Beyond the fact that drug use itself is a crime, such behavior is often associated with other criminal actions, including violence and property crime. As noted in the last chapter, drug use and distribution are related to ganging and gang behavior. There is a continuing perception that drug use is epidemic in the United States, especially among youths. A team of drug use experts contends that our high school students report "a level of involvement in illicit drugs which is greater than has been documented in any other industrialized nation in the world" (Johnston, O'Malley, and Bachman, 1996).

There is ample evidence that many youths are under the influence of alcohol or other drugs at the time they commit delinquent acts (Beck, Kline, and Greenfeld, 1988). While the causal relationship between drugs and delinquency is the matter of some debate, the indisputable correlation between the two (Huizinga, Loeber, and Thornberry, 1995) raises a variety of issues for the juvenile justice system. This chapter will examine the various issues involved in the drugs–delinquency connection—the extent of drug use, the evidence on the causal relationship, and ways to combat the problem. Before examining these topics, however, it is necessary to define some key terms involved in drug research.

Three common terms used in any discussion of the drug problem are **use, abuse,** and **addiction**. While definitions for these ideas vary from source to source, we can identify some uniform components in most definitions. Use and abuse are considered to be synonymous by most authors when juveniles are considered. This is true due to the fact that juveniles are legally barred from the recreational use of any drug, including alcohol. Indeed, even medically prescribed drugs are supposed to be administered by an adult following strict guidelines. Abuse generally refers to the use of any drug beyond that legally prescribed for a medical condition. For juveniles, therefore, any use constitutes abuse. Addiction refers to chronic use of a drug to the point at which the individual develops a need to continue use of the drug, increases the amount used over time, and develops a psychological or physical dependence on the drug (World Health Organization, 1964).

GAUGING THE EXTENT OF DRUG USE

Measuring the extent of drug use is somewhat difficult due to the private nature of the behavior. The only individual involved is the user. There is no victim who calls the police and files a complaint. In essence, the victim and offender are the same person. Consequently, the primary source of information on drug use (the extent of it and changes in it) is individual self-reports of behavior. Such self-report surveys have been conducted on both the general population and groups of known offenders. Data from both sources are considered below.

Drug Use Among Adolescents

Drug use by juveniles has been measured on a yearly basis since the 1970s by the **Monitoring the Future (MTF) Project** carried out by Johnston and associates at the University of Michigan. The MTF Project surveys eighth-, tenth-, and twelfth-grade students every spring (as well as college students and young adults) (Johnston et al., 1996). The project gathers information on a wide variety of behaviors, including levels and types of drug use. In addition, MTF presents drug use information for different time frames, ranging from "ever" using a drug to "daily use" in the past 30 days.

Table 6.1 presents information on the lifetime, annual, past month, and daily prevalence of drug use for high school seniors graduating in 2007. **Prevalence** indicates how many respondents used the drug during the year, as opposed to how many times (**incidence**) that the drug was used. A number of key observations can be made from this information. First, drug use varies greatly by type of drug. Second, only a small fraction of respondents uses any drug other than alcohol or tobacco on a regular basis. This table clearly supports arguments that much drug use—other than marijuana, alcohol, or cigarettes—is experimental.

TABLE 6.1 Lifetime, Annual, Past Month, and Daily Drug Use by 12th Graders, 2007

Drug	Lifetime	Annual	Past Month	Daily Use
Any Illicit Drug	46.8	35.9	21.9	---
Marijuana	41.8	31.7	18.8	5.1
Inhalants	10.5	3.7	1.2	.1
Cocaine	7.8	5.2	2.0	.2
Crack	3.2	1.9	.9	.1
Heroin	1.5	.9	.4	.1
Hallucinogens	8.4	5.4	1.7	.1
Amphetamines	11.4	7.5	3.7	.3
Methamphetamines	3.0	1.7	.6	---
Barbiturates	9.3	6.2	2.7	.2
Alcohol	72.2	66.4	44.4	3.1

Source: Compiled by authors from L.D. Johnston, P.M. O'Malley, J.G. Bachman, and J.E. Schulenberg (2007). *Overall Illicit Drug Use by American Teens Continues Gradual Decline in 2007*. Ann Arbor, MI: University of Michigan. Available at: http://www.monitoringthefuture.org

The most striking finding from the data on daily use is that very few youths use any drug. Only 5 percent claim daily use of marijuana, and roughly 3 percent claim daily alcohol use. Overall, the data suggest that drug use is not the rampant problem portrayed by the media or assumed by the public. Roughly 3 percent or less of the high school seniors used any one drug other than marijuana, alcohol, or amphetamines at least once in the last 30 days in 2007, and daily use was below 1 percent for all categories except marijuana and alcohol. It is only when annual or lifetime figures are considered that drug use begins to appear to be a serious problem, with several categories of drugs being used by 5 percent or more of the high school senior respondents.

Extensive information on drug use can be found at the Monitoring the Future web site: http://www.monitoringthefuture.org/

These self-report figures, however, must be considered cautiously due to the question of respondent representativeness in the MTF. Specifically, MTF data represent the responses from individuals who were attending school at the time of the survey. This ignores the fact that many youths drop out of school. Dropping out is especially great in the inner city, where the drug trade appears to be most concentrated. Johnston, O'Malley, and Bachman (1987) point out that roughly 15 to 20 percent of students drop out and are not included in the senior survey each year; moreover, they contend that dropouts tend to use drugs more often than those who remain in school. This suggests that the data underreports the level of drug use in the population. Given this caveat, the MTF data are useful from the point of view that the survey is conducted annually and provides a standardized set of data that can be compared over time.

Another source of self-report data on youthful drug use is the **National Survey on Drug Use and Health**, which is conducted by the Substance Abuse and Mental Health Services Administration (SAMHSA). The figures from the survey reflect drug use among a sample of youths ages 12 to 17, as compared to the data on students in individual grades in the MTF project. The SAMHSA survey, therefore, includes a larger number of younger respondents. Table 6.2 presents lifetime, annual, and past month use data for the 2007 household survey. The pattern in the results is similar to the MTF data in terms of both use in different time frames and drug categories. Alcohol is the most commonly used substance, followed by tobacco and marijuana. In addition, use is greater when longer time frames are considered. The figures are smaller in most categories compared to the MTF data for high school seniors, primarily due to the inclusion of a wider range of younger respondents.

The data in these tables, particularly those reflecting lifetime or annual use (and to some extent monthly use), often form the basis for claims of a drug problem or epidemic in the country. Use in the past year should not be used as an indicator of a drug "problem" because such use may simply reflect simple experimentation. When attention is focused on a more accurate indicator of serious abuse (such as daily use within the last 30 days, instead of on any use within the last year or even 30 days), the percentages of adolescents reporting frequent use are much lower and much less alarming.

TABLE 6.2 Drug Use by 12-17-Year-Olds, 2007

Drug	Ever Used	Past Year	Past Month
Any Illicit Drug	26.2	18.7	9.5
Marijuana/Hashish	16.2	12.5	6.7
Cocaine	2.1	1.5	.4
Crack	.4	.3	.1
Inhalants	9.6	3.9	1.2
Heroin	.2	.1	0.0
Stimulants	2.9	1.6	.5
Hallucinogens	3.5	2.5	.7
Cigarettes	23.7	15.7	9.8
Alcohol	39.4	31.8	15.9

Source: Compiled from SAMHSA (2008). *2007 National Survey on Drug Use and Health*. Available at: http://www.oas.samhsa.gov/NDSUH/2k7NSDUH/tabs/TOC.htm

Trend data for monthly drug use (see Table 6.3) suggest similar conclusions from the preceding discussion. First, use of more serous drugs has been relatively rare and has remained low throughout the years. Only minor fluctuations in use appear in the data over time. Second, alcohol, tobacco, and marijuana have traditionally dominated the drug use data. Of particular note is that the most prevalently used substance (alcohol) has seen a significant

> The SAMHSA data can be investigated further at http://www.oas.samhsa.gov/nsduh.htm

decrease in use of the past 30 years (from a high of 72% in 1980 to a low of 44% in 2007). On the other hand, marijuana/hashish, the second most commonly used substance, has exhibited wide fluctuations in use.

One major concern with the use of the MTF or the SAMHSA data is over the representativeness of the results. Various researchers argue that the level of drug use is much greater than appears in these sources. They claim that if more representative samples of youths and samples of inner-city residents were used, the figures would be substantially higher. Fagan and Pabon (1990), for example, note that while 30 percent of school students report drug use in the past year, 54 percent of high school dropouts report drug use over the same time period. Similarly, Altschuler and Brounstein (1991) note that while 6 percent of Washington, DC, in-school respondents claim drug use in the past year, 31 percent of the out-of-school respondents make the same claim. Studies such as these illustrate the biased nature of surveys that exclude dropouts or otherwise fail to sample more at-risk populations. At the same time, however, dropout samples are similarly biased toward portraying drug use in its most negative light.

TABLE 6.3 Trends in Past Month Prevalence of Use of Various Drugs
for Twelfth Graders, 1975-2007

	Year							
	1975	1980	1985	1990	1995	2000	2005	2007
Any Illicit Drug	30.7	37.2	29.7	17.2	23.8	24.9	23.1	21.9
Marijuana/Hashish	27.1	33.7	25.7	14.0	21.2	21.6	19.8	18.8
Inhalants	---	1.4	2.2	2.7	3.2	2.2	2.0	1.2
Hallucinogens	4.7	3.7	2.5	2.2	4.4	2.6	1.9	1.7
Cocaine	1.9	5.2	6.7	1.9	1.8	2.1	2.3	2.0
Crack	---	---	---	0.7	1.0	1.0	1.0	0.9
Heroin	0.4	0.2	0.3	0.2	0.6	0.7	0.5	0.4
Amphetamines	8.5	12.1	6.8	3.7	4.0	5.0	3.9	3.7
Barbiturates	4.7	2.9	2.0	1.3	2.2	3.0	3.3	2.7
Alcohol	68.2	72.0	65.9	57.1	51.3	50.0	47.0	44.4

Source: Compiled by authors from L.D. Johnston, P.M. O'Malley, J.G. Bachman, and J.E. Schulenberg (2007). *Overall Illicit Drug Use by American Teens Continues Gradual Decline in 2007*. Ann Arbor, MI: University of Michigan. Available at: http://www.monitoringthefuture.org

Self-report figures, even those based on samples from high-crime areas, suggest that the drug problem has been blown out of proportion. The data show that the use of illicit drugs is not rampant in society. Relatively few individuals use illicit drugs with even a gross measure of regularity (within 30 days). Figures for daily use fall to almost zero for most illicit drugs. This does not mean that adolescent drug use is not a problem. Indeed, any use of an illicit drug by juveniles is a problem.

Concern over drugs is also justified in light of the availability of illicit substances. Besides asking about drug use, the MTF project also asks students about the ease of availability of different drugs (see Table 6.4). While the figures are lowest for eighth-grade respondents, even among that group drugs appear relatively easy to obtain. This is true not only for alcohol (65% report very easy or fairly easy to obtain), cigarettes (60% very or fairly easy), and marijuana (41% very or fairly easy), but also for serious illicit drugs such as powder cocaine, crack cocaine, and amphetamines. The results for twelfth-grade respondents are even more significant: one-quarter of all respondents claim that every substance is either very easy or fairly easy to obtain.

Self-report data provide some insights. One is that the drug problem has been exaggerated. Relatively few youths use drugs on a regular basis, although many may experiment at some point in their lives. Another is that drug use is a greater problem among those youths who have dropped out of school or are otherwise considered at-risk. Perhaps of greater interest is to what extent drug use causes further deviance. Alternative sources of data are needed to shed light on this issue.

TABLE 6.4 Percent Reporting Drugs Very Easy
or Fairly Easy to Obtain, 2004

	8th Graders	10th Graders	12th Graders
Marijuana	41.0	73.3	85.8
LSD	12.3	21.6	33.1
PCP	11.4	18.0	24.2
Cocaine	19.4	31.2	47.8
Crack	20.6	30.6	39.2
Heroin	14.1	18.7	29.6
Other Narcotics	12.4	23.1	40.2
Amphetamines	21.9	35.7	55.4
Barbiturates	18.0	30.0	46.3
Tranquilizers	15.8	25.6	30.1
Alcohol	64.9	84.3	94.2
Cigarettes	60.3	81.4	---

Source: Compiled and computed by authors from L.D. Johnston, P.M. O'Malley, and J.G. Bachman (2004). *Monitoring the Future 2004*. Washington, DC: National Institute on Drug Abuse.

Drug Use Among Offenders

While information on the general population suggests that drug use is not a major problem and that relatively few youths use drugs on a regular basis, data based on offenders presents a different picture. Various data sources suggest that drug use is a critical problem for offenders, including adolescents.

One source for information on drug use among offenders is official data. In 2007, more than 200,000 juveniles were arrested for drug abuse, liquor law, or drunkenness violations in the United States (Federal Bureau of Investigation, 2008). Roughly 14 percent of these violations were committed by juveniles under age 15 (Federal Bureau of Investigation, 2008). Using juvenile court statistics, from 1995 to 2004, cases involving drug law violations among youths increased by 19 percent. Almost 194,000 youths entered juvenile court for drug law violations in 2004. Data on incarcerated youths also can provide information on the use of illicit drugs. Roughly 8,000 youths were placed in residential facilities as a result of a drug law violation in 2003 (Snyder and Sickmund, 2006). Based on a national one-day count of juvenile facilities in 2003, 7 percent of the youths in public facilities and 10 percent of those in private facilities were there due to drug-related offenses (Snyder and Sickmund, 2006). Court and correctional data provide support for the argument that youthful drug use is highly related to contact with the juvenile justice system.

It must be remembered that statistics on youths involved in the juvenile court and institutions represent a worst-case scenario. These youths are not indicative of the majority of juveniles in the population and, therefore, the drug use figures are not applicable to youths not involved in the juvenile justice system. Indeed, this information reflects only those individuals who are caught by the system. It is possible that the use of drugs increases the risk of apprehension. Despite this fact, drug use is integrally related to juvenile justice system involvement.

A Summary of Youthful Drug Use

The fact that relatively few youths use drugs, particularly on a regular basis, does not mean that adolescent drug use is not a

problem. At the same time, high levels of drug use by offending youths do not mean that use is a rampant problem in society. Rather, these figures point out that drugs are used by a small but significant number of youths, particularly by offenders, and that the problem needs to be addressed. Use becomes a greater issue if it engenders further delinquent behavior. The degree to which drug use causes delinquency, however, has been the subject of much debate.

A 17-year-old former heroin addict listens during a biology class for participants in the Hartford Youthful Offender Program in Hartford, Connecticut. She claims that without the program, which gives her a chance to earn her General Equivalency Diploma, she would have been back on the street or ended up in jail for life.

THE DRUGS–DELINQUENCY CONNECTION

Statistics showing drug use among delinquent youths (particularly incarcerated individuals) are often pointed to as proof that drug use causes delinquency. The evidence on the drugs–delinquency connection, however, is unclear. A variety of studies note that there is a high degree of correspondence between drug use and delinquent/criminal behavior (Anglin and Speckart, 1986; Ball, Shaffer, and Nurco, 1983; Bennett and Wright, 1984b; Fagan, Weis, and Cheng, 1990; Greenbaum, 1994; Huizinga, Menard, and Elliott, 1989; Inciardi, Horowitz, and Pottieger, 1993; Johnson et al., 1991; McBride, 1981; Newcomb and Bentler, 1988). What is not clear is which one causes which, or whether they are both the result of something else.

Possible Relationships

The actual relationship between drug use and delinquency can take a variety of forms. White (1990) outlines four possible relationships. First, drug use may cause delinquent activity. This argument typically focuses on the high cost of drugs and the need for youths to commit property crimes in order to secure the funds needed to buy drugs. Indeed, various authors point out that drug users often are involved in property offenses (Anglin and Speckart, 1988; Chaiken and Chaiken, 1982; Collins, Hubbard, and Rachal, 1985; Johnson et al., 1985; National Institute of Justice, 1990). Such an "economic need" argument, however, is only one reason that drug use would cause other forms of deviance. Goldstein (1989) suggests that drugs also may cause crime through their psychopharmacological effects and through systemic violence inherent in the drug market. **Psychopharmacological explanations** suggest that drugs have a direct effect on the user, either physically or psychologically, that impel him or her to act in a certain way. **Systemic violence** refers to violence due to factors such as competition between dealers, retaliation for the sale of bad drugs, the simple need to obtain a drug, or other factors related to the sale and marketing of drugs.

FIGURE 6.1 Possible Relationships Between Drug Use and Delinquency

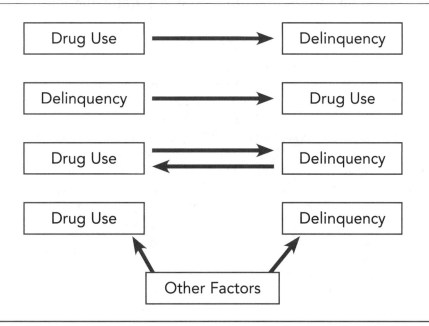

A second approach to the drugs–delinquency relationship is the view that delinquent activity causes drug use (White, 1990). This line of reasoning argues that delinquency leads to association with deviant peers and that it is within these peer groups that drug use appears (Akers et al., 1979; Elliott, Huizinga, and Ageton, 1985; Johnston, O'Malley, and Eveland, 1978; Kandel, 1973). This explanation views drug use as a form of deviance just like other delinquent acts. As youths associate with others who are involved in deviant behavior, they will participate in the same activities as the other youths. If the group is using drugs, the individual will be more prone to use drugs.

A third possible relationship views drug use and delinquency as feeding one another in a **reciprocal relationship**. This approach is a combination of the first two. The final possibility is that there is a **spurious relationship** involving drug use and delinquency. Under this assumption there would be other factors that cause both drug use and delinquency. In essence, the theoretical explanations for why a youth becomes involved in delinquency would also apply to the reasons for drug use. Drug use and delinquency are simply two manifestations of the same basic problems. Identifying which of the four possible relationships between drug use and delinquency is correct is not an easy task. Most attempts have focused on uncovering the time order between the two variables. That is, which came first, drug use or delinquency?

RESEARCH ON THE DRUGS-DELINQUENCY RELATIONSHIP

Delinquency Causes Drug Use

Research on the temporal (time) order of drug use and delinquency reveals a complex relationship. A variety of studies suggest that the dominant direction in the relationship is from delinquent activity to drug use. In a study using longitudinal data on almost 2,000 high school graduates, Johnston and associates (1978) claim that general delinquency predates most drug use. They argue that youthful drug use is an extension of other deviant behavior. This same pattern of drug use following delinquency is uncovered by Inciardi, Horowitz, and Pottieger (1993) in a study of the behavior of serious inner-city delinquents. They claim that drug use most often appears after youths have become involved in minor delinquency. Other authors (Huba and Bentler, 1983; Johnston, O'Malley, and Eveland, 1978; Kandel, Simcha-Fagan, and Davies, 1986; Speckart and Anglin, 1985) also note that delinquent behavior predates actual drug use. That is, the youths commit delinquent acts, join up with other delinquent peers, and enter into drug use along with their peers.

Data from the National Youth Survey (NYS) support this basic argument. The NYS collected data on delinquency, drug use, and demographic factors on a yearly basis from a representative sample of youths. The use of a panel design allows for the inspection of changes in behavior over time and the identification of the temporal order in the data. Elliott,

Huizinga, and Ageton (1985) note that minor delinquency and tobacco use typically precede the use of alcohol and other drugs. Similarly, Huizinga, Menard, and Elliott (1989) show a general progression from minor delinquency to alcohol use, Index offending, marijuana use, and polydrug use, in that order. With the exception of alcohol, the data show that drug use temporally follows more general delinquent behavior. From these studies, drug use is a product and not a cause of deviant behavior.

Drug Use Causes Delinquency

Other studies lend support to the argument that the relationship is in the opposite direction—that drug use precedes and causes delinquency or crime. Ball and associates (1983) report that heroin addicts commit four to six times as many offenses when they are actively using drugs than when not using drugs. Based on subjects in public drug treatment programs, Collins, Hubbard, and Rachal (1985) point out that daily heroin/cocaine users tend to commit substantially more property offenses than nonusers or weekly users. Anglin and Hser (1987) and Anglin and Speckart (1988) note that both official and self-reported criminal activity, particularly property offenses and drug possession/sales, increase with narcotics use. Other studies report a similar trend of elevated criminality during periods of heavy drug use (Nurco et al., 1988; Watts and Wright, 1990).

Two recent analyses also provide support for the argument that drug use precedes delinquency. Huizinga, Loeber, and Thornberry (1995), in a summary of the Denver, Pittsburgh, and Rochester youth studies, note that changes in the type and level of substance abuse typically precede significant changes in the level of other delinquent activity. This relationship was found for males and females as well as for different age and ethnic groups. This analysis is especially important because of the longitudinal nature of the data and the use of more than a single research site. Inciardi and associates (1993) arrive at similar conclusions in their study of serious delinquents in Miami, Florida. They point out that regular drug use (and often drug sales) precede other forms of delinquent behavior. Further, they note that the mean age of onset for drug use is younger than the mean age of onset for offending. The early onset of drug use also predicts early participation in serious delinquency (Inciardi, Horowitz, and Pottieger, 1993).

Reciprocity and Spuriousness

The fact that no consensus has emerged on the correct causal direction between drug use and delinquency suggests that the more plausible explanation is that the relationship is reciprocal. That is, criminal activity leads to drug use, and drug use leads to criminal activity. Support for a reciprocal relationship can be found in many of the same studies presented above. A number of authors note that increased drug use by already delinquent or criminal individuals leads to higher delinquency levels or more serious offending, not to a first offense (Anglin and Hser, 1987; Anglin and Speckart, 1988; Collins, Hubbard, and Rachal, 1985; Huizinga, Loeber, and Thornberry, 1994; Inciardi, Horowitz, and Pottieger, 1993; Nurco et al., 1988). Similarly, Elliott, Huizinga, and Menard (1989) point out that while delinquency precedes drug use, polydrug use is a typical precursor of serious persistent delinquency. Van Kammen and Loeber's (1994) analysis of the Pittsburgh youth study data reports that property offending predicted the onset of drug use. At the same time, however, the initiation of drug use was related to escalating participation in personal offenses. From these studies, it would appear that, regardless of which came first, drug use and delinquency contribute to each other. It appears that drug use leads to crime, and crime leads to drug use.

Similar to the argument for a reciprocal relationship is the view that posits a spurious relationship between drug use and delinquency. This simply means that drug use and crime are contemporaneous—they exist at the same time and vary in a similar fashion, and neither is the ultimate cause of the other. Rather, they are caused by either the same common factors or by different factors. Various authors (Huba and Bentler, 1983; Kandel, Simcha-Fagan, and Davies, 1986; White, Pandina, and LaGrange, 1987) argue that there are common causal factors, such as peer and school influences, that underlie both delinquency and drug use. Carpenter and associates (1988) claim that the spurious nature of the drugs–delinquency relationship is evident in the fact that few youths routinely use drugs and commit delinquent acts. They further note that the majority of drug use and delinquent actions occur in the absence of the other behavior. The more plausible argument, therefore, is for a spurious relationship. Similarly, the same analysis of the NYS data that points out a sequence of behavior beginning with minor offending and ending with polydrug use (Huizinga, Menard, and Elliott, 1989) concludes that the actual cause of the behaviors probably lies with a common set of spurious influences. Other research leads to the same conclusion (Collins, 1989; Elliott, Huizinga, and Ageton, 1985; Fagan and Weis, 1990; Fagan, Weis, and Cheng, 1990; Loeber, 1988; White, 1990).

Summarizing the Relationship

The fact that drug use is related to delinquency cannot be disputed. While the causal relationship is unclear, a strong correlation between the two behaviors means that drug use can be used as a predictor of other delinquent behavior (Elliott and Huizinga, 1984; Kandel, Simcha-Fagan, and Davies, 1986; Newcomb and Bentler, 1988). The research also suggests that each behavior contributes to the other, thereby providing insight for intervention and treatment. It may be possible to attack delinquency by attacking drug use. Drug use in itself is a delinquent act that can bring about action by the juvenile justice system. By acting on it the system is intervening in the lives of youths who are at a higher risk of participating in other delinquent activities.

INTERVENTIONS

Interventions aimed at drug use and abuse can take a variety of forms and fall under the general categories of treatment and prevention. Treatment programs typically are aimed at those individuals who already have established a pattern of continued drug use. In essence, treatment programs are geared toward addicted individuals and can take a variety of forms, including maintenance programs, detoxification programs, therapeutic/residential communities, and outpatient programs. Prevention programs are geared more at keeping individuals from initial involvement with drugs or, at the least, keeping casual users from more frequent and varied drug use. Drug prevention programs for juveniles often include a variety of approaches, such as information dissemination, affective education, and resistance and social skills training. Each of the various treatment and prevention approaches will be examined below.

TREATMENT APPROACHES

What is known about the impact of drug treatment programs comes mainly from the study of programs focusing primarily on adults. This is because there have been relatively few studies of treatment programs for youths and because most juvenile interventions take a more preventive approach. The increased concern over drug use and related problem behavior (such as violence) has resulted in greater attention to

> NIDA provides a great deal of information on drug treatment, including materials on specific programs and drugs. These can be accessed at http://www.nida.nih.gov/infofacts/treatmeth.html

treatment programs for juveniles. While programs may have a different emphasis, many similarities and common features appear across programs. For example, counseling and therapy of one sort or another appear in virtually all of the programs. The following discussion offers examples of the more well-known or effective treatment approaches. Other programs appear elsewhere in this book.

Research on treatment programs has led the National Institute on Drug Abuse (NIDA) to list 13 principles of effective treatment (see Box 6.1). Rather than attempt to offer a prescriptive set of activities for an "ideal" program, NIDA's principles address more generalized issues that can be implemented in different ways. Indeed, the very first principle notes that no one program is effective for all individuals or situations. In general terms, the principles argue that treatment must be responsive to the multiple needs of each individual.

Maintenance and Detoxification Programs

Maintenance programs, a common intervention for addicted individuals, seek to establish a steady state in which the individual does not experience withdrawal symptoms when the drug begins to wear

BOX 6.1

NIDA's 13 Principles of Effective Treatment for Drug Abuse

1. No single program is appropriate for all individuals.
2. Treatment needs to be readily available.
3. Effective treatment attends to multiple needs of the individual.
4. Treatment and service plans must be assessed continuously and modified as necessary.
5. Remaining in treatment for an adequate period of time is critical for effectiveness.
6. Counseling (individual and/or group) and other behavioral therapies are critical components.
7. Medications are an important element of treatment for many patients.
8. Addicted or drug-abusing individuals with coexisting mental disorders should have both disorders treated in an integrated way.
9. Medical detoxification is merely the first stage of addiction treatment and by itself does little to change long-term use.
10. Treatment does not need to be voluntary to be effective.
11. Possible drug use during treatment must be monitored continuously.
12. Treatment programs should provide assessment of HIV/AIDS and other infectious diseases, and counseling to help patients modify or change behaviors.
13. Recovery from drug addition is a long-term process and frequently requires multiple episodes of treatment.

Source: National Institute on Drug Abuse (1999). *Principles of Drug Addiction Treatment: A Research-Based Guide*. Washington, DC: National Institute on Drug Abuse.

off. Consequently, the user will be able to function more normally and participate in everyday activities without the constant need for the drug (Stephens, 1987). The most common maintenance program involves the use of methadone, an oral substitute for heroin. Besides periodic checks (usually urinalysis) to establish abstinence from other drugs, maintenance programs rely heavily on individual and group counseling and the establishment of behavioral guidelines (Anglin and Hser, 1990). Some programs also include incentives/rewards given to clients who test negative for drug use (NIDA, 1999). Evaluations of maintenance programs generally report reduced drug usage and the commission of fewer crimes by patients when they are in the program (Anglin and McGlothlin, 1985; Ball et al., 1987; Hser, Anglin, and Chou, 1988). Unfortunately, the impact of these programs tends to disappear after program participation, and patients return to preprogram levels of drug use and criminal activity when they leave the program (Anglin et al., 1989; McGlothlin and Anglin, 1981).

Often closely aligned with maintenance programs are programs that emphasize **detoxification**. This approach attempts to remove an individual from an addiction by weaning him or her off drugs. Drugs are used over the short term to minimize the pain and discomfort of withdrawal. Detoxification programs target a wide range of drugs, from alcohol to heroin, and can be found in many hospitals and facilities throughout the country. Anglin and Hser (1990) point out that while short-term follow-ups show that detoxification is successful at eliminating drug use, detoxification has not been adequately evaluated over the long term. Unfortunately, some drug users rely on detoxification to reduce the need for massive amounts of drugs to get high. They then return to more normal drug use until they again reach a point at which small amounts are no longer sufficient to serve their needs (Bellis, 1981).

Evaluations of both maintenance and detoxification programs are somewhat mixed. Sells and Simpson (1979) note that they are effective at lowering arrests and illegal activities among juvenile drug abusers. Other positive support is found in the fact that criminal activity is lower among drug users in treatment than among those receiving no intervention (Kaplan 1983; Wish, Toborg, and Bellassai, 1988). NIDA (1999), in its list of effective principles for treatment, notes that the use of medications are an important part of treatment for some individuals. Critics, however, allege that they are crutches that do not solve the problem, but instead lead to a nonproductive lifestyle of methadone, alcohol, other drugs, and petty crime (Stephens, 1987). An additional problem is that many maintenance drugs become simple substitutes for the original drug. A prime example of this is the fact that heroin was developed to solve morphine addiction. Today, instead of curing heroin addiction, methadone addiction has itself become an issue.

Therapeutic/Residential Communities and Outpatient Programs

Another major form of treatment, **therapeutic communities**, emphasizes the provision of a supportive, highly structured, family-like atmosphere within which individuals can be helped to alter their personality and develop social relationships conducive to conforming behavior (Anglin and Hser, 1990). Group sessions, called "games," often involve attention on one member because he or she is a new member of the therapeutic community, is suspected of violating a house rule, or is suspected of using drugs. Pressure is exerted to induce the person to admit the particular problem and the need for support from the group (Stephens, 1987). Group counseling is used to explore the reasons for drug use and to suggest alternative methods for dealing with the factors that lead to substance abuse. Therapeutic communities, such as Synanon, Daytop Village, and Phoenix House, boast positive results—including lower levels of drug use and criminal activity (Anglin and Hser, 1990; Coombs, 1981; DeLeon, 1984; DeLeon and Rosenthal, 1989). The KEY/CREST program combines a residential therapeutic community with post-release assistance in the community. Along with the therapeutic community, clients participate in educational activities, HIV education, a 12-step alcohol program, and other activities aimed at preparing the clients for success outside the institution. The New Vision Therapeutic Community program rests primarily on services while the clients are in prison, with an initial aftercare period upon release. Like the KEY/CREST program, clients undergo individual and group counseling, as well as educational activities.

Evaluations of therapeutic communities and residential treatment programs have revealed success in reducing recidivism and drug use. According to the Office of Justice Programs (2000), these programs are successful when the clients complete the intervention and aftercare. Lipton (1995) concludes that prison-based therapeutic communities "can produce significant reductions in recidivism rates . . . and . . . show consistency of such results over time" (p. 51). It is important to note, however, that even successful programs do not prevent all crime, eliminate all drugs, or graduate all of their initial clients. In a California program, only 28 percent of the offenders completed the program and aftercare, and 22 percent dropped out prior to completing the program (Lipton, 1995).

The final treatment modality, **outpatient drug-free programs**, often follows similar approaches to those in therapeutic communities or residential settings. The greatest difference is the lack of a residential component. Individual and group counseling form the cornerstone of these programs. Programs such as Alcoholics Anonymous bring together current and former addicts to help one another stay off drugs. At meetings, members recount their drug histories and how the group is supporting them in their efforts to abstain from drug use. Other components of outpatient programs may include social skills training, vocational programming, social interaction, referral to other sources of assistance, and possibly short-term drug maintenance (Anglin and Hser, 1990).

Several outpatient drug-free programs exist for youthful offenders. **Multi-dimensional Family Therapy (MDFT)** is centered on the family, peers, and community influences around the youths. Similarly, multi-systemic therapy addresses the multiple sources of inputs to youthful behavior, including the family, schools, peers, and neighborhoods (National Institute on Drug Abuse, 1999). The programs assess the needs of the youths and the youths' families, and provide intensive services to the youths within the different social contexts in which they operate. The intent of the programs is to ensure that youths and their needs do not go unaddressed. Each of these programs have been successful at reducing recidivism and drug use (National Institute on Drug Abuse, 1999; Office of Justice Programs, 2000).

Treatment Summary

There are several problems with the various treatment approaches. First, it is often difficult to motivate addicts and abusers to enter a treatment program. Convincing addicts that they have a problem is often half the battle against the problem. Besides getting drug users into programs, it is also difficult to retain them. Studies of therapeutic communities, for example, have indicated that up to 70 percent of those entering such communities drop out before completing the program (Stephens, 1987; see also Lipton, 1995). One solution to the participation problem may entail mandatory participation as an outcome of either criminal or civil litigation. While research suggests that coerced treatment is less effective than voluntary participation (Anglin, 1988; DeLong, 1972; Maddux, 1988), there is evidence that mandatory treatment does lead to reduced drug use (Anglin and McGlothlin, 1984; Hubbard et al., 1989; Leukefeld and Tims, 1988; National Institute on Drug Abuse, 1999; Visher, 1990). This may be due to the fact that such clients receive more extensive treatment.

Despite various qualifications, treatment appears to be effective at reducing the use of and need for drugs (Visher, 1990). In one summary evaluation of drug treatment, Simpson and Sells (1982) report lower drug use, lower criminal behavior, and improved employment status for clients as long as six years after the end of treatment. Non-treatment control clients fared significantly worse. A National Institute on Drug Abuse (1999) review of treatment programs offers numerous examples of successful programs, although mostly in relation to adult offenders. Conversely, Stephens (1987) suggests that maturing out of the addiction cycle may be the most frequent way out of the drug problem. As addicts age, it is simply harder physically to be a drug addict. As a result, some addicts find it easier to give up drugs than to continue addiction. Walker is also cautious about the ability of treatment to have much impact on the drug problem. He concludes that treatment is quite effective for those individuals who have decided to quit using drugs, but treatment, "as a primary strategy, will not reduce the national drug problem" (Walker, 1998:261).

PREVENTION APPROACHES

The National Institute on Drug Abuse (2004) offers 16 principles of effective drug prevention (see Box 6.2). These include a focus on protective factors; reducing risk factors; including families, peers, and communities in the interventions; dealing with social competence; coupling multiple approaches; and recognizing the long-term needs of the clients (National Institute on Drug Abuse, 2004). Many prevention programs incorporate more than one approach and rely on input from a variety of sources, such as the schools, families, and the community. These approaches can be seen in several of the prevention programs discussed below.

> As with treatment information, NIDA has a wealth of materials available on drug prevention. See http://www.drugabuse.gov/Prevention/Prevopen.html

The "Just Say No" Approach

Perhaps the most direct and simplest prevention programs are those that encourage youths to simply say "no" and resist drug use. During the 1980s, the federal government pushed *"Just Say No"* as the cornerstone of its prevention activities. This approach assumes that juvenile drug use develops out of peer interaction and that use occurs mainly in group situations. Children, therefore, are encouraged to make a personal decision in the face of peer influences to refuse any offer to use illicit drugs. Included in this approach is the basic message that drugs are harmful. The emphasis is on total avoidance of drugs.

The total avoidance of illegal drugs in light of peer pressure through a simple "no" response, however, is somewhat shortsighted. Trebach (1987) compares such a prevention approach to related efforts to tell kids to abstain from any premarital sexual activity. As some children are going to use drugs or engage in sex no matter what adult society says, there is an unrealistic naiveté involved in "Just Say No" and similar campaigns. In addition, there may be a certain amount of hypocrisy associated with a total abstinence crusade. Youths recognize drug use by adults and are influenced by the advertising that is aimed at adults. Some "Just Say No" advocates recognize that kids will use drugs anyway, but justify the approach as a way to convey a message against drugs.

BOX 6.2

NIDA's 16 Principles of Effective Prevention for Drug Abuse

1. Prevention programs should enhance protective factors and reverse or reduce risk factors.

2. Prevention programs should address all forms of drug abuse, alone or in combination, including underage use of legal drugs; the use of illegal drugs; and the inappropriate use of legally obtained substances, prescription medications, or over-the-counter drugs.

3. Prevention programs should address the type of drug abuse problem in the local community, target modifiable risk factors, and strengthen identified protective factors.

4. Prevention programs should be tailored to address risks specific to population or audience characteristics, such as age, gender, and ethnicity.

5. Family-based prevention programs should enhance family bonding and relationships and include parenting skills; practice in developing, discussing and enforcing family policies on substance abuse; and training in drug education and information.

6. Prevention programs can be designed to intervene as early as preschool to address risk factors for drug abuse, such as aggressive behavior, poor social skills, and academic difficulties.

7. Prevention programs for elementary school children should target improving academic and social-emotional learning to address risk factors for drug abuse.

8. Prevention programs for middle or junior high and high school students should increase academic and social competence.

9. Prevention programs aimed at general populations at key transition points, such as the transition to middle school, can produce beneficial effects even among high-risk families and children.

10. Community prevention programs that combine two or more effective programs can be more effective than a single program alone.

11. Community prevention programs reaching populations in multiple settings are most effective when they present consistent, community-wide messages in each setting.

12. When communities adapt programs to match their needs, community norms, or differing cultural requirements, they should retain core elements of the original research-based intervention.

13. Prevention programs should be long-term with repeated interventions to reinforce the original prevention goals.

BOX 6.2 *continued*

14. Prevention programs should include teacher training on good class-room management practices such as rewarding appropriate student behavior.

15. Prevention programs are most effective when they employ interactive techniques, such as peer discussion and parent role-playing, that allow for active involvement in learning about drug abuse and reinforcing skills.

16. Research-based prevention programs can be cost-effective.

Source: National Institute on Drug Abuse (2004). *Lessons from Prevention Research. Info Facts.* Washington, DC: National Institute on Drug Abuse.

Knowledge/Education Programs

A related approach to "Just Say No" programs is the provision of factual knowledge about drugs and their effects. The **knowledge approach** entails providing youths with information on different types of drugs, such as the physical and psychological effects of the drugs, as well as the extent, impact, and possible legal consequences of drug use. In many instances these programs are offered as a part of the normal school curriculum. The basic assumption is that such knowledge will allow the individual to make an informed choice about drug use. It is further assumed that informed youths will opt against using drugs.

Interestingly, evaluations of knowledge/education approaches often suggest that the programs increase drug use by participants. What appears to be happening is that the increased knowledge leads to enhanced curiosity and experimentation by youths in a kind of "I want to find out for myself" attitude (Abadinsky, 1989; Botvin, 1990; Botvin and Dusenbury, 1989; Eiser and Eiser, 1988; Hanson, 1980; Kinder, Pape, and Walfish, 1980; Swadi and Zeitlin, 1987; Weisheit, 1983). Based on information from 143 prevention programs, Tobler (1986) concluded that knowledge programs fail to show any reductions in drug use behavior. The single point on which these programs can demonstrate success is in their ability to increase a subject's knowledge about drugs (Botvin, 1990).

Affective Approaches

Rather than provide information about different substances and issues related directly to drug use, **affective interventions** focus attention on the individual. The assumption is that by building self-esteem, self-awareness, and feelings of self-worth, the youth will be able to make wise choices and resist pressures to use drugs. Few programs, however, rely solely on affective education elements. Programs such as Here's Looking at You 2000 (HLAY 2000), which purports to use an affective approach, typically also include drug information and social skills training. Consequently, it becomes difficult to isolate the impact of affective elements such as self-esteem on subsequent drug involvement.

One well-known program that incorporates a heavy affective component is the Big Brothers/Big Sisters program. This program matches adult mentors with at-risk children in the community. The goal of the program is to provide positive role models to the youths, help build self-esteem, promote healthy attitudes and behaviors, and prepare the youths for daily living. A key component is helping youths feel good about themselves. The Big Brothers/Big Sisters program can be found in more than 500 communities. Evaluations of the initiative show success at reducing drug use, reducing arrests, increasing educational success, and improving the overall quality of life for youths (Office of Justice Programs, 2000). These results are in contrast to other evaluations of affective programs where the interventions have failed to find any significant impact on substance use (Hansen et al., 1988; Kim, 1988; Kim, McLeod, and Shantzis, 1993; Newcomb and Bentler, 1988; Tobler, 1986). It is possible that this failure is due to attempts to look at affective interventions separated from other preventive elements, such as those found in Big Brothers/Big Sisters and similar programs.

Life Skills Training Approaches

Perhaps the failure of affective approaches to have an impact on drug use is the failure to include other elements along with building self-esteem. **Life skills training** often includes affective interventions along with a variety of elements, ranging from basic personal and social skills development (which deal with general life situations and how to deal with them) to the provision of specific resistance skills aimed directly at substance abuse issues. This approach assumes that individuals who use drugs are poorly prepared to address the issues and pressures involved in daily decisionmaking. For example, individuals who find themselves left out of the societal mainstream due to the lack of education and/or job training need to be taught the skills necessary to obtain a job and succeed in an acceptable manner. Individuals who get into trouble because they simply follow the group need to be taught how to be independent, make decisions for themselves, and resist following others into unwise situations. The key resistance skills taught include how to recognize a problematic situation and what alternatives are available to the individual, how to resist outside pressures (such as peers or advertising), how to identify help, how to cope with stress, and how to make wise choices.

Research on life skills or resistance skills training has shown positive results. Perhaps the best example of this impact comes from a series of studies dealing with tobacco, alcohol, and marijuana use by Botvin and associates (see, for example, Botvin and Dusenbury, 1989; Botvin, Renick, and Baker, 1983; Botvin et al., 1984, 1995, 1997, 2003). In these studies, "life skills training" was successful at reducing the number of youths using drugs. Positive results also appear in evaluations of other programs that focus on life skills, social competence, and related topics (see, for example, Eisen et al., 2002; Greenberg and Kusche, 1998; Hawkins et al., 1999). While most of the analyses focus on relatively short-term effects, positive outcomes do appear in longer follow-up assessments.

The D.A.R.E. Program

Perhaps the best-known drug prevention program in existence today is the **Drug Abuse Resistance Education (D.A.R.E.)** program, which incorporates elements of all the previously discussed approaches to prevention. D.A.R.E. is a police-taught, school-based program that began in the Los Angeles United School District in 1983. The program is aimed primarily at elementary students in the fifth or sixth grade, although there are companion programs for younger and older youths as well as for the parents of participating students. The D.A.R.E. curriculum is taught by police officers who have been trained by the program, and it is offered as part of the normal school experience. The topics covered in the program have recently been revised; the current curriculum (see Box 6.3) reflects aspects of affective training, "Just Say No" approaches, peer resistance, and social skills training. The primary focus of the program is on enhancing the social skills of the individual.

Based on its widespread adoption by schools in every state, one would assume that the program has proved successful at combating youthful substance use. Interestingly, this is not the case. Indeed, D.A.R.E. is not even mentioned in NIDA's (2004) guide to proven strategies for preventing drug use. Methodologically rigorous studies fail to find any significant changes in drug use behavior after participation in D.A.R.E. Ringwalt, Ennett, and Holt (1991), in a randomized experiment in 20 North Carolina schools, reported finding no impact on drug use or the intent to use drugs. Clayton, Catterello, and Walden (1991), using data from schools in Lexington, Kentucky, also failed to uncover any impact on participant drug use. In another evaluation, Rosenbaum and associates (1994) examined data from 36 schools in Illinois that were randomly assigned either to receive the D.A.R.E. program or to serve as a control. The outcome of their tests showed no significant difference in substance use between the experimental and control groups after a one-year follow-up. There is also no change in attitudes or

BOX 6.3

Elements of the New D.A.R.E. Curriculum

Elementary School Lessons

Purposes and Overview of D.A.R.E. — introduce D.A.R.E. decision-making model

Tobacco and You — focus on facts and beliefs about tobacco

Smoke Screen — use of decision-making model; discussion of media advertising

Alcohol and You — focus on facts and beliefs about alcohol

The Real Truth — examine alcohol advertisements; discuss inhalants

Friendship Foundations — examine peer pressure and decisionmaking

Putting It Together — application of assertiveness skills

Personal Action — practice decision-making skills in light of peer pressure

Practice! Practice! Practice! — apply assertive refusal skills; affirm healthy choices

Culmination — make public statements about choices to resist drugs and violence

Source: Compiled from D.A.R.E. web site: http://www.dare.com

beliefs as a result of program participation (Rosenbaum et al., 1994). A thorough evaluation of the most recent version of D.A.R.E. has not yet been completed.

Based on these analyses, it appears that D.A.R.E. has little or no impact on subsequent drug use. Why then does D.A.R.E. enjoy such a good reputation, and why should it continue on in our schools? The first part of the question can be answered by pointing out that D.A.R.E. is a relatively nonintrusive intervention that has good intentions and has shown no negative impacts. By using the schools, no specific individuals are singled out or identified. Everyone participates in the program. As part of the educational curriculum, it also gains an immediate legitimacy among students, parents, and the public. Perhaps the best reason why D.A.R.E. should continue in schools deals with the potential it has for

Mark C. Ide

The D.A.R.E. program is probably the best-known drug prevention program for youths. Despite the program's popularity, the majority of methodologically rigorous studies have found that the police-taught, school-based program has little or no impact on subsequent drug use.

engendering positive changes in attitudes and beliefs among youths toward the school, the police, and societal rules. The presence of a police officer in the school for a nonarrest situation opens the door for greater familiarity and understanding between juveniles and the police. It may also produce positive changes in the school environment by promoting other appropriate activities. While the program may not, in itself, bring major change in drug use, D.A.R.E. can contribute to a more general positive school environment that may engender more broad-based changes in attitudes and actions.

Prevention Summary

The evidence on prevention programs suggests that drug use can be impacted by certain types of programs. Resistance/life skills training appears to be the most promising at reducing the level of drug use, although more rigorous and extensive testing needs to be completed. On the other hand, programs based on knowledge provision may result in increased curiosity and experimentation with illicit drugs. Programs that stress self-esteem, self-awareness, and interpersonal growth in the absence of other strategies for dealing with life situations, including drugs (typically referred to as affective education programs), also fail to exhibit any strong influence on drug use (Botvin, 1990; Schaps et al., 1986; Tobler, 1986). Interactive programs are more effective than noninteractive programs (Tobler, 1997). In general, while many prevention programs exist and show promise, most still need to be evaluated with longer follow-up periods and better research designs (particularly using adequate comparison groups).

ALTERNATIVE RESPONSES TO DRUG USE

Responses to drug use do not always reflect pure treatment or prevention. The persistence of drug use in society over time, particularly coupled with the failure or modest impact of most prevention and treatment approaches, has prompted various alternate responses. Among the responses are increased enforcement of drug laws, the development of comprehensive programs that combine legal responses with treatment and prevention, and controversial responses, such as the legalization or decriminalization of drugs.

Increased Enforcement

The typical response in the United States is to invoke the legal process. Aggressive police tactics, strict prosecution, and mandatory sentencing are the norm in most communities. Examples of this include police crackdowns on drug markets, drug interdiction at borders, civil abatement procedures in court, and mandatory prison terms for drug possession or sale. This kind of "get tough" orientation permeates the national drug policy, as evidenced in the 2005 National Drug Control Strategy (see Box 6.4) and the funding that accompanies the strategy. While the strategy appears to be heavily oriented toward prevention and treatment, the reality is that enforcement and interdiction are the primary efforts. The total fiscal year budget for drug control in 2008 was almost $13 billion. Of that amount, $3.5 billion (roughly 23%) is clearly for treatment or prevention. The balance is mainly for arrest, interdiction, prosecution, and punishment.

BOX 6.4

I.   Stopping Use Before it Starts: Education and Community Action

II. Healing America's Drug Users: Getting Treatment Resources Where They are Needed

III. Disrupting the Market: Attacking the Economic Basis of the Drug Trade

Source: The White House (2008). *National Drug Control Strategy*. Washington, DC: The White House.

Enforcement Coupled with Treatment

The fact that many offenders use drugs and come to the juvenile justice system with an established pattern of substance use/abuse places the system in the position of needing to respond to the individual as both an offender and someone who needs help. As a result, both the adult and juvenile justice systems have developed processes that couple enforcement with treatment. Two examples of this are drug courts and the Breaking the Cycle program.

Drug Courts. The drug court movement began in 1989, with the first juvenile **drug court** appearing in 1995. Based on the most recent national statistics, there are 1,938 drug courts in operation, of which 732 are juvenile and/or family drug courts (Bureau of Justice Assistance, 2008). As of 2003, juvenile drug courts had already handled more than 12,000 youths (Office of Justice Programs, 2003).

The underlying philosophy for drug courts is to use the court's authority to prompt participation in and successful completion of treatment aimed at reducing drug use and related criminal behavior. The courts represent a coalition of prosecutors, police, probation, judges, treatment professionals, social service agencies, and other community groups working together to get the offenders off drugs and keep them off drugs (Drug Courts Program Office, 2000). While the drug court process varies from location to location, there is a set of common core strategies that are found throughout most programs (see Box 6.5). Among the common elements are frequent appearances before the court, regular drug testing, treatment assessment, participation in treatment programs, focusing on families, working with schools, aftercare, and providing interventions that are tailored to the individual.

Advocates of drug courts point to a number of potential advantages resulting from the programs. One key advantage is providing treatment to offenders. While most correctional intervention programs, whether residential or nonresidential, offer the opportunity for some types of treatment component, their primary concern with suppression and control often means that treatment is not always available or appropriate. Drug courts, however, are premised upon the need to match offenders with appropriate treatments. The offenders who are admitted to the drug court program are guaranteed to receive some type of treatment. A second advantage is keeping the offender in the community and using community resources to address the offender's needs. The youths are not cut off from their family and community support groups, which are crucial for long-term success.

The literature on the effectiveness of drug court programs presents a mixed picture. Various analyses report that drug court participants recidivate at a significantly lower level than comparison groups (Brewster, 2001; Goldkamp and Wieland, 1993; Gottfredson, Najaka, and Kearley, 2003; Harrell, 1998; Listwan et al., 2003; Spohn et al., 2001). Other analyses, though, find no difference between treatment and comparison groups or higher recidivism for drug court clients (Belenko, Fagan, and Dumanovsky, 1994; Granfield, Eby, and Brewster, 1998; Miethe, Hong, and Reese, 2000).

The popularity of drug courts has resulted in a wealth of information on the approach. One good starting point is the Office of National Drug Control Policy at http://www.whitehousedrugpolicy.gov/enforce/drugcourt.html

BOX 6.5

Juvenile Drug Court Strategies

1. **Collaborative Planning** — Engage all stakeholders in creating an interdisciplinary, coordinated, and systemic approach to working with youth and their families.

2. **Teamwork** — Develop and maintain an interdisciplinary, nonadversarial work team.

3. **Clearly Defined Target Population and Eligibility Criteria** — Define a target population and eligibility criteria that are aligned with the program's goals and objectives.

4. **Judicial Involvement and Supervision** — Schedule frequent judicial reviews and be sensitive to the effect that court proceedings can have on youth and their families.

5. **Monitoring and Evaluation** — Establish a system for program monitoring and evaluation to maintain quality of service, assess program impact, and contribute to knowledge in the field.

6. **Community Partnerships** — Build partnerships with community organizations to expand the range of opportunities available to youth and their families.

7. **Comprehensive Treatment Planning** — Tailor interventions to the complex and varied needs of youth and their families.

8. **Developmentally Appropriate Services** — Tailor treatment to the developmental needs of adolescents.

9. **Gender-Appropriate Services** — Design treatment to address the unique needs of each gender.

10. **Cultural Competence** — Create policies and procedures that are responsive to cultural differences and train personnel to be culturally competent.

11. **Focus on Strengths** — Maintain a focus on the strengths of youth and their families during program planning and in every interaction between the court and those it serves.

12. **Family Engagement** — Recognize and engage the family as a valued partner in all components of the program.

13. **Educational Linkages** — Coordinate with the school system to ensure that each participant enrolls in and attends an educational program that is appropriate to his or her needs.

14. **Drug Testing** — Design drug testing to be frequent, random, and observed. Document testing policies and procedures in writing.

BOX 6.5 *continued*

15. **Goal-Oriented Incentives and Sanctions** — Respond to compliance and noncompliance with incentives and sanctions that are designed to reinforce or modify the behavior of youth and their families.

16. **Confidentiality** — Establish a confidentiality policy and procedures that guard the privacy of the youth while allowing the drug court team to access key information.

Source: Bureau of Justice Assistance (2003). *Juvenile Drug Courts: Strategies in Practice.* Washington, DC: Bureau of Justice Assistance.

Despite the fact that evaluations have not been able to declare drug courts an unqualified success, this approach continues to grow and attract attention. The number of drug courts is growing, particularly in terms of juvenile and family drug courts. One driving force behind the movement is the attraction of combining legal sanctions with treatment into a coordinated response. What is still needed is extensive evaluation of the juvenile drug courts in terms of the impact on general delinquent behavior and the use of drugs in particular.

Breaking the Cycle. The **Breaking the Cycle (BTC) program** takes a similar approach to that found in drug courts. The program seeks to identify offenders with substance abuse problems early in their system processing, assess the appropriate treatment needs of the offender, and establish an integrated set of interventions (sanction, treatment, and rewards) for the individual. The key to the BTC program is coordinating services offered by law enforcement, the courts, corrections, families, schools, social service agencies, communities, and substance abuse treatment providers. The court is a pivotal participant because it can provide sanctions if youths fail to comply with the program. The BTC program has been used in several sites with adult offenders.

Lattimore and colleagues (2005) report on an evaluation of a juvenile BTC program in Lane County, Oregon. The evaluation of the juvenile BTC program provides mixed results (see Lattimore et al., 2005). Comparing program youths to a nonequivalent comparison group, the researchers report greater access to and use of drug treatment interventions by experimental subjects. Participants also report reductions in marijuana use, although there were no reductions in any other drug use, including alcohol use. In addition, while there was little impact on subsequent arrest immediately after program participation, there were clear reductions between six and 12 months after participation (Lattimore et al., 2005).

Evidence from both juvenile drug courts and the juvenile BTC project show that comprehensive interventions in which the juvenile justice system is heavily involved have the potential to reduce drug use and offending. The impact, however, is not uniformly positive. Further study is needed to identify the keys to success. More consistent positive results are required before either approach receives uncritical acceptance.

Ready Availability of Drugs

A proposal at the other end of the political spectrum from those discussed elsewhere in this chapter is the call for the free (or inexpensive) availability of psychoactive drugs. This is a call to legalize or to decriminalize at least the possession of drugs such as heroin and marijuana. Nadelman (1997), for example, argues that drugs should be available on a mail-order basis.

Proponents argue that such action would have several benefits. First, drug addicts would be less likely to suffer adverse health consequences from adulterated drugs or contaminated needles. Second, it could reduce street crime because addicts would not have to steal to obtain the funds to purchase drugs (Goldstein, 1989). Third, it would reduce the possibility of society alienating adolescents. "Youth may generally lose respect for a society that defines them as criminal because they use marijuana" (Stephens, 1987:119). Fourth, legalization would reduce our law enforcement war on drugs, including the disturbing rates of arrest and incarceration of African Americans.

A major concern with the proposal to legalize drugs is that drug use might escalate at an alarming rate. Nadelman argues that this is not a problem because most Americans already resist drugs for reasons other than their status as illegal substances. He notes that 70 percent of Americans resist cigarettes, and 90 percent either do not use drugs at all or use them in moderation. Nadelman concludes that these percentages suggest that Americans "do not really need drug laws to prevent them from entering into destructive relationships with drugs" (Nadelman, 1997:287).

Although legalization may be practical for marijuana, it does not seem to be a realistic possibility for many other psychoactive substances. Current attitudes simply do not favor such a liberal approach. For example, even among high school seniors, 72 percent favor current laws against taking heroin in private, and 44 percent think that smoking marijuana in private should be prohibited (Johnston, O'Malley, and Bachman, 1996). Thus "our value system, rooted in the Protestant ethic, simply will not permit lawmakers to make freely available such powerful mind-altering and euphoria-producing drugs" (Stephens, 1987:120).

SUMMARY: THE RESPONSE OF THE JUVENILE JUSTICE SYSTEM

The juvenile justice system must face several issues concerning drugs and juvenile offenders. First, many of the delinquents committing the worst crimes and the most frequent crimes have drug problems. Statistics clearly demonstrate that offenders tend to have drug problems. It is unclear whether drug use leads to delinquency, delinquency causes drug use, or something else causes both drug use and delinquency. What is clear is that something needs to be done.

The literature on drug treatment and prevention does offer some suggestions for action. As noted earlier, interactive prevention programs fare better than noninteractive programs. Therapeutic communities have had some success in prison settings, especially when followed by aftercare. Multi-dimensional, comprehensive initiatives appear to hold more promise than single-modality programs, and interventions that include the juvenile justice system (such as drug courts) show that coercive programs can have a positive impact.

The juvenile justice system often attempts to deal with less serious drug users by diverting those youths to other programs. The problem with diverting users of alcohol and other drugs to voluntary programs is that such actions may lead to net-widening. That is, more youths are sent to private programs than really need to be sent. In reaction to this problem, some states, such as Washington, simply opt to divest the juvenile court of its jurisdiction over users of alcohol and other drugs. Unfortunately, such a decision can result in complaints "from disgruntled parents who believed that social control—mandated by the court—was essential for straightening out their children" (Schneider, 1988:123-124).

Beyond the problems directly faced by the juvenile justice system, there is the fact that society has failed to take a consistent approach toward drug use. For example, while many drugs are illegal, they are still favored by both youths and adults. This puts parents and drug counselors in a bind. Warnings to avoid drugs completely may fall on unreceptive ears.

On the other hand, condoning some sort of "reasonable" drug use flies in the face of the law. Efforts to label some drugs as dangerous and criminal and others as socially acceptable lead to problems. Adults can buy and use alcohol and tobacco with little or no restraint but have to break the law to obtain even extremely small amounts of controlled substances. This societal "schizophrenia" (Hills, 1980) leads to conflicts in attitudes and hypocrisy in enforcement. Many interventions focus on certain drugs (such as heroin, cocaine, and marijuana) and ignore the serious problems of alcohol and tobacco abuse. Such slighting occurs even though alcohol and tobacco cause harm to more people than any of the so-called dangerous drugs.

In summary, there are no easy answers to the question of how the juvenile justice system should deal with drug offenders. Clear, Clear, and Braga (1997) argue that the criminal and juvenile justice systems must be realistic in their efforts. They take the position that any search for a completely drug-free society is unrealistic. A more realistic vision is to limit drug use as much as possible.

DISCUSSION QUESTIONS

1. You are asked whether drug use causes delinquency. Discuss the possible relationships between drug use and delinquency and take a position on which one is correct. Justify your position.

2. The state legislature has just appointed you to oversee all treatment and prevention programs dealing with drug use. What programs will you keep or institute to fight the drug problem? Why have you selected these programs?

3. Legislation has been proposed to decriminalize drug use in your state. Assuming that this legislation passes, what would you expect to happen to drug use and delinquency? What impact would this have on the juvenile justice system? What other impacts will this have in the state? Provide support for your position.

4. The local police department seeks to continue its D.A.R.E. program. Having just completed a degree in criminal justice, you are called upon for advice. What advice would you offer about this issue?

Chapter 7

POLICING AND JUVENILES

Important Terms

"broken windows" policing

community policing

CompStat

deadly force

disproportionate minority
   contact

juvenile curfew laws

mission distortion

police effectiveness

police use of excessive force

problem-oriented policing

professional policing

racial profiling

restorative justice
   conferences

What You Need to Know

- In 2005, police arrested an estimated 2.1 million persons under age 18. The majority of these (71%) were referred to juvenile court jurisdiction. The police used their discretion to handle and release 20 percent of these youths.

- A new view of the police role is one of community or problem-solving policing. This view tries to include the community as a partner in defining and solving crime and disorder problems.

- "Broken windows" policing places emphasis on policing disorder such as loitering and vagrants because this model sees disorder as a factor associated with street crime. The theory is that if police can reduce disorder, crime will also decrease.

- Still another development is to hold both police managers and officers more accountable for crime and disorder in their precincts or on their beats. This development received greater attention in New York City's CompStat program.

- Research indicates that some departments using traditional police strategies refer to it as community or problem-solving policing. So not all departments are actually following the directions of innovators.

- African Americans generally hold less positive views of the police than whites. Many youths appear to be either indifferent or less than overwhelming in their support of police.

- Research on racial profiling has produced mixed results. It is clear, however, that police views on what constitutes a dangerous neighborhood and on what constitutes disrespect can have at least indirect effects on stops and arrests of young black males.

- Disproportionate minority contact refers to the overrepresentation of any racial group in arrest and court statistics compared to the proportion of that group in the population.

- Research indicates that juvenile curfew laws are not effective in reducing crime.

INTRODUCTION

Policing brings to mind images of arresting suspects, shooting at criminals, writing traffic tickets, testifying in court, driving on patrol, and interrogating murder suspects in the detective bureau. Police still do these things, but they also engage in activities that many people are not aware of. For instance, today police also lead community meetings to discuss the extent and causes of neighborhood crime and disorder. Together with community members they are searching for solutions to urban problems. Police go to homes of juveniles who are on probation to assist probation officers in making curfew checks and try to determine what can be done to help juvenile probationers stay out of trouble and adjust. Police also facilitate **restorative justice conferences,** in which, for instance, a burglary victim meets a juvenile burglar and explains precisely how the burglary impacted the victim. Supporters for both sides are present and, with the help of the police officer leader, they work out an agreement on how the youth can make amends for what he or she did.

So policing today means much more than it did 25 years ago. Back then police were wondering how they could adjust car patrol to reduce crime. They were wondering if more cars would reduce crime or if faster response time would reduce crime. Today police are raising questions about the definition of policing. What is policing? What role do the police have in a democratic society? These questions and the solutions raised so far are having important effects on how police interact with juveniles.

In this chapter we will look at police and juveniles. We will discuss the police role, including such new developments as community policing and CompStat. We will also look at attitudes and the police, including both citizen attitudes toward the police and police attitudes toward citizens, some recent developments in policing, the effectiveness of policing, and improper use of police force.

STATISTICS ON POLICE WORK WITH JUVENILES

The FBI Uniform Crime Reports presents the basic picture of what police do with juvenile offenders. Other than traffic and neglect cases, in 2005, police arrested an estimated 2.1 million persons under age 18. The majority of these (71%) were referred to juvenile court jurisdiction. Twenty percent were handled within the police department and released. Seven percent were referred to criminal or adult court, and the rest were referred to a welfare agency or to another police agency (Snyder, 2008).

Two points are noteworthy. First, the percentage of offenders that police refer to juvenile court (more than 70%) is a significant increase from 1980, when police referred only 58 percent to juvenile court. Second, the fact that 20 percent of juveniles taken into custody are simply handled and released shows the discretion that police have with juveniles. Such discretion can have critical consequences for youths. A youth released in this manner does not have to worry that if he or she commits a new delinquent act a year later the first one will be held against him or her and he or she will be treated as someone with a prior record. The juvenile may be treated as someone without any record. If police impose any racial or other biases into their decisions to handle and release, those racial biases can have serious effects on later decisions by police, prosecutors, and judges. Much of this discretion is hidden and thus difficult to discover.

A highlight of the arrest statistics on juveniles is that in 2005 there were an estimated 1,260 arrests of juveniles for murder. This is a slight increase over the 1,110 juveniles arrested for murder in 2004. However, the 2005 number is down considerably from the peak year of 1993, when there were approximately 3,790 juvenile arrests for murder. In 2005 juvenile arrests for violent crimes were down 25 percent from 1996. Property crime arrests were down 44 percent. Drug abuse violations, however, were up 16 percent (Snyder, 2008).

The overall crime decline that started in the 1990s has yet to be fully explained. Some credit the crime decrease to changes in polic-ing that involved targeting disorder based on a belief that loitering, panhandling, and other types of disorder cause crime (Braga and Bond, 2008). Some credit the decrease to the increase in imprisonment that has been going on for more than 20 years. Others argue that

> One source of information about juvenile arrest statistics is an annual report put out by the Office of Juvenile Justice and Delinquency Prevention, titled *Juvenile Arrests 2005* (published in 2008, this is the latest one available), available at http://www.ojjdp.ncjrs.gov/. Arrest statistics can also be found in the FBI's *Uniform Crime Reports*, available at http://www.fbi.gov/ucr/ucr/htm

broader trends seem to be at work. Zimring (2007), for example, argues that crime also decreased in Canada even though that country did not use the police tactics that New York City used. In the next section we will discuss the police role in general and also devote more attention to the effectiveness of police efforts to reduce disorder as a strategy to reduce crime and delinquency.

THE POLICE ROLE

For much of the twentieth century police tried to be professional crime fighters. This often translated into police driving in one- or two-officer patrol cars until they saw something suspicious or received a radio call to respond to a crime or a call for service. The rationale was that quick response to calls would enable the police to apprehend suspects or deal quickly with problems that citizens reported to central dispatch. Many called this the **professional policing** model. Others have called it "911 policing" because 911 is the emergency phone number used to contact police.

There were several problems with this professional or 911 policing model. One was that increased professionalism did not reduce crime. Studies showed, for example, that simply increasing the extent of patrol in a given sector did not reduce crime. In addition, research showed that quicker response time did not have dramatic effects on crime (Walker, 1998), and that much of a police officer's shift did not even involve crime. Citizens call the police for all types of problems that are not directly crime-related. Some of the actions prompting those calls could escalate into crime, but many of the calls occur because people regard the police as government workers who are available seven days a week, 24 hours a day, and thus should be able to deal with their problems.

Another problem with the professional model is that it built barriers between the police and citizens. When officers sit in one- or two-person cars, they do not have the opportunity to interact with citizens. Interaction can have positive consequences. It can alert police to problems in the neighborhood, or it can produce tips about who might be engaged in either criminal activity or disorder. The old-fashioned foot patrol officer could get to know both neighborhood problems and tips about who might be causing the problems by having opportunities to meet with shopkeepers, pedestrians, and people sitting or standing near corners or other gathering places. Professional policing decreased the number of foot patrol officers and put the police car as a barrier between the officer and citizens.

Community or Problem-Solving Policing

One response to the shortcomings of the professional policing model is **community policing**, which is also called problem-solving or problem-oriented policing. Community policing does not necessarily mean exactly the same thing to everyone who subscribes to it. Some key features do emerge, however, as critical common elements.

One critical factor is problem solving. As Herman Goldstein (1990) has noted, police can and should be problem solvers in the community. Racing at 60 miles per hour in patrol cars to crime scenes is often a case of too little and too late. Even if the police are quick enough to get there and apprehend a suspect still on the scene or catch him or her fleeing the scene, they are too late—a crime has already occurred.

Problem solving, on the other hand, involves an effort to deal with conditions or factors that lead to crime or disorder. If the police can solve the problem, then they prevent crime from happening. A simple example with juveniles is police in one community leading the community to transform a vacant lot into a skateboard park. This solved the disorder problem of kids skating in the street and on sidewalks (Chaiken, 2004).

Another critical element of community policing is community building (Novak et al., 2002). Because the community shares responsibility for policing the community, an important part of community policing is to strengthen the community and its ability to solve problems and prevent and minimize crime, disorder, and other difficulties. Another term for this is establishing partnerships between the police and the public (Schnebly, 2008).

Such problem solving and community building can take numerous forms. One attempt at problem solving and community building is through holding community or neighborhood meetings. Here police meet with community members to identify problems. Citizens might note that an abandoned house or a house in violation of the housing code is a crack house where dealers are conducting business. Alternatively, citizens might complain that a particular street corner or bus stop is a center for gang-related activity. After problem identification, police and citizens together explore possible solutions. In Chicago, citizens decided to conduct marches in gang-related areas to discourage gang activity there. Together with police, Chicago citizens also worked with the bus company to relocate a particular bus stop where school children were being harassed. Citizens and police also sought the help of city housing inspectors and housing courts to close down buildings where drug dealers were conducting business.

In another Chicago neighborhood, citizens found that the local juvenile court was so busy that it was ignoring minor offenders. In response to this problem, the community started an alternative-consequence program. This was a program that gave out community service orders for juveniles accused of misdemeanors such as underage drinking, graffiti, vandalism, shoplifting, and bicycle theft. Youthful offenders usually performed between eight and 100 hours of community service, usually in beautification projects (Skogan and Hartnett, 1997).

In still another Chicago neighborhood, citizens thought that panhandlers, loiterers, and gang members were taking over an important commercial strip. So citizens decided to start Operation Beat Feet, a program in which citizens walked the strip for one to three hours every night. In six months, police reported a 33 percent decrease in five key crimes, compared to the previous year (Skogan and Hartnett, 1997).

In San Diego, California, youths involved in defacing public property with graffiti were directed into voluntary focus groups. These groups helped the youths understand why they had gotten involved in graffiti and taught the kids positive ways to contribute to their communities, such as painting murals at locations frequently targeted with graffiti (Carroll, 2001).

In Indianapolis, police act as facilitators at restorative justice conferences. (For a complete discussion of restorative justice, see Chapter 12.) This program is intended for first-time offenders, age 14 and younger, charged with battery, trespass, mischief, conversion, or felony D theft. If the youth is willing to participate, supporters from both sides (offender and victim) meet in a conference. The coordinator tries to get the group to understand what happened. For example, the coordinator asks the youth about the effects of his or her behavior on the victim and asks the victim how the crime affected him or her. After a thorough exploration of the event, the group tries to work out an agreement to repair the harm that was done. Restitution and community service are key elements of agreements. In Indianapolis, police and others (e.g., neighborhood prosecutors, civilian volunteers) have coordinated restorative justice conferences, which have taken place in police stations, schools, libraries, and community centers (McGarrell et al., 2000).

More than 90 percent of victims in conference cases report being satisfied with the way the case was handled. Ninety-eight percent said they would recommend the conference approach. At six months after the initial incident, only 20 percent of the youths who went through restorative justice conferences recidivated, compared to 34 percent in the control group. One year after the initial incident, 31 percent of the restorative justice conference youths had been rearrested, compared to 41 percent of the control group. Both differences were statistically significant (McGarrell et al., 2000).

In Houston, Texas, community police officers provide a "Knock and Talk" service for truants; they visit truants and talk to them about their truancy problems. In Tacoma, Washington, community police officers deliver truants to a community truancy center (Baker, Sigmon, and Nugent, 2001). In Cleveland, Ohio, police converted houses used as crack houses into police substations. In these so-called "RAPP houses" (named for the Residential Area Policing Program) youths could come in and talk to police officers who were there around the clock (Dunworth, 2000). All of these examples are efforts to both solve problems related to crime and disorder and to enhance the ability of the community to participate in policing itself.

Boston police have taken an approach considerably different from the restorative justice approach used in Indianapolis, but it is still considered to be a problem-solving approach. The problem targeted was violence, specifically homicide. In the Boston Gun Project's Operation Ceasefire, police targeted gangs engaged in violent behavior and used a strategy called "pulling levers," which entailed delivering a message to violent gangs that violence will not be tolerated. In Operation Ceasefire, police hold forums with gang members to announce their intent to apply whatever sanctions they can. Police then arrest gang members for trespassing, public drinking, overt drug use, disorder offenses, probation violations, and outstanding warrants. Evaluators report that Operation Ceasefire "was associated with a 63 percent decrease in youth homicides per month, a 32 percent decrease in shots-fired calls for service per month, a 25 percent decrease in gun assaults per month, and a 44 percent decrease in the number of youth gun assaults per month in the highest risk district" (Braga et al., 2001:3). It should be noted, however, that other research indicates that youth gun homicides had begun to decline in 1995 and that they declined 75 percent in other Massachusetts cities during this period (Fagan, 2002).

In Baton Rouge, Louisiana, police assist probation officers in supervising juveniles and young adults placed on probation for a gun-related offense. Police-probation teams make unscheduled evening visits to probationers about six times per month to check for compliance with probation conditions and to assess needs. In addition to such surveillance, police, probation, and other program participants offer services to address substance abuse, anger management, educational and employment needs, and parental skills (Lizotte and Sheppard, 2001).

Similar to Baton Rouge, St. Louis has a Nightwatch Program in which deputy juvenile probation officers and police officers make random home visits to verify curfew compliance for juvenile probationers. Sanctions such as community service, increased reporting to probation officers, home detention, and regular detention are applied to curfew violators. Rewards such as small gift certificates for products or services are used with compliant youths (Urban, St. Cyr, and Decker, 2003).

The Office of Juvenile Justice and Delinquency Prevention has supported the development of comprehensive, community-wide approaches to gang prevention. These programs involve both suppression and services. Suppression means that police—and often probation—work together in surveillance and information sharing. Service means efforts to provide academic, economic, and social opportunities for gang members. One program targeted older members (17 to 24) of two of the most violent gangs in the Little Village neighborhood of Chicago. Results were favorable, including reduced serious gang violence among the targeted gang members, compared to gang members in a comparison group. Specifically, the program resulted in reduced arrests for serious gang crimes (especially aggravated batteries and assaults) among the targeted youths (Howell, 2000).

Riverside, California, has a gang program that appears to be more comprehensive than the Boston program. Gang youths are supported in attending school and receive job training and opportunities for employment. There is even a stipend for job training. Both probation officers and police make home visits and engage in surveillance efforts that do result in arrests (Howell, 2000). Thus, it appears that suppression and services together are helpful in combating gang delinquency.

Allender (2001) suggests that sometimes the police role in dealing with juvenile gangs may be relatively simple. He suggests that one important thing police can do is simply to notify prosecutors that an arrested juvenile is a gang member. Then the prosecutor can recommend to the judge that sentencing include orders forbidding association with gang members and counseling to discourage gang participation.

Concerns about Community or Problem-Solving Policing

There are some concerns about community or problem-solving policing. One issue is that many practices are labeled community policing that are not actually related to either problem solving or community building. Many police chiefs have claimed that they were practicing community policing simply in order to receive grant money set aside for community policing initiatives or to appear progressive. A second issue is that while the creators of problem-solving policing intended that the police get involved with their community and come up with innovative solutions to crime and disorder problems, many police efforts labeled as problem-solving have been traditional police strategies. A recent study of problem solving in San Diego distinguished between problem solving by police and **problem-oriented policing**. Many officers do engage in problem solving; they "take a thoughtful approach, try to gather some information before proceeding, and often implement a multipronged response to problems" (Cordner and Biebel, 2005:177). The solution, however, may often be either targeted enforcement or saturation patrol or targeted investigation. In other words, the police put additional attention and presence on the problem, but it appears that not many police are engaging in problem-oriented policing in the sense that they are trying to devise tailor-made nontraditional responses and trying to assess impact (Cordner and Biebel, 2005). In other words, police who claim to be practicing problem-solving policing often are not going beyond traditional police tactics to work with communities to come up with innovative solutions to such problems as crime, drug abuse, and disorder.

"Broken Windows" Policing

In **"broken windows" policing**, the police also broaden their concerns and actions, compared to traditional 911 policing. Instead of focusing only on crime, the police pay attention to both crime and disorder. Based on the "broken windows" hypothesis, police consider disorder—for example, rowdy teens hanging out on street corners, "squeegee men" offering to wash car windows for cash "contributions," prostitutes plying their trade, youths or adults trying to jump turnstiles to avoid paying subway fare, "winos" urinating on the street or sleeping in public places like subway stations, and so on—as a serious problem that leads to street crime.

> Disorder demoralizes communities, undermines commerce, leads to the abandonment of public spaces, and undermines public confidence in the ability of government to solve problems; fear drives citizens further from each other and paralyzes their normal, order-sustaining responses, compounding the impact of disorder (Kelling and Coles, 1996:242).

"Broken windows" theory holds that disorder creates fear in citizens, causing them to stay off the streets. The more citizens avoid streets, the more deserted the streets get and the more citizens avoid them. This affects urban trafficking, both auto and pedestrian, hurts business, and can contribute to crime. Some of the strategies used as part of "broken windows" policing are opportunity reduction, problem solving, and crime prevention through environmental design (Kelling and Coles, 1996). Some cities (e.g., Indianapolis) have focused on the "broken windows" model of community policing, while other cities (e.g., St. Petersburg) have focused more on police-community cooperation and problem-solving (Paoline, Myers, and Worden, 2000).

More controversial has been the use of zero-tolerance policing. In New York City, Commissioner William Bratton decided to arrest the aforementioned "squeegee men," subway fare beaters, and panhandlers. Bratton decided on a policy of no—"zero"—tolerance for disorder and minor crimes. It has been found that many of the persons stopped by police for disorder or minor crimes (such as subway fare evasion) are wanted on warrants for more serious crimes. So campaigns against disorder have the advantage of catching a considerable number of street criminals who normally escape apprehension.

We have distinguished community policing from "broken windows" policing, but this distinction is not always clear-cut. In New York City, for example, the get-tough approach to petty offenders was considered to be problem solving. We prefer to consider it distinct from community policing efforts such as those in Chicago where the police attended and promoted community meetings and community problem solving. In New York, the police resorted to what we consider a rather traditional approach—making arrests, with minimal community participation. In Chicago, the police tried to maximize community involvement, and that community participation led to such innovative solutions as citizen marches, alternative dispute resolution, and even getting the bus company to relocate a bus stop.

Questions about "Broken Windows" Theory and Policing

"Broken windows" theory and policing rests on a fundamental assumption: disorder causes crime. The thinking is that if a community allows vagrants to panhandle, prostitutes to cruise streets for customers, and teenagers to congregate on street corners, then law-abiding citizens will retreat, the streets will become even more disorderly, and crime will follow.

There is some support for the hypothesis. For example, the Jersey City POP at Violent Places Project used aggressive disorder enforcement tactics at 24 places noted for violent crime. Results showed significant decreases in total calls for service and total crime incidents (Braga, 2001).

However, there are problems with the "broken windows" hypothesis. The first and most important is that it has not been proven conclusively that disorder causes crime. After a thorough review of the research, Harcourt concludes that "[t]here is little evidence that Mayor Giuliani's quality of life initiative in New York City significantly contributed to the concurrent sharp decline in crime" (Harcourt, 2001:124). Harcourt thinks that the addition of more police officers and consequent enhanced surveillance contributed to the decline in crime in New York City, but fighting disorder had no impact.

Second, sophisticated research shows that common factors cause both disorder and crime. Sampson and Raudenbush (1999), for example, have found that concentrated disadvantage (such factors as poverty, unemployment, and single-female-headed households) and insufficient collective efficacy are the real causes.

Another problem with the hypothesis that disorder causes crime is that "broken windows" policing actually involves a great deal of disorder: disorder by the police in their enforcement tactics. Wilson and Kelling (1982) freely admit that "broken windows"–style police officers "kick ass" and "knock them [gang members] on their ass" (Harcourt, 2001:127). Police are justified in doing just about anything if their suspicions are aroused. This can lead to rampant discrimination and excessive force. For example, allegations of police misconduct increased 68 percent in New York City from 1993 to 1996 (Harcourt, 2001).

Still another problem with the "broken windows" theory of policing is that it makes a simplistic dichotomy between law-abiding and disorderly citizens. It implies that citizens hanging out on the streets and tossing ice cream wrappers on the street are disorderly. The theory makes no allowance for other interpretations of what perhaps appears to be disorder—interpretations such as "artistic ferment, a youth hangout, rebellion, or an alternative lifestyle" (Harcourt, 2001:132). In addition, it focuses on lower-class disorder and ignores upper- or middle-class disorder. It ignores the disorder of paying a housekeeper under the table, tax evasion, insider trading, and noncompliance with environmental regulations. In summary, "broken windows" theory and policing "embraces an unmediated aesthetic of order, cleanliness, and sobriety" (Harcourt, 2001:134).

A final problem with the theory is that it is contrary to a general finding that coercive crime measures do not seem to work but social support is effective in preventing crime (Colvin, Cullen, and Vander Ven, 2002). (For further discussion of the importance of social support, see Chapter 14.) More specifically, the disintegrative shaming practices used in this strategy "stigmatize individuals and push them away from the law-abiding community" (Colvin, Cullen, and Vander Ven, 2002:32). For additional perspectives on community policing, see Boxes 7.1, 7.2, and 7.3.

BOX 7.1

Questioning Community Policing

Most of the experts who write about community policing consider it a positive innovation, but David Garland raises some interesting questions about the focus on quality of life and disorder. Whereas writers such as George Kelling subscribe to the "broken windows" hypothesis that disorder leads to crime, Garland notes that behaviors used to be interpreted quite differently. Now, however,

> "[p]ublic drinking, soft drug use, graffiti, loitering, vagrancy, begging, sleeping rough, being 'uncivil': these cease to be tolerable nuisances or pricks to the middle-class conscience and become the disorderly stuff upon which serious crime feeds. . . . Every minor offence, every act of disorderly conduct—particularly if committed by poor people in public spaces—is now regarded as detrimental to the quality of life" (Garland, 2001:181).

What he means is that the presence of vagrants and street people used to make some people think about the less fortunate and the need for shelters for the homeless and what might be done to address urban poverty. Now the focus is to arrest vagrants and simply get them off the street.

So who is right? Are acts of disorder really precursors to serious crime? Or are such acts "trivia" (Garland, 2001) that are used to "prick . . . conscience"? Does the sight of a beggar cause us to think "worthless panhandler trying to con me out of my hard-earned dollars"? Or does it make us think about the reality of poverty in a consumer society where many can satisfy every whim including cars that cost up to $100,000?

CompStat Policing

Several years ago, New York City started using **CompStat**, a strategic-management process in which police managers are held responsible for the control of crime and the enhancement of the quality of life in New York City. CompStat involves the collection of data on the incidence and location of crimes and other problems. This information is shared and police managers are held responsible for reducing crime and taking care of quality-of-life problems (e.g., the presence of alcoholics and vagrants) in their precincts. The process is now being copied in such cities as Indianapolis, Louisville, and Boston.

The process consists of several steps. First, police must gather accurate and timely information. Crime statistics and information about quality-of-life issues are collected and shared. A second component

BOX 7.2

Community Policing in an Age of the Disappearing Community

Community policing advocates insist that communities are responsible for policing themselves, that they must join efforts with police to make the community safe. Citizens need to participate in community meetings, Neighborhood Watch programs, citizen patrols, and simply the basic task of informing police about neighborhood problems. The police cannot do it alone. Crime and disorder prevention and control should be a joint responsibility. The police and the community can and should work together to define problems, explore possible solutions, and implement actions to address those problems.

A difficulty with this emphasis on the joint responsibility of police and community to define and solve community problems is that the sense of community appears to be disappearing.

In Robert Putnam's metaphor, whereas we used to bowl together in leagues, we are now "bowling alone": "We have been pulled apart from one another and from our communities over the last third of the century" (Putnam, 2000:27). Participation in politics and public affairs, clubs and community associations, churches, unions, and professional societies has been decreasing. To give just one example, in 1975-76 approximately two-thirds of all Americans attended club meetings such as Kiwanis or Rotary, but by 1999 two-thirds of Americans were never attending such meetings (Putnam, 2000).

This decline of social capital (community support) suggests a logical question: Is it reasonable to believe that Americans will participate in community policing efforts in an era of "bowling alone"? If Americans don't even want to bowl together, join clubs together, go to church together, how can police expect them to participate in community meetings or to participate in programs such as Neighborhood Watch to deal with crime, disorder, and other community problems? If, as Putnam suggests, we are watching more television and spending more time on the Internet, then how can police get citizens to turn off their TVs and computers and participate in community policing efforts?

Related to Putnam's concerns, an evaluation of community policing in Houston, Texas, found that the program seemed to favor the interests of homeowners. There was less information about community policing and less participation by less affluent residents. So community policing "can be difficult in places where the community is fragmented by race, class, and lifestyle" (Skogan and Hartnett, 1997:234). In Chicago, however, community policing seemed to enjoy "fairly inclusive recognition, and fairly widespread benefits" (Skogan and Hartnett, 1997).

BOX 7.2 *continued*

So policing experts are calling for greater civic involvement while sociologists such as Putnam are noting the decline of social capital. Should community policing enthusiasts give up or continue their efforts to return policing to its more community-oriented roots?

BOX 7.3

Community Policing: A Conflicting Opinion

Most police and most commentators speak of community policing in glowing terms. The reason for such praise is that it is difficult to criticize efforts to involve the community, especially if such involvement means asking community members to define police priorities and to help come up with solutions for crime and disorder problems.

One dissident voice is Neil Websdale, who did a participant observation study of community policing in Nashville, Tennessee. Websdale contends that community policing is actually a subterfuge to cover up societal neglect of inner cities. Globalization of the economy has resulted in the "economic devastation" of inner-city communities, which contributes to drug use and dealing. Community policing is merely a veneer to cover saturation policing in urban areas. Such policing does nothing to deal with the roots of urban problems and urban crime. Moreover, the residents of inner-city Nashville do not consent to saturation policing but report feeling "under siege" (Websdale, 2001:200). Thus,

> the ideology of community policing fits sweetly with the spread of global capitalism and the joblessness, anomie, and despair left in its chaotic wake. Community policing and global capitalism pose as the forces of democratic progress without ever really asking subject populations what they want (Websdale, 2001:218).

Websdale argues that what residents of inner cities really want is not saturation policing that arrests and incarcerates more and more African Americans. What they want is "gainful employment and the creation of safe, wholesome living conditions where their families can flourish" (Websdale, 2001:219).

What do you think? Do inner-city communities want community policing? Or do they want basic changes in the economy so that more jobs are available?

is rapid deployment: police commanders need to send officers out to address the problem. A third component is effective tactics: police need to focus specific resources on the problem. A fourth component is relentless follow-up and assessment. Police must check to see that crime and other problems are decreasing (Walsh and Vito, 2004).

Although, in New York City, crime and disorder did decrease with CompStat, some questions have been raised about the practice. Some question whether it was CompStat that was responsible for the decrease. Noting that crime went down in other cities at the time that CompStat was being practiced, Moore (2003) argues that other factors were therefore responsible for the decrease. Moore and others also question the aggressive tactics used in New York City, such as rounding up derelicts and so-called "squeegee men." Related to this criticism, Moore also argues that CompStat focuses on arrest and ignores efforts at prevention that could both reduce crime and achieve more overall justice.

Kelling and Sousa (2001) found that "broken windows" policing did decrease violent crime in New York City. Specifically, they found that high rates of misdemeanor arrests in New York City precincts were associated with greater declines in violent crime. Messner and his colleagues (2007) argue that "broken windows" policing in New York City was significantly related to decreases in homicide rates, even controlling for other factors. Corman and Mocan (2005) claim that the increase in the felony arrest rate accounted for almost 30 percent of the decline in homicides while the increase in the minimum wage accounted for 8 percent of the decline.

One of the most impressive studies was a controlled experiment in Lowell, Massachusetts. Police focused on hot spots, locations that had high crime rates. They targeted a random sample of the hot spots with problem-oriented policing. Compared to the control locations that did not receive the disorder policing, robbery decreased 42 percent, nondomestic assault calls decreased 34 percent, and burglary/breaking-and-entering calls decreased 36 percent. Furthermore, litter went down 27 percent at treatment hot spots but increased 11 percent at control hot spots. Incidents of graffiti went down 23 percent at treatment hot spots but increased 19 percent at control hot spots. The authors conclude that tailored police strategies can effectively reduce crime and disorder, in support of the Wilson and Kelling "broken windows" hypothesis (Braga and Bond, 2008).

Other studies, on the other hand, have concluded that "broken windows" policing does not reduce crime. Rosenfeld and his colleagues, for example, found that it did not play a direct role in reducing homicides in New York City (Rosenfeld, Fornango, and Baumer, 2005). Harcourt and Ludwig (2006) argue that analysis of New York City crime data and the Moving to Opportunity experiment in five U.S. cities allows them to conclude that "broken windows" policing did not reduce crime.

At this point, the effects of CompStat and "broken windows" policing on crime seems promising, but there are some who dispute that conclusion. A factor to consider is the racial impact. Part of the "broken windows" policing effort in New York City included arresting persons who were using marijuana in public. Such misdemeanor arrests (MPV: marijuana in public view) increased dramatically, from fewer than 1,000 in 1990 to a peak of 51,000 in the year 2000 (Golub, Johnson, and Dunlap, 2007). What the "broken windows" policing advocates neglect to mention is that these arrests fell disproportionately on minorities, especially young black and Hispanic males. Blacks made up 23 percent of the population but 52 percent of MPV arrests, whereas whites made up 38 percent of the population but only 15 percent of MPV arrests. Note that discrimination is hard to prove because the researchers had no measure of the tendencies of whites versus blacks to actually smoke in public. The authors recommend limiting the practice to public areas in Manhattan and using more appearance tickets (ordering offenders to go to court) instead of arrests (Golub, Johnson, and Dunlap, 2007).

A recent review of what CompStat and non-CompStat police departments were actually practicing showed that both types of departments were pursuing "traditional, police-enforcement strategies" (Weisburd et al., 2003:444). Specifically, both CompStat and non-CompStat departments were emphasizing the following tactics against crime and disorder: increasing arrests for targeted offenders, using check points, targeting repeat offenders, making gun seizures, and improving victim services (Weisburd et al., 2003). CompStat, then, has not been innovative in terms of forcing the police to do new things. The innovation has been directed more at holding upper-level and middle managers accountable for crime and disorder.

Defenders of CompStat argue that the basic ingredients of CompStat policing are its focus on strategic analysis and accountability. In other words, the basics of CompStat are analysis of problems such as crime and disorder, devising strategies to reduce crime and disorder, and measurement to determine if the strategies work. Managers (police chiefs and commanders) are held accountable for results; if they do not reduce crime and disorder, they can and will be replaced (Walsh and Vito, 2004).

One additional note is that similarities can be seen between CompStat policing and the emphasis on accountability currently going on in probation (see Chapter 11). Both of these developments reflect more general trends in both government agencies and business to emphasize strategic management, performance-based objectives, and accountability. Both the public and the private sector see the necessity for government agencies to state their mission and objectives and the need to monitor their activities to see if they are indeed achieving what they set out to achieve. The public demands demonstration that government and business are effective and efficient.

CITIZEN ATTITUDES TOWARD POLICE

Contrary to what many police believe, citizens actually hold rather positive attitudes toward the police. For example, a 2007 Gallup Poll reported that 53 percent of those polled rated the honesty and ethical standards of police either very high or high (*Sourcebook of Criminal Justice Statistics Online*, 2007). In an earlier Gallup Poll respondents rated police below nurses, clergy, druggists, veterinarians, and doctors, but above college teachers, engineers, dentists, psychiatrists, bankers, chiropractors, journalists, lawyers, and others (Maguire and Pastore, 2004). In November of 2001, in the aftermath of the September 11th terrorist attacks, the rating of police jumped; 68 percent of respondents rated police honesty and ethical standards as very high or high (Gallup Organization, 2001). Another survey in 2002 showed that high percentages of the respondents rated the police "excellent" or "pretty good" at solving crime, preventing crime, and being helpful and friendly (Maguire and Pastore, 2004). Almost 60 percent (57%) of the respondents said that they had a "great deal of confidence" or "quite a lot of confidence" in the police as one of the institutions in American society (*Sourcebook of Criminal Justice Statistics Online*, 2002).

Citizens vary considerably, however, in their approval of the police. For example, 56 percent of whites but only 40 percent of blacks rated the honesty and ethical standards of police as high or very high. Similarly, 61 percent of whites but only 43 percent of blacks and 41 percent of Hispanics think that the police treat all races fairly. Less than one-half of young respondents (age 18 to 24 years) think that the police treat all races fairly, compared to more than 50 percent for all other age groups, including 71 percent of senior citizens (age 65 and up). Only 16 percent of whites but 42 percent of blacks and 39 percent of Hispanics fear that the police may stop and arrest them when they are completely innocent (Maguire and Pastore, 2004). In a recent survey in New York City, "blacks were three times more likely than non-blacks to perceive that racially biased policing was widespread, that it was unjustified, and that it had been experienced personally" (Rice and Piquero, 2003:111). Thus, citizen attitudes toward the police are not uniform. Some citizens are more positive, while others are more negative.

> The Sourcebook of Criminal Justice Statistics contains considerable information on public opinion attitude research about criminal justice topics. The Sourcebook is available at http://www.albany.edu/sourcebook/

Of great relevance to the police and juvenile justice is the fact that lower-class youths comprise one group holding negative attitudes toward the police. Anderson (1994) argues that lower-class youths have little faith in the police and subscribe to a street code whereby the "police are most often seen as representing the dominant white society and not caring to protect inner-city residents" (Anderson, 1994:82). As a result of the perception and/or the reality that police do not respond when called, the inner-city youth often relies on self-protection: "taking care of himself" (Anderson, 1994:82) is a critical part of this street code.

A recent study in St. Louis, Missouri, confirms Anderson's argument. This was a qualitative study that used a purposive sample of 75 African-American youths, a number of whom were highly active in delinquency. High percentages of the youths in St. Louis had been harassed or mistreated by the police. About half of both male and female respondents agreed that the police engage in frequent harassment or mistreatment of people. In summary, young men "described being stopped on a regular basis and treated as suspects. They said officers routinely used disrespectful language, engaged in physically intrusive actions such as strip searches and cavity probes, and assumed young men 'got lucky' rather than were innocent when no evidence of criminal wrongdoing was discovered" (Brunson and Miller, 2006:548). Several of the young men reported that if police lacked enough evidence to arrest them, the officers would drive them to another area, let them out, and make them walk home (Brunson, 2007). Simply being a young black male in a disadvantaged neighborhood put these males at risk of police suspicion of criminal activity (Cobbina, Miller, and Brunson, 2008).

A study of more than 5,000 eighth-grade students found that youths were "indifferent" toward the police, that is, they were neither positive nor negative (Taylor et al., 2001). Part of the reason for youths' indifference or negative attitudes toward the police is that youths often have negative experiences with the police. A study in Hartford, Connecticut, for example, found that the 132 youths interviewed reported approximately 400 negative experiences. Thirty-nine percent involved physical encounters (force, hitting, injury), 24 percent involved verbal harassment, and 34 percent were categorized as "other." For example, a 15-year-old Hispanic female reported being thrown against the ground and then against a wall when she was hanging out on the street with friends. A black youth suspected of dealing drugs when he was talking to a friend on the street was grabbed, thrown up against the car, and hit with billy clubs. (He admitted possessing but not dealing drugs.) Another youth was driving and was signaled to pull over. The officer smashed his car window and several officers grabbed, beat, and injured the youth (Borrero, 2001).

It is interesting to speculate about how changes in the nature of policing might affect attitudes toward the police. Recall that Chicago made a major effort to implement community policing. In response, in four of the five experimental districts, residents reported improved police responsiveness to neighborhood concerns, and African-American residents had improved perceptions about police misconduct (Skogan and Hartnett, 1997). In Boston, where Operation Ceasefire meant a tough, deterrent message and approach to violent gang members, interviews with community members indicated that they felt the deterrence strategy was effective but worried about the long-term effects. They were concerned that simply sending troubled youths to prison was not the complete answer and might just increase youths' hostility and hopelessness (Stoutland, 2001).

These variations in attitudes toward the police help to explain the paradox that police often hold negative or cynical views of citizens while citizen attitudes toward the police are actually rather positive. Part of the explanation for this apparent contradiction is that the police are much more likely to come in contact with citizens with less positive views—minority and younger citizens—than with older citizens who hold more positive views. A second explanation for the paradox is that the police often come into contact with citizens at inopportune times—in instances in which citizens have broken the law (even if only a traffic law), been victimized, or witnessed a crime. At such times, citizens are likely to be under stress. They may react with frustration at receiving a speeding ticket or at hearing an officer say that there is little hope of recovering their $400 video recorder that has just been stolen. Citizens may lash out at the available target (i.e., the police officer) much like a frustrated customer reacts to a customer service representative who is not responsible for the problem but has the unpleasant job of trying to rectify it. Repeated contacts with citizens in times of crisis can also lead the police to job burnout (Maslach and Jackson, 1979), cynicism (Niederhoffer, 1967), suspicion (Skolnick, 1966), and/or stress (Crank and Caldero, 1991; Kroes, Margolis, and Hurrell, 1974). In addition, dissatisfaction with a specific police contact leads to lower evaluations of police services in general (Huebner, Schafer, and Bynum, 2004).

One final observation on this matter concerns the fact that any victim of crime views his or her situation as unique while the police view the same situation as routine. The victim often is a first-time victim who is frightened, stunned, and excited about something that is entirely new to him or her. The officer is simply experiencing the third burglary report that night, the twentieth that week, or the one-thousandth in his or her career. Additionally, the officer's realistic judgment that little or nothing can be done to "solve" the crime leads him or her to rush through the encounter with the citizen in order to write up a report so that the victim can file an insurance claim. Based on television or movie stereotypes, the naive citizen may expect the officer to drop everything, spend as much time as possible on the victim's case, and solve it. Realizing that the officer has a very different definition of the situation, the citizen becomes upset and reacts accordingly—possibly accusing the officer of incompetence or laziness. Such negative encounters reinforce officer perceptions of citizens as being negative toward the police, even while the public opinion poll research shows the contrary.

Implications of the Attitudinal Research

Several conclusions can be drawn from this discussion of police attitudes toward citizens and citizen attitudes toward the police. First, both sides could benefit from clarification. The police might benefit from becoming aware that citizens generally are positive about the police. Citizens, on the other hand, need to know why police may be somewhat cynical toward them. Citizens should be aware that police officers have likely seen their problem before and have had contact with some victims who precipitated the crime or were otherwise tainted. More importantly, citizens must be realistic in their expectations of what the police can do. For example, the police often can do little or nothing to recover a stolen television or car. Second, police need to be careful in their dealings with citizens who hold less positive attitudes—namely, youths and minorities. Because these groups may be less favorable in their attitudes toward the police, the police need to target them for more positive treatment. Otherwise, these groups may interpret police indifference and cynicism as evidence of prejudicial attitudes and discriminatory behavior. Furthermore, police sensitivity to the attitudes of youthful and minority citizens can lead to improved police–community relations.

As noted, there has been recent emphasis on the police as problem solvers. Some police experts think that traditional policing can do little more than take reports for many problems. If policing were restructured, however, perhaps more could be done about many of the concerns that citizens have. If police spent less time running from call to call and more time exploring the causes and solutions of various problems, then the police could be more effective and have greater impact (see, e.g., Trojanowicz et al., 1998).

RECENT ISSUES IN POLICING CONCERNING JUVENILES

In addition to the major issue of community policing, several additional issues have arisen in the last few years concerning juveniles: interrogation tactics with juvenile suspects, racial profiling and disproportionate minority contact, curfew laws, intensive supervision, and policing underage drinking.

Interrogation Tactics with Juvenile Suspects

As Chapter 9 points out, the Supreme Court has not ordered police to follow any additional procedures when interrogating juveniles. In other words, the Court has held that a juvenile suspect can waive the privilege against self-incrimination and the right to consult with an attorney and go ahead and agree to be interrogated. Then a court will judge the voluntariness of any confession by looking at all the circumstances of the interrogation and confession.

A recent study by Barry Feld examined the transcripts of 66 police interrogations of juvenile suspects in Minneapolis, Minnesota. Eighty percent of the juveniles waived their *Miranda* rights and agreed to interrogation. On the positive side, police immediately stopped questioning those youths who invoked their rights. On the negative side, police questioned juvenile suspects in much the same manner as they questioned adults. The police often suggested that talking would be beneficial to the suspect, or they phrased the warnings as if they were just a bureaucratic formality instead of a serious constitutional issue with important consequences for the suspect (Feld, 2006). Feld also concludes that the behavior of 16- and 17-year-olds parallels the behavior of most adult suspects; the adult waiver rate is also about 80 percent. So he thinks that 16- and 17-year-olds are about as psychologically mature as adults and understand their rights to the same extent as adults.

An important concern is the danger of false confessions. More than one-third of proven false confessions come from suspects under 18 years of age. Feld thinks that 16- and 17-year-olds are similar to adults, but that younger suspects do need greater protection. He argues for recording all confessions as a safeguard (Feld, 2006).

An intriguing issue about police interrogation techniques is that although the police think they are very good at detecting deception in suspects, research indicates that they are not. Although interrogation experts claim 85 percent accuracy, research puts police accuracy at about 50 percent. What is particularly disturbing about juvenile suspects, moreover, is that juveniles often exhibit behaviors that the interrogation experts claim are deceptive, such as slouching and not making eye contact with the interrogator. Therefore, when a youth is just "being youthful," an interrogator will interpret that behavior as evidence that the youth is lying. Another problem is suggestibility. The desire to please or the tendency to trust authority figures, for example, can influence youths to confess falsely (Meyer and Reppucci, 2007).

In their study of more than 300 police investigators in Baltimore, Meyer and Reppucci (2007) found that police used the same interrogation techniques with children under age 14, youths ages 14 to 17, and adults (age 18 and older). Police believed that children and youths outside the context of interrogation do not understand some words used by adults but then stated that they thought that children, youths, and adults all understand their rights in the interrogation session and the purpose of interrogation. The researchers found that 83 percent of their sample used body language as an indicator of deception despite the problem noted above that youths are likely to slouch and avoid eye contact. Finally, the Baltimore police also reported using coercive and deceptive interrogation techniques with suspects, regardless of age, even though there is greater likelihood of getting inaccurate reports from youthful suspects (Meyer and Reppucci, 2007).

In summary, many juveniles waive their rights, and consent to interrogation. Despite age-related problems with interrogating youthful suspects, many police investigators use techniques that can lead to inaccurate statements and even false confessions from juvenile suspects.

Racial Profiling

One recent issue affecting attitudes toward the police is **racial profiling.** Racial profiling is defined "as the police use of race as the sole basis for initiating law enforcement activity (e.g., stopping, searching, and detaining a person)" (Meehan and Ponder, 2002:403). One form of alleged racial profiling was the practice of stopping African-American drivers for "driving while black" on the New Jersey Turnpike. Police were targeting black drivers for about two-thirds of all traffic stops based on claims that blacks were more likely to be carrying drugs. However, searches of white drivers were in fact producing more contraband than searches of black drivers (Roane, 2001). Similarly, a recent study of profiling in a medium-sized suburban police department found that profiling increased "as African Americans travel farther from 'black' communities and into whiter neighborhoods" (Meehan and Ponder, 2002).

Police need to be especially careful in their dealings with those citizens who hold less positive attitudes toward police. In many cities, young blacks have experienced negative encounters with police and expressed fears about their future.

Mark C. Ide

It should be noted that charges of racial profiling need thorough investigation. A scientific study of New Jersey State Trooper stops of motorists showed that the troopers were stopping black drivers "in approximate proportion to their representation among speeders" (Lange, Johnson, and Voas, 2005:216). Although this does not automatically rule out profiling, it shows that there is a need to have an accurate measure of the composition of violators and not just a measure of the composition of the population in the jurisdiction (Lange, Johnson, and Voas, 2005). Similarly, an observational study in Savannah, Georgia, showed that race affected whether police viewed blacks as suspicious, but such nonbehavioral suspicion did not influence the officer's decision to stop and question (Alpert, MacDonald, and Dunham, 2005).

A recent study in Dade County (Miami), Florida, used both observation and an analysis of 66,000 citizen contact cards that police were required to fill out after a traffic stop. The observation component showed no racial impact. Analysis of the contact cards, however, showed that "in predominantly white and racially mixed areas, black drivers were stopped disproportionately to their representation in the driving population, as estimated through a random sample of not-at-fault drivers in two vehicle crashes" (Alpert, Dunham, and Smith, 2007:48). So part of this study did not support an inference of racial profiling, but the other part did.

More generally, however, Alpert asserts that recent research has shown that blacks and Hispanics are "often overrepresented among stops when compared with the various benchmarks for those groups. Similarly, the research shows that once stopped, blacks and Hispanics are more likely than whites to be searched or arrested" (Alpert, 2007:673). For further discussion of the ethics of profiling, see Box 7.4.

A recent study of "Middleberg," a medium-sized city in illegal drug shipping routes, found that 30 percent of the searches observed by the

BOX 7.4

Racial Profiling: Do Only Outcomes Matter?

Persico and Todd argue that outcomes are the critical consideration in trying to determine if police are engaging in racial profiling. In an analysis of motorists stopped by the Maryland State Police, 63 percent of those stopped were African Americans, and 29 percent were whites. But the hit rates or outcomes, those found in possession of illegal drugs, were not statistically significantly different: 34 percent for African Americans and 32 percent for whites. Persico and Todd argue that this indicates that the Maryland State Police were not discriminating against blacks (Persico and Todd, 2008).

Engel (2008) notes that legal scholars emphasizing due process argue that procedural equity is an important consideration, as well as outcome equity. This approach would be concerned that such a disproportionate number of African Americans were stopped even though the outcomes were not significantly different.

What do you think? Are Persico and Todd correct that equal outcomes translate into a conclusion that the police are treating both racial groups fairly? Or are the legal scholars correct that process is a critical consideration? What do you think minority motorists in Maryland would think if they knew about the difference in stop rates versus equality in outcomes?

Sources: N. Persico and P.E. Todd (2008). "The Hit Rates Test for Racial Bias in Motor-Vehicle Searches." *Justice Quarterly* 25: 37-53; R.S. Engel (2008). "A Critique of the 'Outcome Test' in Racial Profiling Research." *Justice Quarterly* 25: 1-36.

research team were constitutionally suspect but that there was no significant effect of race on these improper searches (Gould and Mastrofski, 2004). Commenting on this study, Harcourt notes that 84 percent of the sample searches involved black suspects and that "it is hard to believe that the police could reach 84% searches of black suspects without some racial profiling" (Harcourt, 2004:369).

An important part of the controversy over profiling is that it can produce negative consequences. Profiling can lower deterrence by lowering trust in the police and willingness to report crime. "Further, hostility between minorities and the police creates an unwillingness to testify at trials, and, when serving on juries, an unwillingness to convict defendants" (Leitzel, 2001).

What is the solution? Leitzel suggests that the police ask themselves the following when considering stopping or searching a minority member: "Would I stop or search this person if he or she were white?" If the answer is no, then the minority individual should not be stopped or searched either, even if, for instance, the neighborhood is predominantly white and blacks stopped in the area have been associated with crime in the past (Leitzel, 2001). A problem with this is that racial stereotyping can be unconscious; the officer may not be aware that he or she is employing a racial stereotype (Graham and Lowery, 2004).

One suggested solution is for the police to record information on stops. Some think that such forced record keeping will decrease profiling. A problem with this suggestion is that police can avoid recording stops and still continue to profile (Meehan and Ponder, 2002).

Based on his assessment of the extent of profiling and the benefits and costs of the practice, Alpert says that now is the time to stop profiling: "Clearly, racial profiling is neither an efficient nor an effective policing tactic, and it can cause a serious collapse in the public's trust and confidence in the police" (Alpert, 2007:676).

Racial profiling raises the broader question of the effect of race on police decisions to arrest and juvenile court decisions to detain, petition, and sentence. This issue is called **disproportionate minority contact** (see Chapter 8 for more on disproportionate minority contact in juvenile court decisions). While black youths ages 10 to 17 made up 16 percent of the U.S. population in 2002, they made up 29 percent of youths referred to juvenile court and 36 percent of those detained (Kempf-Leonard, 2007). This disproportionate contact raises the question of possible unfair police action.

A recent study addressed this question. Using data from the National Incident-Based Reporting System (NIBRS), Pope and Snyder found that in the 17 jurisdictions analyzed there was "no evidence to support the hypothesis that police are more likely to arrest nonwhite juvenile offenders than white juvenile offenders, once other incident attributes are taken into consideration" (Pope and Snyder, 2003:6). Overall, victims identified 69.2 percent of offenders to be white, and 72.7 percent of juvenile offenders arrested were white. The only indication of bias was indirect: "Nonwhite juveniles...are more likely to be arrested when the victim is white than when the victim is nonwhite" (Pope and Snyder, 2003:6).

In a report on disproportionate minority contact in Pittsburgh, Rochester, and Seattle, the authors found evidence of such contact at all three sites. They did not find evidence that differences in offending behavior explained the disproportionate contact. In other words, it is not the case that minorities clearly commit more delinquency and that this explains why police arrest more minorities. Risk factors such as type of neighborhood, family economic status, and youth education problems did substantially reduce the disproportionate minority contact. These findings do not necessarily prove police bias but are consistent with bias if bias does in fact exist (Huizinga et al., 2007).

In a recent analysis of disproportionate minority contact in general, Bishop (2005) reached the opposite conclusion about the police. She noted some of the more subtle ways that race can enter into the policing of juveniles. First, police views of neighborhoods as dangerous or having suspicious persons are related to considerations of race and class. Related to this are high crime rates in urban underclass neighborhoods. A result is that police devote more surveillance to such neighborhoods, which leads to more encounters with juveniles and more arrests. Second, race can have an indirect effect via demeanor in police encounters with juveniles. For example, police can interpret a hostile or less cooperative demeanor as a sign of criminal propensity. Complainant preference can also have an effect. Complainants more often press for arrest of African-American suspects. Bishop thus concludes:

> In sum, the literature indicates that, for a number of reasons, minority youths are more likely than whites to be arrested, referred to court, and detained by police....The overrepresentation of minorities in police arrest data, especially for violent offenses, reinforces racist expectancies (Bishop, 2005:45).

The clear lesson is that race is a factor that needs close attention. Police need to be aware how race can affect decisions to stop and decisions to arrest. They also need to be clear that factors such as a youth's neighborhood and demeanor can bring in race as an indirect influence on those critical decisions. For additional information on the effect of race on arrest decisions, see Box 7.5.

Juvenile Curfew Laws

Juvenile curfew laws have been enacted in numerous cities across the country in an effort to reduce victimization of and by juveniles. The curfew law in Charlotte, North Carolina, included such objectives and also

BOX 7.5

Does the Officer's Race Matter?

In an observational study of Cincinnati, Ohio, police officers, Brown and Frank found that white officers are more likely in general to arrest suspects than black officers. The suspect's race had no effect on white officers' decisions to arrest, but it did have an impact on black officers' decisions. With situational circumstances being equal, the probability that a white officer would arrest a black suspect was 93 percent; the probability that a black officer would arrest a black suspect was 98 percent.

Source: R.A. Brown and J. Frank (2006). "Race and Officer Decision Making: Examining Differences in Arrest Outcomes between Black and White Officers." *Justice Quarterly* 23: 96-126.

strove to "reinforce and promote the role of parents in raising and guiding children" (City of Charlotte Code, cited in Hirschel, Dean, and Dumond, 2001). To accomplish these goals, children under 16 years of age were prohibited from being on the streets from 11:00 P.M. to 6:00 A.M. during the week and from midnight to 6:00 A.M. on Friday and Saturday nights. Other cities with curfews may have different age or time stipulations. Vernon, Connecticut, for example, enacted a curfew for juveniles under 18 and prohibited them being on the streets from 11:00 P.M. to 6:00 A.M. every night of the week (Males, 2000). In one California city, the curfew applied from 11:00 P.M. to 5:00 A.M. on week nights and from 1:00 A.M. to 5:00 A.M. on weekends. Exceptions involved standing in front of their own homes, returning home within one hour of attending certain activities, working, or being in the company of a parent (Stuphen and Ford, 2001).

Research on the effectiveness of curfews indicates that curfew laws do not reduce crime or victimization. For example, after the implementation of the curfew law in Vernon, Connecticut, Part I crimes did decrease, but the decrease "was similar to or less than the crime declines experienced in similar cities and the state as a whole" (Males, 2000:259). A time-series analysis of victimizations in New Orleans showed that the law was "ineffective for reducing victimizations, victimizations of juveniles, and juvenile arrests" (Reynolds, Seydlitz, and Jenkins, 2000:219). In addition, the laws do not appear to reduce subsequent offending by juveniles who are cited for curfew violations. In Charlotte, for example, 40 percent of the youths cited for curfew violations were arrested for an offense following their first curfew violation (Hirschel, Dean, and Dumond, 2001). A national evaluation of 52 counties showed that curfew laws only affected significant decreases in three of 12 crimes (burglaries, larcenies, and simple assaults). The authors concluded that their research "provides, at best extremely weak support for the hypothesis that curfews reduce juvenile crime rates" and that the "results do not encourage the idea that curfews help prevent juvenile crime" (McDowall, Loftin, and Wiersema, 2000:88).

In a review of studies of teen curfews, Adams (2003) identified 10 empirical studies of juvenile curfews. Adams concluded that the weight of the evidence from these 10 studies overall "fails to support the argument that curfews reduce crime and victimization" (p. 155). Adams also questions the fairness of curfew law enforcement, arguing that curfew enforcement relies heavily on officer discretion. Adams worries that curfew enforcement will "fall most heavily on low-income and minority areas" (Adams, 2007:666).

Despite research failing to demonstrate effectiveness, some communities are emphasizing curfew enforcement. One such city is Philadelphia, but the city is trying to reduce the amount of time that officers spend on curfew violators after the arrest by utilizing curfew centers where the police can drop off violators (Adams, 2007).

One reason for the ineffectiveness of curfews is that the hours covered by the laws may not be times evidencing high victimization. In Vernon, Connecticut, for example, it was found that juvenile crime was much more likely to occur in the afternoon (Males, 2000). Nationally, it appears that violent offenses and gang crimes peak at approximately 3:00 P.M. (Sickmund, Snyder, and Poe-Yamagata, 1997). One response to this issue is to have daytime curfews for those youths who are not under the jurisdiction of truancy laws. A recent survey found that 10 percent of the responding jurisdictions had daytime curfews. In fact, some were so restrictive that even a youngster cutting class and not being in the place he was supposed to be in was technically in violation of that city's daytime curfew law (Bannister, Carter, and Schafer, 2001).

Another problem is that curfew enforcement may only ensnare youths who are "already embedded in a criminal lifestyle at an early age" (Hirschel, Dean, and Dumond, 2001:210). As suggested by research in New Orleans, another problem is that juveniles do not necessarily comply with curfew laws. In New Orleans during the first year of the law, more than 3,500 youths were taken into custody just for curfew violations (Reynolds, Seydlitz, and Jenkins, 2000). Most importantly, curfew laws do nothing to improve juveniles' relationships with peers, schools, and family, all of which are important correlates of delinquency. As shown in earlier chapters, parental supervision and attachment to parents are critical factors in preventing delinquency. Curfew laws do nothing to strengthen such supervision or bonding.

One suggestion to salvage some good out of the curfew laws is to use them to identify youths with problems, particularly with regard to problems relating to inadequate parental supervision. This could be done by having a youth service worker screen youths who appear to be experiencing such lack of supervision and refer the youths to appropriate community services (Hirschel, Dean, and Dumond, 2001).

It is interesting that police think curfew laws are effective even though they do not have concrete evidence that the curfews are effective in reducing crime (Bannister, Carter, and Schafer, 2001). Perhaps police enthusiasm for curfews would decrease if they became more familiar with the literature showing that curfews are not effective.

Part of the reality of curfew laws is the panacea phenomenon. As will be noted in Chapter 11 in the discussion of Scared Straight programs, we are often guilty of expecting quick and inexpensive fixes for complicated problems such as delinquency. Unrealistically, we hope that a simple measure such as a curfew law will cure the delinquency problem in our local community. So we pass curfew laws and expect police enforcement of such laws to magically wipe out juvenile crime.

Another reason for the popularity of curfew laws is the "broken windows" theory. The evidence that curfew laws do not decrease crime is further evidence that combating disorder does not always reduce crime (Harcourt, 2001). For a note on curfews and high school proms, see Box 7.6.

Assistance with Intensive Supervision of Probationers

Anchorage, Alaska, tried using police officers to enhance probation officer supervision of juvenile offenders. Anchorage used police officers to turn regular supervision into intensive supervision. This means that the juvenile probationers received additional contacts, contacts with their probation officers, and contacts with police officers. Like many previous intensive supervision programs, there was no reduction in criminal recidivism; there was no significant difference in the percentage of offenders under intensive supervision who committed any new offense or the percentage of offenders under regular supervision who committed any new offense. However, about 30 percent of the intensive supervision offenders had a probation violation, compared to 17 percent of the regular offenders. Thus, increased supervision translates into increased monitoring and detection of technical violations.

It is interesting that Anchorage tried an intensive supervision effort using police when so much prior research on intensive supervision has not been promising. What is promising is a program such as Operation Eiger in Baton Rouge, Louisiana. Here police also help probation officers conduct unscheduled evening visits six times per month, but the program involves addressing needs as well as enforcing probation conditions. Services are provided to deal with substance abuse, anger

BOX 7.6

Curfews and Proms

In 2001 the Georgia legislature enacted a year-round curfew forbidding anyone under 18 from driving after midnight. So, like Cinderella, prom-goers need to be off the road by the stroke of midnight. Breaking this curfew law can mean a penalty of up to one year in jail or a fine of up to $1,000.

Legislators created this law in response to some highly publicized auto deaths of teenagers in the Atlanta area. Unlike the curfew laws discussed in this chapter, this is a safety curfew more than a crime prevention curfew.

In response, schools are planning to end their proms some time before midnight so that students can get home by 12:00. One school will end its prom at 11:30 P.M. to allow for plenty of time to beat the curfew. Police say that they are not making any exceptions for prom night.

What do you think? Should there be an exception for prom night?.

In Hartford, Connecticut, police decided to step up their enforcement of the city's curfew law after a shooting in which one man died and six young people under 18 were wounded. The curfew prohibited anyone under 18 from being on the streets after 9:00 P.M.

Two points are interesting. First, the police did not have the shooter in custody, and there was no indication of his or her age. Second, this shooting took place after an annual parade and occurred at about 6:30 P.M.

It appears that the Hartford police either are not aware of the research on the ineffectiveness of curfews or they choose to ignore that research. What might influence a police chief to enforce a law that has little empirical support? Might other factors be at work?

Source: M. Scott (2002). "Georgia Prom-goers to Face Curfew Thanks to Recent Legislation." *Johnson City Press* (May 1, 2002):6; Associated Press (2008). "Hartford Police to Beef Up Teen Curfew after Shooting." *Johnson City Press*, August 12, 2008:6A.

management, academic difficulties, and employment needs (Lizotte and Sheppard, 2001). Hopefully, this combination of intensive supervision and treatment will have greater success than the program in Alaska using intensive supervision alone.

San Bernardino, California, is another example of a police-probation partnership. There a police officer and a probation officer together make a home visit to all new juvenile probationers. They explain the rules of probation and also search the probationer's residence for weapons and drugs. The program has had some effect in reducing serious crimes in the city, but one concern is **mission distortion** for probation. In other words, probation officers may no longer see themselves as service providers or social workers but may instead over-identify with a law enforcement role (Worrall and Gaines, 2006).

Policing Underage Drinking

The National Minimum Drinking Age Act standardized the legal drinking age at 21 in 1984. Police bear responsibility to enforce this act.

Studies show that youths under age 21 are able to purchase alcohol despite the law. Studies in the 1990s using either actual underage buyers or decoy buyers (individuals over 21 who looked younger than 21) showed that purchase rates ranged from 45 percent to 88 percent. A recent study in a large Midwestern area had an overall sales rate to pseudo-underage buyers of 26 percent (Britt et al., 2006). The authors concluded that there has been progress in reducing such sales over the last decade, and believed that improved training could result in even lower sales.

Police tend to use compliance checks or "Cops in Shops" programs to combat such underage alcohol purchases. Compliance checks are similar to the research just noted: police use underage decoys to try to purchase liquor. Cops in Shops programs put undercover officers in establishments to detect and cite youths who try to purchase alcohol illegally. Police agencies are twice as likely to use compliance checks as Cops in Shops programs (Montgomery, Foley, and Wolfson, 2006). (For further discussion of the issue of the Legal Drinking Age, see Chapter 9.)

POLICE EFFECTIVENESS

In examining **police effectiveness,** it is clear that the police are making a variety of efforts to combat juvenile crime. As noted earlier, police are staffing RAPP houses in Cleveland, facilitating restorative justice conferences in Indianapolis, going to community meetings in Chicago, enforcing curfews all over the country, and participating in demonstration projects such as Operation Ceasefire in Boston.

Overall, how effective are the police in their new efforts against crime and delinquency? For many of these programs, we have already noted specific outcome results. Here a summary is in order.

First, some things simply do not work. Juvenile curfew laws, for example, have been tried in numerous cities. Most evaluations indicate that they are not very effective in the fight against juvenile crime.

Second, a very possible reason that some interventions do not work is that they are simplistic and contrary to what we know. Both the juvenile curfew laws and the Anchorage intensive supervision program, for example, stem from a Scared Straight panacea phenomenon that looks for simple answers: pass a law to keep juveniles off the street or ask a police officer to stop in at a juvenile's house. Human behavior is more complicated than this.

Third, it is critical to avoid unrealistic expectations. In their study of community policing in Chicago, for example, Skogan and Hartnett (1997) found that some neighborhood conditions improved. Every neighborhood had at least one improvement. Victimization declined in two areas, street crime dropped in two others, drug and gang problems declined in two, and graffiti declined in another. Overall, compared to comparison areas, there were positive changes in 27 of the 51 outcomes that the evaluation measured, an overall success rate of 53 percent (Skogan and Hartnett, 1997:244). Skogan and Hartnett emphasize that communities should have realistic expectations from community policing. A success rate of 50 percent appears to be realistic. Expectations of 95 percent or even 75 percent success rates are fanciful.

Fourth, the police are only part of the picture. Eck and Maguire (2000), for example, contend that the decrease in crime in the last 10 years is the result of communities and the nation mobilizing to fight crime. Such mobilization involves police initiatives such as community policing, increased use of prison, demographic trends (the aging of the population and the decrease in the proportion of young males), and the decline of retail drug markets. A realistic perspective on the police impact on crime can be summarized as follows:

> There is one thing that is a myth: The police have a substantial, broad, and independent impact on the nation's crime rate. Rather than think of the police as an isolated institution that has a distinctive impact on crime, perhaps we should think of the police as part of a network of institutions, some of them formal (e.g., courts and schools) and some of them informal (e.g., families and churches), that respond to crime. . . .
>
> When considered in isolation, the effectiveness of any one element of this diverse array of people and organizations may be slight. But collectively, the response might be more dramatic (Eck and Maguire, 2000:247-248).

POLICE USE OF EXCESSIVE FORCE (BRUTALITY)

Police use of excessive force is a sensitive topic and thus it is difficult to gain accurate information about its extent. Like any profession, police will not just open up and reveal professional secrets. They will not readily disclose how frequently and under what circumstances they may use excessive force. So researchers often survey citizens to derive estimates of police use of force.

Based on an observational study of police-citizen encounters about 25 years ago, Albert Reiss reported that teens were the most likely targets of the least damaging type of police brutality, namely, abusive language and commands to "move on." Such commands were particularly frequent in the summer when youths living in the ghetto were likely to spend more time on the streets. Police told both black youths and white youths to leave or go home (Reiss, 1980). More recent research shows that such problems continue, especially for African-American youths. A 1991 survey of more than 300 Cincinnati youths revealed that almost one-half (46.6%) of the black youths reported having been personally hassled by police, compared to only about 10 percent of white youths. In addition, approximately two-thirds of the blacks said that they knew someone who had been hassled (Browning et al., 1994).

As noted previously in the section on attitudes, a study in Hartford, Connecticut, found that the 132 youths interviewed reported approximately 400 negative experiences (Borrero, 2001). Thirty-nine percent involved physical encounters (force, hitting, injury), 24 percent involved verbal harassment, and 34 percent were categorized as "other."

Geller and Toch (1996) argue that the process of stereotyping can be an important factor leading to the use of force against juveniles. A police officer can stereotype a youth as a "typical gang member," and a youth can stereotype a police officer as a "white cop." This stereotyping very easily leads to a process of arrest, resistance or actions interpreted as resistance, and excessive force or actions so interpreted so that a series of self-fulfilling prophecies are set in motion. The problem is to stop the start of such self-fulfilling prophecies.

A hopeful note is that one review concluded that "physical force is infrequently used by the police and that improper force is used even less" (Worden, 1996:46). One problem with this research conclusion is that it may not be in sync with perceptions on the street, especially perceptions in some of the trouble spots of inner-city areas of cities such as New York and Los Angeles. In such locations, contrary perceptions help to trigger the stereotyping process just noted and lead to tragic results.

A national survey on this topic, the Police Public Contact Survey, showed that in 1999 an estimated 43.8 million Americans, 16 or older, had at least one face-to-face contact with a police officer (Langan et al., 2001). More than 400,000 persons (less than 1% of those reporting contact) reported that the police used force or threatened the use of force against them. Most of this was pushing or grabbing. Most of those who experienced force (76%) said the force was excessive. Most persons (85%) involved in force incidents said the officer was white. More than one-half of those who experienced police force said that they had argued with, disobeyed, or resisted the police or used alcohol or other drugs. It should be noted that respondents ages 16 through 19 reported the most frequent experience of force or threat of force by police. About 3 percent of 16-19-year-olds reported force or threat of force, compared to 1.4 percent of 20-29-year-old respondents and less than 1 percent of all age categories 30 or older (Langan et al., 2001). (For a discussion of possible use of force in schools, see Box 7.7.)

BOX 7.7

Police Use of Tasers in Schools

An estimated 1,700 police officers assigned to U.S. schools carry tasers (stun guns) to use against unruly students. Reports indicate that about 24 students in central Florida were shocked, and at least four students have been shocked in the Charlotte, North Carolina, area. One proposal is to ban the use of such stun guns in elementary schools but allow them, but only as a last resort, in middle schools and high schools.

What do you think? Is there a need for such devices in schools? Are they also necessary in elementary schools?

Source: D. Leinwand (2005). "Schools Restrict Use of Tasers." *USA Today* (June 3, 2005):1A.

An observational study of subjects in Indianapolis and St. Petersburg showed that in many instances police could have used more force on resistant suspects but did not do so. On the other hand, in encounters in which the suspect did not resist, officers engaged in behavior that could be perceived as an attempt to increase the level of police response, such as resorting to a threat or low-level physical force (Terrill, 2005).

A study of police use of force in Arizona found that race did not affect use of force overall but was a significant factor in treatment of males in custody. Force was significantly more likely against black and Hispanic males who were not in custody (Schuck, 2003). Race was not a factor, however, in a study of cases of use of force investigated by an internal affairs unit in California. The typical officer investigated was a young male officer with less than a decade of experience who had been investigated before (McElvain and Kposowa, 2004).

Thus, we have conflicting estimates of force and other negative behaviors by police against youths. The national survey indicates about 3 percent of youths experience police force in a typical year. Surveys of youths in two separate cities, Cincinnati and Hartford, report as many as almost 50 percent of certain groups of youths (e.g., blacks) reporting force.

Worden thinks the use of improper force is infrequent, a conclusion supported by the national survey. The hopeful conclusion is that Worden and the national survey are correct. A more pessimistic conclusion is that force is more frequent, especially against minority youths, and that efforts are required to reduce any use of force as much as possible.

A related study sheds some additional light on the issue of police transgressions. Gould and Mastrofski (2004) conducted observation of police behavior in "Middleberg," a medium-sized city in the middle of illicit drug shipment routes. They found that 30 percent of the observed searches (115 over three months) conducted by police were illegal or unconstitutional. This would extrapolate to about 12,000-14,000 unconstitutional searches per year in Middleberg. Thus, a major finding of the research in Middleberg was that "those sworn to uphold the law regularly and repeatedly transgressed constitutional boundaries" (Gould and Mastrofski, 2004:331). One police expert concludes: "The 'dirty secret' of contemporary American criminal justice is that prosecutors and judges know full well the corners that police cut and often turn a blind eye. The success of the entire system depends on convicting the guilty as quickly as possible, even if that means taking liberties with strict due process" (Bayley, 2002:137-138).

Thus, there is police misconduct, ranging from improper searches to improper use of force, and progressing all the way up to the improper use of deadly force. Police administrators must forever be vigilant to reduce such misconduct as much as possible.

Deadly Force

In a review of the literature on **deadly force**, William Geller (1983) describes the typical victim of police shooting as between 17 and 30 years of age. This means that not many juveniles—only the 17-year-olds—are likely to be shot by police officers. All police shootings, however, are not typical; some do involve younger victims. In fact, a test case on the use of deadly force involved the shooting of a 15-year-old youth in Memphis, Tennessee. A Mem-

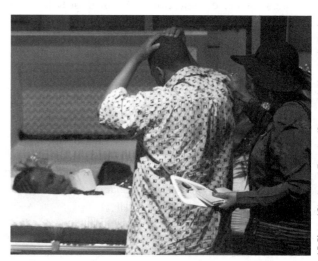

Mourners view the casket of Timothy Thomas during funeral services at the New Prospect Baptist Church in Cincinnati, Ohio. The shooting of the fleeing Thomas, who was wanted on 14 warrants for misdemeanors and traffic violations, led to three days of rioting in the city.

AP Photo/Cincinnati Enquirer/Steven M. Herppich, Pool

phis police officer shot and killed Edward Garner, a 15-year-old eighth-grade student, under that state's common law "fleeing felon" rule, which authorized police to shoot any fleeing felon—even nondangerous ones.

Garner had been prowling inside an empty house and refused to halt in the yard when the police officer warned him to stop. Consequently, the officer shot the youth as he tried to climb a fence to escape. After this incident, the United States Supreme Court ruled that police may not institute a policy to shoot any and all fleeing suspects; rather, they may shoot only those escaping felons who pose a threat to the officer or to others. Box 7.8 presents excerpts from the decision.

This critical case (*Tennessee v. Garner et al.*) ordered police to be much more selective in using deadly force. Research has shown that as a result of the case there has been a decrease both in shooting overall and in the appearance of discrimination in deadly force (Sparger and Giacopassi, 1992). What has happened is that police departments have been forced to devise guidelines for the use of deadly force, and the enforcement of those guidelines has been successful in decreasing police shoot-

BOX 7.8

The U.S. Supreme Court on Deadly Force

In *Tennessee v. Garner et al.*, the U.S. Supreme Court set down guidelines for the constitutional use of deadly force by police officers. Here are some excerpts from the majority opinion by Justice White:

> The use of deadly force to prevent the escape of all felony suspects, whatever the circumstances, is constitutionally unreasonable. It is not better that all felony suspects die than that they escape. Where the suspect poses no immediate threat to the officer and no threat to others, the harm resulting from failing to apprehend him does not justify the use of deadly force to do so. It is no doubt unfortunate when a suspect who is in sight escapes, but the fact that the police arrive a little late or are a little slower afoot does not always justify killing the suspect. A police officer may not seize an unarmed, nondangerous suspect by shooting him dead. . . .
>
> . . . Where the officer has probable cause to believe that the suspect poses a threat of serious physical harm, either to the officer or to others, it is not constitutionally unreasonable to prevent escape by using deadly force. Thus, if the suspect threatens the officer with a weapon or there is probable cause to believe that he has committed a crime involving the infliction or threatened infliction of serious physical harm, deadly force may be used if necessary to prevent escape, and if, where feasible, some warning has been given (*Tennessee v. Garner et al.*, 1985).

ings (Walker and Katz, 2005). However, the problem is not completely gone. In Washington, DC, in 2007, for example, an off-duty police officer shot a 14-year-old who he claimed shot at him first. Although an investigation cleared the officer, the family has filed a sizable lawsuit against the officer (Klein and Leonnig, 2007). More generally, one conclusion about the frequency of deadly force is that it is highly variable; studies that include several departments show considerable differences from one department to another (Skogan, 2004).

A promising area for intervention is hiring practices. Since a recent study (McElvain and Kposowa, 2008) found that educated police officers are less likely to use deadly force, hiring more highly educated officers may be one way for departments to reduce such use of force in the future.

SUMMARY

It is an intriguing time for policing. Both police themselves and outsiders are debating the meaning of policing. Some, like former New York City police commissioner William Bratton, argue that police should take a tough approach (zero tolerance) and arrest even "squeegee men" who harass motorists by foisting unwanted window washing on them. In Boston, this tough approach, called "pulling levers," takes the form of arresting suspected violent gang members for disorder offenses, criminal acts, and outstanding warrants. Other developments in policing, however, take a completely different approach. In Indianapolis, for example, police are coordinating restorative justice conferences in which youths, victims, and supporters on both sides sit down and try to repair the harm done by victimizations. Here offenders learn how they harmed their victims and what they can do to repair that harm.

In other places, such as Chicago, police are attending neighborhood meetings and trying to learn what the community considers to be problems and how those problems should be solved. Problems vary from crack houses operating in residential neighborhoods to gangs harassing youths at bus stops after school.

Whatever specific approaches police are taking, many are also following the lead of CompStat in attempting to specify their mission and objectives more explicitly and trying to measure how closely they are actually achieving their goals. Accountability is a current emphasis in both business and government.

Many cities continue to use juvenile curfew laws in an attempt to reduce juvenile crime. The goal is to reduce both offending and victimization. Apparently these curfew laws and their enforcement continue despite a lack of supporting research evidence.

Perhaps the answer is to combine both approaches. Perhaps violent gang members need the tough (pulling levers) approach while first offenders charged with certain offenses can benefit from a restorative justice conferencing approach. What is clear, however, is that policing is changing and will continue to change. Many police officers undoubtedly continue to drive patrol cars and respond to 911 calls. In many communities, however, more innovative efforts are underway. Hopefully, such innovation will continue to change our ideas and expectations of what the police can and should do to prevent and control delinquency, disorder, and crime.

An important point to remember in any consideration of the police is that policing is only part of the effort to prevent, reduce, or control crime. When crime increases, much of society reacts, and many institutions and actors try to mobilize against crime. It is erroneous to think that the police alone can reduce crime. So instead of focusing only on the police, we should think of them as part of an interrelated network of responders.

> When violent crime grows into a serious social concern, it is not just the police that focus more attention on the problem. Schools, community groups, businesses, health officials, and many other organizations and individuals also respond to crime . . . In summary, as the police mobilize to address crime more effectively, so do many other institutions (Eck and Maguire, 2000:249-250).

So we will repeat our citation of Eck and Maguire at the end of the section on police effectiveness: it is a myth that the "police have a substantial, broad, and independent impact on the nation's crime rate" (Eck and Maguire, 2000:249), but a realistic review of the research shows evidence "for focused policing strategies contributing to the drop in violent crime" (p. 245). It is also important to note that "[s]ome of the policing strategies that have received the most attention (for example, CompStat and zero-tolerance policing in New York City) are the least plausible candidates for contributing to the reduction in violent crime" (Eck and Maguire, 2000:245).

We need to be realistic in our expectations of the police. Surely the police play a role in combating delinquency, but to expect the police to be the only factor—or even the most important factor—is unrealistic. Many factors contribute to delinquency and crime. All the institutions of society must play a part in addressing the problem.

DISCUSSION QUESTIONS

1. Community policing is based on the assumption that the job of the police is to solve the problems that lead to crime. Do you agree or disagree with this assumption? To what extent can society hold the police responsible for the problems that cause crime?

2. Police are trying new types of policing such as community or problem-solving policing, "broken windows" policing, and CompStat. Which approach do you favor? Discuss. Note any possible problems with the various approaches.

3. What do we know about police attitudes toward citizens? About citizen attitudes toward the police? What can be done to improve attitudes on both sides?

4. What do curfew laws seek to accomplish? Are they effective?

5. What do we know about police use of force with juveniles? What can be done to minimize any improper use of force by police?

6. Policing is changing. Would you want to be a police officer in light of all the change that is taking place in policing?

Chapter 8

THE JUVENILE COURT PROCESS

Important Terms

adjudication

blended sentencing

concerned adult role

day-evening centers

detention decision

disposition

drug courts

home detention

informal adjustment

intake decision

legislative waiver

"once an adult, always
  an adult" provisions

petition

plea bargaining

prosecutorial waiver

reverse waiver

secure/nonsecure detention

statutory exclusion

teen courts

token economy programs

transfer (waiver)

zealous advocate role

What You Need to Know

- In 2005, juvenile courts processed almost 1.7 million delinquency cases and an estimated 150,000 petitioned status offense cases. In addition, approximately 6,900 cases were transferred (waived) to adult court.

- The detention decision concerns whether to keep a juvenile in custody or to allow the youth to go home with his or her parents while awaiting further court action. Two options are secure detention and nonsecure detention.

- When an intake officer does not file a petition against a youth but tries to resolve the matter, that is called informal adjustment.

- Two avenues for youths not petitioned to court are teen court and drug court.

- The prosecutor's role in juvenile court may include approving petitions, deciding to prosecute some juveniles in adult courts, and prosecuting juveniles in juvenile court.

- There are several means for youths to be sent to adult court. The most traditional is transfer or waiver, in which the juvenile court judge makes the decision after a hearing.

- Statutory exclusion means that the state legislature rules that certain offenses automatically go to adult court.

- Prosecutorial waiver gives juvenile and adult court concurrent jurisdiction over certain cases. The prosecutor decides which court to use.

- Research on transfer indicates higher recidivism for youths who were transferred to adult criminal court.

- Adjudication and disposition in juvenile courts are the equivalent of conviction and sentencing in adult courts.

- There are several problems concerning attorney representation of juveniles: many youths waive their right to counsel, many attorneys have high caseloads and are poorly paid, and many defense attorneys are unsure whether they should follow the zealous advocate model of defense with juveniles.

- The recent trend in juvenile court appears to be one of increasing punitiveness, although some see signs of a return to an emphasis on rehabilitation.

- A major concern in juvenile court, especially the disposition stage, is the extent of the impact of race on decisions.

INTRODUCTION

Once a police officer takes a youth into custody, it is likely that the police will refer that youth to juvenile court. In both 2006 and 2007, about seven out of 10 youths taken into custody were referred to juvenile court, and a little under 10 percent of juveniles taken into custody were sent directly to adult criminal court. The other arrests were either handled within the police department and released (approximately 20%) or referred to a social welfare agency or another police agency (about 2%) (Federal Bureau of Investigation, n.d.).

When police refer a youth to juvenile court, the court personnel must then make one or more critical decisions: whether to detain (jail) the youth, whether to actually file a petition (charges) against the youth, whether to find (adjudicate) the youth a delinquent, and how to dispose of the petition. These decisions correspond to the adult court decisions of bail versus jail, formal charge versus dismissal, determination of guilt by plea or by trial, and sentencing. An additional decision is the decision to prosecute the youth as an adult in criminal court or retain jurisdiction in juvenile court. Several juvenile court actors—probation officers, defense attorneys, prosecutors, and judges—are involved in these important decisions. While the judge is often the primary decisionmaker, other court personnel play important roles in deciding the fate of juvenile suspects.

This chapter will examine the critical decision points in the juvenile court process: detention, intake, file, transfer (waiver), adjudication, and disposition. We will look at the roles the various court personnel play and should play in the court process. We will describe what happens when a juvenile suspect goes through the juvenile court process and will compare the ideal with the reality. Finally, we will examine some of the controversial issues facing juvenile court today, such as the question of the impact of race on decisionmaking and whether juveniles should have the right to a jury trial.

In 2005 (the latest year for which complete figures were available), juvenile courts processed almost 1.7 million delinquency cases (see Figure 8.1). More than half (56%) of the delinquency cases were petitioned, and approximately 6,900 cases were transferred to adult court via judicial waiver. More than 600,000 youths (623,900) were adjudicated delinquent in juvenile court. Juvenile courts also processed an estimated 150,600 petitioned status offense cases. About 60 percent of these were adjudicated a status offender (see Figure 8.2) (Puzzanchera and Sickmund, 2008). Finally, several thousand youths were processed in adult court as a result of direct file by prosecutors or by statutory exclusion (see below for additional details).

As the figures show, about two-thirds of the adjudicated delinquency cases and more than half of the adjudicated status offense cases were placed on probation. Some nonadjudicated cases also were placed on probation. Significant proportions of adjudicated delinquency and status offense cases (22% and 12%, respectively) were ordered into residential placement (Puzzanchera and Sickmund, 2008).

FIGURE 8.1 Juvenile Court Processing of Delinquency Cases, 2005

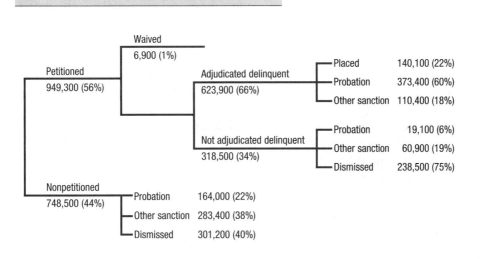

1,697,900 estimated delinquency cases

Waived
6,900 (1%)

Petitioned
949,300 (56%)

Adjudicated delinquent
623,900 (66%)

Placed   140,100 (22%)
Probation   373,400 (60%)
Other sanction   110,400 (18%)

Not adjudicated delinquent
318,500 (34%)

Probation   19,100 (6%)
Other sanction   60,900 (19%)
Dismissed   238,500 (75%)

Nonpetitioned
748,500 (44%)

Probation   164,000 (22%)
Other sanction   283,400 (38%)
Dismissed   301,200 (40%)

Notes: Cases are categorized by their most severe or restrictive sanction. Detail may not add to totals because of rounding. Annual case processing flow diagrams for 1985 through 2005 are available online at http://ojjdp.ncjrs.org/ojstatbb/court/faqs.asp

Source: C. Puzzanchera and M. Sickmund (2008). *Juvenile Court Statistics 2005*. Pittsburgh: National Center for Juvenile Justice. Reprinted with permission.

FIGURE 8.2 Juvenile Court Processing of Petitioned Status Offense Cases, 2005

Total status

Adjudicated a status offender
89,900 (59%)

Placed   10,700 (12%)
Probation   46,300 (52%)
Other sanction   31,900 (36%)

150,600 estimated
petitioned status offense cases

Not adjudicated a status offender
61,700 (41%)

Probation   1,800 (3%)
Other sanction   9,000 (15%)
Dismissed   50,900 (82%)

Notes: Cases are categorized by their most severe or restrictive sanction. Detail may not add to totals because of rounding.

Source: C. Puzzanchera and M. Sickmund (2008). *Juvenile Court Statistics 2005*. Pittsburgh: National Center for Juvenile Justice. Reprinted with permission.

DETENTION

The first decision that juvenile court personnel must make is the **detention decision**. It must be decided whether to keep a juvenile in custody or to allow the youth to go home with his or her parents while awaiting further court action. The detention decision is the juvenile court counterpart of the bail decision in adult court. It is very important because it concerns the freedom of the child and, therefore, resembles the disposition decision. In fact, children sent to detention may stay there for an extensive period of time—perhaps even for a longer time than children sent to state training schools (i.e., youth prisons for juveniles determined to be delinquent). In 2005, approximately 354,000 delinquency cases involved detention. This number represents approximately 20 percent of delinquency cases, about the same proportion detained in 1985. The offense profile of detained delinquency offense cases was 31 percent person offense cases, 27 percent property cases, 10 percent drug cases, and 32 percent public order cases (Puzzanchera and Sickmund, 2008). It should be noted that detention can also be used in some states as a disposition for a brief period of incarceration and as a sanction for violations of probation conditions (Griffin and King, 2005).

For status offense cases, in 2005, detention was used in 8 percent of cases, about the same as 1995. This percentage was similar for whites and blacks. The offense profile of detained status offense cases was 17 percent runaway, 15 percent truancy, 8 percent curfew, 19 percent ungovernability, 23 percent liquor law, and 18 percent miscellaneous. It should be noted that the number of status offense cases involving detention increased from about 7,700 in 1995 to more than 11,900 in 2005 (Puzzanchera and Sickmund, 2008).

Delinquency cases involving black juveniles were more likely to use detention than cases involving white juveniles. Specifically, 18 percent of white delinquency cases and 26 percent of black delinquency cases used detention in 2005 (Puzzanchera and Sickmund, 2008). In one study the average IQ score of detainees was 82.5, well below average (Viljoen, Klaver, and Roesch, 2005).

A cost estimate several years ago was that it cost about $85 to keep one child in detention for one day (Tyler, Darville, and Stalnaker, 2001). Crowding is often a problem; 20 percent of public detention facilities were over capacity in 2002 (Snyder and Sickmund, 2006).

Detention workers or probation officers usually make the initial detention decision. State law may stipulate that a detention hearing be held within a specified period of time so that a judge can rule on the continued need for detention. The Model Juvenile Delinquency Act, a guideline for state codes, stipulates that the detention hearing be held within 36 hours and that certain criteria be used to decide whether to detain a particular youngster (Rossum, Koller, and Manfredi, 1987; see Box 8.1 for the relevant section of the Model Juvenile Delinquency Act).

BOX 8.1

Model Juvenile Delinquency Act

Section 26. [Grounds for Pre-Hearing Detention] A youth taken into custody may be detained if there is probable cause to believe that

(A) The juvenile is a fugitive from justice;

(B) The juvenile has committed a felony while another case was pending;

(C) The juvenile has committed a delinquent act and

   (1) The juvenile will likely fail to appear for further proceedings,

   (2) Detention is required to protect the juvenile from himself or herself,

   (3) The juvenile is a threat to the person or property of others,

   (4) The juvenile will intimidate witnesses or otherwise unlawfully interfere with the administration of justice, or

   (5) There is no person available or capable of caring for the juvenile.

Source: R.A. Rossum, B.J. Koller, and C.P. Manfredi (1987). *Juvenile Justice Reform: A Model for the States*. Clairmont, CA: Rose Institute of State and Local Government and the American Legislative Exchange, p. 33.

A troubling feature of detention hearings is that often they are the first opportunity for the juvenile to meet with an attorney. In one study, more than half of the public defenders did not meet their clients prior to the detention hearing. In one site, an unsupervised law student with no background investigations on the youths represented youths at detention hearings (Puritz et al., 1995). In Pennsylvania, a study found that at detention hearings attorneys did not have much opportunity to confer with their juvenile clients and were not familiar with alternatives to detention (Miller-Wilson and Puritz, 2003). For information on the introduction of weekend court in New York City, see Box 8.2.

As noted in Chapter 10, many youths in the juvenile justice system have a mental health disorder (see Skowyra and Cocozza, 2006). A study of almost 2,000 juvenile detainees in Chicago found approximately 10 percent had thought about committing suicide in the six months prior to being interviewed, and 10 percent had attempted suicide in the past. Cutting and drug overdose were the most common methods used in recent suicide attempts (Abram et al., 2008). For youths with mental health problems, barriers to receiving mental health services can exist. More than half of such detainees believed that their problem would go away or they could solve it on their own, and about one-third were not

BOX 8.2

Weekend Court for Juveniles

As fans of an old television show, "Night Court," would know, New York City has both night court and weekend court for adults, but juveniles had to wait all weekend for court on Mondays. Recently, however, Mayor Michael Bloomberg started weekend court processing for juveniles ages seven to 15. The courts only expect to process about 16 juveniles per weekend. The courts have also begun to use a risk assessment instrument to help decide on detention or release. This instrument helps to decrease the detention of low-risk youths by half and to increase the detention of high-risk youths, also by half.

Source: M. Fernandez (June 9, 2008). "Young Suspects Get a Right Adults Have: A Judge on Weekends." *The New York Times.*

sure where to get help (Abram et al., 2008). Substance use and abuse are also problems. More than three-quarters of detained male juveniles in Cook County (Chicago, Illinois) reported marijuana use in the previous six months, and 4 percent reported cocaine use. Three-quarters of female detainees reported marijuana use, and 10 percent reported cocaine use (McClelland, Teplin, and Abram, 2004). These findings indicate some of the treatment needs in detention facilities. Fortunately, most detention centers do screen for substance abuse, mental health needs, and suicide risk (Snyder and Sickmund, 2006).

Physical health concerns also need attention. For example, testing at the Harris County (Houston, Texas) juvenile detention center in 2006 and 2007 showed that about 10 percent of the boys and about 25 percent of the girls tested positive for a sexually transmitted disease. More positively, only two boys and no girls tested positive for HIV (Schneider, 2008).

Detention Options

Court personnel have several options at the detention decision point. Releasing a child to his or her parents is the most frequently used option; this is the preferred decision in most states (e.g., Alabama Code 12-15-59). **Secure detention**—placing a child in the juvenile equivalent of a local jail—is another alternative. It involves placement in a locked facility of 10, 20, or more youths who are awaiting further court action or are awaiting transfer to a state correctional facility. In some places,

nonsecure detention is another option for youths involved in less serious crimes and for those who do not pose much threat to the community or themselves. Such youngsters may be placed in small group homes that are not locked or not locked as comprehensively as a secure detention facility—hence the term "nonsecure." Youngsters housed in nonsecure detention centers might even go to regular public school classes during the day. Alternatives to detention, such as home detention, will be discussed later in this chapter.

Detention Decisionmaking

As noted above, in 2005, delinquency cases involving black youths were placed in detention more frequently than cases involving white youths. This was true for every year from 1985 to 2005 (Puzzanchera and Sickmund, 2008). Research confirms that minority youths are more likely to be detained than white youths (Bishop, 2005).

Detention Programming

The psychological technique of behavior modification has inspired many detention centers to use **token economy programs.** With this approach, staff members use points or dollar values to reward detained youths for appropriate behavior and withhold or subtract points for inappropriate behavior. Youths earn credits when they follow the rules and they lose credits when they disobey the rules. If they have more credits than losses, they can "purchase" rewards such as snacks, table games, and room privacy at the end of the day and/or on the weekend. (See Box 8.3 for examples of rewards, punishments, and costs.) This type of program is based on psychological principles of conditioning that contend that human behavior is learned through reinforcements.

Given the unique needs of girls in detention, it is critical that detention centers develop gender-specific programs for girls. One issue is that about 70 percent of girls in the juvenile justice system have histories of physical abuse compared to only about 20 percent of the boys (Lederman and Brown, 2000). Programming should also include attention to alcohol, drug, and mental disorders. As noted above, significant proportions of detained juveniles have one or more of these problems.

Positive Programs

Research has found that education should be the cornerstone of detention programming. It is important for detention centers to teach basic academic skills, general education development (GED) test preparation, and also special education, employment readiness training, and

BOX 8.3

Detention Rewards and Fines

How Dollars May Be Earned

1.	School attendance	$10
2.	YMCA activities	$10
3.	Cleaning room (make beds, sweep, mop, etc.)	$5
4.	Extra work (per hour)	$5
5.	Good hygiene	$5
6.	Attending church, etc.	$5
7.	Cleaning unit	$10
8.	Good behavior	$5

Fines for Inappropriate Behaviors

1.	Body Contact (slapping, etc.)	$20
2.	Disrespect (sarcastic or abusive speech, not following rules)	$30
3.	Profanity	$10
4.	Instigating (influencing others to break rules)	$30
5.	Arguing (other youth or staff)	$30
6.	Lying	$40
7.	Complaining (irritating staff with complaints about program, food, other staff, dollars, etc.)	$25
8.	Contraband	$50
9.	Fighting (another resident)	$100
10.	Attempted Escape	$150

Source: Handbook of Procedures, Rules, and Regulations (Jefferson County Detention Center, Birmingham, Alabama). [Items have been renumbered.]

programs about social, cognitive, and life skills such as problem solving and moral reasoning (Stephens and Arnette, 2000). For example, in Jackson, Mississippi, the detention center is actually an extension of the district public school alternative school. In addition to academic programming, the school also offers vocational training and parent training (an "effective parenting" course) (Stephens and Arnette, 2000).

Arizona has been using character education in its detention and correctional facilities since 2001. Based on programs in regular schools, the Character Counts! program teaches character traits that philosophers and religious leaders of all denominations can agree on: trustworthiness, respect, responsibility, fairness, caring, and citizenship. An independent evaluation found an increase in positive behaviors such as taking responsibility and not making excuses (Martinez, 2008).

Often the best programming is to find an alternative to detention. The Maryland Detention Response Unit uses social workers to try to find appropriate community and residential alternatives to detention and to determine the need for mental or educational evaluations. Attorneys also investigate how court-ordered detention can be modified or amended to permit community-based alternatives (National Juvenile Defender Center, 2004).

A survey of youths in secure custody (some were in training schools and some were in detention) gives some indication of what juveniles think about their experiences. The survey showed some problem areas. About one-quarter (26%) of the youths reported staff use of excessive force, half reported seeing staff use excessive force on other inmates, 45 percent said that staff ignored possible trouble, and almost half said that staff said or did something to put an inmate at risk. So it seems that staff often allow or induce juveniles to use force on other juveniles in custody. On the positive side, however, two-thirds of the youths surveyed agreed that they had received help from staff and felt protected by staff (Peterson-Badali and Koegl, 2002).

DETENTION ALTERNATIVES

Because of criticisms of detention programming and because of the high costs of detaining youngsters in secure detention facilities, many jurisdictions have sought alternatives to traditional detention facilities. For example, a few years ago, New York City found that secure detention cost about $58,000 per year per child and that nonsecure detention (foster care and boarding homes) cost about $20,000 per year. Hence, they began using converted stores or lofts as **day-evening centers**. In such cen-

Tables describing the demographic characteristics of youths involved in the juvenile justice system and how juvenile courts process these cases can be investigated at http://www.ojjdp.ncjrs.org/ojstatbb/jcsdb/

ters, mornings involved formal educational programs, early afternoons were devoted to remedial and tutorial work, and late afternoons were reserved for recreational programs (e.g., weekly swimming at YMCA facilities). Two of the four New York City centers also offered evening hours twice a week for children considered to need extra supervision and for those on a waiting list for admission into the day program (Lindner, 1981).

Home Detention

Another popular alternative to traditional detention is **home detention**. This is the juvenile court counterpart of supervised pretrial release for adult criminal defendants. In home detention, the youth awaiting

Many home detention programs use electronic monitoring. With this technology, an electronic anklet functions as a transmitter and is tracked by a receiver installed in the detainee's home. A central monitoring unit is then able to determine the whereabouts of the youth wearing the device.

further juvenile court action is allowed to live at home but is also under the supervision of a detention worker who ensures that the youth is attending school (or working on a job) and maintaining a curfew. The detention worker, often a paraprofessional, may check on the home detention youngster up to four times a day if the worker suspects that the child is getting into new trouble (delinquency). Studies show that 70 to 90 percent of home detention youths do not reoffend and appear in court (Austin, Johnson, and Weitzer, 2005). Similarly, Dallas is now using electronic monitoring for truants instead of detention (Kovach, 2008).

Bail

Bail is not universally available in juvenile court (Rossum, Koller, and Manfredi, 1987:109), but bail for juveniles appears to be an option that is receiving greater attention. New Mexico, for example, authorized bail for serious youthful offenders detained before trial in an adult facility (National Conference of State Legislatures, 1993). This is a reflection of the changing philosophy of juvenile court, from *parens patriae* to punishment. Bail is considered inappropriate in the traditional juvenile court, in which the judge acts like a concerned parent in deciding to detain or release juveniles awaiting further court action. With the changing views of juvenile crime and juvenile court, however, states are beginning to see bail as a reasonable option. The current view that the juvenile is a responsible criminal rather than an immature youth in need of help is consistent with the use of bail as a means to guarantee continued appearance for court hearings.

THE INTAKE DECISION

The second major decision point in juvenile court is the **intake decision**, analogous to the filing decision in adult court. At intake, a court official—either a probation officer or a prosecutor (or both)—decides whether to file a court petition of delinquency, status offense, neglect, abuse, or dependency in a particular case. Traditionally, a probation officer has made the intake decision. The *parens patriae* philosophy of the court dictated this approach because its treatment orientation indicated that the probation officer (ideally a trained social worker) should consider the best interests of the child as well as the legal aspects of the case (as an adult court prosecutor might). That is, an intake probation officer is supposed to resolve every case in light of the considerations of the welfare of the child and the legal demands of the police and victim. This tradition is changing; a number of states even allow prosecutors to make the decision to file certain cases directly in adult criminal court and thereby completely bypass the juvenile court.

Informal Adjustment

One frequent decision of the intake officer is not to file a petition alleging delinquency or a status offense, but instead to try to resolve the matter without resorting to a formal petition against the child. As noted above, almost half (44%) of the 1.7 million delinquency cases coming to juvenile court in 2005 were not petitioned (Puzzanchera and Sickmund, 2008). (Statistics on the number of status offense cases not petitioned are not available.) Many (four out of 10) of the nonpetitioned cases were dismissed; others were handled informally. Informal handling is usually called adjustment at intake or **informal adjustment.** Examples would include requiring a first-time shoplifter to pay restitution to the store or ordering a vandal to paint the public building he or she has defaced. Similarly, intake probation officers often try to counsel troubled family members on a short-term basis or to refer them to counseling services in the community. As a result, a youth involved in runaway behavior, chronic disobedience ("incorrigibility"), or repeated truancy will not be immediately petitioned to court as a status offender. Instead, the youth receives help in dealing with the problem that brought him or her to the attention of court officials.

It is important to note that such informal adjustment practices occur as frequently as 25 percent of the time (Butts, 1994; McCarthy, 1987) and have been part of juvenile court since its inception. With the emphasis on diversion in the 1970s, informal adjustment practices by intake officers took on added dimensions.

Teen Courts

One diversion option to the traditional juvenile court is the use of **teen courts** (sometimes called youth courts). Here the philosophy is based on restorative justice, and youths act as judge, attorney (prosecutor and defense attorney), and jury in cases involving status offenses, misdemeanors, and occasionally a low-level felony. (About one-half of teen courts use adult judges.) The most common penalty is community service. Other sentences include teen court jury duty, writing essays about offending, writing apologies to victims, community service, and monetary restitution. As of 2002, it was estimated that there were more than 800 teen court programs in operation handling more than 100,000 cases per year, making them a primary diversion option (Butts, Buck, and Coggenshall, 2002; National Association of Youth Courts, 2008).

Two studies of the effectiveness of teen courts found no difference between teen courts and comparisons, but three studies found lower recidivism rates in teen court cases than for comparison youths. A recent study of an Illinois teen court found that most of the offenses handled were low-level infractions such as shoplifting (43% of the cases processed), curfew violation, possession of marijuana, disorderly conduct, and so on. Recidivism was only 12 percent after one year and 19 percent after two years (Rasmussen, 2004).

A multi-site study of teen courts in Alaska, Arizona, Maryland, and Missouri found statistically less recidivism for teen court youths in two of the four sites. In Alaska, 6 percent of teen court youths recidivated, compared to 23 percent of non–teen court youths; in Missouri, 9 percent of teen court youths recidivated, compared to 28 percent of non–teen court youths. The authors of the study concluded that "teen courts represent a promising alternative for the juvenile justice system" (Butts, Buck, and Coggenshall, 2002:34). It is also noteworthy that volunteer staff and low budgets mean that teen courts are inexpensive.

Teen court is not intended to deal with serious delinquency, but it appears to be an alternative method for dealing with status offenses, minor delinquent acts such as shoplifting, or problems with alcohol or marijuana. As one author put it, teen court may be a "partial solution to the juvenile justice system's failure to give anything more than a 'slap on the wrist' to first-time offenders" (Rasmussen, 2004:615).

Drug Courts

Another diversion option is juvenile **drug courts** in which the judge, prosecutor, and defense attorney collaborate as a team with drug treatment specialists. Like adult drug courts, juvenile drug courts attempt to intervene in both the criminal activity and the drug usage of clients. The courts use treatment, coordination, and extensive monitoring. The youths must appear in court frequently so that judges can monitor progress and offer encouragement and admonishment to the juveniles. There is frequent drug testing, and there are penalties for failing to test negative. Sanctions for youths that are not following the rules can range from a warning, an order to write a book report or paper or to do household chores, to fines, community service hours, or even detention. There also are incentives such as the dismissal of charges and termination of probation requirements upon graduation. Other rewards include verbal praise and such incentives as gift certificates and tickets to local events. Drug courts usually celebrate completion with a graduation ceremony in court that may include additional features, such as a gift of athletic shoes (Rossman et al., 2004).

There is some indication that drug court supervision in addition to probation or in place of probation may produce better results. The evaluation of a drug court in Phoenix, Arizona, showed that juvenile drug court participants had lower recidivism than the comparison group of regular probationers. On the other hand, only 30 percent of the drug court participants successfully completed the program; 62 percent were put on probation or sent to a state correctional facility (Rodriguez and Webb, 2004).

One problem with drug courts is that they may be reaching the wrong population. If drug courts are actually intended for drug-dependent or addicted youths, they are not capturing many such youths with severe drug problems. "If, on the other hand, juvenile drug courts are designed to deliver prevention services for a broad cross-section of youth involved with alcohol and other drugs, then their current mode of operating may be appropriate, but such a broad mission would raise other questions about the risks of labeling, net-widening, and iatrogenic effects (i.e., the cure may be worse than the disease)" (Butts, Zweig, and Mamalian, 2004:142). Much like the "war" on drugs in general, drug courts often paint a wide stroke that takes in more than is necessary. We worry so much about adolescent drug use that we overreact and do too much.

A study of a juvenile drug court in Charleston, South Carolina, found that it was "more effective than family court services in decreasing rates of adolescent criminal and substance use behavior," but it was not effective in reducing rearrests or reincarceration (Henggeler et al., 2006).

A recent analysis of correctional effectiveness included a section on drug courts, although most of the studies involved adult criminal offenders. One of the included studies involved only juveniles, and one included juveniles and adults. The conclusion was that "there is very strong evidence that drug courts reduce the future criminal activities of offenders" (MacKenzie, 2006:234). However, MacKenzie noted that drug courts include both deterrent and rehabilitative strategies, so it is not clear precisely how drug courts achieve their positive results (MacKenzie, 2006).

A related reform is juvenile mental health courts. About 11 such courts were in operation in 2006, with plans for about 20 additional courts. As with drug courts, the mental health court personnel cooperate with mental health personnel, who are often existing mental health service providers in the community. Some juvenile mental health courts are using evidence-based approaches such as multi-systemic therapy (Cocozza and Shufelt, 2006). Given the newness of this approach, it is too early to assess effectiveness.

A victim-offender mediation program in Texas emphasizing the offender's accountability is still another type of diversion that has been successful. The mediator is often a trained volunteer. An early evaluation found that 29 percent of referrals ended in successful mediation. A few years later the successful mediation rate was 77 percent (Kurlychek, Torbet, and Bozynski, 1999).

Still another new diversion program is the ACT Now truancy reduction program in Pima County, Arizona. This program combines services to get at the root causes of truancy and even misdemeanor prosecution with criminal fines and penalties for parents who do not do enough to get their children to attend school. In those cases where parents were prosecuted, the usual sanction was community service or a $200 fine (Baker, Sigmon, and Nugent, 2001).

These newer programs share several features. Contrasted with diversion programs of 25 years ago, these programs place more emphasis on the accountability of the offender and concern for the victim. Older diversion programs focused on treating the offender without parallel concern for victims. There is also a tendency to involve community members, either teen or adult or both, in the process whereas older diversion programs relied more on expert staff. In general, these programs emphasize both accountability and concern for victims whereas older programs emphasized treatment for the offender.

The Prosecutor's Role

If an intake probation officer decides to file a petition against a child, often that decision requires the approval of an attorney, normally the prosecutor. The prosecutor's approval of the probation officer's decision to file a petition ensures that a legally trained official has reviewed the legal criteria for a properly authorized petition. The prosecutor checks the legal wording of the petition, determines that enough evidence is available for establishing the petition (finding the delinquent or status offender "guilty"), and makes sure that the offense occurred in the court's jurisdiction and that the child was of proper age at the time of the offense.

Because of the importance of such legal criteria, and because of the growing emphasis on more punitive juvenile models, some jurisdictions have turned away from the traditional probation-officer model of intake toward models in which the prosecutor is either the first or the sole intake decisionmaker. Such models are more consistent with more legalistic views of juvenile court in which the state has abandoned the traditional *parens patriae* philosophy. For example, the state of Washington has switched responsibility for the intake decision to the prosecutor for all felony charges and most misdemeanors. There prosecutors make such decisions on the basis of explicit criteria: offense seriousness, prior record, and the age of the youth. Furthermore, informal adjustments are no longer permitted at intake, although police agencies can still "exercise their traditional discretion regarding whether to refer or adjust incidents involving juveniles" (Schneider and Schram, 1986:214). In place of informal adjustments at intake, minor offenses are supposed to be diverted to restitution programs. This action by Washington represents a radical break with traditional juvenile court thinking and practice and is a close approximation of adult processing with its retributive emphasis. (For a diagrammatic comparison of traditional intake and the Washington state practice, see Box 8.4.) Like the legislation in the state of Washington, the Model Juvenile Delinquency Act also stipulates that the prosecutor shall "[d]irectly supervise all matters relating to intake," although the probation officer may continue to make the file-divert decision in misdemeanor cases if the prosecutor so delegates (Rossum, Koller, and Manfredi, 1987:40). Similarly, the National District Attorneys' Association stipulates a very active role for the prosecutor (Shine and Price, 1992), and Louisiana has given the prosecutor greater authority over the intake process (National Conference of State Legislatures, 1993).

BOX 8.4

The Intake Process

Traditional Intake:

Police, parents, school officials, or victims bring youths to attention of Intake	Intake officer files petition	Juvenile Court Hearing
	OR makes an informal adjustment	
	OR diverts to a treatment program	

Prosecutorial Model (e.g., Washington State)

Police, parents, school officials, or victims bring youths to attention of Intake	Prosecutor files a petition	Juvenile Court Hearing
	OR declines to file a petition	
	OR diverts to a restitution program	

A further development is that the prosecutor is now taking on increased responsibility in juvenile cases as increasingly more states are allowing prosecutors to file cases directly in adult criminal court. In addition to traditional waiver (transfer), several mechanisms allow prosecutors to proceed against juveniles in criminal court: concurrent jurisdiction, statutory exclusion, presumptive waiver, reverse waiver, and "once adult/always an adult" statutes. Bishop (2000) estimates that approximately one-quarter million youths under 18 were prosecuted as adults in 1996. (These prosecutor options will be discussed in greater depth later in this chapter.)

Many prosecutors are now pursuing a two-pronged or bifurcated approach with juveniles. The first prong is aggressive prosecution of violent repeat offenders; the second prong is early intervention to prevent further delinquency. One example is Duval County, Florida, where prosecution in one year resulted in more than 750 juveniles being incarcerated as adults in the county jail and another 155 juveniles sentenced to the Florida State Prison. At the same time, minor offenders were sentenced to community service or handled in diversion programs. Prosecutors are now collaborating extensively with other agencies such as schools (Coles and Kelling, 2002).

A number of jurisdictions are pursuing community prosecution. Like some versions of community policing, community prosecution's "overarching goal is to improve the quality of life in a community" (Harp et al., 2004:3). There are three key elements to community prosecution. First, the prosecutor attempts to involve the community in defining and solving problems. Second, problem solving goes beyond traditional enforcement strategies. Third, the prosecutor forms partnerships with law enforcement, probation, schools, and community groups. All this is done in clearly defined target areas, and there is an emphasis on quality-of-life issues, not just serious felonies. Part of the reason for the emphasis on quality-of-life issues is the "broken windows" theory that helped spur the development of community policing efforts (Coles and Kelling, 2002).

An example of community prosecution in action is the Multnomah County (Portland), Oregon, District Attorney's Office. In the mid-1990s, teens had created an unofficial skateboard park in an industrial section of Portland. Business owners complained about litter and about the teen skateboarders grabbing onto trucks for rides on their skateboards. Rather than simply close down the park and prosecute the teens for littering and disorderly conduct, the prosecutor's office met with both sides and an agreement was reached. The teens agreed to stay within a defined area and not litter; the business owners paid for the signs placed around the park and also provided a portable toilet. So the prosecutor's office helped create an innovative solution to a quality-of-life issue that previously would have resulted in prosecution and conviction (Harp et al., 2004).

Research on Intake Decisionmaking

As was the case with police discretion (see Chapter 7), many researchers and analysts have been concerned about the discretion of intake decisionmakers either to file or not file petitions. Of particular concern has been the question of whether race is an important factor in the intake decision and whether racial discrimination occurs at intake. Several conclusions can be drawn from the studies that have been conducted on intake decisionmaking. First, seriousness of the alleged offense clearly influences the decision to file a petition, though it is not necessarily the prime factor. Thus, youths accused of more serious offenses are more likely to be petitioned to court than youths accused of less serious offenses (Bell and Lang, 1985; Cohen and Kluegel, 1978; Fenwick, 1982; McCarthy and Smith, 1986; Minor, Hartmann, and Terry, 1997; Thornberry, 1973). Second, prior record is a factor. Youths with prior records are more likely to be referred (Cohen and Kluegel, 1978; Fenwick, 1982; McCarthy and Smith, 1986; Thornberry, 1973). Third, demeanor often has an effect; uncooperative youths are more likely to be petitioned than cooperative youths (Bell and Lang, 1985; Fenwick, 1982). However, demeanor often is not measured in studies because many researchers rely on official records that do not include any record of the attitude of the child when he or she is interviewed by the court official making the intake decision. Finally, variables such as age, race, class, and gender have produced mixed results. As a result, there is considerable controversy surrounding the impact of each of these variables on the intake decision (for a review and analysis, see Bishop, 2005).

The methodology used in many previous studies was deficient. Specifically, many early studies looked at small, nonrepresentative samples that made it impossible to generalize to courts nationwide. Other studies used only bivariate rather than multivariate statistical analyses of their data. This means that they examined the independent effects of individual variables (such as race) on intake decisions but did not consider the effects on decisions of several variables at once. In addition, many of the studies were conducted years ago, prior to the introduction of due process guarantees in juvenile court and to the relatively recent civil rights movement focusing on eliminating various forms of discrimination.

Furthermore, at least some researchers (e.g., McCarthy and Smith, 1986; Sampson and Laub, 1993) contend that it is misleading to isolate the intake decision apart from the detention, adjudication, and dispositional decisions. They argue that those decisions are basically parts of one complex whole that must be studied together to avoid possible distortions. An analogy would be studying decisions of college football coaches about what play to call on first down but ignoring strategy decisions on the second, third, and fourth downs. Research on first-down strategy is interesting but incomplete. First-down decisions make the most sense when understood in the context of the other downs.

In summary, race appears to have some effect on the intake decision. The research of McCarthy and Smith (1986) indicated some disadvantage for blacks (e.g., greater chance of being petitioned), but Bell and Lang (1985) found a more complex situation. Rodriguez (2005) found that race even affected the selection process for a restorative justice program, with both black and Hispanic/Latino juveniles less likely to be selected.

Sampson and Laub (1993) have placed the discussion of the impact of race on juvenile court decisionmaking in a theoretical context. They see race as linked to structural changes in American society, such as the deindustrialization of central cities and the concomitant rise of the underclass. Their research found that "structural contexts of 'underclass' poverty and racial inequality are significantly related to increased juvenile justice processing" (Sampson and Laub, 1993:305). In simple terms, counties with greater poverty and racial inequality showed higher rates of detention and out-of-home placement of juveniles. Their findings are consistent with the notion that "underclass black males are viewed as a threatening group to middle-class populations and thus will be subjected to increased formal social control by the juvenile justice system" (Sampson and Laub, 1993:306).

Pope (1995) concludes that race is a factor, and he suggests that some changes need to be added to the traditional intake process to ensure that race is not a consideration. One suggestion is training. A second suggestion is to have two intake officers decide each case. A third suggestion is to have a review board examine all the decisions to look for any impact of race. If attention is given to such suggestions to improve court processing and if attention is also given to social and economic factors associated with race problems in the United States, race could cease to be a factor in juvenile court decisionmaking.

PROCESSING JUVENILES IN ADULT CRIMINAL COURT

Many juvenile offenders are now being handled in adult criminal court rather than juvenile court. This is a crucial decision because processing a youth in adult court makes the juvenile subject to adult penalties such as lengthy incarceration in an adult prison as opposed to a relatively short period of incarceration in a juvenile training school. Such a decision also results in the creation of an adult criminal record, which is public and may hinder future opportunities for employment in certain occupations. A juvenile court record, on the other hand, is usually confidential, and, therefore, should not harm the child in any way.

There are several methods that states use to place juveniles into adult court jurisdiction: **transfer** or **waiver**, statutory exclusion, prosecutorial waiver, and lowering the age of juvenile court jurisdiction. Traditionally, waiver or transfer was the primary method of placing juveniles into adult criminal court. In 2004, 46 states and the District of Columbia had statutes allowing judicial waiver (Griffin, 2005).

In 2005, approximately 6,900 juveniles were waived to adult criminal court (Puzzanchera and Sickmund, 2008). This was considerably below the peak number of 12,100 cases waived in 1994. The offense profile of waived cases in 2005 was 51 percent person cases, 27 percent property cases, 12 percent drug cases, and 10 percent public order cases (Puzzanchera and Sickmund, 2008). Juvenile courts are waiving or transferring fewer cases to adult court because the states have been using other means (statutory exclusion and prosecutorial waiver) to prosecute juveniles in adult criminal court. No national statistics exist about how many cases are prosecuted in criminal court via these means (Snyder and Sickmund, 2006).

Statutory exclusion, also called **legislative waiver**, means that state legislatures rule that certain offenses, such as murder, automatically go to adult court. In 2004, 29 states had exclusion laws (Griffin, 2005). In Illinois, the list of offenses excluded from juvenile court jurisdiction includes murder, aggravated sexual assault, robbery with a firearm, drug and weapons offenses committed on or near public housing, and gang-related felonies. The law applies to most juveniles 15 and older but includes 13- and 14-year-olds for murder and sexual assault (Bishop, 2000).

Prosecutorial waiver (direct file/concurrent jurisdiction) is another method for placing juveniles into adult criminal court. State law gives juvenile and adult court concurrent jurisdiction over certain cases. Depending on the offense, the age of the offender, and/or the youth's prior record, the prosecutor decides whether to file the case in juvenile or adult court. In 2004, prosecutorial waiver (concurrent jurisdiction) was available in 15 states and the District of Columbia (Griffin, 2005). For example, in Florida, prosecutors can waive 16- and 17-year-olds charged with any felony, 16- and 17-year-olds charged with a misdemeanor if they have one prior felony and at least one prior misdemeanor, and even 14- and 15-year-olds charged with certain offenses (Bishop, 2000).

Another way to direct juveniles to adult court is for state legislatures to lower the maximum age of juvenile court jurisdiction. As of 2002, three states defined age 16 as the beginning age for criminal court jurisdiction, and 10 states set age 17 as the age for adult court jurisdiction (Bozynski and Szymanski, 2004).

It should be noted that 23 states allow for **reverse waiver**. This means that the criminal courts can return certain cases that they received due to mandatory judicial waiver, legislative exclusion, or prosecutorial waiver back to juvenile court. It is also important to note that 34 states have **"once an adult, always an adult" provisions** (Griffin, 2005). This means that all or certain categories of youths placed in criminal courts must automatically be processed in adult court for any subsequent offenses (Bishop, 2000).

The waiver decision is made at a hearing that is analogous to the preliminary hearing in adult court. At a waiver hearing, the prosecutor must only show probable cause that an offense occurred and that the juvenile committed the offense. The prosecutor does not have to prove guilt beyond a reasonable doubt. Proof of guilt is reserved for the trial in adult court (if waiver is successful) or for the adjudication stage in juvenile court (if the waiver motion fails). The juvenile transfer hearing differs from an adult court preliminary hearing in that the prosecutor must go further and establish that the juvenile is not amenable to juvenile court intervention or that the juvenile is a threat to public safety. An example of nonamenability would be the case of a youth who is already on parole from a state training school for an earlier delinquent act who then commits another serious offense (e.g., armed robbery). If probable cause were established that the youth committed the robbery, then the judge would have to find that the juvenile court had a history of contacts with the boy dating back several years and that one more juvenile court effort to deal with the boy's problems—either through probation or a training school placement—would be futile. An example of a case involving a threat to public safety would be a murder case or an offender with a history of violent offenses.

The Effectiveness of Transfer and Other Methods of Adult Court Processing

Research on transfer and other methods of placing youths into adult court has raised several issues. One concern is what influences the transfer decision; another is that transferred juveniles are receiving harsher sentences than they should. For information on the tragic result of one youth transferred to adult court and sentenced to adult prison, see Box 8.5.

A study of 22 girls who had been tried as adults in Ohio and who were sentenced to an adult prison showed that five had no prior record, 10 had never been placed in residential treatment, and most had histories of sexual and physical abuse, neglect, school difficulties, and chemical dependency. Although the sample was small, it suggested that many of the decisions to transfer these girls to adult court had been "questionable decisions" (Gaarder and Belknap, 2004:509).

A study of 1,042 juveniles prosecuted and sentenced in Pennsylvania adult criminal court between 1997 and 1999 showed that juveniles received harsher sentences in adult court than did young adults, even controlling for legal factors such as offense seriousness and prior record. Specifically, the juveniles were 10 percent more likely to be incarcerated and received a 29 percent increase in sentence length (average sentence length of 2.18 months per juvenile compared to 1.69 months per adult). These "findings suggest that judges may assign greater levels of culpability and dangerousness to transferred juveniles than to young adult offenders" (Kurlychek and Johnson, 2004).

Another issue is the effectiveness of transfer. A recent review of the research on transfer concluded that there is need for more research but that "the bulk of the evidence suggests that transfer laws, at least as currently implemented and publicized, have little or no general deterrent effect in

BOX 8.5

The Results of One Transfer Decision: Rape and Death

Rodney Hulin was convicted of arson at age 16 in Texas and sentenced to adult prison. Within a week of arriving at the Clemens Unit in Brazoria County, Texas, he was raped. During the following months, he was repeatedly beaten, robbed, and forced to perform oral sex. After he was denied protective custody, he became depressed and attempted suicide. After being in a coma for several months, he died. Rodney was small: 5'2" tall and 125 lbs.

Rodney's parents sued. The case was settled out of court.

How serious a crime must be committed for a youth to be transferred to adult court? How serious must the crime be for a youth to be sentenced to an adult prison, where assaults and rapes can occur, especially if the youth is not that strong or not that inclined to defend himself or herself? Based on all the information in the chapter about transfer, is it a positive option?

Adapted from: Human Rights Watch (2001). *No Escape: Male Rape in U.S. Prisons*. Available at: http://www.hrw.org.

preventing serious juvenile crime" (Redding, 2008:3). Research on specific deterrence, on the other hand, is stronger and has clearer implications. Based on six large-scale studies in five jurisdictions, the results are consistent:

> All of the studies found higher recidivism rates among offenders who had been transferred to criminal court, compared with those who were retained in the juvenile system....Thus, the extant research provides sound evidence that transferring juvenile offenders to the criminal court does not engender community protection by reducing recidivism. On the contrary, transfer substantially increases recidivism (Redding, 2008:3).

Based on this research and on research that shows that youths are developmentally different from adults, the American Bar Association (ABA) does not favor prosecuting juveniles as adults.

> The ABA opposes, in principle, the trend toward processing more and younger youths as adults in the criminal justice system and urges policymakers at all levels to take the previously mentioned principles into account in developing and implementing policies involving youth under the age of 18 (cited by Mathis, 2007:S1).

For a historical note on "passive" transfer in the first juvenile court, see Box 8.6.

BOX 8.6

Transfer in the First Juvenile Court: Cook County, Illinois

In the first juvenile court in Cook County, Illinois, there was some confusion about the jurisdiction of the court over older teens. There was also some concern that perhaps it was unconstitutional not to give older teens full due process rights. So the juvenile court judges exercised what is called "passive" transfer. This meant that they did not exercise their jurisdiction over older teens who committed serious crimes while on probation in juvenile court. They simply allowed these teens to be treated as adults in criminal court. They hoped that this strategy would prevent either the state legislature or the Illinois Supreme Court from overruling the law authorizing the juvenile court. The strategy worked; the Illinois Supreme Court did not interfere with the operations of the juvenile court.

Source: Tanehaus, D.S. (2004). *Juvenile Justice in the Making.* New York: Oxford University Press.

Youth and Worker Attitudes

Research on both youth and worker attitudes toward adult court processing indicates that there are some problems with moving juveniles to adult court jurisdiction.

In interviews with 95 serious and chronic adolescent male offenders in Florida (49 of whom had been transferred to criminal court), Bishop found that almost all described juvenile courts favorably but had criticisms of adult court. Most transferred youths believed that criminal court judges did not show interest in them, saw the proceedings as rushed, and, most importantly, had difficulty understanding everything that took place in criminal court. The transferred youths also perceived the criminal courts to be involved in game playing and felt that the public defenders were more interested in talking the youths into accepting pleas. The youths also perceived the courts to be clearly focused on punishment based not so much on what they had done but on judgments that "they were depraved or irredeemable" (Bishop, 2000:137).

In a study of 100 juvenile court personnel in three courts, workers—especially defense attorneys and probation officers—expressed prime concern for rehabilitation. Forty-seven percent of judges, 65 percent of public defenders, 80 percent of private attorneys, and 70 percent of probation officers said that rehabilitation was the paramount concern of judges. However, 40 percent of judges and 64 percent of prosecutors rated balancing the interests of child and society as the paramount concern (Sanborn, 2001).

In other words, although the public and politicians may favor transfer as a way to "get tough" on juvenile crime, not all youths and workers agree that this is the best course of action.

ADJUDICATION AND DISPOSITION

For children not sent to adult criminal court, the next steps after the filing of a petition are **adjudication** and **disposition**. In these decisions, a judge determines whether there is enough evidence to establish the petition and then decides what to do if there is enough evidence. These decisions are comparable to the plea, trial, and sentencing decisions in adult court. Refer back to Figures 8.1 and 8.2 (page 205) for statistics on adjudication and disposition in juvenile court.

Ideally, the determination of the truth of the petition occurs in a rational fashion, with the prosecutor, defense attorney, and judge using their abilities and training to seek justice. In reality, juvenile court sessions often are hectic and hurried, and may reflect the self-interests of the parties involved rather than justice or the best interests of the child. For example, Peter Prescott has described one day in the operations of the Bronx (NY) Family Court as a

> flow of incompetence and indifference. One court officer perpetually frowns, shaking his head in mute consternation at so much exposure to human fallibility. The court clerk, arrogant and disdainful, speaks as little as possible as if in fear of contamination. When he must speak, his tone is dry and contemptuous, his words chopped short: the burden of dealing with these people and their problems! "I've been here two years," a court officer remarks. "Two years too long. But once you're assigned to Family Court, you're stuck because no one wants to come here" (Prescott, 1981:85-86).

An account of the Los Angeles juvenile court system (Humes, 1996) indicates that numerous problems continue to plague juvenile court, an institution marked by both frustration and heroism.

Attorneys in Juvenile Court

There are several problems concerning attorneys in juvenile court. First, many juveniles do not have attorneys. Many juveniles waive their right to an attorney, often because they do not fully understand their rights, especially the importance of the right to an attorney (see, e.g., Brooks and Kamine, 2003). A second critical problem is large caseloads for public defenders in juvenile court. Depending on the state, the case-

Mark C. Ide

Attorneys and other court personnel gather in a courtroom to complete paperwork prior to the presiding of the judge. In the juvenile court setting, many attorneys are reluctant to use the zealous advocate approach that is the norm in U.S. adult courts.

load for the average public defender can range from 360 to 1,000 cases per defender (Jones, 2004). With attorneys being so overworked, many juvenile defendants get the clear impression that "their attorneys do not care about them" (Puritz et al., 1995:47).

Additional problems with public defender systems may include insufficient funding, lack of training, high turnover, low prestige, and low salaries (Feld, 1999). Starting salaries for public defenders in Ohio, for example, were as low as $35,000, and hourly rates for appointed counsel in several counties paid only $50 an hour for in-court work and $40 an hour for out-of-court work (Brooks and Kamine, 2003). Similarly, Georgia only pays appointed attorneys $60 per hour for in-court work, and one county has a cap of $300. Maine pays $50 per hour with a cap of $315. In Louisiana, the state only pays public defenders from $22,000 to $30,000 per year (Jones, 2004).

Many attorneys in juvenile court, both public defenders and private attorneys, are reluctant to utilize the **zealous advocate role** that is (at least theoretically) the norm in adult criminal court. Attorneys in adult criminal courts justify such zealous advocacy (where the attorney fights as hard as possible for all defendants, even defendants who have admitted that they are factually guilty) on the grounds that the system is adversarial and that the adversarial process is best for bringing out the truth. In juvenile court, some attorneys, parents, and judges feel that the adult criminal court norm of zealous advocacy is inappropriate. They may worry that strong advocacy can result in an outcome by which a child who "needs help" will not get it because failure to establish the petition leaves the court with no jurisdiction over the child. As a result, at least some attorneys assume a **concerned adult role** rather than a zealous advocate role, encouraging youths to admit to petitions in cases in which an adversarial approach may have resulted in a dismissal of the petition. Additional problems are that juvenile court is not considered prestigious (it is called "kiddie court") and that judges may pressure attorneys into cooperating rather than being adversarial (Feld, 1999). (For a look at one attorney's thoughts on juvenile court, see Box 8.7.)

BOX 8.7

One Lawyer's Observations about Juvenile Court

Thomas Geraghty has defended children in Cook County, Illinois (Chicago), for 28 years. He believes in juvenile court; he thinks it is preferable to an adult criminal court that has "no special focus on the unique problems associated with the adjudication, support, and treatment of children" (Geraghty, 1998:206). He notes that representing children allows lawyers to get to know children and the external forces such as poverty and child abuse that brought them to juvenile court. Geraghty notes that many of these external factors "are factors that our clients did not create and for which they are in no way responsible" (Geraghty, 1998:236).

He notes the important background details that need to be considered before calls are made for the transfer of youths to adult court or for the elimination of juvenile court. For example, consider a 12-year-old who allegedly shot and killed two teenagers. Investigation showed that this youth was trying to impress two older gang members. More importantly,

> [w]hat came out of this investigation was the story of a child's life. It turned out to be a story of a broken home, a child lost to gang culture despite the efforts of his family and school teachers, and access to a snub-nosed .38 caliber gun. The story of this child's life . . . is the product of all of its parts. Unless we focus our efforts on understanding these stories, in a setting supportive of understanding, we are unlikely to provide justice for children (Geraghty, 1998:241).

A qualitative study indicated that attorneys expressed considerable concern for their youthful clients but that the attorneys were not always sure of the correct course of action. Specifically, interviews with 10 attorneys and 10 clients showed that many of the juveniles did not always understand what was going on either during police interrogation or in court—often they "just didn't get it" (Tobey, Grisso, and Schwartz, 2000:230). For example, one youth waived his *Miranda* rights and talked to the police because he did not understand his right to remain silent. Many of the youths just wanted to "get it over with" (p. 234). Attorneys, in turn, felt that their youthful clients were often passive about decisions such as pleading guilty and thus attorneys "spoke of walking an ethical tightrope regarding who, in fact, was making the decision about such matters" (Tobey, Grisso, and Schwartz, 2000:237).

Buss (2000) agrees that many juveniles do not understand the role of the attorney as zealous advocate. Youths usually see adults as in control, not as advocates willing to listen to their wishes. Lawyers, in turn, may reinforce inaccurate images. Large caseloads prevent lawyers from devoting sufficient attention to juveniles. In addition, attorney hesitation to embrace the role of zealous advocate instead of concerned parent can influence attorneys to be paternalistic toward youthful clients. The result of any misunderstanding of the lawyer's role is that juveniles often are not fully honest with their attorneys. One way to help juvenile defendants to see their attorneys as zealous advocates is to honor confidentiality, especially by respecting confidentiality in relation to parents. If the attorney shows the youth that he or she will not divulge confidences to the youth's parents, that will demonstrate the attorney's undivided loyalty to the youthful defendant. Another important matter is simply to spend more time with youthful clients to counteract any impression that the youth does not matter (Buss, 2000).

Plea Bargaining

As in adult criminal court, the vast majority of cases in juvenile court are resolved by plea bargains (Puritz et al., 1995; Snyder and Sickmund, 2006). Because of the pressure on youths to plead guilty (admit the allegations in the petition) and because of the problems with **plea bargaining** (see, e.g., Newman, 1986), the American Bar Association has recommended that plea bargaining either be made visible or eliminated entirely (Institute of Judicial Administration–American Bar Association, 1980). The ABA maintains that if plea bargaining is retained, the judge should not participate in the process. However, the judge "should require disclosure of the agreement reached and explicitly indicate the conditions under which he or she is willing to honor it" (Institute of Judicial Administration–American Bar Association, 1980:39). If the judge will not accept the plea agreement, he or she should give the juvenile a chance to withdraw his or her plea. Finally, the judge should consult with the juvenile's parents before accepting a plea (Institute of Judicial Administration–American Bar Association, 1980:47). These regulations (or alternatively, the abolition of plea bargaining) would eliminate many of the traditional abuses of the practice.

The issue of plea bargaining may take on increasing importance. Texas, for example, recently revised its laws to allow more determinate sentencing in juvenile court as an alternative to waiving some youths to adult court. Youths subject to this provision can get longer prison sentences and may complete their sentences, when they turn 21, in the adult system. Mears (2000) found that such increased sentencing options gave prosecutors greater leverage in pressuring juveniles to accept plea bargains.

Attorney Effectiveness

Research has shown some disturbing results concerning the effectiveness of defense attorneys in juvenile court. As we will explain, many of the studies show several problems with attorney representation of juvenile clients.

On the positive side, however, Michael Fabricant's (1983) study of juvenile court public defenders in Brooklyn and the Bronx (New York) found that, contrary to stereotypes, public defenders were more effective (or at least as effective) as private attorneys in defending their juvenile clients. Specifically, the public defenders were very effective in obtaining adjournments, avoiding detention, and gaining dismissals. Such indicators of adversarial effectiveness led Fabricant (1983) to conclude that New York City public defenders were not inadequate. This is an impressive finding because they were representing roughly 75 percent of the delinquency and status offense cases in New York City at the time of the study.

In an analysis of six states, Feld (1988) found that in three states many children did not have attorneys. In all six states, however, "unrepresented juveniles seem to fare better than those with lawyers" (Feld, 1988:418). Juveniles with attorneys were more likely to receive placement outside the home or secure confinement than juveniles without attorneys.

In a study of more than 500 juvenile felony court cases in Missouri, Burruss and Kempf-Leonard (2002) also found an adverse effect of attorneys. In other words, "out-of-home placement was more likely to occur if a youth had an attorney, even when other relevant legal and individual factors were the same" (Burruss and Kempf-Leonard, 2002:60). To be more specific, concerning youths charged with felonies in three Missouri courts (one urban, one suburban, and one rural), suburban youths with counsel were almost three times more likely to be removed from home, and rural youths were two and a half times more likely to get out-of-home placement than youths without attorneys. All the urban youths had counsel (Burruss and Kempf-Leonard, 2002). This negative effect of attorney representation raises an interesting point: Would kids be better off without attorneys? Burruss and Kempf-Leonard think not. They think that the negative impact of attorneys in juvenile court may be due to high caseloads, retaining counsel too late in the process, or other court personnel co-opting the attorneys out of an adversarial role.

In a study of two midwestern courts, Guevara, Spohn, and Herz (2004) found that "the presence of an attorney (especially a private attorney) was an aggravating factor. Specifically, youth who appeared with a private attorney were the least likely to have the charges dismissed and the most likely to be securely confined" (p. 366). Most importantly, these findings about the negative impact of private attorneys call "into question the basic and fundamental right to counsel in juvenile court" (Guevara, Spohn, and Herz, 2004:366).

An American Bar Association investigation of Ohio juvenile courts produced several disturbing findings. First, "large numbers of poor youth throughout Ohio go unrepresented, even during some of the most critical proceedings that affect their liberty interest" (Brooks and Kamine, 2003:25). In many counties investigators noted that waiver of counsel was common, with as many as 80 percent of juveniles going without counsel. Second, many attorneys (slightly over 40%) saw their role as representing the "best interest" of the youth rather than being the youth's advocate. In some counties this view of the attorney role was so strong that it did not seem important to have an attorney represent the youth. Third, for many youths who did have attorney representation, the quality of that representation was questionable. The report found that many Ohio youths "receive ineffective assistance of counsel from attorneys who are ill-prepared, insufficiently trained, and/or overwhelmed by high caseloads, insufficient resources and low pay" (Brooks and Kamine, 2003:29). Thus, most cases are handled informally or by plea bargaining, and attorneys had little impact at disposition. One specific problem was low compensation. Starting annual salaries for public defenders were as low as $35,000, and hourly rates for appointed counsel in several counties paid only $50 an hour for in-court work and $40 an hour for out-of-court work. Such low rates do not help to attract or retain competent attorneys (Brooks and Kamine, 2003).

An American Bar Association study in Pennsylvania showed similar problems. Significant numbers of youths did not have representation, and many others had ineffective counsel due to lack of preparation or training. At detention hearings attorneys often had little chance to confer with their juvenile clients and were not familiar with alternatives to detention. Most cases were resolved by pleas, and attorneys saw many courts simply interested in dispensing treatment or punishment. Probation officers made disposition recommendations with little challenge from attorneys. At disposition, many attorneys simply were not acting as advocates for their juvenile clients. The investigators found that probation officers were very influential in the juvenile justice system, to the extent that "the system's over-dependence on [probation's] role has tipped the scales toward a 'best interest' system in delinquency cases in lieu of a system that demands the Commonwealth [of Pennsylvania] prove its case" (Miller-Wilson and Puritz, 2003:59).

Thus, the situation in America's juvenile courts appears to be such that some attorneys are adversarial, some are still traditional and act as concerned adults, and some are in between the two extremes. Furthermore, in some states, many juveniles are not represented by attorneys (Brooks and Kamine, 2003; Feld, 1993; Miller-Wilson and Puritz, 2003).

One frequent problem is simply that many juveniles waive their right to an attorney (Jones, 2004). This state of affairs raises the issue of which is the best approach: zealous advocate, concerned adult, or some compromise between the two alternatives? The chief advantage of the zealous advocate model is that it is probably the best insurance that only truly guilty youths will come under court jurisdiction. Because the attorney does not pressure the child to admit to the petition (plead guilty), there is less danger that the court will attempt some type of intervention program with youths who are not really guilty. An added advantage is that this approach may well generate the most respect from juveniles for the court system. Fewer youths will feel that they have been betrayed or tricked into something that some adult thought was best for them, despite their own wishes.

The biggest danger of the zealous advocate approach is that it may contribute to what Fabricant (1983) calls the contemporary version of benign neglect. That is, because many youths appearing in juvenile court come from families racked with problems, such as low income, public assistance, and/or broken homes, they do need assistance. An adversarial approach may prevent these children from being railroaded into juvenile prisons or other types of intervention due to insufficient legal defense. That adversarial approach, however, does nothing about the real problems faced by these children in their homes and their neighborhoods:

> It must be presumed that these youngsters' fundamental problems will neither be addressed nor resolved through a faithful adherence to process. Just as important, their troubles are likely to be compounded by social indifference. Therefore, a policy of calculated nonintervention may, over time, cause severer and/or increased antisocial behavior from troubled youths who initially are ignored by the court or state (Fabricant, 1983:140).

The advantage of the concerned adult model is that it seeks to address the problems of the child that presumably led the child into delinquency. The problem is that this helping philosophy has been the rationale of the juvenile court since 1899, and, as David Rothman has so aptly phrased it, the rhetoric of individualized attention has always far outstripped the reality of ineffective if not abusive programs (Rothman, 1980).

Jury Trials for Juveniles

Because the U.S. Supreme Court has not mandated the right to a jury trial for all juveniles (see Chapter 9), only 10 states generally allow jury trials as a right for juveniles, and another 11 states allow jury trials in special circumstances (Szymanski, 2002). Some contend that it is critical for juveniles to have the right to a jury trial. For example, Rosenberg (2008) notes that judges find guilt about 25 percent more often than juries do. The American Bar Association agrees that judges may be biased and further states:

> A jury trial gives enhanced visibility to the adjudicative process. A jury trial requires the trial court judge to articulate his or her views of the applicable law in the case through jury instructions, thereby facilitating appellate court review of the legal issues involved. Without the focus on legal issues that such an exercise entails, the danger is great that the applicable law may be misperceived or misapplied and that the error will go uncorrected on appeal (Institute of Judicial Administration—American Bar Association, 1980:53).

Having the right to a jury trial, however, may not make that much difference in juvenile court. In her study of a suburban juvenile court, Mahoney (1985) found that only seven cases out of the 650 actually went to trial. For those seven youths, and for 87 other youths who initially requested a jury trial but later settled without a jury trial, there was no impact of setting (scheduling) a case for trial on outcomes. Thus, "in a handful of serious cases in which a child denies charges, it [a jury trial] may be essential to the cause of justice, but it is unclear how much a jury trial benefits a youth or the community in the great majority of cases (Mahoney, 1985:564). Similarly, recent research in Ohio showed that most attorneys reported that 10 percent or less of cases went to trial; trials were almost nonexistent in some counties (Brooks and Kamine, 2003).

The Recent Emphasis on Punitiveness

Traditionally, the disposition stage of juvenile court has been the epitome of the *parens patriae* philosophy. With the advice of probation officers, social workers, psychologists, and psychiatrists, the judge has tried to act in the best interests of the child. Recently, however, disposition (sentencing) in juvenile justice has taken on an increasingly punitive character.

One indicator of this increasingly explicit focus on punishment is the revision of the purpose clauses of state juvenile codes. In the past, states emphasized prevention, diversion, and treatment. As of 2005, at least six states emphasized "community protection, offender accountability, crime reduction through deterrence, or outright punishment, either predominantly or exclusively," and only four states had traditional child welfare emphases (Griffin, Szymanski, and King, 2005). Sixteen states used the language of balanced and restorative justice, emphasizing public safety, individual accountability to both victims and the community, and offender skill development. Nine states modeled their statutes on the Standard Juvenile Court Act, and six states had a multi-part purpose clause based on the Legislative Guide for Drafting Family and Juvenile Court Acts (Griffin, Szymanski, and King, 2005).

A prime indicator of the trend toward punitiveness is the move by many states to expand provisions for processing juveniles in adult criminal court rather than juvenile court. Between 1998 and 2002, 31 states changed their laws governing the prosecution and sentencing of juveniles in adult criminal courts. For example, 18 states expanded their transfer laws, including the addition of new offenses eligible for transfer. Three states (Illinois, Maryland, and North Carolina) legislated "once an adult, always an adult" laws in which processing in criminal court automatically excludes the juvenile from any juvenile court jurisdiction after that (Griffin, 2005). The overall result is that it is easier to process juveniles as adults in criminal court.

Still another development in this direction is **blended sentencing.** In blended sentencing, either the juvenile court or the adult court imposes a sentence that can involve either the juvenile or the adult correctional system or both systems. The adult sentence may be suspended pending either a violation or the commission of a new crime. Fifteen states have juvenile blended sentencing schemes (the juvenile court imposes sentence), and 17 states have criminal blended sentencing laws (the criminal court imposes sentence) (Griffin, 2005).

One example of a jurisdiction with blended sentencing is New Mexico. That state's "exclusive blend" of sentencing applies to 15-year-olds charged with first-degree murder, 15–17-year-olds charged with serious offenses, or 15–17-year-olds charged with a felony and three prior separate felony adjudications in a two-year period. The juvenile court has jurisdiction and can sentence the youth to a juvenile or an adult sentence. In juvenile-inclusive blended sentencing, the juvenile court has jurisdiction and can sentence to a sanction including both the juvenile correctional system and the adult correctional system. Usually, the adult sanction is suspended unless the youth violates the juvenile sanction (examples of jurisdictions with this are Connecticut, Minnesota, and Montana). Two other options are criminal-exclusive (e.g., California and Florida) and criminal-inclusive blended sentencing (e.g., Arkansas and Missouri), by which the criminal court tries and sentences the youth. In criminal-exclusive systems the sentence can be to juvenile or adult corrections; in criminal-inclusive states the sentence can be to both systems. The other type of blended sentencing is juvenile-contiguous, by which the juvenile court has authority to impose a sanction that goes beyond the age of its jurisdiction. Then differing procedures are used to decide whether the remainder of the sentence is imposed in the adult corrections system (Torbet et al., 1996).

Still another sign of increasing punitiveness is the passing of statutes concerning the confidentiality of juvenile court records and proceedings. Traditionally, such records and court proceedings were closed to the public. The *parens patriae* rationale dictated that this would protect the juvenile from publicity so that a delinquent act would not stigmatize him or her permanently. In the last few years, however, critics have called for publicity to assure community protection, and legislatures have responded. At the end of 2004, 14 states allowed the public to be present for some cases (e.g., cases of older youths charged with a felony) (Snyder and Sickmund, 2006).

A possible consequence of these punitive developments is that the involved states create two ways of processing juveniles. If a youth is older, commits a serious offense, and/or has a prior record, he or she will be treated as an adult or similar to an adult. If a younger youth commits a less serious offense and lacks a prior record, he or she will be handled in a traditional juvenile court. Much of the rationale behind this division of juveniles into quasi-adults and children is the belief that youths have changed. Youths who commit what appear to be willful violent crimes are considered mature and responsible adults who should be held accountable for their actions. Younger youths who commit less serious offenses are still looked on as wayward youths who can be salvaged by the traditional *parens patriae* juvenile court.

Bishop sees some swing of the pendulum away from punishment and back to rehabilitation. First, she notes that although states have modified their purpose clauses to include both public protection and juvenile accountability, "45 maintain allegiance to the juvenile court's traditional benevolent mission" (Bishop, 2006:659). Similarly, three states recently passed laws to improve treatment for committed youths, Mississippi ended its boot camp program, and Tennessee passed a law to expunge juvenile records at age 21. Along with the establishment of teen courts and juvenile mental health courts noted earlier in this chapter, Bishop sees these developments as "indicators of renewed enthusiasm for rehabilitation" (Bishop, 2006:661).

Dispositional Decisionmaking

A major issue in juvenile justice is the question of which factors influence judges in their dispositional (sentencing) decisions. Research indicates several general conclusions. Legal variables such as seriousness of the offense and prior record have a strong influence on dispositions (e.g., Clarke and Koch, 1980; Cohen and Kluegel, 1978; Dannefer and Schutt, 1982; McCarthy and Smith, 1986; Staples, 1987; Thomas and Cage, 1977; Thornberry, 1973). The impact of prior record on dispositions, however, may reflect bias amplification (Dannefer and Schutt, 1982; Sampson, 1986). In other words, prior record may mask the influence of race or social class in police decisionmaking. The impact of offender characteristics such as age, race, social class, and gender has mixed results (for reviews of prior research in this area, especially prior research on the impact of race, see Bishop, 2005; Bishop and Frazier, 1996; Feld, 1999; Guevara, Spohn, and Herz, 2004; Krisberg and Austin, 1993; Leiber and Mack, 2003; McCarthy and Smith, 1986; Pope, 1994; Tracy, 2002).

Usually, the impact of these variables is weaker than the impact of legal variables. One study, however, indicated that "measures of social class and race become increasingly important as direct influences on the final disposition as youths are selected into the system for further processing" (McCarthy and Smith, 1986:58). Another way to put this is that racial bias at early decision points such as detention hearings can have a cumulative effect at disposition such as being sentenced to residential placement (Guevara, Spohn, and Herz, 2004). Leiber and Mack argue that research does suggest a race effect due to decisionmakers perceiving minorities, "especially African-Americans, as either dangerous, delinquent, and/or sexually promiscuous, which in turn had an effect on the case processing of these youth" (Leiber and Mack, 2003:37).

A number of studies report that females receive more severe dispositions than males for minor offenses, especially status offenses, stemming from traditional sex-role expectations. Other studies find leniency for females following the chivalry hypothesis, a paternalistic attitude toward female misbehavior compared to an excusing of boys "sowing their wild oats" (Chesney-Lind, 1977; Chesney-Lind and Shelden, 1992; Cohen and Kluegel, 1979). On the other hand, some studies show no gender bias after controlling for offense type or severity (see Leiber and Mack, 2003).

Prior case processing decisions exert some influence on dispositions. For example, detained youths receive harsher dispositions (Bailey and Peterson, 1981; Chused, 1973; Clarke and Koch, 1980) or are more likely to be formally processed (Frazier and Bishop, 1985; McCarthy, 1987) than youths who are not detained. Moreover, prior case dispositions can affect subsequent dispositions (Henretta, Frazier, and Bishop, 1985, 1986; Thornberry and Christenson, 1984). Finally, some authors report that dispositions vary from one jurisdiction to the next (e.g., Belknap, 1984; Dannefer and Schutt, 1982), while others fail to find such differences (e.g., Staples, 1987).

Specific studies have shed additional light on this issue. Feld's (1993) research on dispositional decisions in Minnesota is pessimistic. He argues that one interpretation of his findings is that

> there is no rationale to dispositional decision making; it consists of little more than hunch, guesswork, and hopes, constrained marginally by the youth's present offense, prior record, and previous dispositions (Feld, 1993:232).

A statewide study of youths in Florida found:

> a consistent pattern of unequal treatment. Nonwhite youths referred for delinquent acts are more likely than comparable white youths to be recommended for petition to court, to be held in pre-adjudicatory detention, to be formally processed in juvenile court, and to receive the most formal or the most restrictive judicial dispositions (Bishop and Frazier, 1996:405-406).

A statewide study of all youths petitioned to juvenile court in Nebraska from 1988 to 1993 (from 5,000 to about 7,000 youths per year) found the disposition decision to be "relatively race-neutral" (Secret and Johnson, 1997:468), but race was related to the detention decision in three years and the detention decision "consistently relates to harsher treatment at the adjudication and disposition stages of juvenile processing" (Secret and Johnson, 1997:474).

A study of juvenile case processing in Texas found "an absence of strong and consistent race and ethnic differentials in juvenile processing in Texas" (Tracy, 2002:175). Based on his research findings, Tracy contends that there is in fact differential involvement of minority youths in delinquency—minorities do commit a disproportionate share of delinquency. So attention needs to be directed to factors that cause such involvement in delinquency rather than squandered on the false issue of disproportionate treatment in juvenile court.

After examining the research on disposition decisions in juvenile court, it appears that the research findings are mixed: some studies find little or no impact of race while other studies reveal a race effect. The race effect may be indirect but nevertheless very real. For example, race may affect the detention decision, which then affects the disposition (see, Bishop, 2005, for a thorough review and analysis of the impact of race). Because the research is often limited to one jurisdiction or state, this may mean that sentencing varies from place to place. Apparently, some jurisdictions have achieved better success than others in making the disposition stage race-neutral. Hopefully, juvenile courts everywhere will make further progress in eliminating race as a factor in juvenile court dispositions.

Where race is still a factor in juvenile court dispositions, it may be that more is needed than simply addressing the problems of juvenile court. Krisberg and Austin (1993), for example, argue that problems in juvenile court dispositions, especially any findings of possible racial disproportionality, cannot be resolved in isolation but are "tied inextricably to the pursuit of social justice. Reforms will continue to fail, as they have in the past, if they do not address the maldistribution of wealth, power, and resources throughout society" (Krisberg and Austin, 1993:110). For a discussion of judicial attitudes as well as changes intended to improve juvenile court dispositions, see Boxes 8.8 and 8.9.

A final comment on the issue of race: it is clear that there is disproportionate minority contact. Minority youths are more likely to be adjudicated delinquent and placed compared to their proportion of the population. Kempf-Leonard thinks that part of the problem is blocked opportunities and that part of the solution is to improve schools, employment opportunities, and neighborhoods (Kempf-Leonard, 2007). Zimring notes that care must be exercised in addressing the problem of disproportionate minority contact so that the solution does not make

BOX 8.8

Judges' Attitudes about Rehabilitation for Juveniles

In a recent survey of judges, one-third agreed with the statement that the possibility of rehabilitation is reduced for juveniles from poor families. Three-quarters agreed that living with both biological parents enhances chances for rehabilitation. More than one-quarter agreed that juveniles living in the suburbs are more likely to be rehabilitated than inner-city youths.

Attitudes like this can have indirect impact on race. If black youths are more likely to be in such categories, and if judges rely on such beliefs in their sentencing, the net result is that judges may consider such youths as less likely to be rehabilitated and give them a harsher disposition (sentence) or transfer them to criminal court.

Source: The complete survey results can be found in: J.M. D'Angelo (2007). "The Complex Nature of Juvenile Court Judges' Transfer Decisions: A Study of Judicial Attitudes." *Social Science Journal* 44:147-159

BOX 8.9

Suggestions for Reducing the Effect of Race on Court Dispositions

Frazier and Bishop (1995) studied 137,028 cases referred to juvenile justice intake units in Florida between 1985 and 1987. They found significant race effects in dispositions even after controlling for the possible effects of other variables such as seriousness of the offense.

They offer several suggestions to reduce the impact of race in juvenile court. First, states should establish policies for reporting, investigating, and responding to individual instances of suspected racial bias. A second suggestion is diversity training for employees. Third, lack of parental cooperation should not be a ban for admission to more informal juvenile justice system options. Fourth, if persons with economic resources can utilize private care instead of harsher system dispositions, then "precisely the same treatment services should be made available at state expense to serve the poor—whether minority or majority race youths" (Frazier and Bishop, 1995:45).

the problem worse. By this he means that one possible approach would be to try to get more white juveniles adjudicated and disposed of (sentenced) in juvenile court. He asks, however, whether this is what society wants or if the better solution is to try and have fewer minority youths adjudicated and sentenced. This latter strategy may not result in perfect proportionality, but a reduction in the number of minority youths adjudicated and sentenced is preferable to having higher percentages of youths adjudicated delinquent and receiving harsh dispositions in juvenile court (Zimring, 2005). A dramatic example is "life without parole" sentences. Black youths make up 60 percent of all youths serving such sentences (Human Rights Watch, 2008). Do we simply want less disproportion, or do we really want fewer "life without parole" sentences across the board? Zimring's preference is for harm reduction over simple reduction of disparity.

SUMMARY

This chapter has examined the critical decision points in juvenile court: intake, detention, waiver and other means of getting youths to adult court, adjudication, and disposition. This review has shown that the ideal of a beneficent court system has not always been reached. Sometimes, for example, detention facilities have been deteriorating physical facilities concealing punitive practices. Even though 40 years have elapsed since the *In re Gault* decision established due process protections for juveniles, attorneys in juvenile court may be confused about their role and often have high caseloads that prevent them from effective representation of juveniles. Many juveniles do not even have attorney representation. Despite the history of civil rights legislation and concern, sometimes race appears to be a factor in juvenile court decisionmaking. Most recently, critics have become concerned about juvenile crime and the adequacy of the juvenile justice system to handle the serious offender. Thus, increased use of waiver, legislative exclusion, and prosecutorial waiver and of other more punitive measures such as blended sentencing have begun to characterize many juvenile court systems. This trend will probably continue.

In light of the ferment in juvenile court and the growing emphasis on harsher measures, concern for the due process rights of juvenile offenders is more critical than ever. In the next chapter, we will discuss due process issues and the rights of juveniles in general.

DISCUSSION QUESTIONS

1. H. Ted Rubin argues that token economies and other detention programs are violations of juvenile detainees' rights because most of the youths have not been adjudicated delinquent. Do you agree, or do you feel that such programs can be justified because they establish order and thereby protect the detainees? Are such practices similar to what "free" youngsters experience everyday in a typical school setting?

2. Much of the research described in this chapter concerns the decisions to detain, petition, and dispose of alleged delinquents. One of the basic issues in all of these decisions is whether the decisionmakers should or should not consider social factors in their decisionmaking. For example, should the attitude of the youth or the quality of parental care influence whether he or she is formally processed or allowed to go home with a warning or a much less severe consequence? Do such social factors have a place in these decisions, or are such social factors so liable to ethnic bias that the decisions should be based solely on legal factors?

3. Do you favor the use of bail in juvenile court? If so, for what sorts of offenders and under what circumstances?

4. Would you consider a career in juvenile detention as an administrator, counselor, teacher, or attendant (guard)?

5. Consider the following: A juvenile is accused of raping a 24-year-old high school teacher. You are a defense attorney and the defendant has asked you to represent him. You are convinced that you could "get the juvenile off" on a technicality. However, several members of your extended family are teachers and feel very strongly about this case. Would you accept the case? Would you pursue the technical defense that would exonerate the defendant, or would you encourage the youth to plead guilty and accept the psychiatric help that an expert feels is needed for the young man?

6. What do you think about the trend toward increased punitiveness (increased criminal court processing of youths, blended sentences, changes in purpose clauses to include punishment and incapacitation as juvenile court objectives, and changes in confidentiality)? Do you favor this trend, or does it represent an abandoning of the ideals of juvenile court?

(continued)

Discussion Questions

7. Suppose that a 13-year-old youth became extremely agitated and angry. He went to his parents' bedroom and got a pistol that was kept there in case an intruder broke in. He then murdered a family member. If this youth had no prior record but also no evidence of psychiatric disturbance, would you favor or oppose processing this youth as an adult in criminal court? How would the factor of a prior record influence your decision? What details of a prior record would most affect your decision? What are your reasons for your position?

8. The use of blended sentences and the increased processing of juveniles in adult court will probably result in an increase in the number of youths being incarcerated in adult prisons or in new youthful offender prisons instead of traditional training schools. What might be some positive and negative consequences of this? How can we prevent a tragedy such as a young man sent to adult prison where he is raped and eventually dies (see Box 8.7)?

Chapter 9

DUE PROCESS AND JUVENILES

Important Terms

Breed v. Jones

consent search

corporal punishment

Fare v. Michael C.

freedom of speech

graduated licensing

In re Gault

In re Winship

Kent v. United States

legal drinking age

McKeiver v. Pennsylvania

New Jersey v. T.L.O.

preventive detention

reasonable doubt standard

Schall v. Martin

school prayer

search and seizure

student search

What You Need to Know

- The U.S. Supreme Court clarified the rights of juvenile defendants in several landmark cases.

- For example, the *Gault* decision ruled that juveniles have the privilege against self-incrimination and the right to the assistance of counsel in cases with the possibility of a decision to put the juvenile in confinement in a locked facility.

- In *McKeiver v. Pennsylvania* the Supreme Court ruled that juveniles do not have the right to trial by jury.

- Reasonable corporal punishment is permissible in schools.

- Students do have limited free speech rights at school, but school officials can exercise broad editorial control over student publications.

- School officials can search students when they have reasonable suspicion to do so.

- Carefully drawn curfew laws have been upheld as constitutional. Excessively vague laws have not been upheld.

- Raising the legal drinking age has had positive effects, although a number of college presidents recently expressed concern that the age (21) affects binge drinking on college campuses.

INTRODUCTION

Juveniles share some—but not all—of the same constitutional rights as adults. While a comprehensive analysis of juvenile rights would require an entire book and is, therefore, beyond the scope of this text, it is important to examine some of the rights pertaining to juveniles. This chapter will first examine the landmark juvenile Supreme Court cases of the 1960s and 1970s (such as *In re Gault*) because those cases fundamentally altered the contours of the juvenile justice system. Then we will examine the Fourth Amendment rights of juveniles in terms of search and seizure by the police. Finally, we will analyze some other important rights of juveniles such as rights in school and rights at home.

THE LANDMARK SUPREME COURT CASES

Between the founding of the juvenile court in 1899 and the *Kent v. United States* case in 1966, the United States Supreme Court basically left the juvenile court alone. In other words, the Supreme Court respected the intentions of juvenile court officials to seek the best interests of the child by allowing juvenile court judges and related personnel a great deal of discretion in attempting to achieve those objectives. In the mid-1960s, however, the Supreme Court was confronted with several cases that indicated that such a hands-off approach was no longer appropriate.

Kent v. United States

In **Kent v. United States** (1966), the Supreme Court was faced with a waiver case appeal wherein a 16-year-old, Morris Kent, had been waived (transferred) to adult criminal court without a hearing, without the assistance of counsel, and without any statement of the reasons for the judge's decision to transfer the matter to the adult court. A judge had decided to transfer Kent, who had been charged with rape, simply on the basis of a review of the youth's social service and probation files. The judge did not allow Kent's privately retained attorney to review any of the files, nor did the judge conduct any hearing on the matter or state the reasons that convinced him to transfer the case. Thus, the waiver decision, a very critical decision that results in the possibility of an adult criminal record and adult penalties, had been made by the judge acting alone, without any concern for Morris Kent's rights.

The Supreme Court justices decided that due process of law entitles a defendant like Morris Kent to certain minimum safeguards, including a hearing, the right to the assistance of an attorney, and a statement of the reasons for transfer if the judge decides to transfer the case to adult court. The Supreme Court reasoned that the juvenile court judge denied

Kent his right to the assistance of an attorney. Without a hearing, Kent's attorney had no opportunity to represent the youth. The denial of the assistance of counsel, a Sixth Amendment right, was compounded by the judge's denial of access to the case files. That denial prevented the attorney from raising any challenges to possible errors in social service or probation staff reports about the defendant.

The *Kent* case is important not so much because it corrected the wrongs done to one individual or because it put some order into the waiver (transfer) procedure, but because it marks the Supreme Court's first major examination of juvenile court processing. This examination found serious shortcomings of both the particular juvenile court that had handled Morris Kent and of juvenile courts in general:

> While there can be no doubt of the original laudable purpose of juvenile courts, studies and critiques in recent years raise serious questions as to whether actual performance measures well enough against theoretical purpose to make tolerable the immunity of the process from the reach of constitutional guaranties applicable to adults. There is much evidence that some juvenile courts, including that of the District of Columbia, lack the personnel, facilities and techniques to perform adequately as representatives of the State in a *parens patriae* capacity, at least with respect to children charged with law violation. There is evidence, in fact, that there may be grounds for concern that the child receives the worst of both worlds: that he gets neither the protections accorded to adults nor the solicitous care and regenerative treatment postulated for children (*Kent v. United States*, 1966).

A final comment on the *Kent* case is that many states are now resorting to prosecutor direct file and statutory exclusion (see Chapter 8 for more details) instead of transfer or waiver to prosecute juveniles as adults in criminal courts. Reliance on these other methods means that the affected juveniles do not get the waiver hearing and protections that *Kent* was intended to guarantee.

In re Gault

The case of **In re Gault** was even more significant. Gerald Gault was a 15-year-old Arizona youth who was arrested for allegedly making obscene phone calls to an adult woman. He was adjudicated a delinquent in a court proceeding that resembled a kangaroo court or a dictatorial tribunal rather than a court of law and was sentenced to the state training school for a possible six-year sentence. The maximum penalty for an adult committing the exact same offense was a $50 fine and two months in jail.

Gault, after being accused, was taken into police custody and detained. Within about a week, he was adjudicated a delinquent and committed to the state training school until he was discharged or turned 21 years of age, whichever came first. All of this occurred without the complainant (the target of the obscene phone calls) ever appearing in court to testify, without any detailed and specific charges being filed (Gault was simply accused of being a "delinquent"), without the assistance of an attorney for Gault (his probation officer "represented" him), and without any transcript of the proceedings. The end result was the possibility of a six-year sentence for what was at worst a nuisance offense.

In reviewing the case, Supreme Court Justice Abe Fortas traced the history of the juvenile court and of the *parens patriae* philosophy and found some fundamental problems. Supposedly, due process guarantees such as the assistance of an attorney were to be relaxed in juvenile court so that youths would receive the treatment benefits promised by both the founders and current advocates of the juvenile court. Instead, as the Court observed in the *Kent* case, the child often received the worst of both worlds: lack of procedural fairness and substandard treatment.

Interestingly, the Supreme Court did not go on to discard the juvenile court philosophy of *parens patriae*. Instead, Justice Fortas observed that due process rights would not hinder juvenile court judges from seeking the best interests of the child but actually would assist them in that effort:

> But recent studies . . . suggest that the appearance as well as the actuality of fairness, impartiality, and orderliness—in short, the essentials of due process—may be a more impressive and more therapeutic attitude so far as the juvenile is concerned (*In re Gault*, 1967).

Judge Fortas went on to rule that juveniles do have certain due process rights in delinquency proceedings in which there is the possibility of confinement in a locked facility. Specifically, such juveniles have the Fifth Amendment privilege against self-incrimination (the right to remain silent) and Sixth Amendment rights to adequate notice of the charges against them, to confront and cross-examine their accusers, and to the assistance of counsel.

In re Winship

In 1970, the Supreme Court went a step further. In the case of **In re Winship**, an appeal of a New York case involving a 12-year-old boy who had stolen $112 from a woman's purse from a locker, the Supreme Court turned its attention to the issue of the standard of proof (how strong a case must be to prove delinquency) in juvenile court. The Court made two rulings. First, the Court ruled that the U.S. Constitution requires that adult criminals be convicted only by the standard of "guilty beyond a reasonable doubt" (the **reasonable doubt standard** of proof). This had been standard practice in adult courts; the Court simply stated that the Constitution mandated what the states had been doing all along. Second, the Court extended the reasonable doubt standard of proof to juvenile delinquency proceedings in which there was the possibility of commitment to a locked facility. As was the case in *In re Gault*, the Court reasoned that this safeguard of the reasonable doubt standard would not detract in any way from the noble intentions of the *parens patriae* philosophy. It also suggested that, rhetoric aside, juvenile training schools were the functional equivalents of adult prisons because both resulted in deprivation of liberty—and any such deprivation of liberty requires due process protections. Finally, the Supreme Court noted that New York State's standard of proof in juvenile proceedings (i.e., guilty by a preponderance of the evidence) was open to inaccurate findings. There was a real possibility that youths could be found delinquent when in fact there was insufficient evidence for such findings.

McKeiver v. Pennsylvania

A year later, in 1971, the Supreme Court took up the issue of a juvenile's right to a jury trial in the case of **McKeiver v. Pennsylvania**. In *McKeiver*, the Supreme Court declined to go so far in extending adult rights as to grant juveniles the right to trial by jury. The Supreme Court decided not to grant juveniles the right to jury trials for several reasons. First, the Court did not want to turn the juvenile court process into a fully adversarial process and end "the idealistic prospect of an intimate, informal protective proceeding" (*McKeiver v. Pennsylvania*, 1971). Second, the Court noted that because bench trials (trials decided by a judge rather than by a jury) for adults often result in accurate determinations of guilt, jury trials are not an absolute necessity for accurate determinations of delinquency. The Court also indicated that it was reluctant to impose a federal requirement of a jury trial because such a mandate could prevent individual states from experimenting with different methods. Finally, the Court noted that it had not reached such total disillusionment with the juvenile justice system to warrant abandoning it.

Barry Feld (1987) contends that the denial of the right of a jury trial to juveniles was an important decision because judges and juries view cases differently. The result of the denial of the right to a jury trial is that it is "easier to convict a youth appearing before a judge in juvenile court than to convict a youth, on the basis of the same evidence, before a jury of detached citizens in a criminal proceeding" (Feld, 1987:530). In other words, Feld believes that judges need less evidence to convict than do juries and that delinquents would fare better before juries.

These cases of *Kent*, *Gault*, *Winship*, and *McKeiver* constituted a philosophical revolution in juvenile court. Together, they forced juvenile courts to at least pay lip service to the notion that juveniles deserve many of the due process safeguards available to adults. Although the *McKeiver* case ruled against extending the right of trial by jury to juveniles, even this case indicated that the Supreme Court would not tolerate the wholesale denial of rights to juveniles. The *McKeiver* case implied that if accurate fact-finding were not available to juveniles, then the Supreme Court might have to impose additional limits on juvenile court discretion.

Still, it must be remembered that a philosophical revolution is not always a revolution in practice. Just because the Supreme Court has ruled that juveniles should be entitled to certain rights, such a pronouncement alone does not guarantee the actual provision of those rights. There is evidence that many children waive their right to counsel and that high caseloads prevent many lawyers representing juveniles from being effective (Miller-Wilson and Puritz, 2003; see also Feld, 1999). Thus, court practices and lack of resources can prevent juveniles from actually benefiting from Supreme Court rulings.

ADDITIONAL SUPREME COURT RULINGS

Since the landmark cases just discussed, the U.S. Supreme Court has decided several cases concerning delinquency proceedings in juvenile court.

Roper v. Simmons: A Ruling on the Death Penalty

In 2005, in *Roper v. Simmons*, the Supreme Court ruled that the death penalty is unconstitutional for juveniles. This case is discussed in detail in Chapter 14.

Breed v. Jones: A Ruling on Waiver

In **Breed v. Jones** (1975), the Court made the waiver process more explicit by ruling that states cannot first adjudicate a juvenile a delinquent and then waive or transfer the youth to adult court. The Court ruled that by doing this in a particular case, the state of California violated the youth's Sixth Amendment protection against double jeopardy (being tried twice for the same crime). The state of California had claimed that double jeopardy was not at issue because the juvenile was only punished once, but the Supreme Court ruled that being tried both in juvenile court and then again in adult court did indeed constitute a violation of the double jeopardy provision.

In a sense, the case of *Breed v. Jones* was not much of a victory for juvenile rights. Prior to the case, juveniles were tried in juvenile court, adjudicated delinquent, and then transferred to adult criminal court where they were tried as adults and sentenced. All that the U.S. Supreme Court ruling accomplished was a procedural change by which the juvenile court would now conduct a waiver or transfer hearing to determine if there was probable cause to believe that the juvenile committed the delinquent act. If the juvenile court finds probable cause and also determines that the juvenile is not amenable to juvenile system intervention (for example, the youth is getting too old for juvenile programs or has been in juvenile programs previously without much success), the juvenile court simply transfers the juvenile to the adult system without any final determination of the charge. A few years ago, one of the authors of this text observed such a waiver hearing, which equaled a full trial on the delinquency petition in every respect except that the judge declared a finding of "probable cause" rather than "delinquent" at the end of the hearing. The practical result of such waivers (transfers) to adult criminal court is the same as if the child had been adjudicated a delinquent. *Breed v. Jones* may be more a case of window dressing rather than an influential juvenile justice case.

Fare v. Michael C.: A Ruling on Interrogation

As noted above, two of the provisions of the *Gault* case were its explicit endorsements of the Fifth Amendment privilege against self-incrimination and the Sixth Amendment right to the assistance of counsel for juveniles. *Gault* applied to juvenile delinquency suspects the *Miranda* rights granted to adult criminal suspects. Like adults, juveniles may waive these two rights and consent to police interrogation without any attorney being present. A voluntary confession can then be used against the juvenile in court.

Gault left it unclear whether a juvenile could waive these so-called *Miranda* rights without first speaking with at least one parent or an attorney. The American Bar Association has gone so far as to recommend mandatory consultation with an attorney prior to any confession to the police (Institute of Judicial Administration–American Bar Association, 1982). Most states, however, simply stipulate that the police give *Miranda* warnings in language that is understandable to juveniles (see Holtz, 1987).

The Supreme Court clarified this issue in the case of **Fare v. Michael C.** (1979). In this case a juvenile murder

Ninth-grader Eric Hainstock is escorted out of a Sauk County (Wisconsin) courtroom in July 2007. Hainstock was charged with first-degree murder and tried as an adult for the shooting death of Weston Schools Principal John Klang.

suspect consented to an interrogation after he was denied the opportunity
to consult with his probation officer. The Court ruled that there is no
constitutional mandate to allow a suspect to speak with his or her probation officer. The rationale of the Court was that the Sixth Amendment
specifies the right to the assistance of counsel, while a probation officer
is basically on the side of the police in seeking to prosecute any juvenile
who has violated his probation. More importantly, the Court ruled that
the child can voluntarily waive his or her privilege against self-incrimination without first speaking to his or her parents and without first consulting an attorney. In such a situation the trial court judge must evaluate the
voluntariness of any confession based on the totality of the circumstances
rather than on any ironclad rule (called a *per se* rule) mandating the
police to bring in at least one parent or an attorney to advise the child
about the wisdom of waiving his or her rights. In evaluating the totality
of the circumstances of the waiver, the trial court must consider such factors as the age, maturity, experience, and intelligence of the youth. Thus,
judges might allow as admissible the waiver of rights by a 17-year-old
high school student with a prior record but probably not the waiver of
rights by a 13-year-old first offender of below-average intelligence.

It is important to note that there is some controversy about the
Supreme Court's wisdom in not requiring more explicit or extensive warnings for juvenile suspects prior to interrogation. First, some
research indicates that not all juveniles clearly understand their rights
when arrested (Huang, 2001). In one study, about one-third of a sample
of institutionalized delinquents thought (erroneously) that they were
required to talk to the police (Robin, 1982). Other research has indicated that more than one-half of the youths tested lacked full understanding of all the *Miranda* warnings, and only about one-fifth adequately
understood all of the warnings (Holtz, 1987:550; see also Grisso and
Schwartz, 2000). Recent neurobiological research confirms difficulties
for minors in understanding and asserting their *Miranda* rights (Juvenile
Law Center, 2004). Second, parents tend not to be the best protectors
of juvenile rights. One study showed that about one-third of the parents
would advise their own children to confess criminal involvement to the
police (Robin, 1982). Due to considerations such as these, some model
juvenile law codes stipulate that police must have juvenile suspects consult with an attorney prior to police interrogation (Institute of Judicial
Administration–American Bar Association, 1982).

Most states follow the "totality of the circumstances" approach outlined in the *Fare* case. A few states put in so-called *per se* rules requiring
that juveniles have the opportunity to confer with a parent, guardian,
attorney, or other interested adult. Unfortunately, a number of states
(Georgia, Louisiana, and Pennsylvania) overturned their *per se* rules
as part of the "get tough" movement (Huang, 2001). However, appellate courts in three states—Alaska, Minnesota, and Wisconsin—have

ordered that police electronically record all juvenile interrogations in order to assure the voluntariness of confessions and prevent police coercion (Ziemer, 2005). The Pennsylvania Supreme Court ruled that a juvenile can waive his or her right to counsel only after a judge questions the juvenile to determine if the juvenile understands the allegations and that a lawyer can be helpful (Burke, 2005).

In *Yarborough, Warden v. Alvarado* (2004), the U.S. Supreme Court ruled that age was not a factor in determining that a juvenile was not in custody for purposes of police questioning. The case involved a two-hour police interview of a 17-year-old murder suspect in a police station without giving the *Miranda* warnings or allowing the boy's parents to be present in the interview room. Based on his statements to the police, the youth was convicted of murder. The court ruled that the lower court made a correct ruling on the noncustodial status of Alvarado based on objective factors such as: (1) the police did not transport the juvenile to the station; (2) his parents were in the lobby, and (3) at the end of the interview the youth went home. The dissent argued, among other factors, that age is an objective factor that the police and courts should consider in determining custody status.

Schall v. Martin: A Ruling on Preventive Detention

In **Schall v. Martin** (1984), the U.S. Supreme Court ruled that a juvenile who is awaiting court action can be held in **preventive detention** if there is adequate concern that the juvenile would commit additional crimes while the primary case is pending further court action. The juvenile, however, does have the right to a hearing on the preventive detention decision and a statement of the reasons for which he or she is being detained. The Court justified its decision on the basis that every state permits such preventive detention for juveniles and on the rationale that such detention protects "both the juvenile and society from the hazards of pretrial crime" (*Schall v. Martin*, 1984). Furthermore, the Court majority reasoned that "juveniles, unlike adults, are always in some form of custody" (*Schall v. Martin*, 1984). The three dissenting justices, on the other hand, noted the impossibility of predicting which juveniles will engage in future crime (this is often labeled the false positive issue) and considered the punitive nature of many detention facilities.

SEARCH AND SEIZURE

Consideration of these landmark U.S. Supreme Court cases demonstrates that juveniles do indeed have basic rights at important stages of the juvenile justice process, especially the waiver (transfer) hearing and the adjudication (trial) stage. Very important are the Fourth Amendment rights of juveniles during investigation or arrest.

The issue of **search and seizure** is a complex one involving a myriad of U.S. Supreme Court interpretations of the Fourth Amendment. This amendment reads:

> The right of the people to be secure in their persons, houses, papers, and effects, against unreasonable searches and seizures, shall not be violated, and no Warrants shall issue, but upon probable cause, supported by Oath or affirmation, and particularly describing the place to be searched, and the persons or things to be seized.

The Fourth Amendment indicates a preference for warrants before the police can search or arrest suspects, but this preference for warrants is riddled with numerous exceptions. This is not the place to describe those exceptions (but see, for example, O'Brien, 1997). Here it is important to examine one question that does affect juveniles: the **consent search** in which a defendant voluntarily allows the police to search someone or one's effects without a search warrant. Since *Schneckloth v. Bustamonte* (1973), the U.S. Supreme Court's ruling on adult consent searches has been that the police may simply ask a person for consent to search the person or his or her house, car, or effects. Unlike the *Miranda* situation, in which the police must advise a person of the right to refuse interrogation, the police do not have to specifically advise an adult suspect that he or she has the right to refuse a search. The police may simply ask an adult, "Do you mind if we take a look around your house?" If the person agrees, then—aware of it or not—the individual has agreed to a consent search. This would be a reasonable search in terms of Fourth Amendment guarantees.

In the case of juveniles, the issue arises whether a juvenile is mature enough to withstand police pressure and intelligent enough to understand his or her rights. The American Bar Association has recommended that juveniles be advised of their right to refuse a consent search and that they also be advised of the opportunity to consult an attorney (Institute of Judicial Administration–American Bar Association, 1982). The ABA felt that these two safeguards would compensate for any youthful susceptibility to police coercion and any lack of sophistication needed to understand fully one's rights. Another set of standards, the American Law Institute Model Code of Pre-arraignment Procedure, stipulates that if a person about to be asked to consent to a search is under 16 years of age, then a parent should be the one who gives consent. The Model Code further advocates that in any consent search situation involving juveniles or adults, the police should advise the individual that he or she "is under no obligation to give such consent and that anything found may be taken and used in evidence" (Wadlington, Whitebread, and

Davis, 1983:301). In other words, the Model Code drafters advocated warnings for consent searches that were similar to the *Miranda* warnings used in interrogation situations. They felt that it should not be assumed that juvenile offenders are aware of their right to refuse a consent search without a clear warning of their right to do so.

A recent Supreme Court case suggests that today's courts are probably inclined to rule on the side of law enforcement rather than to extend offender rights. In *United States v. Mark James Knights* (2002), the Court ruled that a warrantless search of a probationer, supported by reasonable suspicion and authorized by a probation condition, satisfied the Fourth Amendment. This follows *In re Tyrell* (1994), in which a California court ruled that a search of a juvenile on probation (which found marijuana in his pants) did not violate the Fourth Amendment. Police made a patdown search of the youth when they saw a knife on one of two other youths with him. Even though the police did not have probable cause to conduct the search and even though the youth did not consent to the search, the Court felt the police did not violate the juvenile's expectation of privacy because the boy had been placed on probation, which stipulated the condition that he submit to searches by police, probation officers, or school officials. This probation condition erased any reasonable expectation of privacy (*Juvenile Justice Update*, 1995).

RIGHTS IN SCHOOL

Because juveniles spend much of their time in school, many questions about juvenile rights have arisen within the context of school policies and procedures.

Corporal Punishment

In *Ingraham v. Wright*, the U.S. Supreme Court ruled that **corporal punishment** (e.g., paddling) of students is permissible so long as it is reasonable. The reasonableness decision depends on

> the seriousness of the offense, the attitude and past behavior of the child, the nature and severity of the punishment, the age and strength of the child, and the availability of less severe but equally effective means of discipline (*Ingraham v. Wright*, 1977).

The Court noted that corporal punishment could be abused, but observed that common law remedies were effective deterrents to any such abuse of the practice. The Court reasoned that students and their parents could sue school officials or charge them with criminal assault if they went too far in paddling any particular student.

As is often the case, dissenting opinions in Supreme Court cases raise very interesting issues. In fact, dissents sometimes are more note-worthy than the majority or plurality opinions of the Justices. Box 9.1 presents excerpts from the dissenting opinion of Justice White in the case of *Ingraham v. Wright*. These show that there are other sides to the issue of the constitutionality of corporal punishment in schools. The American Bar Association has followed Justice White's dissent and has recommended that "[c]orporal punishment should not be inflicted upon a student. . . ." (Institute for Judicial Administration–American Bar Association, 1982:136). Finally, a review of the research on cor-poral punishment concluded that it should be banned because children who receive corporal punishment are more prone as adults to various deviant acts. Among the later problems are depression, suicide, physical abuse of children and spouses, commission of violent crime, drinking problems, attraction to masochistic sex, and problems attaining a pres-tigious occupation (Straus, 1994).

In a recent Ninth Circuit case, the judges ruled that "no reasonable principal could think it constitutional to intentionally punch, slap, grab, and slam students into lockers" (*P.B. v. Koch*, 1996). (For a note on excessive discipline in schools, see Box 9.2.)

BOX 9.1

Excerpts from Justice White's Dissent in *Ingraham v. Wright*

If there are some punishments that are so barbaric that they may not be imposed for the commission of crimes, designated by our social system as the most thoroughly reprehensible acts an individual can commit, then, *a fortiori*, similar punishments may not be imposed on persons for less cul-pable acts, such as breaches of school discipline. Thus, if it is constitution-ally impermissible to cut off someone's ear for the commission of murder, it must be unconstitutional to cut off a child's ear for being late to class. Although there were no ears cut off in this case, the record reveals beatings so severe that if they were inflicted on a hardened criminal for the commis-sion of a serious crime, they might not pass constitutional muster.

. . .

The essence of the majority's argument is that school children do not need Eighth Amendment protection because corporal punishment is less subject to abuse in the public schools than it is in the prison system. How-

BOX 9.1 *continued*

ever, it cannot be reasonably suggested that just because cruel and unusual punishments may occur less frequently under public scrutiny, they will not occur at all. The mere fact that a public flogging or a public execution would be available for all to see would not render the punishment constitutional if it were otherwise impermissible. Similarly, the majority would not suggest that a prisoner who is placed in a minimum-security prison and permitted to go home to his family on the weekends should be any less entitled to Eighth Amendment protections than his counterpart in a maximum-security prison. In short, if a punishment is so barbaric and inhumane that it goes beyond the tolerance of a civilized society, its openess to public scrutiny should have nothing to do with its constitutionality.

. . .

By holding that the Eighth Amendment protects only criminals, the majority adopts the view that one is entitled to the protections afforded by the Eighth Amendment only if he is punished for acts that are sufficiently opprobrious for society to make them "criminal." This is a curious holding in view of the fact that the more culpable the offender the more likely it is that the punishment will not be disproportionate to the offense, consequently, the less likely it is that the punishment will be cruel and unusual. Conversely, a public school student who is spanked for a mere breach of discipline may sometimes have a strong argument that the punishment does not fit the offense, depending upon the severity of the beating, and therefore that it is cruel and unusual. Yet the majority would afford the student no protection no matter how inhumane and barbaric the punishment inflicted on him might be.

. . .

This tort action [student lawsuits against teachers who abuse corporal punishment] is utterly inadequate to protect against erroneous infliction of punishment for two reasons. First, under Florida law, a student punished for an act he did not commit cannot recover damages from a teacher "proceeding in utmost good faith . . . on the reports and advice of others"; the student has no remedy at all for punishment imposed on the basis of mistaken facts, at least as long as the punishment was reasonable from the point of view of the disciplinarian, uninformed by any prior hearing. The "traditional common-law remedies" on which the majority relies, thus do nothing to protect the student from the danger that concerned the Court in *Goss* [*v. Lopez*]—the risk of reasonable, good-faith mistakes in the school disciplinary process (*Ingraham v. Wright*, 1977).

BOX 9.2

Excessive Discipline/Cruel and Unusual Punishment

Cruel and unusual punishment is an issue in prisons. The parallel issue in schools is excessive discipline. For example, recently a teacher ordered a 10-year-old student to clean a toilet. She had mistakenly concluded that the student intentionally put too much toilet paper in the toilet in order to clog the toilet. She made the boy put his hands in the toilet and pull out the paper. He washed his hands and returned to class.

The case made it to the Tenth Circuit. Judges used the "shock the conscience" test. The judges concluded that the teacher had not acted with malice and so her actions were not deliberate, conscience-shocking actions.

The general lesson from cases such as this is that appeals courts use the standard of shock the conscience. But they interpret

> a very high threshold, and that school personnel's conduct must truly be outrageous. Finally, it is of considerable import that both courts focused primarily on the intent of the school personnel to do harm. Therefore, it is important to ask the question: What inspired the school personnel's action? Unless it was malice or sadism or the injury is substantially severe, there is a strong likelihood the school and its personnel will prevail (Colwell, 2002:3).

What do you think? Did this teacher's actions "shock the conscience"? If not, what would she have to do to shock the conscience?

Source: B. Colwell (2002). "Shocking the Conscience: Excessive Discipline of Elementary and Secondary Students." *School Law Reporter* 44(1):1-3.

Freedom of Speech for Students

Another school rights issue is the First Amendment right to **freedom of speech**. Here the U.S. Supreme Court has upheld the basic principle that students have at least some degree of constitutional protection in that they do not "shed their constitutional rights to freedom of speech or expression at the schoolhouse gate" (*Tinker v. Des Moines Independent Community School District*, 1969). This does not mean that students can say or express anything they wish in whatever manner they wish. What it means is that the right of free speech is to be balanced with the school's interest in education and discipline. Students are entitled to express themselves as long as their expression does not materially and substantially interfere with school discipline or the educational process.

In the *Tinker* case, for example, at issue was the wearing of black armbands by students to protest United States involvement in the Vietnam conflict. The students doing so were suspended and sent home. When the case reached the U.S. Supreme Court, the majority of the justices ruled that the students' First Amendment rights had been violated, noting that the students had expressed themselves without creating any disturbance or interfering with school discipline. Furthermore, the school system had been inconsistent in that it had allowed some students to wear political campaign buttons and others to wear the traditional symbol of Nazism (the swastika). Writing for the majority, Justice Fortas took serious issue with school system prohibition of student expression of only one particular type:

> In our system, state-operated schools may not be enclaves of totalitarianism. School officials do not possess absolute authority over their students. Students in school as well as out of school are "persons" under our Constitution. They are possessed of fundamental rights which the State must respect, just as they themselves must respect their obligations to the State. In our system, students may not be regarded as closed-circuit recipients of only that which the State chooses to communicate. They may not be confined to the expression of those sentiments that are officially approved. In the absence of a specific showing of constitutionally valid reasons to regulate their speech, students are entitled to freedom of expression of their views. . . . (*Tinker v. Des Moines Independent Community School District*, 1969).

This case can be misinterpreted as an outstanding victory for children's rights if some cautions are not noted. First, the Court was probably more concerned with the issue of free speech in general rather than with free speech for children. That is, the ruling in favor of the pupils can probably be traced to the Supreme Court's "long tradition of zealous protection of First Amendment rights" (Davis and Schwartz, 1987:58). Second, the case may be interpreted not so much as a children's rights case as a parents' rights case, because the children in this case shared the same views as their parents on governmental involvement in Vietnam (Davis and Schwartz, 1987). If the views of the students and their parents had not been the same, the ruling may have been otherwise. Finally, the case distinguished between passive expression and disruptive expression of views. Passive speech (for example, wearing armbands) is less disruptive than disturbances or other types of expression. The Court is more likely to uphold such passive speech than more rowdy forms of speech. (For a case about free speech by students on the World Wide Web, see Box 9.3.)

In other First Amendment cases, the Supreme Court has addressed the issue of whether school officials can discipline a student for giving a lascivious speech and who holds editorial control over student publications. In *Bethel School District Number 403 v. Fraser* (1986), the Court

BOX 9.3

Free Speech in Schools: Posting a Web Site

A Pennsylvania middle school student created a web site that had negative comments and pictures about his algebra teacher and school principal. Pictures on the site showed the teacher's head dripping with blood and her face changing into Adolf Hitler. The site also offered money for a hit man to kill the teacher.

In a unanimous decision, the Pennsylvania Supreme Court ruled that school officials could punish the student because the web site created a substantial disruption of school activities. The Court reasoned that there was a nexus between the web site and the school so that the speech could be considered as occurring on-campus. Following the *Fraser* and *Tinker* cases (see text), the Court concluded that "the web site created disorder and significantly and adversely impacted the delivery of instruction" (see http://www.firstamendmentschools.org).

What do you think? Does the school have the legal authority to punish a student for the contents of a web site that the student creates in his or her own home? Should a student be able to create a web site and put highly negative content about teachers on that web site? Should a student be able to devise a web site that criticizes the teaching ability of his or her teachers but does not go so far as to compare the teachers to Hitler or mention anything such as hiring a hit man? What are the limits of free speech for students on web sites?

addressed the issue of "whether the First Amendment prevents a school district from disciplining a high school student for giving a lewd speech at a school assembly." Matthew Fraser nominated a fellow student for a student office by using "an elaborate, graphic, and sexual metaphor." His obscene language violated a school rule, so he was suspended from school for two days. Both the District Court and the Court of Appeals ruled that the school had violated Fraser's First Amendment right to free speech. They reasoned that the speech was basically the same sort of action as the wearing of the protest armbands in the *Tinker* case. The U.S. Supreme Court, however, reversed the lower courts' decision and determined that the school does have a right to ban sexually explicit language, even if it is couched within a political speech, because it is counter to the basic educational mission of the school (see Box 9.4). The Court also limited the degree of freedom students have in expressing themselves in student publications, again pointing out the educational mission of the schools for justification (see Box 9.5).

BOX 9.4

Lewd Speeches in School

In *Bethel School District Number 403 v. Fraser* (1986), the U.S. Supreme Court argued that students do not have an absolute right to free speech under the First Amendment. They refused to equate lewd language given as part of a political statement with the wearing of protest armbands in the *Tinker* case. The justices distinguished the *Fraser* case from *Tinker* in that in the *Tinker* case the speech involved political expression and therefore it merited greater protection whereas

> the penalties imposed in this case were unrelated to any political viewpoint. The First Amendment does not prevent the school officials from determining that to permit a vulgar and lewd speech such as respondent's would undermine the school's basic educational mission. A high school assembly or classroom is no place for a sexually explicit monologue directed towards an unsuspecting audience of teenage students. Accordingly, it was perfectly appropriate for the school to disassociate itself to make the point to the pupils that vulgar speech and lewd conduct is wholly inconsistent with the "fundamental values" of public education (*Bethel School District Number 403 v. Fraser*, 1986).

Further, the Court noted that schools play an important role in preparing students for adult citizenship:

> The process of educating our youth for citizenship in public schools is not confined to books, the curriculum, and the civics class; schools must teach by example the shared values of a civilized social order. Consciously or otherwise, teachers—and indeed the older students—demonstrate the appropriate form of civil discourse and political expression by their conduct and deportment in and out of class. Inescapably, like parents, they are role models. The schools, as instruments of the state, may determine that the essential lessons of civil, mature conduct cannot be conveyed in a school that tolerates lewd, indecent, or offensive speech and conduct such as that indulged in by this confused boy.

> The pervasive sexual innuendo in Fraser's speech was plainly offensive to both teachers and students—indeed to any mature person. By glorifying male sexuality, and in its verbal content, the speech was acutely insulting to teenage girl students. The speech could well be seriously damaging to its less mature audience, many of whom were only 14 years old and on the threshold of awareness of human sexuality. Some students were reported as bewildered by the speech and the reaction of mimicry it provoked (*Bethel School District Number 403 v. Fraser*, 1986).

BOX 9.5

Censorship of Student Publications

In an important First Amendment school case, the Supreme Court ruled that school officials can exercise broad editorial control over student publications:

> Instead, we hold that educators do not offend the First Amendment by exercising editorial control over the style and content of student speech in school-sponsored expressive activities so long as their actions are reasonably related to legitimate pedagogical concerns (*Hazelwood School District v. Kuhlmeier*, 1988).

The case invovled a principal's censorship of a high school newspaper. The principal prevented publication of an article describing three students' experiences during pregnancy and of another article describing student reactions to parental divorce. Writing for the majority, Justice White distinguished the *Tinker* case type of speech as "a student's personal expression that happens to occur on the school premises" from "school-sponsored publications, theatrical productions, and other expressive activities" that are "part of the school curriculum" and "are supervised by faculty members and designed to impart particular knowledge or skills" (*Hazelwood School District v. Kuhlmeier*, 1988). For educational reasons, schools have "greater control" over the latter type of speech.

In his dissent Justice Brennan castigated the majority viewpoint as approving "thought police" and the violation of "the First Amendment's prohibitions against censorship of any student expression that neither disrupts classwork nor invades the rights of others, and against any censorship that is not narrowly tailored to serve its purpose" (*Hazelwood School District v. Kuhlmeier*, 1988). Justice Brennan concluded that "[t]he mere fact of school sponsorship does not . . . license such thought control in the high school, whether through school suppression of disfavored viewpoints or through official assessment of topic sensitivity. . . ." (*Hazelwood School District v. Kuhlmeier*, 1988).

In November of 1995, the U.S. Supreme Court declined to hear a case (denied certiorari) involving the right of a Tennessee junior high school teacher to refuse a research paper on the life of Jesus. In 1991, Brittany Settle, a junior high school student in Dickson County, submitted an outline on the life of Jesus for her research paper assignment. The original assignment noted that the topic must be "interesting, researchable, and decent." The teacher rejected Brittany's outline because, among other factors, she failed to get permission for the topic, the teacher thought that Brittany's strong belief would interfere with objectivity in a research assignment, and the assignment required four sources but Brittany used only one source: the Bible. In the U.S. District Court case, Brittany relied on *Tinker* for the right of free speech. The Court, however, relied on *Hazelwood School District v. Kuhlmeier*:

> The free speech rights of students in the classroom must be limited because effective education depends not only on controlling boisterous conduct, but also on maintaining the focus of the class on the assignment in question . . . Teachers therefore must be given broad discretion to give grades and conduct class discussion based on the content of speech. . . . *Settle v. Dickson County Sch. Bd.*, 1995).

Two additional areas in which freedom of speech in schools has been questioned involve compulsory community service and school prayer. At first glance, the issue of compulsory community service would not appear to be a First Amendment issue. With the advent of programs that require service for high school graduation in several places (such as Dodge City, Kansas; Boston; and the state of Maryland), opponents have argued that such service forces a student to engage in "expressive conduct." That is, the activity serves as an expression of support for the agency receiving the service. For example, a student might object that doing community service at the Girl Scouts sends the message that the student believes in what the Girl Scouts organization represents. This issue was argued in *Steirer v. Bethlehem Area School District* (1994). On appeal the Supreme Court denied certiorari (i.e., the Court declined to consider the case, letting the lower court ruling stand). The Court stated that there was no First Amendment free speech issue because expressive conduct was not clearly at stake. The Court noted that engaging in community service is not the same thing as wearing a black armband or burning a draft card, acts that clearly do express a viewpoint. Despite this ruling, Charters (1994) argues that community service can be seen as fostering an ideological viewpoint and that "students have no civic duty to perform acts of altruism and self-sacrifice the omission of which would justify a school district's withholding a student's diploma" (Charters, 1994:613).

School prayer has become a topic of much debate in recent years. The key to the debate is the issue of whether school prayer represents the promotion of religion by the school. The Supreme Court, in *Lee v. Weisman* (1992), ruled that school officials erred in providing guidelines and permitting prayer at a high school graduation ceremony. However, the U.S. Fifth Circuit Court upheld the right of students to plan and lead prayer at school functions (*Jones v. Clear Creek Independent School District*, 1992). The degree to which prayer in school will be permitted has yet to be determined. Box 9.6 provides some insight into this issue.

BOX 9.6

Prayer at Graduation and at Football Games

"God of the Free, Hope of the Brave:

For the legacy of America where diversity is celebrated and the rights of minorities are protected, we thank You. May these young men and women grow up to enrich it.

For the liberty of America, we thank You. May these new graduates grow up to guard it.

For the political process of America in which all its citizens may participate, for its court system where all may seek justice we thank You. May those we honor this morning always turn to it in trust.

For the destiny of America we thank You. May the graduates of Nathan Bishop Middle School so live that they might help to share it.

May our aspirations for our country and for these young people, who are our hope for the future, be richly fulfilled.

Lee v. Weisman 112 S.Ct. 2649 (1992) at 2652-2653.

A rabbi gave this invocation at graduation for a middle school and a high school in Providence (Rhode Island) in June of 1989. The middle school principal had given the rabbi a guideline for nonsectarian prayers at civic ceremonies and recommended that the invocation and benediction be nonsectarian. The father of one of the students unsuccessfully attempted to get a restraining order prohibiting any invocation or benediction. The District Court held that the actions of the school violated the Establishment Clause of the First Amendment banning governmental advancement of religion. The United States Court of Appeals for the First Circuit affirmed the judgment of the District Court. The case was then appealed to the Supreme Court.

Judge Kennedy's opinion for the court affirmed the lower court decision against the school's actions. Justice Kennedy was concerned about the principal's participation in the composition of the prayer: ". . . our precedents do not permit school officials to assist in composing prayers as an incident to a formal exercise for their students" (at 2657). He was also concerned "with protecting freedom of conscience from subtle coercive pressure in the elementary and secondary public schools" (at 2658). He distinguished a graduation ceremony from prayer at the opening of a legislative session "where adults are free to enter and leave with little comment" (at 2660). He concluded that "the prayer exercises in this case are especially improper because the State has in every practical sense compelled attendance and participation in an explicit religious exercise at an event of singular importance to every student, one the objecting student had no real alternative to avoid" (at 2661). Thus, "the State, in a school setting, in effect required participation in a religious exercise" (at 2659).

Writing for the dissent, Justice Scalia argued that standing silently during a prayer does not automatically imply that the person is joining in the prayer but

BOX 9.6 *continued*

may simply signify "respect for the prayers of others" (at 2682). Justice Scalia ridiculed the argument of subtle coercion, noting that the opinion treats students "as though they were first-graders" instead of individuals "old enough to vote" (at 2682). Theoretically, Justice Scalia lambasted the decision as "the bulldozer of its social engineering" for ignoring historical precedent and laying "waste a tradition that is as old as public-school graduation ceremonies themselves, and that is a component of an even more longstanding American tradition of nonsectarian prayer to God at public celebrations generally" (at 2679). Justice Scalia's reading of history showed that the "history and tradition of our Nation are replete with public ceremonies featuring prayers of thansgiving and petition" (at 2679).

Shortly after the Supreme Court decision, the Fifth Circuit Court ruled that a graduation prayer did not violate the First Amendment because students voted on the prayer, participation was voluntary, and students themselves, rather than a religious official, led the prayer (*Jones v. Clear Creek Independent School District*, 977 F.2d 963 [5th Cir. 1992]). Shortly thereafter, several state legislatures introduced bills authorizing student-initiated prayer in the schools (Rossow and Parkinson, 1994a). In the spring of 1994 Congress passed an education act that would prevent funds from going to schools adopting "policies designed to prevent students from engaging in constitutionally protected prayer or silent reflection" (cited in Underwood, 1994:1040).

Similarly, the Santa Fe School District allowed a student to deliver a "nonsectarian, nonproselytizing" prayer over the public address system before each football game.

Writing for the majority in *Santa Fe Independent School District v. Doe* (2000), Justice Stevens noted that the invocations were authorized by a government policy and took place on government property at a government-sponsored event. In addition, the process of selecting the student to deliver the invocation focused on the majority and denied voicing of minority voices. Justice Stevens ruled that the invocation policy and practice was unconstitutional because

> the realities of the situation plainly reveal that its policy involves both perceived and actual endorsement of religion. In this case, as we found in Lee, the "degree of school involvement" makes it clear that the pregame prayers bear "the imprint of the Sate" and thus put school-age children who objected in an untenable position (at 590).

What do you think? Should prayers such as the one above be permitted at graduation ceremonies? Is such a prayer at graduation improper governmental intrusion into religion? If you were an atheist or a member of a non-mainstream religion, how would you feel during a nonsectarian invocation before a football game? Would it make a difference if each week different students—atheists, Buddhists, Hindus, and so forth—got up to deliver these invocations?

In May of 1997, the United States Court of Appeals for the Eleventh Circuit affirmed the decision of a federal district court that upheld a 1994 Georgia statute authorizing a "moment of quiet reflection" to begin the school day. The statute noted that this moment of quiet reflection "shall not be conducted as a religious service or exercise but shall be considered as an opportunity for a moment of silent reflection on the anticipated activities of the day" (O.C.G.A 20-2-1050, 1996). The judges noted that there was no coercion in the statute:

> All that students must do under this Act is remain silent for 60 seconds; they are not encouraged to pray or forced to remain silent while listening to others' prayers (*Brown v. Gwinnett County School District*, p. 1473).

The court also noted that there was no endorsement of religion in the law and no authorization of any prayer. (For a recent Supreme Court ruling on permitting a religious club to conduct meetings on school premises after school hours, see Box 9.7.)

In 2003 the Secretary of Education issued a directive about constitutionally protected prayer in public elementary and secondary schools (available at http://www.ed.gov/policy/gen/guid/religionandschools/prayer_guidance.html). The guidelines address such issues as prayer during noninstructional time, moments of silence, graduation ceremonies, and organized prayer groups. For example, the directive noted that if a school has a "minute of silence" or other quiet times during the school day, then "[t]eachers and other school employees may neither encourage nor discourage students from praying during such time periods" (p. 4 of Directive). Education law attorneys warn that schools should not follow the guidelines blindly because the guidelines are not necessarily an accurate rendering of case law (Colwell, 2003). Opinion poll research, however, shows that the overwhelming majority of students favor at least some form of prayer being allowed in schools, especially a moment of silence but not necessarily a prayer that mentions Jesus Christ (Ott, 2005).

Student Searches

Another issue involving students is the right of school officials to conduct searches of students versus the students' right of privacy. This issue was highlighted in the Supreme Court case of **New Jersey v. T.L.O.** (1985), which involved the search of a student's purse by an assistant vice principal based on a teacher's suspicion that the student had been smoking in the lavatory in violation of school rules. The Court ruled that such a **student search** was legitimate if it was reasonable in its justification and its extent. By this, the Court meant that:

BOX 9.7

Is the Good News Club Good for School?

The Milford Central School allowed the Good News Club, a private Christian organization for children ages six to 12, to hold weekly meetings in the school cafeteria after school. The club sang songs, heard Bible lessons, memorized scripture, and prayed.

Proponents claimed the First Amendment right of free speech. Opponents were concerned about a violation of the Establishment Clause versus the separation of church and state.

The majority concluded that in denying the club the right to meet, the school board denied the Good News Club its right to free speech. Justice Thomas saw this as viewpoint discrimination and argued that no Establishment Clause interpretation justified that restriction. Justice Thomas wrote that there was no indication that the school board was endorsing religion or creed. Justice Thomas saw the club as similar to organizations like the Boy Scouts that rely on "the invocation of teamwork, loyalty, or patriotism . . . to provide a foundation for their lessons" (*Good News Club v. Milford Central School*, 533 U.S. 98 [2001]).

In their dissent Justices Souter and Ginsberg cited a sample lesson about how "the Bible tells us how we can have our sins forgiven by receiving the Lord Jesus Christ"and "to trust the Lord Jesus to be your savior from sin." Such content led the dissenting Justices to conclude that:

> It is beyond question that Good News intends to use the public school premises not for the mere discussion of subjects from a particular, Christian point of view, but for an evangelical service of worship calling children to commit themselves in an act of Christian conversion.

What do you think? Should religious clubs be allowed to meet on school premises after school hours? Is a club that invites children "to trust the Lord Jesus to be your savior from sin" simply another club that fosters "teamwork" and "loyalty" (in Justice Thomas's terminology)? Or, in the words of the dissent, does opening the school for the Good News Club in effect open the school "for use as a church, synagogue, or mosque"?

According to the Gallup Poll, 72 percent of Americans favor allowing the use of school facilities for religious groups, 66 percent favor daily prayer in the classroom, and 80 percent favor graduation speech prayers (Saad, 2001).

Should students be allowed to hold religious group meetings on school premises?

> Under ordinary circumstances, a search of a student by a
> teacher or other school official will be "justified at its incep-
> tion" when there are reasonable grounds for suspecting that the
> search will turn up evidence that the student has violated or is
> violating either the law or the rules of the school. Such a search
> will be permissible in its scope when the measures adopted are
> reasonably related to the objectives of the search and not exces-
> sively intrusive in light of the age and sex of the student and the
> nature of the infraction (*New Jersey v. T.L.O.*, 1985).

It is important to realize that the Supreme Court explicitly noted that
it was not ruling about a student's right to privacy in lockers or desks,
about whether it would make a difference if the school was acting in
cooperation with or at the suggestion of a police department, or about
whether "individualized suspicion" is such an essential element of the
reasonableness standard for school searches so as to preclude general
searches of students or lockers (*New Jersey v. T.L.O.*, 1985). Thus, the
U.S. Supreme Court left open many of the troubling issues surrounding
searches on school premises, but it did grant school officials considerable latitude to conduct warrantless searches of students. It gave school
officials greater authority to search students than other governmental
officials have to search adults. In the case of *New Jersey v. T.L.O.*, Justices Brennan and Marshall concurred in part but also dissented in part.
Box 9.8 indicates some of their concerns about the majority opinion.

A 1981 action of the Supreme Court sheds additional light on the
Court's attitude toward student searches. Specifically, the Court (*Doe v.
Renfrow*, 1981) that year refused to consider an Indiana case in which
school officials and police used dogs to sniff students and their possessions for marijuana, searched pockets and purses, and even went so far
as to conduct nude body searches of a few students. By refusing to hear
the case, the Supreme Court let stand the lower court ruling that the
school could use a canine team to conduct a general search of classrooms
and could legally search pockets and purses, but went too far in requiring nude body searches (*Doe v. Renfrow*, 1981).

Since the Supreme Court ruling in *New Jersey v. T.L.O.*, two Circuit Court decisions have ruled that strip searches are constitutional. In
one of those cases, a 16-year-old student was strip-searched for drugs
suspected to be hidden in his crotch area (none were found). The Seventh Circuit Court found no violation of *T.L.O.* (*Cornfield by Lewis
v. Consolidated High School District No. 230*, 1993). Two observers
conclude that the courts are trying to assist schools in combating drugs
and violence in our country's schools by authorizing strip searches.
These commentators are fearful that the courts may be taking the wrong
approach: "unfortunately, students appear to be paying the price with
the loss of their privacy and, apparently now, their clothes" (Rossow
and Parkinson, 1994b:1).

BOX 9.8

Excerpts from the Brennan–Marshall Partial Concurrence–Partial Dissent in *New Jersey v. T.L.O.*

In this case, Mr. Choplick [the assistant vice-principal who conducted the search] overreacted to what appeared to be nothing more than a minor infraction—a rule prohibiting smoking in the bathroom of the freshmen's and sophomores' building. It is, of course, true that he actually found evidence of serious wrongdoing by T.L.O., but no one claims that the prior search may be justified by his unexpected discovery. As far as the smoking infraction is concerned, the search for cigarettes merely tended to corroborate a teacher's eyewitness account of T.L.O.'s violation of a minor regulation designed to channel student smoking behavior into designated locations. Because this conduct was neither unlawful nor significantly disruptive of school order or the educational process, the invasion of privacy associated with the forcible opening of T.L.O.'s purse was entirely unjustified at its inception.

. . .

The schoolroom is the first opportunity most citizens have to experience the power of government. Through it passes every citizen and public official, from schoolteachers to policemen and prison guards. The values they learn there, they take with them in life. One of our most cherished ideals is the one contained in the Fourth Amendment: that the Government may not intrude on the personal privacy of its citizens without a warrant or compelling circumstance. The Court's decision today is a curious moral for the Nation's youth. Although the search of T.L.O.'s purse does not trouble today's majority, I submit that we are not dealing with "matters relatively trivial to the welfare of the Nation. There are village tyrants as well as village Hampdens, but none who acts under color of law is beyond the reach of the Constitution. . . ." (*New Jersey v. T.L.O.*, 1985).

The stretching of the right to search students has continued to advance. In 1995 the Supreme Court ruled that public schools could make student athletes undergo random drug testing as a condition for playing on school sports teams (*Vernonia School District v. Acton*, 1995). In *Todd v. Rush County Schools* (1998), the Seventh Circuit relied on *Vernonia* to uphold the actions of an Indiana school district that required students to undergo random, unannounced drug tests (urinalysis) before participating in any extracurricular programs or being able to drive to and from school. In a November 1997 case, the U.S. Court of Appeals for the Seventh Circuit upheld a "medical assessment" of a high school student suspected of having smoked marijuana. The "assessment" involved a school nurse taking the student's blood pressure and pulse. In 1996, the Eighth Circuit upheld a search of all male sixth through twelfth graders. The students had to remove their jackets, shoes, and socks; empty their pockets; and be given a metal detector test after a school bus driver informed the principal that there were fresh cuts on the seats of her bus (*Thompson v. Carthage School District*, 1996). Rossow and Parkinson (1994b) argued that this decision would be welcomed by schools using metal detectors at school entrances.

In *Board of Education of Independent School District No. 92 of Pottawatomie County et al. v. Lindsay Earls et al.* (2002), the Supreme Court ruled that random drug tests of students participating in extracurricular activities such as band or Future Farmers of America are not a violation of the Fourth Amendment. The court noted that schools were concerned about the health risks to students from drug use and made note of the voluntary character of participation in such extracurricular activities. Dissenting Justice Ginsburg, however, argued that such drug testing violates the reasonable subjective expectation of privacy that students have about being forced to submit to urine tests. Justice Ginsburg also noted that participation in extracurricular activities is not completely voluntary but rather "a key component of school life, essential in reality for students applying to college, and, for all participants, a significant contributor to the breadth and quality of the educational experience" (*Board of Education of Independent School District No. 92 of Pottawatomie County et al. v. Lindsay Earls et al.*, 2002).

RIGHTS AT HOME AND IN THE COMMUNITY

Not all questions of juvenile rights have emerged in the context of school. Several issues and cases arise in the home and community.

The Constitutionality of Curfews

Curfew laws have mushroomed in the United States. Cities have enacted curfews to decrease juvenile crime and to protect juveniles from victimization (Davis et al., 1997). Courts have upheld some curfew laws and struck down others. The recent trend seems to be to uphold the laws if they are narrowly drawn and if they provide exceptions for reasonable activities.

A recent case involving a curfew law that was challenged and ruled to be constitutional is *Qutb v. Strauss*. This was a 1993 case that concerned the Dallas, Texas, curfew law. That ordinance prohibited juveniles under age 17 from being on the streets from 11:00 P.M. until 6:00 A.M. on week nights and from midnight until 6:00 A.M. on weekends. Exceptions included being accompanied by a parent, doing an errand for a parent, or attending school, religious, or civic activities. The ordinance also allowed interstate travel or playing on one's own or a neighbor's sidewalk.

The United States Court of Appeals ruled that the law did not violate either equal protection or free association grounds and therefore was not unconstitutional. The Court ruled that the law did serve a compelling state interest, namely, "to reduce juvenile crime and victimization, while promoting juvenile safety and well-being" (*Qutb v. Strauss*, 1993). Here the Court noted that the City of Dallas presented statistics on juvenile crime and victimization during the hours covered by the curfew to substantiate the argument of reducing crime and victimization. Concerning a juvenile's right to free association (a First Amendment right), the Court noted that the law had sufficient exceptions in it so that impositions on association were minor. For example, contrary to arguments that the law prohibited playing midnight basketball, the Court noted that the juvenile could play in such a game as long as it was sponsored by some organization or as long as a parent accompanied the youth to the game.

Similarly drawn curfew laws have stood appeals court challenges, while overly broad laws without exceptions have been struck down. For example, a 1981 case, *Johnson v. City of Opelousas*, was struck down because its only exception was for "emergency errands." Here the judges noted that there was no exception for such associational activities "as religious or school meetings, organized dances, and theater and sporting events, when reasonable and direct travel to or from these activities has to be made during the curfew period" (*Johnson v. City of Opelousas*, 1981).

Thus, clearly drawn curfew laws are withstanding constitutional challenge as long as they allow reasonable exceptions. One author, however, thinks that the constitutional issues merit further review by the Supreme Court in order to clarify some conflicting rulings (*Harvard Law Review*, 2005). In a related matter, the Supreme Court recently struck down Chicago's anti-loitering ordinance as vague. The law prohibited two or more people from loitering for "no apparent purpose." The Court said that the law was too vague to give the public adequate notice of the conduct that is prohibited (*Chicago v. Morales*, 1999).

The Legal Drinking Age

An important children's rights issue is the question of the appropriate age for adolescents to drink alcoholic beverages. In fact, because of the actions of groups such as Mothers Against Drunk Driving (MADD) and because of the threat of reduced federal highway funds, all states prohibit the purchase of alcohol by persons under 21 years of age.

Interestingly, raising the **legal drinking age** to 21 is the flip side of the previous historical trend to lower the drinking age. Not too many years ago, lowering the drinking age was very much the norm, and it was part of a more general trend in both the United States and Canada of lowering the age of privilege-responsibility, including lowering the voting age to 18. In Canada the rationale behind this movement was that because "youths paid taxes, could quit school and work, join the military, vote federally, and drive cars, it was felt that they should be allowed to drink" (Vingilis and DeGenova, 1984:163). In the United States, the military draft provided the added argument that if "boys were old enough to be sent to Viet Nam, . . . they were old enough to drink" (Vingilis and DeGenova, 1984:163). Finally, there was some feeling that if "youth had to use substances, alcohol was society's preferred drug" (Vingilis and DeGenova, 1984:163).

Proponents of a high minimum drinking age argue that it reduces automobile accidents and fatalities, especially for adolescents themselves. They reason that teens need to be protected from their immaturity and impulsiveness because they are inexperienced at both driving and drinking alcohol.

It appears that these arguments make good sense because the research suggests that lowering the drinking age is indeed associated with increases in alcohol-related collisions and with higher fatality rates for nighttime and single-vehicle crashes involving young drivers. Conversely, raising the drinking age is associated with a reduced number of collisions (Vingilis and DeGenova, 1984:166-169). Specifically, the Department of Transportation estimates that raising the legal age for drinking to 21 saved more than 16,000 lives between 1975 and 1996 (Walker, 2001). In related research, it appears that states with the most restrictive graduated driver licensing laws have lower rates of heavy drinking among drivers ages 15 to 17 than states with the least restrictive laws but that there is no comparable difference in binge drinking (SAMHSA, 2004).

The issue, however, is not simple. Some "research indicates that the minimum legal drinking age laws do not deter the majority of teenagers from drinking" (Vingilis and DeGenova, 1984:170). Thus, a reasonable inference from this research on the impact of lowering and raising the drinking age seems to be that it would have some impact but it would not eliminate the problem.

A second problem with raising the drinking age is the question of fairness. That is, the specific issue of raising the drinking age raises the more general issue of the fairness of prohibiting 18-, 19-, and 20-year-olds from drinking, thereby, in effect, treating them as children when the law treats them as adults for other purposes. We have seen, for example, that all states consider 18-year-olds as adults in terms of their responsibility for criminal actions. In fact, one trend in juvenile justice is toward more liberal waiver and related provisions that allow younger and younger juveniles to be tried as adult criminal suspects (subjecting them to the possibility of imprisonment in adult facilities and even capital punishment). The question arises whether it is fair to subject teens to adult criminal court sanctions while at the same time treating them as immature children in terms of their legal ability to drink alcohol. Additional arguments against a high minimum drinking age include the "forbidden fruit" argument, which maintains that it increases the attraction of alcohol, and the "teach-them-to-do-it-right" argument, which contends that parents can use a lower minimum age as an educational device.

Franklin Zimring (1982) argues that it is fair to prohibit 18-year-olds from drinking, but he does not necessarily agree that it is fair to submit adolescents to criminal court sanctions, especially the death penalty. He states several reasons for his view that age 21 is a fair minimum drinking age. First, he believes that 18-year-olds are not mature but that they are in the process of becoming mature adults. Second, he is opposed to a low minimum drinking age because of the leakage problem. Leakage means, for example, that if 18-year-olds can legally purchase alcoholic beverages, then their 16-year-old dates may also drink and be subject to auto accidents and fatalities. Finally, he argues that there are three different aspects to adulthood: liberty, entitlement, and responsibility. Liberty refers to the freedom of choice that adults possess in matters such as making decisions about medical care. An entitlement is a benefit or program offered by government such as the Job Corps, which provides free job training for young persons. Responsibility means "paying the full price for misdeeds and being responsible, as are adults, for self support" (Zimring, 1982:111). It is Zimring's position that it is better to keep the ages for these three aspects of adulthood separate rather than to lump them together. Thus, he sees no inconsistency in permitting adolescents to drive at 16, vote and be drafted at 18, and be able to purchase alcoholic beverages at 21.

Zimring also raises the intriguing issue of raising the drinking age to 25. Based on evidence that single male drivers under 25—not just under 21—are a serious driving risk, he contends that these actuarial facts and logic would argue for an even higher drinking age than 21 to prevent many accidents and fatalities. He notes that there is some precedent for this in that the Constitution does require Senators and the President to be older than 21 years of age. However, Zimring rejects raising the minimum drinking age to 25 because:

> That kind of law is not merely politically implausible and socially divisive, it is also unjust. I have argued elsewhere that our current deferral of liberties can be justified because adolescence merely seems like forever. But using age-grading to defer common liberty into the mid-20's is exploitation in almost every case. Adding four or seven years onto an already long wait is simply too much of a burden. The twenty-first birthday has a long history of serving as the outer boundary for legal disability based on age. There is no good reason to risk the legal incoherence and social division that pushing beyond this limit imposes (Zimring, 1982:124).

Zimring was writing just before the recent push to waive increasingly younger juveniles to adult court, so he did not explicitly address the issues of the age of criminal responsibility and the appropriate age for capital punishment. There are strong indications, however, that he would not favor such actions. For example, he clearly believes that even 19- and 20-year-olds are not fully mature and may need some protection from their youthful mistakes. Thus, Zimring is convinced that our legal policy should be one that "preserves the life chances for those who make serious mistakes, as well as preserving choices for their more fortunate (and more virtuous) contemporaries" (Zimring, 1982:91-92).

Zimring's position is worth considering. Contrary to many contemporary voices, he does not advocate a policy that on the one hand would prohibit drinking until 21, but on the other hand would allow waiver to criminal court at 14. Instead, he takes the more consistent view that persons under 21 are not fully mature and responsible, but that certain aspects of adulthood may be more appropriately begun at 18.

In connection with this issue, Barnum (1987) argues that it is false to justify the existence of a separate juvenile court system on the claim that children are less mature and less responsible for their behavior than adults. Rather, "normal intrinsic cognitive development is sufficient for this capacity [to appreciate what they are doing or what effect it will have] by age two or three" (Barnum, 1987:72). Nevertheless, many think there are developmental differences between children and adults that do justify a separate court for juveniles:

> . . . children are less able to be responsible for themselves, . . . adolescents normally experience transient irresponsibility, and . . . even poorly socialized children may have a better prognosis for rehabilitation than do poorly socialized adults" (Barnum, 1987:78).

In other words, most children do know right from wrong, just as do most adults. However, there are other differences between children and adults that may justify a separate juvenile court system. (For discussion of the related issue of the appropriate age to allow driving, see Box 9.9. For a discussion of the privacy rights of teen drivers versus parental efforts to track teen driving habits, see Box 9.10.)

Perhaps a fitting conclusion to this discussion is Davis and Schwartz's observation that there is a fundamental tension in the law between paternalism (protecting children) and autonomy (granting them responsibility) that will not disappear:

> The law is protective of children, for example, in the areas of contracts, employment, and to a great extent, medical decision making in life-threatening cases. The law grants a measure of autonomy to children or their parents in other areas—for example, abortion decision making (but only to a limited extent), torts (but more as a result of a policy favoring compensation of victims than of a desire to grant children greater responsibility), non-life threatening medical decision making, and emancipation decision making. These disparate results stem from an inherent

conflict in the law—a kind of schizophrenia—between the desire to accord children a greater degree of control over their lives and freedom of choice, and the need, on the other hand, to protect them from others, their surroundings, and, sometimes, from their own folly (Davis and Schwartz, 1987:201).

BOX 9.9

College Presidents Call for a Lower Drinking Age

It appears that societal consensus favors a legal drinking age set at 21. During the summer of 2008, however, more than 100 college presidents called for lowering the drinking age back to 18. The presidents argued that an unintended consequence of the higher age is a culture of binge drinking on campus.

Opponents quickly chimed in, claiming that the higher age had saved about 25,000 American lives between the early 1980s and 2005.

Two economists argue that this claim is not true. Instead, the rate of traffic fatalities had been declining before the change to the age-21 drinking age. Factors behind the decline in fatalities are safer automobiles, better driver education, and improved medical technology. Still another factor is the driving age, not the drinking age. Europe has a lower fatality rate than the United States because people have to wait until age 18 to drive.

Source: Adapted from L. Dean-Mooney (Sept. 15, 2008). "A Lower Age Would Be Unsafe." *U.S. News & World Report*, p. 10; W. Wilkinson (Sept. 29, 2008). "Bottoms Up!" *Forbes*, p. 28.

BOX 9.10

Parental Tracking of Teen Driving

Some parents are installing black boxes in cars that monitor the driving habits of their teenage sons and daughters. The devices record such behaviors as seat-belt use and speed of the car. The devices also make a noise when the driver exceeds safety thresholds while driving.

One teen rights advocate argued that these boxes are an "invasion of privacy" (Davis and O'Donnell, 2005). What do you think? Are automobile black boxes an invasion of privacy or is this simply a reasonable attempt by parents to monitor the driving behavior of teens? Is it legitimate for 16- and 17-year-olds but not for youths 18 or older?

Source: R. Davis and J. O'Donnell (2005). "Some Teenagers Call Tracking Driving an Invasion of Privacy," *USA Today*, 1B.

It is interesting that at present society is lowering the age of criminal responsibility but at the same time insists on making 21 the age of eligibility to purchase alcohol and is pushing for **graduated licensing**. Davis and Schwartz's description of this as "a kind of schizophrenia" seems most fitting.

SUMMARY

This chapter has examined the landmark U.S. Supreme Court cases involving juveniles. The Fourth Amendment rights of juveniles and some of the controversial rights issues in school and in the home were examined. There is no perfectly consistent treatment of juveniles and their rights. Sometimes the law treats them as children, and sometimes it treats them as adults. As Zimring (1982) has pointed out, however, because the issue of juveniles' rights is so complex, perhaps a refusal to come up with one magical age for all children's rights issues is the best solution. Finally, as was noted in the discussion of the landmark Supreme Court cases, the mere stipulation of a right by the Court does not guarantee that police or courts will actually or fully protect that right. Practice is not always the same as philosophy.

DISCUSSION QUESTIONS

1. Has the Supreme Court gone too far or not far enough in protecting the rights of juvenile delinquency suspects? If you were on the Supreme Court, what would you seek to change concerning those rights?

2. Your 15-year-old brother has been arrested for the robbery of a movie video rental store. He is of average intelligence but is immature and impulsive. This is his first arrest. Do you think that he should be allowed to waive his privilege against self-incrimination and his right to confer with an attorney, or do you feel that state law should mandate that an attorney be brought in before the police can conduct any interrogation?

3. Assume that you are the editor of the high school newspaper and that one of your best reporters has just completed a lengthy article on drug use in your school. No names are mentioned in the article; in fact, your reporter has gone to great lengths to protect confidentiality. The principal has read the article and has said that she does not want it published in the school paper. What would you do?

4. Do you agree with the Supreme Court's position that corporal punishment is permissible as a school discipline technique? If you became a teacher or principle, would you use corporal punishment? If so, when and under what circumstances? More generally, how would you feel about your children being subjected to corporal punishment?

5. If you were a high school principal, what would your policy on student searches be? The Supreme Court has recently ruled that drug testing of students in band and clubs is permissible. Would you follow the direction of the Supreme Court and initiate testing of band members and the Future Farmers of America?

6. What is your opinion about compulsory community service? Do you think high schools should be allowed to force students to perform community service as a condition for graduation? Why or why not?

7. What is your opinion about school prayer? Should a school be allowed to invite a priest, minister, rabbi, or other religious leader to graduation to offer a nonsectarian invocation? Should the students be allowed to compose and lead their own invocation at graduation? What do you think about a moment of silence to begin (or end) the school day? Should prayer be permissible at athletic events?

8. What age do you favor as the minimum legal drinking age? How would you feel about the age being set at 25? What do you think about graduated licensing laws? Do you favor or oppose them?

Chapter 10

INSTITUTIONAL/RESIDENTIAL INTERVENTIONS

Important Terms

behavior modification

boot camps

common-sense corrections

cottage system

deinstitutionalization

inmate code

institutional life

program effectiveness

racial tension

shock incarceration

state training schools

victimization

wilderness programs

What You Need to Know

- Almost 100,000 juvenile offenders were in public, private, or tribal residential placement on the date of the most recent census. In addition, about 2,300 juveniles were in adult prisons according to recent data.

- Boot camps can be cost-effective and result in academic progress. They do not reduce recidivism, however, despite the common sense belief that military-type discipline is beneficial.

- Recent statistics indicate that 55 percent of juveniles released from state facilities are rearrested. On the other hand, effective programs can reduce recidivism significantly.

- The most prevalent problem in the juvenile justice system is the presence of mental disorders. Studies show that more than two-thirds of juveniles in the juvenile justice system experience mental disorders.

- Estimates of victimization, including sexual victimization, in juvenile facilities vary; some estimates indicate that almost two-thirds of youths are victimized. A government report noted almost 3,000 allegations of sexual violence in juvenile facilities in 2004.

- Racial tension has been a problem in juvenile facilities. In 2003, minorities constituted 60 percent of the committed juveniles in custody in public and private facilities nationwide.

- Deinstitutionalization or stopping involuntary placements of status offenders continues; in 2003, only 5 percent of institutionalized juveniles were status offenders.

- Many wilderness programs have not been effective, but a recent evaluation showed that such programs with treatment enhancements can reduce recidivism.

INTRODUCTION

This chapter will examine juvenile institutional correctional interventions, both public and private. Although more youths are in community correctional programs, residential programs are a critical component of juvenile corrections.

INSTITUTIONAL CORRECTIONS FOR JUVENILES

On the latest one-day count of juveniles in residential placement in 2003, 96,655 juvenile offenders were in detention, correctional, or shelter facilities. Most (91,831) of these were delinquency offenders. More than 66,000 of the youths were in public facilities, and slightly more than 30,000 (30,321, to be precise) were in private facilities. Seventy-four percent of these youths were committed (after being tried in court), and 25 percent were being detained prior to adjudication. Almost 5,000 of the youths in custody were status offenders (Snyder and Sickmund, 2006). Preliminary statistics show that 92,854 juveniles were in residential placement in 2006, representing a continuing decrease in the custody population (Sickmund, Sladky, and Kang, 2008). The latest information available indicates that the average length of stay was approximately four months and that the average yearly cost of custody in a public institution was $32,488 (Smith, 1998). Many juvenile facilities are outdated, built in the 1970s at best (Roush and McMillen, 2000).

For the latest available statistics on juveniles in custody, go to the "Census of Juveniles in Residential Placement Databook" online at http://www.ojjdp.ncjrs.gov/ojstatbb/cjrp/

According to the most recent report, in 2006, there were 2,364 juveniles in state (adult) prisons. Five states (Connecticut, New York, Florida, North Carolina, and Texas) held more than half of all juveniles in state prisons (Sabol, Minton, and Harrison, 2007).

Although probation handles many more youths, institutions involve a significant minority of the offenders who go through the juvenile justice system. They are the costliest part of the system. One public facility in New York was reported to cost more than $80,000 a year (Singer, 1996). More recently, in three states for which information was available (Missouri, Maryland, and California), the cost of custody ranged from approximately $40,000 to $70,000 a year (McGarvey, 2005).

In 2003 the residential population was 85 percent male and 15 percent female. The racial composition of juvenile offenders in custody was 39 percent white, 38 percent black, and 19 percent Hispanic (the remainder were categorized as "other") (Snyder and Sickmund, 2006).

Preliminary 2006 statistics were almost the same (Sickmund, Sladky, and Kang, 2008). Thus, blacks are overrepresented in juvenile institutions, but there is no clear explanation for the overrepresentation (Sickmund, 2004).

Correctional managers contend that juvenile correctional facilities seek to serve the "best interests of the child," which means that they attempt to provide educational, therapeutic, and recreational programs staffed by concerned caregivers. Critics argue that, at best, the facilities are warehouses or holding tanks where little, if any, positive change takes place. Both past and more recent critics have contended that juvenile facilities harbor as many horror stories as they do children: tales of neglect, abuse, and even death (Human Rights Watch, 2006; Wooden, 1976).

> For the latest available statistics on juveniles in custody in state prisons, go to the web site of the U.S. Department of Justice Bureau of Justice Statistics and check such Bulletins as "Prison and Jail Inmates at Midyear 2006." (A more recent report should be available by the time you read this chapter.) Visit http://www.ojp.usdoj.gov/bjs

This chapter examines various types of institutional and residential interventions with juveniles, including state training schools, youth camps, private placements, and group homes. After describing these various placements, we will examine some of the current issues about their operation, such as the determination of appropriate targets for intervention, effectiveness in reducing recidivism, and client and worker adaptations to the pressures of institutional life. The chapter concludes with information on innovative trends in this area such as deinstitutionalization and wilderness programs.

STATE TRAINING SCHOOLS

State training schools are the juvenile justice system's equivalent of the adult prison; they house those delinquents whom juvenile court judges consider unfit for probation or some other lesser punishment. Some training schools actually resemble adult prisons in terms of their architecture: high walls or fences, locked cell blocks, self-sufficiency (they have their own laundry, hospital, and maintenance facility), and solitary confinement for persistent rule breakers. Other training schools have the so-called **cottage system** of architectural design. Unfortunately, the cottage system is often a far cry from the homelike atmosphere intended by its founders. Cottages are often deteriorating dormitories with decrepit plumbing, heating, and lighting, and an accompanying host of social-cultural problems as well.

Missouri, on the other hand, has developed what many consider a model program. In fact, by emphasizing individual and group treatment in small group dormitory settings, such as a converted school building in St. Louis, Missouri has been awarded an Innovations in American Government Award by Harvard University's Ash Institute (Ash Institute, 2008; McGarvey, 2005).

Training School Programs for Residents

The programming at state training schools is often a combination of academic and vocational education and **behavior modification**. Residents attend school much of the day just like their noninstitutionalized counterparts, but the school run by the prison teaches youths who are usually two to three years below their appropriate grade level in both reading

BOX 10.1

Sample of One Training School's Rules

Below is an actual set of rules and a list of minor rule violations from a southeastern training school:

Rules:
1. There will be no misuse of any property.
2. There is to be no use of vulgar or profane language.
3. There will be no gambling.
4. There will be no tampering with fire and safety equipment.
5. Students will remain in their assigned areas.
6. Students may not borrow, sell, lend, or trade their property.
7. Students are expected to always be courteous.
8. Students are expected to respect privacy and property of others.
9. Students are expected to follow all dress codes.
10. Students are expected to follow instructions of staff.

Minor Rule Violations:
1. Disruptive behavior
2. Failure to follow institutional rules
3. Horseplay
4. Out of assigned area
5. Racial slurs
6. Refusal of a direct order
7. Self-mutilation
8. Sexual slurs
9. Use of obscene language

Source: Student Handbook from a southeastern state.

BOX 10.2

Typical Weekday Daily Schedule at a Residential Placement for Delinquents

6:30 A.M.	Wake Up: dress and clean room
7:00 A.M.	Calisthenics
7:30 A.M.	Hygiene (showers, etc.)
8:00 A.M.	Clean dormitories
8:30 A.M.	Breakfast
9:00 A.M.	Start school
10:30 A.M.	"Rap" half-hour
11:00 A.M.	Return to school
12:00 A.M.	Lunch
12:30 P.M.	"Rap" half-hour
1:00 P.M.	School
3:30 P.M.	Group therapy
5:00 P.M.	Dinner
5:30 P.M.	Work details (kitchen clean-up and dormitory clean-up)
6:00-7:00 P.M.	TV news
7:00-9:00 P.M.	Activities (vary by day: Example: Values Clarification, Occupational Therapy, Recreational Therapy, etc.)
9:00 P.M.	Bedtime for Phase 1 (9:30 P.M. in the summertime)
10:00 P.M.	Bedtime for Phase 2 and above.

Source: Manual from a midwestern residential facility. Note: In this context, to "rap" is to talk freely and frankly.

and mathematics. (For a list of the school rules in one training school, see Box 10.1; for a typical daily schedule, see Box 10.2.)

In addition to standard academic subjects, educational programs may include life skills development, remedial reading and writing, conflict resolution skills development, computer literacy, and learning skills assessment. Additional programming may include groups on anger management and substance abuse resistance and recreation such as sports, crafts, board games, reading, and computer games (Roush and McMillen, 2000).

The behavior modification system usually involves the grading of children at one of several levels. The system includes the daily awarding of points for almost every possible action of the child's day, from getting

BOX 10.3

Typical Institutional Point System

Responsibilities	Points	
1. Get self up on time (6:00 A.M.)	+25	−50
2. Locker neat, orderly, clean room or area with bed made	+50	−100
3. Appropriately dressed	+25	−50
4. Brush teeth and comb hair	+25	−50
5. Daily bath and use deodorant	+25	−100
6. Exercise	+25	−50
7. Acts appropriately: a: Breakfast	+10	−20
b: Lunch	+10	−20
c. Dinner	+10	−20
8. School	+40 per hour	
9. Study hour or watching news	+25 per hour	
10. Daily chores	+50	−100
11. Volunteer work	+60 per hour (120 maximum per day)	
12. See counselor	+25 per hour	
13. Attend group	+50	−100 per hour
14. Attend church or Sunday school services	+25	
15. Bonus points	+100 maximum per day	

Note: A +25 indicates that a resident can earn up to 25 points for performing the specified behavior. A −100 indicates that a resident can have as many as 100 points deducted if the behavior is not performed or not performed properly.

Spending Opportunities

1. Swimming	25 points
2. Recreation room	25 points
3. Parlor games (checkers, cards, etc.)	25 points
4. Telephone calls	20 points
5. Use of television room	25 points
6. Play outside	25 points
7. Group outing off campus	300 points
8. Group outing on campus	200 points
9. Living room	25 points
10. Movies in dorm	100 points
11. Home pass	350 points

Source: Student manual from a southeastern training school.

up on time to getting to bed quietly and on time. The points earned each day can be spent on various privileges, ranging from games, television time, and telephone calls home to off-campus group outings and visits home. The higher the child's level, the more extensive the privileges available. (Box 10.3 gives an actual list of opportunities for earning and spending points at a southeastern training school.) In addition to qualifying for daily privileges, such as television, the points earned also count toward movement from one level to another with additional privilege possibilities. One training school employee characterized the point system as working both as a behavioral control device and as a device to monitor progress within the institution.

Concern for the victim and for crime control has translated into some new programs in juvenile institutions. In California, for example, the Impact of Crime on Victims program combines an educational curriculum with presentations by victims and victims' advocates. In Texas, juvenile murderers receive group psychotherapy and role-playing sessions to help them learn responsibility for their crimes and to imagine what they put their victims through (Bilchik, 1998).

Other Placements

Traditional training schools are not the only means that states use for housing delinquents. In some years, almost 10,000 youths are held in long-term open facilities that allow greater freedom for residents within the facilities and more contacts with the community. The open facilities category of placements includes shelters, halfway houses, group homes, and a few ranches. Group homes are residential facilities for relatively small numbers of youths (perhaps one or two dozen youngsters). The residents often attend regular public schools but participate in group counseling sessions and recreational activities at the group home.

Juvenile court judges also have been known to commit juvenile delinquents to detention centers for a short period of time. Youths are placed on probation, and one condition of probation is a short stay in the local detention facility.

States also utilize private residential placements to house delinquents and some status offenders. In 2003, private facilities held 27,000 delinquent youths and slightly more than 3,200 status offenders. This was almost one-third of all juveniles in placement (Snyder and Sickmund, 2006). Private facilities, like state facilities, range from relatively large institutions to small group homes and even wilderness programs where juveniles camp out. Many were originally started by churches as charitable institutions but have evolved into nonsectarian operations that charge the state thousands of dollars each year for each child they handle.

Boot Camps

A continuing trend is the use of **boot camps** (also called **shock incarceration**). Boot camps are short-term facilities (90-day/120-day/six-month) that are intended to resemble basic training facilities for the military. There is considerable emphasis on discipline and physical training such as marching, running, calisthenics, and other types of conditioning. Usually a "drill instructor" is assigned to each group of offenders. Many boot camp programs also involve aftercare supervision for program graduates. Box 10.4 shows the daily schedule at one boot camp.

The rationale behind boot camps is multifaceted. It is claimed that boot camps can protect the public, reduce prison crowding, reduce costs, punish offenders, hold offenders accountable, deter additional crime, and rehabilitate (counseling and education) (Cronin, 1994).

BOX 10.4

Daily Schedule for Offenders in a New York Boot Camp

A.M.

5:30	Wake up and standing count
5:45-6:30	Calisthenics and drill
6:30-7:00	Run
7:00-8:00	Mandatory breakfast/cleanup
8:15	Standing count and company formation
8:30-11:55	Work/school schedules

P.M.

12:00-12:30	Mandatory lunch and standing count
12:30-3:30	Afternoon work/school schedule
3:30-4:00	Shower
4:00-4:45	Network community meeting
4:45-5:45	Mandatory dinner, prepare for evening
6:00-9:00	School, group counseling, drug counseling, prerelease counseling, decision-making classes
8:00	Count while in programs
9:15-9:30	Squad bay, prepare for bed
9:30	Standing count, lights out

Source: C.L. Clark, D.W. Aziz, and D.L. MacKenzie (1994). *Shock Incarceration in New York: Focus on Treatment*. Washington, DC: U.S. Department of Justice.

The effectiveness of boot camps for both adult and juvenile offenders is mixed. There is some indication that boot camps can reduce state correctional costs and that participants rate their experience in camp as positive, but the evidence shows that boot camps have little or no effect on recidivism (Cronin, 1994; Parent, 2003). It does appear clear, however, that "the military atmosphere alone does not reduce recidivism and increase positive activities during community supervision" (MacKenzie, 1994:66). Ironically, even though many politicians like boot camps because they appear to be "tough," it appears that the educational and rehabilitative programming is what helps the offenders.

An evaluation of three boot camps in Cleveland, Mobile, and Denver offers insights about their advantages and disadvantages. Eligible youths for these camps were youths ages 13 to 17 who had been adjudicated by the juvenile court and were awaiting disposition. Youths considered eligible could not have any history of mental illness or involvement in violent crime but were rated at "high risk" of chronic delinquency and minimal risk of escape.

The graduation rates were positive, ranging from a low of 65 percent at Denver to 87 percent at Mobile and 93 percent at Cleveland. There was significant academic progress at Cleveland and Mobile: from half to two-thirds of the youths at Cleveland improved at least one grade level in various academic skills. In Mobile about 80 percent of the youths improved at least one grade level (Peters, Thomas, and Zamberlan, 1997). A recent long-term follow-up of boot camp participants in California also found no impact on recidivism (Bottcher and Ezell, 2005).

The findings on recidivism, however, were discouraging. There were no significant differences in recidivism between boot camp offenders and the control group offenders at Denver or Mobile. In Cleveland, the experimental youths did worse than the controls. Moreover, at all three sites, survival times—time to the commission of a new offense—were shorter for the youths who went through the boot camps than for control cases (Peters, Thomas, and Zamberlan, 1997).

Concerning cost-effectiveness, the costs per day of the boot camps were similar to one day of institutionalization but more expensive than a day of probation. Costs per offender were lower than controls because boot camp offenders spent less time in the boot camps. The data on annual costs per offender were: Cleveland: $14,021, compared to $25,549 for the Ohio Department of Youth Services; Denver: $8,141, versus $23,425 for a state facility; Mobile; $6,241, versus $11,616 for a state facility (Peters, Thomas, and Zamberlan, 1997:24-25).

Peters and his colleagues conclude that boot camps are not a panacea but they do offer some advantages:

> As an intermediate sanction, boot camps are a useful alternative for offenders for whom probation would be insufficiently punitive, yet for whom long-term incarceration would be excessive. As such, under certain conditions, boot camps can

free bed space for more hardened offenders, thereby reducing the financial burden on correctional budgets (Peters, Thomas, and Zamberlan, 1997).

Boot camps are part of a more general trend in society to "get tough" on crime. One author (Clear, 1994) calls this trend the "penal harm movement"; another team of authors calls it "the punishment paradigm" (Cullen and Wright, 1995). These authors contend that since 1980 the United States has operated on the premise that more punishment is needed to deter crime and incapacitate offenders. Boot camps are one component of the movement, which includes increased use of prisons and jails, lengthier sentences, determinate sentences, career criminal sentencing provisions, increased use of capital punishment, and harsher community sanctions (intensive supervision, house arrest, and electronic monitoring). For juveniles the punishment paradigm has translated into greater prosecution of juveniles in adult court and blended sentences involving the adult correctional system. Thus, boot camps are not an isolated phenomenon but are part of a broader trend in criminal justice focusing on retribution, deterrence, and incapacitation.

AP Photo/Steve Cannon

Demonstrators march on the Florida Capitol to protest how the state has handled the death of a teenager who was punched and kicked by guards at a juvenile detention boot camp. Martin Anderson, 14, died in a Bay County boot camp in January 2006.

A final word on boot camps comes from Cullen and his colleagues (2005), who see the boot camp phenomenon as a clear-cut example of the dangers of "common-sense thinking" in corrections and criminal justice. What they mean is that based on the common-sense thinking that military boot camps "made men out of boys" for the army, many individuals were convinced that correctional boot camps would do the same for juvenile offenders. The research on the lack of success of boot camps, however, shows the dangers of relying on such common-sense thinking: "It is dangerous precisely because it seems so correct, leaves our biases unchallenged, and requires virtually no effort to activate" (Cullen et al., 2005:66). Elsewhere, Cullen argues that boot camp interventions fail because they "are based on a limited theory of crime (rational choice) and do not target the known proximate risk factors for reoffending" (Cullen, 2007:720). The recent incident of a death of a 14-year-old youth in a Florida boot camp influenced that state to close that particular camp, limit intimidation in the remaining four boot camps in the state, and rename their camps "training and respect programs" (*U.S. News and World Report*, 2006: 18).

PROGRAM EFFECTIVENESS

One of the most critical issues facing residential interventions is the effectiveness issue: Do the interventions have any impact on the criminal behavior of their charges? Although much of what follows pertains most directly to publicly run placements (especially state training schools), the problems also affect private placements.

Reviews of Multiple Studies

In the last decade, a number of states have reported recidivism rates for youths released from state juvenile correctional facilities. When rearrest is the measure, on average, 55 percent of released youths recidivate. That figure drops to 33 percent failure when the measure is reconviction or readjudication. With reincarceration as the measure, the failure rate drops to between 12 and 25 percent (Snyder and Sickmund, 2006). These statistics give no information on what sort or what quality of rehabilitation programs took place in these states.

While much of the **program effectiveness** research has focused on specific programs, some researchers have tried to summarize individual program research into a global conclusion on effectiveness. Most of these studies have used the technique of meta-analysis. Meta-analysis is a technique that allows researchers to re-analyze individual studies and arrive at a summary statistic of effectiveness for each individual study that can then be compared to the summary statistics from the other studies.

A meta-analysis of 443 studies published between 1970 and 1987 focused on formal contact with the juvenile justice system as an outcome measure and reported that approximately two-thirds of the study outcomes favored the treatment group over the control group. Behavioral, skill, and multimodal treatment programs resulted in greater effects than other approaches. Deterrence-based programs were not effective (Lipsey, 1992).

Lipsey and Wilson (1998) conducted a meta-analysis of 83 studies of institutional programs for serious offenders and found that there were many instances of programs that had positive effects. The most effective treatment types had an impact on recidivism that was equivalent to reducing a control group baseline recidivism rate of 50 percent to around 30 or 35 percent. If the recidivism rate for these juveniles would have been 50 percent without treatment, the most effective programs reduced it to 30-35 percent. They concluded that this represents a "considerable decrease, especially in light of the fact that it applies to institutionalized offenders, who can be assumed to be relatively serious delinquents" (Lipsey and Wilson, 1998:336). (For a recent review and analysis of effective correctional interventions for both juveniles and adults, see MacKenzie, 2006.) Successful interventions included aggres-

sion replacement training, behavior modification, and a stress inocula-
tion program that helped youths define anger, analyze recent anger
episodes, review self-monitoring data, and construct an individualized
six-item anger hierarchy.

Conclusions about Program Effectiveness

Several cautious conclusions about the effectiveness of institutional
programs for delinquents are in order. First, some research, such as an
evaluation of the Provo program, indicate that community programs are
at least as effective as traditional training schools (Lundman, 1993). The
Provo program was a community program that was an alternative to
sending youths to the Utah training school. Second, research, such as the
evaluation of the Silverlake Project in California, suggests that an innovative and less repressive residential program can be at least as effective
as a traditional training school (Gottfredson, 1987; Lundman, 1993).
Third, even training schools may have an effect in suppressing the average number of crimes youths commit after release, but such institutions
may not be able to deter their charges from committing any crimes after
release. Fourth, this alleged suppression effect may be the result of such
factors as regression toward the mean, simple maturation, or the rehabilitation programs in the training schools instead of the deterrent effect
of a punitive regime in the training school (Lundman, 1993). Finally, the
effectiveness literature suggests that certain interventions can be effective
in reducing recidivism from about 50 percent to 30 or 35 percent. It is
imperative, however, that these interventions follow the principles that
research has identified as effective (Lipsey and Wilson, 1998). We review
those principles in Chapter 11 on community corrections. Examples of
successful strategies that follow effective principles are multisystemic
therapy (MST) and functional family therapy. Multisystemic therapy,
for example, has been shown to reduce days in treatment by about half
at a cost of approximately $6,000 per youth, less than one-fourth of an
eight-month stay in a juvenile facility. One MST program alone, Youth
Villages, served 1,600 Tennessee youths in the year 2000 (Mendel, 2001).
MacKenzie (2006) concludes that there is "strong evidence" about the
effectiveness of moral reconation therapy in reducing recidivism.

Before proceeding to discuss other current issues in juvenile institutions, it is important to note that the measurement of the effectiveness
of treatment programs in such settings assumes that the programs are
in fact carried out as originally intended. Unfortunately, that is not
always true. Although Wooden did his research years ago, his observations on this matter apply today. Specifically, Wooden contended that
institutions were using behavior modification techniques "to manipulate
and control the child for the convenience of the custodians" (Wooden,
1976:101). In a New York facility, "education" actually meant watch-

ing movies on the VCR, especially on Friday (Singer, 1996). According to another report, in a facility referred to as "Cottage Blue," staff were chosen to put together notebooks with lesson plans for each week. These staff members simply pulled pages from the Internet and from workbooks. Notebooks were so badly photocopied that it was impossible to read them (Inderbitzin, 2006a). In what was intended to be a new model facility in Arizona, treatment quickly deteriorated. Staff appeared inconsistent and capricious in such matters as scoring youths' behaviors, staff were disrespectful and interrupted youths in group meetings, a few staff made racially insensitive remarks, and youths were shackled when transported to receive medical treatment. A key educational program did not accomplish its objectives, and substance abuse treatment was not provided. In short, there was a "repeated and systematic violation of the program's fundamental principles and spirit" (Bortner and Williams, 1997:112). Therefore, impressive terms such as "behavior modification," "model program," and "education" do not necessarily translate into humane and progressive interventions. If such interventions are implemented in such negative ways, it is hardly possible to know what results an evaluation study will find or what sort of confidence can be placed in the results.

INSTITUTIONAL LIFE

An important concern in juvenile justice is the effect of **institutional life** on youths. The theory of institutional placements is that they will provide a caring and nurturing environment that will allow the delinquents to change to prosocial behavior in the institution. This will then carry over into future behavior after release. As we shall see, however, the practice often falls far short of the theoretical ideal.

Mental and Substance Disorders

Research shows that the most prevalent problem in the juvenile justice system is mental disorders. Studies show that more than two-thirds of juveniles in the juvenile justice system experience mental disorders. In fact, a study that looked at more than 1,400 youths in three states found that 70 percent of youths in the system met the criteria for at least one mental health disorder. The most common disorders found were disruptive disorders such as conduct disorders, then substance abuse disorders such as alcohol abuse, then anxiety disorders (e.g., obsessive-compulsive disorder), and then mood disorders (e.g., depression) (Shufelt and Cocozza, 2006).

High rates of disorder persist even if conduct and substance abuse disorders are removed from the equation. If conduct disorders were removed, 66 percent of youths still met the criteria for a mental health disorder. If both disorders were removed, almost one-half (45.5%) of youths still met the criteria for having a mental health disorder (Shufelt and Cocozza, 2006).

Girls involved in the juvenile justice system have higher rates of mental disorder than boys. More than 80 percent of girls met the criteria for at least one mental health disorder, compared to 67 percent of boys. Girls were more likely to exhibit internalizing disorders such as anxiety and mood disorders (Shufelt and Cocozza, 2006).

Most importantly, 27 percent of boys and girls in the juvenile justice system had a disorder serious enough to require "significant and immediate treatment" (Shufelt and Cocozza, 2006:4). In short, many juvenile offenders are suffering from mental health disorders, many need immediate attention, and many others need some type of treatment.

Victimization

As is true of adult prisons, probably the most dramatic example of a negative effect of the institution on incarcerated youths is the problem of **victimization,** which ranges from the relatively insignificant act of taking a boy's dessert to forcing a boy to perform fellatio. Such victimization knows no geographic boundaries. In one northern training school, 53 percent of the boys exploited others, and 65 percent were exploited at least on occasion (Bowker, 1980). In a study of six southeastern training schools, more than one-third of the whites, but less than 25 percent of the blacks, reported frequent victimization. In addition, 61 percent of the whites, but less than 50 percent of the blacks, reported that other residents "took advantage of them" in the institution (Bartollas and Sieverdes, 1981:538). It appears that institutionalized girls are less subject to forceful sexual attacks but that "attacks sometimes occur, usually involving adolescent inmates who have expressed an unwillingness to participate in homosexuality and who are zealous in ridiculing inmates who engage in this behavior" (Giallombardo, 1974:160). In one New York facility, some guards formed a "wake-up club," which administered regular beatings to misbehaving or disrespectful youths (Singer, 1996). Although it is difficult to obtain an accurate and up-to-date picture of what victimization takes place across the country, it is safe to say that the institutionalized youngster is deprived of the security that teenagers in positive home environments take for granted.

The Prison Rape Elimination Act (PREA) of 2003 requires facilities to report statistics on sexual violence in both adult and juvenile correctional facilities to the federal Bureau of Justice Statistics. In 2006, juvenile facilities reported 2,025 allegations of sexual violence. Almost 60 percent (57%) involved charges of youth-on-youth violence, and the rest (43%) were staff-on-youth incidents. More than one-third of these incidents occurred in state-operated facilities, and about two-thirds took place in local or privately operated facilities. The overall rate of sexual violence was 16.8 incidents per 1,000 youths (Beck et al., 2008). It must be emphasized that these numbers are based on what officials reported to the federal government. Surveys of residents have been conducted in the last few years, and statistics from them will be available in the future to provide a more complete picture of sexual victimization in youth facilities.

The federal government also reports on the number of deaths in juvenile correctional facilities. In 2005, nine juveniles died in custody; one death was a suicide, and two of the deaths were the result of homicide. For the period 2002-2005, there were 21 suicides and five homicides (Bureau of Justice Statistics, 2007). As the next paragraph shows, however, there are many more acts of suicidal behavior than actual suicides.

A study of juvenile suicide in confinement found 110 such suicides between 1995 and 1999. Of the studies analyzed, 42 percent occurred in training schools or secure facilities, 37 percent in detention facilities, 15 percent in residential treatment centers, and 6 percent in reception/diagnostic centers. Seventy percent of the victims had a history of suicidal behavior; prior suicide attempts were the most frequent type of history. Almost all of the suicides were by hanging, and more than 70 percent of the victims used their bedding materials to commit suicide. The study recommended that youth facilities have a detailed written suicide prevention policy and effective training programs (Hayes, 2004). For further discussion of living conditions in juvenile prison, see Boxes 10.5 and 10.6.

Despite apparent increases in staff victimization, a study of correctional officers in two juvenile detention facilities in Virginia showed low levels of fear of victimization and perceived risk of victimization. In addition, it did not matter whether the guard was working in a therapeutically oriented detention center or a more traditional detention center (Gordon, Moriarty, and Grant, 2003).

A recent study of 500 juveniles in institutions (about half were in traditional institutions such as training schools and about half were in boot camps) focused on the psychological states and perceived environments of the residents. First, juveniles perceived their institutional environments to have high levels of both activity and justice. So the juveniles felt that they had things to do and were being treated fairly, but they also perceived the environments to be restrictive and controlled. Levels of anxiety and depression both decreased over time. Childhood maltreatment (e.g., coming from an abusive home) increased the levels of depression and anxiety. Therefore, it appears that institutional staffs should target therapeutic programming for youths with histories of child maltreatment (Gover and MacKenzie, 2003).

Because some juveniles are transferred to adult court and/or subjected to blended sentencing, a number of youths under 18 are being imprisoned in adult facilities; there were more than 2,300 as of 2006 (Sabol, Minton,

BOX 10.5

Conditions at Cottage Blue:
Much Ado About Nothing or Something?

Gresham Sykes coined the phrase "deprivations of imprisonment" to re-fer to the losses or the pains that prisoners suffer because of incarceration. He listed these deprivations or pains as deprivation or loss of freedom, au-tonomy, goods and services, security, and heterosexual sexual activity (he was writing of adult prisoners, not juveniles) (Sykes and Matza, 1957).

Inderbitzin's study of Cottage Blue points out some of the deprivations, losses, or pains of imprisonment for contemporary juvenile offenders at one facility.

The youths noted deprivation of autonomy in that they had to ask per-mission to shave or shower, to make a phone call, to send a letter, or to get paper and pencil. So they felt like helpless children. They also suffered loss of privacy; they complained about irritating roommates who smelled or wet the bed or were just plain annoying by talking all the time or asking questions all the time. Part of the problem was having to live with youths of different races or different ages.

Concerning what Sykes would call loss of possessions (goods and ser-vices), the youths complained of "inferior" products such as cheap soap or inferior pizza on Friday nights. More generally, they complained of bland food and too much starch in their meals. Another complaint was boredom. So they often asked staff to rent movies or video games for them or to bring them magazines and books.

What do you think of these complaints? How serious are complaints about cheap soap, bland food, or not enough video games? How much attention should staff and administrators in these facilities give to such concerns? Are these complaints trivial, or is it important to make juvenile facilities as posi-tive as possible?

Source: Adapted from M. Inderbitzin (2006). "Lessons from a Juvenile Training School: Survival and Growth." *Journal of Adolescent Research* 21:7-26.

and Harrison, 2007). There is evidence that these young prisoners are at heightened risk of assault, including sexual assault. One reason is that young prisoners often lack the coping skills of older prisoners. One study found that juveniles in adult prisons were 21 times as likely to be assault-ed or injured as teens in the juvenile system (see Benekos and Merlo, 2008). Suicide risk is also higher for such juveniles (Mumola, 2005).

Girls may face special problems. For example, girls have undergone strip searches and cavity searches in the presence of male guards. This tends to reinforce the belief that they do not have control over their own

BOX 10.6

Human Rights Watch: Girls in Custody in New York

In addition to physical abuse, Human Rights Watch documented three cases in the previous five years of staff having sexual intercourse with girls. The investigation also found less serious sexual abuse, including verbal innuendo, male staff observing girls in different states of undress, and unwanted touching. Some staff also made humiliating comments about the past sexual history of girls or the fact that they had a sexually transmitted disease. Some also harassed girls who were lesbians or did not conform to stereotypes. Staff also used frequent strip searches and inspected girls' genitals. Human Rights Watch concluded that the facilities were often failing to serve or even protect the incarcerated girls. Staff and administrative failure to provide meaningful oversight and lack of outside monitoring meant that the girls had no way to seek assistance to stop the abuses.

What needs to be done to protect girls in custody? What must be done to protect girls from sexual abuse, in any form, by male staff members? Is it necessary to have an independent monitor or inspector visit such facilities on a periodic basis, or can facility administrators ensure the safety of the girls?

Source: Adapted from *Custody and Control: Conditions of Confinement in New York's Juvenile Prisons for Girls*. New York: Human Rights Watch.

bodies. Some facilities have not given girls clean clothes and clean towels and washcloths, and some have provided limited hygiene supplies. These abuses and deprivations can be especially important to adolescent girls as they make the transition to womanhood (Acoca, 1998).

A Human Rights Watch investigation found evidence of staff physical abuse of girls in two New York State residential facilities. The investigation alleged that staff frequently applied a technique called "restraint" to girls. Staff would grab a girl from behind, push her on to the floor, push her arms up behind her, and hold or handcuff her. This was used in many situations that did not involve danger or threats—such as talking back or "mouthing off" or not making one's bed correctly. Sometimes the girls got "rug burns" on their faces or all over their bodies. The report noted that excessive force may be especially harmful to girls because past experiences of physical or sexual abuse can lead to intense emotions for them (Human Rights Watch, 2006).

The same investigation also found staff sexual abuse of the residents, ranging from observation of girls in states of undress by male staff, to unwanted touching, all the way to sexual intercourse. Staff abuse also included publicly humiliating comments revealing girls' past sexual histories or their experiences of domestic abuse (Human Rights Watch, 2006).

A recent study of 22 girls in a large women's prison in the Midwest indicated several problem areas for juvenile girls who had been sentenced to adult women's prisons. One problem was lack of recreation time and equipment. Recreation equipment had been ordered for the under-21 unit but had not arrived by the time of the research. No girl reported having been "raped" by an older woman, but some had experienced either name-calling or more serious sexual comments. Four girls indicated that they were in a sexual relationship with an older woman prisoner but that it was consensual. GED education and even college education (an associate degree program in Social Services) were available. Most programs were designed for adult women, but anger management, a Girl Scouts program, and a gang awareness program were specifically targeted at the young prisoners. The authors concluded that their research "raises critical questions about the quality of care given to girls in adult prisons, particularly in programming areas such as education, life skills, recreation, and work training" (Gaarder and Belknap, 2004:75). The authors call for improvements in all these areas, but they add the cautionary note that their ideal solution is to not put any girls or women in women's prisons because "[w]omen's prisons mirror the regulatory mechanisms and treatment of women in society at large, and we seek to dismantle both" (Gaarder and Belknap, 2004:77).

Schaffner (2006) did qualitative research on girls in California detention centers. She argues that many workers, including probation officers, hold inappropriate notions about contemporary girls and even subtly racist attitudes. She argues that juvenile justice needs to implement more gender-specific programming and also address the needs of girls and women who are gay or other in their sexual orientation.

Racial Tension

The statistics on victimization also suggest that **racial tension** is a problem in juvenile institutions. For example, Bartollas and Sieverdes found African-American youths to be both more dominant and more aggressive than white inmates: "Twice as many black as white residents were classified by staff members as highly aggressive toward others; over 40 percent of whites were defined by staff as passive" (Bartollas and Sieverdes, 1981:538). Bartollas and Sieverdes attributed this situation to role reversal in the institution, where white Southern youths found themselves in the novel position of being in the minority. White inmates were outnumbered by black inmates (about 60% of the inmates were black), and about half of the staff members were black. The white youths felt threatened because they were in an environment very different from "the southern culture, [where] whites are used to a position of greater superiority in the free society relative to minority groups than are youth elsewhere in the United States" (Bartollas and Sieverdes, 1981:541). Even a model youth prison in Arizona experienced some racial tensions. It was reported that one staff member called a youth a "taco bender" and another staff member called an African-American youth "colored" (Bortner and Williams, 1997).

The fact that training schools continue to be places with significant proportions of several ethnic groups suggests that racial/ethnic tensions will continue into the foreseeable future. As noted at the beginning of this chapter, in 2003, minorities constituted 61 percent of the juveniles in residential placement. Blacks made up 38 percent of those in placement, and Hispanics accounted for 19 percent of those in placement (Snyder and Sickmund, 2006). Preliminary figures for 2006 showed a similar breakdown: blacks made up 40 percent of juveniles in residential custody, and Hispanics comprised 21 percent (Sickmund, Sladky, and Kang, 2008).

The federal government, through legislation, research, training, and technical assistance, has been attempting to reduce disproportionate minority confinement. One strategy to reduce such disproportionate confinement is using standardized risk assessments at decision points in the juvenile justice system. Such risk assessment structures decisionmaking and thus has the potential to reduce racial bias by court officials (Hsia, Bridges, and McHale, 2004). Another strategy is staff training to make staff more aware of possibly unconscious factors that contribute to disproportionate minority confinement (Bishop, 2005).

The Inmate Code

Another negative effect of institutions is that youths may develop or maintain allegiance to peer norms that run counter to staff efforts to rehabilitate the youngsters. This is the problem of the **inmate code**, which can stress such maxims as "exploit whomever you can," "don't play up to staff," "don't rat on your peers," and "be cool"(Sieverdes and Bartollas, 1986:137). In other words, juvenile inmates develop feelings of distrust and resentment toward staff. These feelings operate in opposition to staff efforts to build trust and openness. There has been some indication that the inmate code is moving away from minding one's own business ("do your own time") to greater exploitation of others:

> In other words, the "old con" who did his/her own time has disappeared from the juvenile correctional system and from most adult correctional systems. Inmates are now more likely to show certain allegiances to other prisoners, especially those in the same racial group or social organization. But, at the same time, this inmate is scheming to manipulate staff and to take advantage of weaker peers (Sieverdes and Bartollas, 1986:143).

As might be expected, research indicates that organizational structure affects the norms and behavior of youthful prisoners. In other words, "[t]he more custodial and punitive settings had inmate cultures that were more violent, more hostile, and more oppositional than those in the treatment-oriented settings (Feld, 1981:336). This finding on the impact of organizational structure on inmate culture suggests that it is possible for administrators to reduce the negative environments in juvenile prisons by opting for an organizational structure that emphasizes treatment over custody. One specific option that administrators can take is to limit the size of juvenile residential placements. Larger populations are more susceptible to custodial climates than smaller populations. Another option is to facilitate communication between treatment staff and custodial staff so that staff members do not exacerbate potential treatment-custody conflicts.

Deprivation of Heterosexual Contact

Another negative effect of institutions is that incarcerated youths are deprived of heterosexual relationships at a time when such relationships are critical in helping the teenager to define himself or herself as a mature sexual adult. Although written about incarcerated girls, Giallombardo's comments on this matter apply equally well (with the appropriate adjustments) to imprisoned boys:

> They are developing images of themselves as adult women, and they are beset with many anxieties concerning their sexuality and acceptance by males. The exclusion of males in their own age group is a source of confusion for adolescent girls. . . . Their confusion is compounded by virtue of the fact that during incarceration they are socialized to view other women as legitimate sex objects (Giallombardo, 1974:244).

In response to this deprivation, many of the girls adjust by participating in kinship role systems and/or homosexual alliances. In the training schools Giallombardo (1974) studied, for example, the girls had affectionate nicknames for one another, wrote love letters to other girls, picked their own special songs, "went steady," and even got married in formal ceremonies (out of staff view). Another study reported that only about 17 percent of the institutionalized girls reported at least one homosexual experience (ranging from kissing to intimate sexual contact) but about half of the girls reported taking a "make-believe family" role (Propper, 1982). Such behavior was clearly not intended by the authorities and has been labeled a "secondary adjustment" (Goffman, 1961:199). The problem with secondary adjustments is that they divert the youths' attention away from the main aspects of the supposedly rehabilitative programs, such as education and counseling, and direct that attention to making life within the training school as pleasant as possible.

As noted above, Schaffner (2006) claims that concern for deprivation of heterosexual contact needs updating. She argues that some girls are gay, transgender, or questioning of their sexual orientation. If juvenile correctional programs are not aware of this, they are missing a critical component of the lives of the offenders they are trying to help. She also thinks that many correctional workers are not aware of contemporary social habits, even of heterosexual girls, and thus can be overly judgmental of behaviors or remarks that should be seen as nothing out of the ordinary for the contemporary culture.

Other problems faced by incarcerated youths include loss of liberty, deprivation of personal possessions, and boredom. Particularly important in terms of possessions is the loss of clothing articles. This is important because it entails a loss of the opportunity to explore various clothing styles. According to Giallombardo (1974), such exploratory behavior is directly related to a girl's sense of identity as well as her popularity.

In one training school, youths had several complaints: loss of autonomy; they felt like helpless children who had to ask permission to shower or get paper and pencil; loss of privacy; they had roommates who smelled bad or talked all the time; loss of desirable possessions; low-quality soap or toothpaste; and bland food. They hoped staff would rent movies or video games for them or bring them books or magazines to break the boredom (Inderbitzin, 2006b).

An important national study on living conditions in juvenile facilities found "substantial and widespread deficiencies" in four matters: living space, security, control of suicidal behavior, and health care (Abt Associates, 1994). Many institutions experience problems concerning crowding, safety and prevention of escapes, suicidal behavior, and health screening. That same report also felt that there was a need to collect systematic data on confined youths' educational and treatment needs. Further evidence that problems continue to exist in juvenile institutions is the publication of a recent American Bar Association manual that offers suggestions for litigation strategies to contest problematic conditions (Puritz and Scali, 1998). It is unfortunate but true that often a lawsuit is the only way that problems in youth prisons become known. For example, it took a lawsuit in Arizona to make it known that one of the state youth prisons maintained "harsh conditions, arbitrary and capricious decision making, and an unduly punitive, unrehabilitative environment" (Bortner and Williams, 1997:3).

NEW DIRECTIONS IN INSTITUTIONAL INTERVENTIONS

Deinstitutionalization of Status Offenders

Since the mid-1970s there has been a movement away from placing status offenders and delinquents in the same state-operated institutions.

It is felt that any mixing of status offenders and delinquents can have harmful consequences on the status offenders. In fact, much of this movement has been one of **deinstitutionalization**: trying to avoid any involuntary placements of status offenders (the practice of some states to deinstitutionalize delinquents as well as status offenders will be discussed in the next section). The strength of this movement is indicated by the fact that 98 percent of the juveniles in public custody in 2003 were delinquents, and only 2 percent were status offenders. This is a considerable decrease from the 7 percent figure in 1985 (Sickmund and Baunach, 1986; Snyder and Sickmund, 2006).

Deinstitutionalization (Closing Training Schools)

Several states, including Massachusetts, Maryland, Pennsylvania, and Utah, have decreased dramatically their use of training schools by closing some of these facilities. In Massachusetts, for example, only about 15 percent of the approximately 800 youths committed to the State Department of Youth services each year are first placed in a locked treatment program. The other 85 percent of the committed youths are placed in community-based programs such as group homes, forestry camps, day treatment programs, outreach-tracking programs, or foster care. Most of the programs have been privatized; private agencies run the programs on a contract basis with the state. In addition, the residential programs are small in size, with no more than 30 youths housed in a facility (Krisberg and Austin, 1993). What this means for most youths is that they spend only about four weeks in secure placement and then are placed in nonsecure treatment programs. In states with heavy reliance on traditional training schools, most youths spend several months in secure confinement and then are placed on aftercare (parole).

The National Council on Crime and Delinquency evaluated the Massachusetts reform and found it to be successful. Compared to other states still relying on traditional training schools, Massachusetts had similar recidivism results, and the effort was cost-effective. More specifically, depending on how long Massachusetts would incarcerate youths in traditional training schools, it would have to spend $10 million to $16.8 million more per year than it was spending in its deinstitutionalization mode (Krisberg, Austin, and Steele, 1989).

An evaluation of the closing of one institution in Maryland, however, found contrary results. Almost three-quarters (72%) of the youths committed to the State Department of Juvenile Services after the institution's closing were rearrested during the one-year follow-up period, whereas only about 45 percent of the youths who had been institutionalized at the training school prior to its closing were rearrested. In a two-and-one-half year follow-up period, 83 percent of the post-closing group were rearrested, compared to 66 percent and 69 percent of the two groups that had been incarcerated at the training school under study. The authors concluded that "the alternatives available when Montrose [the state training school] was closed were less effective in reducing crime than institutionalization would have been" (Gottfredson and Barton, 1993:604). The authors suggest that their findings support the conclusion that "neither institutional nor community-based programs are uniformly effective or ineffective. The *design* [emphasis in original] of the intervention rather than its location appears important" (Gottfredson and Barton, 1993:605). In other words, simply closing traditional training schools is only half of the strategy. The other half is to devise effective programs for the youths that would have been committed to the training schools. It appears that Massachusetts was able to devise such effective alternative programming for its delinquent commitments. Maryland apparently did not come up with effective alternative programming, so the recidivism rates for the group not sent to the training school were disappointing.

Another state that has tried to reduce its institutional population is Missouri. It closed its only training school in 1983 and has tried to keep newer institutions at 33 beds or fewer. To accomplish the goal of reduced placements, Missouri uses such strategies as day treatment programs and trackers. Day treatment is intended for youths released from residential confinement; it involves education, counseling, tutoring, and/or community service. Trackers are personnel, often college students completing a degree in social work or a related field, who monitor and support about 800 youths in community supervision. Trackers offer support, mentoring, and assistance. Missouri also uses nonsecure group homes. One benefit has been cost saving. In 2000, Missouri spent about $94 per every youth ages 10 to 17 in the state, compared to $140 per youth in surrounding states. The state also reports that only about 11 percent of youths released from custody were rearrested or returned to juvenile custody within one year (Mendel, 2001). Mendel (2001) argues that much of the reason for the apparent success of Missouri's emphasis on community programming is the hiring of high-quality staff. At all times youths are overseen by at least two educated and highly trained staff members, compared to other states in which less skilled officers supervise youths. An indication of the success of Missouri is its recent award for innovative programming (Ash Institute, 2008).

Blended Sentencing

The creation of blended sentencing allows either the juvenile court or the adult court to impose a sentence that can involve either the juvenile or the adult correctional system or both (see Chapter 8 for further discussion of blended sentencing). The adult sentence may be suspended pending either a violation or the commission of a new crime. Texas, for example, allows juveniles convicted of certain violent crimes or of habitual offender status to be sentenced to terms of up to 20 years for a second-degree felony and up to 10 years for a third-degree felony (Feld, 1998). One result of blended sentencing will be a growing number of youthful offenders in adult prisons. Note that juvenile offenders in adult prisons may still be considered "minors" for other purposes. In Wisconsin, for example, 17-year-olds in adult prisons are still subject to mandatory education and require parental consent for medical treatment (Torbet et al., 2000).

A study on victimization among youthful inmates in adult prisons is important in light of the development of blended sentencing. Maitland and Sluder interviewed 111 inmates ages 17 to 25. They found that less than 1 percent reported that they had been forced to engage in sexual activity, 3 percent had been forced to give up their money, and 5.5 percent had had a weapon used on them. Less serious victimization experiences, however, were much more frequent. Fifty-nine percent had been verbally harassed, approximately 50 percent had had their property stolen, and 38 percent had been hit, kicked, punched, or slapped. The authors concluded that "young, medium-security prison inmates are most likely to be subjected to less serious forms of victimization by peers during their terms of incarceration" (Maitland and Sluder, 1998:68). Thus, any trend toward putting delinquents in adult prisons when they are 17 or 18 can be expected to produce such victimization results for the youthful offenders so incarcerated.

Another negative aspect of blended sentencing and putting juveniles into criminal court and adult institutions is that the youths may have negative perceptions of how they were processed. In research on criminal court processing of youths in Florida, it was found that the court message to the youths was that their behavior was bad and they were bad. Prison staff also communicated a similar negative message; the youthful prisoners heard that "they were lost causes who could never redeem themselves or return to normal personhood" (Bishop, 2000:153).

Wilderness Programs

Another example of what Cullen and his colleagues (Cullen et al., 2005:66) call **common-sense corrections** is the use of various types of **wilderness programs**, ranging from relatively short stays in outdoor settings to rather long wagon train or ocean ship trips. Both private operators and some states have used this type of programming, which places delinquents in settings where they learn survival skills, limits, and self-esteem. The youths are put in natural settings where they must learn to cook, obtain shelter from the elements, tell directions (read a compass), start fires, and so forth. In the process of accomplishing such tasks, the youths learn to depend on both others and themselves. The thinking is that a successful survival experience in a natural setting will then transfer to the youth's normal environment and he or she will turn to more constructive activities than delinquency. The program, then, is based on common-sense notions (perhaps stemming from experience or familiarity with Boy Scouts and Girl Scouts) that outdoors know-how is beneficial.

A wilderness program in Georgia recently received attention when a 13-year-old boy died. Authorities fired several staff members due to the incident. It is alleged that camp counselors restrained the boy face down and denied him his inhaler (he was asthmatic) (Miller, 2005).

In earlier research, Lipsey and Wilson (1998) concluded that wilderness programs generally had weak effects or no effects on the recidivism rates of the youths who went through the programs compared to control groups. But in a more recent analysis of wilderness and challenge programs for juveniles, they found that programs with more intense physical activities or greater therapeutic enhancements reduced recidivism from 37 percent down to 29 percent (Wilson and Lipsey, 2003).

Adequate basics, such as food, clothing, and shelter, are some of the required criteria for wilderness treatment programs such as RedCliff Ascent's outing in the Wah Wah Mountains of Southwestern Utah. Troubled youths from around the world are sent to such programs in hope that they will straighten out their lives.

In conclusion, simply putting teens through a "survivor's" experience as depicted on television is not enough to reduce delinquency. It appears that the wilderness program must have a therapeutic aspect to be effective (Wilson and Lipsey, 2003). Once again, a common sense belief such as "getting outdoors is what those kids need" is not always accurate (Cullen et al., 2005:66).

SUMMARY

This chapter has examined state and private residential placements, ranging from training schools to wilderness experience programs. An examination of the effectiveness of institutional placements indicates that many children do not really need to be in training schools. Instead, they can be handled in less restrictive settings without any increase in recidivism. This part of the chapter also examined several problematic factors in residential placements, such as victimization, racial tension, and homosexual behavior. Unfortunately, residential placements often translate into horror stories for the children rather than therapeutic havens. Sexual assaults and racial tension have been well-documented components of placements in the past, and they are unlikely to disappear completely. Because of these and related problems, states such as Massachusetts, Maryland, Pennsylvania, and Utah turned to noninstitutional approaches to delinquency, in which fewer youngsters are placed in state training schools. Blended sentencing and increased processing of juvenile offenders in adult court, however, may translate into significant numbers of youthful offenders being incarcerated in adult prisons and to youths serving longer sentences than in the past. The most extreme possibility is that states will abolish juvenile court. If that happens, probably more juveniles will go to adult prisons but some youths will continue to be housed in institutions reserved for offenders under 18.

The only safe prediction is that juvenile corrections will not be the same as it was 25 years ago. It is likely that changes will continue to multiply as society attempts to minimize youth crime.

DISCUSSION QUESTIONS

1. Many are calling for harsher punishment for juvenile offenders, especially violent juvenile offenders. Do you think that persons holding that position are aware of the information on victimization in juvenile training schools (prisons)? Would knowledge of victimization risks in juvenile prisons affect calls for tougher measures for juveniles?

2. Do juveniles deserve prisons that are quite different from adult offenders? Should we continue to model juvenile prisons after schools? Should we drop any pretense of lesser punishment for juveniles and make juvenile facilities very similar to adult prisons?

3. Would you consider a career in juvenile corrections, in either public or private facilities?

4. Should corrections for juveniles go back to its roots and try to emphasize rehabilitation, or should it attempt to incorporate more punitive dimensions? What would the ideal residential program for juveniles look like? How can states prevent some of the abuses noted in this chapter, especially sexual abuse of female inmates?

5. Common sense has led to correctional efforts such as boot camps and wilderness experience programs. Evaluation research often indicates that these common-sense solutions are not all that effective. Why is common sense often a poor guide to public policy?

6. How do you envision juvenile corrections in 10 years? What will juvenile prisons look like a decade from now?

Chapter 11

JUVENILE PROBATION AND COMMUNITY CORRECTIONS

Important Terms

aftercare

"attack" probation

balanced approach

community justice

community service

effectiveness

emphasis on status offenses

goal confusion

motivational interviewing

peacemaking

probation

punitive model

restitution

restorative justice

social history investigation
   (predisposition report)

What You Need to Know

- In 2005, probation handled approximately 600,000 youths who were processed in some way for delinquency or a status offense by the juvenile court.

- In juvenile court, the probation presentence investigation may be called a social history investigation or a predisposition report.

- "Aftercare" is the juvenile court term for parole.

- One current approach in juvenile community corrections is the balanced approach, which attempts to balance offender accountability, competency development, and community safety.

- Police-probation partnerships, including searches of the offender's residence, are an example of a tough approach to juvenile probation.

- Other recent approaches in juvenile probation include restorative justice, peacemaking, and community justice.

- A number of treatment interventions are effective, including cognitive-behavioral and social learning programs.

- Some current concerns about juvenile probation include the problems of goal confusion and some aspects of both restitution and community service.

- Probation managers must attempt to implement programs that are effective in a variety of ways, including reducing recidivism, meeting offender needs, and satisfying the public.

INTRODUCTION

Even before the founding of the first juvenile court in Illinois in 1899, community interventions had been a central weapon of those seeking to fight delinquency. This chapter will examine both traditional and nontraditional community interventions and focus on some of the problems with these approaches to the delinquency problem. The chapter will first describe probation and aftercare for juveniles, highlight some of the current trends in community interventions, and then look at some of the concerns in the field. One of the key issues examined in this chapter is the **effectiveness** issue: Do community interventions have any impact on recidivism? In other words, do community interventions help to reduce the number of offenses committed by the juveniles exposed to the programs, or are the programs ineffective in reducing delinquent activity?

PROBATION

Statistics demonstrate that **probation** continues to be a critical part of the juvenile justice system. In 2005 (the most recent year for which complete data are available), an estimated 373,400 youths who were adjudicated delinquent in juvenile court were placed on probation. This represents well over half (60%) of the 623,900 youths who were adjudicated delinquent. Another 19,100 youths who were not adjudicated delinquent agreed to some form of probation, and another 164,000 youths who were not petitioned agreed to some form of voluntary probation. So probation handled more than 550,000 delinquents altogether in 2005. For status offenses, 46,300 cases resulted in probation, 52 percent of all status offense cases that were adjudicated in juvenile court. So probation was the most common disposition for adjudicated status offenders (Puzzanchera and Sickmund, 2008). (Table 11.1 shows the offenses for which delinquents were placed on probation.) Thus, probation continues to be the workhorse of the juvenile court (Torbet, 1996).

Social History (Predisposition) Investigations

When a child has been adjudicated as either a delinquent or a status offender, usually a probation officer conducts a **social history investigation (predisposition report)** of the youngster and his or her family. Similar to the so-called presentence investigation report in adult courts, social history reports offer judges legal and social information. Legal information includes descriptive material about the delinquency or status offense, including the child's, the victim's, and the police officer's (if a delinquent act) version of the offense, and verified data on the child's prior contacts, if any, with the juvenile court and with the police department's juvenile bureau. Social history information includes verification of the child's age (a critical legal condition for court action) and information on the child's development, family, education, and possible problems such as alcohol or other drug abuse.

TABLE 11.1 Adjudication Offenses for Juvenile Delinquency Probationers

Adjudicated Delinquent Offender Profiles			
Most Serious Offense	**2000**	**2004**	**2005**
Person	23%	24%	26%
Property	40	36	36
Drugs	13	13	13
Public Order	24	27	26
Total	100%	100%	100%
Adjudicated Status Offender Profiles			
Most Serious Offense	**2000**	**2004**	**2005**
Runaway	N/A	11%	12%
Truancy	N/A	38	39
Curfew	N/A	5	4
Ungovernability	N/A	18	20
Liquor law	N/A	23	19
Miscellaneous	N/A	7	6
Total	N/A	100%	100%

Note: Details may not add to total because of rounding.

Source: C. Puzzanchera, A.L. Stahl, T.A. Finnegan, N. Tierney, and H.N. Howard (2004). *Juvenile Court Statistics, 2000*. Pittsburgh: National Center for Juvenile Justice; Stahl, A., C. Puzzanchera, S. Livsey, T.A. Finnegan, N. Tierney, and H.N. Snyder (2007). *Juvenile Court Statistics: 2003-2004*. Pittsburgh: National Center for Juvenile Justice; C. Puzzanchera, and M. Sickmund (2008). *Juvenile Court Statistics, 2005*. Pittsburgh: National Center for Juvenile Justice. Reprinted with permission.

Probation officers gather such information by interviewing the youth; the youth's family, teachers, and other school personnel; the victim; and the police; and by checking various police, court, and school records. They usually collect information on previous arrests from police and court files. Likewise, they may obtain a copy of the child's

For the latest available statistics on juveniles and probation, go to the web site of the Office of Juvenile Justice and Delinquency Prevention and search for the latest report on juvenile court statistics. Go to http://www.ojjdp.ncjrs.gov/ojstatbb/cjrp/

cumulative school record, which contains information on the child's grades, attendance, disciplinary history, and intelligence testing. If necessary, in probation departments that have the resources, the officer may also see to it that a psychologist and/or a psychiatrist examine the child for any suspected emotional problems and to determine the child's intelligence quotient (IQ) more accurately (by an individual IQ test rather than a group test). The probation officer then summarizes all of this information in a report that provides the judge with a more informed basis for the disposition decision.

Some adult courts are now omitting all the social history information. Determinate sentencing in many jurisdictions means that only information about the current charges and the prior record of the accused pertains to sentencing.

Racial disparity can enter into probation reports. A recent examination of more than 200 narrative reports in a western state indicated that probation officers were more likely to note negative personality factors in reports about black youths but were more likely to note negative environmental factors in reports about white youths. Officers were also more likely to assign a higher risk of reoffending to black youths than white youths. There were no racial differences in sentencing recommendations (Bridges and Steen, 1998). Bishop claims that this study "provides some of the most compelling evidence to date of racial stereotyping by juvenile justice officials and of the power of racial stereotypes to influence decision making" (Bishop, 2005:57).

Probation Supervision

Youths who are placed on formal probation supervision in court must follow various conditions, such as reporting regularly to a probation officer, obeying the law, attending school, and remaining within the geographical jurisdiction of the court. Judges may also order specific conditions, such as restitution to the victim(s) of the delinquent act or community service restitution (e.g., performing cleanup work at the local park or playground). Another special condition might be to attend counseling sessions with a social worker, psychologist, or psychiatrist, or require the parents to attend the counseling sessions. A judge might also order a short stay (about one month) in detention as a condition of probation (Schwartz et al., 1987).

If a juvenile follows the conditions of the probation disposition and is adjusting favorably at home, in school, and in the community, then the probation officer can request an early discharge from supervision. If a youngster is not abiding by the conditions and is not adjusting well, then the probation officer may request that the judge order that the youth is in violation of the probation agreement. In that case, the judge can either order the probation to continue (perhaps with additional conditions such as more frequent reporting to the probation officer) or can terminate the probation and place the youth under the supervision of the state youth correctional authority for placement in a public facility or place the youth in a private residential setting.

BOX 11.1

To Register or Not to Register: The Question of Juvenile Sex Offenders

Tennessee does not include persons who committed sex offenses as juveniles on its public sex offender registry. This could result in a 10 percent reduction in federal funding based on provisions of the Adam Walsh Child Protection and Safety Act of 2006.

In Knoxville, Tennessee, over the course of about 10 months, a man raped three women whom he found at coin-operated laundries in the early morning hours. The man had been tried as a sex offender in juvenile court. Tennessee law did not require him to report as a sex offender.

What do you think? Should a juvenile sex offense qualify to place one on a state's sex offender registry? Or does the immaturity and impulsiveness of juveniles (recall the reasoning of the U.S. Supreme Court in the *Roper* case) argue against such placement?

In answering, consider that one juvenile court in Tennessee has started its own Sex Offender Management Task Force, which tries to keep juvenile sex offenders out of state custody by treating them and then reducing the charges so that the youth is not labeled a sex offender for the rest of his or her life. The child is given a complete assessment, and three treatment plans are submitted to the judge who decides which plan to use. Teens who have committed more serious or violent sex offenses are transferred to adult court. Out of a limited sample of 20 offenders, the program reports no new offenses.

What do you think? Should juvenile sex offenders who are younger and commit less serious offenses be given a second chance? Should juvenile court judges have the discretion to not automatically place a juvenile on a sex offender registry and the discretion to transfer more serious offenders to adult court?

Sources: Associated Press (2008). "State Sex Offender Registry Exempts Juvenile Offenses." *Johnson City Press* (August 18, 2008):5A; B. Campbell (2008). "DCS Picks Up Funding of Program that Helps Juvenile Sex Offenders." *Johnson City Press* (September 13, 2008):4A.

AFTERCARE

Many states also have aftercare or parole programs for youths released from state training schools, group homes, or forestry camp placements. **Aftercare** supervision is very similar to probation supervision. In fact, in some states, probation officers also perform aftercare supervision duties. Just as with probation, youths on aftercare status must follow specific conditions and report on a regular basis to a parole officer. If they do not, parole can be revoked and they can be sent back to an institutional placement.

As noted in Chapter 10, recidivism statistics for youths released from institutions cause concern; states are reporting that 55 percent of released youths are arrested for a new offense. (Snyder and Sickmund, 2006). A recent national evaluation of intensive juvenile aftercare proved disappointing. Approximately one-half the youths were arrested for one or more new felonies, and if technical violations (breaking the rules of probation) were included, about 80 percent were rearrested for something. The most disturbing conclusion was that "no statistically significant or substantive differences were seen between IAP [intensive aftercare] and control youth on almost all the recidivism measures" (Wiebush et al., 2005:80). Recidivism measures included percent arrested, number of offenses, severity and frequency of offenses, and time to first arrest. There was some minor evidence that more treatment was associated with less recidivism, but this finding was significant in only one of the study sites. So even a program intended to improve post-release performance did not produce the desired results.

SUPERVISION AND COUNSELING

Probation and aftercare (parole) officers working with juveniles use various combinations of assistance and control (Glaser, 1964) to help youthful offenders avoid further trouble. Some officers act like social workers or counselors as they try to understand the youth and his or her problems and assist the youngster in gaining greater self-insight and self-esteem. Such officers also might attempt some family therapy to help parents better understand the family interaction patterns that have contributed to the child's misbehavior. Other officers assume a tougher role: a quasi-police officer who first threatens the youth with punishment and then monitors the compliance of the child to the court conditions. This "surveillance"(Studt, 1973) type of officer typically believes that deterrence and incapacitation are more important goals than rehabilitation.

Whether oriented toward assistance or control, probation and parole officers tend to use one of several counseling techniques—including reality therapy, client-centered (nondirective) therapy, rational emotive therapy, or behaviorism. Assistance-oriented officers utilize these counseling techniques to a greater extent than control-oriented officers, but even the latter use some of the basic principles of these approaches to interview probationers and to establish some rapport (for more information on counseling techniques, see Van Voorhis, Braswell, and Lester, 2007). Both cognitive techniques (Chavaria, 1997) and behavior modification have proven effective in community interventions with juveniles (Gendreau, Cullen, and Bonta, 1994; MacKenzie, 2006).

Recently, attention has also been focused on offender-agent interactions in the supervision process. Experts are suggesting that motivational interviewing can be effective in probation. **Motivational interviewing** refers to "a style of communication that makes it more likely that offenders will listen, will be engaged in the process, and will be more ready to make changes" (Walters et al., 2007:10).

Motivational interviewing does not mean that officers are to become therapists. It simply recognizes the important role that officers play. It is unrealistic to think that officers can simply refer youthful probationers on their caseloads to therapists or programs, or that officers can simply say, "You need to go to counselor X or program X." If the juvenile offender is not motivated to change and is not motivated to go to the counselor or the program, he or she most likely will not go and will not change. In summary, motivational interviewing recognizes that officers interact with probationers and that those interactions can be crucial in the change process (Walters et al., 2007:10).

A recent study in Maryland evaluated an evidence-based supervision model that included features such as motivational interviewing and other cognitive-behavioral strategies. The program reduced arrest recidivism by 42 percent and technical violations by 20 percent but had no impact on positive drug tests (Taxman, 2008). Taxman's conclusion is that this new model of community supervision—which is a shared decision-making model that involves the offender in the process of determining goals and ways to achieve those goals—can be effective in probation and parole (Taxman, 2008).

CURRENT TRENDS IN COMMUNITY SUPERVISION

Several developments are taking place in community corrections. Many are calling for tougher community corrections with greater attention to punishment and controlling offender risk. Other voices, however, continue to insist that probation and other community interventions need to be more than just strict punishment for crime.

The Balanced Approach

One current approach in juvenile corrections is the **balanced approach**. "This philosophy requires the system to provide balanced attention to the need for competency development, accountability, and community safety and requires efforts to restore, to the greatest extent possible, the victim and community to their precrime status"(Kurlychek, Torbet, and Bozynski, 1999:3). It is thought that restitution and community service send out a message that the offender is responsible for his or her crime and is being held accountable for it. It is considered important that the offender come to realize the harm he or she has caused the victim(s). As of 2004, at least 16 states had juvenile court laws with purpose clauses focusing on the balanced approach (Griffin, Szymanski, and King, 2005; Snyder and Sickmund, 2006).

As you might guess, the balanced approach is actually a combination of traditional rehabilitation, restorative justice, and classical criminology. One example of the balanced approach is Utah's juvenile restitution program, which includes a restitution work fund. Juveniles without jobs or money can perform community service tasks and thereby earn money for their restitution orders. In Boston, Operation Night Light has police and probation officers together on street patrol checking to ensure that probationers are complying with their probation conditions. St. Louis uses deputy juvenile officers and police to make random home visits to check compliance with court-ordered curfews (Urban, St. Cyr, and Decker, 2003). A similar program in Maryland has the probation officers and police targeting selected crime "hot spots" (Kurlychek, Torbet, and Bozynski, 1999).

Another example is the Gang Violence Reduction Program in Chicago, which combines surveillance of violent or potentially violent gang members and the provision of services. Police and probation officers increase their supervision of target youths and provide education, employment, employment training, and some counseling. Evaluation has found decreased serious gang violence and improved perceptions among residents concerning gang crime and police effectiveness in targeting such crime (Howell and Hawkins, 1998).

Pennsylvania has attempted to implement the balanced approach. In fact, the state legislature amended the juvenile law purpose clause in 1995 to include balanced and restorative justice principles. A recent report on outcome measures in 12 Pennsylvania counties for calendar year 2003 provides a snapshot of what the departments have been attempting to do and what they have achieved. Related to the objective of community protection, the counties report that 87 percent of probation cases had no new offenses, and 87 percent also had no serious probation violations. Under the objective of accountability, more than 100,000 hours of community service were completed, with 92 percent of probationers ordered to perform community service actually completing such orders. Almost one-half million dollars of restitution was paid ($479,587), 47 percent of the amount ordered. Eighty-four percent of the probationers ordered to pay restitution paid it in full. In summary, more than 75 percent of the juveniles on probation were attending school or GED classes or were working at case closing. Almost 80 percent were closed as "successful," and only 3 percent were closed as "unsuccessful" (Griffin and Thomas, 2004).

This report on juvenile probation in Pennsylvania contrasts very favorably with a federal (GAO) report on adult probation some 20 years ago.

That report noted the woeful lack of case plans and treatment objectives and unenforced probation conditions for the adult probationers under study. It was a picture of much not even being attempted. Here there is an accountant-like depiction of activity and outcomes. Reports like this can be used to show both legislators and taxpayers that probation is working—that it is accomplishing something. As a recent report on probation noted, "The bottom line is results" (Griffin and Torbet, 2002:134).

On the other hand, it is necessary to keep a certain caution about glowing outcome reports. A focus on outcome reporting can lead to attempts to make the statistics as positive as possible, even if those statistics hide deficiencies. Officers can be tempted to close cases as "successful" even where there is less than complete or desired success. The perfect evaluation would be a controlled or quasi-experiment in which probation is compared to a control group that gets supervision from a nonofficial agency or perhaps no supervision at all. This is especially important in analyzing juvenile probation because many of the youths are first-time offenders or less serious offenders, and a good scare in court might well deter them from future delinquency.

A specific example of the need for caution is the information on community service. The report notes that in Allegheny County alone (Pittsburgh, PA), probationers completed almost 69,000 hours of community service in 2002, the equivalent of more than $350,000 in labor if the youths had been paid the minimum wage for all those hours. (They simply multiply the number of hours worked times the minimum wage to get this estimate of value.)

This estimate of value makes several critical assumptions. One is that the youths actually worked all those hours and worked them fully—not wasting time. A recent report suggests that even regular, paid workers waste about two hours a day at work (drinking coffee, gossiping with coworkers, surfing the Internet, etc.). A second assumption is that those hours and the work were truly necessary, not "make-work" projects that somebody devised to fill the time that the youths were supposed to serve. Did the walls the youths painted really need a fresh coat of paint, or was painting those walls a way to "keep those kids from probation busy"? Finally, the estimate of $350,000 in "free" labor does not include any accounting of how much it costs to supervise the youths; a probation officer or someone else had to make sure the kids got to the work sites and actually did some work. So while reports such as the one from Pennsylvania are encouraging, the actual benefits may not be quite as rosy as depicted.

The Punitive Model: Attack (Tough) Probation

One concern about the balanced approach is whether it in fact "balances" the concerns for competency development, accountability, and community safety, or simply places emphasis on accountability.

Painting a map turned mural, students fill in the black outline to a giant-scale map of Washington State, in a geography class at the Northwest Regional Learning Center (NRLC) in Everett, Washington. The NRLC is a detention school for kids on probation or out on parole through the juvenile justice system and serves as a last chance for some students to earn their high school degree if their former school will not accept them back.

If the balanced approach is not actually balanced, then it might be considered a **punitive model**. This philosophy is quite direct; the offender, even if a juvenile, deserves to be punished.

Miller (1996), for one, argues that the toughening of probation has gone too far. He contends that probation has lost much of its original mission of helping the offender. He argues that probation officers have abandoned any pretense at a social work role and have become "ersatz" (imitation) cops. He says that in this new **"attack probation"** style (a term developed by British criminologist Andrew Rutherford) officers see "their role as one in which to search out any means possible to get the probationer into prison. The motto of this practice was mounted on the office wall of one of California's chief probation officers: 'Trail 'em, Surveil 'em, Nail 'em, and Jail 'em.'" (Miller, 1996:131). In other words, if probation officers are out on the streets at night in "hot spots" (areas with high rates of crime), they are there as quasi-police officers looking for trouble and not as friendly social workers.

As mentioned in Chapter 7 on policing, one recent example of tough probation is police–probation partnerships, as in San Bernardino, California, where a police officer and a probation officer together make a home visit to all new juvenile probationers to explain the rules of probation and search the probationer's residence for weapons and drugs. Although the program has had some effect in reducing serious crimes in the city, one concern is mission distortion for probation—that probation officers may no longer see themselves as service providers or social workers but may instead over-identify with a law enforcement role (Worrall and Gaines, 2006).

A critical question about getting tough is whether such tactics are effective in reducing recidivism. That issue is discussed in the next major section of this chapter. Another interesting question posed by this get-tough movement is whether it is appropriate to use shame tactics in probation. For a discussion of this issue, see Box 11.2.

BOX 11.2

Shame Tactics in Probation and Community Corrections

Shame strategies take several forms. One form of shame penalty is apology. For example, one school vandalizer was forced to apologize in front of the student bodies at the 13 schools he vandalized. Some shame penalties, however, are much more negative, and objections arise that they are stigmatizing rather than reintegrative. For example, some offenders have been required to wear t-shirts or display signs on their car or residence proclaiming their offense ("I am a convicted shoplifter" or "convicted drunk driver"). Karp (1998) contends that such dramatic strategies are ineffective or worse: "Shame penalties that emphasize humiliation are likely to be counterproductive as they drive a wedge between offenders and conventional society" (p. 291). Thus, shame penalties can isolate the offender rather than assist him or her to rejoin the community. He also questions whether shame penalties are effective in modern society, which has an anonymous aspect compared to the potentially more effective informal small group setting (Karp, 1998). In other words, modern America is so big that we do not know our neighbors and thus we do not really experience shame when others (who are strangers) learn that we have done wrong. Shame only has meaning in a small community where people know one another.

Andrew von Hirsch argues against shaming tactics based on an ethical position that such tactics violate the respect that the offender as a human deserves. Von Hirsch argues that punishments should not demean the dignity of the offender. If they destroy the dignity of the offender, they are unacceptable. Thus, von Hirsch is opposed to t-shirts for offenders or bumper stickers that make drunk drivers advertise their offense because there "is no way a person can, with dignity, go about in public with a sign admitting himself or herself to be a moral pariah" (1990:168).

Proponents of identifying labels for offenders would argue that they enhance the punishment value of community corrections. Such marks make probation or parole tougher rather than a lenient "slap on the wrist." Supporters would also argue that there may be deterrent value in the measures. It is embarrassing to wear such markings, and this could serve to deter others from drunk driving or whatever offense results in the added penalty.

What do you think? What kinds of shaming might be effective for juvenile offenders? What are the limits of acceptable strategies?

Renewed Emphasis on Status Offenses

An **emphasis on status offenses** such as truancy is making a comeback in some circles. In 2004, approximately 160,000 status offense cases were petitioned to juvenile court, and about 51,800 juveniles were placed on probation for status offenses (Stahl et al., 2007). About 40 percent of the children were placed on probation due to truancy and about 20 percent for ungovernability. Kern County, California, for example, has instituted a truancy program that uses two deputy probation officers to work with students and families. If initial efforts to resolve truancy fail, the truant youth is referred to one of the deputy probation officers, who then meets with the family at least four times. The officer also makes unannounced home visits, monitors attendance, counsels the youth and his or her parents, and refers the family to appropriate service providers. Tracking continues for one year. If unsuccessful, the case is referred back to the school for possible referral to the district attorney for court action (Garry, 1996). What makes this emphasis on status offenses like truancy new is that status offenses are receiving increased attention due to research that indicates that they are risk factors for serious and violent delinquency. So there is a fear that if these troublesome behaviors are not dealt with, then there is a definite possibility of much worse behavior in the future.

Restorative Justice

Bazemore and Maloney argue that restorative justice should be the theme in a new paradigm for criminal justice, juvenile justice in general, and probation in particular. In contrast to retributive justice, which focuses on vengeance, deterrence, and punishment, **restorative justice** "is concerned with repairing the damage or harm done to victims and the community through a process of negotiation, mediation, victim empowerment, and reparation" (Bazemore and Maloney, 1994:28). In addition to a focus on such repair, restorative justice also emphasizes involving victims, offenders, and community members in the process and rethinking the roles of government and community in trying to achieve justice (Bazemore and Schiff, 2005). As one commentator puts it, "restorative justice is about relationships—how relationships are harmed by crime and how they can be rebuilt to promote recovery and healing for people affected by crime" (Kurki, 2000:266).

As Chapter 12 discusses restorative justice in full, we will end the discussion of restorative justice in probation at this point. We simply note that restorative justice programs can be quite positive. For example, an evaluation of the Community Justice Committee's restorative justice program in Maricopa County, Arizona, showed that 90 percent of the youths referred to the program completed it, and only 20 percent recidivated (that is, had a new complaint filed with juvenile court over the

24-month study period), versus a 32 percent recidivism rate for the comparison, standard diversion program group. Given that the study sample included more than 4,000 program youths and more than 5,000 in the comparison group, the findings are impressive (de Beus and Rodriguez, 2005). Another impressive piece of evidence in support of restorative justice is a meta-analysis of 35 restorative justice programs that found them to be more effective than traditional programs in improving victim and offender satisfaction, increasing compliance with restitution, and reducing recidivism (Latimer, Dowden, and Muise, 2005).

Peacemaking

Like restorative justice, **peacemaking** is a positive philosophy that seeks to go beyond simply criticizing the status quo and beyond a simple focus on recidivism reduction. Peacemaking is a perspective that supports efforts of corrections workers, whether prison counselors or probation officers, to help offenders find greater meaning in their lives. Two proponents, Bo Lozoff and Michael Braswell, contend that all great religions teach four classic virtues: honesty, courage, kindness, and a sense of humor. In this perspective, reductions in recidivism and programs like counseling or vocational training are still important but they are more external. The deeper goal is internal personal change: "The primary goal is to help build a happier, peaceful person right there in the prison [if working with prisoners], a person whose newfound self-honesty and courage can steer him or her to adjust to the biases and shortcomings of a society which does not feel comfortable with ex-offenders" (Lozoff and Braswell, 1989:2).

In a peacemaking perspective, both personal transformation and institutional change are critical, but personal change is seen as the basis of social change. It is critical to begin with yourself. It is also a lifetime task that needs constant work (Braswell, Fuller, and Lozoff, 2001).

Community Justice

Another recent development in community corrections is community justice. The mission of **community justice** is to help community residents "to manage their own affairs, solve their own problems, and live together effectively and safely. This goal is best achieved by giving everyone a stake in the quality of community life" (Clear and Karp, 1998:55). To achieve this mission, community justice involves risk assessment and control of offenders, victim restoration, community contracting, and cost sharing.

Like community policing, community justice is based on the principle that the community has a responsibility to deal with offenders. The community cannot simply assume that probation officers will by themselves take care of offenders and offender problems. The community must allow the offender to make reparation to the victim and also enable the offender "to obtain the assistance, supervision, and supports (including treatment intervention programs) necessary to live in the community crime-free" (Clear and Karp, 1998:54).

Community justice is an ideal that sounds plausible and desirable. One question about community justice is just how open communities are to such an ideal. When talk radio and television commentators focus on prosecutors, judges, and even governors that they consider too soft on crime, one has to ask how much room there is for community justice programs? If a sufficient number of observers think such programs are too lenient, will the programs be given a chance to operate? Programs such as community justice inevitably have failures. Whenever you allow offenders to remain in the community, whether on probation, parole, or some new community justice initiative, a percentage will commit new crimes. If community programs are criticized for such recidivism, public outrage may well force the programs to close or to become much more restrictive in the numbers and types of offenders they serve. Public receptivity to such programs is an important issue.

Another question about community justice is a question raised in the chapter on policing, namely, whether contemporary communities are cohesive enough and have enough resources to support efforts such as community policing or community justice. In other words, are communities willing to do the work required to make community justice succeed? Are people willing to get involved in programs that help victims and help offenders? Or are most people spending so much time on jobs and family that they simply do not have the time or the willingness to help make something like community justice work? As discussed earlier, Putnam (2000) noted that people are having less and less time to give to voluntary organizations such as Kiwanis and Rotary. And even if people are willing to devote time to community justice, do impoverished communities have sufficient resources to assist juvenile offenders in their midst? On the other hand, Vermont has had considerable success in attracting volunteers to serve on reparative boards in that state (Karp, Bazemore, and Chesire, 2004).

Another concern about community justice is that many of the communities with the worst crime problems are problematic communities in other ways as well. Communities with high crime rates also have low employment rates, lower rates of intact families, more problem schools, and fewer support networks. A community justice center may have many caring judges, prosecutors, and defense attorneys, but if the community does not have resources, these caring justice center personnel may not be able to truly assist community residents. Clear and Karp (1998) suggest that cost savings generated by community justice programs be directed to the programs to pay their way. They contend that every person diverted from a prison sentence saves the state about

$45,000 a year; such savings could be used to fund community justice. The problem is that such apparent savings are not necessarily real; one less prisoner does not mean that the prison system can fire a guard making $45,000 a year, for example. Even if such savings did result, the state prison system does not have the legal authority to send $45,000 directly to the community justice center.

A PBS documentary, "Red Hook Justice" (Sugar Pictures, 2004), inadvertently brought home the problem of lack of community resources. A male youth was back in court on a progress check. The judge asked him where he had looked for a summer job. The youth mentioned some fast food places he had applied to but had not heard back from. The judge then asked the youth if he had applied at Company X because X did a lot of hiring. The youth said that X went out of business some months earlier. Apart from the slight embarrassment on the judge's part for mentioning a company that was out of business, this exchange in court shows that well-intentioned judges and probation officers face a structural battle. Many jobs for teens and young adults now exist in suburban sprawl areas far removed from city districts that are the sites of community justice centers.

Based on restorative justice principles and on concepts about corrections of place, one California jurisdiction started an intensive probation program aimed at providing a wide range of services to both probationers and their families. The study design involved random assignment to either the experimental probation program or a control group that was regular probation (one office visit to the probation officer per month and a home visit by the officer every three months).

Evaluation results showed that program youths received significantly more services than control youths. The program youths experienced an average of 14 contacts per month whereas regular probation officers saw their clients once a month. Despite the dramatic differences in services, there were no significant differences in any of the recidivism measures, including arrest measures and incarceration (Lane et al., 2005).

The authors give two possible reasons for the failure of this intensive program to show lower recidivism than regular probation. First, they suspect that many of the regular probationers received more services than the records show. Regular probationers were referred out to quite a few services. Second, youths in both groups were at relatively low risk whereas the effectiveness literature indicates that youths at high or medium risk should be the targets of interventions.

On the positive side, because the intensive program youths did no worse, it can be argued that this research showed that a rehabilitative model can be just as effective as a more traditional model: "...programs focusing on helping offenders may be as useful as those that focus on a more punishment-oriented, surveillance approach" (Lane et al., 2005:47).

Although this project was supposed to be an implementation of some of Clear's ideas of "corrections of place" (Clear and Cadora, 2003), the evaluation did not measure efforts to affect the community such as community development and community service. It appears that what was measured were the services provided to each probationer and the recidivism of the probationers. As a result, we must caution that the final word is not in about the effectiveness of community justice efforts.

Current Trends: What Does the Future Hold?

It is difficult to predict where community corrections will go from here. One possible path is to continue down the "get tough" road. A grim reality is that further financial cutbacks will force probation to do less and less. Another path is to attempt to return probation to a more traditional focus on trying to rehabilitate offenders. Other departments may seek to implement the balanced approach, restorative justice, or community justice (or some combination of such programs). An important issue in deciding on which direction to take is the effectiveness of community corrections. The next two sections will discuss some important findings from the effectiveness literature. The first section will review major findings on the effectiveness of community sanctions such as probation. The second section will review the research on effective treatments. Together these findings give some assistance in thinking about the most appropriate direction for community corrections to take.

EFFECTIVENESS OF JUVENILE PROBATION AND RELATED SANCTIONS

Although national recidivism statistics on juvenile probationers are not readily available and although the research on juvenile probation has not been as extensive as the research on adult probation, there are considerable research findings available to illuminate the effectiveness issue for juvenile probation. Based on research on both juveniles and adults, several conclusions about the effectiveness of community correctional interventions for juveniles seem sound.

One implication of the research is that simply making probation tougher does not work (Cullen, Wright, and Applegate, 1996). The cumulative research on such get-tough measures as Scared Straight programs, boot camps, and intensive supervision has demonstrated that harsher measures, without more treatment elements, do not reduce recidivism. Experimental evaluations of such programs have shown that these tough measures do not reduce recidivism (new arrests or convictions)(Cullen, 2007; MacKenzie, 2006).

Related to this is the finding that often community supervision may be no worse than incarceration—that is, at least as effective as incarceration (see Krisberg and Howell, 1998). In fact, Lipsey and Wilson

(1998) found that among programs that produced consistent evidence of positive effects for serious offenders, noninstitutional programs showed greater reductions in recidivism than institutional programs. This is important. Although offenders released to community supervision commit some new crimes, the fact that they do no worse (and may do better) than offenders sentenced to training schools and then released on traditional aftercare suggests that society can use community supervision knowing that it is not more harmful than incarceration.

Another clear lesson is that the effectiveness of probation varies from place to place. An initial report on the effectiveness of adult felony probation found that the failure rate (new arrests) was 65 percent (Petersilia et al., 1985). Subsequent studies found some rates as low as 22 percent and others in between those two rates (Whitehead, 1991). There are several explanations for such variation. Some locations may be under budgetary pressures and may not have the financial resources to provide much treatment or surveillance of offenders. In adult corrections, for example, an effort to implement results-oriented strategic planning in the Alabama prison system failed because the program did not deal with the central problem: lack of resources. Alabama was only spending about $9,000 per prisoner, compared to a national average of about $27,000 (Moynihan, 2005). Some locations, on the other hand, may be implementing treatment programs that have proven to be effective (for a discussion of such principles, see the next section below). Thus, juvenile probation may be quite effective in some locations but experience serious problems in other locations.

Still another lesson is that intensive supervision can lead to easier detection of technical violations (Petersilia, 1997). In other words, officers are more likely to detect intensive supervision offenders violating the rules of probation such as not reporting to the probation officer, leaving the jurisdiction without permission, breaking curfew, testing positive on a urine drug test, and skipping school. This explains why intensive supervision can be ineffective if the goal is to reduce prison or training school populations. Detection of technical violations often results in revocation of probation. Then the offender is incarcerated as punishment for breaking the conditions of probation. So a sanction (such as intensive supervision) intended to reduce the number of persons being institutionalized can in fact increase the number being institutionalized. This problem can be avoided, however, if a court and correctional agency put in place a system of graduated penalties for technical violations (Altschuler, 1998). A discouraging finding is that some studies have shown that simply being on probation supervision without any officer contacts sometimes is just as effective as being on probation and being seen by an officer (National Council on Crime and Delinquency, 1987). This finding questions whether probation officers have much impact on their clients. One explanation is that perhaps officers are not doing much for their clients. Another explanation is that some offenders do not need much supervision. Perhaps being caught and being placed on probation sent a clear message to these probationers and they have learned their lesson and will not reoffend.

Perhaps the most encouraging finding in recent research is that intensive supervision that includes treatment components can reduce recidivism (Petersilia, 1997). This suggests that although being tough is not enough, addressing offender needs can make a difference. Recall also that a national evaluation of intensive juvenile aftercare did not show effectiveness but that in one of the study sites treatment was associated with less recidivism (Wiebush et al., 2005 [see discussion earlier in this chapter]). Contrary to this claim, a recent study of aftercare with treatment did not show any effectiveness. The study, however, involved a sample of all substance-abusing offenders (Sealock, Gottfredson, and Gallagher, 1997). Because research indicates that treatment is critical, the next section will review the treatment research to show which types of treatment appear to offer promise and which seem to be ineffective.

EFFECTIVE AND INEFFECTIVE TREATMENT INTERVENTIONS WITH OFFENDERS

Although several well-publicized reports claimed that little seemed to be effective in changing offenders and reducing recidivism, there now appears to be considerable consensus that there is knowledge about effective and ineffective interventions. This section will discuss both types of interventions.

Gendreau and his colleagues have spearheaded much of the treatment research. They have concluded that there are several principles of effective interventions. First, interventions need to be intensive and behavioral. Intensive means that the intervention takes up at least 40 percent of the offender's time and goes on for three to nine months. Behavioral interventions are based on the principles of operant conditioning, especially reinforcement. Simply, there must be rewards for desirable behaviors. Some examples are token economies, modeling, and cognitive behavioral interventions, such as problem solving, reasoning, self-control, and self-instructional training. Successful programs target criminogenic needs such as antisocial attitudes, peer associations, substance-abuse problems, and self-control issues rather than non-criminogenic needs such as low self-esteem, anxiety, or depression. The responsivity principle means that attention needs to be paid to matching offenders, therapists, and programs. For example, offenders who prefer structure do better in a more structured program such as a token economy. More anxious offenders do better with therapists who show more interpersonal sensitivity. Programs need to enforce their rules in a firm but fair manner, and positive reinforcers should outnumber punishers by a ratio of at least four to one. Therapists need to be sensitive and adequately trained and supervised. Relapse prevention and advocacy and brokerage with other community agencies are also necessary (Gendreau, 1996; see also Andrews, 2006).

An additional principle is attention to risk; intensive programs should target high- or medium-risk youths rather than low-risk youths and should not mix high- and low-risk offenders (Andrews, 2006). An encouraging note, however, is that there are effective interventions for low-risk youths. For example, a program in Michigan targeted shoplifters. Although not a serious, violent crime, shoplifting accounts for about one-quarter of all property offense petitions in juvenile court. A diversion program using probation officers incorporated such restorative justice components as community service, restitution to charities, and victim apology letters, as well as other elements. The study used random assignment and a two-year follow-up period. Ten percent of the treatment group youth had new petitions filed, versus 25 percent of the control group (Kelley, Kennedy, and Homant, 2003).

Lipsey (1999) has done extensive meta-analysis research on effective programming for juvenile offenders. Recall that meta-analysis is a research technique that studies the overall effects of interventions based on grouping together individual studies. If five studies have looked at the impact of individual counseling programs, for example, meta-analysis would convert the individual findings of each study into an overall effect size for all the studies combined. Using this technique, Lipsey concluded that for noninstitutionalized offenders (e.g., offenders on probation or in other community programs) the interventions of individual counseling, interpersonal skills development, and behavioral programs all had consistent positive effects in reducing recidivism, compared to their respective control groups. In fact, these interventions reduced recidivism of 50 percent in the control groups to 30 percent or lower in the treatment groups (Lipsey, 1999). Such reductions are both significant and important. (For details on the recidivism reductions of various interventions for noninstitutionalized offenders, see Table 11.2. For a summary of the research findings on successful intervention principles, see Box 11.3.) This is only a brief summary of the effectiveness literature but it gives an outline of effective intervention principles.

Additional Factors Related to Effectiveness

The effectiveness research is critical. It is imperative to know what works and what does not work. It is also important, however, to recall some additional factors about successful intervention with offenders.

TABLE 11.2 Most and Least Effective Types of Intervention with Noninstitutionalized Offenders and Estimated Effects on Recidivism

Intervention Type (N)	Estimated Effect Size	Treatment/Control Recidivism Contrast*
Positive Effects, consistent evidence		
Individual counseling (8)	.46	.28/.50
Interpersonal skills (3)	.44	.29/.50
Behavioral problems (7)	.42	.30/.50
Positive Effects, less consistent evidence		
Multiple services (17)	.29	.36/.50
Restitution, Probation/parole (10)	.15	.43/.50
Mixed, but generally positive effects, inconsistent evidence		
Employment-related (4)	.22	.39/.50
Academic programs (2)	.20	.40/.50
Advocacy or casework (6)	.19	.41/.50
Family counseling (8)	.19	.41/.50
Group counseling (9)	.10	.45/.50
Weak or no effects, inconsistent evidence		
Reduced caseload probation/parole (12)	−.04	.52/.50
Weak or no effects, consistent evidence		
Wilderness or challenge (4)	.12	.44/.50
Early release, probation/parole (2)	.03	.48/.50
Deterrence programs (6)	−.06	.53/.50
Vocational programs (4)	−.18	.59/.50

* Recidivism of intervention group in comparison to assumed control group recidivism of .50. For example, individual counseling would produce a recidivism rate of 28 percent compared to the control group without counseling having a recidivism rate of 50 percent.

Numbers in parentheses represent number of studies in that category

Source: M.W. Lipsey (1999). "Can Intervention Rehabilitate Serious Delinquents?" *Annals of the American Academy of Political and Social Science* 564:142-166.

One point to note is that often programs are simply not available for offenders. In adult prisons, only about 40 percent of drug-dependent/ abusing state prisoners had received treatment since admission (Mumola and Karberg, 2006), and only 34 percent of state inmates with a mental health problem had received treatment after admission (James and Glaze, 2006). An assessment of the gap between needs and services provided in Texas found that only 57 percent of those juveniles with high mental health needs received any mental health services. Only one-third of those youths with high needs for substance abuse services received

BOX 11.3

Summary of Research Findings About Successful Correctional Interventions

Research indicates that correctional interventions should:

1. Concentrate on changing negative behaviors by requiring juveniles to recognize and understand thought processes that rationalize negative behaviors.

2. Promote healthy bonds with, and respect for, prosocial members within the juvenile's family, peer, school, and community network.

3. Have a comprehensible and predictable path for client progression and movement. Each program level should be directed toward and directly related to the next step.

4. Have consistent, clear, and graduated consequences for misbehavior and recognition for positive behavior.

5. Recognize that a reasonable degree of attrition must be expected with a delinquent population.

6. Provide an assortment of highly structured programming activities, including education and/or hands-on vocational training and skill development.

7. Facilitate discussions that promote family problem solving.

8. Integrate delinquent and at-risk youths into generally prosocial groups to prevent the development of delinquent peer groups.

To update these principles, in her analysis of effective treatment interventions, Doris MacKenzie emphasizes that punishment and deterrence interventions are not effective. Individual change is critical, especially the offender's cognitive reasoning, antisocial attitudes, and attitudes toward drug use and vocational skills. Most importantly, "[t]here is sufficient evidence to reject the 'nothing works' mantra. Correctional programs do reduce recidivism. Specifically, effective programs provide human service treatment and focus on changing the individual."

Source: M. Kurlychek, P.M. Torbet, and M. Bozynski (1999). *Focus on Accountability: Best Practices for Juvenile Court and Probation*. Washington, DC: U.S. Department of Justice and Delinquency Prevention; D.L. MacKenzie (2006). *What Works in Corrections: Reducing the Criminal Activities of Offenders and Delinquents*. New York: Cambridge University Press, 334-346.

substance abuse treatment (Kelly, Macy, and Mears, 2005). So although research indicates that resolving criminogenic needs such as substance-abuse problems is critical in changing offenders and reducing recidivism, the programs to change such offenders are not always readily available. Another problem is that the public and politicians are reluctant to increase government spending, even for worthy projects.

A second factor that probation officers need to consider is that youths on probation may have more serious or more prevalent problems than official records indicate. In a study of juvenile probationers in Southern Illinois, official records indicated that only 20 percent of the youths were truant and only 6 percent were involved in drug usage, whereas almost one-half of the youths themselves admitted to truancy and 43 percent admitted to drug usage (Cashel, 2003). This reflects the strong possibility that juvenile probationers have problems that are more extensive than officers know.

Another factor to consider is that interventions that would appear to offer benefits for offenders do not always do so. For example, many people assume that part-time employment for teens reduces their chances of committing delinquent acts. These people assume that having a job teaches important life lessons in responsibility. Some recent research, however, shows that employment is not always beneficial. Wright and his colleagues found that the "number of hours employed had an indirect effect in increasing delinquency across the sample" (Wright, Cullen, and Williams, 1997:215). In fact, much of the delinquency of working teens is occupationally related (Wright and Cullen, 2000). So it may not always be productive for probation officers to help teenage probationers get part-time jobs. Instead it may be productive to provide teens with "modest" cash incentives to graduate. In one study such incentives prevented approximately the same amount of crime as a three-strikes law at one-tenth the cost (Wright, Cullen, and Williams, 1997).

This issue is complex, however. Several programs for older adolescents that included an emphasis on employment or advanced skills training had very positive effects. Thus, Krisberg and her colleagues (1995) argue that such programs are effective for older teens.

An Australian study confirmed the oft-repeated observation that workers perceive working with delinquent girls to be more difficult than working with delinquent boys. Baines and Alder interviewed youth workers in Victoria, Australia, and found that perceptions of girls were that they were "more 'devious,' 'full of bullshit,' and 'dramatic' contrasted with their understanding of young men as 'open' and 'honest' and therefore easier to engage" (Baines and Alder, 1996:481). A distressing implication of this study is that workers dislike working with girls. Thus, female offenders, who have very real and serious needs, are not getting the attention and treatment that they need. This is especially distressing given that this "may be a last chance opportunity for many of the young women who are clients of these services" (Baines and Alder, 1996:483).

Another study of officer attitudes toward girls found that many probation officers see girls as manipulative, yet the officers do not take the next appropriate step. They do not try to understand if such manipulative behaviors may be a reasonable response to real problems and then seek out appropriate programs to address the girls' problems. Instead, they just write off the girls (Gaarder, Rodriguez, and Zatz, 2004).

Many also thought that alternative education programs that have distinct school schedules intended for students not doing well in traditional classrooms would be beneficial for delinquents. A recent meta-analysis of alternative schools found that they could have positive effects on school performance and attitude but they did not reduce delinquent behavior (Cox, Davidson, and Bynum, 1995).

Perhaps the most important cautionary note in any discussion of effectiveness is that financial cutbacks often make any debate about effectiveness moot. When state legislators reduce probation budgets, it is simply impossible for probation officers to implement lessons from research findings on effective interventions. In California, for example, a recent report indicated that cutbacks caused caseloads to mushroom to 200 probationers per officer. In response, some offices resorted to computer monitoring of probationers. As a result, the probationers were not receiving any personal contact or supervision. When there are no funds for probation supervision, all the research on effective interventions becomes meaningless. As one youth told Humes, "Probation isn't worth shit!" (Humes, 1996:360). As noted above, a recent national survey of probation agencies confirmed that declining budgets are a reality for many agencies (Lindner and Bonn, 1996). On the positive side, the state of Ohio has had success in using financial incentives to encourage counties to send only the most serious offenders to state training schools and to treat less serious youths without committing them to state training schools (Moon, Applegate, and Latessa, 1997).

CONTINUING CONCERNS IN COMMUNITY CORRECTIONS

As juvenile court and probation enter into their second century of formal existence since the historic founding of the Illinois juvenile court in 1899, several concerns continue. This section will discuss the concerns of goal confusion, restitution, and community service.

Goal Confusion

Goal confusion, also known as "mission distortion" (Worrall and Gaines, 2006), means that judges, probation and aftercare officers, probation directors, state legislators, and juvenile justice experts disagree about the purposes and objectives of juvenile court and community supervision. Part of the reason for such goal confusion is that we have conflicting images of juvenile offenders. At times we see them as "kids gone wrong"—as victims who are not completely evil. At other times we see them as "hostile predators" and "full-fledged" criminals (Morse, 1999). These conflicting images influence how we treat juveniles. Thus, what was once a rather clear institution for supplementing parental concern by means of adult advice and psychological/social work skill has become a matter of controversy. Some courts, officers, and experts still advocate a *parens patriae* and rehabilitation philosophy. In Glaser's (1964) terminology, the emphasis is on assistance to the probationer rather than on controlling the offender. As noted above, however, developments such as "attack" probation, including police–probation partnerships, see the juvenile as a criminal to be patrolled and arrested rather than as a youth in need of assistance. They indicate that many no longer adhere to a pure assistance model. Moreover, advocates of restorative justice argue that it is time to go beyond the stale debates of the past and place new attention on the concerns of the victim. Proponents of the balanced approach would second that suggestion and add that community safety should also be a prime concern.

Restitution

Restitution occurs when juvenile offenders pay for all or part of the damage inflicted on crime victims or property. Restitution can take the form of either the payment of money or the performance of work (chores) for the victim. Restitution may be part of victim–offender reconciliation in which the offender and victim meet to express their concerns and feelings. In some cases probation officers or restitution officers help juveniles find jobs so they can afford to make restitution payments.

The costs of victimization show the importance of restitution to victims. For 2006, the FBI reported that the average dollar value loss per robbery was $1,268, per burglary was $1,834, and per larceny-theft (e.g., shoplifting) was $855. Even thefts of bicycles and coin-operated machines and purse snatching resulted in average losses of $263, $317, and $440, respectively (Federal Bureau of Investigation, 2007).

> For further details on crime trends and costs, go to the FBI's Uniform Crime Reports, available at http://www.fbi.gov/ucr/cius2006. New statistics should be available by the time you are reading this.

Although restitution has many positive features, especially concern for the victim, there are some problems. Some critics think that it is unfair to law-abiding juveniles to help law-breaking youths find jobs. From this viewpoint, job assistance seems like a reward for delinquency. Second, the claims made about the amounts of money paid back to victims are often exaggerated. Victims may be told that all of their losses will be recouped, but actual restitution often falls short.

A recent study in California found that approximately 15 percent of youths in an intensive program and control group youths completed their court-ordered restitution. For the intensive program juveniles, the mean restitution paid was $55 while the mean restitution ordered was $777; for the control group, the mean paid was $42 out of an average order of $321 (Lane et al., 2005). A review of a juvenile restitution program in Vermont showed that only about one-third of the youths were ordered to pay restitution, and enforcement of all conditions (not just restitution) was a problem (Karp et al., 2004). As noted above, almost one-half million dollars of restitution was paid ($479,587) in 12 counties in Pennsylvania in 2003, 47 percent of the amount ordered (Griffin and Thomas, 2004). More positively, in 2006, in Reading, Pennsylvania, almost all of the restitution ordered for juvenile probationers ($204,720 or 94 percent of the $217,787 ordered) was paid (*Reading Eagle*, 2008). Third, restitution advocates often neglect to consider all of the costs involved in administering a restitution program, such as the salaries of those who oversee the program.

Some evaluation research on restitution has been promising. In one study, in two of four sites, about 10 percent fewer offenders sentenced to restitution recidivated than offenders not ordered to pay restitution (Schneider, 1986). Restitution also resulted in clear suppression effects. Those juveniles ordered to pay restitution had lower arrest rates in the year after their sentences compared to the year prior to their sentences (Schneider, 1990). A study of more than 7,000 cases handled informally and more than 6,000 cases placed on formal probation in Utah showed that "the use of restitution is associated with significant reductions in recidivism among certain juvenile offenders" (Butts and Snyder, 1992:4). In a New Hampshire program cited as a model program by the Office of Juvenile Justice and Delinquency Prevention, more than 80 percent of the offenders completed their community service and restitution obligations. The recidivism rate was below 30 percent (Allen, 1994). Recall that a recent meta-analysis of 35 restorative justice programs found them to be more effective in improving victim and offender satisfaction, increasing compliance with restitution, and reducing recidivism than traditional programs (Latimer, Dowden, and Muse, 2005).

Some juveniles have been unable to pay restitution because they could not find jobs or because of family circumstances. To deal with such problems, Utah established a restitution work fund that allows juveniles to work in community service projects. Victims receive restitution from the state fund. Youths have cleaned buses, removed graffiti, cleaned up parks, and worked in public libraries (Kurlychek, Torbet, and Bozynski, 1999).

Community Service

Community service is similar to restitution. It means that offenders perform unpaid work for government or private agencies as payment for crimes without personal victims (e.g., vandalism of public property). Community service could include cutting grass at local parks, doing volunteer work in hospitals, or painting the clubhouse of a Boys Club.

Advocates argue that community service helps delinquents realize the extent of the damage they have done and feel they have paid their debt to society. Proponents also argue that cost benefits result from the "free" labor of the youths. Critics argue that extensive use of community service could take away jobs from law-abiding citizens and that the actual cost benefits of community service are not as impressive as claimed. More specifically, critics contend that the work done is not always necessary (e.g., the clubhouse did not really need a new coat of paint) and that many of the hours of community service labor included such nonproductive activities as learning the job, work breaks, and dawdling if an adult supervisor is not in constant watch over the work. These criticisms do not mean that restitution or community service is worthless but that claims about their worth should be realistic rather than exaggerated.

As noted in the earlier discussion of restorative justice, an important question is whether the community service is simply busy work or has some relationship to the delinquent's offense. If a delinquent can see the connection between his or her community service order and the harm he or she has done, or can see that the community service is a meaningful contribution to the community, he or she is then more likely to see the importance of such service. The offender is then more likely to learn something positive from the community service assignment rather than merely see it as a boring burden to finish as quickly as possible. Community service needs to be taken seriously by both the juvenile justice system and the juvenile so that it is a teaching tool and not just something to keep a youth busy for a few hours a week.

SUMMARY

Probation is under scrutiny. One author has gone so far as to state that in the 1990s probation faced a "crisis of legitimacy" (Corbett, 2002:175). By this Corbett meant that in light of the alarming statistics on juvenile violence at that time, many were questioning whether probation could do anything to stem the tide. Like all government programs, probation is under pressure to show results. Two well-researched studies, one on intensive probation and one on aftercare, showed no differences in recidivism, despite hopes that increased services in both programs would produce such differences. On the other hand, the research on Pennsylvania probation demonstrates that probation agencies can show that they are producing outcomes such as hours of community service, restitution dollars, and probationers who are engaged in meaningful activities such as education. As noted above and also in Chapter

12, restorative justice programs have many positive features, such as paying attention to crime victims and involving the community in the justice process. Tough programs such as Boston's Operation Night Light and San Bernardino's Operation Nightlight offer statistics on homicide reduction and other street crimes that are at least compelling in a public relations sort of way, even if not scientifically compelling.

The future of probation will probably include stating desired outcomes, working on achieving those outcomes, and reporting statistics to demonstrate success for those outcomes. (See Box 11.4 for a contemporary mission statement for probation.) It is clear that probation and other community corrections efforts can state and produce a number of desirable outcomes and thus address demands that probation be accountable for demonstrating clear actions that have some levels of success. It will be interesting to see to what extent probation can blend its traditional emphasis on rehabilitation with current demands to show effective outcomes and to be "tough" on crime and delinquency.

The only safe prediction is that juvenile corrections will not be the same as it was 25 years ago. It is likely that changes will continue to multiply as society attempts to minimize youth crime.

BOX 11.4

A Contemporary Vision Statement for Juvenile Probation

We envision the role of juvenile probation as that of a catalyst for developing safe communities and healthy youth and families. We believe we can fulfill this role by:

- holding offenders accountable,

- building and maintaining community-based partnerships,

- implementing result-based and outcome-driven services and practices,

- advocating for and addressing the needs of victims, offenders, families, and communities,

- obtaining and sustaining sufficient resources, and

- promoting growth and development of all juvenile probation professionals.

Source: P. Griffin and P. Torbet (2002). *Desktop Guide to Good Juvenile Probation Practice.* Pittsburgh: National Center for Juvenile Justice.

DISCUSSION QUESTIONS

1. Many are calling for harsher punishment for juvenile offenders, especially violent juvenile offenders. Do you think that community corrections can supervise such offenders and protect the public? Will the public support community corrections for violent juvenile offenders?

2. Would you consider a career in juvenile corrections, either training schools or community corrections?

3. What measures should community corrections take to best serve juveniles? Give specific suggestions.

4. Should community corrections for juveniles go back to its roots and try to emphasize rehabilitation, or should it attempt to incorporate more punitive dimensions? Do advocates of restorative justice or the balanced approach have the answer to the question of how we can make juvenile probation better? What would the ideal probation program for juveniles look like?

5. Probation is placing increasingly more emphasis on outcomes and outcomes assessment. What are the positive implications of this emphasis? Are there any possible problems with greater attention to outcomes and outcomes assessment?

6. Where do you envision juvenile community corrections in 10 years? What will juvenile probation and aftercare look like a decade from now?

Chapter 12

RESTORATIVE JUSTICE

Important Terms

collective efficacy

community group
conferencing (CGC)

conflict resolution programs

dispute resolution

exchange theory

family group conferencing
(FGC)

neighborhood reparative
boards (NRBs)

net-widening

peacemaking circles

peer mediation

reintegrative shaming

Reintegrative Shaming
Experiments (RISE)

reparative justice

restorative justice

retributive justice

sentencing circles

social disorganization

victim–offender
mediation (VOM)

What You Need to Know

- Restorative justice seeks to repair the harm done to both the victim and the community, while simultaneously changing the behavior of the offender.

- A primary argument used to explain restorative justice is the idea of reintegrative shaming, which argues that shame can be used in a positive fashion to bring offenders back into society.

- Restorative justice takes four primary forms: victim-offender mediation, family group counseling, neighborhood reparative boards, and sentencing/peacemaking circles.

- Victim-offender mediation, also called victim-offender reconciliation programs, involves bringing the victim and offender together with a mediator to try and arrive at an understanding of all positions and find a solution agreeable to both parties.

- Family group conferencing includes family members, friends, and support groups with the victim and offender in trying to find a solution to the issues.

- Neighborhood reparative boards do not require victim participation and require the offender to make amends, restore the victim and community to the pre-offense state, and help the offender understand what he or she did.

- Sentencing circles are open to anyone in the community and are often a part of the court. The sentences can include virtually anything, including jail time.

- Evaluations of restorative justice reveal a great deal of satisfaction among participants and some reduced recidivism, although a great deal of additional research is needed.

INTRODUCTION

Bazemore and Maloney (1994) argue that restorative justice should be the theme in a new paradigm for criminal and juvenile justice in general and probation in particular. In contrast to the dominant theme of retributive justice, which focuses on vengeance, deterrence, and punishment, restorative justice "is concerned with repairing the damage or harm done to victims and the community through a process of negotiation, mediation, victim empowerment, and reparation" (Bazemore and Maloney, 1994:28). As one commentator puts it, "restorative justice is about relationships—how relationships are harmed by crime and how they can be rebuilt to promote recovery and healing for people affected by crime" (Kurki, 2000:266).

This chapter examines the idea of restorative justice as a means of addressing the needs of youthful offenders, victims, and the community. Restorative justice is a major shift from existing practices. Consequently, it is important to define and discuss the philosophical and practical differences between restorative justice and most juvenile justice system activity. This chapter also examines precursors to restorative justice that attempt to shift some problems out of the formal justice system as well as historical practices used by different cultural groups to handle social problems. These various efforts include victim–offender mediation, family-group conferencing, and circle sentencing. This chapter examines the emergence of these and other restorative justice alternatives for addressing the needs of offenders, victims, and the community.

BACKGROUND OF RESTORATIVE JUSTICE

Over the past 30 years there has been an increasing call for programs that pay more attention to the combined needs of victims, offenders, and the community. There is a recognition that juvenile justice processing of offenders is not effective at deterring crime and reducing victimization (McLaughlin et al., 2003). Consequently, there has been a growing demand for new methods of working with offenders. These apparent competing concerns (i.e., finding an alternative to the system for some offenses, assisting the victim, intervening with offenders, and addressing community needs) suggest that any new intervention needs to serve a broader audience. The concept of restorative or **reparative justice** seeks to use interventions that return the victim and offender to their pre-offense states. For offenders, it means assuring that the action will not be repeated. For victims, this means repairing the harm done. For the community, it means returning things to their state prior to the offensive behavior.

Discussions of restorative justice often begin with a comparison between this new idea and that of retributive justice. **Retributive justice** generally focuses on the lawbreaker and the imposition of sanctions for the purposes of deterrence, vengeance, and/or punishment. The formal criminal justice system operates primarily from a retributive justice approach. **Restorative justice** seeks to repair the harm that was done to both the victim and the community, while simultaneously changing the behavior of the offender. Figure 12.1 contrasts some of the basic assumptions underlying both retributive and restorative justice.

A major difference between retributive and restorative justice is the role of victims and the community in addressing the harm caused by the

FIGURE 12.1 Assumptions of Retributive and Restorative Justice

Retributive Justice	Restorative Justice
Crime is an act against the State, a violation of a law, an abstract idea.	Crime is an act against another person or the community.
The criminal justice system controls crime.	Crime control lies primarily in the community.
Offender accountability defined as taking punishment.	Accountability defined as assuming responsibility and taking action to repair harm.
Crime is an individual act with individual responsibility.	Crime has both individual and social dimensions of responsibility.
Punishment is effective. a. Threat of punishment deters crime. b. Punishment changes behavior.	Punishment alone is not effective in changing behavior and is disruptive to community harmony and good relationships.
Victims are peripheral to the process.	Victims are central to the process of resolving crime.
The offender is defined by deficits.	The offender is defined by capacity to make reparations
Focus on establishing blame, on guilt, on past (did he/she do it?).	Focus on problem solving, on liabilities/obligations, on future (what should be done?).
Emphasis on adversarial relationship.	Emphasis on dialog and negotiation.
Imposition of pain to punish and deter/prevent.	Restitution as a means of restoring both parties; goal of reconciliation/restoration.
Community on sideline, represented abstractly by State.	Community as facilitator in restorative process.
Response focused on offenders's past behavior.	Response focused on harmful consequences of offender's behavior; emphasis on the future.
Dependence upon proxy professionals.	Direct involvement by participants.

Source: Adapted from G. Bazemore and M. Umbreit (1994), *Balanced and Restorative Justice: Program Models*. Washington, DC: Office of Juvenile Justice and Delinquency; H. Zehr (1990), *Changing Lives: A New Focus for Crime and Justice*. Scottdale, PA: Herald Press.

criminal/delinquent act. Under retributive justice, a criminal act is viewed as an offense against society or the state, and the victim is nothing more than a witness for the state. Zehr and Mika (2003:41) note that "crime is fundamentally a violation of people and interpersonal relationships." Restorative justice sees crime as an act against the victim and community, and the focus shifts from what is best for the state to repairing the harm that has been committed against the victim and community.

This shift in focus to the victim, community, and harm done means that the typical retributive response to crime of punishment and deterrence is no longer appropriate. Instead, restorative approaches seek to repair the harm done to the victim and community (Zehr and Mika, 2003). This requires a focus on the type of harm done and the desire of the victim and community for actions such as restitution and conciliation. The victim and community must be involved in the process in order to identify the harm and the appropriate responses desired by those victimized.

The entire focus of restorative justice, however, is not on the victim and the community. There is also a belief that the offender is in need of assistance in recognizing the impact of his or her actions and identifying what needs to change in order to avoid such behavior in the future. Rather than focusing on punishment and deterrence as the major approach to dealing with the offender, restorative interventions seek to understand the causes of the behavior and eliminate those factors.

> There are several organizations that offer information on restorative justice. Two of the leaders are the International Institute for Restorative Practices (http://www.restorativepractices.org/) and the Restorative Justice Consortium (http://www.restorativejustice.org.uk/).

A quick review of the assumptions in Figure 12.1 demonstrates the centrality of the harm done to the victim and community and the need for the entire community, including the offender and victim, to participate in repairing the harm. The community, rather than the juvenile justice system alone, should shoulder the burden of dealing with crime (Nicholl, 1999). Braithwaite (2003) points out that restorative justice seeks to restore the victims, restore harmony in society, restore social support for all parties, and restore the offenders.

This is accomplished by bringing together a range of interested parties in a nonconfrontational setting, including the victim and the offender as well as family members or friends, criminal justice system personnel, and members of the general community. The participants, as a group, seek to understand the actions that led to the criminal or antisocial behavior, reveal the feelings and concerns of all parties, negotiate or mediate a solution agreeable to everyone, and assist in implementing that solution (Bazemore and Maloney, 1994). Kurki (2000:266) notes that "restorative justice is about relationships—how relationships are harmed by crime and how they can be rebuilt to promote recovery and healing for people affected by crime."

Precursors to Restorative Justice

The basic elements of restorative justice can be found throughout history. Braithwaite (1999:2) argues that: "Restorative justice has been the dominant model of criminal justice throughout most of human history for all the world's peoples." There was no formal criminal or juvenile justice system as we know it today throughout most of history. There were no authorities to turn to for help if an individual was victimized. Victims and their families were expected to take action themselves to address the problems and repair the harm from the offense. The earliest codified laws, such as the Law of Moses, the Code of Hammurabi, and Roman laws, all outlined the responsibility of individuals to deal with criminal acts committed against them. The development of formal justice systems, particularly the police and criminal courts, shifted the emphasis for taking redress from the victim to the state. It was at this point that the victim became little more than a witness for the state, and the response to crime and delinquency became punishment rather than addressing the harm that was inflicted.

Many restorative justice practices being used today, however, can be traced directly to historical traditions that have survived in indigenous cultures (Weitekamp, 1999). Of particular note are the practices of the Maori in New Zealand, the Aboriginal tribes in Australia, the Inuits in Alaska, and the First Nations tribes in Canada (Crawford and Newburn, 2003). While there is some debate over the degree to which restorative justice comes directly from the traditions of these groups (see Daly, 2002), there is little doubt that the ideas underlying restorative justice are not new in the last quarter century.

In many respects, it could be argued that the very bases for the development of a juvenile court and juvenile justice system are found in restorative justice principles. The *parens patriae* philosophy of the juvenile court focuses not on the offense but the offender and the actions needed to help the youth. The emphasis was not on punishment. Rather, the emphasis was on correcting the deficiencies in the family and community in order that the youth could lead a productive life, while at the same time making society safer. As seen in earlier chapters in this book, the juvenile justice system (at least according to its rhetoric) focuses on fixing problems for the offender and society.

Dispute Resolution

An immediate precursor to restorative justice, particularly in the United States, is dispute resolution or dispute mediation. One can trace modern dispute resolution back to the early 1970s. During this time, a number of jurisdictions started programs to divert minor disputes out of the formal court system. While many programs were adjuncts to prosecutor's offices and the judiciary, others were sponsored by outside groups or organizations. These initial programs provided an arena in which victims and offenders could meet and work out mutually agreeable solutions. The goal, of course, was to avoid going to court.

Dispute resolution is a mechanism for achieving a number of goals simultaneously. First, the parties involved in the situation work together to resolve the problem rather than having some outside authority impose a solution. Second, any dispute that reaches a settlement is one less case with which the formal justice system must contend. This alternative alleviates some congestion in the court system. Third, this informal approach empowers victims by giving them a direct voice in their own matters. Victims retain complete veto power over the final outcome. Finally, dispute resolution provides the victim with a face-to-face encounter with the offender. This meeting enables the victim to vent anger and seek understanding—something that many victims deeply desire.

The basic idea behind dispute resolution is to bring opposing parties together in an attempt to work out a mutually agreeable solution. While dispute resolution programs can vary in terms of the cases they handle or the procedures they use, they typically share five traits in common (Garofalo and Connelly, 1980):

1. A third-party mediator is involved.

2. Disputants usually know each other.

3. Participation must be voluntary.

4. Processes are informal.

5. Disputants are usually referred to the process by someone in the criminal justice system.

First, these programs involve a third-party mediator who monitors participant interaction. This arbitrator keeps the discussion focused and makes suggestions whenever the need arises. Most mediators are volunteers who are not affiliated with the formal justice system. Because of this independence, some people refer to these programs as "neighborhood dispute resolution."

A second characteristic is that many disputants have known each other over a period of time. Often, they are neighbors, friends, or family members (although store owners and customers can utilize such a program). This familiarity can be helpful when trying to forge a compromise. It can also be a challenge because the dispute may be the result of a long-term issue or problem that may not be amenable to a short-term intervention.

Third, most programs insist that participation be completely voluntary. Both disputants must agree to handle the problem through the program. If either party declines to take part, the dispute moves back to the realm of more formal legal action.

Fourth, the actual resolution of a dispute follows a very informal process. Rules of evidence are not enforced, and attorneys are not allowed to attend these sessions. Instead, the process calls for discussion rather than rigid fact-finding. As one might expect, the mediator has a free hand to conduct each meeting as he or she sees fit.

The fifth and final common aspect is that most disputants enroll in the program after being referred to it by a member of the criminal justice system. Most often, the prosecutor has reviewed the case and decided that the interests of justice can be better served in a nontraditional manner.

The approach of dispute resolution programs appeals to a diverse audience. Consequently, they garner support from many corners and have spread rapidly. Prosecutors and judges welcome the chance to reduce overcrowded dockets, and victim advocates see a tremendous potential to help their clients. More than 80 United States cities had dispute resolution programs in place in 1980, with roughly 4,000 trained mediators (Ray, Kestner, and Freedman, 1986). Six years later, that number swelled to 350 programs with 20,000 mediators (Ray, Kestner, and Freedman, 1986). Its popularity is evident in the proliferation of similar arrangements now operating in Canada, Great Britain, Australia, Denmark, Finland, Germany, and many other countries (Umbreit, 1997).

The types of cases found in dispute resolution take a variety of forms. Interpersonal disputes between family members and friends comprise a large portion of the cases brought to mediation. Domestic disputes, harassment, neighborhood nuisances, and landlord/tenant problems make up the bulk of the disputes. Merchant/customer disputes are more evident in programs that rely heavily on prosecutor's offices for referral. Mediation with juveniles is an attempt to keep the youth out of the formal system and eliminate the negative consequences of formal processing (Veevers, 1989).

Dispute resolution and similar programs also appear in a variety of forms in school settings. **Peer mediation programs** bring together disputing parties with a peer mediator to discuss the situation and attempt to resolve the dispute to the satisfaction of both parties. In many cases, there is no clear victim and offender. Instead, the two parties are involved in an argument or disagreement that, left unchecked, could escalate into a physical confrontation. The goal of the mediation is to defuse the situation before it reaches that stage and to keep it from occurring again in the future. Many schools have instituted **conflict resolution programs** and training. While peer mediation may be included in these programs, the most important element of conflict resolution in schools is teaching youths alternative methods for resolving conflicts before they occur. These programs are addressed in more detail in Chapter 13.

The Theoretical Basis of Restorative Practices

The basic argument underlying restorative justice is that reactions to crime and harmful behavior should seek to repair the harm done to the individual and society while simultaneously reintegrating and addressing the needs of the offender. Van Ness and Strong (2006) propose three basic principles inherent in restorative justice:

- Repairing harm (to victim and community)
- Engendering stakeholder involvement (victims, offenders, families, and community)
- Transforming the role of community and government

Within these principles are a variety of more specific goals or dimensions, such as making amends, building relationships, exchanging ideas, and taking ownership of community problems (Bazemore and Schiff, 2005). A number of different theories may be used to underscore the tenets of restorative justice.

The explanation most often proffered is Braithwaite's (1989) reintegrative shaming. **Reintegrative shaming** rests on the assumption that typical processing of offenders through the criminal justice system serves to isolate the offender and stigmatize him or her. This action marginalizes the offender (even more than he or she may already be in society). In addition, it does nothing to correct the behavior or repair the harm done to the victim. Basically, typical system processing serves only to exact a punishment (retribution) for the criminal act.

The underlying premise of Braithwaite's (1989) theory is that shame can be used in a positive fashion to bring the offender back into society. Under reintegrative shaming, the system needs to express its disapproval of the criminal activity while simultaneously forgiving the offender for the action if the offender is willing to learn from the event and make reparations to the victim and society. The key is "reintegration," rather than "stigmatization" (Braithwaite, 1989). The ability to employ reintegrative shaming effectively rests on shifting the sole focus of societal response from the offender to a shared focus on the offending behavior, social disapproval (often by family, friends, and significant others), the needs of the victim and community, and a shared response to make things better (Harris, 2003).

A second theoretical explanation involves exchange theory. **Exchange theory** proceeds from the assumption that equal reciprocity is a cornerstone of social interaction. Parties to a confrontation (such as an offense and subsequent restorative justice program) are looking to establish a balance in the relationship. The offender is expected to make amends for the harm caused, in exchange for reintegration back into society (Bazemore and Schiff, 2005). Under the retributive system of justice, the offender is punished and, while this may be accepted by the victim and community as payment, the punishment can be seen as harmful in itself and not appropriate for truly repairing the harm and ensuring that the problem does not occur again. Bazemore and Schiff (2005) argue that the offender needs to actually make amends in order to be accepted back into society by the victim and the community.

A third theoretical perspective in restorative justice involves the need to develop community resources to address social problems. Many communities display a level of **social disorganization** that mitigates the ability of residents to effect change and control in the area. Restorative justice offers a mechanism to build the social capital necessary to address youthful offenders and the causes of misbehavior (Bazemore and Schiff, 2005). Bazemore and Schiff suggest the need to transform communities into active participants in controlling problem youths and socialize them into proper societal roles. Community members need to feel empowered to do something about problems, that is, they need **collective efficacy**.

It should be apparent that principles of restorative justice rest on a wide array of theories and theoretical perspectives. This is attributable to the fact that restorative justice seeks to do more than just punish offenders, assist victims, or control the community. Instead, it offers opportunities to do all of these things simultaneously, as well as accomplish other related tasks.

TYPES OF RESTORATIVE JUSTICE

Restorative justice takes a variety of different forms, although they all attend to the same basic tenets. Indeed, "restorative justice" is often referred to as "transformative justice," "social justice," "balanced and restorative justice," "peacemaking," or other terms. Braithwaite (2002) notes that many of these terms and programs have been incorporated into the more general idea of restorative justice.

Harris (2003) proposes a model by which to evaluate restorative justice practices (see Figure 12.2). Beyond its use for evaluation, the model contains six aims for any restorative justice program. The four primary aims are:

- Empowerment
- Restoration
- Reintegration
- Emotional and social healing

Empowerment reflects the need for all interested parties to be involved in the process. This provides a sense of legitimacy for both the victim and the offender. *Restoration* simply refers to repairing the harm done to all participants. At the same time, retribution is disavowed as a legitimate response to the behavior. Restorative justice also seeks to *rein-*

tegrate both the offender and the victim into the community, without the stigma of being an offender or being different from the other community members. Finally, there is a clear need to address the *emotional* harm that accompanies the behavior.

FIGURE 12.2 A Model for Evaluating Restorative Practices

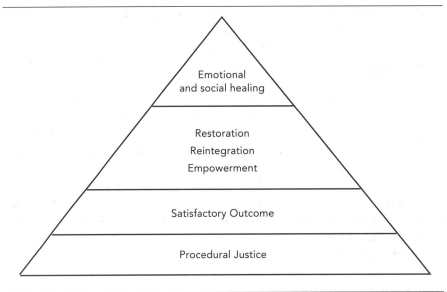

Source: N. Harris (2003). "Evaluating the Practice of Restorative Justice: The Case of Family Group Conferencing." In L. Walgrave (ed.), *Repositioning Restorative Justice.* Portland, OR: Willan.

Achieving these primary aims requires that the restorative approach be grounded on two additional factors:

- Procedural fairness
- Satisfactory outcome

Procedural fairness refers to the fact that the process must respect all the parties involved. The rights (both legal and human) and wishes of all participants must be recognized as legitimate by the participants. There must also be a *satisfactory outcome* reached. This means that all parties agree with the proposed resolution and are willing to follow through with the plan of action. The failure to achieve procedural fairness and a satisfactory outcome from the process itself will make it impossible to fully realize the major aims of restorative justice (Harris, 2003).

Bazemore and Schiff (2005) outline a variety of objectives/foci addressed by different restorative justice processes. As can be seen in Table 12.1, restorative justice seeks to achieve multiple aims, ranging from preventing offending to repairing harm to providing a voice for victims in the formal justice system to rehabilitating the offender. These goals can be realized through various practices and programs located throughout the community and the formal justice system.

TABLE 12.1 Restorative Justice Objectives, Practice,
           and Typical Location

Objective/Focus	Practice	Typical Location/Use
Prevention, peace-making, youth development, community building, family and school discipline	School and neighborhood conferencing, youth development circles, victim awareness education, restorative discipline family support and discussion groups	Schools, neighborhoods, churches, civic groups
Provide decision-making alternative to formal court or other adversarial process for determining obligations for repairing harm	Victim-offender dialogue, family group conferencing, circles, neighborhood accountability boards, other restorative conferencing approaches	Police and community diversion, court diversion, dispositional/ sentencing alternatives, post-dispositional planning, residential alternative discipline, conflict resolution, post-residential reentry
Victim and community input to court or formal decision-making	Written or oral impact statement to court or other entity	Court, probation, residential facilities
Provide reparative sanctions or obligation in response to crime or harmful behavior	Restitution, restorative community service, service to victims, service for surrogate victims, payment to victim service funds	Diversion, court sanction, probation condition, residential program, reentry
Offender treatment/rehabilitation/ education	Victim impact panels, victim awareness education, drunk driving panels, community service learning projects	Probation, residential facilities, diversion program, jails
Victim services and support groups	Volunteer support groups, faith community groups, counseling	Multiple settings
Reentry	Reentry conferences, support circles, restorative community service	Neighborhood and community

Source: G. Bazemore and M. Schiff (2005). *Juvenile Justice Reform and Restorative Justice: Building Theory and Policy from Practice.* Portland, OR: Willan, p. 31. Reprinted with permission.

The degree to which restorative justice programs achieve the results outlined above can vary greatly. Indeed, the diversity in restorative programs can be seen in the extent to which they address the different goals for the varied participants in the restorative process. Figure 12.3 presents a graphic depiction of the types of restorative justice programs and the degree to which they can be considered fully restorative.

The restorative practices typology represents an intersection of three different dimensions—a victim reparation orientation, an offender responsibility focus, and a communities of care domain—all indicated by a separate circle. Each of these dimensions contributes something to address crime and victimization, although each dimension alone offers only limited restoration. Victim reparation, for example, focuses exclusively on the needs of the immediate crime victim through things like victim compensation and victim services, and excludes concerns for the community or the offender. Similarly, the offender responsibility dimension relates to activities that help the offender understand his or her actions and take responsibility. The intersection of different dimensions brings about greater restoration, with the greatest level of restoration occurring where all three dimensions overlap.

FIGURE 12.3 Types and Degrees of Restorative Justice Practice

Source: G. Bazemore and M. Schiff (2005). *Juvenile Justice Reform and Restorative Justice: Building Theory and Policy from Practice.* Portland, OR: Willan, p. 31. Reprinted with permission.

Four broad types of restorative conferencing are victim–offender mediation, family group conferencing, neighborhood reparative boards, and peacemaking/sentencing circles. Each of these approach restorative justice in slightly different ways using the involvement of different individuals and groups (see Table 12.2).

Victim–Offender Mediation

Victim–offender mediation (VOM), also referred to as victim–offender reconciliation programs (VORPs), is a direct outgrowth of the early dispute resolution/dispute mediation programs of the early 1970s and is considered the oldest form of restorative justice (Umbreit, 1999). The first documented VOM program was one run by the Mennonites in Kitchener, Ontario, Canada, in 1973. VOM is typically a post-conviction process (although pre-conviction programs exist) in which the victim and the offender are brought together to discuss a wide range of issues. A trained mediator attends these meetings.

The basic premise of VOM is that the criminal incident and its consequences are complex and beyond the ability of the criminal code to address on its own (Nichol, 1999). Where the formal criminal justice response to crime is to simply impose the sanction outlined in the statutes,

VOM seeks to deal with the needs of both the victim and the offender. Perhaps the most important concern addressed in the VOM meetings is to identify for the offender the types and level of harm suffered by the victim as a result of the crime. The victim is given the opportunity to express his or her concerns about the crime and his or her loss. At the same time, the offender is given the chance to explain why he or she committed the act and the circumstances that may underlie the behavior.

TABLE 12.2 Restorative Conferencing Models Administration and Process

	Victim-offender mediation	Family group conferencing	Neighborhood board	Peacemaking circles
Who normally participates	Mediator, victim, offender (family)	Facilitator, offender family (victim)	Board chair, volunteers, offender, family (victim)	Keeper, offender, volunteers, family, victim and offender supporters
Common permanent structure/staffing	Program coordinator, volunteer mediators (some paid mediators)	Program coordinator, facilitator (volunteers)	Coordinator, volunteer board chair, volunteer board members	Coordinator, volunteer circle members
Facilitation and dominant process	Victims option to speak first; mediator facilitates open-ended dialogue with minimal interference	In most programs facilitator follows script or outline in which offender speaks first, followed by victim and other participants; seeks to move process through phases	Board chair initiates member deliberation after questioning offender and parents, though some variation emerging toward circle or family group conferencing process	Keeper opens session and closes session, person allowed to speak when talking piece is passed to them. Shared leadership and consensus decision-making
Dominant philosophy	Meeting victim and offender needs, healing dialogue as transformative	Family group as essential problem-solver Respectful, normative, disapproval with support; offender empathy and emotion key	Neighborhood social support and community norm affirmation; neighborhood problem-solving focus	Collective healing; community focus; broad problem-solving, community building focus beyond individual offense

Source: G. Bazemore and M. Schiff (2005). *Juvenile Justice Reform and Restorative Justice: Building Theory and Policy from Practice.* Portland, OR: Willan, p. 38. Reprinted with permission.

The aim of this discussion is for the two parties to gain an understanding of the other person as a starting point for identifying a response to the event. The focus of the meetings is on repairing the harm done to the victim, helping the victim heal (both physically and emotionally), restoring the community to the pre-crime state, and reintegrating the offender into society (Umbreit et al., 2003). Among the potential tangible outcomes for the victim may be the offender making monetary restitution or providing service to repair the harm done. Perhaps of equal importance are changes in behavior and attitude on the part of the offender.

Participation in VOM is voluntary for the victim, but the offender may be required by the court to participate as a part of the court process (Umbreit, 1999). Some programs allow for mediation to occur without the need for a face-to-face meeting between the victim and offender. This typically takes place only when the victim desires to participate in mediation but is reluctant to have any further direct contact with the offender.

Victim–offender mediation programs may be a part of the formal criminal justice system or may be run by other agencies that are not directly connected to the system. In some jurisdictions, mediation may be ordered by the judge in lieu of formal sentencing. A successful mediation may mean that the original conviction is vacated or expunged. On the other hand, the failure of an offender to participate in mediation or the failure of the mediation to reach an agreeable resolution may result in the offender being returned to the court for formal sentencing.

More information on VOM can be obtained from the Victim Offender Mediation Association at http://www.voma.org/

Family Group Conferencing

Family group conferencing (FGC) finds its roots in indigenous practices of the Maori in New Zealand. Family group conferencing came to prominence in 1989 when New Zealand, responding to the increasing number of Maori youths being handled in the formal justice system, passed the Children, Young Persons and Their Families Act (Crawford and Newburn, 2003). This Act removed all youths, ages 14-17 (with only a few exceptions for very serious offenders) from formal court processing and mandated that they be diverted to family group conferencing (Kurki, 2000). Since its inception in 1989, FGC has spread to Australia, the United States, Europe, and other countries.

The greatest difference between FGC and VOM is the inclusion of family members, close friends, and other support groups of the victim and offender in the conferences. There is also the possibility of including criminal justice system personnel, including social workers, police officers, and an offender's attorney (Van Ness and Strong, 2006). The basic ideas of FGC were adapted by the police in Wagga-Wagga, Australia, in 1991 into a process known as **community group conferencing (CGC)** (McCold, 2003). One main difference between FGC and CGC is the possible inclusion of a broader set of support groups and community members to the conference (McCold, 2003). Figure 12.4 graphically depicts the potential involvement of different individuals and support groups in FGC and CGC. The expansion of participants from the victim, offender, and mediator in VOM to support persons and community representatives is very important in a variety of ways.

Another difference between FGC and VOM is the absence of a mediator who participates in constructing a resolution to the issues. Instead, FGCs are led by a trained facilitator who serves in various roles. Most often the facilitator will make contact with all participants prior to the conference. At that time he or she will explain the process and the role of each individual. The facilitator will also emphasize the fact that the conference should conclude with a resolution to which all parties are in agreement.

FIGURE 12.4 Parties Involved in Conferencing

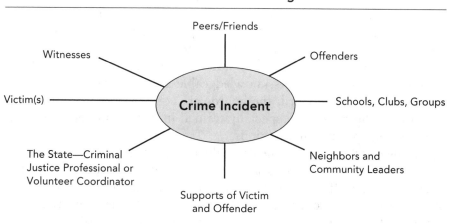

Source: C.G. Nicholl (1999). *Community Policing, Community Justice, and Restorative Justice: Exploring the Links for the Delivery of a Balanced Approach to Public Safety.* Washington, DC: Office of Community Oriented Policing Services.

Once the conference begins, the facilitator leads the participants through a discussion of the facts of the case, the impact of the victimization on the parties, the feelings of all participants toward the action and the offender, and the development of a mutually agreed-upon resolution (Nicholl, 1999). The families and support persons are very important to this process. They are expected to voice their feelings about the harm that was committed, their concern for the victim of the crime, their disappointment about the offender's behavior, and their suggestions for how to resolve the problem. Of great importance is that the support groups are expected to take some responsibility in monitoring the offender and making certain that any agreements are carried out after the conference (Kurki, 2000). Conferences can be held either pretrial or post-trial, and have become a part of police and pretrial diversion programs in many countries (McGarrell et al., 2000; Moore and O'Connell, 1994).

Neighborhood Reparative Boards

Neighborhood reparative boards (NRBs), or neighborhood accountability boards, have existed since the mid-1990s and typically deal with nonviolent youthful offenders. Not unlike other restorative practices, NRBs seek to restore the victims and community to pre-offense states, require the offender to make amends, and aid the offender in understanding the impact of his or her actions on the victim and community. Cases are referred to the boards by the court, most often prior to formal adjudication.

Despite the philosophical similarities between NRBs and other types of restorative conferencing, there are several key differences in how this approach operates. First, victims are not required to participate. Indeed, many early boards frowned on victim participation (Strickland, 2004), although victim participation is becoming more common. Second, while the conferences are often open to the public, actual participation is limited by the board and who they wish to interview. The board questions the offenders and examines statements made by members of the offender's family and others knowledgeable about the event (Bazemore and Umbreit, 2001). Third, the boards are composed of a small group of citizens who have been specially trained in conducting hearings and constructing appropriate sanctions.

At the conclusion of the hearing, the board undertakes private deliberations and outlines a suggested set of actions to be followed by the offender. If the offender agrees with the plan, the board oversees the offender's compliance with the terms and reports to the court about the success or failure of the offender (Bazemore and Umbreit, 2001). Typical conditions of agreements include restitution, apologies, and community service (Karp, 2001).

Peacemaking and Sentencing Circles

The final type of restorative justice program to be discussed is peacemaking and sentencing circles. **Peacemaking circles** are based on Canadian First Nation practices and began formal operation in the early 1990s. Circles invite members from across the community to participate in determining the appropriate sanctions for offenders (Van Ness and Strong, 2006). As a sentencing procedure, this process typically occurs after a case is concluded and the offender is found guilty in court. Participants in circles typically include all of the parties found in FGCs, as well as general community members who wish to be included.

Sentencing circles may function as either a part of the court or separate from the court. In many jurisdictions, this sentencing alternative is used at the discretion of the trial judge and is not provided for under any statutory authority (Crawford and Newburn, 2003). Most cases handled by sentencing circles involve minor offenses, although some programs will consider more serious crimes (Stuart, 1996). Because of the fact that this process takes place post-conviction and can include a wide array of participants, circles normally require a great deal of preparation before they actually convene (Kurki, 2000).

A facilitator is responsible for meeting with all participating parties prior to the actual circle. These meetings are used to explain the process, outline the facts of the case for those who have more limited knowledge, answer any questions the parties may have, and make plans for the actual meeting. In many cases the offender will work on an initial plan to address the harms he or she committed, which will be presented when the circle meets (Nicholl, 1999). This extensive preparation may mean that the circle takes place months after the crime occurred and the court case concluded.

Every participant in the sentencing circle is given the opportunity to speak, express his or her feelings about the crime, and offer opinions and rationales about the outcome of the discussion. The intended outcome of the circle is consensus on a plan of action that may include a wide array of activities. Plans of action may include further meetings between the victim and offender, apologies by the offender, restitution, community service, treatment/rehabilitation programs (such as counseling or drug/alcohol treatment), and/or explicit sentencing recommendations to the trial judge (Nicholl, 1999; Van Ness and Strong, 2006), including possible jail or prison time (Stuart, 1996). The decision of the circles is often binding on the offender (and may be specifically incorporated into the official court record), and a failure to adhere to the decision may result in further criminal justice system processing or being returned to the circle (Van Ness and Strong, 2006).

Beyond the reparative plan for the offender, sentencing circles are meant to bring about action by all parties to the crime. The victim is supposed to receive support and be an active participant in healing himself or herself. The community's role is to identify the factors that lead to the offending behavior and seek ways to eliminate those problems. These causal factors may be specific to the individual offender (such as lack of parental supervision or underage alcohol use) or may be larger social-structural issues (such as unemployment or the presence of gangs in the community).

Summary

While each of the forms of restorative justice take a slightly different approach to repairing the harm done by the criminal act, all are considered restorative because they seek to address the needs of the victim, the offender, and the community. The various approaches (outlined in Figure 12.2) bring about restoration by attempting to build understanding between the parties, identifying the factors at work in the behavior, and arriving at a plan of action that is agreed to by all parties. The extent to which these restorative justice programs are successful is addressed next.

THE IMPACT OF RESTORATIVE JUSTICE

Restorative justice programs are intended to have a number of different possible outcomes, including rehabilitating the offender and repairing the harm done to the victim. Assessing the impact of the interventions, however, is more difficult to do. Many evaluations focus on victim and offender satisfaction with the process and the level of compliance or completion of the agreed-upon settlement. Less common are analyses of the impact of the programs on subsequent offending by the offender.

Satisfaction, Fairness, and Compliance

Assessments of the impact of restorative justice have most often relied on outcomes such as victim satisfaction, feelings of fairness by victims, and compliance with the agreements. With very few exceptions, participants express satisfaction with the restorative process in which they have participated (Braithwaite, 1999). This is true of VOM, FGC, and circle sentencing. Evaluations of VOM typically reveal that between 75 and 100 percent of the participants express satisfaction with the mediation (Kurki, 2000). Similarly high levels of satisfaction arise from FGCs (Bazemore and Umbreit, 2001; Moore and O'Connell, 1994; Umbreit et al., 2003). The level of satisfaction is also reflected in feelings by participants that the process is fair (McCold, 2003; McGarrell et al., 2000; Umbreit, 1999; Umbreit and Coates, 1992; Umbreit et al., 2003). These results contrast greatly with those found in analyses of formal criminal justice system processing, in which victims and offenders report lower satisfaction and feelings of fairness.

An important caveat when considering whether a type of program is effective is that not all projects are implemented with the same degree of success. Some attempts to establish a restorative justice program may be more successful than others. Given this fact, outcomes may also vary from one evaluation to another. Attempting to address this problem, McCold and Wachtel (2002) rated restorative justice programs according to the degree to which they were fully restorative, mostly restorative, or not restorative. They then looked at reports of satisfaction and fairness by victims and offenders. Their results are very illuminating. In general, participants in fully restorative programs report higher levels of satisfaction and perceived fairness, followed by those in mostly restorative programs. Individuals from programs rated as not restorative report the lowest levels of satisfaction and fairness (McCold and Wachtel, 2002).

The success of restorative justice programs is also measured in terms of the ability of the meetings to achieve consensus on a solution and whether the parties carry through with the agreement. Again, there is evidence that most meetings culminate in an agreement and most parties comply with the settlement (Braithwaite, 1999; Kurki, 2000; Schiff, 1999; Umbreit and Coates, 1993). Restitution is a common component of many agreements, and evaluations reveal that 90 percent or more of the offenders in FGC comply with the ordered restitution (Wachtel, 1995). McGarrell and colleagues (2000) note that participants in a conferencing program completed the program at a significantly higher rate than normal diversion clients.

This information on satisfaction and compliance must be tempered somewhat by the fact that participation in the programs is voluntary. The fact that a program is voluntary may mean that only those individuals who are more amenable to the process to begin with are included in the programs. There may be a built-in bias in favor of positive results.

Umbreit and colleagues (2003), for example, point out that only 40 to 60 percent of the victims and offenders who are asked to participate in VOM agree to do so. McCold and Wachtel (1998) report that almost 60 percent of the cases never materialize due to a refusal to participate. Similarly, an analysis of youth conferencing panels in England and Wales finds that only 20 percent of the victims participate (Crawford and Newburn, 2003). There is no way of knowing if positive results are actually a function of the willingness to participate and effect change, rather than of the program itself.

Recidivism

Reducing reoffending is an important restorative goal, particularly in a discussion of juvenile justice. Unfortunately, there is relatively little research on offender recidivism found in the restorative justice literature. There is some evidence, however, that restorative justice programs are able to reduce the level of subsequent offending. In addition, there is a greater emphasis being placed on assessing the impact of restorative justice programming on recidivism.

Most evaluations of recidivism have appeared in relation to VOM programs. Umbreit and Coates (1993), comparing youths who participated in VOM to those undergoing typical juvenile justice processing in three states, report significantly less recidivism on behalf of the VOM sample. In their analysis of restorative justice conferences for youths in Indianapolis, McGarrell and associates (2000) report a 40 percent reduction in recidivism for the program youths, compared to those undergoing normal system processing. Umbreit and colleagues (2001) provide evidence that youths completing VOM projects in two Oregon counties reduced their offending by at least 68 percent in the year after program participation compared to the year before the intervention. Finally, Nugent and associates (1999) note that both the level of reoffending and the seriousness of subsequent offenses is lower for youths who enter and complete VOM programs.

Examinations of recidivism from conferencing are less common, although those that do exist provide some positive assessments. Daly (2003), examining juvenile conferencing in South Australia, finds significantly less recidivism by participants in the conferences. This is particularly true for conferences that are rated as highly restorative. Similarly, Hayes and Daly (2004) uncover reduced recidivism levels after conferencing. The results are strongest for first-time offenders who are participating in the programs. The results also vary by other characteristics of the offenders, suggesting that conferencing is not equally effective with all individuals and cases (Hayes and Daly, 2004). Hayes and Daly (2003) note that reductions in recidivism are strongly related to the ability of a conference to achieve a genuine consensus on a plan of action. Finally, Rodriguez (2005) reports reduced recidivism from FGC, particularly for older offenders and cases involving property crimes.

Discrepant recidivism results appeared in the **Reintegrative Shaming Experiments (RISE)** conducted in Australia. Sherman and Strang (2003) examined the impact of RISE on victims and offenders involved in drunk driving, juvenile property offenses, juvenile shoplifting, and violent youthful offenses. The authors found that conferences reduced recidivism among violent youths by 38 percent. Conversely, there was no impact on either shoplifting or property offenses. Analysis of drunk driving reveals some promising results, but the low number of crimes makes it difficult to evaluate any changes adequately (Sherman and Strang, 2000). Finally, the authors report that the impact of RISE varies across facilitators, suggesting that the training and preparation of these individuals is key to successful conferencing (Sherman and Strang, 2003).

AP Photo/Daily Star, Kari Wheeler

A detainee in the Florida Parishes Juvenile Detention Center works in the center's garden in Goodbee, Louisiana. Detainees are giving back to the community by harvesting the produce and donating it to a local food pantry. Juvenile detainees are experiencing restorative justice with programs that teach new skills and encourage them to give back to the community.

While positive results on recidivism appear in several analyses, a great deal of additional research is needed on the impact of restorative justice programs. This is especially true for FGC and peacemaking circle programs, which have not undergone as extensive evaluations as VOM. There remains a need to identify and understand the conditions under which different restorative justice programs work and do not work (Braithwaite, 2002).

Problems and Issues with Restorative Justice

Despite the growing popularity of restorative justice approaches, there are a number of problems and concerns that remain unanswered. Figure 12.5 presents a number of concerns with restorative justice. Because a full discussion of critical issues is available elsewhere (see Ashworth, 2003; Feld, 1999; Kurki, 2000), only a few of the major concerns are presented here.

FIGURE 12.5 Key Concerns with Restorative Justice

Lack of Victim Participation

Emphasis on Shaming and Not Enough on Reintegration/Reconciliation

Inadequate Preparation

Inability to Engender Participation

Problems with Identifying Appropriate Participants

Problems Recruiting Representative Panels

Coercive Participation (particularly coercion of offenders)

Net-Widening

Inadequate Screening of Cases

Inability of Participants (e.g. Families, Communities) to Meaningfully Contribute

Lack of Neutrality by Participants and/or Facilitator

Inability to Address Serious Violent Crimes

Inability to Address Long-Standing Interpersonal Disputes

Too Victim-Oriented

Inability to Protect Constitutional Rights of Offenders

One problem is that restorative justice programs may be too ambitious in their attempt to solve very complex societal problems (Kurki, 2000). Simply gathering common citizens together to talk about a problem and brainstorm possible solutions is only the beginning of a much more complex process to address major social forces that may cause crime. Many problems involve long-standing interpersonal disputes that may not be amenable to simple mediation or conferencing.

A second concern, related to the first, is that restorative justice has been used primarily with less serious and property crimes. There is a great deal of debate over whether this approach can be used successfully with serious violent offenses (see Bannenberg and Rössner, 2003). This is especially true when offenses such as spouse abuse, sexual assault, aggravated assault, murder, and others are considered. While few programs have directly assessed this question, there is some evidence that restorative justice can be used in more serious personal crime cases. For example, Umbreit and colleagues (2003) report success using VOM with murderers and the families of their victims. Corrado, Cohen, and Odgers (2003) also find positive results (mostly in terms of satisfaction) for a VOM program dealing with serious and violent offenses in British Columbia, Canada. The strongest finding in these studies is the need for very lengthy and extensive preparation prior to the intervention. Despite the fact that most cases involve more minor offenses, Bazemore and Schiff's (2005) survey of juvenile conferencing programs in the United States reveals that a significant percent of programs accept serious personal crimes for settlement (see Table 12.3).

TABLE 12.3 Charges Accepted by Type of Restorative Conferencing
Program (percentages)

Charges	VOM/D	Multiple Practice	Circle	FGC	Board	Total
			Program Type			
Minor assault	79.3	81.8	100.0	67.6	91.7	78.8
Property damage	76.9	77.3	83.3	70.3	61.5	74.5
Personal theft	70.4	81.8	50.0	73.0	92.3	73.1
Business theft	51.9	59.1	33.3	73.0	76.9	59.5
Breaking and entering	41.8	86.4	66.7	45.9	61.5	51.9
Vandalism	50.0	59.1	33.3	48.6	61.5	51.6
Serious assault	40.7	45.5	66.7	29.7	23.1	38.8
Minor drug	14.6	18.2	33.3	32.4	52.8	23.6
Domestic violence	23.1	21.7	33.3	12.8	21.4	21.3
Serious drug	4.9	4.5	16.7	13.5	7.7	8.1
Other*	44.4	36.4	33.3	64.9	23.1	45.6

*Other charges include arson, harassment, loitering, alcohol, behavior issues, auto theft, bomb threat, disorderly conduct, DUI, forgery, weapons, menacing, trespass, possession of stolen property, and various other charges and combination of charges.

Source: G. Bazemore and M. Schiff (2005). *Juvenile Justice Reform and Restorative Justice: Building Theory and Policy from Practice*. Portland, OR: Willan, p. 112. Reprinted with permission.

Third, there exists a concern that, while voluntary, there is an underlying level of coercion in most programs. What makes this truly problematic is that many programs do not allow (or at least frown upon) the presence of defense attorneys, thus raising the issue of an accused's constitutional rights and procedural safeguards (Feld, 1999; Levrant et al., 1999). In some instances, the participation of the offender is actually coerced by the fact that he or she is required to participate under threat of being processed in court. Compounding this problem is the need for the offender to admit to the act during the process. This is especially problematic if the intervention is taking place pre-adjudication.

A fourth concern with restorative justice is over how the "community" is defined and who is allowed to represent the community (Kurki, 2000). This can be a very important concern because the participants help mold the outcome and the expectations for the solution. The participants can bring a wide array of differing expectations. This may not be a problem in smaller, more homogeneous communities, such as Maori or Native American communities, but it can certainly be problematic in large, diverse cities.

Fifth, Feld (1999) notes that there is a distinct imbalance of power in most restorative justice programs. This is especially problematic when juvenile offenders must face not only the victim but also the victim's support groups, members of the criminal justice system, and strangers from the general community. The power differential must be a prime consideration in meetings.

A sixth area of concern deals with the issue of net-widening. **Net-widening** refers to the situation in which the introduction of a new program or intervention serves to bring more people under the umbrella of social control. This is especially problematic when the new programs are intended to take people currently being served in the formal justice system in order to divert them to the new program. The expectation is that the new programs will relieve some of the burden from the formal system while simultaneously offering a better response to the problems. It is not clear the extent to which restorative justice has resulted in net-widening, but there is a legitimate concern that this has occurred.

Despite these and other concerns, restorative justice is receiving a great deal of increased attention. Within a relatively short time frame, restorative programming has spread to countries around the world and is being used with a wide array of problems and events. While used most commonly with youthful offenders and property or minor offenses, advocates are working to include serious and violent acts under the umbrella of restorative justice programming. The increased interest in restorative justice is evident in the proposal made by the Commission on Crime Prevention and Criminal Justice of the United Nation's Economic and Social Council in 2002. This proposal recommends that restorative justice practices be used whenever feasible and sets forth guidelines on that use.

SUMMARY

Restorative justice programs offer another method for handling youths after an offense has occurred. The intent of these programs is multifaceted. The programs attempt to repair the more general harm that has been done to both the victim and the larger community. Equally important is rehabilitating the offender so that he or she does not commit future offenses. There is also a desire to build the community's capacity to address social issues before or as they emerge.

Restorative justice involves various constituencies (Bazemore and Umbreit, 2001; Umbreit, 1997; Van Ness, 1990; Van Ness and Strong, 2006). Under this approach, victims are compensated through restitution, are given a voice in the case handling, and become an integral part of the treatment or intervention provided to the offender. The offender is held accountable for his or her transgressions and may be subjected to a wide array of possible interventions.

The restorative justice model is also very attractive for juvenile justice because it offers a plausible alternative to the get-tough paranoia that is currently popular. It focuses on the victim as well as the offender and the community. It seeks to make the offender more competent and productive in an effort to bond the offender more closely to the community. Finally, the public has a more favorable attitude about such programs with juvenile rather than adult offenders (see Chapter 14 for more details).

Discussion Questions

1. Restorative justice programs are appearing throughout the United States. Do you think this approach is the most appropriate direction for the juvenile justice system to pursue? If so, what form of restorative justice practice should be emphasized (VOM, FGC, NRB, or peacemaking/sentencing circles)? If not, what should be done instead of restorative justice?

2. Advocates of restorative justice point to an array of potential advantages. What features or advantages are there in the restorative justice approach, and which of these should be considered as most important from a juvenile justice perspective?

3. To what extent do you see restorative justice practices meeting the philosophical goals of juvenile justice? Discuss specific features of restorative justice that do and do not correspond to the philosophy of the juvenile justice system.

4. Compare and contrast the different types of restorative justice (i.e., VOM, FGC, NRB, peacemaking/sentencing circles). Which appear to be best suited for use in the juvenile justice system?

Chapter 13

THE VICTIMIZATION OF JUVENILES

Important Terms

abuse

avoidance

child maltreatment

child protective services

Court-Appointed Special
   Advocate (CASA)

cycle of violence

domestic relations court

family courts

guardian *ad litem*

in camera testimony

intraindividual theories

lifestyle explanations

National Child Abuse and
   Neglect Data System (NCANDS)

National Crime Victimization
   Survey (NCVS)

neglect

routine activities theory

social learning approaches

sociocultural explanations

victim-blaming

victim precipitation

What You Need to Know

- Victimization of youths is a very common occurrence and a problem that needs to be addressed by the juvenile justice system.

- According to the NCVS, roughly 5 percent of all youths are victims of a violent crime each year, with a very large portion of that crime taking place at school.

- Counter to popular belief, the killing of students at school is an extremely rare event.

- Youths are also victimized within family settings. Child maltreatment, either as abuse or neglect, is a major problem.

- Youths may adopt an array of responses to victimization, ranging from fear, to avoidance, to carrying weapons and joining a gang.

- Formal agencies that respond to child maltreatment include child protective services, the juvenile court, family court, and the adult criminal justice system.

INTRODUCTION

The juvenile justice system does not deal exclusively with delinquent youths. As has already been seen, the juvenile court is tasked with handling noncriminal misbehavior by juveniles, typically considered as status offenders or unruly/ungovernable. In many jurisdictions, it also has the responsibility of handling youths who are the victims of maltreatment. Beyond the fact that the juvenile justice system must deal with more than just juvenile offenders is the reality that most victims of juvenile offenders are themselves juveniles, and these youths are also in need of assistance.

The present chapter turns the orientation of the book on its head and focuses on youths as victims rather than offenders. Several topics are explored. First, the chapter presents evidence on the extent of juvenile victimization as depicted in both victimization survey data and data on child abuse and neglect. The chapter also discusses explanations for the different forms of victimization. What will become apparent is that there is no single explanation for victimization, just as there is no single explanation for delinquency. Individuals also respond to victimization in different ways, and these methods are explored. Finally, the chapter addresses the role of the juvenile and criminal justice systems in dealing with youthful victims.

THE EXTENT OF VICTIMIZATION

Gauging the extent of victimization can be accomplished through the use of various data collection techniques. Official records, such as the Uniform Crime Reports, provide some indication of the overall extent of victimization in society through counts of offenses brought to the attention of social control agencies. In discussions of victimization, however, most attention turns to surveys that ask respondents about their experiences as a victim of crime. Victim surveys are only about 40 years old and were developed in response to criticisms that official measures underreport the level of crime in society. Consequently, most victim surveys tend to address offenses similar to those found in the Uniform Crime Reports. Victim surveys, however, have been used to address crimes occurring in specific locations, such as in schools and at work, as well as other types of activities, such as abuse and neglect. Beyond victim surveys, organizations such as the American Humane Association and various medical groups also collect information on specific types of victimization.

General Victimization

The most well-known source of victimization data is the **National Crime Victimization Survey (NCVS)**. The current version of the NCVS is the direct descendant of early work in the 1960s and 1970s that explored both the extent of self-reported victimization and the best ways to survey the public. Among the earliest victimization surveys were those commissioned by the 1967 President's Commission on Law Enforcement and Administration of Justice. Those early surveys indicated that, on the average, there was twice as much crime occurring as reflected in police

> Additional information on victims of crimes is available at the NCVS web site at http://www.ojp.usdoj.gov/bjs/cvictgen.htm

records. The NCVS (originally called the National Crime Survey and begun in 1972) provides a great deal of information about the extent of victimization; characteristics of the victim; known information about the offender; data on the time, place, and circumstances of the offense; the economic and physical impact of the crimes; responses by victims; and contact with the criminal justice system.

One important piece of information provided by the NCVS is the breakdown of crimes by victim age and demographic characteristics. Table 13.1 presents estimated 2006 victimization rates for youths ages 12 to 15 and 16 to 19. For these age groups, the estimated rate of all personal crime victimizations is approximately 48 per 1,000 youths ages 12-15 and 53 per 1,000 youths ages 16-19. This means that roughly 5 percent of all youths ages 12-19 are victims of a personal crime in a single year. Note that almost all of these offenses entail physical confrontations with an assailant.

TABLE 13.1 Estimated Victimization Rates for Youthful Age Groups (per 1,000), 2006

	Total		White		Black		Male		Female	
Age	12-15	16-19	12-15	16-19	12-15	16-19	12-15	16-19	12-15	16-19
All personal crimes	47.8	52.8								
Crimes of violence	46.9	51.7	46.3	48.6	49.3	65.0	47.5	53.7	46.3	49.8
Rape/sexual assault	3.4	2.5	3.1	2.5	6.2	3.8	0.5	0.7	6.4	4.3
Robbery	4.0	4.6	4.8	4.4	2.3	6.1	3.6	8.0	4.4	1.1
Aggravated assault	8.3	11.6	7.8	9.8	6.8	16.9	9.0	14.5	7.5	8.5
Simple assault	31.3	33.1	30.6	32.0	34.0	38.3	34.4	30.5	28.0	35.8
Purse snatching/ pocket picking	0.8	1.1	0.7	0.7	0.0	0.0	1.2	1.2	0.5	0.9

Source: Bureau of Justice Statistics (2008). *Criminal Victimization in the United States, 2006—Statistical Tables*. Washington, DC: Bureau of Justice Statistics.

Compared to victimization figures for persons age 25 and older, youths are victimized at much higher rates. Personal crime victimization rates are 36.6 per 1,000 for persons 25-34, 20.6 for person 35-49 years of age, 13.6 for 50-64 years of age, and only 3.9 for those 65 and over (Bureau of Justice Statistics, 2008). What these data show is that youths contribute disproportionately to the ranks of crime victims.

Breakdowns by race and sex (see Table 13.1) reveal some interesting results. In terms of race, black youths and white youths age 12-15 are victimized at similar levels. Older black youths, however, are more often victims of violent crimes and aggravated assault than are older white youths. Comparisons of males and females show only small differences for youths ages 12-15. For older youths, males are more likely to be victims of assault.

The NCVS figures demonstrate that a significant number of youths are victims of crimes ranging from simple larceny to aggravated assault and robbery. A number of other facts are also apparent from the NCVS. First, youths are more likely to be victimized by offenders of the same age, race, and sex as the victim. Second, youths also know the offender more often than do adults. Third, juveniles are less likely to report their victimization experience to the police. Many youths report the offense to someone other than the police.

Whitaker and Bastian (1991) note that many youths are victimized at school. Because youths spend more than one-third of their waking hours at school, it should not be surprising that they experience victimization at school. Unfortunately, victimization at school has only recently become a major concern, mostly due to media portrayals of violence and weapon use on school grounds.

The United States Departments of Education and Justice issue an annual report on school crime and safety based on multiple indicators. Some of the indicators are from the NCVS, and some are from other sources. Students ages 12 through 18 reported almost 1.5 million victimizations (thefts and violent crimes) at school and more than 1.2 million victimizations away from school in 2005 (see Table 13.2). These

Extensive information on crime and victimization at school is compiled each year by the Departments of Justice and Education. Their findings appear at http://nces.ed.gov/programs/crimeindicators/

figures translate into rates of 57 victimizations per 1,000 youths at school and 47 per 1,000 away from school. The fact that both the raw numbers and the rates are higher at school should not be surprising. Youths spend a majority of their waking hours at school during the school year. In addition, schools bring together potential victims with potential offenders, thus enhancing the possibility for victimizations.

Data on victimization of youths at school also provide the ability to inspect differences across demographic dimensions. Table 13.3 shows the percent of students who report being the victims of different types of crimes, as well as breakdowns by gender, race/ethnicity, and grade level.

TABLE 13.2 Characteristics of Juveniles in Correctional Facilities:
Average One Day Count—2003

Type of Crime	At School		Away from School	
	Number	Rate*	Number	Rate*
Theft	868,100	33	610,100	23
Violent Crime	628,200	24	630,900	24
Serious Violence	136,500	5	267,800	10
Total	1,496,300	57	1,241,100	47
* rate per 1,000				

Source: R. Dinkes, E.R. Cataldi, W. Lin-Kelly, and T.D. Snyder (2008). *Indicators of School Crime and Safety: 2007*. Washington, DC: Bureau of Justice Statistics.

The most striking thing about the data is the relative uniformity in the results across almost every student characteristic. The level of victimization reported by males and females is almost identical for all types of offenses. The same is true for different racial/ethnic groups. In terms of grade level (a good proxy for age), the results are very similar for all categories.

TABLE 13.3 Percent Students Reporting Victimization at School
by Selected Characteristics, 2005[a]

Student Characteristics	Total	Theft	Violent[b]	Serious Violent[c]
Total	4.2%	7.1%	1.2%	0.3%
Gender				
Male	4.5	3.0	1.6	0.3
Female	3.9	3.2	0.7	0.3
Race/Ethnicity				
White	4.6	3.4	1.3	0.3
Black	3.9	2.7	1.3	---
Hispanic	3.8	3.0	0.9	0.4
Other	2.2	1.6	---	---
Grade				
6th	4.6	2.8	1.8	---
7th	5.2	2.8	2.8	---
8th	3.6	3.4	1.4	---
9th	4.6	3.7	1.0	---
10th	4.1	3.6	0.5	---
11th	3.6	2.9	0.7	---
12th	3.6	3.3	---	---

[a] Data for students aged 12 to 18.
[b] Violent crimes include rape, sexual assault, robbery, aggravated assault and simple assault.
[c] Serious violent crimes include the violent crimes except for simple assault.

Source: R. Dinkes, E.R. Cataldi, W. Lin-Kelly and T.D. Snyder (2008). *Indicators of School Crime and Safety: 2007*. Washington, DC: Bureau of Justice Statistics.

One attention-grabbing form of victimization at school has been kill-ings of students by other students. The killings in Jonesboro, Arkansas, Columbine High School, and other places attract a great deal of media attention and claims of "crises" facing schools. The reality, however, is that such actions are rare and have been declining. The data in Table 13.4 show that the number of homicides at school is very low, both in terms of absolute levels and relative to the numbers occurring away from school. It is also important to note that the figures in Table 13.4 subsume the multiple homicides that occur in many cases (such as at Columbine). The data clearly demonstrate that youths are safer at school than in the community.

TABLE 13.4 Homicides of Youths At and Away From School

School Year	At School	Away from School
1992-1993	34	3,583
1993-1994	29	3,806
1994-1995	28	3,546
1995-1996	32	3,303
1996-1997	28	2,950
1997-1998	34	2,728
1998-1999	33	2,366
1999-2000	13	2,124
2000-2001	11	2,045
2001-2002	14	1,468
2002-2003	18	1,515
2003-2004	21	1,437
2004-2005	21	1,534
2005-2006	14	-----

Source: R. Dinkes, E.R. Cataldi, W. Lin-Kelly, and T.D. Snyder (2008). *Indicators of School Crime and Safety: 2007*. Washington, DC: Bureau of Justice Statistics.

Victimization at school raises a number of perplexing problems. The most direct concern is the victimization itself. These youths are suffer-ing losses and injuries. A second concern is that when the victimization takes place at school, the schools are failing to protect the youths under their care. This raises potential issues of liability. Third, the level of victimization at school may have a direct impact on the quality of edu-cation received by the students. This may result from students missing days of school because of the offense or fear of being victimized. It also may occur because school officials must spend time trying to establish discipline and control, or because the level of crime makes the staff feel that the students are not interested in receiving an education. Crime and victimization, therefore, may replace educating as the primary concern of the school. Consequently, victimization has both immediate and long-term impacts on students.

Child Maltreatment

Victimization surveys and most official sources of crime data generally miss a major form of victimization against youths, namely child maltreatment. **Child maltreatment** is a term encompassing a variety of actions in which children are harmed, either intentionally or unintentionally. The terms most commonly used for maltreatment are child abuse and child neglect. **Abuse** is the intentional commission of an act upon a child, while **neglect** refers to the omission of a caretaker to provide what a child needs. These can be future delineated into categories such as sexual abuse, physical abuse, and emotional abuse (see Figure 13.1).

FIGURE 13.1 Main Types of Child Maltreatment

Neglect is failure to provide for a child's basic needs. Neglect may be:

- Physical (e.g., failure to provide necessary food or shelter, or lack of appropriate supervision)

- Medical (e.g., failure to provide necessary medical or mental health treatment)

- Educational (e.g., failure to educate a child or attend to special education needs)

- Emotional (e.g., inattention to a child's emotional needs, failure to provide psychological care, or permitting the child to use alcohol or other drugs)

Physical Abuse is physical injury (ranging from minor bruises to severe fractures or death) as a result of punching, beating, kicking, biting, shaking, throwing, stabbing, choking, hitting (with a hand, stick, strap, or other object), burning, or otherwise harming a child. Such injury is considered abuse regardless of whether the caretaker intended to hurt the child.

Sexual Abuse includes activities by a parent or caretaker such as fondling a child's genitals, penetration, incest, rape, sodomy, indecent exposure, and exploitation through prostitution or the production of pornographic materials.

Emotional Abuse is a pattern of behavior that impairs a child's emotional development or sense of self-worth. This may include constant criticism, threats, or rejection, as well as withholding love, support, or guidance. Emotional abuse is often difficult to prove and, therefore, Child Protective Services may not be able to intervene without evidence of harm to the child. Emotional abuse is almost always present when other forms are identified.

Source: Child Welfare Gateway Information (2006). *What Is Child Abuse and Neglect?* Washington, DC: U.S. Department of Health and Human Services. Found at: http://www.childwelfare.gov/pubs/factsheets/whatiscan.cfm

What makes child maltreatment especially noteworthy is the fact that the offender is typically a parent or other relative. While not a new phenomenon, it is only since the 1960s that child abuse and neglect have been seen as a social problem. Prior to that time, these types of actions were primarily considered private problems that were best dealt with by the family.

> More information on what constitutes child maltreatment can be found at http://www.childwelfare.gov/pubs/factsheets/whatiscan.cfm

Measuring child abuse and neglect is difficult due to the nature of the actions and the victim–offender relationship. First, abuse and neglect typically do not take place in public. Instead, they occur at home where there are no witnesses besides the victim, offender, and other family members. Second, in many cases, the victim may not recognize the action by the parent as wrong. The child is either too immature to understand the nature of what is happening, cannot adequately verbalize the events, or does not know who to tell about the abuse or neglect. Third, despite the abuse, children often still express love and affection for the parent/relative and may not want to do something that will get the offender into trouble. As a result, the child will not report, and may even deny, the existence of maltreatment.

Due to these problems, no firm figures on abuse and neglect are available. What is known is that the problem is widespread. One source of data on child abuse and neglect is child protective services (CPS) agencies in each state. Data from these agencies are collected and compiled by the **National Child Abuse and Neglect Data System (NCANDS)**. In 2006, there were more than 1 million documented cases of child abuse or neglect in the United States (see Table 13.5) (Administration on Children, Youth, and Families, 2008). Almost two-thirds of the maltreated children (64.1%) experienced some form of neglect. Only 16 percent experienced physical abuse, while almost 9 percent experienced sexual abuse and 7 percent psychological maltreatment (Administration on Children, Youth, and Families, 2008). Victimization rates were similar for males and females. In terms of race/ethnicity, the rate of victimization for African Americans and other minority youths was roughly twice that of white youths (Administration on Children, Youth, and Families, 2008). Unfortunately, child maltreatment often leads to the death of the victim, According to NCANDS data, 1,376 children were killed in 2006 as a result of maltreatment.

The figures for the extent of abuse and neglect are only estimates. There is no accurate count for this type of victimization. The fact that most such acts occur behind closed doors between relatives means that we may never have a complete picture of the problem. What can be concluded is that these are baseline figures and that the real extent of abuse and neglect is probably much higher.

TABLE 13.5 Number and Rate of Child Maltreatment, 2006

Type	Number	Rate	%*
Physical Abuse	142,041	1.9	16.0
Neglect	567,787	7.7	64.1
Medical Neglect	19,180	0.3	2.2
Sex Abuse	78,120	1.1	8.8
Psychological Maltreatment	58,577	0.8	6.6
Other Abuse	133,978	1.8	15.1
Unknown	10,221	0.1	1.2
Fatalities	1,376	<0.1	

* does not equal 100 due to multiple types in some incidents

Source: Administration on Children, Youth, and Families (2008). *Child Maltreatment, 2006*. Washington, DC: U.S. Department of Health and Human Services.

EXPLAINING JUVENILE VICTIMIZATION

Attempts to explain why an individual is a victim can take a variety of forms. Certainly, one way to explain victimization is to turn the equation over and focus on the offender. The various theories addressed earlier in this text (Chapters 3 and 4) follow this more traditional approach to understanding unacceptable behavior. Because the perpetrator is the one who has violated the law, it is natural to focus attention on that individual, rather than the victim. There must be something about the offender that led to the victimization. The realm of victimology, however, does not rely exclusively on the theories already presented in this text. Rather, attempts to explain juvenile victimization range from those that attempt to blame the victim for the action to others targeted at specific forms of victimization.

From Victim-Blaming to Lifestyle

Early research on victims paid considerable attention to who the victims were and the circumstances surrounding the events. Throughout these works was an underlying theme that individuals became victims because of something they did, did not do, or could not do. For example, von Hentig (1941) outlined 13 categories of victims, including the young, females, the elderly, minorities, and mentally defective individuals. What made these people victims was the fact that they were somehow vulnerable. Some people cannot physically ward off an attack, others do not recognize they are being victimized, and others see themselves outside the societal mainstream and accept the victimization. Mendelsohn (1956) took this argument one step further in a classification relying on the culpability of the victim. "Victims with minor guilt" place themselves into a position in which victimization is possible. The "victim more guilty than the offender" actively initiates the event that causes the victimization. Similarly, the "most guilty victim" starts out as an offender and ends up the victim.

This line of reasoning reached its apex with the work of Wolfgang (1958) and Amir (1971). Both of these authors argued that substantial numbers of offenses are victim-precipitated. **Victim precipitation** posits that the victim is actively involved in the offense. Wolfgang (1958) stated that

> victim-precipitated [homicide] cases are those in which the victim was the first to show and use a deadly weapon, to strike a blow in an altercation— in short, the first to commence the interplay of resort to physical violence (p. 252).

The victim, therefore, holds some responsibility for his or her own status due to his or her actions or inactions. Amir (1971) extended this argument to rape offenses by claiming that how the victim acted, where she was, how she dressed, and similar factors placed the victim in the role of contributing to her own victimization. While these early ideas of victim culpability have been referred to as **victim-blaming** and subjected to much criticism (see Curtis, 1974; Franklin and Franklin, 1976; Weis and Borges, 1973), the idea that the actions of individuals may contribute to their victimization has not been completely discounted.

Today, **lifestyle explanations** and **routine activities theory** are commonly employed to show how individual behavior contributes to victimization. These theories argue that where individuals go, who they go with, and when they go all define their lifestyle and their chances of victimization (Cohen and Felson, 1979; Hindelang, Gottfredson, and Garofalo, 1978). If one's choices for behavior places him or her in an area where crime is common, at a time when there is no one to provide protection, then the chances for victimization are enhanced. That person's lifestyle, therefore, contributes to becoming a victim.

Examples and support for a lifestyle explanation of juvenile victimization are plentiful. The fact that juveniles are disproportionately represented among offenders would suggest that juveniles would also be the victims for a variety of reasons. First, other youths are available to victimize—at school, out-of-doors in the neighborhood, in play groups, and as acquaintances. Second, juvenile offenders will view other youths as more physically vulnerable than most adults. Third, interaction with other youths provides knowledge and opportunities for offending. Fourth, individuals who engage in deviant behavior are themselves at higher risk of being a victim (Clark and Lab, 1995; Esbensen and Huizinga, 1991; Lauritsen et al., 1991). In essence, the juvenile lifestyle includes more youths to victimize than adults. As youths either find themselves or place themselves in situations in which delinquency is more likely, they will invariably be victimized.

Explanations of Child Abuse and Neglect

Where the lifestyle approach emphasizes the behavior and choices of the victim as contributors to victimization, explanations of child maltreatment focus exclusively on the offender and society. The victim is not considered culpable. In general, explanations for child maltreatment can be divided into three categories: intraindividual theories, sociocultural explanations, and social learning theories (Doerner and Lab, 2008). **Intraindividual theories** view child maltreatment as an internal flaw or defect of the abuser. The key is to identify the flaw and intervene to avoid future abusive behavior (Belsky, 1978). Abusers are considered to exhibit some form of psychopathological condition (Steele and Pollock, 1974), such as role reversal. Under role reversal, the abuser/parent expects the child to provide nurturance and love to the parent, rather than having to supply those things to the victim/child. Intraindividual theories have been used to absolve society of any responsibility for child abuse and lay the blame on a few "sick" individuals.

Sociocultural explanations shift the emphasis from the individual to society and the environment. The abuser may be stressed by any number of factors, such as unemployment, conflicts at work or home, family size, social isolation, and economic problems (Belsky, 1978; Garbarino and Gilliam, 1980; Gelles, 1980; Gil, 1971). This stress leads the individual to strike out against someone or something that cannot retaliate. Where a spouse, other adults, or an employer will not tolerate inappropriate action, a child has neither the physical stature nor the social standing to resist maltreatment. A child, therefore, becomes the recipient of abuse as a proxy outlet for stress.

Social learning approaches to child maltreatment rest on the assumption that an individual has learned to be abusive by observing past abusive behavior. This observation includes the possibility that the abuser was himself or herself abused as a child. The idea that a child who is abused or who witnesses abuse will grow up to be an abuser is often referred to as the **cycle of violence** (Schwartz, 1989; Straus, 1983). Following basic social learning tenets, a child who observes abusive behavior that is not sanctioned, particularly if it is perpetrated by a respected significant adult, is more likely to model his or her future behavior accordingly. This same argument has been used as an explanation of spousal abuse (U.S. Attorney General's Task Force, 1984). Widom (1989, 1995), following abused/neglected youths and a control group into adulthood, reports a significant relationship between abuse/neglect as a child and deviant behavior of various types later in life. Researchers of the cycle of violence theory point out a variety of methodological problems and issues and call for further research before the theory is accepted as a causal factor in abuse and deviant behavior (see Gelles and Cornell, 1990; Pagelow, 1984; Simons et al., 1995).

Explanations for child abuse and neglect are still in their infancy. Indeed, scholarly interest in this form of victimization is relatively new, with most work dating since the 1960s. Consequently, little consensus exists on the scope of the problem, explanations for maltreatment, or how to best attack the problem. This state of affairs will persist until further research is completed.

RESPONSES TO VICTIMIZATION

Victimization, whether direct or vicarious, has the potential of eliciting a number of responses from the victim. While victims may view the responses as beneficial, they are often debilitating and may lead the victims into criminal or delinquent behavior. Responses can range from taking direct action at the time of an offense to raised levels of fear of crime to various actions aimed at reducing the risk of initial or further victimization. Carrying weapons for protection or joining gangs may be responses chosen by youthful victims. In both cases, however, the response may be illegal and/or lead to more victimization.

Immediate Responses

One response to victimization is for the victim to take action at the time of the offense. According to the National Crime Victimization Survey (NCVS), almost 60 percent of youthful victims invoke some self-protective action (Bureau of Justice Statistics, 2008). Where the NCVS breaks down self-protective action by age group, it does not do so for individual forms of response. Using information for all respondents on type of self-protective behavior (see Table 13.6), it is apparent that most measures are not confrontational in nature. The most common responses to violent crimes are to resist or capture the offender (22.9%), run away or hide from the offender (14.8%), get help/give alarm (12.3%), or try to persuade or appease the offender (13.0%). Less than 10 percent of victims directly attack or threaten an offender (Bureau of Justice Statistics, 2008).

Fear of Crime as a Response

Whether or not a victim takes an action at the time of an offense, there will probably be some changes in beliefs or behavior subsequent to the victimization experience. While many studies show that roughly 40 to 50 percent of the population is fearful of crime (Hindelang, 1975; Skogan and Maxfield, 1981; Toseland, 1982), there is relatively little research that assesses fear among juveniles. This is particularly interesting because youths are among the most victimized.

TABLE 13.6 Percent of Victims Taking Self-Protective Measures in
Violent Victimizations and Type of Measures Taken

Measure	Percent
Attacked offender with weapon	1.2
Attacked offender without weapon	8.7
Threatened offender with weapon	0.5
Threatened offender without weapon	2.5
Resisted or captured offender	22.9
Scared or warned offender	10.8
Persuaded or appeased offender	13.0
Ran away or hid	14.8
Got help or gave alarm	12.3
Screamed from pain or fear	3.8
Took another method	9.3

Source: Bureau of Justice Statistics (2008). *Criminal Victimization in the United States, 2006.* Statistical Tables. Washington, DC: Bureau of Justice Statistics.

When research does look at youths, fear does not appear to be a minor concern. Lab and Clark (1994), in their study of junior and senior high school students, found that 30 percent of the students claimed to fear being attacked at school, independent of whether they had ever been victimized in the past. Interestingly, fear was higher for younger respondents. Similarly, the NCVS reports that 6 percent of youths are fearful of being attacked at school (Dinkes et al., 2008).

Fear can be debilitating, regardless of whether it is a result of past victimization. Fear leads some people to avoid other persons and places. It makes others decide to carry a weapon for protection, and still others to join groups to fight crime. The very fact that fear can cause people to change their normal routine is evidence that it is something to be addressed. This is not to suggest that fear is always a bad thing. Indeed, to the extent that fear alters a person's behavior and chances of being victimized, fear is a useful tool.

Avoidance

One common reaction to actual or potential victimization and fear is **avoidance** of certain places or people. Avoidance is possibly the leading response to fear of victimization (Gates and Rohe, 1987; Skogan, 1981). Two analyses designed to identify citizen responses to fear and victimization (Lab, 1990; Lavrakas and Lewis, 1981) found that avoidance behavior is common. Reasonable avoidance behavior for a youth may include staying away from a playground where gang members are known to hang out or refraining from walking alone at night in an area with a high crime rate.

Unfortunately, there are some instances in which avoidance is not a viable alternative. For youths, victimization at school raises the option of staying home from school or avoiding certain places at school. Avoidance at school, however, means that school work is missed, the student is distracted from work while at school, and/or there is discomfort and inconvenience involved in avoiding important parts of the school (such as a restroom or the cafeteria). In their study of in-school victimization, Lab and Clark (1994) reported that 9 percent of the students stayed home at least once over a six-month time period due to fear of being assaulted at school, and 5 percent avoided school for fear of having something stolen. While the majority of students do not avoid school or places at school, there is a small but significant percent of students who feel they must stay away from important parts of the school. Using the NCVS School Crime Supplement data to identify the predictors of avoidance behavior by students, Lab and Whitehead (1994) reported that fear is by far the most important consideration, even surpassing actual victimization experiences.

Resorting to Weapons

An inescapable fact about youths in recent years is their ability to obtain and use weapons. Nationally, one-fifth of the population reports having bought a gun for their own protection or to protect their homes. Eleven percent (11%) report actually carrying (or having carried) a weapon for protection (Saad, 2001). Surveys of students show that weapons are an everyday occurrence in and around many schools. One national survey reveals that 17 percent of youths carried weapons at least once in the past month, with 6 percent claiming to have carried them at school (DeVoe et al., 2004). Similarly, a survey of New York City high school students revealed

A Hancock City (Michigan) police officer uses a hand-held metal detector to search incoming Hancock Middle School students for weapons. The school district's superintendent said the measure was put in place after a written threat of a shooting was discovered in a boys' bathroom.

that, in schools without metal detectors, almost 14 percent of the students carried a weapon inside school at least once within a 30-day period ("Violence-Related Attitudes," 1993). Finally, Lab and Clark (1994) reported that 24 percent of their respondents carried a weapon for protection at school at least once during the preceding six months. According to most studies, the most frequent weapon being carried is a knife or razor. Guns are not the most prevalent weapon.

The carrying of weapons for self-protection is problematic for a number of reasons. First, most of these items are illegal for youths to possess. Second, possession of weapons by any individual on school grounds is illegal. Third, the presence of a weapon has the potential of escalating any confrontation to much higher levels and mitigates the possibility of defusing a situation. Fourth, a weapon may result in the victim being hurt more than if no weapon was available. Finally, accepting the premise that you meet force with force portends a mind-set wherein force becomes the solution of choice, rather than a solution of last resort.

Gangs as Protection

In times of crisis or turmoil, it is natural for people to seek out support from those around them. Most victims will turn to family members for such assistance. Another source of support is close friends and peers. For many youths, the friends and peers include gang members. This is particularly true for youths in large inner-city areas. The response to victimization, therefore, may entail joining a gang for protection. Some youths see joining a gang as a means of restoring a feeling of security. If a youth is victimized by gang members, either directly or by mistake, joining a gang further becomes a self-defense mechanism.

Joining gangs as a response to victimization, however, is a double-edged sword. While the gang may supply some sense of protection, it typically demands participation in illegal behavior and conflict with other gangs and individuals. These demands often result in further victimization of the individual, rather than protection from victimization. At the same time that gang membership may alleviate victimization, joining a gang can also contribute to ongoing victimization, albeit as a member of a group and not just as an individual.

Summary of Victimization Responses

Juveniles can respond to victimization in a variety of ways. At the same time, many of the potential responses have negative aspects that can exacerbate problems for the youth. Fear, which may serve as a protective measure, can lead to withdrawal from other people and the community. It can also prompt a youth to stay home from school or avoid certain places at school. Still other victims may purchase and carry weapons for protection. Victimization also may drive a youth to join a gang as a means of feeling safe. While each of these may appear reasonable, they can lead to further victimization, more serious situations, and, certainly, a deterioration in the general quality of life.

THE ROLE OF FORMAL SOCIAL CONTROL AGENCIES

Various social control agencies can become involved in youthful victimization. Most social control agencies, however, focus on juvenile victims of abuse and neglect and ignore the victim status as it emerges from other forms of offending. Clearly, a juvenile who loses money due to a theft or is hurt from an assault tends to be considered a witness more so than a victim by the justice system. Assistance to these victims is relatively limited to mediation and similar programs already discussed. On the other hand, victims of abuse and neglect receive a great deal of attention by various formal control agencies, particularly child protective services and the different court systems.

Perhaps the only agency that will have contact with all forms of youthful victims will be the police. This is because they are typically the ones called whenever someone is in need of help. The police, however, are geared toward identifying offenders, making arrests, and preparing cases for prosecution. Except for initial contacts, providing immediate protection, referrals to other sources of assistance, and work with prevention programs, law enforcement officers spend little time dealing with the victim. This is true whether the victim is an adult or a juvenile. Consequently, the balance of this section looks at how other system components deal with youthful victims.

Child Protective Services

An alternative point of system entry besides the police that has been established for the purposes of protecting youths is child protective services. **Child protective services** are mandated in every state as a direct result of the Child Abuse Prevention and Treatment Act of 1974 (Wiehe, 1992). This federal act required states to set up rules for the reporting and handling of abused children. States not conforming to the Act would be denied various forms of federal funding. Because the exact nature of how a state would provide protective services was left to the state, these services appear under various state agencies such as Social Services and Departments of Human Services.

Child protective service agencies fill a variety of roles and have diverse powers in different states. First, in virtually all jurisdictions, these agencies are responsible for accepting reports of abuse and neglect cases and undertaking or coordinating the investigation of such allegations. While many investigations are done by employees of the child protective service, others may be assigned to other agencies, such as the police or prosecutor's office. A second common function of child protective services is the removal of children from suspected (or documented) abusive situations. This removal may last for only a short time or can last for an extended period, depending on the facts of the case. The protection of the child from further possible harm is the goal of any decision to remove a child from his or her parents. Child protective services often provide oversight to foster care, adoption, and other forms of custodial arrangements for the state.

Finally, child protective services focus on the preservation of the family unit. Underlying this approach is the belief that the family setting is the most appropriate for raising a child. Stabilizing the family situation, removing the problematic elements in the home, and improving the quality of life for the child guide the decisions made by the agency. Given this preoccupation with family preservation, most child protective agencies do not need court orders or sanctions to work with families. Much like diversion programs or informal probation, child protective services will work with families to solve problems without resorting to formal court procedures if all parties agree. In some cases the agency will actually provide the recommended intervention, and in others the agency may act as more of a referral source than service provider.

Child protective services reach a large number of victims and families each year. Almost 3.6 million children were the recipients of preventive measures in 2006. This is almost 48 children out of

Members of The Fundamentalist Church of Jesus Christ of Latter-day Saints are assisted by law enforcement officials as they board a bus used to relocate them. Child protective services workers raided the compound in April 2008 in a massive custody case that swept 439 children from a polygamist sect's West Texas ranch into foster care, All but a few dozen cases against parents were dropped, but Texas Child Protective Services maintains that 12 girls in the sect were sexually abused in underage "spiritual" marriages performed with their parents' consent, and maintains that nearly two-thirds of the 146 families it investigated had children who were abused or neglected.

AP Photo/Tony Gutierrez

every 1,000 in the United States (National Child Abuse and Neglect Data System, 2008). In addition, more than 1.3 million youths received post-investigative services, of which an estimated 533,000 were victims of crimes (National Child Abuse and Neglect Data System, 2008). Roughly 312,000 youths were removed from their homes in 2006 as a result of abuse or neglect (National Child Abuse and Neglect Data System, 2008). These figures reveal two things. First, CPS agencies reach a substantial number of abuse and neglect victims. Second, these agencies handle many youths for an array of problems beyond just victimization.

Child protective services personnel work very closely with different courts. While these agencies often generate cases for the criminal and juvenile courts, the courts also call on these services for assistance as cases work their way through the system. This referral from the courts to protective services can range from taking custody of children when parents are incarcerated for a crime to investigating allegations of abuse and neglect that emerge in the course of divorce proceedings.

The Juvenile Court

The juvenile court deals with a wide variety of issues related to youths. Besides handling delinquents and status offenders, it faces cases of dependency, abuse, and neglect. In these cases, the court must consider the protection and needs of the juvenile victim, the needs of the entire family unit, and the possible sanctioning and needs of the (typically adult) offender.

Cases of abuse and neglect force the juvenile court to assume a more conflict orientation than presumed under the *parens patriae* philosophy. Because of the diverse issues in abuse and neglect cases, many juvenile courts are affiliated with (or even part of) what are more generally known as **family courts**. Larger family courts may designate certain judges to handle delinquency matters and others to deal with abuse and neglect cases. These latter cases typically follow a more rigorous set of procedural guidelines, including evidentiary safeguards, the presence of attorneys, and formal examination and cross-examination of witnesses. This is required because of the due process rights of the accused.

In every case of abuse and neglect, the primary concern of the juvenile court is the well-being of the juvenile and the family unit. Other youths in the home also become a focal point along with the individual victim, based on the assumption that they are potential victims. Because abuse and neglect cases place the interests of the child in conflict with that of an accused parent, the court typically appoints someone to be an advocate for the needs and interests of the child. Two common names for such an advocate would be a **Court-Appointed Special Advocate (CASA)** or a **guardian *ad litem***. The CASA program began in Seattle in the late 1970s and has since spread to all states (National CASA, 2008). According to National CASA (2008), there are almost 60,000 CASA volunteers handling 243,000 children in the United States. These advocates usually serve in a voluntary capacity, although some courts provide office space, supplies, and travel expenses. The exact role and responsibility of a CASA volunteer and a guardian *ad litem* varies across jurisdictions, although their general duty is to protect the interests of the child in virtually any legal proceeding (see Box 13.1). These individuals typically receive training in the functioning of the juvenile court, the needs of youths, the availability of resources, and how to investigate the circumstances of the case.

Court-appointed advocates often fulfill some of the same functions as other actors in the criminal and juvenile justice systems. These

BOX 13.1

Excerpts from Ohio's Guardian ad Litem Statute

2151.281 Guardian ad litem.

(A) The court shall appoint a guardian ad litem, subject to rules adopted by the supreme court, to protect the interest of a child in any proceeding concerning an alleged or adjudicated delinquent child or unruly child when either of the following applies:

(1) The child has no parent, guardian, or legal custodian.

(2) The court finds that there is a conflict of interest between the child and the child's parent, guardian, or legal custodian.

(B)(1) The court shall appoint a guardian ad litem, subject to rules adopted by the supreme court, to protect the interest of a child in any proceeding concerning an alleged abused or neglected child…

(2) The guardian ad litem appointed for an alleged or adjudicated abused or neglected child may bring a civil action against any person who is required by division (A)(1) or (4) of section 2151.421 of the Revised Code to file a report of child abuse or child neglect that is known or reasonably suspected or believed to have occurred if that person knows, or has reasonable cause to suspect or believe based on facts that would cause a reasonable person in a similar position to suspect or believe, as applicable, that the child… is the subject of child abuse or child neglect and does not file the required report and if the child suffers any injury or harm as a result of the child abuse or child neglect that is known or reasonably suspected or believed to have occurred or suffers additional injury or harm after the failure to file the report…

(I) The guardian ad litem for an alleged or adjudicated abused, neglected, or dependent child shall perform whatever functions are necessary to protect the best interest of the child, including, but not limited to, investigation, mediation, monitoring court proceedings, and monitoring the services provided the child by the public children services agency or private child placing agency that has temporary or permanent custody of the child, and shall file any motions and other court papers that are in the best interest of the child…

Source: Anderson's Ohio Online Docs. Available at: http://codes.ohio.gov/orc/2151.81

individuals, because of their focus on youths, can undertake a more thorough investigation of a case than can an overburdened police force. They can also spend the time to identify potential sources of treatment for the child, offender, and family that is not a role of law enforcement investigators. In some places these individuals also serve in the place of an attorney on the child's behalf. One key difference, however, between an attorney and a CASA volunteer or guardian *ad litem* involves their orientation toward the case. Whereas an attorney argues in accordance with the client's wishes, a court-appointed advocate is supposed to argue in the best interests of the child, even if that conflicts with the desires of the child (Sagatun and Edwards, 1995). These court volunteers, therefore, provide a service that may not be available in their absence.

The juvenile court can impose a variety of conditions on the child victim and the family. Among these are emergency temporary custody orders, permanent custody decisions (including adoption), individual and family counseling, mandatory treatment programs, and the incarceration of offenders. In making these decisions, the juvenile court judge must rely on information from a variety of sources. Court-appointed advocates are one source of vital information and recommendations. As in adjudication decisions in which the judge relies on probation personnel for an appropriate disposition, the judge typically follows the recommendation of court-appointed advocates in cases of abuse and neglect.

> More information about CASA can be found at the national web site at http://www.nationalcasa.org/

CASA volunteers have had a big impact on abuse and neglect cases. An evaluation conducted by the Department of Justice's Inspector General (2006) noted that cases in which CASA was involved tended to receive more and longer services and arrive at better position outcomes than cases without their intervention (see Table 13.7). The only surprise was the fact that cases involving CASA had a lower rate of family reunification. The reason for this is probably due to the fact that CASA handles more complex and difficult cases.

TABLE 13.7 Outcomes of CASA Involvement

Youths spend a longer time in foster care.

More youths are placed in foster care.

Youths receive more case services.

More cases are permanently closed before the youth reaches the age of majority.

Less likelihood youths will reenter the juvenile justice system.

Higher likelihood of a successful "permanent plan" being implemented.

Lower chance of family reunification—more adoptions.

Source: U.S. Department of Justice (2006). *National CASA Program—Audit Report 07-04*. Washington, DC: U.S. Department of Justice, Office of the Inspector General.

The Criminal Court

The criminal court holds a difficult position when faced with youthful victims, particularly abuse and neglect victims. This is because of its orientation toward determining guilt or innocence of the accused and imposing sentences on the convicted. The victim in the criminal court holds no more stature than does any witness. It is the state that is the aggrieved party and the state that is pursuing the prosecution of the offender (Doerner and Lab, 2008). As a consequence of this situation, the criminal court focuses on providing the accused with his or her due process rights. Besides the victim's role as a witness, the court's only other concern for a victim is to protect him or her from further harm.

A juvenile victim in the criminal court is especially problematic due to his or her lack of maturity. The process can be very traumatic for a child, particularly if the accused is an abusive or neglectful parent. In the past, many cases never reached trial, or the prosecution was unsuccessful due to problems with youthful victims/witnesses. In recent years, however, criminal courts have started to make accommodations for youthful victims. For example, some jurisdictions provide victim counselors as a means of minimizing the trauma of a court appearance and assisting youths with recall problems (Burgess and Lazlo, 1976; Geiselman, Bornstein, and Saywitz, 1992). These counselors can serve in a fashion and capacity similar to CASA workers and guardians *ad litem*. Other courts have relaxed the hearsay rule (Levine and Battistoni, 1991) or allowed **in camera testimony** (Bjerregaard, 1989; Melton, 1980) as means of entering testimony while protecting the victim. The relaxed hearsay rule allows third-party testimony, such as from a counselor or psychiatrist. *In camera* testimony entails testimony outside the courtroom, such as in a judge's chambers or by means of closed-circuit television or on tape. While these efforts are not allowed in all jurisdictions, they are gaining acceptance as a way to protect the youthful victim while still prosecuting the accused.

On a related note, both juvenile and adult victims hold few rights in the criminal court. As noted earlier, there have been some accommodations made for juveniles as witnesses. Other inroads to the court appear in legislation that provides victims with rights such as the right to be informed about court proceedings, the right to protection from intimidation, and the right to address the court at the time of sentencing (Doerner and Lab, 2005). Unfortunately, there is little discussion of youthful victims in any of the arguments for these changes or in the enacting legislation.

Domestic Relations Court

A final court in which juvenile victims may find themselves is a **domestic relations court**. These are civil courts devoted to the issues involved in divorce, child support, and related matters. As with juvenile courts, domestic relations may be configured as a special court within a larger family court setting in some jurisdictions. Youthful victims appear in these courts primarily in cases in which allegations of abuse or neglect are made by one parent against another. The child does not have a separate standing in the court, despite the possibility of abuse or neglect. When such allegations are made, the court will order an investigation (often by protective services agencies) for the purpose of making a determination with regard to the question before the court (i.e., divorce, support payments, etc.). It is possible that the court will provide a CASA worker or a guardian *ad litem* to the child when such allegations are made. If evidence of abuse or neglect is uncovered in the case, those issues are turned over to the criminal or juvenile courts for action. Therefore, while youthful victimization may emerge in domestic relations courts, those problems are outside of the court's jurisdiction and will be turned over to another court.

SUMMARY: THE NEED TO RECOGNIZE THE VICTIM

Addressing children as victims of crime has long been a component of the juvenile justice system and, to a minimal extent, other courts, but this fails to garner much attention in discussions of juvenile justice. This is unfortunate because most youthful offenders prey on other youths, and significant numbers of youths are victims of abuse and neglect. While the juvenile court has long standing in the areas of abuse and neglect, youthful victims have few coping mechanisms available for dealing with other forms of victimization. This is especially true outside the juvenile justice system. To what can this anonymity of juvenile victimization be attributed? One major source of blame has to be the fact that too often the emphasis on juvenile offenders ignores the other half of the offense dyad—the juvenile victim. We have attempted to begin to rectify this shortcoming in this chapter. It is also important, however, that more emphasis be placed on research and programming for juvenile victims. Without those efforts, juvenile victims will continue to receive little attention.

DISCUSSION QUESTIONS

1. You have recently been hired to work for an agency that deals with abused and neglected youths. Research your state statutes and report on the legal definitions of abuse and neglect, and what is mandated in terms of dealing with these victims (such as mandatory reporting, treatment, etc.). What gaps do you see in the statutes? What changes would you make?

2. You have been asked to draw up new legislation dealing with child abuse and neglect. Define the terms, outline the issues you would include in the legislation, and discuss the role you see for the juvenile court and how, if at all, it would alter the court's philosophy.

3. Discuss the responses youths make when victimized. What are the positive and negative consequences of the various responses? What types of services are available to handle victimized juveniles (not including abuse and neglect)? What services are in your town? What services would you like to see initiated?

4. Your local Parent Teacher Association (PTA) is clamoring for increased security measures at school. The PTA wants to prevent homicides and other violent crimes. What information should the PTA and the school be aware of in order to make reasonable choices?

Chapter 14

FUTURE DIRECTIONS IN JUVENILE JUSTICE

Important Terms

capital punishment

criminalized juvenile court

divestiture

jurisdiction over status offenders

political economy

positive youth development

restorative justice juvenile court

Roper v. Simmons

spiritual dimension in corrections

therapeutic jurisprudence

youth justice system

What You Need to Know

- Reform proposals for juvenile court include re-emphasizing and reinvigorating the rehabilitative orientation of juvenile court, changing juvenile court into a scaled-down version of criminal court, and abolishing juvenile court.

- Another model is to adopt a restorative justice model for juvenile court.

- Social issues that affect juveniles include race (disproportionate minority confinement and contacts), the need to rebuild community, the role of the family, character education, and the political economy.

- In *Roper v. Simmons* (2005), the U.S. Supreme Court ruled that the death penalty is unconstitutional for juveniles. Like the dissenting Justice Scalia, some would argue that the death penalty is appropriate for juveniles.

- A recent estimate is that there are about 2,500 juveniles serving Life Without Parole sentences. Critics argue that the same reasoning used by the majority of the Supreme Court in *Roper* applies to Life Without Parole: incomplete adolescent psychological development and impulsiveness argue that juveniles are not fully responsible.

- There is some confusion over the proper role of juvenile court concerning status offenders. Petitioned cases are increasing while many call for ending jurisdiction.

- Although many would like an easy solution, that is not possible. The answer is to address the problems of youths who break the law.

INTRODUCTION

The juvenile court is in trouble. Critics point out numerous problems and suggest either change or elimination. State legislators and prosecutors have taken away many of the clients of juvenile court. New state laws mandate handling many juveniles in adult criminal court. Prosecutors today have increased authority to direct juveniles to adult court. It is likely that these trends will continue and there will be little or nothing left of juvenile court.

This chapter will examine several proposals about the future of juvenile court. One drastic proposal is to abolish juvenile court. Other proposals call for new types of courts. We will outline these proposals and assess them. This chapter will also look at some broader issues affecting the treatment of juvenile offenders. For example, we will look at the role of community and family in dealing with delinquency. We will question whether steps can be taken to improve the ways in which both community and family try to prevent delinquency.

PROPOSALS FOR REFORMING JUVENILE COURT

Rehabilitating the Rehabilitative Parens Patriae Court

One approach to the problems of the juvenile court is try to return to the rehabilitative and *parens patriae* roots of the court. Reformers who support this option think that the failures of juvenile court are failures of implementation: the juvenile court has not delivered the rehabilitation that it initially promised. A major factor behind this failure of implementation is lack of funding. Legislators have not provided the money needed to help youths obtain education, individual counseling, family counseling, and vocational training.

If juvenile courts received adequate funding and if they followed the advice of the research on effective rehabilitation programs (see Chapters 10 and 11 for summaries of those findings), then juvenile court could be the ideal youth court envisioned by the Progressives at the beginning of the twentieth century. Juvenile court judges could act like concerned parents trying to help children.

A leader in the drive to get juvenile court to deliver rehabilitation is Lipsey (1999). Lipsey has done meta-analysis research on effective interventions. He believes that such research shows that there are effective interventions for both institutionalized and noninstitutionalized offenders. The best programs have the capability to "reduce recidivism by 40-50 percent, that is, to cut recidivism rates to very nearly half of what they would be without such programming" (Lipsey, 1999:163).

Furthermore, these programs "do not entail exceptional efforts or costs" (Lipsey, 1999:163); they are doable and affordable. (For a recent review of effective correctional interventions for both juveniles and adults, see MacKenzie, 2006.)

Krisberg uses the term "redemption" and offers the moral argument that we need to be concerned about redeeming all children:

> Moreover, it is patently clear that most of us would seek a justice system that is founded on core principles of charity and redemption if it were our own children who were in trouble. This, of course, is the key issue. If we recognize the truth that all children are our children, the search for the juvenile justice ideal is our only moral choice (Krisberg, 2005:196).

Corbett (2001) agrees with the call to implement the findings on effective interventions and adds that it is important to focus on early intervention instead of late intervention. Parent training, for example, has been shown to be effective. Another suggestion is to emphasize "the paying of just debts": "Restitution and community service programs repay and restore victims and harmed communities and counter the prevalent notion that juvenile offenders are immune from any real penalties . . ." (Corbett, 2001:149). He also suggests that probation officers should act as moral educators who help juveniles build character. He maintains that setting an example is crucial: "Every occasion where self-restraint is exercised in the face of a probationer's provocation, where kindness and courtesy is extended to a probationer's family in defiance of the juvenile's expectation, and every effort by the officer to insure fair treatment in dispositional and revocational proceedings are opportunities for character building and moral education" (Corbett, 2001:149). His final suggestion is to attempt violence prevention through anger management skills training and similar social skills education programs.

Howell (2003) advocates both early intervention and the use of proven rehabilitation principles. He also urges the use of verified risk assessment techniques so that the court can identify and focus on youths most likely to become serious, violent, and chronic offenders, rather than wasting efforts on the least serious offenders who will not offend again. He supports graduated sanctions, gender-specific programming for girls, and the elimination of transfer to adult court.

Probably the most debatable point in Howell's suggestions is his call to end transfer. His rationale is that the "criminal justice system does not have the capacity to treat or protect juveniles, and incarcerating juveniles in adult facilities is not effective in deterring future crime" (Howell, 2003:309). Although Howell bases his suggestion on research evidence, it appears that the political mood is to "get tough" with juveniles, and transfer is one strategy that addresses that political mood.

A slight variation of this focus on the return to rehabilitation is the concept of **positive youth development**. Proponents of this concept argue that most youths can grow up properly and stay out of trouble if they can be attached to the proper social resources, especially prosocial, caring adults. For youths under juvenile court supervision, probation would include linking the youth with an adult mentor, involving the youth in a community engagement project and in appropriate recreation, and ensuring that the youth has some sort of paid employment. This would be different from the current philosophy of juvenile court that sees minor offenders as not really needing anything until they escalate into more serious delinquency (Butts, Mayer, and Ruth, 2005). For a review and analysis of early intervention efforts in general, see Farrington and Welsh (2007).

Bishop claims that many states have actually passed legislation to continue rehabilitation in juvenile court. Purpose clauses continue to include treatment as a primary purpose of the court. Three states have recently passed legislation to improve individualized treatment plans for youths in custody, four states have passed laws providing mental health assessment and treatment, and several states have passed laws to establish teen courts and other diversion programs. Still other states operate drug and/or mental health courts with a clear treatment focus. Mississippi ended its boot camp program, and Connecticut raised the age of jurisdiction from 16 to 18. Bishop argues that such legislative actions are evidence that "the juvenile justice system is less punitive and more treatment-oriented than is commonly assumed" (Bishop, 2006:659).

None of these suggestions requires a radical reshaping of probation or the juvenile justice system. The suggestions build on the history and tradition of probation as caring individuals (probation officers in the tradition of probation founder John Augustus). What Corbett proposes is that today's officers utilize both social science findings (e.g., parent education and anger management training) and common sense, such as setting a character-building example, to attempt to induce juveniles to become prosocial.

A final note in favor of a rehabilitative juvenile court is that public opinion supports it. For example, in a survey of 1,308 Florida residents, Mears and his colleagues found that more than 80 percent of the public disapproves of abolishing the juvenile justice system. In fact, even "many conservatives. . . view violent juvenile offenders as capable of being rehabilitated" (Mears et al., 2007:249). (For an additional suggestion of Mears and his colleagues, see Box 14.1.)

A Critic of the Rehabilitative Juvenile Court

Barry Feld points out flaws with the argument that juvenile court failure is simply a failure of implementation and that all that is needed is a rededication to the original rehabilitative ideals of juvenile court. Feld agrees that adequate funds have not been devoted to juvenile court,

BOX 14.1

A Uniform Upper Age for Juvenile Court

Mears and his colleagues suggest that the time is right to revisit the question of the upper age limit in juvenile court and to settle on one uniform age for all the states. As Chapter 1 noted, states vary in their upper age limits, with most states having 18 as the age at which adult criminal court jurisdiction begins (except for transfer).

Mears and his colleagues first note that the *Roper* capital punishment decision would fit with the age of 18. That decision relied heavily on psychological research demonstrating that most juveniles under 18 are not fully developed psychologically. Second, their research on public opinion in Florida found that there is considerable variation in public opinion about age and juvenile court jurisdiction. About one-third said that 17 or older should be the lowest age for trying youths as adults, 28 percent said 16, 13 percent said 15, and 28 percent said 14 or lower.

Mears and his colleagues think that the current variation in ages needs to end; states should have a uniform age that is consistent with the psychological research on adolescent development (Mears et al., 2007).

What do you think? Should the states be uniform in setting the upper age limit for juvenile court? If so, which age is best? As noted above, public opinion is divided on the opposite question about the appropriate lower limit for treating juveniles as adults.

Source: Adapted from D.P. Mears, C. Hay, M. Gertz, and C. Mancini (2007). "Public Opinion and the Foundation of the Juvenile Court." *Criminology* 45:223-257.

but he argues that funds will always be inadequate. One reason is that there is "pervasive public antipathy" to helping the poor, disadvantaged, disproportionately minority youths who are the clients of juvenile court. Another reason is that because committing a crime is the condition for receiving "help" from juvenile court, there is a built-in punishment focus. Feld argues that providing for children is a societal responsibility, not just a responsibility of juvenile court. In fact, the mere existence of juvenile court is an excuse or alibi for not providing for poor, minority youths. In Feld's words:

> A society collectively provides for the welfare of its children by supporting families, communities, schools, and social institutions that nurture all young people and not by cynically incarcerating its most disadvantaged children "for their own good" (Feld, 1999:296).

Feld also argues that juvenile court does not provide procedural fairness to children. Traditionally, some of the procedural protections of adult court, such as the right to jury trial, have been denied to children on the justification that the juvenile court was not a punitive court like adult court. Even worse than denying procedural protections, juvenile courts have treated children in similar circumstances who commit similar offenses in unequal and disparate fashion. This individualized handling was originally justified on the supposed rehabilitative foundation of juvenile court. However, because juvenile court is punitive and does not provide rehabilitation, this denial of due process safeguards makes juvenile court unfair and unjust.

In summary, Feld thinks that efforts to return the juvenile court to its rehabilitative ideal are doomed to failure: "The current juvenile court provides neither therapy nor justice and cannot be rehabilitated" (Feld, 1999:297).

Interestingly, it appears that Feld has more recently become a bit uncertain about his position. Instead of advocating the end of juvenile court, in 2007 he concluded that juvenile courts "do less harm than when states process children in the adult criminal justice system" (Feld, 2007:256). However, he continues to maintain that the juvenile court is failing to achieve its rehabilitative goals. In addition, black youths are experiencing unfair treatment. They are receiving severe adult sentences if transferred to adult court and are disproportionately confined if kept in the juvenile system. Feld thinks that politicians use juvenile court to exploit the crime issue: "Politicians and the public view the juvenile courts' clients as young criminals of color and refuse to commit resources necessary to improve their life conditions or to create a juvenile system that provides real justice" (Feld, 2007:255).

A Criminalized Juvenile Court

A second solution to the problems of juvenile court is to "criminalize" juvenile court: to attempt to make it a scaled-down version of adult criminal court. In order to do this, two things need to be done. First, a **criminalized juvenile court** would entail providing juveniles with all the procedural protections of criminal court. Thus, children would have the right to a jury trial and would have fully adversarial defense attorneys, not attorneys who often slip into the role of a concerned parent trading off zealous advocacy for promises of treatment. A second action that needs to be taken to transform juvenile court into a criminal court for youths would be to scale down penalties out of concern for the reduced culpability of children. Sentences would be shorter in such a juvenile court compared to adult criminal court. This reform was suggested about 30 years ago by the American Bar Association and the Institute of Judicial Administration. The suggestion was published in the Juvenile

Justice Standards (Institute of Judicial Administration–American Bar Association, 1982).

The major problem with the suggestion for a criminalized juvenile court is that it may not satisfy calls for a more punitive approach to juvenile offenders. Critics of the current juvenile justice system do not want reduced penalties; they want adult penalties for what they perceive as adult offenses: "adult crime, adult time," in the words of one governor (see Vandervort and Ladd, 2001:229). Such critics contend that violent offenses indicate culpability and should be punished with lengthy prison terms, and that is not the vision of the Juvenile Justice Standards.

Abolishing Juvenile Court

Prior to his second thoughts noted above, Feld argued that the problems of juvenile court are too extensive and too fundamental to try to reform it. Now is the time to abandon the sinking ship by abolishing juvenile court. Because juvenile court provides neither help nor crime control, now is the time to abolish it. In its place Feld proposed adult criminal court for all, both juveniles and adults.

Adult court would mean that juveniles would receive adult procedural protections. Juveniles would have the right to a jury trial, and defense attorneys would act as zealous adversaries. In addition, Feld argued that juveniles should still get shorter sentences because shorter sentences have been a saving feature of juvenile court and they "enable most young offenders to survive the mistakes of adolescence with a semblance of their life chances intact" (Feld, 1999:304). He argued that adult courts could "discount" sentences for youths. Specifically, 14-year-olds would receive 25 to 33 percent of the adult penalty; 16-year-olds, 50 to 66 percent; and 18-year-olds, the full adult penalty.

Feld failed to note that adult court sentencing for juveniles would also require some type of protection of the youth's record. The state of New York, for example, has a "youthful offender" provision that makes convictions and sentences under its provisions like juvenile court adjudications and dispositions in that they do not count against the individual. In other words, one benefit of juvenile court is that a youth can legally say that he or she has not been "arrested" or "convicted"; instead, he or she has been "taken into custody' and "adjudicated." Such legal protections against arrest and conviction records can be extremely important if one is applying for a job, graduate school, or the military.

Vandervort and Ladd (2001) raised a serious objection to Feld's proposal. They argue that Michigan has changed its juvenile code to the point that many juveniles are now handled in adult court, and the results have been harmful for juveniles. They contend that procedural rights are eroding in adult court. A juvenile transferred to adult court actually receives fewer due process protections in adult court than he or she would have in juvenile court. Juveniles are simply getting punishment in adult court, not treatment. Their conclusion is far more pessimistic than Feld's:

> Realistically, the adult criminal system has little or nothing positive to offer young people, it serves few, if any, elements of the public's interest, other than the impulse for retribution (Vandervort and Ladd, 2001:230).

One example illustrates their point. In 1997, Nathaniel Abraham, then 11 years old, was charged with murder. The juvenile court trial judge suppressed Nathaniel's confession to the police because the youth did not understand the *Miranda* warnings. The trial judge also chose a juvenile disposition; Nathaniel could only be under juvenile justice system control until age 21. The appellate court reversed the judge's ruling on understanding *Miranda* because it felt that the trial judge had placed too much emphasis on the child's youth and emotional impairment and not enough emphasis on the facts of the crime. Likewise, both the governor and other politicians criticized the judge's sentence; this is when the governor invoked the slogan "adult crime, adult time" (Vandervort and Ladd, 2001:229).

Another problem with Feld's suggestion of discounted sentencing for youths in adult court is that even discounted sentences might not be much of a bargain. Recall that Feld suggests that 16-year-olds should receive a youth discount of 50 to 66 percent. If a life sentence is equivalent to a sentence of 50 years, a 16-year-old (see the case of *LeBlanc* discussed below) processed in adult court would actually stay in prison until age 41 (half of 50 is 25 plus 16 equals age 41) or age 49 (66% of 50 plus 16). Thus, even with a youth "discount," youths processed in adult court would pay a heavy price if they left juvenile court, for which the maximum age for jurisdiction is 21.

Exemplifying the deficiencies of Feld's suggestion is the case of *In re LeBlanc*. LeBlanc was a 16-year-old who was charged with murdering his father. He had lived an exemplary life and been a good student but was immature mentally. He was waived to adult court where the likely sentence was life in prison. If he had been kept in juvenile court, he could be confined only until age 21, and he would have received high school and college education. The only possible "benefit" of adult court processing would be that the adult correctional system would teach LeBlanc a trade, but the lengthy prison sentence meant that "it would be decidedly unlikely that he would ever have been able to use that trade beyond the walls of the prison in which he would be housed" (Vandervort and Ladd, 2001:250).

Research, too, shows problems with adult court processing. Bishop and her colleagues interviewed juveniles who had been transferred to adult court in Florida. Juveniles were negative about adult court and adult corrections. They did not fully understand what transpired in adult court and perceived the process to be one of gamesmanship. They felt that criminal court judges had "little interest in them or their problems" whereas juvenile court judges "expressed interest in their problems and concern for their well-being" (Bishop, 2000:136). Similarly, the juveniles felt that juvenile correctional staff "cared for them, understood what troubled them, and believed in their potential . . .," whereas they perceived staff in adult correctional facilities as hostile, derisive, and uncaring workers who thought the juveniles were incapable of change (Bishop, 2000:144).

Kerbs (1999) notes two other problems with Feld's suggestion to switch juveniles to adult criminal court. First, politicians are not saying "discount"; they are crying out "adult crime, adult time." Politicians are mouthing a simplistic formula that suggests that they regard youthful offenders as simply younger but fully responsible offenders. Second, Kerbs fears that African-American juveniles transferred to adult court will continue to receive unfair treatment compared to whites—"unequal justice under law" (Kerbs, 1999:120). Thus, there is reason to believe that abolishing juvenile court would not have the positive effects Feld envisioned and might well produce very negative effects.

Creating a New Juvenile Court

Still another suggestion is to make a new juvenile court. Claude Noriega (2000) suggests that we create a new juvenile court that has two branches: one for children and one for adolescents. The children's court would be rehabilitative and would presume that children are inculpable, that is, they do not have criminal responsibility. The adolescent court would presume partial culpability and would be more punitive than the children's court. Of course, adult court would continue to presume that adults are culpable and would be the most punitive of the three courts.

Waiver would be by judicial hearing only. There would be no prosecutorial or legislative waiver, and waiver would be only to the next step. Thus, children could only be waived to adolescent court, and only adolescents could be waived to adult court. Juveniles (children and adolescents) would not be allowed to waive their right to counsel. Noriega's reasoning for this is that children and adolescents are generally presumed not competent; they are not allowed to enter into contracts, cannot drink alcohol, and cannot vote or drive (until late adolescence).

This is an interesting proposal. Noriega disagrees with Feld that abolishing juvenile court is the best course of action. Noriega argues that abolishing juvenile court will not guarantee that adult courts treat children/adolescents properly. He argues that it will be hard to treat a juvenile as a juvenile after he has been designated an "adult" and that it will be difficult to actually give discounts, à la Feld, to juveniles in adult court "as if they were getting their sentence on sale from Kmart" (Noriega, 2000:692-693).

An attractive feature of this proposal is that it offers a more complex and realistic view of development. Instead of assuming that one day a juvenile is a child and the next day he is an adult, it recognizes the intermediate stage of adolescence. Noriega is also probably more realistic than Feld about the actual results of abolishing juvenile court and letting adult court handle juvenile matters. Adult courts are probably not going to be as caring and protective or concerned about youth discounts as Feld hopes.

Unfortunately, Noriega just gives a sketchy outline. He says that states should have a children's court and an adolescent's court. He does not give us specific age limits for each. Nor does he specify punishment limits (e.g., incarceration terms) for each. Still another problem is that this could result in yet another bureaucracy—adolescent court and adolescent corrections—when the current juvenile and adult bureaucracies both have myriad problems. To note just one issue, will states be willing to create a new adolescent court and corrections system (assuming the current juvenile court becomes children's court)? Will they be willing to hire more personnel? Build more courtrooms? Build more prisons? As Garland (2001—and see below) so aptly points out, the recent trend has been to cut back the welfare state in general. Noriega's proposal goes against that trend; governmental bodies are looking to cut expenditures, not embrace new spending initiatives.

A "Youth Justice System" within Adult Criminal Court

Jeffrey Butts (2000) offers still another variation: a **youth justice system** within adult court. As we observed at the beginning of the chapter, Butts notes that the juvenile justice system is disappearing before our very eyes. Presumptive waiver provisions, mandatory waiver, blended sentencing, mandatory minimums and other sentencing guidelines, open hearings, and the use of juvenile records in adult court (e.g., to count as first or second strikes in three-strikes cases) are all nails in the coffin of the traditional juvenile court. Thus "[i]t is too late to save the traditional [juvenile justice] system because the traditional system is already gone" (Butts, 2000:52). He also notes that widespread opposition to the idea of delinquency dictates the end of delinquency cases in juvenile court. When the public hears "delinquent," they think "weak and lenient" (Butts, 2000:55).

His suggestion is to transfer all delinquency matters to adult court but to create a separate arm of adult court to deal with criminal acts allegedly committed by juveniles. He argues that adult courts are creating new specialized courts such as drug courts and mental health courts that do specialized intake and treatment. He thinks that specialized youth justice courts could do the same for juveniles. The benefit would be to stop fighting over which court—juvenile or adult—gets which offender and to start focusing "on ensuring the quality of the process used for all youth" (Butts, 2000:56). Because Butts is proposing a specialized court like drug and mental health courts, his proposal can be considered an extension of the movement called **therapeutic jurisprudence**: "an interdisciplinary perspective that urges us to consider the therapeutic and antitherapeutic consequences of legal rules, of legal procedures, and of the roles of lawyers, judges, and others acting within the legal arena" (Wexler, 2002:205).

Butts is accurate that many of the changes in juvenile court in the last 10 years have taken away many of the clientele (via some type of waiver/transfer). He is also accurate that some of the new drug courts and mental health courts (therapeutic jurisprudence) have made significant strides in dealing with their particular clients. A major question, however, is whether most jurisdictions would in fact start such courts and would devote the resources needed to allow them to carry out their mission. Creating new youth services courts in the adult system without adequate funding and resources would be a sham.

A Restorative Justice Juvenile Court

Gordon Bazemore (1999) suggests that now is the time to take the "fork in the road," to try a new path for juvenile court. As noted in Chapter 12, Bazemore is one of the main proponents for adopting a restorative justice model in the juvenile justice system.

In Pittsburgh, young offenders are involved in service projects such as home repair for the elderly and voter registration drives. In Utah, offenders are paying victim restitution out of wages from public service jobs. In Oregon, offender work crews cut firewood and deliver it to the elderly. More than 150 cities are utilizing victim–offender mediation. In Colorado and Florida, offenders work with Habitat for Humanity building homes for lower-income families. In Florida, probation officers are walking neighborhood beats to help promote local guardianship of communities. In Boston and in Florida, probation officers are helping police monitor probationers at night.

What all of these efforts have in common is a restorative justice focus that emphasizes the victim and the community. The approach is "focused less on achieving public safety by incarcerating individual offenders and more on reducing fear, building youth-adult relationships, and increasing the capacity of community groups and institutions to prevent crime and safely monitor offenders in the community" (Bazemore, 1999:98).

This represents a radical rethinking of the role of juvenile court. Instead of sanctioning and supervising offenders, the role of the **restorative justice**

juvenile court would be to build community so that neighborhoods can better respond to—but also prevent—delinquency. Communities would be more involved in sentencing through community panels or conferences or dispute resolution programs. Communities would return to their role of being responsible for youths. Bazemore argues that the community must address socialization needs with "caring adults who spend time with young people not because they are paid to do so but because they share a commitment to the idea that youth development is a community responsibility" (Bazemore, 1999:101).

A positive feature of Bazemore's proposal is that it is not a hypothetical proposal; many restorative justice programs are already in place. As noted, numerous communities already are working at restorative justice. A major question, however, is how far restorative justice can go. How willing are citizens to assume the responsibilities that restorative justice would give them in deciding cases and monitoring sanctions such as community service? If people are not available to staff the restorative justice programs, they will not work. Proving that it is possible to implement such programs, Vermont has a system of 49 restorative justice boards with almost 300 volunteer board members in operation (Karp, Bazemore, and Chesire, 2004). These boards use 30- to 60-minute meetings to negotiate restorative justice contracts between victims and offenders. So it is possible to implement such programs.

A recent survey of juvenile court judges found overall support for victim involvement in the juvenile court process. For example, 60 percent of the judges agreed that victims should have input into the sanctioning and dispositional decisions of juvenile court, and 44 percent thought that victims should have input into diversion decisions. Focus group discussions with judges, however, showed some ambivalence about victim involvement. Some judges thought that involving victims in juvenile court decisions might introduce some bias into juvenile court. Some judges thought that greater victim involvement might detract from judges' attempts to remain neutral in juvenile court (Bazemore and Leip, 2000).

On the one hand, restorative justice is a reality in many juvenile courts. As of a few years ago, Bazemore and Schiff (2005) noted that there were well over 700 restorative justice programs, some adult and some juvenile, in operation across the country. While most of these programs do address the core restorative justice principle of repairing harm, not all of the programs have addressed community and government role transformation. In other words, many operate within the traditional framework of government programs rather than trying to achieve community-building. So a probation department may start a restitution program or a community service program or even some type of victim-offender mediation, but it may not take the next step of involving community members to a much greater extent in seeking justice and making both victims and offenders whole once again (Bazemore and Schiff, 2005).

Zimring's Caution

Franklin Zimring (2000) adds a cautionary note to the various proposals about keeping, abolishing, or modifying juvenile court. He reminds us that even juvenile court is in the business of imposing punishment. As rehabilitative as the intentions of the founders may have been, the truth, as noted in *In re Gault*, is that juvenile court "dispositions" often deprive youths of their freedom. For Zimring, this truth of punishment means that a crucial element, even if we abolish juvenile court, is reduced punishment. In other words, even if all juveniles went to adult court, there still would be a legitimate issue of deciding on lesser punishments for such offenders. Second, Zimring points out that the United States is inconsistent about juveniles. It prohibits them from voting until age 18 and from drinking until age 21 because they are considered immature yet submits them to adult court and punishment at increasingly lower ages. Zimring agrees that youths are immature and argues that states need to address this inconsistency and not just ignore it.

Summary

Juvenile justice is at a crossroads. Critics have pointed out serious flaws with juvenile court, and many states have already removed many youths from juvenile court jurisdiction. In light of the criticisms of juvenile court and the legislation sending more juveniles to adult court, now is the time to rethink the nature and goals of juvenile court. On the other hand, the research on effectiveness suggests that there are effective interventions that can reduce recidivism. And Bishop (2006) points out that perhaps the turn away from rehabilitation has been exaggerated. Now is the time to consider proposals such as those delineated above and decide on the best course of action.

BROADER ISSUES

Beyond the need to make changes in juvenile court, there are additional issues that need to be addressed if American society is to help juveniles grow into mature, responsible, law-abiding adults. We will note several such issues here and show how they relate to juvenile justice. We will consider the issues of race and juvenile court, the possible decline of community and social capital, the role and needs of American families, and the political economy.

Race and Juvenile Court

Several sources note that race is a problem in juvenile justice. The harshest criticism is that the public is not as concerned about disadvantaged children as middle- and upper-class children (Feld, 1999; see below). The consensus is that the juvenile justice system has a problem of disproportionate minority contacts (see, e.g., Bishop, 2005). In 2002, for example, although they comprised only about 11 percent of the population, blacks made up 29 percent of juvenile referrals to juvenile court, 29 percent of those adjudicated, about one-third of those placed out of the home, and one-third of those waived to criminal court (Kempf-Leonard, 2007). In 2004, blacks made up 32 percent of those adjudicated, 36 percent of those placed out of home, and 41 percent of those waived to criminal court (Stahl et al., 2007:62-63).

A number of writers argue that juvenile justice must fight the influence of racism. The federal government, for example, has made the elimination of disproportionate minority confinement in juvenile correctional facilities a priority.

Feld (1999) summarized several studies that looked at sentencing in juvenile court. The studies indicated that legal variables—present offense and prior record—account "for virtually all the variance in juvenile court sentences that can be explained" (Feld, 1999:266). "However, after controlling for legal and offense variables, the individualized justice of juvenile courts produces racial disparities in the sentencing of minority offenders" (Feld, 1999:266). To give but one example, in California, African-American youths made up 8.7 percent of the youth population but 37 percent of juveniles in confinement (Feld, 1999). The existence of racial disparity is an additional reason for Feld's call to abolish juvenile court.

Ferguson (2000) contends that racism occurs prior to the juvenile justice system; it starts in school:

> Schools mirror and reinforce the practices and ideological systems of other institutions in the society. The racial bias in the punishing systems of the school reflects the practices of the criminal justice system (Ferguson, 2000:231).

Ferguson gives as evidence the remark of a vice-principal about a small 10-year-old boy: "That one has a jail cell with his name on it" (cited in Ferguson, 2000:1). Another indicator of the pervasiveness of racial prejudice and discrimination in American society is that many black kids feel that to succeed in school they must "act white": "being a 'good' student is equivalent to losing one's racial cultural identity" (Ferguson, 2000:203).

Perhaps most disturbing of all is Feld's (1999) assertion that there is pervasive public antipathy to the problems of disadvantaged and minority children. If society does not really care for poor minority children, then it may not matter all that much which court—juvenile rehabilitative, juvenile criminal, or adult criminal—is designated to process juvenile delinquency. Unless society is truly committed to the problems of all youths, and especially disadvantaged youths, then youth crime will persist.

As noted in Chapter 8, a dissident voice about this issue is Tracy (2002), who contends that much of the claim for disproportionate handling of African-American juveniles in the juvenile justice system rests on flimsy evidence. Tracy's own research in Texas did not find "strong and consistent race and ethnic differentials in juvenile processing" (Tracy, 2002:175). Tracy thinks that there is differential minority involvement in delinquency, and this differential involvement needs to be addressed. In other words, "if a greater prevalence of minority youth commit delinquent offenses, then there will be more such youth available for processing at each point of the juvenile justice process compared to Anglo youth" (Tracy, 2002:176).

A recent analysis of three major studies of delinquency in Pittsburgh, Rochester, and Seattle found clear evidence of greater contact/referral of minorities in the juvenile justice system. This differential minority contact cannot be accounted for by higher offending by minorities. However, the researchers could not conclude that differential minority contact proves racial bias (Huizinga et al., 2007). This report suggests that race continues to be an issue that merits concern in the juvenile justice system.

Similarly, a recent review of the research on juvenile justice system processing concludes that race is still a factor in processing (Bishop, 2005). One reason for the influence of race is at the very heart of the juvenile justice system. As noted in Chapter 2, juvenile court was founded to treat children with problems. This intent put discretion into the system. Because officials have discretion, they often focus on minority juveniles because they think that minority youths need the help that the juvenile justice system is supposed to offer. So the positive intention of offering assistance to minority children has resulted in a disproportionate share of minority youths being subjected to juvenile court processing and dispositions such as placement. While the intent may have been positive, the result has been a disproportionate share of minorities at all stages of the juvenile justice system, starting with police and ending with custodial placements (Bishop, 2005).

This is not the place for a thorough analysis of racism in the juvenile justice system. We simply note that many analysts see disproportionate processing of minority youths while Tracy argues that the problem is disproportionate involvement. Even Tracy would agree that it is important to eliminate any traces of racism or perceived racial inequities in juvenile court so that all youths will regard the juvenile justice system as fair. Without the perception of fair treatment, minority youths will be suspicious and resentful, and those emotions doom any hope of reclaiming problem youths.

The Need to Rebuild Community

As noted in the discussion of community policing in Chapter 7, Robert Putnam (2000) argues that we are "bowling alone"; that is, social capital is eroding. In other words, civic participation and other measures of community involvement are declining. If accurate, this decline of social capital has implications for juvenile justice.

One measure of the decline of community is religious participation. Between the 1960s and the 1990s, church membership declined by approximately 10 percent. Similarly, church attendance has declined by approximately 10-12 percent over the last quarter century, most markedly from the mid-1980s to the mid-1990s (Putnam, 2000). Participation in civic clubs has also declined. In 1975-76, about two-thirds (64%) of Americans had attended at least one club meeting in the previous year. That slipped to about 38 percent by 1999 (Putnam, 2000).

What do Americans do with their time now? One major activity is television watching. Eight out of 10 Americans now report that most evenings they watch television (Putnam, 2000). In fact, "[m]ost studies estimate that the average American now watches roughly four hours per day, very nearly the highest viewership anywhere in the world" (Putnam, 2000:222). Along with other electronic media, television has

> . . . rendered our leisure more private and passive. More and more of our time and money are spent on goods and services consumed individually, rather than those consumed collectively. Americans' leisure time can increasingly be measured—as do strategic marketers—in terms of 'eyeballs,' since watching things (especially electronic screens) occupies more and more of our time, while doing things (especially with other people) occupies less and less (Putnam, 2000:245).

As noted in Chapter 7, if community is in fact declining, then the future of community policing is not as optimistic as its proponents proclaim. Decline of community would have other repercussions as well. If community is declining and if that decline cannot be stopped, then restorative justice efforts also will face difficulties. If we want citizens to participate in restorative justice conferencing, victim–offender mediation programs, sentencing circles, and other restorative justice programs (see the earlier section on restorative justice), we need a solid community base as the foundation for those efforts. If people do not join together socially, how can we realistically expect them to come together for restorative justice initiatives?

A more fundamental issue is that the decline of community may even make delinquency worse and increase the need for juvenile justice interventions. If civic clubs are disbanding due to lack of interest and participation, we can expect reduced sponsorship of youth sports teams, scout troops, and Boys and Girls Clubs. Many civic clubs sponsor such programs for neighborhood youths. If the clubs are disappearing, either the parents will have to pick up the tab or the youth teams and programs will not survive.

There is hope, however. Putnam points out, for example, that Americans seem to want to reverse the trend of declining civic participation and social capital: "We tell pollsters that we wish we lived in a more civil, more trustworthy, more collectively caring community" (Putnam, 2000:403). He offers some steps that could be effective in restoring social capital. One is for employers to be more family- and community-friendly. Some firms, for example, offer release time to some employees to volunteer for community service such as serving on United Way campaigns. Because part-time workers participate more in community, Putnam urges employers to make greater allowance for part-time employment opportunities. He urges urban planners to design living areas that are more pedestrian-friendly and urges church leaders to revivify spiritual community. He calls for electronic entertainment that fosters community engagement rather than passive sitting in front of television sets. He suggests using the arts to foster community. He urges greater civics education and other efforts to foster political participation (Putnam, 2000).

The challenge is great. Many forces are at work to isolate us from our neighbors. Contemporary trends, such as the proliferation of personal computers, Internet usage, personal mp3 players, and a TV and DVD player for each household member, are all working to drive us apart. In the 1950s, even television watching was a family activity. There was only one television set and only three major networks. Today we have multiple sets in even the poorest of households and hundreds of cable or satellite stations to choose from. Families may watch the Super Bowl together, but little else.

It is important not to idealize a past that was far from perfect. The 1950s were not idyllic for African Americans who had to sit at the back of the bus and could not get into the college of their choice. Nor were they idyllic for women who could not enter jobs and professions that they aspired to. However, it is important to note that we need to restore social capital. If we wish to prevent delinquency and to pursue new avenues such as restorative justice, then citizens must be willing to contribute to their communities. As noted above, states such as Vermont are proving that there are citizens willing to step up and serve on restorative justice boards; that is, there are people willing to do something about delinquency and victimization (Karp, Bazemore, and Chesire, 2004).

Bazemore and Schiff have a different opinion about Putnam's argument that individuals are abandoning community clubs like Kiwanis and Rotary and spending increasingly more time in solitary/individual pursuits, such as surfing the web or playing video games. They think that there is truth in Putnam's assessment, but they also think that there is a real hunger for community. Bazemore and Schiff feel that many citizens are frustrated with justice systems for professionalizing and taking over tasks and responsibilities that are really community responsibilities. It is hoped that restorative justice practices can build on community resolve "to deal with what can no longer be viewed simply as individual problems of offenders or victims" (Bazemore and Schiff, 2005:351). In other words, Bazemore and Schiff think that the community really wants to be involved and that restorative justice programs can be successful in the difficult task of reengaging citizens in the juvenile justice process (Bazemore and Schiff, 2005).

The Role of the Family

Where Putnam argues that community life is eroding, William Bennett (2001) argues that the American family is in rapid decline. He points to what he considers alarming levels of divorce, births of out-of-wedlock children, single-parent families, and cohabiting couples as evidence of his claim.

Bennett believes that a decline in values is responsible for the "collapse" of the American family. He thinks that America's sense of community and religion has given way to "a radical individualistic ethos," "a fierce assault directed against marriage and the family," and "the rise of a consumerist mentality" (Bennett, 2001:16-17). He contends that the media has given much impetus to this decline. He argues, for example, that on many daytime television talk shows "indecent exposure is celebrated as a virtue, perversions are made to seem commonplace, and modesty and discretion are frowned upon" (Bennett, 2001:32). Bennett's (2001) solution is to return to family values and to resist the erosion of values.

An interesting counterpoint to Bennett's position is Mintz's argument that we are overly protective of youths, and such overprotection does not allow children the opportunities to grow and mature. He argues, for example, that binge drinking in college can be traced to not allowing children the opportunity to learn to drink responsibly. Similarly, as kids have increasingly less free time and less free space, we deny them opportunities to learn, explore, and grow.

Mintz also argues that nostalgia is no answer; there is no way to return to a Disneyland or *Music Man* version of Main Street in small-town America where the biggest threat was a pool hall coming to town:

> It is not possible to recreate a "walled garden" of childhood innocence, no matter how hard we might try. No V-chip, Internet filtering software, or CD-rating system will immunize children from the influence of contemporary culture. Since we cannot insulate children from all malign influences, it is essential that we prepare them to deal responsibly with the pressures and choice they face. That task requires knowledge, not sheltering. In a risk-filled world, naiveté is vulnerability (Mintz, 2004:382).

So the challenge is to both protect children but at the same time give them opportunities to explore and grow:

> Our challenge is to reverse the process of age segmentation, to provide the young with challenging alternatives to a world of malls, instant messaging, music videos, and play dates. Huck Finn was an abused child, whose father, the town drunk, beat him for going to school and learning to read. Who would envy Huck's battered childhood? Yet he enjoyed something too many children are denied and which adults can provide: opportunities to undertake odysseys of self-discovery outside the goal-driven, overstructured realities of contemporary childhood (Mintz, 2004:383-384).

Character Education

Similar to Bennett, Christina Hoff Sommers (2000) thinks that faulty character education is a major cause of delinquency and other problems. Sommers states that there are two approaches to educating the young, especially boys. Aristotle argued for moral education analogous to physical training. Just as exercise leads to muscle strength, practicing goodness leads to moral character. Parents and schools need to discipline children to get them to behave well.

The Rousseauian approach, on the other hand, thinks that children are naturally good, and no external code should be imposed on the child. Teachers, therefore, should not preach to students but should allow their natural goodness to shine forth. One recent example of this philosophy is values clarification, a program that simply tried to help children discover their own values. An even more recent example is the self-esteem movement, which puts each student on a pedestal. Instead of studying great persons, students are encouraged to celebrate their own wondrous gifts.

Sommers thinks that the Rousseauian approach has won out in American schools and that it is simply wrong. She thinks that most parents, however, opt for Aristotle's approach: "throughout the world, mothers and fathers never cease to work at habituating children to the exercise of self-control, temperance, honesty, courage" (Sommers, 2000:191).

As evidence, Sommers notes that Eric Harris and Dylan Klebold, the perpetrators of the Columbine High School violence in 1999, had written disturbingly violent stories. A teacher had notified school officials, but the school took no action because there was more concern about violating free speech than about correcting inappropriate speech. In Sommers's description, in most schools, "[i]t has become the style not to interfere with the child's self-expression and autonomy" (Sommers, 2000:200).

Character education does not mean preaching. Rather, "[w]e teach by who we are" (Tigner, 2000). The world's great teachers—Socrates, Jesus, Buddha—taught with their persons, and we must do the same. Sommers makes us ask ourselves a question: Does failure to teach morality in school lead to violence such as the Columbine High School massacre? If we taught the Victorian virtues of "honesty, integrity, courage, decency, politeness" (Sommers, 2000:196), rather than pursuing the Rousseau-like path of self-expression, would delinquency decrease?

Social Support for Families

Others agree that family is critical for child and adolescent development and delinquency prevention. Many think, however, that society is not as supportive of families as it could be. The problem is not that parents are abandoning family values, but that there are social, economic, and political forces at work that weaken the ability of families to do their job. The answer is to provide more assistance to families.

Alida Merlo noted that 13 percent of American children live in conditions that are considered to make them "high-risk" children. About one-third of U.S. children live in one-parent families, about 20 percent live in a home headed by a high school dropout, about 20 percent grow up in poverty, almost 30 percent live with parents who do not have a full-time job, about 12 percent of families receive public assistance, and about 15 percent of children do not have health insurance (Merlo, 2000). In 1996, about 1,000 children died of maltreatment (abuse or neglect), yet in "all the political rhetoric about preventing youth violence, any reference to these fatalities, or the conditions that may increase their likelihood, is conspicuously absent" (Merlo, 2000:649). The proponents of tough juvenile policies also ignore the developmental stages that youths go through and instead simply assume that adolescents are completely adult in all respects. Merlo concludes that we need "a moratorium on punitive, reactionary juvenile justice reform" in favor of "a more rational, less political, more observant, more humane manner" (Merlo, 2000:658-659).

Merlo is right for two reasons. First, she is right because it is simply wrong to ignore these high-risk children. The second reason is that there is an "emerging consensus" that "coercion causes crime and social support prevents crime" (Colvin, Cullen, and Vander Ven, 2002:19). To be more specific, the research clearly shows that childhood conduct disorders can lead to delinquency, especially for high-rate offenders. It is also clear that "supportive programs—programs that invest in at-risk children and in at-risk families—work to reduce crime" (Cullen, Wright, and Chamlin, 1999:198-199). Social support for families includes such assistance as parent-effectiveness training, paid family leave, health care insurance, and visiting nurse programs.

In conclusion, a number of conservative and liberal writers agree that there are important problems pertaining to families and their ability to raise healthy and law-abiding children. Conservatives argue that families need to return to traditional values and character education, whereas liberals argue that families need more social and economic support to help them to do their job.

The Political Economy and Juvenile Court

David Garland (2001) makes an intriguing and complex assessment of today's criminal justice policy. He argues that the **political economy**—social, political, and economic changes in the last 30 years—have had important effects on how we view and treat crime, criminals, and delinquents.

First, over the last half of the twentieth century, there has been a dramatic increase in crime and delinquency. A number of changes led to this increase. One was the growth of the consumer economy with its spread of portable consumer goods. Very simply, people today have more "stuff"—stereos, TVs, cameras, laptop computers—so there are more opportunities to steal goods, whether by shoplifting or burglary. Similarly, there are more families with both spouses working, and that means that there are more empty homes to burglarize during the day. The growth of the suburbs also means more spread-out neighborhoods and fewer "knowing eyes"—fewer guardians—to keep a lookout on one another's homes. Finally, a questioning of traditional authority has led to less social control.

At the same time, the so-called welfare state was expanding, and government bureaucracies were growing. Then problems developed. Race riots, civil rights demonstrations, and anti-war protests caused concern. More practically, recession in the 1970s raised questions about the ability to pay for ever-expanding benefit programs. President Ronald Reagan in the United States and Prime Minister Margaret Thatcher in Britain represented "[h]ostility toward 'tax and spend' government, undeserving welfare recipients, 'soft on crime' policies, unelected trade unions who were running the country, the break-up of the family, the breakdown of law and order . . ."(Garland, 2001:97). Reagan and Thatcher both allowed market forces to take precedence in their respective economies with the same result: "the rapid collapse of industrial production and the re-emergence of structural unemployment on a massive scale not seen since the 1930s" (Garland, 2001:98). This decline of factories and factory jobs meant higher unemployment, which Garland thinks contributed to increased crime.

Crime can be viewed as a matter of individual choice and responsibility, not as something socially generated:

> Crime came to be seen instead as a problem of indiscipline, a lack of self-control or social control, a matter of wicked individuals who needed to be deterred and who deserved to be punished. Instead of indicating need or deprivation, crime was

a matter of anti-social cultures or personalities, and of rational individual choice in the face of lax law enforcement and lenient punishment regimes (Garland, 2001:102).

Accompanying this was a questioning of the state's ability (via policing and corrections) to control the crime problem. Governments see the necessity of recognizing less-than-omnipotent power to control crime, yet they fear the political consequences of admitting powerlessness over crime. So for politicians there is a perceived "need to find popular and effective measures that will not be viewed as signs of weakness or an abandonment of the state's responsibility to the public" (Garland, 2001:111). Unfortunately, the public often has unrealistic expectations and ideas about crime control, expectations that demand results at any cost. Concretely, the public demands that

> criminals should be prosecuted to the full extent of the law, the guilty should always be punished, dangerous individuals should never be released, prisoners should serve their full terms, and an offender's sentence should precisely reflect his offense. And somehow, at the same time, the innocent should always be acquitted, the rule of law upheld, and expenditure held within reasonable levels (Garland, 2001:112).

To summarize, forces such as the proliferation of consumer goods and the decline of guardianship (watchers) were increasing crime at the same time that government funds were decreasing the provision of treatment programs for delinquents and criminals (due to such factors as the globalization of the economy). Thus, popular sentiment was developing against the poor in general and against delinquents and criminals in particular. Governments were waging war on crime and tending to incarcerate more and more and treat less and less. In juvenile court, this movement has translated into increasing transfer of youths to adult court, sentencing youthful offenders to adult corrections or blended corrections (a combination of juvenile and adult sanctions), and even use of the death penalty for juveniles.

The net result is that instead of devising initiatives to help these groups, politicians are practicing welfare reform for the poor and tough justice for youthful delinquents. These policies coincide with economic realities in twenty-first-century America (and Britain), and they also comfort the middle and upper classes with their fear of street crime—no matter how exaggerated that paranoia may be.

Garland does not have the answers to the scene he so well describes. Inattention to the real needs of youths (especially poor youths) is not a new phenomenon in the United States. In the mid-nineteenth century, for example, the Children's Aid Society in New York City dealt with the urban poor by getting rid of them rather than by actually dealing with the poverty that afflicted them. Specifically, Charles Loring Brace, founder of the Children's Aid Society, began the "orphan trains" that shipped New York City youths west to farmers and whomever else would accept these youths. This practice grew, even though many of the youths suffered abuse in their new environments equal to or worse than what they had suffered at the hands of their own parents in New York. The policy was attractive because it visibly removed problem youths from New York and put them out of sight—in placements out west (O'Connor, 2001).

Part of the solution may mean a re-ordering of priorities. If the global economy means that there is only a limited amount of money available for social spending programs in our postmodern economy, perhaps we need to re-evaluate our entitlement programs. Just as Western democracies re-evaluated welfare spending in the 1990s and enacted "welfare reform," perhaps we need to re-evaluate other entitlement programs to see if we are spending enough money on programs that benefit youths.

Perhaps the easiest way to follow Garland's suggestions, however, is to use his analysis to clarify some of the true purposes of the current system. He argues that the current passion for punishment is politically generated. It coincides with many of the social and economic changes of the last 25 years and addresses much of the fear of crime generated by the proliferation of consumer goods, the reduction of guardianship in sprawling suburban housing developments spawned by the interstate highway system, the absence of anyone home during working hours due to dual-income households, and a perception that traditional values are eroding. Garland clearly shows that much of America's passion for punishment is a grasping for straws in the face of threatening changes and perceptions of high crime rates.

Reintroducing the Spiritual Dimension into Corrections

As noted above, some think that the answer to delinquency is character education. Going even further than this, Ron Powers (2002) argues that the basic problem facing today's youths is apocalyptic nihilism. By this he means that American youths face a gnawing gap in their lives, that they seek "a community that satisfied their longing for worth-proving ritual, meaningful action in the service of a cause, and psychological intimacy" (Powers, 2002:65). Similarly, Staples (2000) argues that one explanation for school violence is the emptiness of our consumer culture, which does not satisfy the deeper longings of the heart. In Staples's words, both youths and adults possess a "fundamental yearning for significance through engagement in the processes of reflection, creativity, compassion, and the gift of self to others" (Staples, 2000:33). So Powers, Staples, and others believe that youths are searching for a deeper sense of meaning in their lives.

Instead of providing such meaning, American policy offers problem youths punishment. The answer, says Powers, is "respectful inclusion: through a reintegration of our young into the intimate circles of family and community life. We must face the fact that having ceased to exploit children as laborers, we now exploit them as consumers. We must find ways to offer them useful functions tailored to their evolving capacities" (Powers, 2002:74).

John Whitehead and Michael Braswell (2000) argue that what is needed is to re-introduce the **spiritual dimension in corrections.** This would entail efforts of corrections workers, whether prison counselors, chaplains, or probation officers, to help offenders find greater meaning in their lives.

Both residential institutions and probation can try to address the spiritual needs of juvenile offenders. Prisons and jails have always had chaplains and religious services as part of their programming. That can and should continue, but institutions and probation/parole can take additional steps to incorporate the spiritual dimension into correctional practice.

First, correctional workers—correctional counselors, probation officers, parole officers, correctional officers—can all attempt to help offenders focus on the question of meaning in their lives. In group sessions and individual reporting, these workers can encourage offenders to think about the meaning of their lives.

Second, correctional workers have the simple but potentially profound example of their own lives. They can come to work each and every day showing a sense of purpose and meaning in their lives and in their interactions with prisoners that will influence those who come in contact with them. All of us can attest to persons who show by the example of their lives that there is something that energizes them and inspires them despite the difficulties they face. This is in stark contrast to workers who exert a negative influence in the prison or in the parole office. For example, in one women's prison, some guards came in and plopped down in front of the television set to watch hours of sports programming (Girshick, 1999), and in some Canadian correctional facilities, guard supervisors were found to create an environment rife with sexual harassment (McMahon, 1999). At the very least, workers need to refrain from abuse, harassment, and anything else that detracts from prison as a place where offenders can think about the meaning of their lives.

A concrete suggestion is to adopt an intervention strategy such as the "Making Life Choices" program, which is a participatory learning strategy that focuses "on creating contexts in which young people themselves can discover their own competence for influencing the direction of their lives" (Ferrer-Wreder et al., 2002:170). The goal is "accepting control and responsibility of one's life" (Ferrer-Wreder et al., 2002:171).

A similar suggestion is to start faith-based training schools for juveniles. The State of Florida has started faith-based prisons for adult prisoners, and the federal government started some faith-based programming in 2002 (Camp et al., 2006). As of this writing, definitive results are not yet available. One concern about faith-based prisons is that they could divert money away from important programs for all prisoners, such as education and vocational training (Jablecki, 2005).

One reason for raising the issue of introducing the spiritual dimension into corrections is that there is evidence that it matters. In a recent study of offenders ages 15 to 24, Benda (2002) found that religion was inversely related to carrying a weapon, violence, the use of illicit drugs, and the selling of illicit drugs. Religion was measured by church attendance, religious expressions, and forgiveness.

So one task of corrections may be to help that segment of offenders who are open to asking and seeking answers to the perennial questions about life: Why am I here? What is the meaning of life? What is happiness? Should I just seek more money and prestige, or are there other more important goals in life? Do I just consider myself, or should I think about others? Am I

AP Photo/Michael Conroy

Inmates watch as Indiana Governor Mitch Daniels speaks at an open house for the first Faith- and Character-Based Purposeful Living Units at the Correctional Industrial Facility in Pendleton, Indiana. The character development program, based in part on religion to transform inmates from a criminal way of life to one of lawful responsibility, has also been tested at the Indiana's Plainfield Juvenile Correctional Facility.

making moral or immoral choices? As one thinker puts it, am I seeking "significance through engagement in the processes of reflection, creativity, compassion, and the gift of self to others" (Staples, 2000:33)? None of this should lead to proselytizing or to erasing the separation of church and state. No correctional worker should impose his or her religious beliefs on inmates or probationers.

Some may object that attempting to inject the spiritual into correctional practice is too ambitious a project. If corrections cannot accomplish the basic objective of keeping offenders crime-free, then how can it be expected to help offenders become better persons spiritually? However, this objection may have it backwards. Perhaps one reason that corrections has had such an uninspiring record with recidivism is that it makes no effort to help offenders in a search for meaning and purpose in their lives. If the implicit objective of corrections is that offenders only need to buy into the American Dream, and if that dream is questionable and uninspiring and one that ignores the deeper potential of human living, then it may be no surprise that probation does little to improve recidivism.

A final note is that recent research has shown the importance of religion in delinquency causation. In a recent study of boot camp inmates, Benda (2002) found that religion was clearly correlated (inversely) with crimes against persons. In fact, religion was the fifth largest correlate in the model. So the more religious these inmates, the less likely they were to be involved in violence. Similarly, an analysis of the National Youth Survey found that religiosity affected adolescent use of illicit drugs (Jang and Johnson, 2001). These studies confirm the importance of religion and suggest its usefulness in preventing delinquency.

CAPITAL PUNISHMENT FOR JUVENILES

In 2006, there were 17,399 homicides in the United States; 1,111 of these were committed by juveniles (Federal Bureau of Investigation, 2007). This is dramatically lower than the approximately 3,800 juveniles who were arrested for murder in 1993, the peak year for murders by juveniles (Snyder, 2005). Despite this decrease, however, we will probably see continued media attention on juveniles who kill.

For adult murderers, **capital punishment** has been debated for years (see, e.g., van den Haag and Conrad, 1983, and Costanzo, 1997, for further discussion). The questions in the debate have been both philosophical and empirical. Some of the philosophical questions involve the moral issue of the state taking a human life (for viewpoints on this issue, see Boxes 14.2 and 14.3) and the morality of capital punishment in the

BOX 14.2

Some Arguments against Capital Punishment

Two voices against capital punishment are Mark Costanzo and Donald Cabana.

One of Costanzo's arguments is that if society considers killing to be wrong, then it is just as wrong for the state to kill as it is for an individual to kill. The only exceptions are "self-defense, imminent danger, or the protection of society" (Costanzo, 1997:135). None of these exceptions apply to the capital offender because he "has already been captured and waits in a prison cell safely isolated from the community" (Costanzo, 1997:136).

Costanzo is very empathetic to the victim's family but he argues that an execution will not bring back the victim for the family. Furthermore, an execution is "a state-sanctioned killing [that] will debase us all and create a

BOX 14.2 *continued*

new set of victims: the murderer's family" (Costanzo, 1997:143). This is to be avoided because, for one thing, the murderer's family members are innocent of wrongdoing. An interesting suggestion of Costanzo's is to stop trying to abolish the death penalty, at least for a period of time. Instead, opponents should try a "detour" strategy of trying to get state lawmakers to limit the death penalty to multiple or serial murder cases. There are several advantages to this strategy. First, because it would reduce the number of capital punishment cases, it would save both court trial time and appellate time. Second, it would reduce the possibility of mistakes because the evidence in multiple murder cases is "often overwhelming" (Costanzo, 1997:155). Third, it would reduce racial bias because most serial killers are white. The overall result would be that "[w]e could finally claim that only the worst of the worst are executed" (Costanzo, 1997:155).

Finally, Costanzo aptly expresses the argument of many that killing a murderer seems an extremely illogical way for society to convey the message that killing is wrong:

> Killing is an odd way to show that killing is wrong, an odd way to show that society is just and humane. . . . we also send the message that killing is an acceptable way of solving the problem of violence, that a life should be extinguished if we have the power to take it and the offender has taken a life. We lend legal authority to the dangerous idea that if someone has committed a depraved crime, we should treat him or her as a nonhuman who can be killed without remorse (Costanzo, 1997:166-167).

Donald Cabana is a former warden who carried out a number of executions in the state of Mississippi. He has written about the execution of one man, Connie Evans, whom he executed and had come to know was a changed individual:

> This was not the same cold-blooded murderer who had arrived on death row six years before. His tears were not just those of a young man fearful of what lay beyond death's door; I was convinced they were also tears of genuine sorrow and pain for the tragic hurt and sadness he had caused so many people.

Cabana argued to the governor for a stay but there were no legal grounds to do so. Cabana had to carry out the execution even though he felt that ". . . as a society we were supposed to be better than the Connie Ray Evanses of the world" (Cabana, 1996:15). Cabana eventually resigned his warden's position and went on to become a college professor.

BOX 14.3

An Argument in Favor of Capital Punishment

Ernest van den Haag is one of the leading proponents of the death penalty. Here are some of his arguments in favor of the death penalty.

First, he thinks that many critics of the death penalty are cowards who are afraid to impose the penalty:

> Aware of human frailty they shudder at the gravity of the decision and refuse to make it. The irrevocability of a verdict of death is contrary to the modern spirit that likes to pretend that nothing ever is definitive, that everything is open-ended, that doubts must always be entertained and revisions made. Such an attitude may be proper for inquiring philosophers and scientists. But not for courts. They can evade decisions on life and death only by giving up their paramount duties: to do justice, to secure the lives of the citizens, and to vindicate the norms society holds inviolable (van den Haag, 1978:67-68).

Second, van den Haag argues that murder—the most serious crime—cries out for the most serious penalty—execution. Otherwise, society is failing to carry out the proper affirmation of common values:

> In all societies, the degree of social disapproval of wicked acts is expressed in the degree of punishment threatened. Thus, punishments both proclaim and enforce social values according to the importance given to them. There is no other way for society to affirm its values. To refuse to punish any crime with death, then, is to avow that the negative weight of a crime can never exceed the positive value of the life of the person who committed it. I find that proposition implausible (van den Haag, 1978:68).

Third, van den Haag is not persuaded by arguments that the death penalty is wrong because it is carried out in a discriminatory fashion. If discriminatory use of the death penalty is a problem, eliminate the discrimination, not the death penalty. Furthermore, van den Haag cautions against any unfounded cries of discrimination:

> It is true that most of those currently under sentence of death are poor and a disproportionate number are black. But most murderers (indeed, most criminals) are poor and a disproportionate number are black. (So too are a disproportionate number of murder victims.) One must expect therefore that most of our prison population, including those on death row, are poor and a disproportionate number black (van den Haag and Conrad, 1983:206-207).

BOX 14.3 *continued*

Finally, van den Haag thinks that the average person favors capital punishment while the average college-educated judge opposes it. There are two reasons for this:

> First, the college-educated, including judges, usually do not move in circles in which violence, including murder, is a daily threat. Not feeling threatened by murder, they can afford to treat it leniently. . . . Second, . . . [S]tudents tend to absorb and to be victimized by the intellectual fashions of their college days. Uneducated people more often accept tradition and their own experience. . . . The idea of the criminal as a sick victim of society thrives among intellectuals. The fashion in intellectual circles for the last fifty years has been to regard criminals as victims of society, sick people who should be treated and rehabilitated. People who are executed cannot be rehabilitated (van den Haag and Conrad, 1983:159).

face of the possibility of mistakes (i.e., executing someone who has been mistakenly convicted). The empirical questions include the deterrent impact of capital punishment (does it prevent individuals from committing murder because they fear being sentenced to die?) and the issue of racial or class bias (is the death penalty more likely to be imposed on minorities than on whites?). These same issues apply to the question of the appropriateness of the death penalty for juveniles.

In 2005, the Supreme Court ruled that the death penalty is unconstitutional for juveniles. In *Roper v. Simmons* (2005), writing for the majority, Justice Arthur Kennedy wrote that "[t]he Eighth and Fourteenth Amendments forbid imposition of the death penalty on offenders who were under the age of 18 when their crimes were committed." The ruling came in a case in which Christopher Simmons, age 17, with two accomplices, broke and entered a home at 2:00 A.M. took a woman captive, drove away, and threw the woman from a railroad trestle into a river.

The majority opinion reasoned that the juvenile death penalty is rejected by the majority of the states and is used infrequently in states that authorize it. This suggests that today American society views juveniles as less culpable than adults. The majority went on to cite scientific evidence that juveniles under 18 are less mature and responsible than adults, more susceptible to peer pressure, and have character that is less well formed than that of an adult. The majority recognizes that there is no perfect decision about the appropriate age for the death penalty but that a line has to be drawn somewhere. They choose age 18. "The age of 18 is the point where society draws the line for many purposes between childhood and adulthood" (*Roper v. Simmons*, 2005).

Dissenting, Justice Antonin Scalia pointed out that only 18 states actually prohibit executions for juveniles. Unlike the majority, Justice Scalia argued that one cannot reason that states without the death penalty prohibit it for juveniles; he contended that those states should not be considered because they have not addressed the issue of the appropriate age for the death penalty. He also noted that psychological studies about maturity and recklessness give us a picture of juveniles in general. Some particular juveniles, however, may be culpable and may commit particularly heinous crimes that merit the death penalty. He thinks that a jury can and should decide whether a particular juvenile is indeed culpable and has committed a crime that is so horrible as to deserve capital punishment. (See Box 14.4 for quotes from the majority opinion and from Justice Scalia's dissent.)

Mirah Horowitz (2000) argues that there should be no death penalty for juveniles for several reasons. First, she claims that reasoning ability, maturity, and experience levels are lower for juveniles than for adults. Second, subjecting juveniles to the death penalty is arbitrary in that it is contrary to other laws that assume that children under 18 need protection and are not ready for certain responsibilities or privileges such as the right to vote, to sit on juries, to consent to treatment, and to marry. To subject juveniles to the death penalty but deny them these other privileges "seems hypocritical when society does not trust them with the civic responsibilities of an adult" (Horowitz, 2000:166). Horowitz also thinks that juveniles have greater potential for rehabilitation than adults. Part of this is the fact that they have a greater proportion of their lives still ahead of them. Another part of her argument is that many juveniles have not had a chance to get away from the abuse or other problems they have suffered. Society should offer them at least one chance to develop apart from a negative home environment. Finally, Horowitz contends that considerations of deterrence and retribution often do not apply to juveniles. In general, youth impulsiveness, poor judgment, and feelings of invincibility prevent them from regarding even the death penalty with the rational calculation necessary for an adequate deterrent impact. Specific problems such as history of abuse, substance abuse issues, mental illness, low intelligence, and even brain damage detract from the full capability necessary for fair deterrence or punishment.

Horowitz thinks the solution is simple: stop executing juveniles. Instead, juveniles who kill should be sentenced to prison with the possibility of parole. This would give youths who kill "the chance to reverse the violent patterns that may have been established in their lives," and it would allow us "to address the societal problems that cause them to be violent in the first place" (Horowitz, 2000:175).

The Supreme Court's *Roper* decision has ended the debate over the death penalty for practical purposes. An unintended consequence of the decision is an increase in the number of juveniles serving Life Without

BOX 14.4

Majority and Dissenting Opinions in the *Roper* Case

Justice Kennedy's Majority Opinion:

The susceptibility of juveniles to immature and irresponsible behavior means "their irresponsible conduct is not as morally reprehensible as that of an adult." *Thompson, supra*, at 835 (plurality opinion). Their own vulnerability and comparative lack of control over their immediate surroundings mean juveniles have a greater claim than adults to be forgiven for failing to escape negative influences in their whole environment. See *Stanford*, 492 U.S., at 395 (Brennan, J. dissenting). The reality that juveniles still struggle to define their identity means it is less supportable to conclude that even a heinous crime committed by a juvenile is evidence of irretrievably depraved character. From a moral standpoint it would be misguided to equate the failings of a minor with those of an adult, for a greater possibility exists that a minor's character deficiencies will be reformed."

Justice Scalia's Dissent:

"Murder, however, is more than just risky or antisocial behavior. It is entirely consistent to believe that young people often act impetuously and lack judgment, but, at the same time, to believe that those who commit premeditated murder are—at least sometimes—just as culpable as adults. Christopher Simmons, who was only seven months shy of his 18th birthday when he murdered Shirley Crook, described to his friends *beforehand*—'[i]n chilling, callous terms,'. . . the murder he planned to commit. He then broke into the home of an innocent woman, bound her with duct tape and electrical wire, and threw her off a bridge alive and conscious."

What do you think? Is Justice Kennedy correct that minors are still immature and struggling with their identity? Is there greater chance that they can be reformed? Or is Justice Scalia correct that some individual juveniles are just as culpable as adults—that some youths commit heinous crimes and should be held fully accountable for them? Do you agree with Justice Kennedy that all youths should be ineligible for the death penalty, or do you agree with Justice Scalia that some youths may deserve the death penalty?

Parole sentences. Contrary to the suggestion of Horowitz, many states are incarcerating juveniles for life with no hope of parole. The next section discusses this issue.

Life Without Parole for Juveniles

The most recent estimate is that there are 2,484 persons serving Life Without Parole (LWOP) sentences who were under 18 when they committed their crimes; this is up from 2,225 in 2005 (Human Rights Watch, 2008). Youths serving such sentences are 97 percent male and 60 percent black. Sixteen percent were 15 or younger at the time of their crimes (Human Rights Watch, 2008). Some of these juveniles were sentenced prior to *Roper*, and some were sentenced after *Roper* made it impossible to sentence a juvenile to death.

Box 14.5 lists the top 10 states in the use of Life Without Parole sentences for juveniles. Unlike the death penalty, LWOP is not as concentrated in the South but has been given out quite frequently in Pennsylvania, Michigan, and California. On the flip side, Colorado banned such sentences in 2006, five additional states are in the process of banning them, and eight states besides Colorado prohibit them (Fagan, 2007).

BOX 14.5

Top Ten States (plus 4):
Life Without Parole Sentences for Juveniles

(Numbers of juveniles serving Life Without Parole sentences in parentheses)
Pennsylvania (444)
Louisiana (334)
Michigan (316)
Florida (266)
California (227)
Missouri (116)
Illinois (103)
Arkansas (73)
Alabama (62)
Massachusetts (53)

Next Four:

Colorado (48)
Oklahoma (48)
Virginia (48)
North Carolina (44)

Source: Adapted from Human Rights Watch (2008). *The Rest of Their Lives: Life Without Parole for Youth Offenders in the United States in 2008*. New York: Human Rights Watch.

The growth in the use of Life Without Parole sentences for juveniles is expected given the *Roper* decision banning the death penalty for juveniles. Absent the death penalty, Life Without Parole is arguably the harshest sentence a state can impose. So if a juvenile is convicted of a heinous murder, it is logical that judges, responding to prosecutors, juries, the public, and the press, would impose the harshest alternative available: Life Without Parole.

Critics, however, see problems. One problem is unfair implementation. For example, in 11 states black youths who are arrested for murder are more likely to be sentenced to such a sentence than white youths arrested for murder (Human Rights Watch, 2008). Human Rights Watch reports that in both California and Connecticut the ratio of black youths arrested for murder sentenced to LWOP is more than five times higher than that for white youths arrested for murder. Just as some criticized racial discrimination in the administration of the death penalty, critics see racial problems continuing in the use of Life Without Parole sentences.

Critics also point to other problems in meting out Life Without Parole sentences to juveniles. First, the majority—59 percent—of juveniles with LWOP sentences are first-time offenders with no prior adult criminal record or juvenile adjudication record. Second, it is estimated that a quarter (26%) of the juveniles with LWOP sentences were convicted of felony murder. That is, they were an accomplice; for example, their co-defendant actually committed the murder during another felony crime. Third, frequently the juvenile committed the crime with an adult and in many cases the adult received a more lenient sentence.

Another problem is that youths sentenced to Life Without Parole are experiencing severe trauma in prison, including knifings, threats, and suicidal thoughts (Human Rights Watch, 2008).

Still another criticism is that while sentences usually serve multiple goals, including rehabilitation, LWOP has no rehabilitative aspects. It simply gives up on any hope of change for the offender. With juveniles, however, there is usually considerable chance for change.

Perhaps the most serious criticism of Life Without Parole sentences for juveniles is the question of responsibility. Barry Feld, for example, argues that the reasoning behind the *Roper* decision that made the death penalty unconstitutional for juveniles applies with equal vigor to LWOP sentences. If a juvenile is too immature and too susceptible to peer pressure to be executed, argues Feld, the same logic dictates that he or she is not mature enough for a sentence of Life Without Parole. In Feld's words: "Adolescents' personalities are in transition and it is unjust and irrational to continue harshly to punish a fifty- or sixty-year old person for the crime that an irresponsible child committed several decades earlier" (Feld, 2008:36).

A number of authorities concur with Feld that Life Without Parole is overly harsh for juveniles. Human Rights Watch, for example, notes that the United States is "an international anomaly" as the only country in the world that imposes LWOP sentences on juveniles (Human Rights Watch, 2008:8). Michael Tonry argues that Life Without Parole is one of several American inhumane policies that is "unimaginable in most other Western countries" (Tonry, 2008:3).

Still another problem is the problem of mistakes. This is due to "the inability of judges and juries to accurately render individualized assessments about whether a teenager's immaturity and developmental deficits attenuates his or her culpability" (Fagan, 2007:742). Part of the problem is that juries sometimes treat youthful age as a factor characterizing juveniles as more dangerous rather than seeing incomplete development as making them less responsible.

LWOP for juveniles has not attracted the same outcry that capital punishment for juveniles did. The death penalty is dramatic because it is so extreme. Life Without Parole can be seen as a considerable improvement over the death penalty and can lull juvenile justice/reform advocates into a sense of victory that they have stopped a horrible injustice. However, if Barry Feld is correct that the same reasoning that destroys the justification for a juvenile death penalty also destroys that for a juvenile LWOP, then juvenile justice advocates need to get ready for another fight—the fight to overturn Life Without Parole for juveniles.

JURISDICTION OVER STATUS OFFENSES

Also related to the fundamental issue of the philosophy and continued existence of juvenile court is the issue of **divestiture**, that is, eliminating juvenile court **jurisdiction over status offenders**. Assuming that a state chooses not to eliminate juvenile court completely, should it continue to exercise control over disobedient, runaway, and truant adolescents? As noted, the state of Washington has opted to continue juvenile court but to eliminate jurisdiction over status offenses. Maine has written full divestiture into law. Most states have retained jurisdiction but implemented policies of deinstitutionalization (stopped confining status offenders in state institutions). In many places, private drug treatment and mental health facilities have stepped in to fill the void that juvenile court previously occupied (Feld, 1999).

Despite such efforts, status offenses and status offenders continue to take up a considerable portion of juvenile court time and effort. In 2004, juvenile courts handled an estimated 159,400 petitioned status offense cases, an increase of more than 39 percent over 1995. Truancy cases increased more than 35 percent between 1995 and 2004, while runaway cases, curfew cases, ungovernable cases, and liquor law cases each increased less than 20 percent. Despite more than a decade of discussion about ending juvenile court jurisdiction over status offenses, approximately 12,300 youths were adjudicated status offenders and placed in out-of-home placements in 2004 (Stahl et al., 2007). The 2003 census of juveniles in custody showed 4,824 youths in custody for a status offense (Snyder and Sickmund, 2006).

Arguments for Ending Jurisdiction

There are several arguments in favor of complete divestiture. First, it allows the juvenile court more time and resources to deal with juvenile delinquents—especially violent and chronic delinquents. Because the court does not have to process or supervise status offenders, probation officers, prosecutors, public defenders, judges, and correctional program employees are able to focus on more serious delinquents. Second, the elimination of status offense jurisdiction prevents any possible violations of the due process rights of status offenders, such as being prosecuted for very vague charges. For example, how disobedient does a child have to be before he or she is "incorrigible," or how truant before he or she is eligible for a truancy petition? Status offense statutes typically are unclear and vague. Third, elimination of this jurisdiction recognizes the reality that juvenile courts are not adequately staffed and equipped to deal with status offenders. Most probation officers often have only bachelor's degrees and are not qualified to do the social work and psychological counseling necessary to assist troubled teenagers and their families. Thus, status offenders should be diverted to private agencies with trained social workers and counselors who are better equipped to handle the complex problems of these youths and their families. Furthermore, eliminating juvenile court jurisdiction would force any intervention to be voluntary, which some argue is the proper way to deal with status offenders.

Another argument for elimination is that jurisdiction over status offenses has "weakened the responsibility of schools and agencies to arrange out-of-court interventive services and solutions" (Rubin, 1985:63). What Rubin means is that status offense laws have allowed schools to run inadequate and boring programs that promote truancy and, in turn, blame parents and children for the problem. Instead of petitioning youths to juvenile court, schools should be improving instructional programs or offering innovative approaches such as alternative schools where children attend school half a day and then work half a day for pay. In other words, prosecuting status offenders often is a blame-the-victim approach that ignores the real causes of the problems: inferior schools, ineffective parents, and insensitive communities (see Rubin, 1985, and Schur, 1973, for further discussion of this issue). (For a viewpoint of child welfare caseworkers on this issue, see Box 14.5.)

Meda Chesney-Lind (1987) believes that status offenses are intricately intertwined with the place of women in American society. She questions whether the concern over maintaining jurisdiction is one of concern or control:

> What is really at stake here is not "protection" of youth so much as it is the right of young women to defy patriarchy. Such defiance by male youth is winked at, both today and in the past, but from girls such behavior is totally unacceptable (Chesney-Lind, 1987:21).

Much of the concern, therefore, about status offenders is not so much for the children as for maintaining a patriarchal society. Thus, like the critics of the child savers discussed in Chapter 2, Chesney-Lind questions the intentions of those concerned with the protection of status offenders.

Arguments for Continuing Jurisdiction

Some still think, however, that juvenile court jurisdiction over status offenses is both desirable and necessary. Proponents of continued jurisdiction contend that parents and schools need the court backing to impress adolescents with the need to obey their parents, attend school, and not run away from home. Concerning truancy, Rubin argues that repeal of status offense jurisdiction would "effectively eradicate compulsory education" and that "children will be free to roam the streets with impunity" (Rubin, 1985:65). Furthermore, such total freedom would "deny children the necessary preparation for achievement in a complex technological society" (Rubin, 1985:65). Second, proponents of court jurisdiction argue that private agencies in the community will not handle (or will not be able to handle) all of the status offense cases if the juvenile court cannot intervene. Private agencies intervene only with willing clients, and many status offenders taken to such agencies simply refuse assistance. Moreover, some agencies do not provide the services they claim to provide (Schneider, 1985).

Proponents also contend that status offenders often escalate into delinquent activity, and note that truants are linked with daytime burglary and vandalism (Baker, Sigmon, and Nugent, 2001). Therefore, they claim, early intervention can prevent current and future delinquency. However, the escalation hypothesis is controversial. Some proportion of status offenders do indeed escalate or progress, but most do not (Lab, 1984; Rojek and Erickson, 1982; Shannon, 1982). Hence, it is questionable whether all status offenders should be subject to juvenile court jurisdiction. A similar argument is that many status offenders become involved in very dangerous situations that can cause serious harm to the child. For example, one study of runaways found that more than 50 percent dealt drugs and about 20 percent (including 19% of the male runaways) engaged in acts of prostitution to support themselves (Miller et al., 1980). Research on street children has shown that many turn to theft, prostituting, rolling johns, and selling drugs to survive (Hagan and McCarthy, 1997). Proponents of court jurisdiction argue that courts might prevent some children from running away and becoming involved in associated dangerous behaviors. A related argument is that because states intervene "to protect adults from their own harmful conduct" (Ryan, 1987:64), they should protect juveniles from the harmful consequences of their actions.

Another argument in favor of continued jurisdiction is that it prevents status offenders from being processed as delinquents. That is, where divestiture has occurred, there is some evidence of treating status offenders as minor delinquents (Schneider, 1985). Finally, there is concern that total removal of status offense jurisdiction

There are differing opinions as to whether juvenile courts should continue having jurisdiction over status offenses. Status offenses, such as cigarette smoking, are forms of juvenile misbehavior that would not constitute a criminal act for an adult.

from juvenile court "changes the character of the court and may substantially weaken attempts to consider the child status of delinquent" (Mahoney, 1987:29). In other words, Mahoney fears that removal of status offense jurisdiction, with a concentration on delinquency only, may lead to a view of the juvenile court as concerned with crime only and, hence, a belief that adult criminal courts can exercise that function. Thus, removal of status offense jurisdiction may very well be the beginning of the end of the juvenile court.

At present, the debate over divestiture has changed. In the Justice Department's research and writing on delinquency, there is little mention of status offenses as such. Instead of debate about divestiture, the Office of Juvenile Justice and Delinquency Prevention emphasizes prevention strategies that help youngsters at risk of becoming delinquent by building up protective factors. Such protective factors include caring parents who supervise their children, personal attributes such as conventional beliefs and conflict resolution skills, and schools that have caring teachers and help youths succeed in school (Coordinating Council on Juvenile Justice and Delinquency Prevention, 1996). The Coordinating Council is concerned with such programs as truancy reduction programs that have the police round up truants so that parents can be notified and come pick up their children (see also Chapter 7). Also mentioned are mentoring programs including Bigs in Blue, which matches high-risk youths with police officer mentors who try to help youths cope with peer pressure and also do well in school. Noted as well are conflict resolution programs in schools and community efforts such as community policing cooperative arrangements that attack community risk factors such as easy availability of drugs and firearms (Coordinating Council on Juvenile Justice and Delinquency Prevention, 1996; see also Baker, Sigmon, and Nugent, 2001).

Unlike a decade ago, the emphasis is not so much on the status offender as a distinct problem, but on those risk factors that can lead to serious, violent, or chronic delinquency. Attention to reducing risk factors and enhancing protective factors is considered to be the way to prevent such problematic delinquency.

CONCLUSION

Most of the proposals for the future of the juvenile justice system have some merit. The authors of these proposals care about juveniles and about how the juvenile court system should attempt to prevent and control delinquency.

The suggestion to get the juvenile justice system to return to its *parens patriae* roots—to attempt to get juvenile court to truly implement rehabilitation efforts based on valid empirical research findings—is a positive one. The goal is noble: genuine assistance for juveniles. Obstacles include funding problems, lack of societal commitment to the disadvantaged youths that are the clientele of juvenile court, vestiges of racism, and punitive strains in some politicians.

Bazemore's call to make a drastic change and pursue the path of restorative justice is also positive. Advantages of this proposal are that it can appeal to both liberals and conservatives. Both parties like the fact that restorative justice puts renewed emphasis on the victim. Restitution, for example, is desirable because it restores the victim to the condition he or she was in prior to the crime. Perhaps the major question about this proposal is whether citizens will commit to participate. Putnam's (2000) concerns about the decline of community in America raise the question that citizens are not as civically involved today as they were even 50 years ago. A number of communities, including the state of Vermont (Karp, Bazemore, and Chesire, 2004), have implemented restorative justice practices, though, so this does not appear to be a pipedream.

Feld's earlier call for the end of juvenile court is controversial. His proposal is not as drastic as it seems at first hearing because he tempers it with important caveats. He would provide due process protections, such as fully adversarial attorneys, for all juveniles handled in adult court. Likewise his call for discounted sentencing would keep juveniles from serving full adult prison terms. A major concern with his proposal is the exact value of the discounts. A 10 percent discount off of a 50-year sentence—leaving 45 years for a juvenile—would be a virtually meaningless change. A 75 percent discount would be meaningful. Probably the major question about Feld's proposal is whether moving all juvenile cases to adult court would simply translate into complete abandonment of the concept of differential treatment for juveniles due to immaturity and inexperience and a very rapid track toward treating juveniles exactly like adults. Bishop's (2000) research on the experiences of youths transferred to adult court in Florida supports the probability of such abandonment of concern for children. The transferred youths she interviewed had negative evaluations of both adult court and adult correctional facilities while juveniles in the juvenile system felt positively about juvenile court and juvenile correctional staff. As noted earlier in this chapter, it now appears that Feld has at least partially backed off from his call for abandonment because his current view is that the juvenile court is less harmful than adult court processing of juveniles (Feld, 2007).

Perhaps one way to prevent the suggestion to abolish juvenile court from resulting in an abandonment of the noble goals of juvenile court is to follow Butts's advice. If we are going to move all juveniles to adult court, then start a youth justice court within the confines of adult court similar to drug courts and mental health courts. These specialized courts (also known as the therapeutic jurisprudence movement [Braithwaite, 2002; Wexler, 2002]) recognize the distinctive needs of special populations. If there is only one adult court, everyone who goes to it will be treated the same. If there are specialized courts under the adult court umbrella, then there will be consideration for special needs such as drug addiction, mental illness, and youthful immaturity and reduced responsibility.

Some of the broader suggestions noted in this chapter also merit mention in this concluding section. For instance, Garland's analysis that the decline of the rehabilitative ideal is tied in with broader economic changes such as the globalizing economy and the eroding of the welfare state deserves serious attention. This analysis suggests that trying to return juvenile court to its rehabilitative roots and even trying to set up youth justice courts that address youth needs within the adult court system are both doomed to failure for the simple reason that the true problem is decreasing availability of funding. The real solution is to somehow change the economic forces that work to reduce the funds available for treatment efforts, whether in juvenile or adult court. As mentioned earlier, one issue that might be addressed is spending on the elderly (e.g., Social Security) versus spending on children. The problem is that the elderly are a significant and growing constituency. As the "baby boomers" age into senior citizen status, they will become an even greater voting bloc. Even though many senior citizens have pension plans, they are reluctant to reduce their entitlements (Social Security), which prevents those government funds from being available for delinquency prevention in particular and youth programs in general.

Character education or the reintroduction of the spiritual dimension into juvenile corrections also merits serious consideration. If Staples (2000) is correct that problems such as school violence stem, at least in part, from excessive emphasis on the consumer culture and inattention to the search for meaning, creativity, and engagement, then superficial changes in juvenile court are not critical. If such terms as "character education" or a "search for the spiritual" are simply ploys to avoid funding meaningful programs for youths in trouble, then they are hypocritical and dangerous. However, if calls for character education and the reintroduction of the spiritual dimension go along with education, job training, substance abuse counseling, and other efforts to address all the needs of problem youths, both material and spiritual, then they hold promise. Critics of our consumer culture are accurate that there is more to life than purchasing increasingly more goods.

The founders of the juvenile court had it at least half right: kids do need help. That was true back in 1899 and is as true today in the twenty-first century. The problem is that in seeking solutions for youth problems and problem youths we prefer to ignore this truth and seek refuge in simplistic slogans like "adult time" and "Scared Straight." We are a lot like dieters seeking to lose weight; we want the easy way out. Just as persons trying to lose weight have to face the hard facts of diet and exercise, American society has to face the facts of delinquency. There is no easy solution. Whatever proposal for the future of juvenile court wins out, it will not be an answer unless it addresses the problems of youths who break the law.

DISCUSSION QUESTIONS

1. Discuss the reform proposals for juvenile court. Which proposal(s) do you favor? Why? What might the consequences be of abolishing juvenile court?

2. How does the status of community life affect juvenile delinquency and juvenile justice? How much does reform of the juvenile justice system depend on strong communities? Is Putnam correct that community life seems to be having problems as individuals seem to turn to more solitary pursuits? Can this trend be reversed?

3. How do current political and economic events affect juvenile justice? For example, do you think that the war on terrorism will have any effects on juvenile justice?

4. Do you favor the death penalty for juveniles? Discuss this in light of the recent Supreme Court decision making the juvenile death penalty unconstitutional.

5. Discuss Life Without Parole for juveniles. Do you agree with Barry Feld that the Supreme Court's reasoning in the *Roper* case about capital punishment for juveniles also applies to Life Without Parole for juveniles? Or is the death penalty unique?

6. What role, if any, should juvenile court have with status offenders?

REFERENCES

Abadinsky, H. (1989). *Drug Abuse: An Introduction.* Chicago: Nelson-Hall.

Abrahamsen, D. (1944). *Crisis and the Human Mind.* New York: Columbia University Press.

Abram, K.M., J.Y. Choe, J.J. Washburn, L.A. Teplin, D.C. King, and M.K. Dulcan (2008). "Suicidal Ideation and Behaviors among Youths in Juvenile Detention." *Journal of the American Academy of Child and Adolescent Psychiatry* 47:301-308.

Abram, K.M., L.D. Paskar, J.J. Washburn, and L.A. Teplin (2008). "Perceived Barriers to Mental Health Services among Youths in Detention." *Journal of the American Academy of Child and Adolescent Psychiatry* 47:291-300.

Abt Associates (1994). *Conditions of Confinement: Juvenile Detention and Corrections Facilities: Research Report.* Washington, DC: U.S. Department of Justice.

Acoca, L. (1998). "Outside/Inside: The Violation of American Girls at Home, on the Streets, and in the Juvenile Justice System." *Crime & Delinquency* 44:561-589.

Adams, K. (2003). "The Effectiveness of Juvenile Curfews at Crime Prevention." *Annals of the American Academy of Political and Social Science* 587:136-159.

Adams, K. (2007). "Abolish Juvenile Curfews." *Criminology & Public Policy* 6:663-670.

Adams, L.R. (1974). "The Adequacy of Differential Association Theory." *Journal of Research in Crime and Delinquency* 11:1-8.

Administration on Children, Youth, and Families (2008). *Child Maltreatment, 2006.* Washington, DC: U.S. Department of Health and Human Services.

Ageton, S., and D.S. Elliott (1973). "The Effects of Legal Processing on Self-concept." Mimeograph. Boulder, CO: Institute of Behavioral Science, University of Colorado.

Agnew, R. (1984). "Goal Achievement and Delinquency." *Sociology and Social Research* 68:435-451.

Agnew, R. (1992). "Foundation for a General Strain Theory of Crime and Delinquency." *Criminology* 30:47-87.

Agnew, R. (1994). "The Techniques of Neutralization and Violence." *Criminology* 32:555-580.

Agnew, R. (1997). "Stability and Change in Crime Over the Life Course: A Strain Theory Explanation." In T.P. Thornberry (ed.), *Developmental Theories of Crime and Delinquency.* New Brunswick, NJ: Transaction.

Agnew, R., and A.A.R. Peters (1986). "The Techniques of Neutralization: An Analysis of Predisposing and Situational Factors." *Criminal Justice and Behavior* 13:81-97.

Agnew, R., and H.R. White (1992). "An Empirical Test of General Strain Theory." *Criminology* 30:475-499.

Aichorn, A. (1963). *Wayward Youth*. New York: Viking.

Akers, R.L. (1990). "Rational Choice, Deterrence, and Social Learning Theory in Criminology: The Path Not Taken." *Journal of Criminal Law and Criminology* 81:653-676.

Akers, R.L. (1991). "Self-control as a General Theory of Crime." *Journal of Quantitative Criminology* 7:201-211.

Akers, R.L., M.K. Krohn, L. Lonza-Kaduce, and M. Radosevich (1979). "Social Learning and Deviant Behavior: A Specific Test of a General Theory." *American Sociological Review* 44:636-655.

Allen, P. (1994). *OJJDP Model Programs 1993*. Washington, DC: U.S. Department of Justice.

Allender, D.M. (2001). "Gangs in Middle America: Are They a Threat?" *FBI Law Enforcement Bulletin* 70(12):1-9.

Alpert, G.P. (2007). "Eliminate Race as the Only Reason for Police-Citizen Encounters." *Criminology & Public Policy* 6:671-678.

Alpert, G.P., R.G. Dunham, and M.R. Smith (2007). "Investigating Racial Profiling by the Miami-Dade Police Department: A Multimethod Approach." *Criminology & Public Policy* 6:25-56.

Alpert, G.P., J.M. MacDonald, and R.G. Dunham (2005). "Police Suspicion and Discretionary Decision Making during Citizen Stops." *Criminology* 43:407-434.

Altschuler, D.M. (1998). "Intermediate Sanctions and Community Treatment for Serious and Violent Juvenile Offenders." In R. Loeber and D.P. Farrington (eds.), *Serious and Violent Juvenile Offenders: Risk Factors and Successful Interventions* (pp. 367-385). Thousand Oaks, CA: Sage.

Altschuler, D., and P.J. Brounstein (1991). "Patterns of Drug Use, Drug Trafficking, and Other Delinquency among Inner City Adolescent Males in Washington, DC." *Criminology* 29:589-622.

American Dietetics Association (1984). "Position Paper of the American Dietetics Association on Diet and Criminal Behavior." *Journal of the American Dietetics Association* 85:361-362.

Amir, M. (1971). *Patterns in Forcible Rape*. Chicago: University of Chicago Press.

Anderson, E. (1994). "The Code of the Streets." *Atlantic Monthly* 273(5):81-94.

Andrews, D.A. (2006). "Enhancing Adherence to Risk-Need-Responsivity: Making Quality a Matter of Policy." *Criminology & Public Policy* 5:595-602.

Anglin, M.D. (1988). "The Efficacy of Civil Commitment in Treating Narcotics Addiction." *Journal of Drug Issues* 18:527-547.

Anglin, M.D., and Y. Hser (1987). "Addicted Women and Crime." *Criminology* 25:359-397.

Anglin, M.D., and Y. Hser (1990). "Treatment of Drug Abuse." In M. Tonry and J.Q. Wilson (eds.), *Drugs and Crime* (pp. 393-460). Chicago: University of Chicago Press.

Anglin, M.D., and W.H. McGlothlin (1984). "Outcome of Narcotic Addict Treatment in California." In F.M. Tims and J.P. Ludford (eds.), *Drug Abuse Treatment Evaluation: Strategies, Progress and Prospects* (pp. 106-128). Washington, DC: National Institute on Drug Abuse.

Anglin, M.D., and W.H. McGlothlin (1985). "Methadone Maintenance in California: A Decade's Experience." In L. Brill and C. Winnick (eds.), *Yearbook of Substance Use and Abuse* (pp. 219-280). New York: Human Sciences Press.

Anglin, M.D., and G.R. Speckhart (1986). "Narcotics Use, Property Crime, and Dealing: Structural Dynamics Across the Addiction Career." *Journal of Quantitative Criminology* 2:355-375.

Anglin, M.D., and G.R. Speckhart (1988). "Narcotics Use and Crime: A Multisample, Multimethod Analysis." *Criminology* 26:197-233.

Anglin, M.D., G.R. Speckhart, M.W. Booth, and T.M. Ryan (1989). "Consequences and Costs of Shutting Off Methadone." *Addictive Behaviors* 14:307-326.

Aries, P. (1962). *Centuries of Childhood*. New York: Knopf.

Ash Institute (2008). *Division of Youth Services Honored as Innovations in American Government Award Winner* (September 9, 2008). Cambridge, MA: Harvard University Press. Available at: http://content.knowledgeplex.org/streams/ksg/Ash-Institute/09.09.08_DYS.pdf

Ashworth, A. (2003). "Is Restorative Justice the Way Forward for Criminal Justice?" In E. McLaughlin, R. Fergusson, G. Hughes, and L. Westmarland (eds.), *Restorative Justice: Critical Issues*. Thousand Oaks, CA: Sage.

Associated Press (2008a). "Hartford Police to Beef Up Teen Curfew after Shooting." *Johnson City Press* (August 12, 2008):6A.

Associated Press (2008b). "State Sex Offender Registry Exempts Juvenile Offenses." *Johnson City Press* (August 18, 2008):5A.

Austin, J., K.D. Johnson, and R. Weitzer (2005). *Alternatives to the Secure Detention and Confinement of Juvenile Offenders*. Washington, DC: U.S. Department of Justice.

Bailey, W.C., and R.D. Peterson (1981). "Legal Versus Extra-Legal Determinants of Juvenile Court Dispositions." *Juvenile and Family Court Journal* 32:41-59.

Baines, M., and C. Alder (1996). "Are Girls More Difficult to Work With? Youth Workers' Perspectives in Juvenile Justice and Related Areas." *Crime & Delinquency* 42:467-485.

Baker, M.L., J.N. Sigmon, and M.E. Nugent (2001). *Truancy Reduction: Keeping Students in School*. Washington, DC: Office of Juvenile Justice and Delinquency Prevention.

Ball, J.C., E. Corty, R. Bond, and A. Tommasello (1987). "The Reduction of Intravenous Heroin Use, Nonopiate Abuse and Crime During Methadone Maintenance Treatment—Further Findings." Paper presented at the Annual Meeting of the Committee on Problems on Drug Dependency, Philadelphia, PA.

Ball, J.C., J.W. Shaffer, and D.N. Nurco (1983). "The Day-to-Day Criminality of Heroin Addicts in Baltimore: A Study in the Continuity of Offense Rates." *Drug and Alcohol Dependence* 12:119-142.

Bandura, A., and R.H. Walters (1963). *Social Learning and Personality Development*. New York: Holt, Rhinehart and Winston.

Bannenberg, B., and D. Rössner (2003). "New Developments in Restorative Justice to Handle Family Violence." In E. Weitkamp and H. Kerner (eds.), *Restorative Justice in Context: International Practice and Directions* (pp. 51-79). Portland, OR: Willan.

Bannister, A.J., D.L. Carter, and J. Schafer (2001). "A National Police Survey on Juvenile Curfews." *Journal of Criminal Justice* 29:233-240.

Barnum, R. (1987). "The Development of Responsibility: Implications for Juvenile Justice." In F.X. Hartman (ed.), *From Children to Citizens: Volume II: The Role of the Juvenile Court* (pp. 67-79). New York: Springer-Verlag.

Bartollas, C., and C.M. Sieverdes (1981). "The Victimized White in a Juvenile Correctional System." *Crime & Delinquency* 27:534-543.

Bayley, D.H. (2002). "Law Enforcement and the Rule of Law: Is There a Tradeoff?" *Criminology & Public Policy* 2:133-154.

Bazemore, G. (1999). "The Fork in the Road to Juvenile Court Reform." *Annals of the American Academy of Political and Social Science* 564:81-108.

Bazemore, G., and L. Leip (2000). "Victim Participation in the New Juvenile Court: Tracking Judicial Attitudes Toward Restorative Justice Reforms." *Justice System Journal* 21(2):199-226.

Bazemore, G., and D. Maloney (1994). "Rehabilitating Community Service: Toward Restorative Service in a Balanced Justice System." *Federal Probation* 58:24-35.

Bazemore, G., and M. Schiff (2005). *Juvenile Justice Reform and Restorative Justice: Building Theory and Policy from Practice.* Portland, OR: Willan.

Bazemore, G., and M. Umbreit (2001). *A Comparison of Four Restorative Conferencing Models.* Washington, DC: U.S. Department of Justice, Office of Juvenile Justice and Delinquency Prevention.

Beck, A.J., D.B. Adams, and P. Guerino (2008). "Sexual Violence Reported by Juvenile Correctional Authorities, 2005-2006." *Bureau of Justice Statistics Special Report.* Washington, DC: U.S. Department of Justice.

Beck, A.J., S.A. Kline, and L.A. Greenfield (1988). "Survey of Youth in Custody, 1987." *Bureau of Justice Statistics Special Report.* Washington, DC: US Department of Justice.

Beldon, E. (1920). *Courts in the U.S. Hearing Children's Cases.* Washington, DC: U.S. Children's Bureau.

Belenko, S., J.A. Fagan, and T. Dumanovsky (1994). "The Effects of Level Sanctions on Recidivism in Special Drug Courts." *Justice System Journal* 17:53-80.

Belknap, J. (1984). "The Effect of Local Policy on the Sentencing Patterns of State Wards." *Justice Quarterly* 1:549-561.

Belknap, J. (1987). "Routine Activity Theory and the Risk of Rape: Analyzing Ten Years of National Crime Survey Data." *Criminal Justice Policy Review* 2:337-356.

Bell, D., and K. Lang (1985). "The Intake Dispositions of Juvenile Offenders." *Journal of Research in Crime and Delinquency* 22:309-328.

Bellis, D.J. (1981). *Heroin and Politicians: The Failure of Public Policy to Control Addiction in America.* Westport, CT: Greenwood.

Belsky, J. (1978). "Three Theoretical Models of Child Abuse: A Critical Review." *Child Abuse & Neglect* 2:37-49.

Benda, B.B. (2002). "Religion and Violent Offenders in Boot Camp: A Structural Equation Model." *Journal of Research in Crime and Delinquency* 39:91-121.

Benekos, P.J., and A.V. Merlo (2008). "Juvenile Justice: The Legacy of Punitive Policy." *Youth Violence and Juvenile Justice* 6:28-46.

Bennett, T. (1986). "Situational Crime Prevention from the Offender's Perspective." In K. Heal and G. Laycock (eds.), *Situational Crime Prevention: From Theory to Practice.* London: Her Majesty's Stationery Office.

Bennett, T., and R. Wright (1984a). *Burglars on Burglary.* Brookfield, VT: Gower.

Bennett, T., and R. Wright (1984b). "The Relationship Between Alcohol and Burglary." *British Journal of Addiction* 79:431-437.

Bennett, W.J. (2001). *The Broken Hearth: Reversing the Moral Collapse of the American Family.* New York: Doubleday.

Bentham, J. (1948). *An Introduction to the Principles of Morals and Legislation.* New York: Hafner.

Bergseth, K.J., and J.A. Bouffard (2007). "The Long-term Impact of Restorative Justice Programming for Juvenile Offenders." *Journal of Criminal Justice* 35:433-451.

Bilchik, S. (1998). *A Juvenile Justice System for the 21st Century.* Washington, DC: U.S. Department of Justice.

Bishop, D.M. (2000). "Juvenile Offenders in the Adult Criminal Justice System." In M. Tonry (ed.), *Crime and Justice: A Review of Research,* Vol. 27 (pp. 81-167). Chicago: University of Chicago Press.

Bishop, D.M. (2004). "Injustice and Irrationality in Contemporary Youth Policy." *Criminology & Public Policy* 4:633-644.

Bishop, D.M. (2005). "The Role of Race and Ethnicity in Juvenile Justice Processing." In D.F. Hawkins and K. Kempf-Leonard (eds.), *Our Children, Their Children: Confronting Racial and Ethnic Differences in American Juvenile Justice* (pp. 23-82). Chicago: University of Chicago Press.

Bishop, D.M. (2006). "Public Opinion and Juvenile Policy: Myths and Misconceptions—Reaction Essay." *Criminology & Public Policy* 5:653-664.

Bishop, D.M., and C.E. Frazier (1996). "Race Effects in Juvenile Justice Decision-Making: Findings of a Statewide Analysis." *Journal of Criminal Law and Criminology* 86:392-414.

Bjerregaard, B. (1989). "Televised Testimony as an Alternative in Child Sexual Abuse Cases." *Criminal Law Bulletin* 25:164-175.

Bjerregaard, B., and A.J. Lizotte (1995). "Gun Ownership and Gang Membership." *Journal of Criminal Law and Criminology* 86:37-58.

Bjerregaard, B., and C. Smith (1993). "Gender Differences in Gang Participation, Delinquency, and Substance Use." *Journal of Quantitative Criminology* 4:329-355.

Bloch, H.A., and A. Niederhoffer (1958). *The Gang: A Study in Adolescent Behavior.* New York: Philosophical Library.

Bonnett, P.L., and C.L. Pfeiffer (1978). "Biochemical Diagnosis for Delinquent Behavior." In L.J. Hippchen (ed.), *Ecologic-Biochemical Approaches to Treatment of Delinquents and Criminals* (pp. 183-205). New York: Van Nostrand Reinhold.

Bookin-Weiner, H., and R. Horowitz (1983). "The End of the Youth Gang: Fad or Fact?" *Criminology* 21:585-602.

Booth, A., and D.W. Osgood (1993). "The Influence of Testosterone on Deviance in Adulthood: Assessing and Explaining the Relationship." *Criminology* 31:93-118.

Bordua, D.J. (1958). "Juvenile Delinquency and 'Anomie': An Attempt at Replication." *Social Problems* 6:230-238.

Borrero, M. (2001). "The Widening Mistrust between Youth and Police." *Families in Society: The Journal of Contemporary Human Services* 82:399.

Bortner, M.A., and L.M. Williams (1997). *Youth in Prison: We the People of Unit Four.* New York: Routledge.

Bottcher, J., and M.E. Ezell (2005). "Examining the Effectiveness of Boot Camps: A Randomized Experiment with a Long-term Follow-up." *Journal of Research in Crime and Delinquency* 42:309-332.

Botvin, G.J. (1990). "Substance Abuse Prevention: Theory, Practice and Effectiveness." In M. Tonry and J.Q. Wilson (eds.), *Drugs and Crime* (pp. 461-520). Chicago: University of Chicago Press.

Botvin, G.J., E. Baker, L. Dusenbury, E. Botvin, and T. Diaz (1995). "Long-term Follow-up Results of a Randomized Drug-Abuse Prevention Trial in a White Middle Class Population." *Journal of the American Medical Association* 273:1106-1112.

Botvin, G.J., E. Baker, N. Renick, A.D. Filazzola, and E. Botvin (1984). "A Cognitive-Behavioral Approach to Substance Abuse Prevention." *Addictive Behaviors* 9:137-147.

Botvin, G.J., and L. Dusenbury (1989). "Substance Abuse Prevention and the Promotion of Competence." In L.A. Bond and B.E. Compas (eds.), *Primary Prevention and Promotion in the Schools* (pp. 146-178). Newbury Park, CA: Sage.

Botvin, G.J., J.A. Epstein, E. Baker, T. Diaz, and M. Ifill-Williams (1997). "School-based Drug Abuse Prevention with Inner-city Minority Youth." *Journal of Child and Adolescent Substance Abuse* 6:5-19.

Botvin, G.J., K.W. Griffin, E. Paul, and A.P. Macaulay (2003). "Preventing Tobacco and Alcohol Use among Elementary School Students Through Life Skills Training." *Journal of Child and Adolescent Substance Abuse* 12:1-18.

Botvin, G.J., N. Renick, and E. Baker (1983). "The Effects of Scheduling Format and Booster Sessions on a Broad Spectrum Psychological Approach to Smoking Prevention." *Journal of Behavioral Medicine* 6:359-379.

Bowker, L.H. (1980). *Prison Victimization.* New York: Elsevier.

Bowker, L.H., and M.W. Klein (1983). "The Etiology of Female Juvenile Delinquency and Gang Membership: A Test of Psychological and Social Structural Explanations." *Adolescence* 18:739-751.

Bozynski, M., and L. Szymanski (2004). "National Overviews." *State Juvenile Justice Profiles.* Pittsburgh: National Center for Juvenile Justice. Available at: http://www.ncjj.org/stateprofiles/

Braga, A.A. (2001). "The Effects of Hot Spots Policing on Crime." *Annals of the American Academy of Political and Social Science* 578:104-125.

Braga, A.A., and B.J. Bond (2008). "Policing Crime and Disorder Hot Spots: A Randomized Controlled Trial." *Criminology* 46:577-607.

Braga, A.A., D.M. Kennedy, A.M. Piehl, and E.J. Waring (2001). *The Boston Gun Project: Impact Evaluation Findings*. Washington, DC: National Institute of Justice.

Braithwaite, J. (1989). *Crime, Shame and Reintegration*. Cambridge, England: Cambridge University Press.

Braithwaite, J. (1999). "Restorative Justice: Assessing Optimistic and Pessimistic Accounts." In M. Tonry (ed.), *Crime and Justice: A Review of Research,* Vol. 25. Chicago: University of Chicago Press.

Braithwaite, J. (2002). *Restorative Justice and Responsive Regulation*. New York: Oxford University Press.

Braithwaite, J. (2003). "Restorative Justice and a Better Future." In E. McLaughlin, R. Fergusson, G. Hughes, and L. Westmarland (eds.), *Restorative Justice: Critical Issues*. Thousand Oaks, CA: Sage.

Braswell, M., J. Fuller, and B. Lozoff (2001). *Corrections, Peacemaking, and Restorative Justice: Transforming Individuals and Institutions*. Cincinnati: Anderson.

Brennan, P.A., S.A. Mednick, and J. Volavka (1995). "Biomedical Factors in Crime." In J.Q. Wilson and J. Petersilia (eds.), *Crime* (pp. 65-90). San Francisco: ICS Press.

Brenzel, B.M. (1983). *Daughters of the State: A Social Portrait of the First Reform School for Girls in North America, 1856-1903*. Cambridge, MA: MIT Press.

Brewster, M.P. (2001). "An Evaluation of the Chester County (PA) Drug Court Program." *Journal of Drug Issues* 31:171-206.

Bridges, G.S., and S. Steen (1998). "Racial Disparities in Official Assessments of Juvenile Offenders: Attributional Stereotypes as Mediating Mechanisms." *American Sociological Review* 63:554-570.

Britt, H., T.L. Toomey, W. Dunsmuir, and A.C. Wagenaar (2006). "Propensity for and Correlates of Alcohol Sales to Underage Youth." *Journal of Alcohol and Drug Education* 50(2):25-42.

Brooks, K., and D. Kamine (2003). *Justice Cut Short: An Assessment of Access to Counsel and Quality of Representation in Delinquency Proceedings in Ohio*. Columbus: Ohio State Bar Association. Available at: http://www.juvenilecoalition.org/legal_representation/ohio_report_2003/ohio_report_2003.pdf

Brown, R.A., and J. Frank (2006). "Race and Officer Decision Making: Examining Differences in Arrest Outcomes between Black and White Officers." *Justice Quarterly* 23:96-126.

Brown, W.K. (1978). "Black Gangs as Family Extension." *International Journal of Offender Therapy and Comparative Criminology* 22:39-45.

Browning, S.L., F.T. Cullen, L. Cao, R. Kopache, and T.J. Stevenson (1994). "Race and Getting Hassled by the Police: A Research Note." *Police Studies* 17(1):1-11.

Brunner, H.G. (1996). "MAOA Deficiency and Abnormal Behavior. Perspectives on an Association." In G.R. Bock and J.A. Goode (eds.), *Genetics of Criminal and Antisocial Behavior* (pp. 155-163). Chichester, England: John Wiley and Sons.

Brunson, R.K. (2007). "'Police Don't Like Black People': African-American Young Men's Accumulated Police Experiences." *Criminology & Public Policy* 6:71-102.

Brunson, R.K., and J. Miller (2006). "Gender, Race, and Urban Policing: The Experience of African American Youths." *Gender and Society* 20:531-552.

Bureau of Justice Assistance (2003). *Juvenile Drug Courts: Strategies in Practice.* Washington, DC: Bureau of Justice Assistance. Available at: http://www.ncjrs. gov/pdffiles1/bja/197866.pdf

Bureau of Justice Assistance (2005). *Gang Resistance Education and Training.* Washington, DC: Bureau of Justice Assistance. Available at: http://great-online.org

Bureau of Justice Assistance (2008). *Summary of Drug Court Activity by State and County.* Washington, DC: Bureau of Justice Assistance. Available at: http://spa. american.edu/justice/documents/2150.pdf

Bureau of Justice Statistics (2007). *State Juvenile Correctional Facility Deaths, 2002-2005 —Statistical Tables.* Washington, DC: Bureau of Justice Statistics.

Bureau of Justice Statistics (2008). *Criminal Victimization in the United States, 2006— Statistical Tables.* Washington, DC: Bureau of Justice Statistics.

Burgess, A.W., and A.T. Laszlo (1976). "When the Prosecutrix Is a Child: The Victim Consultant in Cases of Sexual Assault." In E.C. Viano (ed.), *Victims & Society.* Washington, DC: Visage Press.

Burgess, R.L., and R.L. Akers (1966). "A Differential Association-Reinforcement Theory of Criminal Behavior." *Social Problems* 14:128-147.

Burke, M.N. (2005). "Juvenile Justice Supreme Court Provides Uniformity in Juvenile Procedure Rules." *Pennsylvania Law Weekly* 28(17):5.

Burruss, G.W., and K. Kempf-Leonard (2002). "The Questionable Advantage of Defense Counsel in Juvenile Court." *Justice Quarterly* 19:37-68.

Bursik, R.J., and H.G. Grasmick (1993). *Neighborhoods and Crime: The Dimensions of Effective Community Control.* New York: Lexington.

Buss, E. (2000). "The Role of Lawyers in Promoting Juveniles' Competence as Defendants." In T. Grisso and R.G. Schwartz (eds.), *Youth on Trial: A Developmental Perspective on Juvenile Justice* (pp. 243-265). Chicago: University of Chicago Press.

Butts, J.A. (1994). "Offenders in Juvenile Court, 1992." *Juvenile Justice Bulletin.* Washington, DC: U.S. Department of Justice.

Butts, J.A. (2000). "Can We Do Without Juvenile Justice?" *Criminal Justice* 15(1):50-57.

Butts, J.A., J. Buck, and M.B. Coggershall (2002). *The Impact of Teen Court on Young Offenders.* Washington, DC: Urban Institute Press.

Butts, J.A., S. Mayer, and G. Ruth (2005). *Focusing Juvenile Justice on Positive Youth Development—Issue Brief.* Chicago: Chapin Hall Center for Children.

Butts, J.A., and H.N. Snyder (1992). *Restitution and Juvenile Recidivism.* Washington, DC: U.S. Department of Justice.

Butts, J.A., J.M. Zweig, and C. Mamalian (2004). "Defining the Mission of Juvenile Drug Courts." In J.A. Butts and J. Roman (eds.), *Juvenile Drug Courts and Teen Substance Abuse* (pp. 137-184). Washington, DC: Urban Institute Press.

Cabana, D.A. (1996). *Death at Midnight: The Confession of an Executioner.* Boston: Northeastern University Press.

Camp, S.D., J. Klein-Saffran, O. Kwon, D.M. Daggett, and V. Joseph (2006). "An Exploration into Participation in a Faith-based Prison Program." *Criminology & Public Policy* 5:529-550.

Campbell, A. (1984). "Girls' Talk: The Social Representation of Aggression by Female Gang Members." *Criminal Justice and Behavior* 11:139-156.

Campbell, A. (1990). "Female Participation in Gangs." In C.R. Huff (ed.), *Gangs in America* (pp. 163-182). Newbury Park, CA: Sage.

Campbell, B. (2008). "DCS Picks Up Funding of Program that Helps Juvenile Sex Offenders." *Johnson City Press* (September 13, 2008):4A.

Carpenter, C., B. Glassner, B.D. Johnson, and J. Loughlin (1988). *Kids, Drugs, and Crime.* Lexington, MA: Lexington Books.

Carroll, B.P. (2001). "Major Case Management: Key Components." *FBI Law Enforcement Bulletin* 70(6):1-4.

Cashel, M.L. (2003). "Validity of Self-reports of Delinquency and Socio-Emotional Functioning among Youth on Probation." *Journal of Offender Rehabilitation* 37:11-23.

Cavan, R.S., and T.N. Ferdinand (1981). *Juvenile Delinquency*, 4th ed. New York: Harper and Row.

Chaiken, J.M., and M.R. Chaiken (1982). *Varieties of Criminal Behavior.* Santa Monica, CA: RAND.

Chaiken, M.R. (2004). *Community Policing Beyond the Big Cities.* Washington, DC: National Institute of Justice.

Charters, C.A. (1994). "Volunteer Work Assumes a New Role in Public High School: *Steirer v. Bethlehem Area School District.*" *Journal of Law and Education* 23:607-613.

Chavaria, F.P. (1997). "Probation and Cognitive Skills." *Federal Probation* 61:57-60.

Chesney-Lind, M. (1977). "Judicial Paternalism and the Female Status Offender: Training Women to Know Their Place." *Crime & Delinquency* 23:121-130.

Chesney-Lind, M. (1987). "Girls' Crime and Woman's Place: Toward a Feminist Model of Female Delinquency." Paper presented at the Annual Meeting of the American Society of Criminology, New Orleans, LA.

Chesney-Lind, M., and R.G. Shelden (1992). *Girls, Delinquency, and Juvenile Justice.* Pacific Grove, CA: Brooks/Cole.

Child Welfare Gateway Information (2006). *What Is Child Abuse and Neglect?* Washington, DC: U.S. Department of Health and Human Services. Available at: http://www.childwelfare.gov/pubs/factsheets/whatiscan.cfm

Chilton, R.J. (1964). "Continuities in Delinquency Area Research: A Comparison of Studies for Baltimore, Detroit and Indianapolis." *American Sociological Review* 129:71-83.

Chin, K. (1990). *Chinese Subculture and Criminality: Nontraditional Crime Groups in America.* Westport, CT: Greenwood.

Chin, K., J. Fagan, and R.J. Kelly (1992). "Patterns of Chinese Gang Extortion." *Justice Quarterly* 9:625-646.

Christiansen, K.O. (1974). "Seriousness of Criminality and Concordance among Danish Twins." In R. Hood (ed.), *Crime, Criminology, and Public Policy.* New York: Free Press.

Chused, R. (1973). "The Juvenile Court Process: A Study of Three New Jersey Counties." *Rutgers Law Review* 26:488-615.

Clark, C.L., D.W. Aziz, and D.L. MacKenzie (1994). *Shock Incarceration in New York: Focus on Treatment.* Washington, DC: U.S. Department of Justice.

Clark, R.D., and S.P. Lab (1995). "The Relationship between Victimization and Offending among Junior and Senior High School Students." Paper presented at the Annual Meeting of the Academy of Criminal Justice Sciences, Boston, MA.

Clarke, J.P., and L.L. Tifft (1966). "Polygraph and Interview Validation of Self-reported Deviant Behavior." *American Sociological Review* 31:516-523.

Clarke, R.V., and M. Felson (1993). *Routine Activities and Rational Choice.* New Brunswick, NJ: Transaction.

Clarke, S.H., and G.G. Koch (1980). "Juvenile Court: Therapy or Crime Control, and Do Lawyers Make a Difference." *Law and Society Review* 14:263-308.

Clayton, R.R., A. Cattarello, and K.P. Walden (1991). "Sensation Seeking as a Potential Mediating Variable for School-based Prevention Interventions: A Two-year Follow-up of DARE." *Journal of Health Communications* 3:229-239.

Clear, T.R. (1994). *Harm in American Penology: Offenders, Victims, and Their Communities.* Albany, NY: SUNY Press.

Clear, T.R., and E. Cadora (2003). *Community Justice.* Belmont, CA: Wadsworth.

Clear, T.R., V.B. Clear, and A.A. Braga (1997). "Correctional Alternatives for Drug Offenders in an Era of Overcrowding." In M. McShane and F.P. Williams (eds.), *Criminal Justice: Contemporary Literature in Theory and Practice* (pp. 24-44). New York: Garland.

Clear, T.R., and D.R. Karp (1998). "Community Justice: An Essay." *Corrections Management Quarterly* 2(3):49-60.

Cloward, R., and L. Ohlin (1960). *Delinquency and Opportunity: A Theory of Delinquent Gangs.* New York: Free Press.

Cobbina, J.E., J. Miller, and R.K. Brunson (2008). "Gender, Neighborhood Danger, and Risk-Avoidance Strategies among Urban African-American Youths." *Criminology* 46:673-707.

Cocozza, J.J., and J.L. Shufelt (2006). *Juvenile Mental Health Courts: An Emerging Strategy.* Delmar, NY: The National Center for Mental Health and Juvenile Justice.

Cohen, A.K. (1955). *Delinquent Boys: The Culture of the Gang.* Glencoe, IL: Free Press.

Cohen, L.E., and J.R. Kluegel (1978). "Determinants of Juvenile Court Dispositions: Ascriptive and Achieved Factors in Two Metropolitan Courts." *American Sociological Review* 44:588-608.

Cohen, L.E., and J.R. Kluegel (1979). "Selecting Delinquents for Adjudication: An Analysis of Intake Screening Decisions in Two Metropolitan Juvenile Courts." *Journal of Research in Crime and Delinquency* 16:143-163.

Cohen, L.E., and M. Felson (1979). "Social Changes and Crime Rate Trends: A Routine Activities Approach." *American Sociological Review* 44:588-608.

Coles, C.M., and G.L. Kelling (2002). "New Trends in Prosecutors' Approaches to Youthful Offenders." In G.S. Katzman (ed.), *Securing Our Children's Future: New Approaches to Juvenile Justice and Youth Violence* (pp. 28-83). Washington, DC: Brookings Institution Press.

Collins, J.J. (1989). "Alcohol and Interpersonal Violence: Less than Meets the Eye." In N.A. Wiener and M.E. Wolfgang (eds.), *Pathways to Criminal Violence* (pp. 49-67). Newbury Park, CA: Sage.

Collins, J.J., R.L. Hubbard, and J.V. Rachal (1985). "Expensive Drug Use and Illegal Income: A Test of Explanatory Hypotheses." *Criminology* 23:743-764.

Colvin, M., F.T. Cullen, and T. Vander Ven (2002). "Coercion, Social Support, and Crime: An Emerging Theoretical Consensus." *Criminology* 40:19-42.

Colwell, B. (2002). "Shocking the Conscience: Excessive Discipline of Elementary and Secondary Students." *School Law Reporter* 44(1):1-3.

Colwell, B. (2003). "Student Speech at Graduation: When Does It Violate the Establishment Clause?" *School Law Reporter* 45(5):75-78.

Conger, R.D., and R.L. Simons (1997). "Life-course Contingencies in the Development of Adolescent Antisocial Behavior: A Matching Law Approach." In T.P. Thornberry (ed.), *Advances in Criminological Theory* (pp. 55-99). New York: Aldine.

Cook, P.J., M.H. Moore, and A.A. Braga (2002). "Gun Control." In J.Q. Wilson and J. Petersilia (eds.), *Crime: Public Policies for Crime Control* (pp. 291-330). Oakland, CA: ICS Press.

Cooley, C.H. (1902). *Human Nature and the Social Order.* New York: Scribner.

Coombs, R.H. (1981). "Back on the Streets: Therapeutic Communities' Impact upon Drug Abusers." *American Journal of Alcohol Abuse* 8:185-201.

Cooper, C.N. (1967). "The Chicago YMCA Detached Workers: Current Status of an Action Program." In M.W. Klein (ed.), *Juvenile Gangs in Context* (pp. 183-193). Englewood Cliffs, NJ: Prentice Hall.

Coordinating Council on Juvenile Justice and Delinquency Prevention (1996). *Combating Violence and Delinquency: The National Juvenile Justice Action Plan: Report.* Washington, DC: U.S. Department of Justice.

Corbett, R.P. (2001). "Juvenile Probation on the Eve of the Next Millennium." In J.L. Victor and J. Naughton (eds.), *Annual Edition: Criminal Justice* 01/02 (pp. 141-151). Guilford, CT: Dushkin.

Corbett, R.P. (2002). "Reinventing Probation and Reducing Youth Violence." In G.S. Katzmann (ed.), *Securing Our Children's Future: New Approaches to Juvenile Justice and Youth Violence* (pp. 175-199). Washington, DC: Brookings Institution Press.

Cordner, G., and E.P. Biebel (2005). "Problem-Oriented Policing in Practice." *Criminology & Public Policy* 4:155-180.

Corman, H., and N. Mocan (2005). "Carrots, Sticks, and Broken Windows." *Journal of Law and Economics* 48:235-265.

Cornish, D.B., and R.V. Clarke (1986). *The Reasoning Criminal.* New York: Springer-Verlag.

Corrado, R.R., I.M. Cohen, and C. Odgers (2003). "Multi-problem Violent Youths: A Challenge for the Restorative Justice Paradigm." In E.G.M. Weitekamp and H. Kerner (eds.), *Restorative Justice in Context: International Practice and Directions.* Portland, OR: Willan.

Corriero, M.A. (2006). *Judging Children as Children: A Proposal for a Juvenile Justice System.* Philadelphia: Temple University Press.

Cortes, J.B. (1972). *Delinquency and Crime.* New York: Seminar Press.

Costanzo, M. (1997). *Just Revenge: Costs and Consequences of the Death Penalty.* New York: St. Martin's Press.

Cox, S.M., W.S. Davidson, and T.S. Bynum (1995). "A Meta-Analytic Assessment of Delinquency-Related Outcomes of Alternative Education Programs." *Crime & Delinquency* 41:219-234.

Crank, J.P., and M. Caldero (1991). "The Production of Occupational Stress in Medium-sized Police Agencies: A Survey of Line Officers in Eight Municipal Departments." *Journal of Criminal Justice* 19:339-349.

Crawford, A., and T. Newburn (2003). *Youth Offending and Restorative Justice: Implementing Reform in Youth Justice*. Portland, OR: Willan.

Cromwell, P.F., J.N. Olson, and D.W. Avary (1991). *Breaking and Entering: An Ethnographic Analysis of Burglary*. Newbury Park, CA: Sage.

Cronin, R.C. (1994). *Boot Camps for Adult and Juvenile Offenders: Overview and Update*. Washington, DC: National Institute of Justice.

Crowe, R.R. (1972). "The Adopted Offspring of Women Criminal Offenders." *Archives of General Psychiatry* 27:600-603.

Cullen, F.T. (2007). "Make Rehabilitation Corrections' Guiding Paradigm." *Criminology & Public Policy* 6:717-728.

Cullen, F.T., K.R. Blevins, J.S. Trager, and P. Gendreau (2005). "The Rise and Fall of Boot Camps: A Case Study in Common Sense Corrections." *Journal of Offender Rehabilitation* 40:53-70.

Cullen, F.T., and J.P. Wright (1995). "The Future of Corrections." In B. Maguire and P. Radosh (eds.), *The Past, Present, and Future of American Criminal Justice* (pp. 198-219). New York: General Hall.

Cullen, F.T., J.P. Wright, and B.K. Applegate (1996). "Control in the Community: The Limits of Reform." In A.T. Harland (ed.), *Choosing Correctional Options that Work: Defining the Demand and Evaluating the Supply* (pp. 69-116). Thousand Oaks, CA: Sage.

Cullen, F.T., J.P. Wright, and M.B. Chamlin (1999). "Social Support and Social Reform: A Progressive Crime Control Agenda." *Crime & Delinquency* 45:188-207.

Cummings, S. (1993). "Anatomy of a Wilding Gang." In S. Cummings and D.J. Monti (eds.), *Gangs: The Origins and Impact of Contemporary Youth Gangs in the United States* (pp. 49-73). Albany, NY: SUNY Press.

Cummings, S., and D.J. Monti (1993). "Public Policy and Gangs: Social Science and the Urban Underclass." In S. Cummings and D.J. Monti (eds.), *Gangs: The Origins and Impact of Contemporary Youth Gangs in the United States* (pp. 305-320). Albany, NY: SUNY Press.

Curley, T. (1997). "Easing Teens into the Driver's Seat." *USA Today* (April 21, 1997):3A.

Curry, G.D., and S.H. Decker (1998). *Confronting Gangs: Crime and Community*. Los Angeles: Roxbury.

Curry, G.D., R.A. Ball, and S.H. Decker (1996). "Estimating the National Scope of Gang Crime from Law Enforcement Data." *Research in Brief*. Washington, DC: U.S. Department of Justice, Office of Justice Programs, National Institute of Justice.

Curry, G.D., R.J. Fox, R.A. Ball, and D. Stone (1993). *National Assessment of Law Enforcement Anti-Gang Information Resources—Final Report*. Washington, DC: U.S. Department of Justice, Office of Justice Programs, National Institute of Justice.

Curtis, L.A. (1974). *Criminal Violence: National Patterns and Behavior*. Lexington, MA: D.C. Heath.

Daly, K. (2002). "Restorative Justice: The Real Story." *Punishment and Society* 4:5-79.

Daly, K. (2003). "Making Variation a Virtue: Evaluating the Potential and Limits of Restorative Justice." In E.G.M. Weitekamp and H. Kerner (eds.), *Restorative Justice in Context: International Practices and Directions*. Portland, OR: Willan.

D'Angelo, J.M. (2007). "The Complex Nature of Juvenile Court Judges' Transfer Decisions: A Study of Judicial Attitudes." *Social Science Journal* 44:147-159.

Dannefer, D., and R.K. Schutt (1982). "Race and Juvenile Justice Processing in Court and Police Agencies." *American Journal of Sociology* 87:1113-1132.

Davis, R., and J. O'Donnell (2005). ""Black Boxes for Cars Slow to Catch On: Some Teenagers Call Tracking Driving an Invasion of Privacy." *USA Today* (June 3, 2005):1B. Available at: http://www.usatoday.com/educate/reading/black_boxes.pdf

Davis, S.M., and M.D. Schwartz (1987). *Children's Rights and the Law*. Lexington, MA: D.C. Heath.

Davis, S.M., E.S. Scott, W. Wadlington, and C.H. Whitebread (1997). *Children in the Legal System: Cases and Materials*, 2nd ed. Westbury, NY: Foundation Press.

de Beus, K., and N. Rodriguez (2007). "Restorative Justice Practice: An Examination of Program Completion and Recidivism." *Journal of Criminal Justice* 35:337-347.

Dean-Mooney, L. (2008). "A Lower Age Would Be Unsafe." *U.S. News & World Report* (September 15, 2008):10.

Decker, S., S. Pennel, and A. Caldwell (1997). *Illegal Firearms: Access and Use by Arrestees*. Washington, DC: National Institute of Justice.

Decker, S., and B. Van Winkle (1994). "Slinging Dope: The Role of Gangs and Gang Members in Drug Sales." *Justice Quarterly* 11:583-604.

Decker, S., R. Wright, and R. Logie (1993). "Perceptual Deterrence among Active Residential Burglars: A Research Note." *Criminology* 31:135-147.

DeFleur, M.L., and R. Quinney (1966). "A Reformulation of Sutherland's Differential Association Theory and a Strategy for Empirical Verification." *Journal of Research in Crime and Delinquency* 3:1-22.

DeLeon, G. (1984). "Program-based Evaluation Research in Therapeutic Communities." In F.M. Tims and J.P. Ludford (eds.), *Drug Abuse Treatment Evaluation: Strategies, Progress and Prospects* (pp. 69-87). Washington, DC: National Institute on Drug Abuse.

DeLeon, G., and M.S. Rosenthal (1989). "Treatment in Residential Therapeutic Communities." In T.B. Karasu (ed.), *Treatment of Psychiatric Disorders: A Task Force Report of the American Psychiatric Association,* Vol. 2 (pp. 1379-1396). Washington, DC: American Psychiatric Association.

DeLong, J.V. (1972). "Treatment and Rehabilitation." *Dealing with Drug Abuse: A Report to the Ford Foundation* (pp. 173-254). New York: Praeger.

Dentler, R.A., and L.J. Monroe (1961). "Social Correlates of Early Adolescent Theft." *American Sociological Review* 26:733-743.

DeVoe, J.F., K. Peter, P. Kaufman, A. Miller, M. Noonan, T.D. Snyder, and K. Baum (2004). *Indicators of School Crime and Safety, 2004*. Washington, DC: Bureau of Justice Statistics.

Dinkes, R., E.R. Cataldi, W. Lin-Kelly, and T.D. Snyder (2008). *Indicators of School Crime and Safety, 2007*. Washington, DC: Bureau of Justice Statistics.

Doerner, W.G., and S.P. Lab (2008). *Victimology*, 5th ed. Newark, NJ: LexisNexis Matthew Bender.

Drug Courts Program Office (2000). *About the Drug Courts Program Office.* Washington, DC: U.S. Department of Justice.

Dunworth, T. (2000). *National Evaluation of the Youth Firearms Initiative.* Washington, DC: U.S. Department of Justice.

Durkheim, E. (1933). *The Division of Labor in Society.* (Translated by G. Supson.) New York: Free Press.

Eck, J., and J. Maguire (2000). "Have Changes in Policing Reduced Violent Crime? An Assessment of the Evidence." In A. Blumstein and J. Wallman (eds.), *The Crime Drop in America* (pp. 207-265). Cambridge, England: Cambridge University Press.

Egley, A., J.C. Howell, and A.K. Major (2004). "Recent Patterns of Gang Problems in the United States: Results from the 1996-2002 National Youth Gang Survey." In F. Esbensen, S.G. Tibbetts, and L. Gaines (eds.), *American Youth Gangs at the Millennium* (pp. 90-108). Long Grove, IL: Waveland.

Egley, A., and C.E. O'Donnell (2008). *Highlights of the 2006 National Youth Gang Survey.* Washington, DC: Office of Juvenile Justice and Delinquency Prevention.

Ehrenkranz, J., E. Bliss, and M.H. Sheard (1974). "Plasma Testosterone: Correlation with Aggressive Behavior and Social Dominance in Man." *Psychosomatic Medicine* 36:469-475.

Eisen, M., G.L. Zellman, H.A. Massett, and D.L. Murray (2002). "Evaluating the Lions-Quest 'Skills for Adolescence' Drug Education Program: First Year Behavior Outcomes." *Addictive Behaviors* 27:619-632.

Eiser, C., and J.R. Eiser (1988). *Drug Education in Schools.* New York: Springer-Verlag.

Elliott, D.S. (1985). "The Assumption that Theories can be Combined with Increased Explanatory Power: Theoretical Integrations." In R.F. Meier (ed.), *Theoretical Methods in Criminology* (pp. 123-150). Beverly Hills: Sage.

Elliott, D.S., S.S. Ageton, and R.J. Canter (1979). *The Prevalence and Incidence of Delinquent Behavior: 1976-1980.* Boulder, CO: Behavioral Research Institute.

Elliott, D.S., and D. Huizinga (1984). *The Relationship between Delinquent Behavior and ADM Problems.* Boulder, CO: Behavioral Research Institute.

Elliott, D.S., D. Huizinga, and S.S. Ageton (1985). *Explaining Delinquency and Drug Use.* Beverly Hills: Sage.

Elliott, D.S., D. Huizinga, and S. Menard (1989). *Multiple Problem Youth: Delinquency, Substance Use and Mental Health Problems.* New York: Springer-Verlag.

Ellis, L. (1982). "Genetics and Criminal Behavior: Evidence through the End of the 1970s." *Criminology* 20:42-66.

Empey, L.T. (1982). *American Delinquency: Its Meaning and Construction.* Homewood, IL: Dorsey Press.

Engel, R.S. (2008). "A Critique of the 'Outcome Test' in Racial Profiling Research." *Justice Quarterly* 25:1-36.

Erikson, E.H. (1968). *Identity, Youth and Crisis.* New York: Norton.

Erickson, M.L. (1971). "The Group Context of Delinquent Behavior." *Social Problems* 19:114-129.

Erickson, M.L. (1973). "Group Violations and Official Delinquency: The Group Hazard Hypothesis." *Criminology* 11:127-160.

Esbensen, F., and D. Huizinga (1991). "Juvenile Victimization and Delinquency." *Youth and Society* 23:202-228.

Esbensen, F., and D. Huizinga (1993). "Gangs, Drugs and Delinquency in a Survey of Urban Youth." *Criminology* 31:565-590.

Esbensen, F., and D.W. Osgood (1997). "National Evaluation of G.R.E.A.T." *NIJ Research in Brief*. Washington, DC: National Institute of Justice.

Esbensen, F., D. Peterson, T.J. Taylor, A. Freng, and D.W. Osgood (2004). "Gang Prevention: A Case Study of a Primary Prevention Program." In F. Esbensen, S.G. Tibbetts, and L. Gaines (eds.), *American Youth Gangs at the Millennium* (pp. 351-274). Long Grove, IL: Waveland.

Eysenck, H.J., and G.H. Gudjonsson (1989). *The Causes and Cures of Criminality*. New York: Plenum.

Fabricant, M. (1983). *Juveniles in the Family Courts*. Lexington, MA: Lexington Books.

Fagan, J. (1990). "Social Process of Delinquency and Drug Use among Urban Gangs." In C.R. Huff (ed.), *Gangs in America* (pp. 183-219). Newbury Park, CA: Sage.

Fagan, J. (2002). "Policing Guns and Youth Violence." *Children, Youth and Gun Violence* 12:133-151.

Fagan, J. (2007). "End Natural Life Sentences for Juveniles." *Criminology & Public Policy* 6:735-746.

Fagan, J., and E. Pabon (1990). "Contributions of Delinquency and Substance Use to School Dropout Among Inner-city Youths." *Youth and Society* 21:306-354.

Fagan, J., and J.G. Weis (1990). *Drug Use and Delinquency among Inner City Youth*. New York: Springer-Verlag.

Fagan, J., J.G. Weis, and Y. Cheng (1990). "Delinquency and Substance Use among Inner City Students." *Journal of Drug Issues* 20:351-402.

Farrington, D.P., and B.C. Welsh (2007). *Saving Children from a Life of Crime: Early Risk Factors and Effective Interventions*. New York: Oxford University Press.

Fattah, E.A. (1993). "The Rational Choice/Opportunity Perspectives as a Vehicle for Integrating Criminological and Victimological Theories." In R.V. Clarke and M. Felson (eds.), *Routine Activity and Rational Choice* (pp. 225-258). New Brunswick, NJ: Transaction.

Faust, F.L., and P.J. Brantingham (1979). *Juvenile Justice Philosophy: Readings, Cases and Comments*. St. Paul, MN: West.

Federal Bureau of Investigation (n.d.). *Uniform Crime Reports*. Washington, DC: U.S. Department of Justice. Available at: http://www.fbi.gov/ucr/ucr.htm

Federal Bureau of Investigation (2007). *Crime in the United States, 2006*. Washington, DC: Federal Bureau of Investigation. Available at: http://www.fbi.gov/ucr/cius2006/index.html

Federal Bureau of Investigation (2008). *Crime in the United States, 2007*. Washington, DC: Federal Bureau of Investigation. Available at: http://www.fbi.gov/ucr/cius2007/index.html

Feld, B.C. (1981). "Legislative Policies toward the Serious Juvenile Offender: On the Virtues of Automatic Adulthood." *Crime & Delinquency* 27:497-521.

Feld, B.C. (1987). "The Juvenile Court Meets the Principle of the Offense: Legislative Changes in Juvenile Waiver Statutes." *The Journal of Criminal Law and Criminology* 78:471-533.

Feld, B.C. (1988). "*In re Gault* Revisited: A Cross-State Comparison of the Right to Counsel in Juvenile Court." *Crime & Delinquency* 34:393-424.

Feld, B.C. (1993). *Justice for Children: The Right to Counsel and the Juvenile Courts.* Boston: Northeastern University Press.

Feld, B.C. (1998). "Juvenile and Criminal Justice Systems' Responses to Youth Violence." In M. Tonry and M.H. Moore (eds.), *Youth Violence* (pp. 189-261). Chicago: University of Chicago Press.

Feld, B.C. (1999). *Bad Kids: Race and the Transformation of the Juvenile Court.* New York: Oxford University Press.

Feld, B.C. (2006). "Juveniles' Competence to Exercise *Miranda* Rights: An Empirical Study of Policy and Practice." *Minnesota Law Review* 91:26-100.

Feld, B.C. (2007). "A Century of Juvenile Justice: A Work in Progress or a Revolution that Failed?" *Northern Kentucky Law Review* 34:189-256.

Feld, B.C. (2008). "A Slower Form of Death: Implications of *Roper v. Simmons* for Juveniles Sentenced to Life Without Parole." *Notre Dame Journal of Law, Ethics & Public Policy* 22(1):9-65.

Fenwick, C.R. (1982). "Juvenile Court Intake Decision Making: The Importance of Family Affiliation." *Journal of Criminal Justice* 10:443-453.

Ferguson, A.A. (2000). *Bad Boys: Public Schools in the Making of Black Masculinity.* Ann Arbor, MI: University of Michigan Press.

Fernandez, M. (2008). "Young Suspects Get a Right Adults Have: A Judge on Weekends." *New York Times* (June 9, 2008). Available at: http://www.nytimes.com/2008/06/09/nyregion/09juvenile.html

Ferrer-Wreder, L., C.C. Lorente, E. Briones, J. Bussell, S. Berman, and O. Arrufat (2002). "Promoting Identity Development in Marginalized Youth." *Journal of Adolescent Research* 17:168-187.

Feyerhem, W. (1980). "The Group Hazard Hypothesis: A Reexamination." *Journal of Research in Crime and Delinquency* 17:58-68.

Fishman, L.T. (1988). "The Vice Queens: An Ethnographic Study of Black Female Gang Behavior." Paper presented at the Annual Meeting of the American Society of Criminology, Chicago, IL.

Foster, J.D., S. Dinitz, and W.C. Reckless (1972). "Perceptions of Stigma Public Intervention for Delinquent Behavior." *Social Problems* 20:202-209.

Fox, J.R. (1985). "Mission Impossible? Social Work Practice with Black Urban Youth Gangs." *Social Work* 30:25-31.

Franklin II, C.W., and A.P. Franklin (1976). "Victimology Revisited: A Critique and Suggestions for Future Direction." *Criminology* 14:177-214.

Frazier, C.E., and D.M. Bishop (1985). "The Pretrial Detention of Juveniles and Its Impact on Case Dispositions." *Journal of Criminal Law and Criminology* 76:1132-1152.

Frazier, C.E., and D.M. Bishop (1995). "Reflections on Race Effects in Juvenile Justice." In K. Kempf-Leonard, C.E. Pope, and W.H. Feyerherm (eds.), *Minorities in Juvenile Justice* (pp. 16-46). Thousand Oaks, CA: Sage.

Gaarder, E., and J. Belknap (2004). "Little Women: Girls in Adult Prison." *Women & Criminal Justice* 15(2):51-80.

Gaarder, E., N. Rodriguez, and M. Zatz (2004). "Criers, Liars, and Manipulators: Probation Officers' Views of Girls." *Justice Quarterly* 21:547-578.

Gallup Organization (2001). "Firefighters Top Gallup's 'Honesty and Ethics' List." *The Gallup Poll Monthly* 435:46-48.

Garbarino, J., and G. Gilliam (1980). *Understanding Abusive Families*. Lexington, MA: Lexington Books.

Garland, D. (2001). *The Culture of Control: Crime and Social Order in Contemporary Society*. Chicago: University of Chicago Press.

Garofalo, J., and K.J. Connelly (1980). "Dispute Resolution Centers, Part I: Major Features and Processes." *Criminal Justice Abstracts* 12:416-436.

Garry, E.M. (1996). *Truancy: First Step to a Lifetime of Problems*. Washington, DC: U.S. Department of Justice.

Gates, L.B., and W.M. Rohe (1987). "Fear and Reactions to Crime: A Revised Model." *Urban Affairs Quarterly* 22:425-453.

Gay, B.W., and J.W. Marquart (1993). "Jamaican Posses: A New Form of Organized Crime." *Journal of Crime and Justice* 16:139-170.

Geary, D.P. (1983). "Nutrition, Chemicals and Criminal Behavior: Some Psychological Aspects of Anti-social Conduct." *Juvenile and Family Court Journal* 34:9-13.

Geiselman, R.E., G. Bornstein, and K.J. Saywitz (1992). *New Approach to Interviewing Children: A Test of Its Effectiveness*. Washington, DC: U.S. Department of Justice.

Geller, W.A. (1983). "Deadly Force: What We Know." In C.B. Klockars (ed.), *Thinking about Police: Contemporary Readings* (pp. 313-331). New York: McGraw-Hill.

Geller, W.A., and H. Toch (1996). "Understanding and Controlling Police Abuse of Force." In W.A. Geller and H. Toch (eds.), *Police Violence: Understanding and Controlling Police Abuse of Force* (pp. 292-328). New Haven, CT: Yale University Press.

Gelles, R.J. (1980). "Violence in the Family: A Review of Research in the 70's." *Journal of Marriage and the Family* 42:873-885.

Gelles, R.J., and C.P. Cornell (1990). *Intimate Violence in Families*. Beverly Hills: Sage.

Gendreau, P. (1996). "The Principles of Effective Intervention with Offenders." In A.T. Harland (ed.), *Choosing Correctional Options That Work: Defining the Demand and Evaluating the Supply* (pp. 117-130). Thousand Oaks, CA: Sage.

Gendreau, P., F.T. Cullen, and J. Bonta (1994). "Intensive Rehabilitation Supervision: The Next Generation in Community Corrections?" *Federal Probation* 58(1):72-78.

Geraghty, T.F. (1998). "Justice for Children: How Do We Get There?" *Journal of Criminal Law and Criminology* 88:190-241.

Giallombardo, R. (1974). *The Social Work of Imprisoned Girls*. New York: John Wiley.

Gil, D. (1971). *Violence Against Children: Physical Child Abuse in the United States*. Cambridge, MA: Harvard University Press.

Giordano, P.C., S.A. Cernkovich, and M.D. Pugh (1986). "Friendship and Delinquency." *American Journal of Sociology* 91:1170-1202.

Girshick, L.B. (1999). *No Safe Haven: Stories of Women in Prison.* Boston: Northeastern University Press.

Glaser, D. (1956). "Criminality Theories and Behavioral Images." *American Journal of Sociology* 61:434-444.

Glaser, D. (1964). *The Effectiveness of a Prison and Parole System.* Indianapolis: Bobbs-Merrill.

Glasser, W. (1965). *Reality Therapy.* New York: Harper and Row.

Glueck, S., and E. Glueck (1956). *Physique and Delinquency.* New York: Harper.

Goddard, H.H. (1920). *Efficiency and Levels of Intelligence.* Princeton, NJ: Princeton University Press.

Goffman, E. (1961). *Asylums: Essays on the Situation of Mental Patients and Other Inmates.* Garden City, NY: Anchor Books.

Gold, M. (1970). *Delinquent Behavior in an American City.* Belmont, CA: Brooks/Cole.

Goldkamp, J.S., and D. Weiland (1993). "Assessing the Impact of Dade County's Felony Drug Court." *NIJ Research in Brief.* Washington, DC: U.S. Department of Justice.

Goldman, D., J. Lappalainen, and N. Ozaki (1996). "Direct Analysis of Candidate Genes in Impulsive Behavior." In G.R. Bock and J.A. Goode (eds.), *Genetics of Criminal and Antisocial Behavior* (pp. 139-152). Chicester, England: John Wiley and Sons.

Goldstein, A.P. (1993). "Gang Intervention: A Historical Review." In A.P. Goldstein and C.R. Huff (eds.), *The Gang Intervention Handbook* (pp. 21-51). Champaign, IL: Research Press.

Goldstein, H. (1990). *Problem-Oriented Policing.* New York: McGraw-Hill.

Goldstein, P.J. (1989). "Drugs and Violent Crime." In N.A. Weiner and M.E. Wolfgang (eds.), *Pathways to Criminal Violence* (pp. 16-48). Newbury Park, CA: Sage.

Golub, A., B.D. Johnson, and E. Dunlap (2007). "The Race/Ethnicity Disparity in Misdemeanor Marijuana Arrests in New York City." *Criminology & Public Policy* 6:131-164.

Gordon, J.A., L.J. Moriarty, and P.H. Grant (2003). "Juvenile Correctional Officers' Perceived Fear and Risk of Victimization: Examining Individual and Collective Levels of Victimization in Two Juvenile Correctional Centers in Virginia." *Criminal Justice and Behavior* 30:62-84.

Goring, C. (1913). *The English Convict: A Statistical Study.* Montclair, NJ: Patterson Smith.

Gottfredson, D.C., and W.H. Barton (1993). "Deinstitutionalization of Juvenile Offenders." *Criminology* 31:591-611.

Gottfredson, D.C., S.S. Najaka, and B. Kearley (2003). "Effectiveness of Drug Treatment Courts: Evidence from a Randomized Trial." *Criminology & Public Policy* 2:171-198.

Gottfredson, D.M. (1987). "Prediction and Classification in Criminal Justice Decision Making." In D.M. Gottfredson and M. Tonry (eds.), *Prediction and Classification: Criminal Justice Decision Making* (pp. 1-20). Chicago: University of Chicago Press.

Gottfredson, M.R., and T. Hirschi (1990). *A General Theory of Crime.* Stanford, CA: Stanford University Press.

Gould, J.B., and S.D. Mastrofski (2004). "Suspect Searches: Assessing Police Behavior under the U.S. Constitution." *Criminology & Public Policy* 3:315-362.

Gover, A.R., and D.L. MacKenzie (2003). "Child Maltreatment and Adjustment to Juvenile Correctional Institutions." *Criminal Justice and Behavior* 30:374-396.

Graham, S., and B.S. Lowery (2004). "Priming Unconscious Racial Stereotypes about Adolescent Offenders." *Law and Human Behavior* 28:483-504.

Granfield, R., C. Eby, and T. Brewster (1998). "An Examination of the Denver Drug Court: The Impact of a Treatment-oriented Drug-offender System." *Law and Policy* 20:183-202.

Grasmick, H.G., C.R. Tittle, R.J. Bursik, and B.J. Ameklev (1993). "Testing the Core Empirical Implications of Gottfredson and Hirschi's General Theory of Crime." *Journal of Research in Crime and Delinquency* 30:5-29.

Gray, G.E., and L.K. Gray (1983). "Diet and Juvenile Delinquency." *Nutrition Today* 18:14-21.

Greenbaum, S. (1994). "Drugs, Delinquency and Other Data." *Juvenile Justice* 2(1):2-8.

Greenberg, M.T., and C. Kusche (1998). *Promoting Alternative Thinking Strategies (PATHS): Blueprints for Violence Prevention.* Boulder, CO: Institute of Behavioral Science.

Griffin, P. (2005). "National Overviews." *State Juvenile Justice Profiles.* Pittsburgh: National Center for Juvenile Justice. Available at: http://www.ncjj.org/stateprofiles/

Griffin, P. (2007). "National Overviews." *State Juvenile Justice Profiles.* Pittsburgh: National Center for Juvenile Justice. Available at: http://www.ncjj.org/stateprofiles/

Griffin, P., and M. King (2005). "National Overviews." *State Juvenile Justice Profiles.* Pittsburgh: National Center for Juvenile Justice. Available at: http://www.ncjj.org/stateprofiles/

Griffin, P., and D. Thomas (2004). "The Good News: Measuring Juvenile Outcomes at Case Closing." *Pennsylvania Progress* 10(2):1-6.

Griffin, P., and P. Torbet (2002). *Desktop Guide to Good Juvenile Probation Practice.* Pittsburgh: National Center for Juvenile Justice.

Griffin, P., L. Szymanski, and M. King (2005). "National Overviews." *State Juvenile Justice Profiles.* Pittsburgh: National Center for Juvenile Justice. Available at: http://www.ncjj.org/stateprofiles/

Griffin, P., L. Szymanski, and M. King (2006). "National Overviews." *State Juvenile Justice Profiles.* Pittsburgh: National Center for Juvenile Justice. Available at: http://www.ncjj.org/stateprofiles/

Grisso, T.P., and R.G. Schwartz (2000). *Youth on Trial: A Developmental Perspective on Juvenile Justice.* Chicago: University of Chicago Press.

Guevara, L., C. Spohn, and D. Herz (2004). "Race, Legal Representation, and Juvenile Justice: Issues and Concerns." *Crime & Delinquency* 50:344-371.

Hagan, J., and B. McCarthy, in collaboration with P. Parker and J. Climenhage (1997). *Mean Streets: Youth Crime and Homelessness.* New York: Cambridge University Press.

Hagedorn, J.M. (1988). *People and Folks: Gangs, Crime and the Underclass in a Rustbelt City.* Chicago: Lakeview Press.

Hagedorn, J.M. (1994). "Homeboys, Dope Fiends, Legits, and New Jacks." *Criminology* 32:197-220.

Hansen, D.J. (1980). "Drug Education: Does it Work?" In F.S. Scarpitti and S.K. Datesman (eds.), *Drugs and Youth Culture* (pp. 251-282). Beverly Hills: Sage.

Hansen, W.B., C.A. Johnson, B.R. Flay, J.W. Graham, and J.L. Sobel (1988). "Affective and Social Influences Approaches to the Prevention of Multiple Substance Abuse among Seventh Grade Students: Results from Project SMART." *Preventive Medicine* 17:135-154.

Harcourt, B.E. (2001). *Illusion of Order: The False Promise of Broken Windows Policing*. Cambridge, MA: Harvard University Press.

Harcourt, B.E. (2004). "Unconstitutional Police Searches and Collective Responsibility." *Criminology & Public Policy* 3:363-378.

Harcourt, B.E., and J. Ludwig (2006). "Broken Windows: New Evidence from New York City and a Five-City Social Experiment." *University of Chicago Law Review* 73:271-320.

Harding, R.W. (1993). "Gun Use in Crime, Rational Choice, and Social Learning Theory." In R.V. Clarke and M. Felson (eds.), *Routine Activity and Rational Choice* (pp. 85-102). New Brunswick, NJ: Transaction.

Hardt, R.H., and S. Peterson-Hardt (1977). "On Determining the Quality of Delinquency Self-report Method." *Journal of Research in Crime and Delinquency* 14:247-261.

Harp, C., M. Kuykendall, M. Cunningham, and T. Ware (2004). *Juvenile Delinquency and Community Prosecution: New Strategies for Old Problems*. Alexandria, VA: American Prosecutors Research Institute.

Harrell, A. (1998). "Drug Courts and the Role of Graduated Sanctions." *NIJ Research Preview*. Washington, DC: National Institute of Justice.

Harrell, E. (2005). "Violence by Gang Members, 1993-2003." *Crime Data Brief*. Washington, DC: Bureau of Justice Statistics.

Harris, J.A. (1999). "Review and Methodological Considerations in Research on Testosterone and Aggression." *Aggression and Violent Behavior* 4:273-291.

Harris, N. (2003). "Evaluating the Practice of Restorative Justice: The Case of Family Group Conferencing." In L. Walgrave (ed.), *Repositioning Restorative Justice*. Portland, OR: Willan.

Harvard Law Review (2005). "Juvenile Curfews and the Major Confusion over Minor Rights." *Harvard Law Review* 118:2400-2421.

Hawkins, J.D., R.F. Catalano, R. Kosterman, R. Abbott, and K.G. Hill (1999). "Preventing Adolescent Health-risk Behaviors by Strengthening Protection During Childhood." *Archives of Pediatric and Adolescent Medicine* 153:226-234.

Hayes, H., and K. Daly (2004). "Conferencing and Re-offending in Queensland." *Australian and New Zealand Journal of Criminology* 37:167-191.

Hayes, L.M. (2004). *Juvenile Suicide in Confinement: A National Survey*. Baltimore, MD: National Center on Institutions and Alternatives.

Henggeler, S.W., C.A. Halliday-Boykins, P.B. Cunningham, J. Randall, S.B. Shapiro, and J.E. Chapman (2006). "Juvenile Drug Court: Enhancing Outcomes by Integrating Evidence-based Treatments." *Journal of Consulting and Clinical Psychology* 74:42-54.

Henretta, J.C., C.E. Frazier, and D.M. Bishop (1985). "Juvenile Justice Decision-Making: An Analysis of the Effects of Prior Case Outcomes." Paper presented at the Annual Meeting of the American Society of Criminology, San Diego, CA.

Henretta, J.C., C.E. Frazier, and D.M. Bishop (1986). "The Effect of Prior Case Outcomes on Juvenile Justice Decision-Making." *Social Forces* 65:554-562.

Herrnstein, R.J., and C. Murray (1994). *The Bell Curve: Intelligence and Class Structure in American Life*. New York: Free Press.

Hills, S.L. (1980). *Demystifying Social Deviance*. New York: McGraw-Hill.

Hindelang, M.J. (1971). "The Social versus Solitary Nature of Delinquent Involvement." *British Journal of Criminology* 11:167-175.

Hindelang, M.J. (1973). "Causes of Delinquency: A Partial Replication and Extension." *Social Problems* 20:470-487.

Hindelang, M.J. (1975). *Public Opinion Regarding Crime, Criminal Justice, and Related Topics*. Washington, DC: U.S. Department of Justice.

Hindelang, M.J., M.R. Gottfredson, and J. Garofalo (1978). *Victims of Personal Crime: An Empirical Foundation for a Theory of Personal Victimization*. Cambridge, MA: Ballinger.

Hindelang, M.J., T. Hirschi, and J.G. Weis (1981). *Measuring Delinquency*. Beverly Hills: Sage.

Hippchen, L.J. (1978). *Ecologic-Biochemical Approaches to Treatment of Delinquents and Criminals*. New York: Van Nostrand Reinhold.

Hippchen, L.J. (1981). "Some Possible Biochemical Aspects of Criminal Behavior." *International Journal of Biosocial Research* 2:37-48.

Hirschel, J.D., C.W. Dean, and D. Dumond (2001). "Juvenile Curfews and Race: A Cautionary Note." *Criminal Justice Policy Review* 12:197-214.

Hirschi, T. (1969). *Causes of Delinquency*. Berkeley: University of California Press.

Hirschi, T., and M.J. Hindelang (1977). "Intelligence and Delinquency: A Revisionist Review." *American Sociological Review* 42:572-587.

Holtz, L.E. (1987). "*Miranda* in a Juvenile Setting: A Child's Right to Silence." *The Journal of Criminal Law and Criminology* 78:534-556.

Hooten, E. (1931). *Crime and Man*. Cambridge, MA: Harvard University Press.

Hope, T. (1997). "Inequality and the Future of Community Crime Prevention." In S.P. Lab (ed.), *Crime Prevention at a Crossroads* (pp. 143-158). Cincinnati: Anderson.

Horney, J. (1978). "Menstrual Cycles and Criminal Responsibility." *Law and Human Behavior* 2:25-36.

Horowitz, M.A. (2000). "Kids Who Kill: A Critique of How the American Legal System Deals with Juveniles Who Commit Homicide." *Law and Contemporary Problems* 63:133-177.

Horowitz, R. (1983). *Honor and the American Dream: Culture and Identity in a Chicano Community*. New Brunswick, NJ: Rutgers University Press.

Howell, J.C. (1997a). "Youth Gangs." *OJJDP Fact Sheet* #72. Washington, DC: Office of Juvenile Justice and Delinquency Prevention.

Howell, J.C. (1997b). *Youth Gang Homicides and Drug Trafficking*. Washington, DC: Office of Juvenile Justice and Delinquency Prevention.

Howell, J.C. (2000). *Youth Gang Programs and Strategies: Summary*. Washington, DC: Office of Juvenile Justice and Delinquency Prevention.

Howell, J.C. (2003). *Preventing and Reducing Juvenile Delinquency: A Comprehensive Framework*. Thousand Oaks, CA: Sage.

Howell, J.C., and J.D. Hawkins (1998). "Prevention of Youth Violence." In M. Tonry and M.H. Moore, *Youth Violence* (pp. 189-261). Chicago: University of Chicago Press.

Hser, Y., M.D. Anglin, and C. Chou (1988). "Evaluation of Drug Abuse Treatment: A Repeated Measure Design Assessing Methadone Maintenance." *Evaluation Review* 12:547-570.

Hsia, H.M., G.S. Bridges, and R. McHale (2004). *Disproportionate Minority Confinement 2002 Update: Summary*. Washington, DC: U.S. Department of Justice.

Huang, D.T. (2001). "Less Unequal Footing: State Courts' Per Se Rules for Juvenile Waivers During Interrogation and the Case for Their Implementation." *Cornell Law Review* 86:437.

Huba, G.J., and P.M. Bentler (1983). "Causal Models of the Development of Law Abidance and its Relationship to Psychosocial Factors and Drug Use." In W.S. Laufer and J.M. Day (eds.), *Personality Theory, Moral Development and Criminal Behavior* (pp. 165-215). Lexington, MA: D.C. Heath.

Hubbard, R.L., M.E. Marsden, J.V. Rachal, H.J. Harwood, E.R. Cavanaugh, and H.M. Ginzbury (1989). *Drug Abuse Treatment: A National Study of Effectiveness*. Chapel Hill, NC: University of North Carolina Press.

Huebner, B.M., J.A. Shafer, and T.S. Bynum (2004). "African American and White Perceptions of Police Service: Within- and Between-Group Variation." *Journal of Criminal Justice* 32:123-135.

Huff, C.R. (1990). "Denial, Overreaction, and Misidentification: A Postscript on Public Policy." In C.R. Huff (ed.), *Gangs in America* (pp. 310-317). Newbury Park, CA: Sage.

Huff, C.R. (1993). "Gangs in the United States." In A.P. Goldstien and C.R. Huff (eds.), *The Gang Intervention Handbook* (pp. 3-20). Champaign, IL: Research Press.

Huizinga, D., R. Loeber, and T.P. Thornberry (1995). *Urban Delinquency and Substance Abuse: Research Summary*. Washington, DC: Office of Juvenile Justice and Delinquency Prevention.

Huizinga, D., S. Menard, and D. Elliot (1989). "Delinquency and Drug Use: Temporal and Developmental Patterns." *Justice Quarterly* 6:419-456.

Huizinga, D., T.P. Thornberry, K.E. Knight, P.J. Lovegrove, R. Loeber, K. Hill, and D.P. Farrington (2007). "Disproportionate Minority Contact in the Juvenile Justice System: A Study of Differential Minority Arrest/Referral to Court in Three Cities." An unpublished report submitted to the Office of Juvenile Justice and Delinquency Prevention. Available from the National Criminal Justice Reference Service.

Human Rights Watch (2001). *No Escape: Male Rape in United States Prisons*. New York: Human Rights Watch.

Human Rights Watch (2006). *Custody and Control: Conditions of Confinement in New York's Juvenile Prisons for Girls*. New York: Human Rights Watch.

Human Rights Watch (2008). *The Rest of Their Lives: Life Without Parole for Youth Offenders in the United States in 2008*. New York: Human Rights Watch.

Humes, E. (1996). *No Matter How Loud I Shout: A Year in the Life of Juvenile Court*. New York: Simon & Schuster.

Hunter, A. (1985) "Private, Parochial and Public School Orders: The Problem of Crime and Incivility in Urban Communities." In G.D. Suttles and M.N. Zald (eds.), *The Challenge of Social Control: Citizenship and Institution Building in Modern Society.* Norwood, NJ: Ablex.

Hurst, Y.G. (2007). "Juvenile Attitudes toward the Police." *Criminal Justice Review* 32:121-141.

Hurst, Y.G., and J. Frank (2000). "How Kids View Cops: The Nature of Juvenile Attitudes toward the Police." *Journal of Criminal Justice* 28:189-202.

Hutchings, B., and S.A. Mednick (1977). "Criminality in Adoptees and Their Adoptive and Biological Parents: A Pilot Study." In S.A. Mednick and K.O. Christiansen (eds.), *Biosocial Bases of Criminal Behavior* (pp. 127-141). New York: Gardner Press.

Hutchinson, R., and C. Kyle (1993). "Hispanic Street Gangs in Chicago's Public Schools." In S. Cummings and D.J. Monti (eds.), *Gangs: The Origins and Impact of Contemporary Youth Gangs in the United States* (pp. 113-136). Albany, NY: SUNY Press.

Inciardi, J.A., R. Horowitz, and A.E. Pottieger (1993). *Street Kids, Street Drugs, Street Crime: An Examination of Drug Use and Serious Delinquency in Miami.* Belmont, CA: Wadsworth.

Inderbitzin, M. (2006a). "A Look from the Inside: Balancing Custody and Treatment in a Juvenile Maximum-Security Facility." *International Journal of Offender Therapy and Comparative Criminology* 51:348-362.

Inderbitzin, M. (2006b). "Lessons from a Juvenile Training School: Survival and Growth." *Journal of Adolescent Research* 21:7-26.

Institute of Judicial Administration—American Bar Association (1980). *Juvenile Justice Standards Project: Standards Relating to Adjudication*, 2nd ed. Cambridge, MA: Ballinger.

Institute of Judicial Administration—American Bar Association (1982). *Juvenile Justice Standards Project: Standards for Juvenile Justice: A Summary and Analysis*, 2nd ed. Cambridge, MA: Ballinger.

Jablecki, L.T. (2005). "A Critique of Faith-based Prison Programs." *The Humanist* 65:11-16.

James, D.J., and L.E. Glaze (2006). "Mental Health Problems of Prison and Jail Inmates." *Bureau of Justice Statistics Special Report.* Washington, DC: U.S. Department of Justice.

Jang, S.J., and B.R. Johnson (2001). "Neighborhood Disorder, Individual Religiosity, and Adolescent Use of Illicit Drugs: A Test of Multilevel Hypotheses." *Criminology* 39:109-144.

Jankowski, M.S. (1991). *Islands in the Street: Gangs and American Urban Society.* Berkeley, CA: University of California Press.

Jeffery, C.R. (1965). "Criminal Behavior and Learning Theory." *Journal of Criminal Law, Criminology and Police Science* 56:294-300.

Jensen, G.F. (1972). "Delinquent and Adolescent Self-Conceptions: A Study of the Personal Relevance of Infractions." *Social Problems* 20:84-103.

Jensen, G.F., and D. Brownfield (1983). "Parents and Drugs." *Criminology* 21:543-554.

Jensen, G.F., and D. Brownfield (1986). "Gender, Lifestyles and Victimization: Beyond Routine Activity." *Violence and Victims* 1:85-99.

Joe, D., and N. Robinson (1980). "Chinatown's Immigrant Gangs: The New Young Warrior Class." *Criminology* 18:337-345.

Johnson, B.D., P.J. Goldstein, E. Prebel, J. Schmeidler, D.S. Lipton, B. Sprunt, and T. Miller (1985). *Taking Care of Business: The Economics of Crime by Heroin Abusers.* Lexington, MA: Lexington Books.

Johnson, B.D., E.D. Wish, J. Schmeidler, and D. Huizinga (1991). "Concentration of Delinquent Offending: Serious Drug Involvement and High Delinquency Rates." *Journal of Drug Issues* 21:205-229.

Johnson, K. (2005). "U.S. Gang Membership May be Higher than Reported." *USA Today.* Available at: http://www.usatoday.com/news/nation/2005-08-03-gangs-under-estimated_x.htm

Johnston, L.D., P.M. O'Malley, and J.G. Bachman (1987). *National Trends in Drug Use and Related Factors among American High School Students and Young Adults, 1975-1986.* Rockville, MD: National Institute on Drug Abuse.

Johnston, L.D., P.M. O'Malley, and J.G. Bachman (1996). *National Survey Results on Drug Use from the Monitoring the Future Study, 1975-1995.* Washington, DC: U.S. Department of Health and Human Services.

Johnston, L.D., P.M. O'Malley, J.G. Bachman, and J.E. Schulenberg (2007). *Overall Illicit Drug Use by American Teens Continues Gradual Decline in 2007.* Ann Arbor, MI: University of Michigan. Available at: http://www.monitoringthefuture.org

Johnston, L.D., P.M. O'Malley, and L.K. Eveland (1978). "Drugs and Delinquency: A Search for Causal Connections." In D.B. Kandel (ed.), *Longitudinal Research on Drug Use: Empirical Findings and Methodological Issues* (pp. 137-156). Washington, DC: Hemisphere.

Johnstone, J.W.C. (1981). "Youth Gangs and Black Suburbs." *Pacific Sociological Review* 58:355-375.

Jones, J.B. (2004). *Access to Counsel.* Washington, DC: U.S. Department of Justice.

Juvenile Justice Update (1995). "Juveniles Subject to Warrantless Search as a Probation Condition Have No Expectation of Privacy." *Juvenile Justice Update* (April/May) 2:8.

Juvenile Law Center (2005). "Amicus Brief for *In re Christopher K., a Minor.*" Available at: http://www.jlc.org

Kandel, D.B. (1973). "Adolescent Marijuana Use: Role of Parents and Peers." *Science* 181:1067-1070.

Kandel, D.B., O. Simcha-Fagan, and M. Davies (1986). "Risk Factors for Delinquency and Illicit Drug Use from Adolescence to Young Adulthood." *Journal of Drug Issues* 16:67-90.

Kanter, D., and W. Bennett (1968). "Orientation of Street-Corner Workers and Their Effects on Gangs." In S. Wheeler (ed.), *Controlling Delinquents.* New York: Wiley.

Kaplan, J. (1983). *The Hardest Drug: Heroin and Drug Policy.* Chicago: University of Chicago Press.

Karp, D.R. (1998). "The Judicial and Judicious Use of Shame Penalties." *Crime & Delinquency* 44:277-294.

Karp, D.R. (2001). "The Offender/Community Encounter: Stakeholder Involvement in the Vermont Reparative Boards." In D.R. Karp and T. Clear (eds.), *What Is Community Justice? Case Studies of Restorative Justice and Community Supervision* (pp. 61-86). Thousand Oaks, CA: Sage.

Karp, D.R., G. Bazemore, and J.D. Chesire (2004). "The Role and Attitudes of Restorative Board Members: A Case Study of Volunteers in Community Justice." *Crime & Delinquency* 50:487-515.

Karp, D.R., M. Sweet, A. Kirshenbaum, and G. Bazemore (2004). "Reluctant Participants in Restorative Justice? Youthful Offenders and Their Parents." *Contemporary Justice Review* 7:199-216.

Katz, C.M., and V.J. Webb (2003). *Police Response to Gangs: A Multi-Site Study—Final Report*. Washington, DC: National Institute of Justice.

Katz, J., and W.J. Chambliss (1995). "Biology and Crime." In J.F. Sheley (ed.), *Criminology: A Contemporary Handbook* (pp. 275-304). Belmont, CA: Wadsworth.

Kaufman, P., X. Chen, S.P. Choy, K.A. Chandler, C.D. Chapman, M.R. Rand, and C. Ringel (1998). *Indicators of School Crime and Safety, 1998*. Washington, DC: Office of Educational Research and Improvement.

Kelley, T.M., D.B. Kennedy, and R.J. Homant (2003). "Evaluation of an Individualized Treatment Program for Adolescent Shoplifters." *Adolescence* 38:725-733.

Kelling, G. (1975). "Leadership in the Gang." In D.S. Cartwright, B. Tomson, and H. Schwartz (eds.), *Gang Delinquency* (pp. 111-126). Monterey: Brooks/Cole.

Kelling, G.L., and C.M. Coles (1996). *Fixing Broken Windows: Restoring Order and Reducing Crime in Our Communities*. New York: Touchstone.

Kelling, G.L., and W. Sousa (2001). "Do Police Matter? An Analysis of the Impact of New York City's Police Reforms." *Civic Report No. 22*. New York: Manhattan Institute.

Kelly, W.R., T.S. Macy, and D.P. Mears (2005). "Juvenile Referrals in Texas: An Assessment of the Criminogenic Needs and the Gap between Needs and Services." *Prison Journal* 85:467-489.

Kempf-Leonard, K. (2007). "Minority Youths and Juvenile Justice: Disproportionate Minority Contact After Nearly 20 Years of Reform Efforts." *Youth Violence and Juvenile Justice* 5:71-87.

Kennedy, D. (1998). "Pulling Levers: Getting Deterrence Right." *National Institute of Justice Journal* 236:2-8.

Kennedy, L.W., and D.R. Forde (1990). "Routine Activities and Crime: An Analysis of Victimization Data in Canada." *Criminology* 28:137-152.

Kerbs, J.J. (1999). "(Un)equal Justice: Juvenile Court Abolition and African Americans." *Annals of the American Academy of Political and Social Science* 564:109-125.

Kim, S. (1988). "A Short- and Long-term Evaluation of Here's Looking at You Alcohol Education Program." *Journal of Drug Education* 18:235-242.

Kim, S., J.H. McLeod, and C. Shantzis (1993). "An Outcome Evaluation of Here's Looking at You 2000." *Journal of Drug Education* 23:67-81.

Kinder, B.N., N.E. Pape, and S. Walfish (1980). "Drug and Alcohol Education Programs: A Review of Outcome Studies." *International Journal of the Addictions* 15:1035-1054.

King, M., and L. Szymanski (2006). "National Overviews." *State Juvenile Justice Profiles*. Pittsburgh: National Center for Juvenile Justice. Available at: http://www.ncjj.org/stateprofiles/

Klein, A., and C.D. Leonnig (2007). "Officers in District Shooting Defended: 22-Year Veteran Who Killed Teen Has 'Stellar History.'" *Washington Post* (October 7, 2007):C01.

Klein, M.W. (1969). "Gang Cohesiveness, Delinquency, and a Street-work Program." *Journal of Research in Crime and Delinquency* 6:135-166.

Klein, M.W. (1971). *Street Gangs and Street Workers*. Englewood Cliffs, NJ: Prentice Hall.

Klein, M.W. (1995). The American Street Gang: Its Nature, Prevalence and Control. New York: Oxford University Press.

Klein, M.W., and C.L. Maxson (1989). "Street Gang Violence." In N.A. Weiner and M.E. Wolfgang (eds.), *Violent Crime, Violent Criminals* (pp. 198-234). Newbury Park, CA: Sage.

Klein, M.W., and C.L. Maxson (2006). *Street Gang Patterns and Policies*. New York: Oxford University Press.

Klein, M.W, C.L. Maxson, and L.C. Cunningham (1991). "Crack, Street Gangs, and Violence." *Criminology* 29:623-650.

Kohlberg, L. (1981). *The Philosophy of Moral Development*. San Francisco: Harper and Row.

Kornhauser, R.R. (1978). *Social Sources of Delinquency*. Chicago: University of Chicago Press.

Kovach, G.C. (2008). "To Curb Truancy, Dallas Tries Electronic Monitoring." *New York Times* (May 12, 2008). Available at: http://www.nytimes.com/2008/05/12/education/12dallas.html?_r=1&partner=rssnyt&emc=rss&oref=slogin

Kreuz, L.E., and R.M. Rose (1972). "Assessment of Aggressive Behavior and Plasma Testosterone in a Young Criminal Population." *Psychosomatic Medicine* 34:321-332.

Krisberg, B. (2005). *Juvenile Justice: Redeeming Our Children*. Thousand Oaks, CA: Sage.

Krisberg, B., and J. Austin (1978). *The Children of Ishmael*. Palo Alto, CA: Mayfield.

Krisberg, B., and J. Austin (1993). *Reinventing Juvenile Justice*. Newbury Park, CA: Sage.

Krisberg, B., J. Austin, and P.A. Steele (1989). *Unlocking Juvenile Corrections: Evaluating the Massachusetts Department of Youth Services*. San Francisco: National Council on Crime and Delinquency.

Krisberg, B., E. Currie, D. Onek, and R.G. Wiebush (1995). "Graduated Sanctions for Serious, Violent, and Chronic Juvenile Offenders." In J.C. Howell, B. Krisberg, J.D. Hawkins, and J.J. Wilson (eds.), *Serious, Violent, and Chronic Juvenile Offenders: A Sourcebook* (pp. 142-170). Thousand Oaks, CA: Sage.

Krisberg, B., and J.C. Howell (1998). "The Impact of the Juvenile Justice System and Prospects for Graduated Sanctions in a Comprehensive Strategy." In R. Loeber and D.P. Farrington (eds.), *Serious and Violent Juvenile Offenders: Risk Factors and Successful Interventions* (pp. 313-345). Thousand Oaks, CA: Sage.

Kroes, W.H., B.L. Margolis, and J.J. Hurrell (1974). "Job Stress in Policemen." *Journal of Police Science and Administration* 2:145-155.

Krohn, M., and J. Massey (1980). "Social Control and Delinquent Behavior: An Examination of the Elements of the Social Bond." *Sociological Quarterly* 21:529-543.

Kurki, L. (2000). "Restorative and Community Justice in the United States." In M. Tonry (ed.), *Crime and Justice: A Review of Research,* Vol. 27 (pp. 235-303). Chicago: University of Chicago Press.

Kurlychek, M., and B.D. Johnson (2004). "The Juvenile Penalty: A Comparison of Juvenile and Yong Adult Sentencing Outcomes in Criminal Court." *Criminology* 42:485-515.

Kurlychek, M., P.M. Torbet, and M. Bozynski (1999). *Focus on Accountability: Best Practices for Juvenile Court and Probation.* Washington, DC: U.S. Department of Justice and Delinquency Prevention.

Lab, S.P. (1984). "Patterns in Juvenile Misbehavior." *Crime & Delinquency* 30:293-308.

Lab, S.P. (1990). "Citizen Crime Prevention: Domains and Participation." *Justice Quarterly* 7:467-492.

Lab, S.P., and R.B. Allen (1984). "Self-report and Official Measures: A Further Examination of the Validity Issue." *Journal of Criminal Justice* 12:445-456.

Lab, S.P., and R.D. Clark (1994). "Gauging Crime and Control in the Schools." Paper presented at the Annual Meeting of the American Society of Criminology, Miami, FL.

Lab, S.P., and R.D. Clark (1996). *Discipline, Control and School Crime: Identifying Effective Intervention Strategies—Final Report.* Washington, DC: National Institute of Justice.

Lab, S.P., and J.T. Whitehead (1994). "Avoidance Behavior as a Response to In-School Victimization." *Journal of Security Administration* 17:32-45.

Lander, B. (1954). *Towards an Understanding of Juvenile Delinquency.* New York: Columbia University Press.

Lane, J., S. Turner, T. Fain, and A. Sehgal (2005). "Evaluating an Experimental Intensive Probation Program: Supervision and Official Outcomes." *Crime & Delinquency* 51:26-52.

Langan, P.A., L.A. Greenfield, S.K. Smith, M.R. Durose, and J.J. Levin (2001). *Contacts between Police and the Public: Findings from the 1999 National Survey.* Washington, DC: U.S. Department of Justice.

Lange, J.E., M.B. Johnson, and R.B. Voas (2005). "Testing the Racial Profiling Hypothesis for Seemingly Disparate Traffic Stops on the New Jersey Turnpike." *Justice Quarterly* 22:193-223.

Latimer, J., C. Dowden, and D. Muise (2005). "The Effectiveness of Restorative Justice Practices: A Meta-Analysis." Ottawa, Canada: Canada Department of Justice. Cited in N. Rodriguez (2007). "Restorative Justice at Work: Examining the Impact of Restorative Justice Resolutions on Juvenile Recidivism." *Crime & Delinquency* 53:355-379.

Lattimore, P.K., C.P. Krebs, P. Graham, and A.J. Cowell (2005). *Evaluation of the Juvenile Breaking the Cycle Program—Final Report.* Washington, DC: National Institute of Justice.

Lauritsen, J.L., R.J. Sampson, and J.H. Laub (1991). "The Link between Offending and Victimization among Adolescents." *Criminology* 29:265-292.

Lavrakas, P.J., and D.A. Lewis (1981). "The Conceptualization and Measurement of Citizen Crime Prevention Behaviors." *Journal of Research in Crime and Delinquency* 17:254-272.

LeBlanc, M. (1997). "A Generic Control Theory of the Criminal Phenomenon: The Structural Dynamic Statements of an Integrative Multilayered Control Theory." In T.P. Thornberry (ed.), *Developmental Theories of Crime and Delinquency* (pp. 215-285). New Brunswick, NJ: Transaction.

Lederman, C.S., and E.N. Brown (2000). "Entangled in the Shadows: Girls in the Juvenile Justice System." *Buffalo Law Review* 48:909-925.

Leiber, M.J., and K.Y. Mack (2003). "The Individual and Joint Effects of Race, Gender, and Family Status on Juvenile Justice Decision-Making." *Journal of Research in Crime and Delinquency* 40:34-70.

Leitzel, J. (2001). "Race and Policing." *Society* (March/April):38-42.

Leinwand, D. (2005). "Schools Restrict Use of Tasers." *USA Today* (June 3, 2005):1A.

Lemert, E.M. (1951). *Social Pathology: A Systematic Approach to the Theory of Sociopathic Behavior*. New York: McGraw-Hill.

Lester, D., and M. Braswell (1987). *Correctional Counseling*. Cincinnati: Anderson.

Leukefeld, C.G., and F.M. Tims (1988). *Compulsory Treatment of Drug Abuse: Research and Clinical Practice*. Rockville, MD: National Institute on Drug Abuse.

Levine, M., and L. Battistoni (1991). "The Corroboration Requirement in Child Sex Abuse Cases." *Behavioral Sciences and the Law* 9:3-20.

Levrant, S., F.T. Cullen, B. Fulton, and J.F. Wozniak (1999). "Reconsidering Restorative Justice: The Corruption of Benevolence Revisited?" *Crime & Delinquency* 45:3-27.

Lilly, J.R., F.T. Cullen, and R.A. Ball (1995). *Criminological Theory: Context and Consequences*, 2nd ed. Thousand Oaks, CA: Sage.

Lindner, C. (1981). "The Utilization of Day-Evening Centers as an Alternative to Secure Detention of Juveniles." *Journal of Probation and Parole* 13:12-18.

Lindner, C., and R.L. Bonn (1996). "Probation Officer Victimization and Fieldwork Practices: Results of a National Study." *Federal Probation* 60(2):16-23.

Lipsett, P. (1968). "The Juvenile Offender's Perception." *Crime & Delinquency* 14:49-62.

Lipsey, M.W. (1992). "Juvenile Delinquency Treatment: A Meta-Analytic Inquiry into the Viability of Effects." In T. Cook, H. Cooper, D. Corday, H. Hartman, L. Hedges, R. Light, T. Louis, and F. Mosteller (eds.), *Meta-Analysis for Explanation: A Casebook* (pp. 83-127). New York: Russell Sage Foundation.

Lipsey, M.W. (1999). "Can Intervention Rehabilitate Serious Delinquents?" *Annals of the American Academy of Political and Social Science* 564:142-166.

Lipsey, M.W., and F.T. Cullen (2007). "The Effectiveness of Correctional Rehabilitation: A Review of Systematic Reviews." *Annual Review of Law and Social Science* 3:299-320.

Lipsey, M.W., and D.B. Wilson (1998). "Effective Intervention for Serious Juvenile Offenders: A Synthesis of Research." In R. Loeber and D.P. Farrington (eds.), *Serious and Violent Juvenile Offenders: Risk Factors and Successful Intervention* (pp. 313-345). Thousand Oaks, CA: Sage.

Lipton, D.L. (1995). *The Effectiveness of Treatment for Drug Abusers under Criminal Justice Supervision*. Washington, DC: U.S. Department of Justice.

Listwan, S.J., C.L. Jonson, F.T. Cullen, and E.J. Latessa (2008). "Cracks in the Penal Harm Movement: Evidence from the Field." *Criminology & Public Policy* 7:423-465.

Listwan, S.J., J.L. Sundt, A.M. Holsinger, and E.J. Latessa (2003). "The Effects of Drug Court Programming on Recidivism: The Cincinnati Experience." *Crime & Delinquency* 49:389-411.

Lizotte, A., and D. Sheppard (2001). "Gun Use by Male Juveniles: Research and Prevention." *Juvenile Justice Bulletin.* Washington, DC: U.S. Department of Justice.

Loeber, R. (1988). "Natural Histories of Conduct Problems, Delinquency and Related Substance Abuse." In B.B. Lahey and A.E. Kazdin (eds.), *Advances in Clinical Child Psychology,* Vol. 11 (pp. 73-124). New York: Plenum.

Lombroso, C. (1876). *On Criminal Man.* Milan, Italy: Hoepli.

Lowney, J. (1984). "The Wall Gang: A Study of Interpersonal Process and Deviance among Twenty-three Middle-class Youths." *Adolescence* 19:527-538.

Lozoff, B., and M. Braswell (1989). *Inner Corrections: Finding Peace and Peace Making.* Cincinnati: Anderson.

Lundman, R.J. (1993). *Prevention and Control of Juvenile Delinquency,* 2nd ed. New York: Oxford University Press.

Lyons, M.J. (1996). "A Twin Study of Self-reported Criminal Behavior." In G.R. Bock and J.A. Goode (eds.), *Genetics of Criminal and Antisocial Behavior* (pp. 61-69). Chichester, England: John Wiley and Sons.

Mack, J.W. (1909). "The Juvenile Court." *Harvard Law Review* 23:104-119.

MacKenzie, D.L. (1994). "Results of a Multisite Study of Boot Camp Prisons." *Federal Probation* 58(2):60-66.

MacKenzie, D.L. (2006). *What Works in Corrections: Reducing the Criminal Activities of Offenders and Delinquents.* New York: Cambridge University Press.

Maddux, J.F. (1988). "Clinical Experience in Civil Commitment." In C.G. Leukefeld and F.M. Tims (eds.), *Compulsory Treatment of Drug Abuse: Research and Clinical Practice* (pp. 35-56). Washington, DC: National Institute on Drug Abuse.

Maguire, K., and A.L. Pastore (2004). *Sourcebook of Criminal Justice Statistics, 2003.* Washington, DC: Bureau of Justice Statistics. Available at: http://www.albany.edu/sourcebook/

Mahoney, A.R. (1985). "Jury Trial for Juveniles: Right or Ritual?" *Justice Quarterly* 2:553-565.

Mahoney, A.R. (1987). *Juvenile Justice in Context.* Boston: Northeastern University Press.

Maitland, A.S., and R.D. Sluder (1998). "Victimization and Youthful Prison Inmates: An Empirical Analysis." *Prison Journal* 78:55-73.

Males, M.A. (2000). "Vernon, Connecticut's Juvenile Curfew: The Circumstances of Youths Cited and Effects on Crime." *Criminal Justice Policy Review* 11:254-267.

Marcos, A.L., S.J. Bahr, and R.E. Johnson (1986). "Test of a Bonding/Differential Association Theory of Adolescent Drug Use." *Social Forces* 65:135-161.

Martinez, J.Y. (2008). "Character Education in Juvenile Detention." *Corrections Today* 70:150-154.

Maslach, C., and S.E. Jackson (1979). "Burned-out Cops and Their Families." *Psychology Today* 12(12):59-62.

Massey, J.L., and M.D. Krohn (1986). "A Longitudinal Examination of an Integrated Social Process Model of Deviant Behavior." *Social Forces* 65:106-134.

Mathis, K.J. (2007). "American Bar Association: Adult Justice System is the Wrong Answer for Most Juveniles." *American Journal of Preventive Medicine* 32:S1-S2.

Mause, L. (1974). *The History of Childhood*. New York: Psychohistory Press.

Maxson, C.L. (1995). "Street Gangs and Drug Roles in Two Suburban Cities." *NIJ Research in Brief*. Washington, DC: National Institute of Justice.

Maxson, C.L., K. Woods, and M.W. Klein (1996). "Street Gang Migration: How Big a Threat?" *NIJ Journal* 230:26-31.

Mays, G.L., K. Fuller, and L.T. Winfree (1994). "Gangs and Gang Activity in Southern New Mexico: A Descriptive Look at a Growing Rural Problem." *Journal of Crime and Justice* 17:25-44.

McBride, D. (1981). "Drugs and Violence." In J.A. Inciardi (ed.), *The Drugs/Crime Connection* (pp. 105-124). Beverly Hills: Sage.

McCarthy, B.R. (1987). "Preventive Detention and Pretrial Custody in the Juvenile Court." *Journal of Criminal Justice* 15:185-200.

McCarthy, B.R., and B.L. Smith (1986). "The Conceptualization of Discrimination in the Juvenile Justice Process: The Impact of Administrative Factors and Screening Decisions on Juvenile Court Dispositions." *Criminology* 24:41-64.

McClelland, G.M., L.A. Teplin, and K.M. Abram (2004). "Detection and Prevalence of Substance Use among Juvenile Detainees." *Juvenile Justice Bulletin*. Washington, DC: U.S. Department of Justice, Office of Juvenile Justice and Delinquency Prevention.

McCold, P. (2003). "A Survey of Assessment Research on Mediation and Conferencing." In L. Walgrave (ed.), *Repositioning Restorative Justice* (pp. 67-120). Portland, OR: Willan.

McCold, P., and T. Wachtel (1998). *Restorative Policing Experiment: The Bethlehem, Pennsylvania, Police Family Group Conferencing Project*. Pipersville, PA: Community Service Foundation.

McCold, P., and T. Wachtel (2002). "Restorative Justice Theory Validation." In E.G.M. Weitekamp and H. Kernere (eds.), *Restorative Justice: Theoretical Foundations*. Portland, OR: Willan.

McDowall, D., C. Loftin, and B. Wiersema (2000). "The Impact of Youth Curfew Laws on Juvenile Crime Rates." *Crime & Delinquency* 46:76-91.

McElvain, J.P., and A.J. Kposowa (2008). "Police Officer Characteristics and the Likelihood of Using Deadly Force." *Criminal Justice and Behavior* 35:505-521.

McGarrell, E.F., K. Olivares, K. Crawford, and N. Kroovand (2000). *Returning Justice to the Community: The Indianapolis Juvenile Restorative Justice Experiment*. Indianapolis: Hudson Institute.

McGarvey, A. (2005). "A Culture of Caring." *The American Prospect* (September): A12-A14.

McGlothlin, W.H., and M.D. Anglin (1981). "Shutting Off Methadone: Costs and Benefits." *Archives of General Psychiatry* 38:885-892.

McLaughlin, E., R. Fergusson, G. Hughes, and L. Westmarland (2003). "Introduction: Justice in the Round—Contextualizing Restorative Justice." In E. McLaughlin, R. Fergusson, G. Hughes, and L. Westmarland (eds.), *Restorative Justice: Critical Issues*. Thousand Oaks, CA: Sage.

McMahon, M. (1999). *Women on Guard: Discrimination and Harassment in Corrections*. Toronto, Canada: University of Toronto Press.

Mead, G.H. (1934). *Mind, Self and Society*. Chicago: University of Chicago Press.

Mears, D.P. (2000). "Assessing the Effectiveness of Juvenile Justice Reforms: A Closer Look at the Criteria and the Impacts on Diverse Stakeholders." *Law and Policy* 22:175-202.

Mears, D.P., C. Hay, M. Gertz, and C. Mancini (2007). "Public Opinion and the Foundation of the Juvenile Court." *Criminology* 45:223-257.

Mednick, S.A., and K.O. Christiansen (1977). *Biosocial Bases of Criminal Behavior*. New York: Gardner.

Meehan, P.J., and M.C. Ponder (2002). "Race and Place: The Ecology of Racial Profiling African American Motorists." *Justice Quarterly* 18:399-430.

Megargee, E.I., and M.J. Bohn (1979). *Classifying Criminal Offenders: A New System Based on the MMPI*. Beverly Hills: Sage.

Melton, G.B. (1980). "Psycholegal Issues in Child Victims' Interaction with the Legal System." *Victimology* 5:274-284.

Mendel, R.A. (2001). *Guiding Lights for Reform in Juvenile Justice*. Washington, DC: American Youth Policy Forum.

Mendelsohn, B. (1956). "The Victimology." *Etudes Internationale de Psycho-sociologie Criminelle* (July):23-26.

Merlo, A.V. (2000). "Juvenile Justice at the Crossroads: Presidential Address to the Academy of Criminal Justice Sciences." *Justice Quarterly* 17:639-661.

Merton, R.K. (1938). "Social Structure and Anomie." *American Sociological Review* 3:672-682.

Messner, S.F., S. Galea, K.J. Tardiff, M. Tracy, A. Bucciarelli, T.M. Piper, V. Frye, and D. Vlahov (2007). "Policing, Drugs, and the Homicide Decline in New York City in the 1990s." *Criminology* 45:385-412.

Meyer, J.R., and N.D. Reppucci (2007). "Police Practices and Perceptions Regarding Juvenile Interrogation and Interrogative Suggestibility." *Behavioral Sciences and the Law* 25:757-780.

Miethe, T.D., L. Hong, and E. Reese (2000). "Reintegrative Shaming and Recidivism Risks in Drug Court: Explanations for Some Unexpected Findings." *Crime & Delinquency* 46:522-541.

Miethe, T.D., M.C. Stafford, and J.S. Long (1987). "Social Differentiation in Criminal Victimization: A Test of Routine Activities Lifestyle Theory." *American Sociological Review* 52:184-194.

Miller, D., D. Miller, F. Hoffman, and R. Duggan (1980). *Runaways—Illegal Aliens in their Own Land: Implications for Service*. New York: Praeger.

Miller, J. (2000). *One of the Guys? Girls, Gangs and Gender*. New York: Oxford University Press.

Miller, J.G. (1996). *Search and Destroy: African-American Males in the Criminal Justice System.* New York: Cambridge University Press.

Miller, J.Y. (2005). "6 Aides Lose Jobs after a Boy Dies." *Atlanta Journal-Constitution* (May 14):A9-A10.

Miller, W.B. (1958). "Lower Class Culture as a Generating Milieu of Gang Delinquency." *Journal of Social Issues* 15:5-19.

Miller, W.B. (1966). "Violent Crime in City Gangs." *Annals* 343:97-112.

Miller, W.B. (1975). *Violence by Youth Gangs and Youth Groups as a Crime Problem in Major American Cities.* Washington, DC: National Institute for Juvenile Justice and Delinquency Prevention.

Miller, W.B. (1982). *Crime by Youth Gangs and Groups in the United States.* Washington, DC: Office of Juvenile Justice and Delinquency Prevention.

Miller, W.B., H. Gertz, and H.S.G. Cutter (1961). "Aggression in a Boys' Street-corner Group." *Psychiatry* 24:283-298.

Miller-Wilson, L.S., and P. Puritz (2003). *Pennsylvania: An Assessment of Access to Counsel and Quality of Representation in Delinquency Proceedings.* Washington, DC, and Philadelphia: American Bar Association Juvenile Justice Center and Juvenile Law Center in Collaboration with the National Juvenile Defender Center and the Northeast Juvenile Defender Center. Available at: http://www.jic.org/Resources/pdfs/assess/PA%20assess.pdf

Minor, K.I., D.J. Hartmann, and S. Terry (1997). "Predictors of Juvenile Court Actions and Recidivism." *Crime & Delinquency* 18:295-318.

Minor, W.W. (1981). "Techniques of Neutralization: A Reconceptualization and Empirical Examination." *Journal of Research in Crime and Delinquency* 18:295-318.

Mintz, S. (2004). *Huck's Raft: A History of American Childhood.* Cambridge, MA: Belknap.

Moffitt, T.E. (1997). "Adolescence-Limited and Life-Course-Persistent Offending: A Complementary Pair of Developmental Theories." In T.P. Thornberry (ed.), *Developmental Theories of Crime and Delinquency* (pp. 11-54). New Brunswick, NJ: Transaction.

Montgomery, J.M., D.L. Foley, and M. Wolfson (2006). "Enforcing the Minimum Drinking Age: State, Local and Agency Characteristics Associated with Compliance Checks and Cops in Shops Programs." *Addiction* 101:223-231.

Monti, D.J. (1993). "Origins and Problems of Gang Research in the United States." In S. Cummings and D.J. Monti (eds.), *Gangs: The Origins and Impact of Contemporary Youth Gangs in the United States* (pp. 3-26). Albany, NY: SUNY Press.

Moon, M.M., B.K. Applegate, and E.J. Latessa (1997). "RECLAIM Ohio: A Politically Viable Alternative to Treating Youthful Felony Offenders." *Crime & Delinquency* 43:438-456.

Moore, D., and T. O'Connell (1994). "Family Conferencing in Wagga Wagga: A Communitarian Model of Justice." In C. Adler and J. Wundersitz (eds.), *Family Conferencing and Juvenile Justice: The Way Forward or Misplaced Optimism?* Canberra, Australia: Australian Institute of Criminology.

Moore, J. (1988). "Introduction: Gangs and the Underclass: A Comparative Perspective." In J.M. Hagedorn (ed.), *People and Folks: Gangs, Crime and the Underclass in a Rustbelt City* (pp. 3-18). Chicago: Lake View Press.

Moore, J. (1991). *Going Down to the Barrio: Homeboys and Homegirls in Change.* Philadelphia: Temple University Press.

Moore, J. (1993). "Gangs, Drugs, and Violence." In S. Cummings and D.J. Monti (eds.), *Gangs: The Origins and Impact of Contemporary Youth Gangs in the United States* (pp. 27-46). Albany, NY: SUNY Press.

Moore, J., and J. Hagedorn (2001). "Female Gangs: A Focus on Research." *OJJDP Juvenile Justice Bulletin.* Washington, DC: Office of Juvenile Justice and Delinquency Prevention.

Moore, M.H. (2003). "Sizing up COMPSTAT: An Important Administrative Innovation in Policing." *Criminology & Public Policy* 2(3):469-494.

Morales, A. (1992). "A Clinical Model for the Prevention of Gang Violence and Homicide." In R.C. Cervantes (ed.), *Substance Abuse and Gang Violence* (pp. 105-118). Newbury Park, CA: Sage.

Morse, S. (1999). "Delinquency and Desert." *Annals of the American Academy of Political and Social Science* 564:56-80.

Moynihan, D.P. (2005). "The Impact of Managing for Results Mandates in Corrections: Lessons from Three States." *Criminal Justice Policy Review* 16:18-37.

Mumola, C.J. (2005). "Suicide and Homicide in State Prisons and Local Jails." *Bureau of Justice Statistics Special Report.* Washington, DC: U.S. Department of Justice.

Mumola, C.J., and J.C. Karberg (2006). "Drug Use and Dependence, State and Federal Prisoners, 2004." *Bureau of Justice Statistics Special Report.* Washington, DC: U.S. Department of Justice.

Nadelmann, E.A. (1997). "Thinking Seriously about Alternatives to Drug Prohibition." In M. McShane and F.P. Williams (eds.), *Criminal Justice: Drug Use and Drug Policy* (pp. 269-316). New York: Garland.

Nassi, A., and S.I. Abramowitz (1976). "From Phrenology to Psychosurgery and Back Again: Biological Studies of Criminality." *American Journal of Orthopsychiatry* 46:591-607.

National Alliance of Gang Investigators Associations (2005). *National Gang Threat Assessment.* Washington, DC: Bureau of Justice Assistance.

National Association of Youth Courts (2008). *Youth Courts.* Baltimore: National Association of Youth Courts. Available at: http://www.youthcourt.net/

National CASA (2008). *Court Appointed Special Advocates for Children.* Available at: http://www.nationalcasa.org/index.asp

National Child Abuse and Neglect Data System (2008). *Child Maltreatment, 2006.* Washington, DC: U.S. Department of Health and Human Services.

National Conference of State Legislatures (1993). *1993 State Legislature Summary.* Washington, DC: National Conference of State Legislatures.

National Dairy Council (1985). "Diet and Behavior." *Dairy Council Digest* 56:19-24.

National Institute on Drug Abuse (1999). *Principles of Drug Addiction Treatment: A Research-Based Guide.* Washington, DC: National Institute on Drug Abuse.

National Institute on Drug Abuse (2004). *Lessons from Prevention Research. Info Facts.* Washington, DC: National Institute on Drug Abuse.

National Institute of Justice (1990). *Drugs and Crime: 1989 Drug Use Forecasting Report*. Washington, DC: National Institute of Justice.

National Juvenile Defender Center (2004). *The Use and Abuse of Juvenile Detention: Understanding Detention and Its Uses*. Washington, DC: National Juvenile Defender Center.

National Youth Gang Center (2000). *1998 National Youth Gang Survey: Summary*. Washington, DC: Office of Juvenile Justice and Delinquency Prevention.

National Youth Gang Center (2007). *National Youth Gang Survey Analysis*. Washington, DC: Office of Juvenile Justice and Delinquency Prevention. Available at: http://www.iir.com/nygc/nygsa/

Newcomb, M.D., and P.M. Bentler (1988). *Consequences of Adolescent Drug Use*. Newbury Park, CA: Sage.

Newman, D.J. (1986). *Introduction to Criminal Justice*, 3rd ed. New York: Random House.

Newman, H.H., F.H. Freeman, and K.J. Holzinger (1937). *Twins: A Study of Heredity and Environment*. Chicago: University of Chicago Press.

Nicholl, C.G. (1999). *Community Policing, Community Justice, and Restorative Justice: Exploring the Links for the Delivery of a Balanced Approach to Public Safety*. Washington, DC: Office of Community Oriented Policing Services.

Niederhoffer, A. (1967). *Behind the Shield: The Police in Urban Society*. Garden City, NY: Anchor Books.

Noriega, C. (2000). "Stick a Fork in It: Is Juvenile Justice Done?" *New York Law School Journal of Human Rights* 16:669-698.

Novak, K.J., J. Frank, B.W. Smith, and R.S. Engel (2002). "Revisiting the Decision to Arrest: Comparing Beat and Community Officers." *Crime & Delinquency* 48:70-98.

Nugent, W.R., M.S. Umbreit, L. Wiinamaki, and J. Paddock (1999). "Participation in Victim-Offender Mediation and Severity of Subsequent Delinquent Behavior: Successful Replications?" *Journal of Research in Social Work Practice* 11:5-23.

Nurco, D.N., T.W. Kinlock, T.E. Hanlon, and J.C. Ball (1988). "Nonnarcotic Drug Use Over an Addition Career—A Study of Heroin Addicts in Baltimore and New York City." *Comprehensive Psychiatry* 29:450-459.

O'Brien, D.M. (1997). *Constitutional Law and Politics* (Vol. 2), 3rd ed. New York: W.W. Norton.

O'Brien, R.M. (1985). *Crime and Victimization Data*. Beverly Hills: Sage.

O'Connor, S. (2001). *Orphan Trains: The Story of Charles Loring Brace and the Children He Saved and Failed*. Boston: Houghton Mifflin.

Office of Justice Programs (2000). *Promising Strategies to Reduce Substance Abuse*. Washington, DC: Office of Justice Programs.

Office of Justice Programs (2003). *Juvenile Family Drug Courts: Summary of Drug Court Activity by State and County*. Washington, DC: Office of Justice Programs.

Office of Juvenile Justice and Delinquency Prevention (1999). *Promising Strategies to Reduce Gun Violence*. Washington, DC: Office of Juvenile Justice and Delinquency Prevention.

Ott, B. (2005). "School Prayer: Teen Support Hinges on Type." *Gallup Poll Tuesday Briefing* (July 26, 2005):1-2.

Padilla, F. (1993). "The Working Gang." In S. Cummings and D.J. Monti (eds.), *Gangs: The Origins and Impact of Contemporary Youth Gangs in the United States* (pp. 173-192). Albany, NY: SUNY Press.

Pagelow, M.D. (1984). *Family Violence.* New York: Greenwood Press.

Palamara, F., F.T. Cullen, and J.C. Gersten (1986). "The Effect of Police and Mental Health Intervention on Juvenile Deviance: Specifying Contingencies in the Impact of Formal Reaction." *Journal of Health and Social Behavior* 27:90-105.

Paoline, E.A., S.M. Myers, and R.E. Worden (2000). "Police Culture, Individualism, and Community Policing: Evidence from Two Departments." *Justice Quarterly* 17:575-605.

Parent, D.G. (2003). *Correctional Boot Camps: Lessons from a Decade of Research.* Washington, DC: National Institute of Justice.

Parsloe, P. (1978). *Juvenile Justice in Britain and the U.S.: The Balance of Needs and Rights.* London: Routledge and Kegan Paul.

Pastore, A.L., and K. Maguire (2008). *Sourcebook of Criminal Justice Statistics, 2007.* Washington, DC: Bureau of Justice Statistics. Available at: http://www.albany.edu/sourcebook/

Pearson, F.S., D.S. Lipton, C.M. Cleland, and D.S. Yee (2002). "The Effects of Behavioral/Cognitive Behavioral Programs on Recidivism." *Crime & Delinquency* 48:476-496.

Persico, N., and P.E. Todd (2008). "The Hit Rates Test for Racial Bias in Motor-Vehicle Searches." *Justice Quarterly* 25:37-53.

Peters, M., D. Thomas, and C. Zamberlan (1997). *Boot Camps for Juvenile Offenders: Program Summary.* Washington, DC: U.S. Department of Justice.

Petersilia, J. (1997). "Probation in the United States." In M. Tonry (ed.), *Crime and Justice: A Review of Research,* Vol. 22 (pp. 149-200). Chicago: University of Chicago Press.

Petersilia, J., S. Turner, J. Kahan, and J. Peterson (1985). "Executive Summary of Rand's Study, 'Granting Felons Probation: Public Risks and Alternatives.'" *Crime & Delinquency* 3:379-392.

Peterson-Badali, M., and C.J. Koegl (2002). "Juvenile Offenders' Experiences of Incarceration: The Role of Correctional Staff in Peer-on-Peer Violence." *Journal of Criminal Justice* 30:41-49.

Pinderhughes, H. (1993). "'Down with the Program': Racial Attitude and Group Violence among Youth in Bensonhurst and Gravesend." In S. Cummings and D.J. Monti (eds.), *Gangs: The Origins and Impact of Contemporary Youth Gangs in the United States* (pp. 75-94). Albany, NY: SUNY Press.

Piquero, A.R., R. MacIntosh, and M. Hickman (2000). "Does Self-control Affect Survey Response?" *Criminology* 38:897-930.

Pisciotta, A.W. (1979). "The Theory and Practice of the New York House of Refuge, 1857-1935." Unpublished Ph.D. dissertation, Florida State University.

Pisciotta, A.W. (1982). "Saving the Children: The Promise and Practice of Parens Patriae, 1838-98." *Crime & Delinquency* 28:410-425.

Pisciotta, A.W. (1983). "Race, Sex and Rehabilitation: A Study of Differential Treatment in the Juvenile Reformatory, 1825-1900." *Crime & Delinquency* 29:254-269.

Platt, A.M. (1977). *The Child Savers: The Invention of Delinquency.* Chicago: University of Chicago Press.

Podolsky, E. (1964). "The Chemistry of Murder." *Pakistan Medical Journal* 15:9-14.

Poole, E.D., and R.M. Regoli (1979). "Parental Support, Delinquent Friends and Delinquency." *Journal of Criminal Law and Criminology* 70:188-193.

Pope, C.E. (1994). "Racial Disparities in the Juvenile Justice System." *Overcrowded Times* 5(6):1,5-7.

Pope, C.E. (1995). "Equity Within the Juvenile Justice System: Directions for the Future." In K.K. Leonard, C.E. Pope, and W.H. Feyerherm (eds.), *Minorities and the Juvenile Justice System* (pp. 201-216). Thousand Oaks, CA: Sage.

Pope, C.E., and H.N. Snyder (2003). *Race as a Factor in Juvenile Arrests.* Washington, DC: U.S. Department of Justice.

Powers, R. (2002). "The Apocalypse of Adolescence." *Atlantic Monthly* (March) 89:58-74.

Prescott, P.S. (1981). *The Child Savers: Juvenile Justice Observed.* New York: Knopf.

President's Commission on Law Enforcement and Administration of Justice (1967). *Task Force Report: Juvenile Delinquency and Youth Crime.* Washington, DC: U.S. Government Printing Office.

Propper, A.M. (1982). "Make-Believe Families and Homosexuality among Imprisoned Girls." *Criminology* 20:127-138.

Puritz, P., S. Burrell, R. Schwartz, M. Soler, and L. Warboys (1995). *A Call for Justice: An Assessment of Access to Counsel and Quality of Representation in Delinquency Proceedings.* Washington, DC: American Bar Association Juvenile Justice Center.

Puritz, P., and M.A. Scali (1998). *Beyond the Walls: Improving Conditions of Confinement for Youth in Custody.* Washington, DC: Office of Juvenile Justice and Delinquency Prevention.

Putnam, R.D. (2000). *Bowling Alone: The Collapse and Revival of American Community.* New York: Simon & Schuster.

Puzzanchera, C., and M. Sickmund (2008). *Juvenile Court Statistics, 2005.* Pittsburgh: National Center for Juvenile Justice.

Puzzanchera, C., A.L. Stahl, T.A. Finnegan, N. Tierney, and H.N. Howard (2004). *Juvenile Court Statistics, 2000.* Pittsburgh: National Center for Juvenile Justice.

Quicker, J.C. (1974). "The Effect of Goal Discrepancy on Delinquency." *Social Problems* 22:76-86.

Rada, R.T., D.R. Laws, and R. Kellner (1976). "Plasma Testosterone Levels in the Rapist." *Psychosomatic Medicine* 38:257-268.

Raine, A., P.H. Venables, and M. Williams (1995). "High Autonomic Arousal and Electrodermal Orienting at Age 15 Years as Protective Factors against Criminal Behavior at Age 29 Years." *American Journal of Psychiatry* 152:1595-1600.

Rasmussen, A. (2004). "Teen Court Referral, Sentencing, and Subsequent Recidivism: Two Proportional Hazards Models and a Little Speculation." *Crime & Delinquency* 50:615-635.

Ray, L., P. Kestner, and L. Freedman (1986). "Dispute Resolution: From Examination to Experimentation." *Michigan Bar Journal* 65:898-903.

Reading Eagle (2008). "Juveniles Pay Off Fines by Serving Community." *Reading Eagle* (January 26, 2008):N/A.

Reckless, W.C. (1962). "A Non-causal Explanation: Containment Theory." *Excerpta Criminologica* 1:131-134.

Reckless, W.C. (1967). *The Crime Problem.* New York: Appleton, Century, Crofts.

Redding, R.E. (2008). "Juvenile Transfer Laws: An Effective Deterrent to Delinquency?" *OJJDP Juvenile Justice Bulletin.* Washington, DC: Office of Juvenile Justice and Delinquency Prevention.

Reiss, A.J., Jr. (1980). "Police Brutality." In R.J. Lundman (ed.), *Police Behavior: A Sociological Perspective* (pp. 274-296). New York: Oxford University Press.

Reiss, A.J., Jr., and A.L. Rhodes (1961). "The Distribution of Juvenile Delinquency in the Social Class Structure." *American Sociological Review* 26:720-732.

Reiss, A.J., Jr., and J.A. Roth (1993). *Understanding and Preventing Violence* (Vol. 1). Washington, DC: National Academy Press.

Rengert, G.F., and J. Wasilchick (1985). *Suburban Burglary: A Time and a Place for Everything.* Springfield, IL: Charles C Thomas.

Reppetto, T.A. (1974). *Residential Crime.* Cambridge, MA: Ballinger.

Reynolds, K.M., R. Seydlitz, and P. Jenkins (2000). "Do Juvenile Curfew Laws Work? A Time-series Analysis of the New Orleans Law." *Justice Quarterly* 17:205-230.

Rice, S.K., and A.R. Piquero (2005). "Perceptions of Discrimination and Justice in New York City." *Policing* 28:98-117.

Rich, J.M., and J.L. DeVitis (1985). *Theories of Moral Development.* Springfield, IL: Charles C Thomas.

Ringwalt, C.L., S.T. Ennett, and K.D. Holt (1991). "An Outcome Evaluation of Project D.A.R.E." *Health Education Research: Theory and Practice* 6:327-337.

Roane, K.R. (2001). "A Risky Trip Through White Man's Pass." *U.S. News and World Report* 130:24.

Robin, G.D. (1967). "Gang Member Delinquency in Philadelphia." In M.W. LeKlein (ed.), *Juvenile Gangs in Context* (pp. 15-24). Englewood Cliffs, NJ: Prentice Hall.

Robin, G.D. (1982). "Juvenile Interrogations and Confessions." *Journal of Police Science and Administration* 10:224-228.

Rodriguez, N. (2005). "Restorative Justice, Communities, and Delinquency: Whom Do We Reintegrate?" *Criminology & Public Policy* 4:103-130.

Rodriguez, N., and V.J. Webb (2004). "Multiple Measures of Juvenile Drug Court Effectiveness: Results of a Quasi-Experimental Design." *Crime & Delinquency* 50:292-314.

Rojek, D.G., and M.L. Erickson (1982). "Juvenile Diversion: A Study of Community Cooptation." In D.G. Rojek and G.F. Jensen (eds.), *Readings in Juvenile Delinquency* (pp. 316-321). Lexington, MA: D.C. Heath.

Roncek, D.W., and P.A. Maier (1991). "Bars, Blocks, and Crimes Revisited: Linking the Theory of Routine Activities to the Empiricism of 'Hot Spots.'" *Criminology* 29:725-753.

Rosenbaum, D.P., R.L. Flewelling, S.L. Bailey, C.L. Ringwalt, and D.L. Wilkinson (1994). "Cops in the Classroom: A Longitudinal Evaluation of Drug Abuse Resistance Education (DARE)." *Journal of Research in Crime and Delinquency* 31:3-31.

Rosenberg, I.M. (2008). "Gault Turns 40: Reflections on Ambiguity." *Criminal Law Bulletin* 44:330-354.

Rosenfeld, R., R. Fornango, and E. Baumer (2005). "Did Ceasefire, COMPSTAT and Exile Reduce Homicide?" *Criminology & Public Policy* 4:419-450.

Rossman, S.B., J.A. Butts, J. Roman, C. DeStefano, and R. White (2004). "What Juvenile Drug Courts Do and How They Do It." In J.A. Butts and J. Roman (eds.), *Juvenile Drug Courts and Teen Substance Abuse* (pp. 55-106). Washington, DC: Urban Institute Press.

Rossow, L.F., and J.R. Parkinson (1994a). "State Legislators React to *Jones v. Clear Creek* and Bishop Knox Behavior." *School Law Reporter* 36(5):1-2.

Rossow, L.F., and J.R. Parkinson (1994b). "Yet Another Student Strip Search: Cornfield By *Lewis v. Consolidated High School District No. 230.*" *School Law Reporter* 36(3):1-2.

Rossum, R.A., B.J. Koller, and C.P. Manfredi (1987). *Juvenile Justice Reform: A Model for the States.* Clairmont, CA: Rose Institute of State and Local Government and the American Legislative Exchange.

Rothman, D.J. (1971). *The Discovery of the Asylum: Social Order and Disorder in the New Republic.* Boston: Little, Brown.

Rothman, D.J. (1980). *Conscience and Convenience: The Asylum and Its Alternatives in Progressive America.* Boston: Little, Brown.

Roush, D.M., and M. McMillen (2000). *Construction, Operations, and Staff Training for Juvenile Confinement Facilities.* Washington, DC: Office of Juvenile Justice and Delinquency Prevention.

Rowe, D.C. (2002). *Biology and Crime.* Los Angeles: Roxbury.

Rubin, H.T. (1985). *Juvenile Justice: Policy, Practice, and Law*, 2nd ed. New York: Random House.

Rutter, M. (1996). "Introduction: Concepts of Antisocial Behavior, of Cause and of Genetic Influences." In G.R. Bock and J.A. Goode (eds.), *Genetics of Criminal and Antisocial Behavior* (pp. 1-14). Chichester, England: John Wiley and Sons.

Ryan, C.M. (1987). "Juvenile Court Jurisdiction: Intervention and Intrusion." In F.X. Hartmann (ed.), *From Children to Citizens: Volume II: The Role of the Juvenile Court* (pp. 56-64). New York: Springer-Verlag.

Ryerson, E. (1978). *The Best-Laid Plans: America's Juvenile Court Experiment.* New York: Hill and Wang.

Saad, L. (2001). "Fear of Crime at Record Lows." *Gallup Poll Monthly* 433:2-10.

Sabol, W.J., T.D. Minton, and P.M. Harrison (2007). "Prison and Jail Inmates at Midyear 2006." *Bureau of Justice Statistics Bulletin.* Washington, DC: U.S. Department of Justice.

Sagatun, I.J., and L.P. Edwards (1995). *Child Abuse and the Legal System.* Chicago: Nelson-Hall.

SAMHSA (2004). *Graduated Driver Licensing and Drinking among Young Drivers.* Washington, DC: Substance Abuse and Mental Health Services Administration. Available at: http://www.drugabusestatistics.samhsa.gov

SAMHSA (2008). *2007 National Survey on Drug Use and Health: Detailed Tables.* Washington, DC: Substance Abuse and Mental Health Services Administration. Available at: http://www.oas.samhsa.gov/NSDUH/2k7NSDUH/tabs/TOC.htm

Sampson, R.J. (1986). "Effects of Socioeconomic Context on Official Reaction to Juvenile Delinquency." *American Sociological Review* 51:876-885.

Sampson, R.J., and J.H. Laub (1993). *Crime in the Making: Pathways and Turning Points through Life.* Cambridge, MA: Harvard University Press.

Sampson, R.J., and S.W. Raudenbush (1999). "Systematic Social Observation of Public Spaces: A New Look at Disorder in Urban Neighborhoods." *American Journal of Sociology* 105:603-651.

Sanborn, J. (2001). "A Parens Patriae Figure or Impartial Fact Finder: Policy Questions and Conflicts for the Juvenile Court Judge." *Criminal Justice Policy Review* 12:311-332.

Sanders, W.B. (1994). *Gangbangs and Drive-bys: Grounded Culture and Juvenile Gang Violence.* New York: Aldine de Gruyter.

Schaffner, L. (2006). *Girls in Trouble with the Law.* New Brunswick, NJ: Rutgers University Press.

Schaps, E., J.M. Moskowitz, J.H. Malvin, and G.A. Schaeffer (1986). "Evaluation of Seven School-based Prevention Programs: A Final Report of the Napa Project." *International Journal of the Addictions* 21:1081-1112.

Schauss, A.G. (1980). *Diet, Crime and Delinquency.* Berkeley, CA: Parker House.

Schiff, A. (1999). "The Impact of Restorative Interventions on Juvenile Offenders." In G. Bazemore and L. Walgrave (eds.), *Restorative Juvenile Justice: Repairing the Harm of Youth Crime.* Monsey, NY: Criminal Justice Press.

Schlossman, S.L. (1977). *Love and the American Delinquent: The Theory and Practice of "Progressive" Juvenile Justice, 1825-1920.* Chicago: University of Chicago Press.

Schnebly, S.M. (2008). "The Influence of Community-Oriented Policing on Crime-Reporting Behavior." *Justice Quarterly* 25:223-251.

Schneider, A.L. (1985). *The Impact of Deinstitutionalization on Recidivism and Secure Confinement of Status Offenders.* Washington, DC: U.S. Department of Justice.

Schneider, A.L. (1986). "Restitution and Recidivism Rates of Juvenile Offenders: Results from Four Experimental Studies." *Criminology* 24:533-552.

Schneider, A.L. (1988). "A Comparative Analysis of Juvenile Court Responses to Drug and Alcohol Offenses." *Crime & Delinquency* 34:103-124.

Schneider, A.L. (1990). *Deterrence and Juvenile Crime: Results from a National Policy Experiment.* New York: Springer-Verlag.

Schneider, A.L., and D.D. Schram (1986). "The Washington State Juvenile Justice Reform: A Review of Findings." *Criminal Justice Policy Review* 2:211-235.

Schneider, M.E. (2008). "HIV Rates Are Low in High-Risk Adolescent Group Studied." *Pediatric News* 42:10.

Schrag, C. (1971). *Crime and Justice: American Style*. Washington, DC: U.S. Government Printing Office.

Schuck, A.M. (2003). "The Masking of Racial and Ethnic Disparity in Police Use of Physical Force: The Effects of Gender and Custody Status." *Journal of Criminal Justice* 32:557-564.

Schulsinger, F. (1972). "Psychopathy: Heredity and Environment." *International Journal of Mental Health* 1:190-206.

Schur, E.M. (1973). *Radical Nonintervention: Rethinking the Delinquency Problem*. Englewood Cliffs, NJ: Prentice Hall.

Schwartz, I.M., G. Fishman, R. Rawson Hatfield, B.A. Krisberg, and Z. Eisikovits (1987). "Juvenile Detention: The Hidden Closets Revisited." *Justice Quarterly* 4:219-235.

Schwartz, M.D. (1989). "Family Violence as a Cause of Crime: Rethinking Our Priorities." *Criminal Justice Policy Review* 3:115-132.

Schwartz, M., and S.S. Tangri (1965). "A Note on Self-concept as an Insulator Against Delinquency." *American Sociological Review* 30:922-926.

Scott, M. (2002). "Georgia Prom-goers to Face Curfew Thanks to Recent Legislation." *Johnson City Press* (May 1, 2002):6.

Sealock, M.D., D.C. Gottfredson, and C.A. Gallagher (1997). "Delinquency and Social Reform: A Radical Perspective." In L. Empey (ed.), *Juvenile Justice* (pp. 245-290). Charlottesville: University of Virginia Press.

Secret, P.E., and J.B. Johnson (1997). "The Effect of Race on Juvenile Justice Decision Making in Nebraska: Detention, Adjudication, and Disposition, 1988-1993." *Justice Quarterly* 14:445-478.

Sells, S.B., and D.D. Simpson (1979). "Evaluation of Treatment Outcomes for Youths in the Drug Abuse Reporting Program (DARP): A Follow-up Study." In G.M. Beschner and A.S. Friedman (eds.), *Youth Drug Abuse* (pp. 571-628). Lexington, MA: Lexington Books.

Shah, S.A., and L.H. Roth (1974). "Biological and Psychophysiological Factors in Criminality." In D. Glaser (ed.), *Handbook of Criminology* (pp. 101-173). New York: Rand McNally.

Shannon, L.W. (1982). *Assessing the Relationship of Adult Criminal Careers to Juvenile Careers*. Iowa City: Iowa Urban Community Research Center.

Shaw, C.R., and H.D. McKay (1942). *Juvenile Delinquency and Urban Areas*. Chicago: University of Chicago Press.

Shaw, C.R., F.M. Zorbaugh, H.D. McKay, and L.S. Cottrell (1929). *Delinquency Areas*. Chicago: University of Chicago Press.

Sheldon, W.H. (1949). *Varieties of Delinquent Youth: An Introduction to Correctional Psychiatry*. New York: Harper and Brothers.

Sheley, J.F., and J.D. Wright (1993). *Gun Acquisition and Possession in Selected Juvenile Samples*. Washington, DC: Office of Juvenile Justice and Delinquency Prevention.

Sheppard, D., H. Grant, W. Rowe, and N. Jacobs (2000). "Fighting Juvenile Gun Violence." *OJJDP Juvenile Justice Bulletin*. Washington, DC: Office of Juvenile Justice and Delinquency Prevention.

Sherman, L.W. (2007). "Use Probation to Prevent Murder." *Criminology & Public Policy* 6:843-850.

Sherman, L.W., and H. Strang (2000). *Recidivism Patterns in the Canberra Reintegrative Shaming Experiments (RISE)*. Canberra, Australia: Center for Restorative Justice, Australian National University.

Sherman, L.W., H. Strang, and D. Woods (2003). "Captains of Restorative Justice: Experience, Legitimacy and Recidivism by Type of Offence." In E.G.M. Weitekamp and H. Kerner (eds.), *Restorative Justice in Context: International Practice and Directions* (pp. 229-256). Portland, OR: Willan.

Shine, J., and D. Price (1992). "Prosecutors and Juvenile Justice: New Roles and Perspectives." In I.M. Schwartz (ed.), *Juvenile Justice and Public Policy: Toward a National Agenda* (pp. 101-133). New York: Lexington Books.

Short, J.F. (1960). "Differential Association as a Hypothesis: Problems of Empirical Testing." *Social Problems* 8:14-25.

Short, J.F., and I. Nye (1958). "Extent of Unrecorded Delinquency: Tentative Conclusions." *Journal of Criminal Law, Criminology and Police Science* 49:296-302.

Short, J.F., and F.L. Strodbeck (1965). *Group Process and Gang Delinquency*. Chicago: University of Chicago Press.

Shufelt, J.S., and J.C. Cocozza (2006). *Youth with Mental Health Disorders in the Juvenile Justice System: Results from a Multi-State Prevalence Study*. Delmar, NY: National Center for Mental Health and Juvenile Justice.

Sickmund, M. (2004). *Juveniles in Corrections*. Washington, DC: U.S. Department of Justice.

Sickmund, M., and P.J. Baunach (1986). "Children in Custody: Public Juvenile Facilities, 1985." *Bureau of Justice Statistics Bulletin*. Washington, DC: U.S. Department of Justice.

Sickmund, M., T.J. Sladky, and W. Kang (2008). "Census of Juveniles in Residential Placement Databook." Washington, DC: U.S. Department of Justice, Office of Justice Programs. Available at: http://www.ojjdp.ncjrs.org/ojstatbb/cjrp/

Sickmund, M., H.N. Snyder, and E. Poe-Yamagata (1997). *Juvenile Offenders and Victims: 1997 Update on Violence*. Washington, DC: Office of Juvenile Justice and Delinquency Prevention.

Sieverdes, C., and C. Bartollas (1986). "Security Level and Adjustment Patterns in Juvenile Institutions." *Journal of Criminal Justice* 14:135-145.

Simons, R.L., C. Wu, C. Johnson, and R.D. Conger (1995). "A Test of Various Perspectives on the Intergenerational Transmission of Domestic Violence." *Criminology* 33:141-171.

Simpson, D.D., and S.B. Sells (1982). "Effectiveness of Treatment for Drug Abuse: An Overview of the DARP Research Program." *Advances in Alcohol and Substance Abuse* 2:7-29.

Simpson, E.L. (1974). "Moral Development Research: A Case Study of Scientific Cultural Bias." *Human Development* 17:81-106.

Singer, S.I. (1996). *Recriminalizing Delinquency: Violent Juvenile Crime and Juvenile Justice Reform*. New York: Cambridge University Press.

Skinner, B.F. (1953). *Science and Human Behavior*. New York: Macmillan.

Skogan, W.G. (1981). "On Attitudes and Behavior." In D.A. Lewis (ed.), *Reactions to Crime*. Beverly Hills: Sage.

Skogan, W.G., and S.M. Hartnett (1997). *Community Policing, Chicago Style*. New York: Oxford University Press.

Skogan, W.G., and M.G. Maxfield (1981). *Coping with Crime: Individual and Neighborhood Reactions*. Beverly Hills: Sage.

Skogan, W.G., and T.L. Meares (2004). "To Better Serve and Protect: Improving Police Practices." *Annals of the American Academy of Political and Social Science* 593:66-83.

Skolnick, J. (1966). *Justice Without Trial*. New York: John Wiley and Sons.

Skolnick, J., R. Bluthenthal, and T. Correl (1993). "Gang Organization and Migration." In S. Cummings and D.J. Monti (eds.), *Gangs: The Origins and Impact of Contemporary Youth Gangs in the United States* (pp. 193-218). Albany, NY: SUNY Press.

Skowyra, K., and J.J. Cocozza (2006). "A Blueprint for Change: Improving the System Response to Youth with Mental Health Needs Involved with the Juvenile Justice System." *National Center for Mental Health and Juvenile Justice Research and Program Brief*. Delmar, NY: National Center for Mental Health and Juvenile Justice.

Smith, B. (1998). "Children in Custody: 20-Year Trends in Juvenile Detention, Correctional, and Shelter Facilities." *Crime & Delinquency* 44:526-543.

Snyder, E. (1971). "The Impact of the Juvenile Court Hearing on the Child." *Crime & Delinquency* 32:97-133.

Snyder, H.N. (2000). "Juvenile Arrests, 1999." *OJJDP Juvenile Justice Bulletin*. Washington, DC: U.S. Department of Justice, Office of Juvenile Justice and Delinquency Prevention.

Snyder, H.N. (2005). "Juvenile Arrests, 2003." *OJJDP Juvenile Justice Bulletin*. Washington, DC: U.S. Department of Justice, Office of Juvenile Justice and Delinquency Prevention.

Snyder, H.N. (2008). "Juvenile Arrests, 2005." *OJJDP Juvenile Justice Bulletin*. Washington, DC: U.S. Department of Justice, Office of Juvenile Justice and Delinquency Prevention.

Snyder, H.N., and M. Sickmund (2006). *Juvenile Offenders and Victims: 2006 National Report*. Pittsburgh: National Center for Juvenile Justice.

Sommers, C.H. (2000). *The War Against Boys: How Misguided Feminism Is Harming Our Young Men*. New York: Touchstone.

Sourcebook of Criminal Justice Statistics Online(2002). Available at: http://www.albany.edu/sourcebook2002

Sourcebook of Criminal Justice Statistics Online (2007). Available at: http://www.albany.edu/sourcebook2007

Sparger, J.R., and D.J. Giacopassi (1992). "Memphis Revisited: A Reexamination of Police Shootings after the *Garner* Decision." *Justice Quarterly* 9:211-225.

Speckart, G.R., and M.D. Anglin (1985). "Narcotics and Crime: A Causal Modeling Approach." *Journal of Quantitative Criminology* 2:3-28.

Spergel, I.A. (1966). *Street Gang Work: Theory and Practice*. Reading, MA: Addison-Wesley.

Spergel, I.A. (1984). "Violent Gangs in Chicago: In Search of Social Policy." *Social Service Review* 58:199-226.

Spergel, I.A. (1986). "The Violent Gang Problem in Chicago: A Local Community Approach." *Social Service Review* 60:94-131.

Spergel, I.A., and G.D. Curry (1993). "The National Youth Gang Survey: A Research and Development Process." In A.P. Goldstein and C.R. Huff (eds.), *The Gang Intervention Handbook* (pp. 359-400). Champaign, IL: Research Press.

Spergel, I.A., G.D. Curry, R. Chance, C. Kane, R. Ross, A. Alexander, E. Simmons, and S. Oh (1990). *National Youth Gang Suppression and Intervention Program: Executive Summary, Stage 1: Assessment.* Arlington, VA: National Youth Gang Information Center.

Spergel, I.A., K.M. Wa, and R.V. Sosa (2001). *Evaluation of the Bloomington-Normal Comprehensive Gang Program—Final Report.* Washington, DC: Office of Juvenile Justice and Delinquency Prevention.

Spergel, I.A., K.M. Wa, and R.V. Sosa (2002). *Evaluation of the Mesa Gang Intervention Program (MGIP)—Final Report.* Washington, DC: Office of Juvenile Justice and Delinquency Prevention.

Spergel, I.A., K.M. Wa, and R.V. Sosa (2003). *Evaluation of the Riverside Comprehensive Community-wide Approach to Gang Prevention, Intervention and Suppression—Final Report.* Washington, DC: Office of Juvenile Justice and Delinquency Prevention.

Spergel, I.A., K.M. Wa, and R.V. Sosa (2004a). *Evaluation of the Tucson Comprehensive Community-wide Approach to Gang Prevention, Intervention and Suppression—Final Report.* Washington, DC: Office of Juvenile Justice and Delinquency Prevention.

Spergel, I.A., K.M. Wa, and R.V. Sosa (2004b). *Evaluation of the San Antonio Comprehensive Community-wide Approach to Gang Prevention, Intervention and Suppression—Final Report.* Washington, DC: Office of Juvenile Justice and Delinquency Prevention.

Spohn, C., R.K. Piper, T. Martin, and E.D. Frenzel (2001). "Drug Courts and Recidivism: The Results of an Evaluation Using Two Comparison Groups and Multiple Indicators of Recidivism." *Journal of Drug Issues* 31:149-176.

Stahl, A., T. Finnegan, and W. Kang (2003). *Easy Access to Juvenile Court Statistics: 1985-2000.* Washington, DC: U.S. Department of Justice. Available at: http://ojjdp. ncjrs.org/ojstatbb/ezajcs/

Stahl, A., C. Puzzanchera, S. Livsey, A. Sladky, T.A. Finnegan, N. Tierney, and H.N. Snyder (2007). *Juvenile Court Statistics: 2003-2004.* Pittsburgh: National Center for Juvenile Justice.

Staples, J.S. (2000). "Violence in Schools: Rage against a Broken World." *Annals of the American Academy of Political and Social Science* 567:30-41.

Staples, W.G. (1987). "Law and Social Control in Juvenile Justice Dispositions." *Journal of Research in Crime and Delinquency* 24:7-22.

Starbuck, D., J.C. Howell, and D.J. Lindquist (2001). "Hybrid and Other Modern Gangs." *OJJDP Juvenile Justice Bulletin.* Washington, DC: Office of Juvenile Justice and Delinquency Prevention.

Steele, B.F., and C.B. Pollock (1974). "A Psychiatric Study of Parents Who Abuse Infants and Small Children." In R.E. Helfer and C.H. Kempe (eds.), *The Battered Child*, 2nd ed (pp. 80-133). Chicago: University of Chicago Press.

Stephens, R.C. (1987). *Mind-Altering Drugs: Use, Abuse, and Treatment*. Newbury Park, CA: Sage.

Stephens, R.D., and J.L. Arnette (2000). *From the Courthouse to the Schoolhouse: Making Successful Transitions*. Washington, DC: Office of Juvenile Justice and Delinquency Prevention.

Stoutland, S.E. (2001). "The Multiple Dimensions of Trust in Resident/Police Relations." *Journal of Research in Crime and Delinquency* 38:226-253.

Straus, M.A. (1983). "Ordinary Violence, Child Abuse, and Wife Battering: What Do They Have in Common?" In D. Finkelhor, R.J. Gelles, G.T. Hotaling, and M.A. Straus (eds.), *The Dark Side of Families: Current Family Violence Research*. Beverly Hills: Sage.

Straus, M.A. (1994). *Beating the Devil Out of Them: Corporal Punishment in American Families*. New York: Lexington Books.

Street, D., R.D. Vinter, and C. Perrow (1966). *Organization for Treatment: A Comparative Study of Institutions for Delinquents*. New York: Free Press.

Strickland, R.A. (2004). *Restorative Justice*. New York: Peter Lang.

Stuart, B. (1996). "Circle Sentencing: Turning Swords into Ploughshares." In B. Galaway and J. Hudson (eds.), *Restorative Justice: International Perspectives*. Monsey, NY: Criminal Justice Press.

Studt, E. (1973). *Surveillance and Service in Parole: A Report of the Parole Action Study*. Washington, DC: National Institute of Corrections.

Stuphen, R.D., and J. Ford (2001). "The Effectiveness and Enforcement of a Teen Curfew Law." *Journal of Sociology and Social Welfare* 28:55-78.

Sullivan, C., M.Q. Grant, and J.D. Grant (1957). "The Development of Interpersonal Maturity: Applications to Delinquency." *Psychiatry* 20:373-385.

Sutherland, E.H. (1939). *Principles of Criminology*, 3rd ed. Philadelphia: Lippincott.

Sutherland, E.H., and D.R. Cressey (1974). *Criminology*, 9th ed. Philadelphia: Lippincott.

Swadi, H., and H. Zeitlin (1987). "Drug Education to School Children: Does it Really Work?" *British Journal of Addiction* 82:741-746.

Sykes, G.M., and D. Matza (1957). "Techniques of Neutralization: A Theory of Delinquency." *American Sociological Review* 22:664-670.

Szymanski, L.A. (2002). "Juvenile Delinquents' Right to a Jury Trial." *NCJJ Snapshot* 7(9). (September). Pittsburgh: National Center for Juvenile Justice.

Tanehaus, D.S. (2004). *Juvenile Justice in the Making*. New York: Oxford University Press.

Tangri, S.S., and M. Schwartz (1967). "Delinquency Research and the Self-concept Variable." *Journal of Criminal Law, Criminology and Police Science* 58:182-190.

Tannenbaum, F. (1938). *Crime and the Community*. New York: Columbia University Press.

Taxman, F.S. (2008). "No Illusions: Offender and Organizational Change in Maryland's Proactive Community Supervision Efforts." *Criminology & Public Policy* 7(2):275-302.

Taylor, M., and C. Nee (1988). "The Role of Cues in Simulated Residential Burglary." *British Journal of Criminology* 28:396-407.

Taylor, T.J., K.B. Turner, F. Esbensen, and T. Winfree (2001). "Coppin' an Attitude: Attitudinal Differences among Juveniles toward Police." *Journal of Criminal Justice* 29:295-305.

Tennenbaum, D.J. (1977). "Personality and Criminality: A Summary and Implications of the Literature." *Journal of Criminal Justice* 5:225-235.

Terrill, W. (2005). "Police Use of Force: A Transactional Approach." *Justice Quarterly* 22:107-138.

Thomas, C.W., and R. Cage (1977). "The Effect of Social Characteristics on Juvenile Court Dispositions." *Sociological Quarterly* 18:237-252.

Thornberry, T.P. (1973). "Race, Socioeconomic Status and Sentencing in the Juvenile Justice System." *Journal of Criminal Law and Criminology* 64:90-98.

Thornberry, T.P. (1987). "Toward an Interactional Theory of Delinquency." *Criminology* 25:863-892.

Thornberry, T.P. (1998). "Membership in Youth Gangs and Involvement in Serious and Violent Offending." In R. Loeber and D.P. Farrington (eds.), *Serious and Violent Offenders*. Newbury Park, CA: Sage.

Thornberry, T.P., and J.H. Burch (1997). *Gang Members and Delinquent Behavior*. Washington, DC: Office of Juvenile Justice and Delinquency Prevention.

Thornberry, T.P., and R.L. Christenson (1984). "Unemployment and Criminal Involvement: An Investigation of Reciprocal Causal Structures." *American Sociological Review* 49:398-411.

Thornberry, T.P., M.D. Krohn, A.J. Lizotte, and D. Chard-Wierschem (1993). "The Role of Juvenile Gangs in Facilitating Delinquent Behavior." *Journal of Research in Crime and Delinquency* 30:55-87.

Thornberry, T.P., A.J. Lizotte, M.D. Krohn, M. Farnworth, and S.J. Jang (1994). "Delinquent Peers, Beliefs, and Delinquent Behavior: A Longitudinal Test of Interactional Theory." *Criminology* 32:47-84.

Thrasher, F.M. (1936). *The Gang*. Chicago: University of Chicago Press.

Thurman, Q.C. (1984). "Deviance and the Neutralization of Moral Commitment: An Empirical Analysis." *Deviant Behavior* 5:291-304.

Tigner, S.S. (2000). "Cultivating Virtue?" *Journal of Education* 182(2):11-18.

Tittle, C., W. Villemez, and D. Smith (1978). "The Myth of Social Class and Criminality: An Empirical Assessment of the Empirical Evidence." *American Sociological Review* 43:643-656.

Tobey, A., T. Grisso, and R. Schwartz (2000). "Youths' Trial Participation as Seen by Youths and Their Attorneys: An Exploration of Competence-based Issues." In T. Grisso and R.G. Schwartz (eds.), *Youth on Trial: A Developmental Perspective on Juvenile Justice* (pp. 225-242). Chicago: University of Chicago Press.

Tobler, N.S. (1986). "Meta-Analysis of 143 Adolescent Drug Prevention Programs: Quantitative Outcome Results of Program Participants Compared to a Control or Comparison Group." *Journal of Drug Issues* 16:537-567.

Tobler, N.S. (1997). "Meta-Analysis of Adolescent Drug Prevention Programs: Results of the 1993 Meta-Analysis." In W.J. Bukoski (ed.), *Meta-Analysis of Drug Abuse Prevention Programs* (pp. 5-68). Rockville, MD: National Institute on Drug Abuse.

Tonry, M. (2008). "Crime and Human Rights—How Political Paranoia, Protestant Fundamentalism, and Constitutional Obsolescence Combined to Devastate Black America: The American Society of Criminology 2007 Presidential Address." *Criminology* 46:1-33.

Torbet, P.M. (1996). *Juvenile Probation: The Workhorse of the Juvenile Justice System.* Washington, DC: U.S. Department of Justice.

Torbet, P., R. Gable, H. Hurst, I. Montgomery, L. Szymanski, and D. Thomas (1996). *State Responses to Serious and Violent Juvenile Crime.* Washington, DC: Office of Juvenile Justice and Delinquency Prevention.

Torbet, P., P. Griffin, H. Hurst, and L.R. MacKenzie (2000). *Juveniles Facing Criminal Sanctions: Three States that Changed the Rules.* Washington, DC: U.S. Department of Justice.

Toseland, R.W. (1982). "Fear of Crime: Who is Most Vulnerable?" *Journal of Criminal Justice* 10:199-210.

Toy, C. (1992). "A Short History of Asian Gangs in San Francisco." *Justice Quarterly* 9:647-666.

Tracy, P.E. (2002). *Decision Making and Juvenile Justice: An Analysis of Bias in Case Processing.* Westport, CT: Praeger.

Trasler, G. (1993). "Conscience, Opportunity, Rational Choice, and Crime." In R.V. Clarke and M. Felson (eds.), *Routine Activity and Rational Choice* (pp. 305-322). New Brunswick, NJ: Transaction.

Trebach, A.S. (1987). *The Great Drug War and Radical Proposals that Could Make America Safe Again.* New York: Macmillan.

Trojanowicz, R., V.E. Kappeler, L.K. Gaines, and B. Bucqueroux (1998). *Community Policing: A Contemporary Perspective*, 2nd ed. Cincinnati: Anderson.

Tyler, J., R. Darville, and K. Stalnaker (1988). "Juvenile Boot Camps: A Descriptive Analysis of Program Diversity and Effectiveness." *Social Science Journal* 38:445.

Umbreit, M.S. (1997). "Victim-Offender Dialogue: From the Margins to the Mainstream Throughout the World." *The Crime Victims Report* 1:35-36,48.

Umbreit, M.S. (1999). "Avoiding the Marginalization and McDonaldization of Victim Offender Mediation: A Case Study in Moving toward the Mainstream." In G. Bazemore and L. Walgrave (eds.), *Restorative Juvenile Justice: Repairing the Harm of Youth Crime* (pp. 213-234). Monsey, NY: Criminal Justice Press.

Umbreit, M.S., and R.B. Coates (1992). *Victim Offender Mediation: An Analysis of Programs in Four States of the U.S.* St. Paul, MN: Center for Restorative Justice and Peacemaking.

Umbreit, M.S., R.B. Coates, and B. Vos (2001). *Juvenile Offender Mediation in Six Oregon Counties.* Salem, OR: Oregon Dispute Resolution Commission.

Umbreit, M.S., B. Vos, R.B. Coates, and K.A. Brown (2003). *Facing Violence: The Path of Restorative Justice and Dialogue.* Monsey, NY: Criminal Justice Press.

Underwood, J. (1994). "Prayer in the Schools." *Schools and the Courts* 20 (May):1039-1050.

Urban, L.S., J.L. St. Cyr, and S.H. Decker (2003). "Goal Conflict in the Juvenile Court: The Evolution of Sentencing Practices in the United States." *Journal of Contemporary Criminal Justice* 19:454-479.

U.S. Attorney General's Task Force (1984). *Family Violence*. Washington, DC: U.S. Government Printing Office.

U.S. Bureau of the Census (2005). *Annual Population Estimates*. Washington, DC: U.S. Bureau of the Census. Available at: http://www.census.gov/popest/states/NST-ann-est.html

U.S. Department of Education (2003). *Guidance on Constitutionally Protected Prayer in Public Elementary and Secondary Schools*. Washington, DC: U.S. Department of Education. Available at: http://www.ed.gov/policy/gen/guid/religionandschools/prayer_guidance.html

U.S. Department of Justice (1997). *Criminal Victimization in the United States, 1995*. Washington, DC: Bureau of Justice Statistics.

U.S. Department of Justice (2006). *National CASA Program—Audit Report 07-04*. Washington, DC: U.S. Department of Justice, Office of the Inspector General.

Valdez, A. (2000). *Gangs: A Guide to Understanding Street Gangs*, 3rd ed. San Clemente, CA: LawTech.

van den Haag, E. (1978). "In Defense of the Death Penalty: A Legal-Practical-Moral Analysis." *Criminal Law Bulletin* 14:51-68.

van den Haag, E., and P. Conrad (1983). *The Death Penalty: A Debate*. New York: Plenum.

Vandervort, F.E., and W.E. Ladd (2001). "The Worst of All Possible Worlds: Michigan's Juvenile Justice System and International Standards for the Treatment of Children." *University of Detroit Mercy Law Review* 78:202-258.

Van Kammen, W.B., and R. Loeber (1994). "Are Fluctuations in Delinquent Activities Related to the Onset and Offset in Juvenile Illegal Drug Use and Drug Dealing?" *The Journal of Drug Issues* 24:9-24.

Van Ness, D.W. (1990). "Restorative Justice." In B. Galaway and J. Hudson (eds.), *Criminal Justice, Restitution, and Reconciliation*. Monsey, NY: Criminal Justice Press.

Van Ness, D.W., and K.H. Strong (2006). *Restoring Justice: An Introduction to Restorative Justice*, 3rd ed. Newark, NJ: LexisNexis Matthew Bender.

Van Voorhis, P., M. Braswell, and D. Lester (2007). *Correctional Counseling and Rehabilitation*, 6th ed. Newark, NJ: LexisNexis Matthew Bender.

Veevers, J. (1989). "Pre-court Diversion for Juvenile Offenders." In M. Wright and B. Galaway (eds.), *Mediation and Criminal Justice: Victims, Offenders and Community*. Newbury Park, CA: Sage.

Vigil, J.D. (1993). "The Established Gang." In S. Cummings and D.J. Monti (eds.), *Gangs: The Origins and Impact of Contemporary Youth Gangs in the United States* (pp. 95-112). Albany, NY: SUNY Press.

Vigil, J.D. (1997). "Learning from Gangs: The Mexican American Experience." *ERIC Digest*, Document No. RC020943.

Viljoen, J.L., J. Klaver, and R. Roesch (2005). "Legal Decisions of Preadolescent and Adolescent Defendants: Predictors of Confessions, Pleas, Communication with Attorneys, and Appeals." *Law and Human Behavior* 29:253-277.

Vingilis, E.R., and K. DeGenova (1984). "Youth and the Forbidden Fruit: Experiences with Changes in Legal Drinking Age in North America." *Journal of Criminal Justice* 12:161-172.

"Violence-Related Attitudes and Behaviors of High School Students—New York City, 1992." (1993). *Journal of School Health* 63:438-440.

Virkkunen, M., D. Goldman, and M. Linnoila (1996). "Serotonin in Alcoholic Violent Offenders." In G.R. Bock and J.A. Goode (eds.), *Genetics of Criminal and Antisocial Behavior* (pp. 168-176). Chichester, England: John Wiley and Sons.

Visher, C.A. (1990). "Incorporating Drug Treatment in Criminal Sanctions." *NIJ Reports* #221. Washington, DC: National Institute of Justice.

Vold, G.B., and T.J. Bernard (1986). *Theoretical Criminology*, 3rd ed. New York: Oxford University Press.

von Hentig, H. (1941). "Remarks on the Interaction of Perpetrator and Victim." *Journal of Criminal Law, Criminology and Police Science* 31:303-309.

von Hirsch, A. (1990). "The Ethics of Community-based Sanctions." *Crime & Delinquency* 36:162-173.

Wachtel, T. (1995). "Family Group Conferencing: Restorative Justice in Practice." *Juvenile Justice Update* 1(4):1-2,13-14.

Wadlington, W., C.H. Whitebread, and S.M. Davis (1983). *Cases and Materials on Children in the Legal System*. Mineola, NY: Foundation Press.

Waldo, G.P., and S. Dinitz (1967). "Personality Attributes of the Criminal: An Analysis of Research Studies, 1950-1965." *Journal of Research in Crime and Delinquency* 4:185-202.

Walker, S. (1998). *Sense and Nonsense about Crime and Drugs: A Policy Guide*, 4th ed. Belmont, CA: Wadsworth.

Walker, S. (2001). *Sense and Nonsense about Crime and Drugs: A Policy Guide*, 5th ed. Belmont, CA: Wadsworth.

Walker, S. (2006). *Sense and Nonsense about Crime and Drugs: A Policy Guide*, 6th ed. Belmont, CA: Wadsworth.

Walker, S., and C.M. Katz (2005). *The Police in America: An Introduction*. Boston: McGraw-Hill.

Walsh, W.F., and G.F. Vito (2004). "The Meaning of CompStat: Analysis and Response." *Journal of Contemporary Criminal Justice* 20:51-69.

Walters, G.D. (1992). "A Meta-Analysis of the Gene-Crime Relationship." *Criminology* 30:595-613.

Walters, S.T., M.D. Clark, R. Gingerich, and M.L. Meltzer (2007). *A Guide for Probation and Parole: Motivating Offenders to Change*. Washington, DC: U.S. Department of Justice, National Institute of Corrections.

Watts, W.D., and L.S. Wright (1990). "The Relationship of Alcohol, Tobacco, Marijuana, and Other Illegal Drug Use to Delinquency among Mexican-American, Black, and White Adolescent Males." *Adolescence* 25:171-181.

Websdale, N. (2001). *Policing the Poor: From Slave Plantation to Public Housing*. Boston: Northeastern University Press.

Weis, K., and S.S. Borges (1973). "Victimology and Rape: The Case of the Legitimate Victim." *Issues in Criminology* 8:71-115.

Weisburd, D., S.D. Mastrofski, A.M. McNally, R. Greenspan, and J.J. Willis (2003). "Reforming to Preserve: CompStat and Strategic Problem Solving in American Policing." *Criminology & Public Policy* 2:421-456.

Weisel, D.L., and T.O. Shelley (2004). *Specialized Gang Units: Form and Function in Community Policing—Final Report.* Washington, DC: National Institute of Justice.

Weisheit, R.A. (1983). "The Social Context of Alcohol and Drug Education: Implications for Program Evaluations." *Journal of Alcohol and Drug Education* 29:72-81.

Weitekamp, E.G.M. (1999). "The History of Restorative Justice." In G. Bazemore and L. Walgrave (eds.), *Restorative Juvenile Justice: Repairing the Harm of Youth Crime.* Monsey, NY: Criminal Justice Press.

Wexler, D.B. (2002). "Some Reflections on Therapeutic Jurisprudence and the Practice of Criminal Law." *Criminal Law Bulletin* 38:205-215.

Whitaker, C., and L. Bastian (1991). *Teenage Victims: A National Crime Survey Report.* Washington, DC: U.S. Department of Justice.

White, G.F. (1990). "The Drug Use-Delinquency Connection in Adolescence." In R. Weisheit (ed.), *Drugs, Crime and the Criminal Justice System.* Cincinnati: Anderson.

White, H.R., R.J. Pandina, and R.L. LaGrange (1987). "Longitudinal Predictors of Serious Substance Use and Delinquency." *Criminology* 25:715-740.

White House, The (2008). *National Drug Control Strategy.* Washington, DC: The White House.

Whitehead, J.T. (1991). "The Effectiveness of Felony Probation: Results from an Eastern State." *Justice Quarterly* 8:525-543.

Whitehead, J.T., and M.C. Braswell (2000). "The Future of Probation: Reintroducing the Spiritual Dimension into Correctional Practice." *Criminal Justice Review* 25:207-233.

Wiatrowski, M., D. Griswold, and M. Roberts (1981). "Social Control Theory and Delinquency." *American Sociological Review* 46:525-541.

Widom, C.S. (1989). "Child Abuse, Neglect and Violent Criminal Behavior." *Criminology* 27:251-271.

Widom, C.S. (1995). "Childhood Victimization and Violent Behavior." Paper presented at the Annual Conference on Criminal Justice Research and Evaluation, Washington, DC.

Wiebush, R.G., D. Wagner, B. McNulty, Y. Wang, and T.N. Le (2005). *Implementation and Outcome Evaluation of the Intensive Aftercare Program—Final Report.* Washington, DC: Office of Juvenile Justice and Delinquency Prevention.

Wiehe, V.R. (1992). *Working with Child Abuse and Neglect.* Itasca, IL: F.E. Peacock.

Wilkinson, W. (2008). "Bottoms Up!" *Forbes* (September 29, 2008):28.

Williams, N., and S. Williams (1970). *The Moral Development of Children.* London: Macmillan.

Wilson, J.Q., and R.J. Herrnstein (1985). *Crime and Human Nature.* New York: Simon & Schuster.

Wilson, J.Q., and G.L. Kelling (1982). "Broken Windows: The Police and Neighborhood Safety." *Atlantic Monthly* 249(3):29-38.

Wilson, S.J., and M.W. Lipsey (2003). "Wilderness Challenge Programs for Delinquent Youth: A Meta-Analysis of Outcome Evaluations." *Evaluation and Program Planning* 23:1-12.

Wish, E.D., M.A. Toborg, and J.P. Bellassai (1988). *Identifying Drug Users and Monitoring Them During Conditional Release*. Washington, DC: U.S. Department of Justice.

Witkin, G. (ed.) (2006). "Florida Boots Harsh Tactics." *U.S. News and World Report* (May 8, 2006):18

Wolfgang, M.E. (1958). *Patterns in Criminal Homicide*. Montclair, NJ: Patterson Smith. Reprinted 1975.

Wood, P.B., B. Pfefferbaum, and B.J. Arneklev (1993). "Risk-taking and Self-control: Social Psychological Correlates of Delinquency." *Journal of Crime and Justice* 16:111-130.

Wooden, K. (1976). *Weeping in the Playtime of Others: America's Incarcerated Children*. New York: McGraw-Hill.

Wooden, W.S., and R. Blazak (2001). *Renegade Kids, Suburban Outlaws: From Youth Culture to Delinquency*, 2nd ed. Belmont, CA: Wadsworth.

Worden, R.E. (1996). "The Causes of Police Brutality: Theory and Evidence on Police Use of Force." In W.A. Geller and H. Toch (eds.), *Police Violence: Understanding and Controlling Police Abuse of Force* (pp. 23-51). New Haven, CT: Yale University Press.

World Health Organization (1964). *WHO Expert Committee on Addiction Producing Drugs: 13th Report*. #23. Geneva: World Health Organization.

Worrall, J.L., and L.K. Gaines (2006). "The Effect of Police-Probation Partnerships on Juvenile Arrests." *Journal of Criminal Justice* 34:579-589.

Wright, J.P., and F.T. Cullen (2000). "Juvenile Involvement in Occupational Delinquency." *Criminology* 38:863-892.

Wright, J.P, F.T. Cullen, and N. Williams (1997). "Working While in School and Delinquent Involvement: Implications for Social Policy." *Crime & Delinquency* 43:203-221.

Wright, R.T., and S.H. Decker (1994). *Burglars on the Job: Streetlife and Residential Break-ins*. Boston: Northeastern University Press.

Yablonsky, L. (1962). *The Violent Gang*. New York: Macmillan.

Zatz, M.S. (1985). "Los Cholos: Legal Processing of Chicano Gang Members." *Social Problems* 33:13-30.

Zehr, H. (1990). *Changing Lenses: A New Focus for Crime and Justice*. Scottdale, PA: Herald Press.

Zehr, H., and H. Mika (2003). "Fundamental Concepts of Restorative Justice." In E. McLaughlin, R. Fergusson, G. Hughes, and L. Westmarland (eds.), *Restorative Justice: Critical Issues*. Thousand Oaks, CA: Sage.

Zevitz, R. (1993). "Youth Gangs in a Small Midwestern City: Insider's Perspectives." *Journal of Crime and Justice* 16:149-166.

Ziemer, D. (2005). "Juvenile Interrogations Must Be Recorded." *Wisconsin Law Journal* (July 13, 2005). Available at: http://www.wislawjournal.com/article.cfm/2005/07/13/recording

Zimring, F.E. (1982). *The Changing Legal World of Adolescence*. New York: Free Press.

Zimring, F.E. (2000). "Penal Proportionality for the Young Offender: Notes on Immaturity, Capacity, and Diminished Responsibility." In T. Grisso and R.G. Schwartz (eds.), *Youth on Trial: A Developmental Perspective on Juvenile Justice* (pp. 271-289). Chicago: University of Chicago Press.

Zimring, F.E. (2005). "Minimizing Harm from Minority Disproportion in American Juvenile Justice." In D.F. Hawkins and K. Kempf-Leonard (eds.), *Our Children, Their Children: Confronting Racial and Ethnic Differences in American Juvenile Justice* (pp. 413-427). Chicago: University of Chicago Press.

Zimring, F.E. (2007). *The Great American Crime Decline.* New York: Oxford University Press.

Court Cases and Statutes

Bethel School District No. 403 v. Fraser, 478 U.S. 675, 106 S.Ct. 3159, 92 L.Ed.2d 549 (1986).

Board of Education of Independent School District No. 92 of Pottawatomie County et al. v. Lindsay Earls et al., 536 U.S. 822 (2002).

Breed v. Jones, 421 U.S. 519, 95 S.Ct. 1779, 44 L.Ed.2d 346 (1975).

Brown v. Gwinnett County School District, 112 F.3d 1464 (11th Cir. 1997).

Chicago v. Morales, 527 U.S. 41 (1999).

Commonwealth v. Fisher, 213 Pa. 48 (1905).

Cornfield by Lewis v. Consolidated High School District No. 230, 991 F.3d 1316, 1326-1327 (7th Cir. 1993).

Doe v. Renfrow, 451 U.S. 1022 (1981).

Ex parte Crouse, 4 Wheaton (Pa.) 9 (1838).

Fare v. Michael C., 442 U.S. 707, 99 S.Ct. 2560, 61 L.Ed.2d 197 (1979).

Good News Club v. Milford Central School, 533 U.S. 98 (2001).

Hazelwood School District v. Kuhlmeier, 484 U.S. 260, 108 S.Ct. 562, 98 L.Ed.2d 592 (1988).

Ingraham v. Wright, 430 U.S. 651, 97 S.Ct. 1401, 51 L.Ed.2d 711 (1977).

In re Gault, 387 U.S. 1, 87 S.Ct. 1428, 18 L.Ed.2d 527 (1967).

In re LeBlanc, 171 Mich. App. 405, 412 (1988).

In re Tyrell, 8 Cal.4th 68 (1994).

In re Winship, 397 U.S. 358, 90 S.Ct. 1068, 25 L.Ed.2d 368 (1970).

Gonzalez v. Mailliard, Civ. No. 50424, N.D. Cal. 2/9/71, Appeal U.S. No. 70-120 4/9/71 (1971).

Johnson v. City of Opelousas, 658 F.2d 1065 (5th Cir. 1981).

Jones v. Clear Creek Independent School District, 977 F.2d 963 (5th Cir. 1992).

Kent v. United States, 383 U.S. 541, 86 S.Ct. 1045, 16 L.Ed.2d 84 (1966).

Lee v. Weisman, 112 S.Ct. 2649 (1992).

McKeiver v. Pennsylvania, 403 U.S. 528, 91 S.Ct. 1976, 29 L.Ed.2d 647 (1971).

New Jersey v. T.L.O., 469 U.S. 325 (1985).

P.B. v. Koch, 96 F.3d 1298 (9th Cir. 1993).

People v. Turner, 55 Ill. 280 (1870).

Qutb v. Strauss, 11 F.3d 488 (5th Cir. 1993).

Roper v. Simmons, 543 U.S. 551 (2005).

Santa Fe Independent School District v. Doe, 530 U.S. 290 (2000).

Schall v. Martin, 467 U.S. 253, 104 S.Ct. 2403, 81 L.Ed.2d 207 (1984).

Schneckloth v. Bustamonte, 412 U.S. 218, 93 S.Ct. 2041, 36 L.Ed.2d 854 (1973).

Settle v. Dickson County School Board, 53 F.3d 152 (6th Cir. 1995).

Stanford v. Kentucky, 492 U.S. 361 (1989).

Steirer v. Bethlehem Area School District, 987 F.2d 989 (3rd Cir. 1994).

Tennessee v. Garner et al., 83 U.S. 1035, 105 S.Ct. 1694, 85 L.Ed.2d 1 (1985).

Thompson v. Carthage School District, 87 F.3d 979 (8th Cir. 1996).

Tinker v. Des Moines Independent Community Schools District, 393 U.S. 503, 89 S.Ct. 733, 21 L.Ed.2d 731 (1969).

Todd v. Rush County Schools, 133 F.3d 984 (7th Cir. 1998).

United States v. Mark James Knights, 278 F.3d 920 (9th Cir. 2002).

Vernonia School District v. Acton, 515 U.S. 646 (1995).

Yarborough, Warden v. Alvarado, 541 U.S. 652 (2004).

GLOSSARY

A

abandonment: the permanent desertion of a child; an acceptable practice from the fourth to the thirteenth centuries when a child was an economic burden to a household.

abuse: any nonaccidental infliction of injury that seriously impairs a child's physical or mental health.

adjudication: the process of determining whether there is enough evidence to find a youth to be a delinquent, a status offender, or a dependent.

affective interventions: an approach to drug use prevention that focuses attention on the individual in order to build self-esteem, self-awareness, and feelings of self-worth.

aftercare: mandatory programming for youths after release from training schools or other placements, similar to parole in adult courts.

apprenticeship: a situation in which one is bound by indenture to serve another for a prescribed period with a view to learning an art or trade.

anomie: Emil Durkheim's concept of the state of normlessness in society.

atavistic: a term describing ape-like physical qualities of the head and body that were supposed by Cesare Lombroso to be indicative of the individual's developmental state.

"attack" (tough) probation: also known as "tough probation," the trend to make probation supervision stricter (tougher) by devoting less emphasis on assistance and counseling and greater attention to monitoring the conditions of probation. Attack probation can refer to intensive supervision, electronic monitoring of offender movements, and shame tactics.

avoidance: a common reaction to actual or potential victimization in which an individual stays away from particular locations where or individuals by whom victimization is anticipated.

B

balanced approach: a recent approach in juvenile corrections that places emphasis on the offender, the victim, and community safety. One aim is to restore the victim and the community, as much as possible, to his or her pre-crime status.

behavior modification: a therapeutic approach based on the work of B.F. Skinner and Hans J. Eysenck that entails the use of reinforcements to increase the probability of desired behaviors and a lack of reinforcement, or punishment stimuli, to decrease the probability of undesirable behaviors.

biosociology: also known as sociobiology, the idea that the biological makeup of the organism and the surrounding environment are intimately related.

blended sentencing: a development in juvenile justice in which either the juvenile court or the adult court imposes a sentence that can involve either the juvenile or the adult correctional system or both.

bond to society (also called **social bond**): in Travis Hirschi's control theory, the connections an individual has to the social order; the four elements of the bond are attachment, commitment, involvement, and belief.

boot camp: a short-term program that resembles basic military training by emphasizing physical training and discipline; boot camps often include educational and rehabilitative components.

Boston Gun Project: a project that targeted firearms use by gangs by using a "pulling levers" (zero-tolerance) approach.

Breaking the Cycle (BTC) program: a program that seeks to identify offenders with substance abuse problems early in their system processing, assess the appropriate treatment needs of the offender, and establish an integrated set of interventions (sanction, treatment, and rewards) for the individual.

"broken windows" policing: policing strategies based on the belief that signs of urban decay, such as broken windows, in a neighborhood serve to make the neighborhood more conducive to crime and more fear-inducing; police attend to both crime and disorder.

C

capital punishment: the death penalty. The Supreme Court recently ruled that capital punishment is unconstitutional for juveniles.

Chancery Court: a body concerned with property matters in feudal England; responsible for overseeing the financial affairs of orphaned juveniles who were not yet capable of handling their own matters.

Chicago School: a perspective explaining deviance as the natural outgrowth of the location in which it occurs; named for the work performed by social scientists at the University of Chicago.

child maltreatment: a variety of actions in which children are harmed, either intentionally or unintentionally.

child protective services: a state's method of handling child abuse cases; usually responsible for accepting and investigating reports of abuse and neglect and for removing children from potential or actual abusive situations.

child saver: Anthony Platt's term for a person involved in the development of the juvenile court during the Progressive Era.

Classicism: a school of thought that sees humankind as having free will, that is, humans calculate the pros and cons of an activity before choosing what to do (compare to **Positivism**).

collective efficacy: the empowerment of the community to do something about problems (e.g., crime).

common-sense corrections: the use of various types of wilderness programs, ranging from relatively short stays in outdoor settings to long wagon train or ocean ship trips.

community group conferencing (CGC): a strategy involving the community of people most affected by the crime in deciding the resolution of a criminal or delinquent act. It is much like family group conferencing, except that it includes a broader set of support groups and community members; see **family group conferencing.**

community justice: an approach to justice that focuses on helping community residents manage their own affairs, solve their own problems, and live together effectively and safely.

community policing: problem-oriented policing that relies on input from the public to define problems and establish police policy.

community service: the practice of having offenders perform unpaid work for government or private agencies as payment for crimes without personal victims.

Community-Wide Approach to Gang Prevention, Intervention, and Suppression Program: a program aimed to initiate a comprehensive set of strategies: mobilizing communities, providing youth opportunities, suppressing gang violence, providing social intervention (services) and street outreach, and facilitating organizational change and development in community agencies.

CompStat: a management process in which police managers are held accountable for the control of crime and the enhancement of the quality of life in their areas. Statistics are collected to help pinpoint where problems are, and police managers then try to reduce crime and improve quality of life indicators in those areas.

concerned adult role: a role assumed by some attorneys in juvenile cases in which the attorney acts as a "concerned adult" rather than a zealous advocate, sometimes encouraging youths to admit to petitions in cases in which an adversarial approach may have resulted in a dismissal of the petition.

concordance: similarity among groups in a study.

conflict resolution programs: programs in which the most important element is teaching youths alternative methods for resolving conflicts before they occur.

consent search: a search in which a defendant voluntarily allows the police to search person or effects without a search warrant.

containment theory: Walter Reckless's social control theory holding that behavior is controlled through outer containment (influences of family, peers, etc.) and inner containment (strengths within an individual), working in opposition to external pushes, external pressures, and external pulls.

corporal punishment: physical punishment.

cottage system: a training school design that attempts to simulate home life more closely than would a prison-like institution; it divides the larger prison into smaller "cottages" for living.

Court-Appointed Special Advocate (CASA): a voluntary advocate for children in child abuse and neglect cases.

criminalized juvenile court: a suggested reform of juvenile court that advocates providing juveniles with all the procedural protections of adult criminal court and offering reduced penalties for juvenile offenders.

culture conflict: the conflict resulting when one set of cultural or subcultural practices necessitates violating the norms of a coexisting culture.

cycle of violence: the idea that a child who is abused or who witnesses abuse will grow up to be an abuser.

D

dark figure of crime: crimes that are unreported to the police.

day-evening center: a detention alternative in which a center was formed to devote time to formal education and remedial and tutorial work in the day and recreational programs in the evening.

deadly force: police actions that have the potential to cause the death of the offender.

deinstitutionalization: the practice of avoiding any involuntary residential placements of status offenders; also, the general idea of removing any youths from institutional control.

delinquency: in general, conduct that subjects a juvenile individual to the jurisdiction of the juvenile court (for more on the various definitions comprised under this term, see Chapter 1).

detached worker program: a program designed to place system workers into the environment of the gang.

detention decision: the decision whether to keep a juvenile in custody or to allow the youth to go home while awaiting further court action.

determinism: a theory or doctrine holding that acts of the will, occurrences in nature, and social or psychological phenomena are causally determined by preceding events or natural laws.

detoxification: a treatment approach that attempts to remove an individual from an addiction by weaning him or her off drugs.

developmental theories: theories that explain the changes and stability that characterize the trajectory of an individual's behavior or time.

differential association: Edwin Sutherland's theory suggesting that criminal behavior is learned when an individual encounters an excess of definitions favoring deviant definitions over those that conform to the law.

differential identification: a concept proposing that personal association is not always necessary for the transmission of behavioral cues; fictional presentations provide information concerning acceptable behavior.

differential reinforcement: a theory that proposes that an individual can learn from a variety of sources, both social and nonsocial, and that the differing levels of reinforcement received will help shape future behavior.

disposition: the process of determining what intervention to give a juvenile offender upon his or her adjudication as a delinquent.

disproportionate minority contact: the fact that minority youths are more likely to be arrested or adjudicated delinquent compared to their proportion of the population.

dispute resolution: bringing together adversarial parties in an attempt to arrive at a mutually agreeable solution.

diversion: attempting to find alternative forms of dealing with problem youth outside of normal system processing.

divestiture: elimination of juvenile court jurisdiction over status offenses.

domestic relations court: a civil court devoted to issues involved in divorce, child support, and related matters.

dowry: the money, goods, or estate that a woman would bring to her husband in marriage.

drift: the concept that individuals are pushed and pulled toward different modes of activity at different times in their lives (that is, a person can "drift" in and out of crime).

Drug Abuse Resistance Education (D.A.R.E.) program: a school-based, police-taught program aimed at elementary students that attempts to reduce drug use by focusing on enhancing the social skills of the individual.

drug courts: specialized courts that attempt to help drug offenders stop using drugs by providing services and judicial supervision.

E

ecological fallacy: the fallacy of attributing results based on grouped data to the individual level.

ecological perspective: an approach that seeks to explain deviance as a natural outgrowth of the location in which it occurs.

effectiveness: whether interventions have an impact on any measure of the crime problem.

ego: in Freudian theory, the social identity of an individual; actual behavior; conscious activity.

elaboration model: a perspective that takes components of various theories in order to construct a single explanation that incorporates the best parts of the individual theories.

emphasis on status offenses: a focus on status offenses such as truancy; see **status offense**.

enhancement model: a model of the delinquency–gang relationship that strikes a middle ground in which gangs recruit delinquency-prone youths and enhance their deviance.

exchange theory: a theory that proceeds from the assumption that equal reciprocity is a cornerstone of social interaction. Parties to a confrontation (such as an offense and subsequent restorative justice program) seek to establish a balance in the relationship.

F

family court: a court designated to deal with family matters.

family group conferencing (FGC): a strategy involving the community of people most affected by the crime in deciding the resolution of a criminal or delinquent act.

focal concerns: the concerns designated by Walter Miller to represent the cultural values of the lower class; they include, trouble, toughness, smartness, excitement, fate, and autonomy.

foray: an attack, usually by two or three youths, upon one or more rival gang members (e.g., a drive-by shooting).

free will: the tenet that people choose to act the way that they do after calculating the pros and cons of an activity.

freedom of speech: the right to speak freely without censorship or limitation; for students, the Supreme Court has ruled that the right of free speech is to be balanced with the school's interest in education and discipline.

G

gang: in general, a group that exhibits characteristics that set them apart from other affiliations of juveniles, often involved in deviant activity (for more on the various definitions comprised under this term, see Chapter 5).

Gang Resistance Education and Training (G.R.E.A.T.) Program: a program operated by the Bureau of Alcohol, Tobacco, Firearms, and Explosives in which local police officers present a curriculum to middle-school children designed to induce them to resist the pressure to join a gang.

ganging: the process of developing gangs.

general strain theory: Robert Agnew's theory positing that the removal of valued stimuli or the presentation of negative stimuli can lead to strain and, perhaps, deviance.

generic control theory: a theory that proposes that control can come from several sources that vary over time and situation; four categories of control mechanisms are bonding, unfolding, modeling, and constraining.

goal confusion: the state of affairs in which judges, probation and aftercare officers, probation directors, state legislators, juvenile justice experts, and others in the system disagree about the objectives of juvenile court and community supervision.

graduated licensing: a strategy in which young drivers acquire on-the-road driving experience in lower-risk settings, then learning time is increased and drivers are gradually introduced to more difficult driving situations; they "graduate" to greater driving responsibility as they master the previous steps.

group hazard hypothesis: a contention that delinquency committed in groups has a greater chance of being detected and acted upon by the juvenile and criminal justice systems.

guardian ad litem: an individual appointed by the court to serve as an advocate for a child in a child abuse or neglect case (also see **Court-Appointed Special Advocate**).

H

hedonistic calculus: the belief that individuals seek to maximize pleasure.

home detention: programs that supervise juveniles at home instead of in custody while they are awaiting further court action.

houses of refuge: early institutions for children that were designed to separate the youth from the detrimental environment of the city.

hybrid gangs: gangs that are mixed racially or ethnically or gangs whose members may belong to more than one gang.

I

I-levels: See **interpersonal maturity levels**.

in camera testimony: testimony given outside the courtroom, often used for the testimony of children in abuse and neglect cases.

id: in Freudian theory, unconscious desires, drives, instincts.

incidence: how many times something (e.g., a drug) was used.

Index crime: an offense included in Part I of the Uniform Crime Reports. The eight crimes included are murder, rape, robbery, aggravated assault, burglary, larceny, motor vehicle theft, and arson.

infanticide: the deliberate killing of young children, a common practice prior to the fourth century when a child was an economic burden to a household.

informal adjustment: informal handling of an offense without the filing of a petition (e.g., a probation intake officer orders the payment of restitution).

inmate code: a group of peer norms or a code of behavior among inmates that may or may not conflict with the norms expected by treatment professionals and correctional staff.

inner containment: direct control over the individual from inside sources.

institutional life: refers to the demands of daily life in institutions such as detention centers and state training schools where all aspects of life are regulated. Inmates typically make adjustments to such institutions that often work against the objectives of staff.

intake decision: the decision whether to file a court petition of delinquent, status offense, abuse or dependency.

intelligence quotient (IQ): a test, developed by Alfred Binet. that provides a numerical representation of the mental ability of an individual [the formula is IQ = (mental age/chronological age) x 100].

Interpersonal Maturity Levels (I-levels): developed by Sullivan et al., the seven levels that reflect the progressive development of social and interpersonal skills.

interstitial areas: areas that are deteriorating and in a state of disorganization.

intraindividual theory: in explanations of child maltreatment, a theory that views child maltreatment as an internal defect of the abuser.

invasion, domination, and succession: the phenomenon in which inner-city areas undergo constant change. Over a period of time, one underprivileged group invades an area and then gains some degree of dominance there, and then that group leaves the area for more desirable outer zones, allowing new groups of underprivileged people to take their place.

involuntary servitude: selling or trading a youth to another for service.

J

jurisdiction over status offenders: the juvenile court's prerogative to exercise control over juveniles who have committed status offenses (e.g., disobedient, runaway, and truant adolescents); see **status offense**.

"Just Say No": a school- and media-based program designed to encourage children to make a personal decision to refuse any offer to use illicit drugs in the face of peer influences.

juvenile: a minor. (The precise definition of a juvenile varies from jurisdiction to jurisdiction, currently ranging from under age 16 to under age 18.)

juvenile curfew laws: laws that states that juveniles must stay inside their houses at specific times, enacted in an effort to reduce victimization of and by juveniles.

K

knowledge approach: an approach to drug use prevention that entails providing youths with information on different types of drugs and the possible legal consequences of using them.

L

labeling: the contention that the fact of being labeled deviant by society leads an individual to act in accordance with that label.

legal drinking age: the age at which a person is allowed to legally purchase and consume alcohol.

legislative waiver: state laws that provide for automatic transfer of juvenile to adult court, as opposed to judicial waiver or transfer (see **waiver**).

life-course theories: see **developmental theories**.

life skills training: educational programs that include basic personal and social skills development (which deal with general life situations and how to deal with them) as well as specific resistance skills aimed directly at substance abuse issues.

lifestyle explanations: see **routine activities theory**.

looking-glass self: the idea that individuals view themselves in the way other people look at them.

M

maintenance program: a drug treatment program that seeks to establish a state in which the individual does not experience withdrawal systems.

medical model: a perspective that approaches the deviant act as a symptom of a larger problem (or "disease").

meta-analysis: a statistical technique that uses data from a number of studies to compute a common statistic in order to compare results across studies.

Minnesota Multiphasic Personality Inventory (MMPI): a 556-question inventory that serves as a standardized method for tapping personality traits in individuals.

mission distortion: in probation, the phenomenon describing what happened when probation officers no longer see themselves as service providers or social workers but instead over-identify with a law enforcement role.

modeling: a form of learning that entails copying the behavior of others.

modes of adaptation: according to Merton, the various ways of adapting to strain; the five modes of adaptation are conformity, innovation, ritualism, retreatism, and rebellion.

Monitoring the Future (MTF) Project: a self-report survey, administered annually to high school seniors, college students, and young adults, that includes both serious and less serious offenses, such as robbery, aggravated assault, hitting teachers, use of weapons, group fighting, and drug usage.

moral development: Kohlberg's theory that individuals progress through six stages of "moral development," which are arranged into three levels: preconventional, conventional, and postconventional (principled).

motivational interviewing: a style of communication designed to make it more likely that offenders will listen, will be engaged in the process, and will be more ready to make changes.

Multi-dimensional Family Therapy (MDFT): therapy centered on the family, peers, and community influences around youths.

multiple causation: the belief that delinquency is caused by multiple factors in conjunction with one another.

N

National Child Abuse and Neglect Data System (NCANDS): a voluntary national data collection and analysis system created in response to the requirements of the Child Abuse Prevention and Treatment Act.

National Crime Victimization Survey (NCVS): a victim survey administered by the U.S. Census Bureau.

National Incident-Based Reporting System (NIBRS): a system that collects detailed information on 22 categories of offenses with 46 specific crimes rather than just the eight Index offenses. It reports on all of the offenses that occur during a criminal incident., and includes a wide array of information not found in traditional UCR data.

National Survey on Drug Use and Health: a survey of the prevalence, patterns, and consequences of alcohol, tobacco, and illegal drug use and abuse of the general U.S. civilian noninstitutionalized population, age 12 and older, conducted by the Substance Abuse and Mental Health Services Administration (SAMHSA).

National Youth Gang Survey (NYGS): a survey administered by Spergel and Curry (1993) that identified the five common gang-intervention strategies of suppression, social intervention, organization change and development, community organization, and opportunities provision.

National Youth Survey (NYS): a self-report survey administered to 11- to 17-year-old youths that taps information on Index offenses.

nature–nurture controversy: the debate as to whether intelligence is inherited (nature) or whether it is an outcome of growth in the environment (nurture).

near group: an assembly of individuals characterized by a relatively short lifetime, little formal organization, a lack of consensus between members, a small core of continuous participants, self-appointed leadership, and limited cohesion.

neglect: the failure to provide life's essentials (e.g., food, shelter, clothing, etc.) to a child.

Neoclassicism: the middle ground between classicism and positivism, the contention that humankind exercises some degree of free will, but that choices are limited by a large number of factors both within and outside of the individual (also called **soft determinism**).

neighborhood reparative boards (NRBs): boards made up of community members that seek to restore victims and community to pre-offense states, require the offender to make amends, and aid the offender in understanding the impact of his or her actions on the victim and community.

net-widening: the practice of handling youths (or other offenders) who normally would have been left alone.

neurotransmitters: chemicals involved in the transmission of electrical impulses through the nervous system.

nonsecure detention: the placement of a delinquent youth in a small group home that is not as securely locked to await further court action (compare to **secure detention**).

nullification: a refusal to enforce the law or impose a punishment.

O

offense rate: the number of offenses per 100,000 persons.

"once an adult, always an adult" provisions: state laws that mandate that certain juvenile offenders be processed in adult court after an initial processing in adult criminal court.

operant conditioning: the reinforcement of behavior through a complex system of rewards.

orthomolecular factors: chemicals that are introduced to the body or altered through diet or other influences.

outer containment: direct control over the individual from outside sources.

outpatient drug-free program: a nonresidential form of drug treatment that emphasizes the provision of a supportive, highly structured, family-like atmosphere within which a patient can be helped to alter his or her personality and develop social relationships conducive to conforming behavior.

P

panel design: a study design in which the same set of individuals are interviewed repeatedly over an extended number of years.

parens patriae: a legal doctrine under which the state is seen as a parent.

peacemaking: a perspective that supports efforts of corrections workers, whether prison counselors or probation officers, to help offenders find greater meaning in their lives.

peer mediation: a program in which disputants in a matter are brought together with a third-party peer (youth) mediator in an effort to resolve the dispute to the satisfaction of both parties.

petition: the document filed in juvenile court alleging that a juvenile is a delinquent, status offender, or dependent.

physiognomy: the idea that facial features are related to behavior.

plea bargaining: negotiation between the prosecutor and the defense attorney concerning the petition (charge) and/or the disposition (sentence).

police brutality: police use of excessive force.

police discretion: the authority of police to enforce or not enforce the law, or how to enforce the law.

police effectiveness: whether police are accomplishing their objectives such as controlling crime, improving the quality of life, or solving problems.

police use of excessive force: intentional use of brutality by police

political economy: Writers such as Garland contend that both politics and economics affect the operation of the criminal and juvenile justice systems. For example, Garland argues that current political and economic pressures dictate less emphasis on rehabilitation and greater emphasis on punishment, deterrence, and incapacitation.

positive youth development: the concept that most youths can grow up properly and stay out of trouble if they can be attached to the proper social resources, especially prosocial, caring adults.

Positivism: a school of thought based upon determinism, wherein what an individual does is determined by factors beyond the control of the individual (compare to **Classicism**).

prevalence: how many respondents report the use of something (e.g., a drug).

preventive detention: detention to prevent further delinquency while awaiting court action on an earlier charge.

primary deviance: those actions that are rationalized or otherwise dealt with as functions of a socially acceptable role (compare to **secondary deviance**).

probation: a type of community corrections in which an offender is under the supervision of a probation officer. The court orders the offender to follow certain rules and to report regularly to a probation officer.

problem-oriented policing: addressing the underlying causes of problems (such as delinquency) rather than simply addressing the symptoms.

professional policing: also known as the 911 model of policing, a model of policing that emphasizes rapid response to citizen calls for service. This model includes greater emphasis on police patrol in cruisers rather than foot patrol.

program effectiveness: the question of whether programs achieve their objectives.

prosecutorial waiver: a waiver or transfer by the prosecutor of a juvenile case to adult court.

psychoanalysis: pioneered by Freud, an approach to understanding human behavior, the major premise of which is that unconscious, and perhaps instinctual, factors account for much of the behavior displayed by individuals.

psychopharmacological perspective: the perspective that drugs have a direct causal impact on crime by inducing the user to act out in a certain way.

pulling levers: an approach wherein the police strictly enforce any and all codes and regulations (i.e., zero tolerance) in an attempt to change the behavior of a target group.

punitive model (attack probation): a philosophy of probation that emphasizes punishment such as curfew enforcement rather than a more rehabilitation-oriented model that emphasizes treatment of the underlying problems of the probationer.

R

racial profiling: the practice of using race as the sole indicator of suspicion of criminal activity.

racial tension: discord based on differences in racial background.

radical nonintervention: the practice of leaving youths alone as much as possible in order to avoid labeling (see **labeling**).

rational choice theory: the theory that potential offenders make choices based on various factors in the physical and social environments.

reactive hypoglycemia: changes in the blood sugar level, both higher and lower, as a result of dietary intake.

reasonable doubt standard: the standard of proof used in both adult criminal cases and juvenile delinquency cases: doubt based on reason that a reasonable man or women might entertain.

reciprocal relationship: a relationship in which two behaviors being studied (e.g., drug use and delinquency) feed one another.

reintegrative shaming: an idea postulated by Braithwaite that offers shaming as a key mechanism for showing societal disapproval. The shaming needs to be imposed in such a fashion as to draw the offending party into conforming society.

Reintegrative Shaming Experiments (RISE): a study conducted in Australia that compared the effects of standard court processing with the effects of conferencing on victims and offenders involved in drunk driving, juvenile property offenses, juvenile shoplifting, and violent youthful offenses.

reparative justice: see **restorative justice**.

restitution: the practice of offenders paying for all or part of the damage inflicted on persons or property damaged by the offense.

restorative justice: a model of justice that is concerned with repairing the damage or harm inflicted through processes of negotiation, mediation, empowerment, and reparation.

restorative justice conferences: meetings in which victims and offenders face one another in an attempt at restorative justice, for example, a burglary victim meets a juvenile burglar and explains precisely how the burglary impacted the victim. Supporters for both sides are present and, with the help of a leader, they work out an agreement on how the offender can make amends.

restorative justice juvenile court: a juvenile court focused on building community so that neighborhoods can better respond to and prevent delinquency. With such a court, communities would be more involved in sentencing through community panels or conferences or dispute resolution programs.

retributive justice: justice that focuses on the lawbreaker and the imposition of sanctions for the purposes of deterrence, vengeance, and/or punishment.

reverse waiver: the act of the adult criminal court returning certain cases received from juvenile court via waiver back to the juvenile court.

right to intervention: *Commonwealth v. Fisher* determined that a juvenile has a right to intervention rather than a right to freedom; the juvenile court was granted a free hand in dealing with youths.

role-taking: the process in which an individual (a child) assumes the role of a person or character whom they have observed (see **modeling**).

routine activities theory: a perspective that assumes that the normal, day-to-day behavior of individuals contributes to deviant events; that is, the convergence of motivated offenders, suitable targets, and an absence of guardians allows for the commission of crime.

rumble: a gang fight.

S

school prayer: prayer that takes place in the school setting; it is debated whether school prayer represents the promotion of religion by the school.

search and seizure: can include searches of persons, places, and things and actions such as taking into custody (arrest); Fourth Amendment protects against unreasonable searches and seizures.

secondary deviance: deviance that occurs when deviant behavior is used as a means of adjusting to society's reactions (compare to **primary deviance**).

secure detention: the placement of a youth in a locked facility with other youths who are awaiting either further court action or transfer to a state correctional facility.

selection model: a model of the delinquency–gang relationship that maintains that gangs recruit or attract already delinquent youths.

self-control theory: Gottfredson and Hirschi's theory holding that self-control, internalized by individuals early in life, is what constrains a person from involvement in deviant behavior.

JUVENILE JUSTICE: AN INTRODUCTION

self-report measures: surveys that attempt to gauge the level of delinquency by asking individuals to tell of their own participation in deviant activity.

sentencing circles: a community-directed process, conducted in partnership with the criminal justice system, to develop consensus on an appropriate sentencing plan that addresses the concerns of all interested parties; the process takes place post-conviction to determine a sentence.

shock incarceration: alternatives to traditional incarceration in which participants are involved in an intensive curriculum of discipline, work, strenuous physical activities, education, and other programs; boot camps are a common form.

Short–Nye instrument: developed by James Short and Ivan Nye, this early self-report survey asked youths to note the frequency with which they committed each of 23 items, dominated by status and minor offenses.

social bond: see **bond to society**.

social control theories: theories that seek to find factors that keep an individual from becoming deviant.

social disorganization: the state of a community in which the people in that community are unable to exert control over those living there.

social facilitation model: a model of the delinquency–gang relationship that maintains that belonging to a gang is the cause of increased deviance.

social history investigation: an investigation performed by a probation officer into the legal and social history of a delinquent youth and his or her family, similar to a presentence investigation in adult court.

social learning approach: in explanations of child maltreatment, an approach that contends that an individual learns to be abusive or neglectful by observing past behavior of that type.

sociocultural explanation: in explanations of child maltreatment, an explanation that emphasizes the role of society and the environment in leading to deviant behavior.

soft determinism: (see **neoclassicism**).

somatotypes: physiques (e.g., ectomorph, endomorph, and mesomorph) supposedly corresponding to particular temperaments.

spiritual dimension in corrections: a suggestion that corrections should go beyond providing education and counseling to also focus on such issues as the meaning of life and the importance of personal values in one's life.

spiritualistic/demonological explanations: the belief that deviant acts are the result of the battle between good and evil, God and the devil.

spurious relationship: a relationship in which two occurrences have no causal connection yet it may be inferred that they do, due to a certain third factor that causes both behaviors being studied (e.g., drug use and delinquency).

state training schools: residential placement centers for juveniles who have been adjudicated delinquent. They are youth prisons that may have a cottage structure and educational programming.

status offense: an action illegal only for persons of a certain status (i.e., juveniles); an action for which only a juvenile can be held accountable (e.g., runaway behavior, truancy).

statutory exclusion: a state legislature's rule that certain offenses, such as murder, automatically go to adult court; see **legislative waiver.**

STEP Act: California's Street Terrorism Enforcement and Prevention Act of 1988, which effectively criminalizes membership in a street gang.

strain theory: Robert Merton's theory that deviance results from a disjuncture between the goals approved by a culture and the means approved for reaching those goals.

student search: search of a student's possessions or person in a school.

subculture: a smaller part of a larger culture that exists within and is part of the larger culture.

subculture of violence: a value system that accepts the use of violence to solve problems.

superego: in Freudian theory, learned values, behaviors; moral character of the individual; outlines the acceptable and unacceptable; may be conscious or unconscious.

symbolic interactionism: the process through which an individual creates his or her self-image through interaction with the outside world.

systemic violence: violence due to factors related to the sale and marketing of drugs.

T

tautological: leading to circular reasoning.

techniques of neutralization: techniques outlined by Sykes and Matza that allow a juvenile to accommodate deviant behavior while maintaining a positive self-image.

teen courts: a diversion option in which youths act as judge, prosecutor, defense attorney, and jury in minor cases such as status offenses and misdemeanors. The most common penalty is community service.

theory: an attempt to answer the question "why?"

therapeutic community: a residential form of drug treatment that emphasizes the provision of a supportive, highly structured, family-like atmosphere within which a patient can be helped to alter their personality and develop social relationships conducive to conforming behavior.

therapeutic jurisprudence: courts that go beyond adjudicating and sentencing issues to consider the therapeutic role that the court can take. A prime example is drug courts, which attempt to use the court setting to motivate the offender and offer the offender services that will help solve his/her drug problem.

token economy programs: a behavior modification strategy, often used in training schools and other residential facilities, in which point or dollar values are assigned to particular behaviors and are used as a way of rewarding appropriate behavior.

training school: an institution that houses delinquents considered to be unfit for probation or another lesser punishment.

transfer: see **waiver**.

transfer of evil: moving the attribution of evil from the act to the actor.

U

Uniform Crime Reports (UCR): data collected yearly by the Federal Bureau of Investigation, which provides information on 29 categories of offenses known to the police. It includes two offense subgroups: the first eight offenses are known as the Part I crimes or Index crimes; all remaining offenses fall within the Part II category.

use, abuse, and addiction: three common terms used in discussing the drug problem. *Use* means the utilization of a drug. *Abuse* refers to the use of any drug beyond that legally prescribed for a medical condition. *Addiction* refers to chronic use of a drug to the point at which the individual develops a need to continue use of the drug, increases the amount used over time, and develops a psychological or physical dependence on the drug.

V

victim-blaming: assigning some of the responsibility for a victimization to the victim.

victim precipitation: a situation in a victimization experience in which the victim may have struck the first blow or somehow initiated the victimization.

victimization: in general, being victimized by a crime or delinquent act such as assault or theft. In reference to institutional life, victimization refers to an assault (physical or sexual) or theft experienced in a facility such as a state training school.

victim-offender mediation (VOM): a formal mediation program in which victim and offender are clearly identified and the participation of the offender is often a requirement of the court; also known as Victim-Offender Reconciliation Programs (VORPs).

W

waiver: the process by which an individual who is legally a juvenile is sent to the adult criminal system for disposition and handling (also called **judicial waiver** or **transfer**).

wet nursing: the practice of employing a surrogate mother to care for and suckle a child.

wilderness program: a program in which youths undergo an outdoor experience that is designed to teach self-reliance, independence, and self-worth.

wilding gang: a middle-class gang that strikes out at what its members perceive to be inequalities and infringements on their rights by other ethnic groups.

Y

youth justice system: a suggestion to process juveniles in adult courts that are a type of therapeutic jurisprudence. These juvenile courts would be similar to drug courts in their emphasis on treatment within a court framework.

Z

zealous advocate role: defense attorney role that emphasizes strong tactics to prove the juvenile defendant innocent or get the least severe penalty (contrasted to the concerned adult model in which the attorney acts like a parent seeking the best treatment outcome for the youth).

SUBJECT INDEX

A

Abandonment of children, 27
Abolition of juvenile court, 383-385
Abuse, 359-361, 363-364
Accommodation of deviant behavior, 82, 83
Accountability, 216
ACT Now truancy reduction program (Arizona), 216
Adam Walsh Child Protection and Safety Act of 2006, 305
Adaptation, modes of, 86-87
Addiction, 134. *See also* Drug abuse
Adjudication and disposition
   attorney effectiveness, 229-231
   attorneys in juvenile court, 225-228
   deprivation of freedom from, 389
   dispositional decisionmaking, 234-238
   jury trials, 231-232
   plea bargaining, 228
   predisposition report for, 302-304
   punitiveness, 232-234
Adolescent court, 385-386
Adoption studies, 55-56
Adult courts, transfer to, 204.
   See also Transfer (waiver) to adult criminal court
   from adolescent court, 385
   Breed v. Jones (1975), 246-247
   criminal court, victimization of juveniles, and, 372-373
   evaluation of, 415
   expanding use of, 233
   juvenile courts versus, 220-225
   Kent v. United States (1966), 242-243
   minimum age for, 6-8
   passive, 223-224
   prosecutor's role in, 218

race of juvenile offender and, 385
statistics on, 204-205
"youth justice system" for, 386-387
"Adult crime, adult time," 383, 384, 385, 416
Affective interventions, to drug-use prevention, 152-153
African-Americans. *See* Blacks
Aftercare, 148, 305-308, 318
Age
   citizen attitudes toward police and, 180
   of gang members, 110
   for legal drinking, 267-272
   uniform, for juvenile court, 381
   victimization categorized by, 355-356
   at which criminal courts gain jurisdiction over young offenders, 6-8
Age distribution
   for juvenile arrests (*Uniform Crime Reports*), 9-11
   in self-reporting data, 20
Age of juvenile offenders. *See also* Drug abuse
   alcohol abuse and, 193, 267-272
   FBI data on, 10
   in gangs, 110
   self-report statistics on, 20
   for transfer to adult court, 6-8, 220, 221
   Uniform Crime Reports data on, 9, 11
Aggressive behavior, 57
AIDS/HIV, 146, 148
Alaskan natives, juvenile arrest statistics for, 10, 11
Alcoholics Anonymous, 148
Alcohol use
   deviant behavior linked to, 58
   self-reports on, 18, 19
   as status offense, 4, 267-272
   12-step programs for, 148

491

United States v. Mark James Knights
(2002), 251
waiver ruling, 246-247
Yarborough, Warden v. Alvarado
(2004), 249

E

Early childhood, in psychoanalysis, 63
Early interventions, 379
Ecological fallacy, 76-77
Ecological perspective, in sociological
explanation of delinquency, 74-77
Economic globalization, 177, 399, 415
Ectomorph, 53
Education approach, to drug-use
prevention, 152
Effectiveness
of institutional interventions, 285-287
of juvenile probation and related
sanctions, 316-318
of policing, 193-194
questions about, 302
of treatment interventions with
offenders, 318-323
Ego, in psychoanalysis, 61-63
Eighth Amendment, 405
Elaboration model, 96
Electronencephalography (EEG), 58
Electronic monitoring, 212
Elmira Reformatory, 33
Emancipation for juveniles, 270
Emotional healing, in restorative
justice, 338
Employment readiness programs,
209-210
Empowerment, in restorative justice,
337
Endomorph, 53
Enforcement, as drug-use prevention
strategy, 157-161
Enhancement model, gangs and, 119
Entitlement programs, 269, 399, 416
Entrepreneurship, in gangs, 112, 115
Ethnicity, of gang members, 111-112,
117, 122
Evidence, rules of, 34
Evidence-based supervision model, 307
Evil, transfer of, in labeling
perspective, 93
Excessive discipline, 254. *See also*
Corporal punishment

Excessive force, police use of, 194-199,
211
Exchange theory, 336-337
Execution. *See* Capital punishment
Ex parte Crouse (1838), 36, 37
Exploitive use of juveniles, 41
External pressures/external pulls
to deviant behavior, 91

F

Fairness, in restorative justice, 346-347
Faith and Character-Based Purposeful
Living Units (Indiana), 401
Faith-based training schools, 400-401
Family courts, 370
Family group conferencing (FGC), 341,
342-343
Family issues, in future of juvenile
justice, 394-397
Fare v. Michael C. (1979), 247-249
FBI Supplemental Homicide Reports,
120
Fear, as response to victimization,
364-365
Federal Bureau of Investigation (FBI),
9-10, 120, 324
"Feeble-mindedness" of criminals, 69
Females
chivalry hypothesis and, 235
delinquency rates of, 15
dispositional decisionmaking and,
235
dowries and, 27
early institutions for, 33-34, 41
as gang members, 112, 116
gender-specific programs for, 209,
292, 379
infanticide of, 27
intervention effectiveness with,
322-323
juvenile arrest statistics for, 10, 11
with mental disorders, 288
status offenses and, 412
victimization of, 290-292
as victims, 355-356, 360
Fifth Amendment (self-incrimination
protection), 244
Financial gain, gangs and, 123
Firearms
Boston Gun Project, 127, 170, 200
"drive-by" shootings and, 121
gangs and, 118, 121-122

NAME INDEX